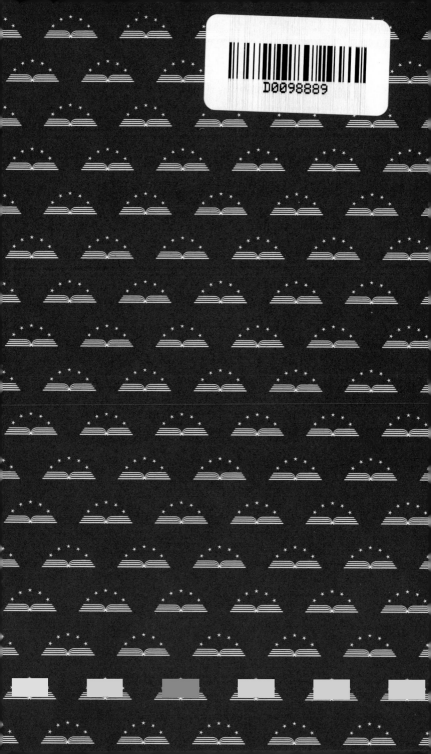

THE
LINCOLN
ANTHOLOGY

THE
LINCOLN
ANTHOLOGY

Great Writers on

His Life and Legacy from

1860 to Now

EDITED BY HAROLD HOLZER

A SPECIAL PUBLICATION OF
The Library of America

Chronology copyright © 1989 by Literary Classics of the United States, Inc., New York, NY. Originally published in Abraham Lincoln, *Speeches and Writings 1832–1865*, edited by Don E. Fehrenbacher.

Some of the material in this volume is reprinted with the permission of holders of copyright and publishing rights. Acknowledgments are on page 935

Distributed to the trade by Penguin Putnam Inc. and in Canada by Penguin Books Canada, Ltd.

Design by Francesca Belanger

Library of Congress Control Number: 2008934337

ISBN: 978-1-59853-033-9 (trade edition)
ISBN: 978-1-59853-043-8 (slipcase edition)

The Library of America—192s

First Printing

Printed in the United States of America

The Lincoln Anthology:
Great Writers on His Life and Legacy from 1860 to Now
is published with support from

THE NATIONAL ENDOWMENT
FOR THE HUMANITIES

and

THE BODMAN FOUNDATION

Contents

List of Illustrations

Introduction

Writing—the art of communicating thoughts to the mind, through the eye—is the great invention of the world. Great in the astonishing range of analysis and combination which necessarily underlies the most crude and general conception of it—great, very great in enabling us to converse with the dead, the absent, and the unborn, at all distances of time and of space.

> —*Abraham Lincoln, Lecture on Discoveries and Inventions, February 11, 1859*

Why, if the old Greeks had had this man, what trilogies of plays—what epics—would have been made out of him! How the rhapsodes would have recited him! How quickly that quaint tall form would have enter'd into the region where men vitalize gods, and gods divinify men! But Lincoln, his times, his death—great as any, any age—belong altogether to our own, and are autochthonic.

> —*Walt Whitman, 1882*

This book is a conversation, held across "all distances of time and of space," about Abraham Lincoln and his complex and protean legacy. It brings together a highly diverse array of writers—journalists, biographers, satirists, essayists, novelists, clergymen, poets, playwrights, historians, memoirists, and statesmen—who have explored the fertile terrain between history and folklore, memory and imagination, rhapsodies and denunciations, to write about Lincoln. Inevitably, it is also a book about his country: the nation that made his rise possible, the nation that he saved, and the nation that, 200 years after his birth, now remembers him anew. The writers collected here share Whitman's awareness that "Lincoln, his times, his death" are "autochthonic"—meaning "indigenous, native, aboriginal"—which is to say, wholly and distinctly American.

Eulogizing the recently slain President in April 1865, Ralph

Waldo Emerson said of the man who had left his native soil but once, to briefly tour the Canadian side of Niagara Falls: "He was thoroughly American, had never crossed the sea, had never been spoiled by English insularity or French dissipation; a quite native, aboriginal man, as an acorn from an oak; no aping of foreigners, no frivolous accomplishments . . ." A few months later, James Russell Lowell was even more emphatic: "New birth of our new soil, the first American." Generations later, in 2000, Richard Slotkin could still imagine the young hero of his novel *Abe* boasting as only an American can: "*I am Abraham Lincoln—the Bull of the Lick from Pigeon Crick! Half-horse, half-alligator, and blood-nephew to the meanest son of a bitch west of the mountains. The universal sky is my shake roof and I stake my claim to the whole American republic.*"

In his own time, and in the years since, Lincoln emerged as, and has remained, nothing less than the ideal American hero: the self-made Everyman who triumphed over poverty and obscurity through hard work, relentless study, intense determination, and unyielding honesty; a man of the people who dedicated himself to ensuring that others would have a fair chance to succeed in what he called the race of life; a president who bore the unimaginable burdens and sorrows of leading his country through four years of brutally fratricidal war while enjoying the exhilaration that came with breaking the chains of slavery, and who, in the hour of victory, without a trace of malice in his heart, died a martyr's death. Like every mythic image built on a historic person, the legend distills a more complex underlying reality. But as the pages that follow will show, his is a legacy of extraordinary resonance and universality, incubated in journalism, eulogy, and political oratory, nurtured in biography and historical writing, challenged and reasserted in poetry, fiction, and drama, and explored afresh by successive generations of writers as a renewable source for inspiration—the DNA for the connective tissue that Americans still invoke to sanctify the past and bless the future.

Ten months after he spoke about writing as "the art of communicating," Lincoln was becoming a serious contender for national office, and many Americans understandably clamored for information about his origins. So little was known about him that his first biographers turned to the potential candidate himself to provide details, and he obliged by supplying the bare essentials that have been fleshed out so vigorously ever since. Thus, when Jesse W. Fell, an Illinois Republican, asked for help on behalf of a Pennsylvania writer named Joseph J. Lewis, Lincoln responded on December 20, 1859, by sending Fell "a little sketch" in which he managed to distill his entire history, along with a physical description, into just four paragraphs of text. "There is not much of it," Lincoln conceded, "for the reason, I suppose, that there is not much of me." In his groundbreaking biographical report, which appeared in the *Chester County Times* on February 11, 1860, Lewis extrapolated that Lincoln was "a strictly moral and temperate man," a man "of frank and engaging manners, of kind and genial nature, unaffectedly modest, social in disposition, ready in conversation . . . a firm friend and yet not implacable to an enemy, a consistent politician, a good citizen and an honest patriot." (After his nomination Lincoln provided John L. Scripps, a Chicago newspaper editor, with a longer, third-person sketch that Scripps used in writing his own *Life of Abraham Lincoln*.)

And so the Lincoln image took form, through both his own words and the words of other writers, a literary interaction that would continue as his speeches and writings gained wider circulation and as more campaign biographies appeared. In the century and a half since, no American has been the subject of more biography and hagiography, analysis and revisionism, in prose and verse alike, from writers in this country and from around the world, than the man almost no one knew on the eve of his election to the White House. While much of this immense outpouring has been laudatory, Lincoln has also received his share of harsh criticism. In his own time and since, writers have assailed his character and his politics, and pointedly questioned Whitman's vision of Lincoln the sublime. Hailed as a liberator and the savior of democracy, he has also been denounced as a bloodthirsty tyrant and a false messiah. And as writers over time have recalled, interpreted, and debated Lincoln, politicians—Republicans and Democrats alike—have striven to seize, embrace, and adapt his enduring hold on the American consciousness and to make his memory into a talisman that would bring them popular approval and electoral success.

The aim of this anthology is to bring together insightful and imaginative writing about Abraham Lincoln from the past 150 years, writing that explores and illuminates how various images of Lincoln—emancipator, self-made American, champion of democracy, savior of the Union—have been, in the words of the historian Merrill Peterson, "developed, entwined, embellished, revised, and recast, through several generations." In selecting the contents, the emphasis has been placed on enduring works by novelists, poets, dramatists, and other imaginative writers, as well as perceptive and significant engagements with Lincoln's legacy by influential public figures (Carl Schurz, Booker T. Washington, Woodrow Wilson, Mario Cuomo) and public intellectuals (Jacques Barzun, Reinhold Niebuhr, Garry Wills). While most of the writers in the anthology are American, an international perspective is provided by selections from, among others, Karl Marx, Henrik Ibsen, Victor Hugo, H. G. Wells, and Donggill Kim.

Whether international or American in origin, the writings collected here demonstrate how Lincoln's literary image reflects the intriguing and seemingly incongruous paradoxes of his character: the man of great sadness who had a rollicking sense of humor; the warrior of steely resolve who also could show mercy toward condemned soldiers and defeated enemies; the strong backwoods giant whose features eventually became a haunting canvas of profound suffering; the man of understandable modesty about his homeliness, who nonetheless displayed an almost eager willingness to sit for painters, sculptors, and photographers; the Kentucky-born advocate of colonization and white supremacy who emancipated millions and eventually advocated black suffrage; a man capable of boisterous frontier camaraderie as well as magisterial eloquence, steadfast honesty and sharp-elbowed political maneuvering; a man as grand as the heroic statue that sits inside the Lincoln Memorial, yet as democratic as the profile on the commonplace copper penny. All of these contradictions lead in the end to an inescapable sense of mys-

tery, as Langston Hughes understood in contemplating the
Memorial in 1932:

> Let's go see old Abe
> Sitting in the marble and the moonlight,
> Sitting lonely in the marble and the moonlight,
> Quiet for ten thousand centuries, old Abe.
> Quiet for a million, million years.
>
> Quiet—
>
> And yet a voice forever
> Against the
> Timeless wall
> Of time—
> Old Abe.

That Lincoln would become a subject of such enduring fascination to generations of American writers could hardly have
been foreseen on February 27, 1860, when, introduced by the
famous poet and newspaper editor William Cullen Bryant, he
delivered from the rostrum of Cooper Union in New York City
the address that made him a national figure. As a self-educated
westerner, Lincoln was alien to the literary and cultural elites of
New York and New England, who generally favored New York
senator William H. Seward for the Republican presidential nomination. For much of his presidency Lincoln was frequently
criticized, both publicly and privately, either as a weak and indecisive leader incapable of choosing clear policies or appointing
effective military commanders, or as a dangerous despot who
disregarded the constitutional limits on executive power. Whatever admiration he did win from established American writers
for his wartime leadership was often mixed with condescension
regarding his informal frontier manners, his fondness for popular humorists such as Artemus Ward, Orpheus C. Kerr, and
Petroleum V. Nasby, and his inability to conform to established
standards of presidential decorum. Yet Lincoln eventually found
literary advocates in James Russell Lowell and Harriet Beecher
Stowe, the latter describing him in 1864 as "in the strictest sense

a man of the working classes . . . his position now . . . is a sign to all who live by labor that their day is coming."

Then came Appomattox and, just five days later, Ford's Theatre. Lincoln was shot on Good Friday, and the first sermons preached in his memory were heard on Easter Sunday (which coincided that year with Passover), circumstances that greatly contributed to his apotheosis as a martyr who redeemed a suffering nation with his sacrifice. Edward Everett Hale compared Lincoln to Jesus; Henry Ward Beecher and the nation's rabbis likened him to Moses leading the chosen people out of bondage and to within sight of a promised land he himself was fated not to enter. Bryant, Lowell, and Julia Ward Howe offered poetical tributes, joined by such now-obscure poets as Edmund Clarence Stedman and Richard Henry Stoddard, whose memorial offerings deserve rediscovery as testaments to the passions of the hour.

"Why Scripps" said he, on one occasion, "it is a great piece of folly to attempt to make anything out of my early life. It can all be condensed into a single sentence, and that sentence you will find in Gray's Elegy: 'The short and simple annals of the poor.' That's my life, and that's all you or any one else can make of it."

> —*John L. Scripps, author of an 1860 Lincoln campaign*
> *biography, in a letter to William H. Herndon, June 24, 1865*

The decades following Lincoln's death saw an outpouring of reminiscences by those who had known him, beginning with journalist Noah Brooks and continuing with the entertaining memoirs of the former White House clerk William O. Stoddard. With the invaluable assistance of Lincoln's son Robert and exclusive access to Lincoln's papers, former presidential secretaries John G. Nicolay and John Hay wrote a ten-volume "court history" of his administration, carefully designed to enshrine Lincoln's reputation as a wise and great statesman. A far different course was embarked upon by William H. Herndon, Lincoln's Springfield law partner from 1844 to 1861. Angered by the popular tendency to idealize and mythologize his friend, Herndon resolved in 1865 to combine his own firsthand recollections and perceptions with "*solid facts & well attested truths*" about Lincoln's early life, and he spent nearly two years interviewing and corresponding with dozens of people who had known Lincoln and his family long before in Kentucky, Indiana, and Illinois.

After years of delay and with the help of a collaborator, *Herndon's Lincoln* appeared in 1889, challenging pious and sentimental views of Lincoln by describing his dedication to logic and reason, his unrelenting ambition, and his lack of orthodox religious belief. Perhaps the most influential of all early Lincoln biographers, Herndon is generally remembered as a demythologizer, yet paradoxically he is the source for the most romantic (and one of the most disputed) of all Lincoln stories, the tale of his desperate love for a doomed prairie girl named Ann Rutledge. Few pieces in this anthology have the strange power of Herndon's controversial 1866 lecture on Lincoln, Ann, and the pioneers of their New Salem village, in which Herndon breathlessly recounts the precise hour, day, and location on which he uncovered the hidden key to Lincoln's melancholy character and then loses himself in an extended rhapsody extolling the sublime beauty of the Sangamon valley. Lincoln's widow cursed Herndon for suggesting he had ever loved another woman, but his former partner had etched an indelible image that seemed to explain Lincoln's persistent sadness, albeit little else.

You are the children of Abraham Lincoln. We are at best only his step-children, children by adoption, children by force of circumstance and necessity.

—*Frederick Douglass, April 14, 1876*

Some of the most insightful posthumous appraisals of Lincoln came from two of his contemporaries, each of whom in his own way was Lincoln's somewhat unlikely counterpart. Frederick Douglass was, like Lincoln, a self-educated, self-made man who overcame great obstacles to forge a famous public career in oratory and political activism. A frequent critic of Lincoln's administration until the Emancipation Proclamation, Douglass became the first African American to confer with an American president on matters of policy. When asked to deliver the oration at the dedication of the Freedmen's Monument in Washington, D.C., in 1876, Douglass gave a speech on Lincoln, race, and emancipation remarkable for its candor, nuance, perception, and conviction. Describing Lincoln as "preeminently the white man's president, entirely devoted to the welfare of white men," Douglass proceeded to assess Lincoln's actions in the highly appropriate context of politics and public opinion. "Viewed from the genuine abolition ground," he said, "Mr. Lincoln seemed tardy, cold, dull, and indifferent: but measuring him by the sentiment of his country, a sentiment he was bound as a statesman to consult, he was swift, zealous, radical, and determined."

Unlike Douglass, Walt Whitman never spoke with Lincoln, though he would long treasure the memory of his sightings of the President on the streets of the wartime capital. Each a revolutionary figure in his chosen form of writing, Whitman and Lincoln are arguably the two great literary geniuses of 19th-century American democracy. While mainly associated with Lincoln through his poetry, especially the sublime elegy "When Lilacs Last in the Dooryard Bloom'd," Whitman also contemplated his hero in prose as unique and unmistakable as his verse. Citing a commentator on Shakespeare who praised the playwright's ability to thoroughly blend "the ideal with the practical or realistic" (Lincoln's love for Shakespeare's plays was well known), Whitman wrote: "If this be so, I should say that what Shakspere did in poetic expression, Abraham Lincoln essentially did in his personal and official life. I should say the invisible foundations and vertebra of his character, more than any man's in history, were mystical, abstract, moral and spiritual—while upon all of them was built, and out of all of them radiated, under the control of the average of circumstances, what the vulgar call *horse-sense*, and a life often bent by temporary but most urgent materialistic and political reasons."

As the 19th century drew to a close, the abandonment of Reconstruction and the increasing desire among white Americans for an end to sectional conflict pushed slavery and emancipation into the background of historical memory and caused Lincoln's martyrdom to be increasingly recalled as a sacrifice to

North-South rapprochement. The desire for sectional reconciliation was expressed by Richard Watson Gilder in his poem "To the Spirit of Abraham Lincoln (Reunion at Gettysburg Twenty-Five Years After the Battle)"; by the American novelist Winston Churchill, who has his fictitious Lincoln reunite the Confederate heroine with her Unionist lover at the climax of his historical romance *The Crisis* (1901); and by Theodore Roosevelt, who in his 1909 centenary address at the Lincoln birthplace memorial in Hodgenville, Kentucky, spoke of how as time passed "all of us, wherever we dwell, grow to feel an equal pride in the valor and self-devotion, alike of the men who wore the blue and the men who wore the gray."

Lincoln also evolved into an ideal held up to every American child, and especially to every boy. Bayard Taylor stressed the proximity of his example in an 1870 picture book, *The Ballad of Abraham Lincoln*: "His arm was strong, his heart was bold, / His deeds were wise and true; / He did not live in days of old, / But here at home with you." Writing in 1888, Noah Brooks assured his juvenile readers that the young Lincoln "never played cards, nor gambled, nor smoked, nor used profane language, nor addicted himself to any of the rude vices of the time." And in "Lincoln—the Boy" (1907), James Whitcomb Riley blended sentiment and inspiration: "With love-light in his eyes and shade / Of prescient tears:—Because / Only of such a boy were made / The loving man he was."

Generational change began to reshape Lincoln's legacy at the turn of the century. Increasingly those who wrote about him were not contemporaries with firsthand knowledge, or even adult memories of his administration and the Civil War, but persons for whom Lincoln was at best a childhood recollection, such as the bestselling biographer Ida Tarbell, President Theodore Roosevelt and President Woodrow Wilson, and the former slave Booker T. Washington. For a new generation of poets such as Edwin Markham, Edwin Arlington Robinson, Vachel Lindsay, and John Gould Fletcher, Lincoln was less a person, or a martyr, than a figure of myth, a force of nature, a haunting spirit forged from, and part of, national memory.

The passage of time also affected Lincoln's role in contemporary politics. Until the end of the 19th century, Lincoln and the Union victory in the Civil War were the closely held symbols of the Republican party. (Grover Cleveland, the only Democrat to be elected president after 1856 and before 1912, was also the only elected president between Lincoln and Theodore Roosevelt who had not served as an officer in the Union Army.) When William Jennings Bryan sought to claim Lincoln for the populist Democrats at the turn of the century, the Republican press reacted as if Lincoln had been assassinated for a second time. Fortunately for the Republicans, Theodore Roosevelt, who as a child had watched Lincoln's funeral procession in New York, became perhaps the most ardent Lincoln admirer ever to sit in the presidential chair. For luck, he wore a ring containing a lock of Lincoln's hair, kept his portrait in a place of prominence on his desk, and avidly listened to the recollections of his Secretary of State—Lincoln's old junior secretary, John Hay.

Not surprisingly, when Theodore Roosevelt spoke of Lincoln, he often described a man much like himself, a progressive nationalist and practical reformer who followed his own course despite criticism from both radicals and conservatives. Later, when Roosevelt returned to the political arena in 1912 to challenge his own hand-picked White House successor, William Howard Taft, the beleaguered incumbent successfully sought the endorsement of Lincoln's rigidly anti-Roosevelt surviving son, Robert. In the end, both men lost to Woodrow Wilson, who sought to lay claim to Lincoln's legacy for the Democrats even as he imposed Jim Crow segregation on the federal bureaucracy. Despite the eloquence of his 1916 address at Hodgenville, Wilson's bid to wrest Lincoln from the Republicans faltered, perhaps because of the tragic outcome of his own term as a president waging a controversial war.

Abraham Lincoln was a Southern poor white, of illegitimate birth, poorly educated and unusually ugly, awkward, ill-dressed . . . he was big enough to be inconsistent—cruel, merciful; peace-loving, a fighter; despising Negroes and letting them fight and vote; protecting slavery and freeing slaves. He was a man—a big, inconsistent, brave man.   —*W.E.B. Du Bois, May 1922*

The grim circumstances of entrenched segregation and deadly racial violence that confronted blacks in the early decades of the 20th century tested African-American loyalty to the Republican party and its greatest symbol. After an exceptionally vicious race riot exploded in 1908 in Springfield, Lincoln's old Illinois hometown, a "Lincoln Conference on the Negro Question" was held that led to the founding of the NAACP. More than a decade later, W.E.B. Du Bois had become disenchanted with the racial policies of both parties and used the pages of the NAACP magazine *The Crisis* to speak frankly about the complexities of Lincoln's record on race and slavery. In the face of the predictable storm of protest aroused by his iconoclasm, Du Bois carefully restated his case for a qualified admiration, saying that he revered Lincoln the more "because up out of his contradictions and inconsistencies he fought his way to the pinnacles of earth and his fight was within as well as without."

Sharper still were the cruel ironies attending the dedication of the Lincoln Memorial on May 30, 1922. At a ceremony where African-American spectators were herded into a segregated area at the back of the crowd, Chief Justice William Howard Taft gave an address that never mentioned slavery, while President Warren Harding assured his audience that Lincoln saw emancipation only as a measure to preserve the union. Robert R. Moton, successor to Booker T. Washington as principal of the Tuskegee Institute, was chosen to speak on behalf of his race, and he drafted a speech warning that the memorial would prove "but a hollow mockery, a symbol of hypocrisy" unless the nation rededicated itself to the pursuit of justice and equality. After submitting his draft to the event's organizers, Moton was advised to mute his criticism of the status quo. He did so, and his original draft, never spoken, has remained unpublished until now.

Lincoln? did he gather
the feel of the American dream
and its kindred over the earth?
                              —*Carl Sandburg, 1936*

No writer did more to shape the memory of Lincoln in the first half of the 20th century than the poet turned popular biographer Carl Sandburg. A socialist who became an enthusiastic supporter of Franklin D. Roosevelt and the New Deal, Sandburg saw in Lincoln a perpetual tribune of the common people, a faithful son of the democratic frontier whose example would always remind Americans of their duty to confront tyranny and injustice. Sandburg's influence can be clearly seen in *Abe Lincoln in Illinois*, the highly successful 1938 stage drama (and 1940 film) written by Robert E. Sherwood. A friend of the working man who reluctantly seeks office in order to confront the inescapable evil of slavery, Sherwood's Lincoln was the perfect hero for an America moving from the New Deal toward a perilous confrontation with fascism. Not surprisingly, Sherwood went on to become a speechwriter for Franklin D. Roosevelt, the Democrat who finally broke the Republicans' monopoly control of Lincoln memory. Having already enlisted Lincoln as an ally in the struggle to overcome the Great Depression, Roosevelt readily made him a fellow warrior in the looming battle against the Axis. (One of his most memorable appropriations of Lincoln memory was his comparison of Charles Lindbergh, his isolationist adversary, to Lincoln's wartime foe, the notorious Copperhead leader Clement L. Vallandigham—who, ironically, was a Democrat.) Sherwood and FDR alike helped forge a new image of Lincoln as a man who had to be prodded into action, but once roused, saved the nation. It fit the moment perfectly, even if few who knew the relentlessly ambitious Lincoln in life would have recognized the counter-myth of the reluctant leader created so many years after his death. Roosevelt's claim on Lincoln has been reasserted by Democrats ever since, most notably by one of his successors as governor of New York, Mario Cuomo.

Manic-depressive Lincoln, national hero!
—Delmore Schwartz, 1959

The memory of Lincoln in the second half of the 20th century was profoundly shaped by a perspective radically different from Sandburg's, that of the literary critic Edmund Wilson. In his influential study of Civil War literature, *Patriotic Gore* (1962), Wilson offered a provocative psychological reading of Lincoln's 1838 Springfield Lyceum Address, arguing that the rising politician was consumed from a young age by the ambition to play a great and heroic role in history, an obsession that drove him to become the very "towering genius" against whom he had warned his Lyceum audience. Lincoln might well have avoided war in 1861, Wilson insisted, if not for his quest to ascend into the national pantheon as the savior of the Union the Founders had created. In his introduction to *Patriotic Gore*, he compared Lincoln to Bismarck and Lenin; each man had become "an uncompromising dictator" while creating a great new modern power. Rejecting any notion of American exceptionalism, he judged the Union victory in the Civil War and the American role in the ongoing Cold War to be equally amoral exercises of national power, akin to the instinctual struggles of hungry sea slugs. *Patriotic Gore* would inspire a generation of psychobiographers to further explore Lincoln's inner world. Both its psychological and political critique would find fictional expression in Gore Vidal's controversial bestseller *Lincoln* (1984). One of a series of historical novels intended as a chronicle of how the American republic turned into an empire, *Lincoln* explicitly embraced the idea that Lincoln had willed his own death in atonement for the war he had so resolutely waged.

In 1963 Martin Luther King Jr. stood before the Lincoln Memorial and began his speech to the March on Washington by invoking the "great American, in whose symbolic shadow we stand today" who had signed the Emancipation Proclamation. Five years later, in the era of the Black Power movement, the image of a heroic Lincoln came under attack when Lerone Bennett Jr., a senior editor at *Ebony*, rhetorically asked "Was

Abe Lincoln a White Supremacist?" and answered with an un-equivocal affirmative. "Lincoln must be seen as the embodiment, not the transcendence, of the American tradition," he wrote, "which is, as we all know, a racist tradition." Like Edmund Wilson, Bennett sought not only to challenge accepted history but also to free his readers from what he considered a profoundly misleading mythic inheritance.

Along with other African-American writers such as Vincent Harding, Bennett transformed the anti-Lincoln tradition, which had previously been defined by white writers who blamed Lincoln for the destruction of state sovereignty, the brutal ascendancy of industrial capitalism, and the triumph of militant American nationalism. Bennett's unsparing critique of Lincoln's racial policies also marked a new stage in the distinct African-American tradition of Lincoln memory that had evolved alongside the predominant white tradition. For many decades in which most white Americans recalled Lincoln as a figure of reunion and reconciliation, and as an exemplar of the self-made man, black Americans remembered him, first and foremost, as an emancipator. In time, he became a symbol of both freedom attained and freedom denied. The memory of Lincoln was used time and again to remind Americans of what was still owed to the people he had freed, but the memory of how emancipation had delivered only partial liberation also became a measure of how much Lincoln, and the American democracy he represented and exemplified, had withheld from those who sought the full measure of freedom.

> I have walked up and down the
> valleys
> of his astounding face
> I have witnessed all the golgothas
> I have climbed the steep declivities
> of all his dreams
> —*Marsden Hartley, 1939*

At the beginning of the 21st century imaginative writing about Lincoln shows a renewed vitality. In *The March* E. L. Doctorow skillfully treats familiar themes—Lincoln's exhaustion at the end of the war, the psychological burden of his strained marriage—while in *Abe* Richard Slotkin sends the young Lincoln down the Mississippi on a journey clearly designed to evoke *Adventures of Huckleberry Finn*. And in *Mr. Lincoln's Wars* Adam Braver takes the risk of bringing Lincoln closer to the present by the use of modern vernacular and, in the novel's final chapter, envisioning him as character from a 20th-century hard-boiled novel who teeters on the brink of neo-noir cynicism and despair while contemplating a life of legal drudgery in the service of the cheats and chiselers of central Illinois.

Yet perhaps the most surprising turn in the recent course of Lincoln memory came in the world of politics. On February 10, 2007, two days before Lincoln's 198th birthday, another Illinois politician—like Lincoln a tall, lanky lawyer who had served for eight years in the state legislature—stood outside the Springfield state house, across the square from the site where Lincoln had delivered his lecture on discoveries and inventions in 1859, and announced his candidacy for President of the United States. Senator Barack Obama did not hesitate to imply that his election would do much to complete the "unfinished work" Lincoln had acknowledged at Gettysburg in 1863. At this writing, it is certain that Senator Obama has already made history by becoming the first black candidate to win the presidential nomination of a major American political party.

His evocation of Lincoln as he began his quest for the presidency testifies powerfully to Lincoln's astonishing durability as a symbol of aspiration and expectation, the irresistible totem of American hope, however difficult to fulfill. No doubt in years to come there will be yet further shifts and turns in how we see Lincoln, and through him, ourselves. There will always be something more to be said, to be *written*, about the man Whitman called "that quaint tall form." Let the conversation across "all distances of time and of space" continue.

HAROLD HOLZER
August 2008

Portrait by Mathew Brady, New York City, taken February 27, 1860, the day Lincoln gave his address at Cooper Union. *Courtesy of the Library of Congress.*

William Cullen Bryant

Bryant (1794–1878) had been a published poet for more than 50 years, and the editor of the anti-slavery *New York Evening Post* for 30, when he rose at the new Manhattan college, the Cooper Union, to introduce a little-known Illinois Republican named Abraham Lincoln to an audience of 1,500 on February 27, 1860. Lincoln's well-received lecture, which Bryant reprinted in full—and lavishly praised—in his influential newspaper the following afternoon, helped to successfully introduce the western presidential aspirant to the vote-rich Northeast, and it is widely credited with propelling Lincoln toward his party's nomination three months later. While there is no evidence that Lincoln ever read Bryant's most famous poem, "Thanatopsis" (1817), its focus on the comforts Nature offers after death was echoed in one of the future President's own attempts at poetry, "My Childhood-Home I See Again" (1846): "Where things decayed, and loved ones lost / In dreamy shadows rise."

Introduction of Abraham Lincoln at Cooper Union

It is a grateful office that I perform in introducing to you an eminent citizen of the West, hitherto known to you only by reputation, who has consented to address a New York assembly this evening. A powerful auxiliary, my friends, is the great West in that battle which we are fighting in behalf of freedom against slavery and in behalf of civilization against barbarism, for the occupation of some of the fairest regions of our continent now first opened to colonization. [Applause.] I recognise an agency higher and wiser than that of man, in causing the broad and fertile region which forms the northern part of the valley of the Mississippi to be rapidly filled with a population of hardy freemen, who till their own acres with their own hands, and who would be ashamed to subsist by the labor of slaves. [Applause.] These children of the West form a living bulwark against the advance of slavery, and from them is recruited the vanguard of the mighty armies of liberty. [Loud applause.] One of them I present to you this evening, a gallant soldier of the political campaign of 1856, [applause] in which he rendered good service to the Republican cause, and the great champion of that cause in Illinois two years later, when he and his friends would have won the victory but for the unjust apportionment law, by which a minority of the population are allowed to elect a majority of the legislature. I need only to pronounce the name of Abraham Lincoln of Illinois—[loud cheers]—I have only to pronounce his name, to secure your profoundest attention.

February 27, 1860

William Dean Howells

Decades before he won fame as a pioneer in realistic fiction, Howells (1837–1920), then a young Ohio newspaper editor, was hired to write one of the earliest campaign biographies of the Republican presidential nominee, from which this selection is excerpted. Such books were crucial political tools in an era in which the candidates themselves did no personal campaigning, and Howells' pro-Lincoln effort was the most important of the genre. Yet when the publisher claimed that it had been "authorized" by the candidate, an "astounded" Lincoln protested: "I *authorize* nothing—will be *responsible* for *nothing*." Still, he later made more than a dozen handwritten corrections to the first edition, leaving the impression that everything he left uncorrected could be taken as factual. (The selection below contains some of these corrections.) Howells was rewarded in 1861 with an appointment as the American consul in Venice, but never met his most famous subject face-to-face, later admitting he "missed the greatest chance of my life."

FROM
Life of Abraham Lincoln

Chapter VI.

The period over which Lincoln's Congressional career extends, is one of the most interesting of our history.

Mr. Polk's favorite scheme of a war of glory and aggrandizement, had been in full course of unsatisfactory experiment. Our little army in Mexico had conquered a peace as rapidly as possible. The battles of Palo Alto, Reseca de la Palma, Monterey, Buena Vista, Cerro Gordo, and the rest, had been fought to the triumph and honor of the American arms. Everywhere, the people had regarded these successes with patriotic pride. They had felt a yet deeper interest in them because the volunteer system had taken the war out of the hands of mercenaries, and made it, in some sort, the crusade of Anglo-Saxon civilization and vigor against the semi-barbarism and effeteness of the Mexican and Spanish races.

Yet, notwithstanding the popular character thus given to the army, the war itself had not increased in popularity. People, in their sober second thought, rejected the specious creed, "Our country, right or wrong," and many looked forward earnestly and anxiously to a conclusion of hostilities.

The elections of Congressmen had taken place, and in the Thirtieth Congress, which assembled on the 6th of December, 1847, the people, by a majority of seven Whigs in the House, pronounced against the war, though hardly more than a year had elapsed since their Representatives, by a vote of one hundred and twenty-two to fourteen, had declared war to exist through the act of Mexico.

In those days, great men shaped the destinies of the nation. In the Senate sat ~~Clay~~, Calhoun, Benton, Webster, Corwin. In the House were Palfrey, Winthrop, Wilmot, Giddings, Adams. *Mr. Clay was not in the Senate at that time.*

The new member from Illinois, who had distinguished himself in 1844 as the friend of Clay and the enemy of Texan annexation, took his seat among these great men as a representative of the purest Whig principles; he was opposed to the war, as Corwin was; he was anti-slavery, as Clay was; he favored internal improvements, as all the great Whigs did.

And as Abraham Lincoln never sat astride of any fence, unless in his rail-splitting days; as water was never carried on both of his square shoulders; as his prayers to Heaven have never been made with reference to a compromise with other powers; so, throughout his Congressional career, you find him the bold advocate of the principles which he believed to be right. He never dodged a vote. He never minced matters with his opponents. He had not been fifteen days in the House when he made known what manner of man he was.

On the 22d of December he offered a series of resolutions,*

---

*The following are the resolutions, which it is judged best to print here in full:

"*Whereas*, the President of the United States, in his Message of making the most damaging inquiries of the President, as to the verity of certain statements in his messages of May and December. Mr. Polk had represented that the Mexicans were the first aggressors in the existing hostilities, by an invasion of American soil, and an effusion of American blood, after rejecting the friendly overtures made by this country.

Mr. Lincoln's resolutions demanded to know whether the spot on which American blood had been shed, was not Mexican, or at least, disputed territory; whether the Mexicans who shed this blood had not been driven from their homes by the approach of our arms; whether the Americans killed were not

---

May 11, 1846, has declared that 'the Mexican government refused to receive him, [the envoy of the United States,] or listen to his propositions, but, after a long-continued series of menaces, have at last invaded *our territory*, and shed the blood of our fellow-citizens on *our own soil*.'

"And again, in his Message of December 8, 1846, that 'we had ample cause of war against Mexico long before the breaking out of hostilities; but even then we forbore to take redress into our own hands, until Mexico basely became the aggressor, by invading *our soil* in hostile array, and shedding the blood of our citizens.'

"And yet again, in his Message of December 7, 1847, 'The Mexican government refused even to hear the terms of adjustment which he (our minister of peace) was authorized to propose, and finally, under wholly unjustifiable pretexts, involved the two countries in war, by invading the territory of the State of Texas, striking the first blow, and shedding the blood of our citizens on *our own soil*.'

"And whereas this House is desirous to obtain a full knowledge of all the facts which go to establish whether the particular spot on which the blood of our citizens was so shed, was, or was not, at that times, *our own soil*. Therefore, "*Resolved, by the House of Representatives*, That the President of the United States be respectfully requested to inform this House—

"1st. Whether the spot on which the blood of our citizens was shed, as in his memorial declared, was, or was not within the territory of Spain, at least, after the treaty of 1819, until the Mexican revolution.

"2d. Whether that spot is, or is not within the territory which was wrested from Spain by the revolutionary government of Mexico.

"3d. Whether that spot is, or is not within a settlement of people, which settlement has existed ever since long before the Texas Revolution, and until its inhabitants fled before the approach of the United States army.

armed soldiers sent into Mexican territory, by order of the President of the United States.

Parliamentary strategy defeated the proposed inquiry, the resolutions going over under the rules.

On the 12th of January, Mr. Lincoln made a speech* on the reference of different parts of the President's message. In this speech he justified a previous vote of sentiment, declaring that the war had been "unnecessarily and unconstitutionally commenced by the President of the United States." That vote had been pressed upon the opposition of the House, by the President's friends, in order to force an expression of opinion which should seem unjust to that functionary. Discussing this point, Mr. Lincoln coolly argued to conclusions the most injurious to the administration; showing that even though the President had attempted to construe a vote of supplies for the army into a vote applauding his official course, the opposition had remained

---

"4th. Whether that settlement is, or is not isolated from any and all other settlements of the Gulf and the Rio Grande on the south and west, and of wide uninhabited regions on the north and east.

"5th. Whether the people of that settlement, or a majority of them, have ever submitted themselves to the government or laws of Texas, or of the United States, of consent or of compulsion, either of accepting office or voting at elections, or paying taxes, or serving on juries, or having process served on them or in any other way.

"6th. Whether the people of that settlement did or did not flee at the approaching of the United States army, leaving unprotected their homes and their growing crops *before* the blood was shed, as in the message stated; and whether the first blood so shed was, or was not shed within the inclosure of one of the people who had thus fled from it.

"7th. Whether our *citizens* whose blood was shed, as in his message declared, were, or were not, at that time, armed officers and soldiers sent into that settlement by the military order of the President, through the Secretary of War.

"8th. Whether the military force of the United States was, or was not so sent into that settlement after General Taylor had more than once intimated to the War Department that, in his opinion, no such movement was necessary to the defense or protection of Texas."—*Congressional Globe*, vol. xviii, 1st session, 30th Congress, page 64.

Globe Appendix, vol. xix, page 93.

silent, until Mr. Polk's friends forced this matter upon them. Mr. Lincoln then took up the arguments of the President's message, one by one, and exposed their fallacy; and following the line of inquiry marked out by his resolutions of December, proved that the first American blood shed by Mexicans, was in retaliation for injuries received from us, and that hostilities had commenced on Mexican soil. The speech was characterized by all the excellences of Lincoln's later style—boldness, trenchant logic, and dry humor.

He next appears in the debates,* as briefly advocating a measure to give bounty lands to the surviving volunteer soldiers of the war of 1812, and arguing the propriety of permitting all soldiers holding land warrants, to locate their lands in different parcels, instead of requiring the location to be made in one body.

As Lincoln is a man who never talks unless he has something particular to say, (rare and inestimable virtue!) a period of some three months elapsed before he made another speech in Congress. On the 20th of June, 1848, the Civil and Diplomatic Appropriation bill being under consideration, he addressed to the House and the country, a clear and solid argument in favor of the improvement of rivers and harbors.† As a Western man, and as a man whom his own boating experiences had furnished with actual knowledge of the perils of snags and sawyers, he had always been in favor of a measure which commended itself at once to the heart and the pocket of the West. As the representative of a State with many hundred miles of Mississippi river, and vast river interests, he argued to show that an enlightened system of internal improvements, must be of national as well as local benefit.‡ The prevailing Democratic errors on this subject, as Mr. Lincoln succinctly stated them, were as follows:

"That internal improvements ought not to be made by the General Government:

"1. Because they would overwhelm the Treasury.

*Globe, vol. xviii, page 550.

†Globe Appendix, vol. xix, page 709.

‡This speech will be found printed at length in the appendix to the present biography.

"2. Because, while their *burdens* would be general, their *benefits* would be *local* and *partial*, involving an obnoxious inequality; and,

"3. Because they would be unconstitutional.

"4. Because the States may do enough by the levy and collection of tonnage duties; or, if not,

"5. That the Constitution may be amended.

"The sum," said Lincoln, "of these positions is, Do nothing at all, lest you do something wrong."

He then proceeded to assail each of the positions, demolishing them one after another. That admirable simplicity of diction which dashes straight at the heart of a subject, and that singular good sense which teaches a man to stop when he is done, are no less the characteristics of this effort than of all the other speeches of Mr. Lincoln.

Of a different manner, but illustrating a phase of his mind equally marked, is the speech he made in the House on the 27th of July,* when he discussed the political questions of the day with reference to the Presidential contest between General Taylor and Mr. Cass. It abounds in broad ridicule and broad drollery—the most effective and the most good-natured. Severe and sarcastic enough, when treating a false principle, it seems never to have been one of Lincoln's traits to indulge in bitter personalities. His only enemies, therefore, are those who hate his principles.

On the 21st of December, 1848, Mr. Gott, of New York, offered a resolution in the House, instructing the Committee on the District of Columbia to report a bill for the abolition of the slave-trade in that District. There were men in Congress then who had not forgotten the traditions of the Republican fathers, and who were indignant that slaves should be bought and sold in the shadow of the capital—that the slave-trader should make the political metropolis of the Republic a depot on the line of his abominable traffic.

As soon as the resolution of Mr. Gott was read, a motion was made to lay it on the table, which was lost by a vote of eighty-one to eighty-five. A hot struggle ensued; but the resolution was

Globe Appendix, vol. xix, page 1041.

adopted. An immediate attempt to reconsider proved ineffectual. The action upon reconsideration was postponed from day to day, until the 10th of January following, when Mr. Lincoln proposed that the committee should be instructed to report a bill forbidding the sale, beyond the District of Columbia, of any slave born within its limits, or the removal of slaves from the District, except such servants as were in attendance upon their masters temporarily residing at Washington; establishing an apprenticeship of twenty-one years for all slaves born within the District subsequent to the year 1850; providing for their emancipation at the expiration of the apprenticeship; authorizing the United States to buy and emancipate all slaves within the District, whose owners should desire to set them free in that manner; finally submitting the bill to a vote of the citizens of the District for approval.

It is well known that the efforts to abolish the slave-trade in the District of Columbia have resulted in nothing.* The wise, humane, and temperate measure of Mr. Lincoln shared the fate of all the rest.

Another great measure of the Congress in which Mr. Lincoln figured, was the Wilmot Proviso—now a favorite Republican measure—and so pervading, with its distinctive principle (opposition to slavery extension) the whole Republican soul, that, whether in or out of platforms, it remains the life and strength of the party. To this measure Mr. Lincoln was fully committed. Indeed, it is a peculiarity of this man, that he has *always* acted decidedly one way or the other. He thought the Mexican war wrong. He opposed it with his whole heart and strength. He thought the Wilmot Proviso right, and he says he "had the pleasure of voting for it, in one way or another, *about forty times.*"

---

*Mr. Lincoln's proposition had received the approval of Mayor Seaton, of Washington, who informed him that it would meet the approbation of the leading citizens. Afterward, Southern Congressmen visited the Mayor and persuaded him to withdraw the moral support given to the measure. When this had been done, the chief hope of success was destroyed, and the bill, of which Mr. Lincoln gave notice, was never introduced.

Mr. Lincoln was one of those who advocated the nomination of General Taylor, in the National Whig Convention of 1848. Returning to Illinois after the adjournment of Congress, he took the stump for his favorite candidate, and was active throughout that famous canvass. In 1849, he retired from Congress, firmly declining re-nomination, and resumed the practice of his profession.

The position which he maintained in the House of Representatives was eminently respectable. His name appears oftener in the ayes and noes, than in the debates; he spoke therefore with the more force and effect when he felt called upon to express his opinion.

The impression that his Congressional speeches give you, is the same left by all others that he has made. You feel that he has not argued to gain a point, but to show the truth; that it is not Lincoln he wishes to sustain, but Lincoln's principles.

Chapter VII.

Peace to the old Whig party, which is dead! When a man has ceased to live, we are cheaply magnanimous in the exaltation of his virtues, and we repair whatever wrong we did him when alive by remorselessly abusing every one who hints that he may have been an imperceptible trifle lower than the angels.

It is with such post-mortem greatness of soul that the leaders of the Democracy have cherished the memory of the Whig party, and gone about the stump, clad in moral sackcloth and craped hats.

If you will believe these stricken mourners, virtue went out with that lamented organization; and there is but one true man unhanged in America, and he is a stoutish giant, somewhat under the middle size.

In speaking, therefore, of the Whig party, you have first to avoid offense to the gentlemen who reviled its great men in their lifetime, and who have a fondness for throwing the honored dust of the past into the eyes of the present. Then, respect is due to the feelings of those Republicans who abandoned the

Whig party only after the last consolations of religion had been administered, and who still remember it with sincere regret.

The prejudices of another class of our friends must be treated with decent regard. Very many old Democrats in the Republican ranks are earnestly persuaded that in former times they were right in their opposition to the Whigs.

Yet one more variety of opinion must be consulted—the opinion that the Whig party had survived its usefulness, and that all which was good in it has now entered upon a higher and purer state of existence in the Republican organization.

Doubtless it would be better not to mention the Whig party at all. Unfortunately for the ends of strict prudence, the story of Abraham Lincoln's life involves allusion to it, since he was once a Whig, and became a Republican, and not a Democrat. But as every Republican is a code of by-laws unto himself—subject only to the Chicago platform—perhaps we may venture to reverently speak of the shade which still, it is said, revisits the glimpses of Boston; and to recount the events which preceded its becoming a shade.

So early as 1848 the dismemberment of the Whig party commenced. It had been distinguished by many of the characteristics of the Republican party, among which is the reserved right of each member of the organization to think and act for himself, on his own responsibility, as already intimated. Whenever its leaders deflected from the straight line of principle, their followers called them to account; and a persistence in the advocacy of measures repugnant to the individual sense of right, caused disaffection.

Many sincere and earnest men, who supported Henry Clay with ardor, ceased to be Whigs when General Taylor was nominated, because they conceived that his nomination was a departure from the Clay Whig principles of opposition to the Mexican war and the acquisition of slave territory.

This is not the place to pronounce upon the wisdom or justice of their course. Others, as sincere and earnest as they, supported General Taylor, and continued to act with the Whig party throughout the Fillmore administration.

The assimilation of the two great parties on the slavery

question in 1852, widened the distance between the Whigs and the Free Soilers, and the former were, in the opinion of the latter, demoralized before the election in which they suffered so total an overthrow, though they continued steadfast in their devotion to the Whig name until 1854, when the first organization of the Republicans took place, under the name of the Anti-Nebraska party.

The Whig Free Soilers were eager and glad to fraternize with their old friends; and all greeted with enthusiasm the vast accessions which the new party received from the men who had given spiritual vitality to the Democracy.

Those members of both the old parties, who were particularly sensible to the attractions of office, those whom no proslavery aggression could render superior to the luxury of a feeble or selfish acquiescence, also coalesced, and now constitute, with a few sincere political reminiscences, the Democracy of the North.

Up to the time of the repeal of the Missouri Compromise, Abraham Lincoln remained a Whig, both from conviction and affection.

In 1848, he had made speeches in favor of the election of General Taylor, in Maryland, in Massachusetts, and in Illinois. In his own Congressional district, where his word has always been platform enough, the success of his canvass was declared by a majority of fifteen hundred for Taylor.

After his retirement from Congress, he devoted himself, with greater earnestness than ever before, to the duties of his profession, and extended his business and repute. He did not reappear in the political arena until 1852, when his name was placed on the Scott electoral ticket.

In the canvass of that year, so disastrous to the Whig party throughout the country, Lincoln appeared several times before the people of his State as the advocate of Scott's claims for the Presidency. But the prospect was everywhere so disheartening, and in Illinois the cause was so utterly desperate, that the energies of the Whigs were paralyzed, and Lincoln did less in this Presidential struggle than any in which he had ever engaged.

During that lethargy which preceded the dissolution of his

party, he had almost relinquished political aspirations. Successful in his profession, happy in his home, secure in the affection of his neighbors, with books, competence, and leisure—ambition could not tempt him. It required the more thrilling voice of danger to freedom, to call the veteran of so many good fights into the field. The call was made.

It would be useless to recount here the history of the Missouri Compromise, and the circumstances attending the violation of that compact, though that history is properly a part of the biography of every public man in the country. Throughout the fierce contest which preceded the repeal of the Compromise, and the storm of indignation which followed that repeal, the whole story was brought vividly before the people, and can not now have faded from their recollection. Those to whom it is yet strange, will find it briefly and faithfully related in the speech of Abraham Lincoln, made in reply to Douglas, at Peoria, in October, 1854.*

*Printed in full in this volume. Douglas and Lincoln had previously met at Springfield, where the latter played David to the abbreviated Goliah of the former. The following spirited sketch of the scene is by the editor of the Chicago *Press and Tribune*, who was present:

"The affair came off on the fourth day of October, 1854. The State Fair had been in progress two days, and the capital was full of all manner of men. The Nebraska bill had been passed on the previous twenty-second of May. Mr. Douglas had returned to Illinois to meet an outraged constituency. He had made a fragmentary speech in Chicago, the people filling up each hiatus in a peculiar and good-humored way. He called the people a mob—they called him a rowdy. The 'mob' had the best of it, both then and at the election which succeeded. The notoriety of all these events had stirred up the politics of the State from bottom to top. Hundreds of politicians had met at Springfield, expecting a tournament of an unusual character—Douglas, Breese, Koerner, Lincoln, Trumbull, Matteson, Yates, Codding, John Calhoun, (of the order of the candle-box,) John M. Palmer, the whole house of the McConnells, Singleton, (known to fame in the Mormon war,) Thomas L. Harris, and a host of others. Several speeches were made before, and several after, the passage between Lincoln and Douglas, but that was justly held to be *the* event of the season.

"We do not remember whether a challenge to debate passed between the friends of the speakers or not, but there was a perfectly amicable

The people were glad to hear the voice of their favorite once more, and Lincoln's canvass of Illinois was most triumphant. The legislative elections were held, and those who denounced the repeal of the Missouri Compromise, were found to be in the majority.

———————————

understanding between Lincoln and Douglas, that the former should speak two or three hours, and the latter reply in just as little or as much time as he chose. Mr. Lincoln took the stand at two o'clock—a large crowd in attendance, and Mr. Douglas seated on a small platform in front of the desk. The first half hour of Mr. Lincoln's speech was taken up with compliments to his distinguished friend Judge Douglas, and dry allusions to the political events of the past few years. His distinguished friend, Judge Douglas, had taken his seat, as solemn as the Cock-Lane ghost, evidently with the design of not moving a muscle till it came his turn to speak. The laughter provoked by Lincoln's exordium, however, soon began to make him uneasy; and when Mr. L. arrived at his (Douglas's) speech, pronouncing the Missouri Compromise 'a sacred thing, which no ruthless hand would ever be reckless enough to disturb,' he opened his lips far enough to remark, 'A first-rate speech!' This was the beginning of an amusing colloquy.

"'Yes,' continued Mr. Lincoln, 'so affectionate was my friend's regard for this Compromise line, that when Texas was admitted into the Union, and it was found that a strip extended north of 36° 30′, he actually introduced a bill extending the line and prohibiting slavery in the northern edge of the new State.'

"'And you voted against the bill,' said Douglas.

"'Precisely so,' replied Lincoln; 'I was in favor of running the line *a great deal further south*.'

"'About this time,' the speaker continued, 'my distinguished friend introduced me to a particular friend of his, one David Wilmot, of Pennsylvania.' [Laughter.]

"'I thought,' said Douglas, 'you would find him congenial company.'

"'So I did,' replied Lincoln. 'I had the pleasure of voting for his proviso, in one way and another, about forty times. It was a *Democratic* measure then, I believe. At any rate, General Cass scolded honest John Davis, of Massachasetts, soundly, for talking away the last hours of the session, so that he (Cass) couldn't crowd it through. *A propos* of General Cass: if I am not greatly mistaken, he has a prior claim to my distinguished friend, to the authorship of Popular Sovereignty. The old general has an infirmity for writing letters. Shortly after the scolding he gave John Davis, he wrote his Nicholson letter'—

The election of a United States Senator took place the following winter, and General Shields was superseded. This gentleman, who, listening to the seductive persuasions of his voiceful colleague, was said to have voted for the repeal of the Compromise against his own convictions, was a candidate for re-election. On the part of the opposition majority there were

---

"Douglas (solemnly)—'God Almighty placed man on the earth, and told him to choose between good and evil. That was the origin of the Nebraska bill!'

"Lincoln—'Well, the priority of invention being settled, let us award all credit to Judge Douglas for being the first to discover it.'

"It would be impossible, in these limits, to give an idea of the strength of Mr. Lincoln's argument. We deemed it by far the ablest effort of the campaign, from whatever source. The occasion was a great one, and the speaker was every way equal to it. The effect produced on the listeners was magnetic. No one who was present will ever forget the power and vehemence of the following passage:

"My distinguished friend says it is an insult to the emigrants to Kansas and Nebraska to suppose they are not able to govern themselves. We must not slur over an argument of this kind because it happens to tickle the ear. It must be met and answered. I admit that the emigrant to Kansas and Nebraska is competent to govern *himself*, but,' the speaker rising to his full hight, '*I deny his right to govern any other person* WITHOUT THAT PERSON'S CONSENT.' The applause which followed this triumphant refutation of a cunning falsehood, was but an earnest of the victory at the polls which followed just one month from that day.

"When Mr. Lincoln had concluded, Mr. Douglas strode hastily to the stand. As usual, he employed ten minutes in telling how grossly he had been abused. Recollecting himself, he added, 'though in a perfectly courteous manner'—abused in a perfectly courteous manner! He then devoted half an hour to showing that it was indispensably necessary to California emigrants, Santa Fè traders and others, to have organic acts provided for the Territories of Kansas and Nebraska—that being precisely the point which nobody disputed. Having established this premise to his satisfaction, Mr. Douglas launched forth into an argument wholly apart from the positions taken by Mr. Lincoln. He had about half finished at six o'clock, when an adjournment to tea was effected. The speaker insisted strenuously upon his right to resume in the evening, but we believe the second part of that speech has not been delivered to this day."

two candidates, Lincoln and Trumbull. The great body of the opposition voted steadily for the former on several ballots; but some Democrats who had been elected on the anti-Nebraska issue, continued to cast their votes for Trumbull.

Lincoln feared that this dissension might result in the election of a less positive man than Trumbull, and with his usual unselfishness, appealed to his friends to vote for Trumbull, adjuring them by their friendship to him to make this concession of individual preference. His appeal was not in vain, and Trumbull was elected Senator.

This, however, was not the ~~first~~ sacrifice which he made to conciliation and union. The ~~anti-Nebraska~~ party of ~~the same year offered~~ him the nomination for Governor; but in the existing state of organizations, he declined for the sake of the cause *only Republicans 1856 probably would have given.* which all had espoused. It occurs in politics that a force which suddenly rallies about a principle, may be disheartened by the choice of a leader whom recent animosities have rendered obnoxious. Lincoln, as a Whig, had been one of the most decided and powerful opponents of Democracy in Illinois. The period since his opposition to many Democratic members of the anti-Nebraska party had ceased was very brief, and old feelings of antagonism had not died away. He perceived that the advancement of himself might impede the advancement of his principles. Doubtless, he could be elected Governor of Illinois, but the victory which bore him into office might be less brilliant and useful than that which could be achieved under another. He therefore withdrew his name, and threw his influence in favor of Governor Bissell, who had been a Democrat, and who was triumphantly elected.

It must be remembered that the Republican party ~~had, as yet, no definite existence~~ in Illinois. The anti-*was just being formed* Nebraska party was the temporary name of the Whigs, Democrats, and Free Soilers, who opposed the repeal of the Missouri Compromise. It is true that a Mass State Convention, with a view to forming a permanent organization, had been held at Springfield, in October; but many anti-Nebraska men, who still adhered to old names, had not taken part in it. The following resolutions were adopted at this Convention:

"1. *Resolved*, That we believe this truth to be self-evident, that when parties become subversive of the ends for which they are established, or incapable of restoring the Government to the true principles of the Constitution, it is the right and duty of the people to dissolve the political bands by which they may have been connected therewith, and to orga- nize new parties upon such principles and with such views as the circumstances and exigencies of the nation may demand.

Not the resolutions of that convention. See debates at Ottawa, Freeport & Galesburg.

"2. *Resolved*, That the times imperatively demand the reorganization of parties, and, repudiating all previous party attachments, names, and predilections, we unite ourselves together in defense of the liberty and Consti- tution of the country, and will hereafter co-operate as the Republican party, pledged to the accomplishment of the fol- lowing purposes: To bring the administration of the Govern- ment back to the control of first principles; to restore Ne- braska and Kansas to the position of free territories; that, as the Constitution of the United States vests in the States, and not in Congress, the power to legislate for the extradition of fugitives from labor, to repeal and entirely abrogate the Fugi- tive Slave law; to restrict slavery to those states in which it exists; to prohibit the admission of any more slave states into the Union; to abolish slavery in the District of Columbia; to exclude slavery from all the territories over which the Gen- eral Government has exclusive jurisdiction; and to resist the acquirement of any more territories unless the practice of slavery therein forever shall have been prohibited.

"3. *Resolved*, That in furtherance of these principles we will use such Constitutional and lawful means as shall seem best adapted to their accomplishment, and that we will sup- port no man for office, under the General or State Govern- ment, who is not positively and fully committed to the sup- port of these principles, and whose personal character and conduct is not a guarantee that he is reliable, and who shall not have abjured old party allegiance and ties."

In the course of the first debate between Douglas and

Lincoln, which was held at Ottawa, in August, 1858, Douglas read these resolutions, declaring that Lincoln had participated in the Convention, and assisted in their adoption. Lincoln met this earliest of a series of misrepresentations with prompt denial, and proved that he was not a member of the Convention.

The actual Republican party of Illinois, dates its formation from a period somewhat later; and Lincoln was one of the first members of the present organization. Not so ultra, probably, as the indignant men who framed the resolutions quoted, he was quite as firmly opposed to slavery. In the speech from which he read, in reply to the charge of Douglas, he gives with Wesleyan point, the reason why indifference to slavery should be abhorred:

"This *declared* indifference, but, as I must think, covert *real* zeal for the spread of slavery, I can not but hate. I hate it because of the monstrous injustice of slavery itself. I hate it because it deprives our republican example of its just influence in the world—enables the enemies of free institutions, with plausibility, to taunt us as hypocrites—causes the real friends of freedom to doubt our sincerity, and especially because it forces so many really good men among ourselves into an open war with the very fundamental principles of civil liberty—criticising the Declaration of Independence, and insisting that there is no right principle of action but *self-interest*."

1860

Henry Villard

A Bavarian-born journalist, Villard (1835–1900) reported on the 1858 Lincoln-Douglas Senate race for the New York *Staats Zeitung* and after Lincoln's election in 1860 returned to Springfield as correspondent for the pro-Democratic *New York Herald*. In a series of frank, often critical, but increasingly favorable reports, he created a rich and ultimately endearing portrait of Lincoln's final months at home during the fall and winter of 1860–61. Villard then traveled east with Lincoln en route to the inauguration but stopped in New York after tiring of the hoopla surrounding the President-elect—thus missing the most dramatic and controversial story of the journey, Lincoln's clandestine nighttime transit through hostile Baltimore. He later married the daughter of abolitionist William Lloyd Garrison, grew wealthy in the western railroad business, and in 1881 bought William Cullen Bryant's old paper, the *New York Evening Post*.

FROM
Lincoln on the Eve of '61

Small as the number of attendants has been for some days—not over 160 per day—the receptions of the President are nevertheless highly interesting and worthy of detailed notice. They are held daily from ten A.M. to 12 Noon and from three P.M. to half-past five P.M. in the Governor's room at the State House, which has been for some time given up to the wants of Mr. Lincoln.

The appointed hour having arrived, the crowd moved up stairs into the second storey, in the southeast corner of which the reception room is located. Passing through a rather dark sort of doorway, the clear voice and often ringing laughter of the President usually guide them to the right door. The boldest of the party having knocked, a ready "Come in" invites them to enter. On opening the door, the tall, lean form of "Old Abe" directly confronts the leader of the party. Seizing the latter's

hand with a hearty shake, Lincoln leads him in, and bids the rest
to follow suit with an encouraging "Get in, all of you." The
whole party being in, he will ask for their names, and then immediately start a running conversation. Although he is naturally
more listened to than talked to, he does not allow a pause to
become protracted. He is never at a loss as to the subjects that
please the different classes of visitors and there is a certain
quaintness and originality about all he has to say, so that one
cannot help feeling interested. His "talk" is not brilliant. His
phrases are not ceremoniously set, but pervaded with a humor-
ousness and, at times, with a grotesque joviality, that will always
please. I think it would be hard to find one who tells better
jokes, enjoys them better and laughs oftener than Abraham
Lincoln.

The room of the Governor of the State of Illinois cannot be
said to indicate the vast territorial extent of that commonwealth.
It is altogether inadequate for the accommodation of Mr. Lincoln's visitors. Twenty persons will not find standing room in it,
and the simultaneous presence of a dozen only will cause inconvenience. The room is furnished with a sofa, half-a-dozen arm-
chairs, a table and a desk, the latter being assigned to the private
secretary, who is always present during visiting hours. These,
together with countless letters and files of newspapers, and quite
an assortment of odd presents, constitute the only adornments
of the apartment. No restrictions, whatever, being exercised as
to visitors, the crowd, that daily waits on the President, is always
of a motley description. Everybody who lives in this vicinity or
passes through this place, goes to take a look at "Old Abe."
Muddy boots and hickory shirts are just as frequent as broadcloth, fine linen, etc. The ladies, however, are usually dressed up
in their very best, although they cannot hope to make an impression on old married Lincoln. Offensively democratic exhi-
bitions of free manners occur every once in a while. Churlish
fellows will obtrude themselves with their hats on, lighted cigars
and their pantaloons tucked into their boots. Dropping into
chairs they sit puffing away and trying to gorgonize the President with their silent stares, until their boorish curiosity is fully
satisfied. Formal presentations are dispensed with in most cases.

Nearly everyone finds his own way in and introduces himself. Sometimes half a dozen rustics rush in, break their way through other visitors up to the object of their search and after calling their names and touching the Presidential fingers, back out again.

November 19

His old friends, who have been used to a great indifference as to the "outer man" on his part, say that "Abe is putting on airs." By this, they refer to the fact that he is now wearing a brand new hat and suit and that he has commenced cultivating the—with him—unusual adornment of whiskers.

But, these late outward embellishments to the contrary notwithstanding, a Broadway tailor would probably feel no more tempted to consider Lincoln as coming up to his artistic requirements of a model man than Peter Cooper. The angularity of the Presidential form, and its habitual *laissez aller*, preclude a like possibility. We venture to say that Fifth Avenue snobs, if unaware who he was, would be horrified at walking across the street with him. And yet, there is something about the man that makes one at once forget these exterior short-comings and feel attracted toward him.

The President-elect being the very embodiment of good humor, it seems as though from this fact, much that happens about him partakes of a comical character. Some days ago, a tall Missourian marched into the reception room. Seeing the tall form of the President rise before him, and not knowing what to say, he ejaculated "I reckon one is about as big as the other." "Let us measure" was the instantaneous reply; and the Missourian was actually placed against the wall, told "to be honest, and stand flat on his heels," and his height measured with a stick.

Mr. Lincoln's personal appearance is the subject of daily remark among those who have known him formerly. Always cadaverous, his aspect is now almost ghostly. His position is wearing him terribly. Letters threatening his life are daily received from the South, occasionally, also, a note of warning from some Southerner who does not like his principles, but would regret violence. But these trouble him little compared with the apprehended difficulty of conciliating the South without destroying the integrity of his own party. The present aspect of the country, I think, augurs one of the most difficult terms which any President has yet been called to weather; and I doubt Mr. Lincoln's capacity for the task of bringing light and peace out of the chaos that will surround him. A man of good heart and good intention, he is not firm. The times demand a Jackson.

November 20

Today's work was the hardest "Old Abe" did since his election. He had hardly appeared at the State House when he was beset by an eager crowd that had been on the lookout for him ever since daylight. They gave him no time to occupy himself the usual two hours previous to the morning receptions with his private secretary, but clung to his coat tails with an obstinacy worthy of a better cause. He had to admit them at once into his apartment, and then submit for nearly ten long, weary hours to the importunities of a steady tide of callers. Limited as the space required by the lean proportions of the President is, he found it a most difficult task to find sufficient standing room. By constant entreaties to make room he maintained himself in close proximity to the door, which position he had chosen with a view to facilitating the inevitable hand shakings. But he found to his intense bodily inconvenience that this deference to the comfort of his callers was not the most practical plan he might have adopted. The curious defiled past him, after squeezing the Presidential fingers, into the room, and settled either on the sofa or chairs or remained standing for protracted observations. Only after having stared with open mouths to their heart's content—many employed hours in that agreeable pastime—would they move out of the room and enable others to gain admittance. A tight jam prevailed, therefore, all day around the President, who found himself frequently "driven to the wall."

Many Sangamon country youths brought their sweethearts along and presented them to "Old Abe," who was at times surrounded by robust beauty. Place seekers were in despair all day. In vain, they tried to gain the Presidential ear. It was monopolized from early morning until late in the evening by the "people."

Although "Old Abe" had been nearly tortured to death during the daytime, the people gave him no rest after dark; even at his private residence, at half-past six, he was once more crowded upon in his parlor, and had to undergo another agony of presentations. The whole lower story of the building was filled all the evening with well dressed ladies and gentlemen, whose comfort was, however, greatly diminished by the constant influx of an ill-mannered populace. Mrs. Lincoln had to endure as many importunities as the head of the family. She often had to hear callers ask each other, "Is that the old woman?" The President's offspring, however, seemed to enjoy the fuss hugely. The cheering outside was always responded to by their juvenile yells.

As predicted by me some days ago, the Republican jollification of today was, as to display of enthusiasm and number of attendance, a comparative failure, although held at the capital of the State and the home of the President-elect. The American people are known not to be able to foster a protracted excitement on one particular subject. Having been treated *ad nauseam* to wide awake processions, meetings, speeches, fireworks, etc., during the campaign, they are now sick of all such empty demonstrations, and wish to see no more of them for some time. The aggregate number of attendants from abroad did not exceed two thousand, and that of actual participants fell below five hundred.

November 1860

Artemus Ward

An itinerant newspaper printer born in Maine, Charles Farrar Browne (1834–1867) introduced his "Artemus Ward" alter ego—a Yankee writer who composed humorous dispatches in dialect—in the *Cleveland Plain Dealer* in 1858. By the time he moved to New York during the 1860 campaign year, Artemus Ward had all but eclipsed his creator, becoming one of the country's most popular satirists, first in *Vanity Fair* and then in wildly popular books. Lincoln adored Ward and his rival contemporary humorists "Orpheus C. Kerr" (a play on "office seeker") and "Petroleum V. Nasby," and like many Americans, found their writings restorative during the most anxious days of the Civil War. His relentlessly humorless Secretary of the Treasury, Salmon P. Chase, remembered that Lincoln opened the historic Cabinet meeting of September 22, 1862, at which the President announced his decision to issue the Emancipation Proclamation, by reading a chapter from Artemus Ward's new book, "which he thought very funny. Read it, and seemed to enjoy it very much." Only then did the President assume a "graver tone" and announce his momentous plans to his Cabinet officers. Lincoln undoubtedly also read this pre-inaugural depiction of a backwoods President-elect besieged by job-seekers.

Artemus Ward
On His Visit to Abe Lincoln

I hiv no politics. Nary a one. I'm not in the bisniss. If I was I spose I should holler versiffrusly in the streets at nite and go home to Betsey Jane smellin of coal ile and gin, in the mornin. I should go to the Poles arly. I should stay there all day. I should see to it that my nabers was thar. I should git carriges to take the kripples, the infirm and the indignant thar. I should be on guard agin frauds and sich. I should be on the look out for the infamus lise of the enemy, got up jes be4 elecshun for perlitical effeck. When all was over and my candydate was elected, I should move heving & arth—so to speak—until I got orifice, which if I didn't git a orifice I should turn round & abooze the Administration with all my mite and maine. But I'm not in the bisniss. I'm in a far more respectful bisniss nor whot pollertics is. I wouldn't giv two cents to be a Congresser. The wuss insult I ever received was when sertin citizens of Baldinsville axed me to run fur the Legislater. Sez I, "My frends, dostest think I'd stoop to that there?" They turned as white as a sheet. I spoke in my most orfullest tones, & they knowd *I* wasn't to be trifled with. They slunked out of site to onct.

There4, hevin no politics, I made bold to visit Old Abe at his humstid in Springfield. I found the old feller in his parler, surrounded by a perfeck swarm of orifice seekers. Knowin he had been capting of a flat boat on the roarin Mississippy I thought I'd address him in sailor lingo, so sez I "Old Abe, ahoy! Let out yer main-suls, reef hum the forecastle & throw yer jib-poop overboard! Shiver my timbers, my harty!" [N. B. This is ginuine mariner langwidge. I know, becawz I've seen sailor plays acted out by them New York theater fellers.) Old Abe lookt up quite cross & sez, "Send in yer petition by & by. I cant possibly look at it now. Indeed. I can't. It's onpossible, sir!"

"Mr. Linkin, who do you spect I air?" sed I.

"A orifice-seeker, to be sure?" sed he.

"Wall, sir," sed I, "you's never more mistaken in your life. You hain't gut a orifiss I'd take under no circumstances. I'm A. Ward. Wax figgers is my perfeshun. I'm the father of Twins, and they look like me—*both of them*. I cum to pay a frendly visit to the President eleck of the United States. If so be you wants to see me say so—if not, say so, & I'm orf like a jug handle."

"Mr. Ward, sit down. I am glad to see you, Sir."

"Repose in Abraham's Buzzum!" sed one of the orifice seekers, his idee bein to git orf a goak at my expence.

"Wall," sez I, "ef all you fellers repose in that there Buzzum thare'll be mity poor nussin for sum of you!" whereupon Old Abe buttoned his weskit clear up and blusht like a maiding of sweet 16. Jest at this pint of the conversation another swarm of orifice seekers arrove & cum pilin into the parler. Sum wanted post orifices, sum wanted collectorships, sum wanted furrin missions, and all wanted sumthin. I thought Old Abe would go crazy. He hadn't more than had time to shake hands with 'em, before another tremenjis crowd cum porein onto his premises. His house and dooryard was now perfeckly overflowed with orifice seekers, all clameruss for a immejit interview with Old ABE. One man from Ohio, who had about seven inches of corn whiskey into him, mistook me fur Old ABE and addresst me as "The Pra-hayrie Flower of the West!" Thinks I *you* want a offis putty bad. Another man with a goldheded cane and a red nose told Old ABE he was "a seckind WASHINGTON & the Pride of the Boundliss West!"

Sez I, "Square, you wouldn't take a small post-offis if you could git it, would you?"

Sez he, "a patrit is abuv them things, sir!"

"There's a putty big crop of patrits this season, aint there Square?" sez I, when *another* crowd of offis seekers pored in. The house, door-yard, barn & woodshed was now all full, and when *another* crowd cum I told 'em not to go away for want of room as the hog-pen was still empty. One patrit from a small town in Mishygan went up on top the house, got into the chimney and slid down into the parler where Old ABE was endeverin to keep the hungry pack of offiss-seekers from chawin him up alive without benefit of clergy. The minit he reached the fire place he jumpt up, brusht the soot out of his eyes, and yelled: "Don't make eny pintment at the Spunkville postoffice till you've read my papers. All the respectful men in our town is signers to that there dockyment!"

"Good God!" cride Old ABE, "they cum upon me from the skize—down the chimneys, and from the bowels of the yearth!" He hadn't more'n got them words out of his delikit mouth before two fat offiss-seekers from Wisconsin, in endeverin to crawl atween his legs for the purpuss of applyin for the tollgate-ship at Milwawky, upsot the President eleck & he would hev gone sprawlin into the fire-place if I hadn't caught him in these arms. But I hadn't more'n stood him up strate, before another man cum crashin down the chimney, his head strikin me vilently agin the inards and prostratin my voluptoous form onto the floor. "Mr. LINKIN," shoutid the infatooated being, "my papers is signed by every clergyman in our town, and likewise the skoolmaster!"

Sez I, "you egrejis ass," gittin up & brushin the dust from my eyes, "I'll sign your papers with this bunch of bones, if you don't be a little more keerful how you make my bread baskit a depot in the futer. How do you like that air perfumery?" sez I, shuving my fist under his nose. "Them's the kind of papers I'll giv you! Them's the papers *you* want?"

"But I workt hard for the ticket; I toiled night and day! The patrit should be rewarded!"

"Virtoo," sed I, holdin' the infatooated man by the coat-collar, "virtoo, sir, is its own reward. Look at me!" He did look at me, and qualed be4 my gase. "The fact is," I continued, lookin' round upon the hungry crowd, "there is scacely a offiss for every ile lamp carrid round durin' this campane. I wish thare was. I wish thare was furrin missions to be filled on varis lonely Islands where eppydemics rage incessantly, and if I was in Old Abe's place I'd send every mother's son of you to them. What air you here for?" I continnered, warmin up considerable, "can't you giv Abe a minit's peace? Don't you see he's worrid most to death! Go home, you miserable men, go home & till the sile! Go to peddlin tinware—go to choppin wood—go to bilin' sope —stuff sassengers—black boots—git a clerkship on sum respect-able manure cart—go round as original Swiss Bell Ringers— becum 'origenal and only' Campbell Minstrels—go to lecturin at 50 dollars a nite—imbark in the peanut bizniss—*write for the Ledger*—saw off your legs and go round givin concerts, with techin appeals to a charitable public, printed on your handbills— anything for a honest livin', but don't come round here drivin old Abe crazy by your outrajus cuttings up! Go home. Stand not upon the order of your goin', but go to onct! If in five minits from this time," sez I, pullin' out my new sixteen dollar huntin cased watch, and brandishin' it before their eyes, "Ef in five minits from this time a single sole of you remains on these here premises, I'll go out to my cage near by, and let my Boy Con-structor loose! & if he gits amung you, you'll think Old Solfer-ino has cum again and no mistake!" You ought to hev seen them scamper, Mr. Fair. They run orf as tho Satun hisself was arter them with a red hot ten pronged pitchfork. In five minits the premises was clear.

"How kin I ever repay you, Mr. WARD, for your kindness?" sed Old ABE advancin and shakin me warmly by the hand. "How kin I ever repay you, sir?"

"By givin' the whole country a good, sound administration. By poerin' ile upon the troubled waters, North and South! By pursooin' a patriotic, firm, and just course, and then if any State wants to secede, let 'em Sesesh!"

"How 'bout my Cabnit Ministre, WARD?" sed ABE.

"Fill it up with Showmen, sir! Showmen is devoid of politics. They hain't got a darn principle! They know how to cater to the public. They know what the public wants, North & South. Showmen, sir, is honest men. Ef you doubt their literary ability, look at their posters, and see small bills! Ef you want a Cabinit as is a Cabinit fill it up with showmen, but don't call on me. The moral wax figger perfeshun mustn't be permitted to go down while there's a drop of blood in these vains! A. LINKIN, I wish you well! Ef POWERS or WALCUTT wus to pick out a model for a beautiful man, I scacely think they'd sculp you; but ef you do the fair thing by your country you'll make as putty a angel as any of us, or any other man! A. LINKIN, use the talents which Nature has put into you judishusly and firmly, and all will be well! A. LINKIN, adoo!"

He shook me cordyully by the hand—we exchanged picters, so we could gaze upon each others' liniments when far away from one another—he at the hellum of the ship of State, and I at the hellum of the show bizniss—admittance only 15 cents.

December 8, 1860

Ralph Waldo Emerson

Emerson (1803–1882) probably met Lincoln for the first time in 1853, when the poet-philosopher traveled to Springfield, Illinois, to deliver lectures on "The Anglo-Saxon" and "Power." Lincoln's friend Orville H. Browning praised Emerson's language as "chaste, strong and vigorous," but accustomed to western-style gesticulation, added: "his action nothing." A frequent attendee at such events, Lincoln likely heard Emerson's talks at the Hall of Representatives in the State House—where five years later he would deliver his "House Divided" address—and may have joined a post-event supper in the speaker's honor at a local church. The two men met again in the White House on February 2, 1862, when Emerson offered advice on the vexing case of convicted slave trader Nathaniel Gordon. Lincoln ordered a stay of execution, but when it lapsed allowed Gordon to be executed later in the month. Emerson, a dedicated abolitionist who was not always favorable toward Lincoln, wrote these observations at the time.

FROM
The Journals

Visit to Washington.

31 January, 1862.

At Washington, 31 January, 1 Feb, 2d, & 3d, saw Sumner, who on the 2d, carried me to Mr Chase, Mr Bates, Mr Stanton, Mr Welles, Mr Seward, Lord Lyons, and President Lincoln. The President impressed me more favorably than I had hoped. A frank, sincere, well-meaning man, with a lawyer's habit of mind, good clear statement of his fact, correct enough, not vulgar, as described; but with a sort of boyish cheerfulness, or that kind of sincerity & jolly good meaning that our class meetings on Commencement Days show, in telling our old stories over. When he has made his remark, he looks up at you with great satisfaction, & shows all his white teeth, & laughs. He argued to Sumner the whole case of Gordon, the slave-trader, point by point, and added that he was not quite satisfied yet, & meant to refresh his memory by looking again at the evidence.

All this showed a fidelity & conscientiousness very honorable to him.

When I was introduced to him, he said, "O Mr Emerson, I once heard you say in a lecture, that a Kentuckian seems to say by his air & manners, *"Here am I; if you don't like me, the worse for you."*

————

Mr S. said, "Will you go & call on the President? I usually call on him at this hour." Of course, I was glad to go.

We found in the President's chamber his two little sons,— boys of 7 & 8 years perhaps,—whom the barber was dressing & "whiskeying their hair," as he said, not much to the apparent contentment of the boys, when the cologne got into their eyes. The eldest boy immediately told Mr Seward, "he could not guess what they had got." Mr Seward "bet a quarter of a dollar that he could.—Was it a rabbit? was it a bird? was it a pig?" he guessed always wrong, & *paid his quarter* to the youngest, before the eldest declared it was a rabbit. But he sent away the mulatto to find the President, & the boys disappeared. The President came, and Mr Seward said, "You have not been to Church to-day." "No," he said, "and, if he must make a frank confession, he had been reading for the first time Mr Sumner's speech (on the Trent affair)." Something was said of newspapers, & of the story that appeared in the journals, of some one who selected all the articles which Marcy should read, &c, &c,

The President incidentally remarked, that for the N.Y. Herald, he certainly ought to be much obliged to it for the part it had taken for the Govt. in the Mason & Slidell business. Then Seward said somewhat to explain the apparent steady malignity of the "London Times." It was all an affair of the great interests of markets. The great capitalists had got this or that stock: as soon as anything happens that affects their value, this value must be made real, and the "Times" must say just what is required to sell those values. &c. &c. The Government had little or no voice in the matter. "But what news today?" "Mr Fox has sent none. Send for Mr Fox." The servant could not find Mr Fox.

The President said, he had the most satisfactory communication from Lord Lyons; also had been notified by him, that he had received the order of the Bath, & he, the President, had received two communications from the French minister. France, on the moment of hearing the surrender of the prisoners, had ordered a message of gratification to be sent, without waiting to read the grounds: then, when the dispatches had been read, had hastened to send a fresh message of thanks & gratulation. Spain also had sent a message of the same kind. He was glad of this that Spain had done. For he knew, that, though Cuba sympathized with secession, Spain's interest lay the other way. Spain knew that the Secessionists wished to conquer Cuba.

Mr Seward told the President somewhat of Dr Pyne's sermon, & the President said, he intended to show his respect for him some time by going to hear him.

We left the President, & returned to Mr Seward's house.

February 1862

Nathaniel Hawthorne

Hawthorne (1804–1864) published the novels and stories that brought him fame in the decade before the Civil War, and then he spent seven years in Europe before returning to the United States in 1860. He visited the White House with a delegation in 1862 and wrote home proudly on March 16: "I have shaken hands with Uncle Abe." Hawthorne, a New England Democrat and longtime friend of former President Franklin Pierce, recounted his trip to the capital and to the Union lines in northern Virginia in a lengthy article for *Atlantic Monthly*. When James Fields, the magazine's editor, objected to his candid personal description of the President, Hawthorne omitted the passage rather than alter it, protesting to Fields that he thought it "the only part of the article really worth publishing," and adding: "Upon my honor, it seems to me to have a historical value— but let it go." The suppressed section is restored in the excerpt printed below; it begins "and in lounged a tall, loose-jointed figure . . ." (page 33.26) and ends ". . . on the immaculate page of the Atlantic" (page 36.11). In the 1862 magazine version, the footnote on page 37 appeared where the offending passage had been removed, with the beginning of the note changed to: "We are compelled to omit two or three pages, in which the author describes the interview, and gives his idea of the personal appearance and deportment of the President. The sketch appears to have been written . . ." (All of the footnotes in the article were written by Hawthorne himself as a form of ironic commentary.)

FROM
Chiefly About War-Matters by a Peaceable Man

Of course, there was one other personage, in the class of statesmen, whom I should have been truly mortified to leave Washington without seeing; since (temporarily, at least, and by force of circumstances) he was the man of men. But a private grief had built up a barrier about him, impeding the customary free intercourse of Americans with their chief-magistrate; so that I might have come away without a glimpse of his very remarkable physiognomy, save for a semi-official opportunity of which I was glad to take advantage. The fact is, we were invited to annex ourselves, as supernumeraries, to a deputation that was about to wait upon the President, from a Massachusetts whip-factory, with a present of a splendid whip.

Our immediate party consisted only of four or five, (including Major Ben Perley Poore, with his note-book and pencil,) but we were joined by several other persons, who seemed to have been lounging about the precincts of the White House, under the spacious porch, or within the hall, and who swarmed in with us to take the chances of a presentation. Nine o'clock had been appointed as the time for receiving the deputation, and we were punctual to the moment, but not so the President, who sent us word that he was eating his breakfast, and would come as soon as he could. His appetite, we were glad to think, must have been a pretty fair one; for we waited about half-an-hour, in one of the ante-chambers, and then were ushered into a reception-room, in one corner of which sat the Secretaries of War and of the Treasury, expecting, like ourselves, the termination of the presidential breakfast. During this interval, there were several new additions to our groupe, one or two of whom were in a working-garb; so that we formed a very miscellaneous collection of people, mostly unknown to each other, and without any common sponsor, but all with an equal right to look our head-servant in the face. By-and-by, there was a little stir on the staircase and in the passage-way; and in lounged a tall, loose-jointed figure, of an exaggerated Yankee port and demeanor, whom, (as being about the homeliest man I ever saw, yet by no means repulsive or disagreeable,) it was impossible not to recognize as Uncle Abe.

Unquestionably, Western man though he be, and Kentuckian by birth, President Lincoln is the essential representative of all Yankees, and the veritable specimen, physically, of what the world seems determined to regard as our characteristic qualities. It is the strangest, and yet the fittest thing in the jumble of human vicissitudes, that he, out of so many millions, unlooked-for, unselected by any intelligible process that could be based upon his genuine qualities, unknown to those who chose him, and unsuspected of what endowments may adapt him for his tremendous responsibility, should have found the way open for him to fling his lank personality into the chair of state—where, I presume, it was his first impulse to throw his legs on the council-table, and tell the cabinet-ministers a story. There is no describing his lengthy awkwardness, nor the uncouthness of his movement; and yet it seemed as if I had been in the habit of seeing him daily, and had shaken hands with him a thousand times in some village-street; so true was he to the aspect of the pattern American, though with a certain extravagance which, possibly, I exaggerated still further by the delighted eagerness with which I took it in. If put to guess his calling and livelihood, I should have taken him for a country-schoolmaster, as soon as anything else. He was dressed in a rusty black frock-coat and pantaloons, unbrushed, and worn so faithfully that the suit had adapted itself to the curves and angularities of his figure, and had grown to be an outer skin of the man. He had shabby slippers on his feet. His hair was black, still unmixed with gray, stiff, somewhat bushy, and had apparently been acquainted with neither brush nor comb, that morning, after the disarrangement of the pillow; and as to a night-cap, Uncle Abe probably knows nothing of such effeminacies. His complexion is dark and sallow, betokening, I fear, an insalubrious atmosphere around the White House; he has thick black eyebrows and an impending brow; his nose is large, and the lines about his mouth are very strongly defined.

The whole physiognomy is as coarse a one as you would meet anywhere in the length and breadth of the States; but, withal, it is redeemed, illuminated, softened, and brightened, by a kindly though serious look out of his eyes, and an expression of homely sagacity, that seems weighted with rich results of village-experience. A great deal of native sense; no bookish cultivation, no refinement; honest at heart, and thoroughly so, and yet, in some sort, sly—at least, endowed with a sort of tact and wisdom that are akin to craft, and would impel him, I think, to take an antagonist in flank, rather than to make a bull-run at him right in front. But, on the whole, I liked this sallow, queer, sagacious visage, with the homely human sympathies that warmed it; and, for my small share in the matter, would as lief have Uncle Abe for a ruler as any man whom it would have been practicable to put in his place.

Immediately on his entrance, the President accosted our Member of Congress, who had us in charge, and, with a comical twist of his face, made some jocular remark about the length of his breakfast. He then greeted us all round, not waiting for an introduction, but shaking and squeezing everybody's hand with the utmost cordiality, whether the individual's name was announced to him or not. His manner towards us was wholly without pretence, but yet had a kind of natural dignity, quite sufficient to keep the forwardest of us from clapping him on the shoulder and asking for a story. A mutual acquaintance being established, our leader took the whip out of its case, and began to read the address of presentation. The whip was an exceedingly long one, its handle wrought in ivory, (by some artist in the Massachusetts state-prison, I believe,) and ornamented with a medallion of the President, and other equally beautiful devices; and along its whole length, there was a succession of golden bands and ferules. The address was shorter than the whip, but equally well made, consisting chiefly of an explanatory description of these artistic designs, and closing with a hint that the gift was a suggestive and emblematic one, and that the President would recognize the use to which such an instrument should be put.

This suggestion gave Uncle Abe rather a delicate task in his reply, because, slight as the matter seemed, it apparently called for some declaration, or intimation, or faint foreshadowing of policy in reference to the conduct of the war, and the final treatment of the rebels. But the President's Yankee aptness and not-to-be-caughtness stood him in good stead, and he jerked or wriggled himself out of the dilemma with an uncouth dexterity that was entirely in character; although, without his gesticulation of eye and mouth—and especially the flourish of the whip, with which he imagined himself touching up a pair of fat horses—I doubt whether his words would be worth recording, even if I could remember them. The gist of the reply was, that he accepted the whip as an emblem of peace, not punishment; and this great affair over, we retired out of the presence in high good humor, only regretting that we could not have seen the President sit down and fold up his legs, (which is said to be a most extraordinary spectacle,) or have heard him tell one of those delectable stories for which he is so celebrated. A good many of them are afloat upon the common talk of Washington, and are certainly the aptest, pithiest, and funniest little things imaginable; though, to be sure, they smack of the frontier freedom, and would not always bear repetition in a drawing-room, or on the immaculate page of the Atlantic.

Good Heavens, what liberties have I been taking with one of the potentates of the earth, and the man on whose conduct more important consequencies depend, than on that of any other historical personage of the century! But with whom is an American citizen entitled to take a liberty, if not with his own chief-magistrate? However, lest the above allusions to President Lincoln's little peculiarities (already well-known to the country and to the world) should be mis-interpreted, I deem it proper to say a word or two, in regard to him, of unfeigned respect and measurable confidence. He is evidently a man of keen faculties, and, what is still more to the purpose, of powerful character. As to his integrity, the people have that intuition of it which is never deceived. Before he actually entered upon his great office, and for a considerable time afterwards, there is no reason to suppose that he adequately estimated the gigantic task about to be imposed on him, or, at least, had any distinct idea how it was to be managed; and, I presume, there may have been more than one veteran politician who proposed to himself to take the power out of President Lincoln's hands into his own, leaving our honest friend only the public responsibility for the good or ill-success of the career. The extremely imperfect developement of his statesmanly qualities, at that period, may have justified such designs. But the President is teachable by events, and has now spent a year in a very arduous course of education; he has a flexible mind, capable of much expansion, and convertible towards far loftier studies and activities than those of his early life; and, if he came to Washington as a backwoods humorist, he has already transformed himself into as good a statesman (to speak moderately) as his prime-minister.*

*We hesitated to admit the above sketch, and shall probably regret our decision in its favor. It appears to have been written in a benign spirit, and perhaps conveys a not inaccurate impression of its august subject; but it lacks *reverence*, and it pains us to see a gentleman of ripe age, and who has spent years under the corrective influence of foreign institutions, falling into the characteristic and most ominous fault of Young America.

July 1862

James Sloan Gibbons

A New York banker, abolitionist, and writer on financial subjects, Gibbons (1810–1892) reportedly found his inspiration for the lyrics to this immensely popular wartime song while striding behind a squad of soldiers marching in rhythmic cadence along the streets of New York City. The verse was first published in the *New York Evening Post* on July 16, 1862—two weeks after Lincoln had issued a call for another 300,000 volunteers—and it was quickly reprinted in Boston, Chicago, Washington, and other Northern cities. Set to music by several composers, the song sold a remarkable 500,000 copies of sheet music and did much to establish a new, patriarchal image as "Father Abraham" for the former "Honest Abe." Not everyone succumbed to its undisguised attempt to rally Union morale and manpower after the failure of the Peninsula Campaign; in a racist parody, the English magazine *Punch* countered: "Three hundred thousand might be called a pretty tidy figure. / We've nearly sent you white enough, why don't you take the nigger?" Gibbons, who wrote the verse anonymously, was not identified as their author until 1887.

Three Hundred Thousand More

We are coming, Father Abraam, three hundred thousand
    more,
From Mississippi's winding stream and from New England's
    shore;
We leave our ploughs and workshops, our wives and children
    dear,
With hearts too full for utterance, with but a silent tear;
We dare not look behind us, but steadfastly before—
We are coming, Father Abraam—three hundred thousand
    more!

If you look across the hill-tops that meet the northern sky,
Long moving lines of rising dust your vision may descry;
And now the wind, an instant, tears the cloudy veil aside,

And floats aloft our spangled flag in glory and in pride;
And bayonets in the sunlight gleam, and bands brave music
  pour—
We are coming, Father Abraam—three hundred thousand
  more!

If you look up all our valleys, where the growing harvests
  shine,
You may see our sturdy farmer-boys fast forming into line;
And children from their mother's knees are pulling at the
  weeds,
And learning how to reap and sow, against their country's
  needs;
And a farewell group stands weeping at every cottage door—
We are coming, Father Abraam—three hundred thousand
  more!

You have called us, and we're coming, by Richmond's bloody
  tide
To lay us down for freedom's sake, our brothers' bones
  beside;
Or from foul treason's savage grasp to wrench the murderous
  blade,
And in the face of foreign foes its fragments to parade,
Six hundred thousand loyal men and true have gone before—
We are coming, Father Abraam—three hundred thousand
  more!

July 16, 1862

Horace Greeley

Greeley (1811–1872) had an often fractious relationship with Lincoln. The founding editor of the powerful pro-Republican *New York Tribune* had flirted with the idea of endorsing his opponent, Democrat Stephen A. Douglas, in the Senate campaign of 1858 after Douglas broke with the Buchanan administration over Kansas policy. Two years later, Greeley supported Edward Bates over Lincoln for the presidential nomination, though he warmly supported the eventual nominee. After the election, Greeley tried to exert influence over patronage, but Lincoln not only ignored the newspaperman's recommendations, but remained pointedly neutral when Greeley unsuccessfully attempted to win the Senate seat previously held by the incoming Secretary of State, William H. Seward. During the Civil War, Greeley was a frequent critic of the Lincoln administration. This famous 1862 editorial in the *Tribune* is best remembered for the public reply it inspired from Lincoln, which included the frequently quoted sentence: "My paramount object in this struggle *is* to save the Union, and is *not* either to save or to destroy slavery." In truth, by the time Greeley's editorial appeared, Lincoln had already drafted the preliminary Emancipation Proclamation, but had decided to withhold it until after a Union military victory.

The Prayer of Twenty Millions

To Abraham Lincoln, President of the United States:

Dear Sir:—I do not intrude to tell you—for you must know already—that a great portion of those who triumphed in your election, and of all who desire the unqualified suppression of the Rebellion now desolating our country, are sorely disappointed and deeply pained by the policy you seem to be pursuing with regard to the slaves of Rebels. I write only to set succinctly and unmistakably before you what we require, what we think we have a right to expect, and of what we complain.

I. We require of you, as the first servant of the Republic, charged especially and pre-eminently with this duty, that you

EXECUTE THE LAWS. Most emphatically do we demand that such laws as have been recently enacted, which therefore may fairly be presumed to embody the *present* will, and to be dictated by the *present* needs of the *Republic*, and which, after due consideration, have received your personal sanction, shall by you be carried into full effect, and that you publicly and decisively, instruct your subordinates that such laws exist, that they are binding on all functionaries and citizens, and that they are to be obeyed to the letter.

II. We think you are strangely and disastrously remiss in the discharge of your official and imperative duty with regard to the emancipating provisions of the new Confiscation Act. Those provisions were designed to fight Slavery with Liberty. They prescribe that men loyal to the Union, and willing to shed their blood in her behalf, shall no longer be held, with the nation's consent, in bondage to persistent, malignant traitors, who for twenty years have been plotting, and for sixteen months have been fighting to divide and destroy our country. Why these traitors should be treated with tenderness by you, to the prejudice of the dearest rights of loyal men, we cannot conceive.

III. We think you are unduly influenced by the counsels, the representations, the menaces, of certain fossil politicians hailing from the Border Slave States. Knowing well that the heartily, unconditionally loyal portion of the white citizens of those States, do not expect nor desire that slavery shall be upheld to the prejudice of the Union, (for the truth of which we appeal not only to every Republican residing in those States, but to such eminent loyalists as H. Winter Davis, Parson Brownlow, the Union Central Committee of Baltimore, and to the Nashville *Union*,) we ask you to consider that slavery is everywhere the inciting cause, and sustaining base of treason: the most slave-holding sections of Maryland and Delaware being this day, though under the Union flag, in full sympathy with the Rebellion, while the free labor portions of Tennessee, and of Texas, though writhing under the bloody heel of treason, are unconquerably loyal to the Union. So emphatically is this the case, that a most intelligent Union banker of Baltimore recently avowed his confident belief that a majority of the present Legislature of

Maryland, though elected as and still professing to be Unionists, are at heart desirous of the triumph of the Jeff. Davis conspiracy; and when asked how they could be won back to loyalty,
replied—"Only by the complete Abolition of Slavery." It seems
to us the most obvious truth, that whatever strengthens or forti-
fies slavery in the Border States strengthens also treason, and
drives home the wedge intended to divide the Union. Had you
from the first refused to recognize in those States, as here, any
other than unconditional loyalty—that which stands for the
Union, whatever may become of slavery—those States would
have been, and would be, far more helpful and less troublesome
to the defenders of the Union, than they have been, or now
are.

IV. We think timid counsels in such a crisis calculated to
prove perilous, and probably disastrous. It is the duty of a government as wantonly, wickedly assailed by Rebellion as ours has
been, to oppose force to force in a defiant, dauntless spirit. It
cannot afford to temporize with traitors nor with semi-traitors.
It must not bribe them to behave themselves, nor make them
fair promises in the hope of disarming their causeless hostility.
Representing a brave and high-spirited people, it can afford to
forfeit anything else better than its own self-respect, or their
admiring confidence. For our Government even to seek, after
war has been made on it, to dispel the affected apprehensions of
armed traitors that their cherished privileges may be assailed by
it, is to invite, insult and encourage hopes of its own downfall.
The rush to arms of Ohio, Indiana, Illinois, is the true answer at
once to the rebel raids of John Morgan, and the traitorous sophistries of Berrah Magoffin.

V. We complain that the Union cause has suffered, and is
now suffering immensely, from mistaken deference to Rebel
Slavery. Had you, Sir, in your Inaugural Address, unmistakably
given notice that, in case the Rebellion already commenced
were persisted in, and your efforts to preserve the Union and
enforce the laws, should be resisted by armed force *you would
recognize no loyal person as rightfully held in slavery by a traitor*, we
believe the Rebellion would therein have received a staggering
if not fatal blow. At that moment, according to the returns of

the most recent elections, the Unionists were a large majority of the voters of the slave States. But they were composed in good part of the aged, the feeble, the wealthy, the timid—the young, the reckless, the aspiring, the adventurous, had already been largely lured by the gamblers and negro-traders, the politicians by trade and the conspirators by instinct, into the toils of treason. Had you then proclaimed that rebellion would strike the shackles from the slaves of every traitor, the wealthy and the cautious would have been supplied with a powerful inducement to remain loyal. As it was, every coward in the South soon became a traitor from fear; for loyalty was perilous, while treason seemed comparatively safe. Hence, the boasted unanimity of the South—a unanimity based on Rebel terrorism, and the fact that immunity and safety were found on that side, danger and probable death on ours. The Rebels from the first have been eager to confiscate, imprison, scourge and kill; we have fought wolves with the devices of sheep. The result is just what might have been expected. Tens of thousands are fighting in the Rebel ranks to-day whose original bias and natural leanings would have led them into ours.

VI. We complain that the Confiscation Act which you approved is habitually disregarded by your Generals, and that no word of rebuke for them from you has yet reached the public ear. Fremont's Proclamation and Hunter's Order favoring Emancipation were promptly annulled to you; while Halleck's No. 3, forbidding fugitives from slavery to Rebels to come within his lines—an order as unmilitary as inhuman, and which received the hearty approbation of every traitor in America—with scores of like tendency have never provoked even your remonstrance. We complain that the officers of your armies have habitually repelled, rather than invited the approach of slaves who would have gladly taken the risks of escaping from the Rebel masters to our camps, bringing intelligence often of inestimable value to the Union cause. We complain that those who have thus escaped to us, avowing a willingness to do for us whatever might be required, have been brutally and madly repulsed, and often surrendered to be scourged, maimed and tortured by the ruffian traitors, who pretend to own them. We complain that a large proportion of our regular Army Officers, with many of the Volunteers, evince far more solicitude to uphold slavery than to put down the Rebellion. And finally, we complain that you, Mr. President, elected as a Republican, knowing well what an abomination Slavery is, and how emphatically it is the core and essence of this atrocious Rebellion, seem never to interfere with those atrocities, and never give a direction to your military subordinates, which does not appear to have been conceived in the interest of slavery rather than of freedom.

VII. Let me call your attention to the recent tragedy in New Orleans, whereof the facts are obtained entirely through pro-slavery channels. A considerable body of resolute, able-bodied men, held in slavery by two Rebel sugar-planters in defiance of the Confiscation Act, which you have approved, left plantations thirty miles distant, and made their way to the great mart of the south-west, which they knew to be in the undisputed possession of the Union forces. They made their way safely and quietly through thirty miles of Rebel territory, expecting to find freedom under the protection of our flag. Whether they had or had not heard of the passage of the Confiscation Act, they reasoned logically that we could not kill them for deserting the service of their lifelong oppressors, who had through treason become our implacable enemies. They came to us for liberty and protection, for which they were willing to render their best service; they met with hostility, captivity, and murder. The barking of the base curs of slavery in this quarter deceives no one—not even themselves. They say, indeed, that the negroes had no right to appear in New Orleans armed (with their implements of daily labor in the canefield); but no one doubts that they would gladly have laid these down if assured that they should be free. They were set upon and maimed, captured and killed, because they sought the benefit of that Act of Congress which they may not specifically have heard of, but which was none the less the law of land—which they had a clear *right* to the benefit of—which it was *somebody's* duty to publish far and wide, in order that so many as possible should be impelled to desist from serving Rebels and the Rebellion, and come over to the side of the Union. They sought their liberty in strict accordance with the law of the land—they were butchered or reenslaved, for so doing, by the help of the Union soldiers enlisted to fight against slave-holding treason. It was *somebody's* fault that they were murdered —if others shall hereafter suffer in like manner, in default of explicit and public direction to your Generals that they are to be recognized and obey the Confiscation Act, the world will lay the blame on you. Whether you will choose to bear it through future history and at the bar of God, I will not judge. I can only hope.

VIII. On the face of this wide earth, Mr. President, there is not one disinterested, determined, intelligent champion of the Union cause who does not feel that all attempts to put down the Rebellion and at the same time uphold its inciting cause are preposterous and futile—that the Rebellion, if crushed out to-morrow, would be renewed within a year if slavery were left in full vigor—that Army Officers who remain to this day devoted to slavery can at best be but half-way loyal to the Union—and that every hour of deference to slavery is an hour of added and deepened peril to the Union. I appeal to the testimony of your ambassadors in Europe. It is freely at your service, not at mine. Ask them to tell you candidly whether the seeming subserviency of your policy to the slaveholding, slavery-upholding interest, is not the perplexity, the despair of statesmen of all parties, and be admonished by the general answer.

IX. I close as I began with the statement that what an im-mense majority of the loyal millions of your countrymen re-quire of you is a frank, declared, unqualified, ungrudging execu-tion of the laws of the land, more especially of the Confiscation Act. That Act gives freedom to the slaves of Rebels coming within our lines, or whom those lines may at any time inclose— we ask you to render it due obedience by publicly requiring all your subordinates to recognize and obey it. The Rebels are everywhere using the late anti-negro riots in the North, as they have long used your officers' treatment of negroes in the South, to convince the slaves that they have nothing to hope from a Union success—that we mean in that case to sell them into a bitterer bondage to defray the cost of the war. Let them impress this as a truth on the great mass of their ignorant and credulous bondmen, and the Union will never be restored—never. We cannot conquer ten millions of people united in solid phalanx against us, powerfully aided by Northern sympathizers and European allies. We must have scouts, guides, spies, cooks, teamsters, diggers, and choppers, from the blacks of the South, whether we allow them to fight for us or not, or we shall be baffled and repelled. As one of the millions who would gladly have avoided this struggle at any sacrifice but that of principal and honor, but who now feel that the triumph of the Union is indispensable not only to the existence of our country, but to the well-being of mankind, I entreat you to render a hearty and unequivocal obedience to the law of the land.

Yours,

Horace Greeley.

New York, August 19, 1862

Karl Marx

During Lincoln's presidency Marx (1818–1883) was living in London and working on his magnum opus *Capital* while writing occasional articles for the press. Along with his friend and collaborator Friedrich Engels, Marx saw the American Civil War as a crucial struggle between the Northern working class and the Southern slave oligarchy and became a passionate supporter of the Union cause. The article below was written for the Viennese newspaper *Die Presse* and reflects his mixed assessment of Lincoln's leadership during the first 18 months of the war.

On Events in North America

October 7, 1862

The brief campaign in Maryland has decided the fate of the American Civil War, even though the fortunes of war of both contending parties may yet be in the balance for a shorter or longer period of time. It has already been pointed out in this newspaper that the struggle for the border slave states is the struggle for the domination of the Union, and in this conflict, the Confederacy, although it began under the most favorable circumstances, which have never again recurred, has been defeated.

Maryland was rightly considered the head, and Kentucky the arm, of the slaveholders' party in the border states. Maryland's metropolis, Baltimore, has hitherto been kept "loyal" only by means of a state of siege. It was an accepted dogma, not only in the South but also in the North, that the appearance of the Confederates in Maryland would serve as the signal for a popular mass rising against "Lincoln's satellites." The question here was not only one of military success, but of a moral demonstration that would electrify the Southern elements in all the border states and draw them forcibly into their vortex.

With the occupation of Maryland, Washington would fall, Philadelphia would be endangered, and New York no longer

47

safe. The simultaneous invasion of Kentucky, the most important border state because of its population, position, and economic sources, was, considered by itself, only a diversion. If, however, it had been supported by decisive successes in Maryland, it would have led to suppression of the Union party in Tennessee, outflanked Missouri, secured Arkansas and Texas, threatened New Orleans, and, above all, carried the war to Ohio, the central state of the North, whose possession would assure control of the North as much as that of Georgia would that of the South. A Confederate army in Ohio would cut off the western parts of the Northern states from the eastern, and fight the enemy from its own center. After the defeat of the main rebel army in Maryland, the invasion of Kentucky, carried out with little energy, and nowhere meeting with popular sympathy, shrank to an insignificant guerrilla move. Even the capture of Louisville now only caused the "giants of the West"—the bands of troops from Iowa, Illinois, Indiana, and Ohio—to unite into an "avalanche" comparable to the one that came crashing down on the South during the first glorious Kentucky campaign.

Thus the Maryland campaign showed that the waves of Secession lacked the powerful thrust to strike across the Potomac and into the Ohio. The South was limited to the defensive; whereas any possibility for success lay *only in the offensive*. Deprived of the border states, squeezed between the Mississippi in the West and the Atlantic Ocean in the East, it has won nothing—except a graveyard.

One must not for a moment forget that the Southerners possessed, and politically dominated, the border states at the time they raised the banner of rebellion. What they demanded was the territories. With the loss of the territories, they lost the border states.

And yet the invasion of Maryland was risked under the most favorable circumstances. A series of ignominious and unheard-of defeats on the part of the North; the Federal Army demoralized; "Stonewall" Jackson the hero of the day; Lincoln and his administration a general laughingstock; the Democratic party in the North newly strengthened and already counting on a "Jefferson Davis" presidential candidacy; France and England

at the point of loudly proclaiming the legitimacy of the slaveholders, whom they had already recognized within themselves!
"*E pur si muove.*" Nevertheless, in world history reason does
conquer.

More important than the Maryland campaign is Lincoln's
Proclamation. The figure of Lincoln is *sui generis* in the annals
of history. No initiative, no idealistic eloquence, no buskin, no
historic drapery. He always presents the most important act in
the most insignificant form possible. Others, when dealing with
square feet of land, proclaim it a "struggle for ideas." Lincoln,
even when he is dealing with ideas, proclaims their "square
feet." Hesitant, resistant, unwilling, he sings the bravura aria of
his role as though he begged pardon for the circumstances that
force him "to be a lion." The most awesome decrees, which will
always remain historically remarkable, that he hurls at the enemy
all resemble, and are intended to resemble, the trite summonses
that one lawyer sends to an opposing lawyer, the legal chicaneries
and pettifogging stipulations of an *actiones juris*. His most recent
proclamation—the Emancipation Proclamation—the most significant document in American history since the founding of
the Union and one which tears up the old American Constitution, bears the same character.

Nothing is easier than to point out, as do the English Pindars
of slavery—the *Times*, the *Saturday Review*, and *tutti quanti*—what
is aesthetically repulsive, logically inadequate, officially bur-
lesque, and politically contradictory in Lincoln's major actions
and policies. Nevertheless, in the history of the United States
and of humanity, Lincoln will take his place directly next to
Washington! Nowadays, when the most insignificant event on
this side of the Atlantic Ocean takes on an air of melodrama, is
it entirely without significance that in the New World what is
significant should appear dressed in a workaday coat?

Lincoln is not the offspring of a people's revolution. The ordinary play of the electoral system, unaware of the great tasks it
was destined to fulfill, bore him to the summit—a plebeian, who
made his way from stone-splitter to senator in Illinois, a man
without intellectual brilliance, without special greatness of character, without exceptional importance—an average man of good

will. Never has the New World scored a greater victory than in the demonstration that with its political and social organization, average men of good will suffice to do that which in the Old World would have required heroes to do!

Hegel once remarked that in reality comedy is above tragedy, the humor of reason above its pathos. If Lincoln does not possess the pathos of historical action, he does, as an average man of the people, possess its humor. At what moment did he issue the Proclamation that, as of January 1, 1863, slavery is abolished in the Confederacy? At the very moment when, in its Congress at Richmond, the Confederacy, as an independent state, decided on "peace negotiations." At the very moment when the slaveholders of the border states believed that, with the incursion of the Southerners into Kentucky, the "peculiar institution" would be about as secure as their control over their *Landsmann*, President Abraham Lincoln at Washington.

October 12, 1862

George Templeton Strong

A successful lawyer in New York City, Strong (1820–1875) began keeping a diary in 1835 while attending Columbia College. For 40 years he maintained the detailed and eloquent journal of both his activities and private thoughts that amounted to some 4.5 million words by the time of his death. Strong voted for Lincoln in the 1860 election and in 1861 became the treasurer of the newly formed Sanitary Commission, a civilian organization established to care for sick and wounded Union soldiers. In the entries printed below, written after the bloody Union repulse at Fredericksburg, Strong expresses the anxiety, shared by many opponents of slavery, that Lincoln would rescind the Emancipation Proclamation before it was scheduled to take effect on January 1, 1863.

FROM

The Diaries

*D*ecember 18. Our loss at Fredericksburg is crawling up to 17,000. It is generally held that Stanton forced Burnside to this movement against his earnest remonstrance and protest. Perhaps Stanton didn't. Who knows? But there is universal bitter wrath against him throughout this community, a deeper feeling more intensely uttered than any I ever saw prevailing here. Lincoln comes in for a share of it. Unless Stanton be speedily shelved, something will burst somewhere. The general indignation is fast growing revolutionary. The most thorough Republicans, the most loyal Administration men, express it most fiercely and seem to share the personal vindictiveness of the men and women whose sons or brothers or friends have been uselessly sacrificed to the vanity of the political schemes of this meddling murderous quack. His name is likely to be a hissing, till it is forgotten, and the Honest Old Abe must take care lest his own fare no better. A year ago we laughed at the Honest Old Abe's grotesque genial Western jocosities, but they nauseate us now. If these things go on, we shall have pressure on him to resign and make way for Hamlin, as for one about whom no-body knows anything and who may therefore be a change for the better, none for the worse being conceivable. "O Abraham, *O mon Roi!*"

December 21, SUNDAY. Seward has tendered his resignation! Whether it will be accepted and if so, who will succeed him, and whether other changes in the Cabinet are to follow, we don't yet know. Edward Everett and Charles Sumner are named as candidates for the succession. I do not think Seward a loss to government. He is an adroit, shifty, clever politician, in whose career I have never detected the least indication of principle. He believes in majorities, and it would seem, in nothing else. He has used anti-Masonry, law reform, the common school system, and anti-slavery as means to secure votes, without possessing an honest conviction in regard to any of them.

December 24, WEDNESDAY. The little tempest in the Cabinet has cleared up. Nobody resigns after all. Burnside comes out with a frank, honest, manly report, taking on himself whatever blame attaches to the repulse before Fredericksburg. I regret one passage, in which he says he was unwilling to be entrusted with the command of the army when McClellan was relieved, because he felt himself unequal to the place. But the paper as a whole is honorable to him and of good omen for the country. We are sure now of *one* fact, and we are sure of very few. We have one man in high place who is single-minded and unselfish and sincere. His identification is great gain, even admitting his ability to be third-rate.

Christmas is a great institution, especially in time of trouble and disaster and impending ruin. *Gloria in Excelsis Deo et in Terra Pax* are words of permanent meaning, independent of chance and change, and that meaning is most distinctly felt when war and revolution are shaking the foundations of society and threat-ening respectable citizens like myself with speedy insolvency.

December 27. Public affairs unchanged. Will Uncle Abe Lin-coln stand firm and issue his promised proclamation on the first of January, 1863? Nobody knows, but I think he will. Charles J. Stillé of Philadelphia has published a clever pamphlet, com-paring our general condition as to blunders, imbecility, failures, popular discontent, financial embarrassment, and so on with that of shabby old England during the first years of her Peninsular War. He makes out a strong case in our favor. It is a valuable paper, and we must have it reprinted here, for there are many feeble knees in this community that want to be confirmed and corroborated. It had an excellent effect on Bidwell; a bad case of typhoid despondency in a state of chronic collapse and utter prostration. He rallied a little after reading it, and was heard to remark that "we might possibly come out all right after all."

Jefferson Davis's precious proclamation!! Butler and all Butler's commissioned officers to be hanged, whenever caught. Ditto all armed Negroes, and all white officers commanding them. This is the first great blunder Jeff has committed since the war began. It's evidence not only of barbarism but of weakness, and will disgust his foreign admirers (if anything can) and strengthen the backbone of the North at the same time. If he attempts to carry it out, retaliation becomes a duty, and we can play at extermination quite as well as Jeff Davis.

George Wright, who was here Christmas evening, recounted a talk with some South Carolina woman about the policy of forming nigger regiments. The lady was furious. "Just think how infamous it is that our *gentlemen* should have to go out and fight niggers, and that every nigger they shoot is a thousand dollars out of their own pockets! Was there ever anything so outrageous?" "And then," said Wright, "she was so mad that she just jumped straight up and down a minute or two." No wonder. The liberating proclamation we hope for next Thursday, January 1, 1863, may possibly prove a *brutum fulmen*, "a pope's bull against the comet" (a clever mot of Abe Lincoln's), but the enlisting, arming, and drilling of a few thousand muscular athletic buck niggers, every one of whom knows he will be certainly hanged and probably tortured besides if made prisoner, is a material addition to the national force. How strange that patriotic, loyal people should deny its expediency. This generation is certainly overshadowed by a superstition, not yet quite exploded, that slaveholding rights possess peculiar sanctity and inviolability, that everybody who doubts their justice is an Abolitionist, and that an Abolitionist is a social pariah, a reprobate and caitiff, a leper whom all decent people are bound to avoid and denounce. We shall feel otherwise ten years hence, unless subjugated meanwhile by the pluck and ferocity of the slaveholders' rebellion, and look back on Northern reverence for slavery and slaveholders A.D. 1862, even after the long experience of war with treason arrayed in support of slavery, as we now regard the gross superstitions of ten centuries ago, or the existing superstitions of the Mandingoes and the Zulu Kaffirs. I trust we may not have to remember it as a signal instance of judicial blindness, a paralyzing visitation of divine vengeance on a whole people at the very moment when their national existence depended on their seeing the truth and asserting it.

December 30. We know Banks's destination now. He has relieved Butler at New Orleans. Is this wise? Perhaps they expect to take Charleston or Mobile and want Butler to do the same, organizing work there which he has done so successfully at New Orleans. But today's story is that Secretary Stanton goes out and Butler succeeds him. That would be a gain, I think. . . .

There is a report of nineteen colored chattels hanged in Charleston. If true, the presumption is that this large amount of property was thus sacrificed because it exhibited symptoms of contumacy and insubordination, produced by the expected proclamation of January first—day after tomorrow!!! A critical day that will be. Will Lincoln's backbone carry him through the work he is pledged then to do? It is generally supposed that he intends to redeem his pledge, but nobody knows, and I am not sanguine on the subject. If he come out fair and square, he will do the "biggest thing" an Illinois jury-lawyer has ever had a chance of doing, and take high place among the men who have controlled the destinies of nations. If he postpone or dilute his action, his name will be a byword and a hissing till the annals of the nineteenth century are forgotten.

1862

Ralph Waldo Emerson

Emerson made this journal entry sometime in the summer of 1863. His remark about Lincoln writing letters to "any . . . saucy Party committee that writes to him" may refer to the public letters Lincoln sent on June 12 and June 29, 1863, in response to anti-administration resolutions adopted by Democratic meetings in New York and Ohio.

FROM
The Journals

Lincoln We must accept the results of universal suffrage, & not try to make it appear that we can elect fine gentlemen. We shall have coarse men, with a fair chance of worth & of manly ability, but not polite men, not men to please the English or French.

You cannot refine Mr Lincoln's taste, or extend his horizon; he will not walk dignifiedly through the traditional part of the President of America, but will pop out his head at each railroad station & make a little speech, & get into an argument with Squire A. & Judge B. he will write letters to Horace Greeley, and any Editor or Reporter or saucy Party committee that writes to him, & cheapen himself. But this we must be ready for, and let the clown appear, & hug ourselves that we are well off, if we have got good nature, honest meaning, & fidelity to public interest, with bad manners, instead of an elegant roué & malignant selfseeker.

c. July 1863

James Russell Lowell

A poet and literary critic known for works such as *The Vision of Sir Launfal* and *A Fable for Critics*, Lowell (1819–1891) was also a professor of Romance languages at Harvard and served as the founding editor of *Atlantic Monthly* (1857–1861). He admired and often praised Lincoln, but occasionally dealt out sharp criticism as well, worrying initially that the new President was too "provincial" to respond adequately to the monumental crisis facing the country. This wide-ranging essay, inspired by Lincoln's 1863 annual message to Congress (the 19th-century equivalent of today's State of the Union address), appeared in the January 1864 *North American Review*, the magazine where Lowell had just become co-editor. On January 16, 1864, Lincoln wrote to the magazine's publishers expressing his hope that Lowell's essay "will be of value to the country," and then added: "I fear I am not quite worthy of all which is therein kindly said of me personally." The President then commented on a particular sentence (see pp. 74.28–75.1): "In what is there expressed, the writer has not correctly understood me. I have never had a theory that secession could absolve States or people from their obligations. Precisely the contrary is asserted in the inaugural address; and it was because of my belief in the continuation of these *obligations*, that I was puzzled, for a time, as to denying the legal *rights* of those citizens who remained individually innocent of treason or rebellion. But I mean no more now than to merely call attention to this point." Lincoln's letter appeared in the April 1864 *North American Review*.

The President's Policy

There have been many painful crises since the impatient vanity of South Carolina hurried ten prosperous Commonwealths into a crime whose assured retribution was to leave them either at the mercy of the nation they had wronged, or of the anarchy they had summoned but could not control, when no thoughtful American opened his morning paper without dreading to find that he had no longer a country to love and honor. Whatever the result of the convulsion whose first shocks were beginning to be felt, there would still be enough square miles of earth for elbow-room; but that ineffable sentiment made up of memory and hope, of instinct and tradition, which swells every man's heart and shapes his thought, though perhaps never present to his consciousness, would be gone from it, leaving it common earth and nothing more. Men might gather rich crops from it, but that ideal harvest of priceless associations would be reaped no longer; that fine virtue which sent up messages of courage and security from every sod of it would have evaporated beyond recall. We should be irrevocably cut off from our past, and be forced to splice the ragged ends of our lives upon whatever new conditions chance might twist for us.

We confess that we had our doubts at first whether the patriotism of our people were not too narrowly provincial to embrace the proportions of national peril. We had an only too natural distrust of immense public meetings and enthusiastic cheers, and we knew that the plotters of rebellion had roused a fanaticism of caste in the Southern States sure to hold out longer than that fanaticism of the flag which was preached in the North, for hatred has deeper roots than sentiment, though we knew also that frenzy would pass through its natural stages, to end in dejection, as surely in Carolina as in New York.

That a reaction should follow the holiday enthusiasm with which the war was entered on, that it should follow soon, and that the slackening of public spirit should be proportionate to the previous over-tension, might well be foreseen by all who had studied human nature or history. Men acting gregariously are always in extremes; as they are one moment capable of higher courage, so they are liable, the next, to baser depression, and it is often a matter of chance whether numbers shall multiply confidence or discouragement. Nor does deception lead more surely to distrust of men, than self-deception to suspicion of principles. The only faith that wears well and holds its color in all weathers is that which is woven of conviction and set with the sharp mordant of experience. Enthusiasm is good material for the orator, but the statesman needs something more durable to work in,—must be able to rely on the deliberate reason and consequent firmness of the people, without which that presence of mind, no less essential in times of moral than of material peril, will be wanting at the critical moment. Would this fervor of the Free States hold out? Was it kindled by a just feeling of the value of constitutional liberty? Had it body enough to withstand the inevitable dampening of checks, reverses, delays? Had our population intelligence enough to comprehend that the choice was between order and anarchy, between the equilibrium of a government by law and the tussle of misrule by *pronunciamiento*? Could a war be maintained without the ordinary stimulus of hatred and plunder, and with the impersonal loyalty of principle? These were serious questions, and with no precedent to aid in answering them.

At the beginning of the war there was, indeed, occasion for the most anxious apprehension. A President known to be infected with the political heresies, and suspected of sympathy with the treason, of the Southern conspirators, had just surrendered the reins, we will not say of power, but of chaos, to a successor known only as the representative of a party whose leaders, with long training in opposition, had none in the conduct of affairs; an empty treasury was called on to supply resources beyond precedent in the history of finance; the trees were yet growing and the iron unmined with which a navy was to be built and armored; officers without discipline were to make a mob into an army; and, above all, the public opinion of Europe, echoed and reinforced with every vague hint and every specious argument of despondency by a powerful faction at home, was either contemptuously sceptical or actively hostile. It would be hard to over-estimate the force of this latter element of disintegration and discouragement among a people where every citizen at home, and every soldier in the field, is a reader of newspapers. The pedlers of rumor in the North were the most effective allies of the rebellion. A nation can be liable to no more insidious treachery than that of the telegraph, sending hourly its electric thrill of panic along the remotest nerves of the community, till the excited imagination makes every real danger loom heightened with its unreal double. The armies of Jefferson Davis have been more effectually strengthened by the phantom

regiments of Northern newspapers, than by the merciless dra-
goonery of his conscription.

And even if we look only at more palpable difficulties, the
problem to be solved by our civil war was so vast, both in its
immediate relations and its future consequences; the conditions
of its solution were so intricate and so greatly dependent on
incalculable and uncontrollable contingencies; so many of the
data, whether for hope or fear, were, from their novelty, incapable of arrangement under any of the categories of historical
precedent,—that there were moments of crisis when the firmest
believer in the strength and sufficiency of the democratic theory
of government might well hold his breath in vague apprehension of disaster. Our teachers of political philosophy, solemnly
arguing from the precedent of some petty Grecian, Italian, or
Flemish city, whose long periods of aristocracy were broken
now and then by awkward parentheses of mob, had always
taught us that democracies were incapable of the sentiment of
loyalty, of concentrated and prolonged effort, of far-reaching
conceptions; were absorbed in material interests; impatient of
regular, and much more of exceptional restraint; had no natural
nucleus of gravitation, nor any forces but centrifugal; were
always on the verge of civil war, and slunk at last into the natural
almshouse of bankrupt popular government, a military despotism. Here was indeed a dreary outlook for persons who knew
democracy, not by rubbing shoulders with it lifelong, but merely
from books, and America only by the report of some fellow-
Briton, who, having eaten a bad dinner or lost a carpetbag here,
had written to the Times demanding redress, and drawing a
mournful inference of democratic instability. Nor were men
wanting among ourselves who had so steeped their brains in
London literature as to mistake Cockneyism for European culture, and contempt of their country for cosmopolitan breadth
of view, and who, owing all they had and all they were to democracy, thought it had an air of high-breeding to join in the
shallow epicedium that our bubble had burst. Others took up
the Tory gabble, that all the political and military genius was on
the side of the Rebels, and even yet are not weary of repeating
it, when there is not one of Jefferson Davis's prophecies as to the

course of events, whether at home or abroad, but has been utterly falsified by the event, when his finance has literally gone to
rags, and when even the journals of his own capital are beginning
to inquire how it is, that, while their armies are always victorious, the territory of the Confederacy is steadily diminishing.

But beside any disheartening influences which might affect
the timid or the despondent, there were reasons enough of settled
gravity against any over-confidence of hope. A war—which,
whether we consider the expanse of the territory at stake, the
hosts brought into the field, or the reach of the principles involved, may fairly be reckoned the most momentous of modern
times—was to be waged by a people divided at home, unnerved
by fifty years of peace, under a chief magistrate without experience and without reputation, whose every measure was sure to
be cunningly hampered by a jealous and unscrupulous minority,
and who, while dealing with unheard-of complications at home,
must soothe a hostile neutrality abroad, waiting only a pretext
to become war. All this was to be done without warning and
without preparation, while at the same time a social revolution
was to be accomplished in the political condition of four millions
of people, by softening the prejudices, allaying the fears, and
gradually obtaining the co-operation, of their unwilling liberators. Surely, if ever there were an occasion when the heightened
imagination of the historian might see Destiny visibly intervening in human affairs, here was a knot worthy of her shears.
Never, perhaps, was any system of government tried by so continuous and searching a strain as ours during the last three years;
never has any shown itself stronger; and never could that strength
be so directly traced to the virtue and intelligence of the people,
—to that general enlightenment and prompt efficiency of public opinion possible only under the influence of a political framework like our own. We find it hard to understand how even a
foreigner should be blind to the grandeur of the combat of ideas
that has been going on here,—to the heroic energy, persistency,
and self-reliance of a nation proving that it knows how much
dearer greatness is than mere power; and we own that it is impossible for us to conceive the mental and moral condition of
the American who does not feel his spirit braced and heightened

by being even a spectator of such qualities and achievements. That a steady purpose and a definite aim have been given to the jarring forces which, at the beginning of the war, spent themselves in the discussion of schemes which could only become operative, if at all, after the war was over; that a popular excitement has been slowly intensified into an earnest national will; that a somewhat impracticable moral sentiment has been made the unconscious instrument of a practical moral end; that the treason of covert enemies, the jealousy of rivals, the unwise zeal of friends, have been made not only useless for mischief, but even useful for good; that the conscientious sensitiveness of England to the horrors of civil conflict has been prevented from complicating a domestic with a foreign war;—all these results, any one of which might suffice to prove greatness in a ruler, have been mainly due to the good sense, the good humor, the sagacity, the large-mindedness, and the unselfish honesty of the unknown man whom a blind fortune, as it seemed, had lifted from the crowd to the most dangerous and difficult eminence of modern times. It is by presence of mind in untried emergencies that the native metal of a man is tested; it is by the sagacity to see, and the fearless honesty to admit, whatever of truth there may be in an adverse opinion, in order more convincingly to expose the fallacy that lurks behind it, that a reasoner at length gains for his mere statement of a fact the force of argument; it is by a wise forecast which allows hostile combinations to go so far as by the inevitable reaction to become elements of his own power, that a politician proves his genius for state-craft; and especially it is by so gently guiding public sentiment that he seems to follow it, by so yielding doubtful points that he can be firm without seeming obstinate in essential ones, and thus gain the advantages of compromise without the weakness of concession, by so instinctively comprehending the temper and prejudices of a people as to make them gradually conscious of the superior wisdom of his freedom from temper and prejudice,—it is by qualities such as these that a magistrate shows himself worthy to be chief in a commonwealth of freemen. And it is for qualities such as these that we firmly believe history will rank Mr. Lincoln among the most prudent of statesmen and the most successful of rulers. If we wish to appreciate him, we have only to conceive the inevitable chaos in which we should now be weltering, had a weak man or an unwise one been chosen in his stead.

"Bare is back," says the Norse proverb, "without brother behind it"; and this is, by analogy, true of an elective magistracy. The hereditary ruler in any critical emergency may reckon on the inexhaustible resources of *prestige*, of sentiment, of superstition, of dependent interest, while the new man must slowly and painfully create all these out of the unwilling material around him, by superiority of character, by patient singleness of purpose, by sagacious presentiment of popular tendencies and instinctive sympathy with the national character. Mr. Lincoln's task was one of peculiar and exceptional difficulty. Long habit had accustomed the American people to the notion of a party in power, and of a President as its creature and organ, while the more vital fact, that the executive for the time being represents the abstract idea of government as a permanent principle superior to all party and all private interest, had gradually become unfamiliar. They had so long seen the public policy more or less directed by views of party, and often even of personal advantage, as to be ready to suspect the motives of a chief magistrate compelled, for the first time in our history, to feel himself the head and hand of a great nation, and to act upon the fundamental maxim, laid down by all publicists, that the first duty of a government is to defend and maintain its own existence. Accordingly, a powerful weapon seemed to be put into the hands of the opposition by the necessity under which the administration found itself of applying this old truth to new relations. They were not slow in turning it to use, but the patriotism and common sense of the people were more than a match for any sophistry of mere party. The radical mistake of the leaders of the opposition was in forgetting that they had a country, and expecting a similar obliviousness on the part of the people. In the undisturbed possession of office for so many years, they had come to consider the government as a kind of public Gift Enterprise conducted by themselves, and whose profits were nominally to be shared among the holders of their tickets, though all the prizes had a trick of falling to the lot of the managers. Amid the tumult of war, when the life of the nation was at stake, when the principles of despotism and freedom were grappling in deadly conflict, they had no higher conception of the crisis than such as would serve the purpose of a contested election; no thought but of advertising the tickets for the next drawing of that private speculation which they miscalled the Democratic party. But they were too little in sympathy with the American people to understand them, or the motives by which they were governed. It became more and more clear that, in embarrassing the administration, their design was to cripple the country; that, by a strict construction of the Constitution, they meant nothing more than the locking up of the only arsenal whence effective arms could be drawn to defend the nation. Fortunately, insincerity by its very nature, by its necessary want of conviction, must erelong betray itself by its inconsistencies. It was hard to believe that men had any real horror of sectional war, who were busy in fomenting jealousies between East and West; that they could be in favor of a war for the Union as it was, who were for accepting the violent amendments of Rebellion; that they could be heartily opposed to insurrection in the South who threatened government with forcible resistance in the North; or that they were humanely anxious to stay the effusion of blood, who did not scruple to stir up the mob of our chief city to murder and arson, and to compliment the patriotism of assassins with arms in their hands. Believers, if they believed anything, in the divine right of Sham, they brought the petty engineering of the caucus to cope with the resistless march of events, and hoped to stay the steady drift of the nation's purpose, always setting deeper and stronger in one direction, with the scoop-nets that had served their turn so well in dipping fish from the turbid eddies of politics. They have given an example of the shortest and easiest way of reducing a great party to an inconsiderable faction.

The change which three years have brought about is too remarkable to be passed over without comment, too weighty in its lesson not to be laid to heart. Never did a President enter upon office with less means at his command, outside his own strength of heart and steadiness of understanding, for inspiring confidence in the people, and so winning it for himself, than Mr.

Lincoln. All that was known of him was that he was a good stump-speaker, nominated for his *availability*,—that is, because he had no history,—and chosen by a party with whose more extreme opinions he was not in sympathy. It might well be feared that a man past fifty, against whom the ingenuity of hostile partisans could rake up no accusation, must be lacking in manliness of character, in decision of principle, in strength of will,—that a man who was at best only the representative of a party, and who yet did not fairly represent even that,—would fail of political, much more of popular, support. And certainly no one ever entered upon office with so few resources of power in the past, and so many materials of weakness in the present, as Mr. Lincoln. Even in that half of the Union which acknowledged him as President, there was a large, and at that time dangerous minority, that hardly admitted his claim to the office, and even in the party that elected him there was also a large minority that suspected him of being secretly a communicant with the church of Laodicea. All that he did was sure to be virulently attacked as ultra by one side; all that he left undone, to be stigmatized as proof of lukewarmness and backsliding by the other. Meanwhile he was to carry on a truly colossal war by means of both; he was to disengage the country from diplomatic entanglements of unprecedented peril undisturbed by the help or the hinderance of either, and to win from the crowning dangers of his administration, in the confidence of the people, the means of his safety and their own. He has contrived to do it, and perhaps none of our Presidents since Washington has stood so firm in the confidence of the people as he does after three years of stormy administration.

Mr. Lincoln's policy was a tentative one, and rightly so. He laid down no programme which must compel him to be either inconsistent or unwise, no cast-iron theorem to which circumstances must be fitted as they rose, or else be useless to his ends. He seemed to have chosen Mazarin's motto, *Le temps et moi*. The *moi*, to be sure, was not very prominent at first; but it has grown more and more so, till the world is beginning to be persuaded that it stands for a character of marked individuality and capacity for affairs. Time was his prime-minister, and, we began to think at one period, his general-in-chief also. At first he was so slow that he tired out all those who see no evidence of progress but in blowing up the engine; then he was so fast, that he took the breath away from those who think there is no getting on safely while there is a spark of fire under the boilers. God is the only being who has time enough; but a prudent man, who knows how to seize occasion, can commonly make a shift to find as much as he needs. Mr. Lincoln, as it seems to us in reviewing his career, though we have sometimes in our impatience thought otherwise, has always waited, as a wise man should, till the right moment brought up all his reserves. *Semper nocuit differre paratis*, is a sound axiom, but the really efficacious man will also be sure to know when he is *not* ready, and be firm against all persuasion and reproach till he is.

One would be apt to think, from some of the criticisms made on Mr. Lincoln's course by those who mainly agree with him in principle, that the chief object of a statesman should be rather to proclaim his adhesion to certain doctrines, than to achieve their triumph by quietly accomplishing his ends. In our opinion, there is no more unsafe politician than a conscientiously rigid *doctrinaire*, nothing more sure to end in disaster than a theoretic scheme of policy that admits of no pliability for contingencies. True, there is a popular image of an impossible He, in whose plastic hands the submissive destinies of mankind become as wax, and to whose commanding necessity the toughest facts yield with the graceful pliancy of fiction; but in real life we commonly find that the men who control circumstances, as it is called, are those who have learned to allow for the influence of their eddies, and have the nerve to turn them to account at the happy instant. Mr. Lincoln's perilous task has been to carry a rather shackly raft through the rapids, making fast the unrulier logs as he could snatch opportunity, and the country is to be congratulated that he did not think it his duty to run straight at all hazards, but cautiously to assure himself with his setting-pole where the main current was, and keep steadily to that. He is still in wild water, but we have faith that his skill and sureness of eye will bring him out right at last.

A curious, and, as we think, not inapt parallel, might be

drawn between Mr. Lincoln and one of the most striking figures in modern history,—Henry IV. of France. The career of the latter may be more picturesque, as that of a daring captain always is; but in all its vicissitudes there is nothing more romantic than that sudden change, as by a rub of Aladdin's lamp, from the attorney's office in a country town of Illinois to the helm of a great nation in times like these. The analogy between the characters and circumstances of the two men is in many respects singularly close. Succeeding to a rebellion rather than a crown, Henry's chief material dependence was the Huguenot party, whose doctrines sat upon him with a looseness distasteful certainly, if not suspicious, to the more fanatical among them. King only in name over the greater part of France, and with his capital barred against him, it yet gradually became clear to the more far-seeing even of the Catholic party, that he was the only centre of order and legitimate authority round which France could reorganize itself. While preachers who held the divine right of kings made the churches of Paris ring with declamations in favor of democracy rather than submit to the heretic dog of a Béarnois,—much as our *soi-disant* Democrats have lately been preaching the divine right of slavery, and denouncing the heresies of the Declaration of Independence,—Henry bore both parties in hand till he was convinced that only one course of action could possibly combine his own interests and those of France. Meanwhile the Protestants believed somewhat doubtfully that he was theirs, the Catholics hoped somewhat doubtfully that he would be theirs, and Henry himself turned aside remonstrance, advice, and curiosity alike with a jest or a proverb (if a little *high*, he liked them none the worse), joking continually as his manner was. We have seen Mr. Lincoln contemptuously compared to Sancho Panza by persons incapable of appreciating one of the deepest pieces of wisdom in the profoundest romance ever written; namely, that, while Don Quixote was incomparable in theoretic and ideal statesmanship, Sancho, with his stock of proverbs, the ready money of human experience, made the best possible practical governor. Henry IV. was as full of wise saws and modern instances as Mr. Lincoln, but beneath all this was the thoughtful, practical, humane, and thoroughly earnest man, around whom the fragments of France were to gather themselves till she took her place again as a planet of the first magnitude in the European system. In one respect Mr. Lincoln was more fortunate than Henry. However some may think him wanting in zeal, the most fanatical can find no taint of apostasy in any measure of his, nor can the most bitter charge him with being influenced by motives of personal interest. The leading distinction between the policies of the two is one of circumstances. Henry went over to the nation; Mr. Lincoln has steadily drawn the nation over to him. One left a united France; the other, we hope and believe, will leave a reunited America. We leave our readers to trace the farther points of difference and resemblance for themselves, merely suggesting a general similarity which has often occurred to us. One only point of melancholy interest we will allow ourselves to touch upon. That Mr. Lincoln is not handsome nor elegant, we learn from certain English tourists who would consider similar revelations in regard to Queen Victoria as thoroughly American in their want of *bienséance*. It is no concern of ours, nor does it affect his fitness for the high place he so worthily occupies; but he is certainly as fortunate as Henry in the matter of good looks, if we may trust contemporary evidence. Mr. Lincoln has also been reproached with Americanism by some not unfriendly British critics; but, with all deference, we cannot say that we like him any the worse for it, or see in it any reason why he should govern Americans the less wisely.

The most perplexing complications that Mr. Lincoln's government has had to deal with have been the danger of rupture with the two leading commercial countries of Europe, and the treatment of the slavery question. In regard to the former, the peril may be considered as nearly past, and the latter has been withdrawing steadily, ever since the war began, from the noisy debating-ground of faction to the quieter region of practical solution by convincingness of facts and consequent advance of opinion which we are content to call Fate.

As respects our foreign relations, the most serious, or at least the most obvious, cause of anxiety has all along been the irritation and ill-will that have been growing up between us and England. The sore points on both sides have been skilfully exasperated by interested and unscrupulous persons, who saw in a war between the two countries the only hope of profitable return for their investment in Confederate stock, whether political or financial. The always supercilious, often insulting, and sometimes even brutal tone of British journals and public men, has certainly not tended to soothe whatever resentment might exist in America.

> "Perhaps it was right to dissemble your love,
>   But why did you kick me down stairs?"

We have no reason to complain that England, as a necessary consequence of her clubs, has become a great society for the minding of other people's business, and we can smile good-naturedly when she lectures other nations on the sins of arrogance and conceit; but we may justly consider it a breach of the political *convenances* which are expected to regulate the intercourse of one well-bred government with another, when men holding places in the ministry allow themselves to dictate our domestic policy, to instruct us in our duty, and to stigmatize as unholy a war for the rescue of whatever a high-minded people should hold most vital and most sacred. Was it in good taste, that we may use the mildest term, for Earl Russell to expound our own Constitution to President Lincoln, or to make a new and fallacious application of an old phrase for our benefit, and tell us that the Rebels were fighting for independence and we for empire? As if all wars for independence were by nature just and deserving of sympathy, and all wars for empire ignoble and worthy only of reprobation, or as if these easy phrases in any way characterized this terrible struggle,—terrible not so truly in any superficial sense, as from the essential and deadly enmity of the principles that underlie it. His Lordship's bit of borrowed rhetoric would justify Smith O'Brien, Nana Sahib, and the Maori chieftains, while it would condemn nearly every war in which England has ever been engaged. Was it so very presumptuous in us to think that it would be decorous in English statesmen if they spared time enough to acquire some kind of knowledge, though of the most elementary kind, in regard to this country and the questions at issue here, before they pronounced so off-hand a judgment? Or is political information expected to come Dogberry-fashion in England, like reading and writing, by nature?

And now all respectable England is wondering at our irritability, and sees a quite satisfactory explanation of it in our national vanity. *Suave mari magno*, it is pleasant, sitting in the easy-chairs of Downing Street, to sprinkle pepper on the raw wounds of a kindred people struggling for life, and philosophical to find in self-conceit the cause of our instinctive resentment. Surely we were of all nations the least liable to any temptation of vanity at a time when the gravest anxiety and the keenest sorrow were never absent from our hearts. Nor is conceit the exclusive attribute of any one nation. The earliest of English travellers, Sir John Mandeville, took a less provincial view of the matter when he said, "that in whatever part of the earth men dwell, whether above or beneath, it seemeth always to them that dwell there that they go more right than any other folk."

It is time for Englishmen to consider whether there was nothing in the spirit of their press and of their leading public men calculated to rouse a just indignation, and to cause a permanent estrangement on the part of any nation capable of self-respect, and sensitively jealous, as ours then was, of foreign interference. Was there nothing in the indecent haste with which belligerent rights were conceded to the Rebels, nothing in the abrupt tone assumed in the Trent case, nothing in the fitting out of Confederate privateers, that might stir the blood of a people already overcharged with doubt, suspicion, and terrible responsibility? The laity in any country do not stop to consider points of law, but they have an instinctive appreciation of the *animus* that actuates the policy of a foreign nation; and in our own case they remembered that the British authorities in Canada did not wait till diplomacy could send home to England for her slow official tinder-box to fire the "Caroline." Add to this, what every sensible American knew, that the moral support of England was equal to an army of two hundred thousand men to the Rebels, while it insured us another year or two of exhausting war. Even if we must come to grief, the openly expressed satisfaction of a disinterested acquaintance, and his triumphant "I told you so's," are not soothing to the best-regulated nerves; but in regard to the bearing of England toward ourselves, it was not so much the spite of her words (though the time might have been more tastefully chosen) as the actual power for evil in them that we felt as a deadly wrong. Perhaps the most immediate and efficient cause of mere irritation was the sudden and unaccountable change of manner on the other side of the water. Only six months before, the Prince of Wales had come over to call us cousins; and everywhere it was nothing but "our American brethren," that great offshoot of British institutions in the New World, so almost identical with them in laws, language, and literature,—this last of the alliterative compliments being so bitterly true, that perhaps it will not be retracted even now. To this outburst of long-repressed affection we responded with genuine warmth, if with a little of the awkwardness of a poor relation bewildered with the sudden tightening of the ties of consanguinity when it is rumored that he has come into a large estate. Then came the rebellion, and, *presto!* a flaw in our titles was discovered, the plate we were promised at the family table is flung at our head, and we were again the scum of creation, intolerably vulgar, at once cowardly and overbearing,—no relations of theirs, after all, but a dreggy hybrid of the basest bloods of Europe. Panurge was not quicker to call Friar John his *former* friend. We could not help thinking of Walter Mapes's jingling paraphrase of Petronius,—

> "Dummodo sim splendidis vestibus ornatus,
> Et multa familia sim circumvallatus,
> Prudens sum et sapiens et morigeratus,
> Et tuus nepos sum et tu meus cognatus,"—

which we may freely render thus:

> So long as I was prosperous, I'd dinners by the dozen,
> Was well-bred, witty, virtuous, and everybody's cousin:
> If luck should turn, as well she may, her fancy is so flexile,
> Will virtue, cousinship, and all return with her from exile?

There was nothing in all this to exasperate a philosopher, much to make him smile rather; but the earth's surface is not chiefly inhabited by philosophers, and we revive the recollection of it now in perfect good humor, merely by way of suggesting to our *ci-devant* British cousins, that it would have been easier for them to hold their tongues than for us to keep our tempers under the circumstances.

The English Cabinet made a blunder, unquestionably, in taking it so hastily for granted that the United States had fallen forever from their position as a first-rate power, and it was natural that they should vent a little of their vexation on the people whose inexplicable obstinacy in maintaining freedom and order, and in resisting degradation, was likely to convict them of their mistake. But if bearing a grudge be the sure mark of a small mind in the individual, can it be a proof of high spirit in a nation? If the result of the present estrangement between the two countries shall be to make us more independent of British criticism, so much the better; but if it is to make us insensible to the value of British opinion, in matters where it gives us the judgment of an impartial and cultivated outsider, if we are to shut ourselves out from the advantages of English culture, the loss will be ours, and not theirs. Because the door of the old homestead has been once slammed in our faces, shall we in a huff reject all future advances of conciliation, and cut ourselves foolishly off from any share in the humanizing influences of the place, with its ineffable riches of association, its heirlooms of immemorial culture, its historic monuments, ours no less than theirs, its noble gallery of ancestral portraits? We have only to succeed, and England will not only respect, but, for the first time, begin to understand us. And let us not, in our justifiable indignation at wanton insult, forget that England is not the England only of the snobs who dread the democracy they do not comprehend, but the England of history, of heroes, statesmen, and poets, whose names are dear, and their influence as salutary to us as to her.

Undoubtedly, slavery was the most delicate and embarrassing question with which Mr. Lincoln was called on to deal, and it was one which no man in his position, whatever his opinions, could evade; for, though he might withstand the clamor of partisans, he must sooner or later yield to the persistent importunacy of circumstances, which thrust the problem upon him at every turn and in every shape. He must solve the riddle of this new Sphinx, or be devoured. Though Mr. Lincoln's policy in this critical affair has not been such as to satisfy those who demand an heroic treatment for even the most trifling occasion, and who will not cut their coat according to their cloth, unless they can borrow the scissors of Atropos, it has been at least not unworthy of the long-headed king of Ithaca. Mr. Lincoln had the choice of Bassanio offered him. Which of the three caskets held the prize which was to redeem the fortunes of the country? There was the golden one whose showy speciousness might have tempted a vain man; the silver of compromise, which might have decided the choice of a merely acute one; and, the leaden,—dull and homely-looking, as prudence always is,—yet with something about it sure to attract the eye of practical wisdom. Mr. Lincoln dallied with his decision perhaps longer than seemed needful to those on whom its awful responsibility was not to rest, but when he made it, it was worthy of his cautious but sure-footed understanding. The moral of the Sphinx-riddle, and it is a deep one, lies in the childish simplicity of the solution. Those who fail in guessing it, fail because they are over-ingenious, and cast about for an answer that shall suit their own notion of the gravity of the occasion and of their own dignity, rather than the occasion itself.

In a matter which must be finally settled by public opinion, and in regard to which the ferment of prejudice and passion on both sides has not yet subsided to that equilibrium of compromise from which alone a sound public opinion can result, it is proper enough for the private citizen to press his own convictions with all possible force of argument and persuasion; but the popular magistrate, whose judgment must become action, and whose action involves the whole country, is bound to wait till the sentiment of the people is so far advanced toward his own point of view, that what he does shall find support in it, instead of merely confusing it with new elements of division. It was not unnatural that men earnestly devoted to the saving of their country, and profoundly convinced that slavery was its only real enemy, should demand a decided policy round which all patriots might

rally,—and this might have been the wisest course for an absolute ruler. But in the then unsettled state of the public mind, with
a large party decrying even resistance to the slaveholders' rebellion as not only unwise, but even unlawful; with a majority, perhaps, even of the would-be loyal so long accustomed to regard
the Constitution as a deed of gift conveying to the South their
own judgment as to policy and instinct as to right, that they were
in doubt at first whether their loyalty were due to the country or
to slavery; and with a respectable body of honest and influential
men who still believed in the possibility of conciliation,—Mr.
Lincoln judged wisely, that, in laying down a policy in deference
to one party, he should be giving to the other the very fulcrum
for which their disloyalty had been waiting.

It behooved a clear-headed man in his position not to yield
so far to an honest indignation against the brokers of treason in
the North, as to lose sight of the materials for misleading which
were their stock in trade, and to forget that it is not the falsehood of sophistry which is to be feared, but the grain of truth
mingled with it to make it specious,—that it is not the knavery
of the leaders so much as the honesty of the followers they may
seduce, that gives them power for evil. It was especially his duty
to do nothing which might help the people to forget the true
cause of the war in fruitless disputes about its inevitable consequences.

The doctrine of State rights can be so handled by an adroit
demagogue as easily to confound the distinction between liberty
and lawlessness in the minds of ignorant persons, accustomed
always to be influenced by the sound of certain words, rather than
to reflect upon the principles which give them meaning. For,
though Secession involves the manifest absurdity of denying to a
State the right of making war against any foreign power while
permitting it against the United States; though it supposes a
compact of mutual concessions and guaranties among States without any arbiter in case of dissension; though it contradicts common sense in assuming that the men who framed our government did not know what they meant when they substituted
Union for Confederation; though it falsifies history, which shows
that the main opposition to the adoption of the Constitution

was based on the argument that it did not allow that independence in the several States which alone would justify them in seceding;—yet, as slavery was universally admitted to be a reserved right, an inference could be drawn from any direct attack upon it (though only in self-defence) to a natural right of resistance, logical enough to satisfy minds untrained to detect fallacy, as the majority of men always are, and now too much disturbed by the disorder of the times, to consider that the order of events had any legitimate bearing on the argument. Though Mr. Lincoln was too sagacious to give the Northern allies of the Rebels the occasion they desired and even strove to provoke, yet from the beginning of the war the most persistent efforts have been made to confuse the public mind as to its origin and motives, and to drag the people of the loyal States down from the national position they had instinctively taken to the old level of party squabbles and antipathies. The wholly unprovoked rebellion of an oligarchy proclaiming negro slavery the corner-stone of free institutions, and in the first flush of over-hasty confidence venturing to parade the logical sequence of their leading dogma, "that slavery is right in principle, and has nothing to do with difference of complexion," has been represented as a legitimate and gallant attempt to maintain the true principles of democracy. The rightful endeavor of an established government, the least onerous that ever existed, to defend itself against a treacherous attack on its very existence, has been cunningly made to seem the wicked effort of a fanatical clique to force its doctrines on an oppressed population.

Even so long ago as when Mr. Lincoln, not yet convinced of the danger and magnitude of the crisis, was endeavoring to persuade himself of Union majorities at the South, and to carry on a war that was half peace in the hope of a peace that would have been all war,—while he was still enforcing the Fugitive Slave Law, under some theory that Secession, however it might absolve States from their obligations, could not escheat them of their claims under the Constitution, and that slaveholders in rebellion had alone among mortals the privilege of having their cake and eating it at the same time,—the enemies of free government were striving to persuade the people that the war was an

Abolition crusade. To rebel without reason was proclaimed as one of the rights of man, while it was carefully kept out of sight that to suppress rebellion is the first duty of government. All the evils that have come upon the country have been attributed to the Abolitionists, though it is hard to see how any party can become permanently powerful except in one of two ways,—either by the greater truth of its principles, or the extravagance of the party opposed to it. To fancy the ship of state, riding safe at her constitutional moorings, suddenly engulfed by a huge kraken of Abolitionism, rising from unknown depths and grasping it with slimy tentacles, is to look at the natural history of the matter with the eyes of Pontoppidan. To believe that the leaders in the Southern treason feared any danger from Abolitionism, would be to deny them ordinary intelligence, though there can be little doubt that they made use of it to stir the passions and excite the fears of their deluded accomplices. They rebelled, not because they thought slavery weak, but because they believed it strong enough, not to overthrow the government, but to get possession of it; for it becomes daily clearer that they used rebellion only as a means of revolution, and if they got revolution, though not in the shape they looked for, is the American people to save them from its consequences at the cost of its own existence? The election of Mr. Lincoln, which it was clearly in their power to prevent had they wished, was the occasion merely, and not the cause, of their revolt. Abolitionism, till within a year or two, was the despised heresy of a few earnest persons, without political weight enough to carry the election of a parish constable; and their cardinal principle was disunion, because they were convinced that within the Union the position of slavery was impregnable. In spite of the proverb, great effects do not follow from small causes,—that is, disproportionately small,—but from adequate causes acting under certain required conditions. To contrast the size of the oak with that of the parent acorn, as if the poor seed had paid all costs from its slender strong-box, may serve for a child's wonder; but the real miracle lies in that divine league which bound all the forces of nature to the service of the tiny germ in fulfilling its destiny. Everything has been at work for the past ten years in the cause of antislavery, but Garrison and Phillips have been far less successful propagandists than the slaveholders themselves, with the constantly-growing arrogance of their pretensions and encroachments. They have forced the question upon the attention of every voter in the Free States, by defiantly putting freedom and democracy on the defensive. But, even after the Kansas outrages, there was no wide-spread desire on the part of the North to commit aggressions, though there was a growing determination to resist them. The popular unanimity in favor of the war three years ago was but in small measure the result of antislavery sentiment, far less of any zeal for abolition. But every month of the war, every movement of the allies of slavery in the Free States, has been making Abolitionists by the thousand. The masses of any people, however intelligent, are very little moved by abstract principles of humanity and justice, until those principles are interpreted for them by the stinging commentary of some infringement upon their own rights, and then their instincts and passions, once aroused, do indeed derive an incalculable reinforcement of impulse and intensity from those higher ideas, those sublime traditions, which have no motive political force till they are allied with a sense of immediate personal wrong or imminent peril. Then at last the stars in their courses begin to fight against Sisera. Had any one doubted before that the rights of human nature are unitary, that oppression is of one hue the world over, no matter what the color of the oppressed,—had any one failed to see what the real essence of the contest was,—the efforts of the advocates of slavery among ourselves to throw discredit upon the fundamental axioms of the Declaration of Independence and the radical doctrines of Christianity, could not fail to sharpen his eyes. This quarrel, it is plain, is not between Northern fanaticism and Southern institutions, but between downright slavery and upright freedom, between despotism and democracy, between the Old World and the New.

The progress of three years has outstripped the expectation of the most sanguine, and that of our arms, great as it undoubtedly is, is trifling in comparison with the advance of opinion. The great strength of slavery was a superstition, which is fast losing its hold on the public mind. When it was first proposed to raise negro regiments, there were many even patriotic men who felt as the West Saxons did at seeing their high-priest hurl his lance against the temple of their idol. They were sure something terrible, they knew not what, would follow. But the earth stood firm, the heavens gave no sign, and presently they joined in making a bonfire of their bugbear. That we should employ the material of the rebellion for its own destruction, seems now the merest truism. In the same way men's minds are growing wonted to the thought of emancipation; and great as are the difficulties which must necessarily accompany and follow so vast a measure, we have no doubt that they will be successfully overcome. The point of interest and importance is, that the feeling of the country in regard to slavery is no whim of sentiment, but a settled conviction, and that the tendency of opinion is unmistakably and irrevocably in one direction, no less in the Border Slave States than in the Free. The chances of the war, which at one time seemed against us, are now greatly in our favor. The nation is more thoroughly united against any shameful or illusory peace than it ever was on any other question, and the very extent of the territory to be subdued, which was the most serious cause of misgiving, is no longer an element of strength, but of disintegration, to the conspiracy. The Rebel leaders can make no concessions; the country is unanimously resolved that the war shall be prosecuted, at whatever cost; and if the war go on, will it leave slavery with any formidable strength in the South? and without that, need there be any fear of effective opposition in the North?

While every day was bringing the people nearer to the conclusion which all thinking men saw to be inevitable from the beginning, it was wise in Mr. Lincoln to leave the shaping of his policy to events. In this country, where the rough and ready understanding of the people is sure at last to be the controlling power, a profound common-sense is the best genius for statesmanship. Hitherto the wisdom of the President's measures has been justified by the fact that they have always resulted in more firmly uniting public opinion. It is a curious comment on the sincerity of political professions, that the party calling itself Democratic should have been the last to recognize the real

movement and tendency of the popular mind. The same gentlemen who two years ago were introducing resolutions in Congress against coercion, are introducing them now in favor of the
war, but against subjugation. Next year they may be in favor of
emancipation, but against abolition. It does not seem to have
occurred to them that the one point of difference between a
civil and a foreign war is, that in the former one of the parties
must by the very nature of the case be put down, and the other
left in possession of the government. Unless the country is to be
divided, no compromise is possible, and, if one side must yield,
shall it be the nation or the conspirators? A government may
make, and any wise government would make, concessions to
men who have risen against real grievances; but to make them
in favor of a rebellion that had no juster cause than the personal
ambition of a few bad men, would be to abdicate. Southern
politicians, however, have always been so dexterous in drawing
nice distinctions, that they may find some consolation inappre-
ciable by obtuser minds in being coerced instead of subjugated.

If Mr. Lincoln continue to act with the firmness and prudence which have hitherto distinguished him, we think he has
little to fear from the efforts of the opposition. Men without
sincere convictions are hardly likely to have a well-defined and
settled policy, and the blunders they have hitherto committed
must make them cautious. If their personal hostility to the President be unabated, we may safely count on their leniency to the
opinion of majorities, and the drift of public sentiment is too
strong to be mistaken. They have at last discovered that there is
such a thing as Country, which has a meaning for men's minds
and a hold upon their hearts; they may make the further discovery, that this is a revolution that has been forced on us, and not
merely a civil war. In any event, an opposition is a wholesome
thing; and we are only sorry that this is not a more wholesome
opposition.

We believe it is the general judgment of the country on the
acts of the present administration, that they have been, in the
main, judicious and well-timed. The only doubt about some of
them seems to be as to their constitutionality. It has been sometimes objected to our form of government, that it was faulty in

having a written constitution which could not adapt itself to the needs of the time as they arose. But we think it rather a theoretic than a practical objection; for in point of fact there has been hardly a leading measure of any administration that has not been attacked as unconstitutional, and which was not carried nevertheless. Purchase of Louisiana, Embargo, Removal of the Deposits, Annexation of Texas, not to speak of others less important,—on the unconstitutionality of all these, powerful parties have appealed to the country, and invariably the decision has been against them. The will of the people for the time being has always carried it. In the present instance, we purposely refrain from any allusion to the moral aspects of the question. We prefer to leave the issue to experience and common sense. Has any sane man ever doubted on which side the chances were in this contest? Can any sane man who has watched the steady advances of opinion, forced onward slowly by the immitigable logic of facts, doubt what the decision of the people will be in this matter? The Southern conspirators have played a desperate stake, and, if they had won, would have bent the whole policy of the country to the interests of slavery. Filibustering would have been nationalized, and the slave-trade re-established as the most beneficent form of missionary enterprise. But if they lose? They have, of their own choice, put the chance into our hands of making this continent the empire of a great homogeneous population, substantially one in race, language, and religion,—the most prosperous and powerful of nations. Is there a doubt what the decision of a victorious people will be? If we were base enough to decline the great commission which Destiny lays on us, should we not deserve to be ranked with those dastards whom the stern Florentine condemns as hateful alike to God and God's enemies?

We would not be understood as speaking lightly of the respect due to constitutional forms, all the more essential under a government like ours and in times like these. But where undue respect for the form will lose us the substance, and where the substance, as in this case, is nothing less than the country itself, to be over-scrupulous would be unwise. Who are most tender in their solicitude that we keep sacred the letter of the law, in order that its spirit may not keep us alive? Mr. Jefferson Davis and those who, in the Free States, would have been his associates, but must content themselves with being his political *guerilleros*. If Davis had succeeded, would he have had any scruples of constitutional delicacy? And if he has not succeeded, is it not mainly owing to measures which his disappointed partisans denounce as unconstitutional?

We cannot bring ourselves to think that Mr. Lincoln has done anything that would furnish a precedent dangerous to our liberties, or in any way overstepped the just limits of his constitutional discretion. If his course has been unusual, it was because the danger was equally so. It cannot be so truly said that he has strained his prerogative, as that the imperious necessity has exercised its own. Surely the framers of the Constitution never dreamed that they were making a strait waistcoat, in which the nation was to lie helpless while traitors were left free to do their will. In times like these, men seldom settle precisely the principles on which they *shall* act, but rather adjust those on which they *have* acted to the lines of precedent as well as they can after the event. This is what the English Parliament did in the Act of Settlement. Congress, after all, will only be called on for the official draft of an enactment, the terms of which have been already decided by agencies beyond their control. Even while they are debating, the current is sweeping them on toward new relations of policy. At worst, a new precedent is pretty sure of pardon, if it successfully meet a new occasion. It is a harmless pleasantry to call Mr. Lincoln "Abraham the First,"—we remember when a similar title was applied to President Jackson; and it will not be easy, we suspect, to persuade a people who have more liberty than they know what to do with, that they are the victims of despotic tyranny.

Mr. Lincoln probably thought it more convenient, to say the least, to have a country left without a constitution, than a constitution without a country. We have no doubt we shall save both; for if we take care of the one, the other will take care of itself. Sensible men, and it is the sensible men in any country who at last shape its policy, will be apt to doubt whether it is true conservatism, after the fire is got under, to insist on keeping up the flaw in the chimney by which it made its way into the house. Radicalism may be a very dangerous thing, and so is calomel, but not when it is the only means of saving the life of the patient. Names are of great influence in ordinary times, when they are backed by the *vis inertiæ* of life-long prejudice, but they have little power in comparison with a sense of interest; and though, in peaceful times, it may be highly respectable to be conservative merely for the sake of being so, though without very clear notions of anything in particular to be conserved, what we want now is the prompt decision that will not hesitate between the bale of silk and the ship when a leak is to be stopped. If we succeed in saving the great landmarks of freedom, there will be no difficulty in settling our constitutional boundaries again. We have no sympathy to spare for the pretended anxieties of men who, only two years gone, were willing that Jefferson Davis should break all the ten commandments together, and would now impeach Mr. Lincoln for a scratch on the surface of the tables where they are engraved.

We cannot well understand the theory which seems to allow the Rebels some special claim to protection by the very Constitution which they rose in arms to destroy. Still less can we understand the apprehensions of many persons lest the institution of slavery should receive some detriment, as if it were the balance-wheel of our system, instead of its single element of disturbance. We admit that we always have thought, and think still, that the great object of the war should be the restoration of the Union at all hazards, and at any sacrifice short of honor. And however many honest men may scruple as to law, there can be no doubt that we are put under bonds of honor by the President's proclamation. If the destruction of slavery is to be a consequence of the war, shall we regret it? If it be needful to the successful prosecution of the war, shall any one oppose it? Is it out of the question to be constitutional, without putting the slaveholders back precisely where they were before they began the rebellion? This seems to be the ground taken by the opposition, but it becomes more and more certain that the people, instructed by the experience of the past three years, will never consent to any plan of adjustment that does not include emancipation.

If Congress need any other precedent than *salus populi suprema lex* for giving the form and force of law to the public will, they may find one in the act of Parliament which abolished the feudal privileges of the Highland chiefs in 1747. A great occasion is not to be quibbled with, but to be met with that clear-sighted courage which deprives all objections of their force, if it does not silence them. To stop short of the only measure that can by any possibility be final and decisive, would be to pronounce rebellion a harmless eccentricity. To interpret the Constitution has hitherto been the exclusive prerogative of Slavery: it will be strange if Freedom cannot find a clause in it that will serve her purpose. To scruple at disarming our deadliest foe, would be mere infatuation. We can conceive of nothing parallel, except to have had it decided that the arrest of Guy Fawkes and the confiscation of his materials were a violation of Magna Charta; that he should be put back in the cellar of Westminster palace, his gunpowder, his matches, his dark-lantern, restored to him, with handsome damages for his trouble, and Parliament assembled overhead to give him another chance for the free exercise of his constitutional rights.

We believe, and our belief is warranted by experience, that all measures will be found to have been constitutional at last on which the people are overwhelmingly united. We must not lose sight of the fact, that whatever is *extra*-constitutional is not necessarily *un*constitutional. The recent proclamation of amnesty will, we have no doubt, in due time bring a vast accession of strength to the emancipationists from the slaveholding States themselves. The danger of slavery has always been in the poor whites of the South; and wherever freedom of the press penetrates,—and it always accompanies our armies,—the evil thing is doomed. Let no one who remembers what has taken place in Maryland and Missouri think such anticipations visionary. The people of the South have been also put to school during these three years, under a sharper schoolmistress, too, than even ours has been, and the deadliest enemies of slavery will be found among those who have suffered most from its indirect evils. It is only by its extinction—for without it no secure union would be possible—that the sufferings and losses of the war can be repaid. That extinction accomplished, our wounds will not be long in healing. Apart from the slaveholding class, which is numerically small, and would be socially insignificant without its privileges, there are no such mutual antipathies between the two sections as the conspirators, to suit their own purposes, have asserted, and even done their best to excite. We do not like the Southerners less for the gallantry and devotion they have shown even in a bad cause, and they have learned to respect the same qualities in us. There is no longer the nonsensical talk about Cavaliers and Puritans, nor does the one gallant Southron any longer pine for ten Yankees as the victims of his avenging steel. As for subjugation, when people are beaten they are beaten, and every nation has had its turn. No sensible man in the North would insist on any terms except such as are essential to assure the stability of peace. To talk of the South as our future Poland is to talk without book; for no region rich, prosperous, and free could ever become so. It is a geographical as well as a moral absurdity. With peace restored, slavery rooted out, and harmony sure to follow, we shall realize a power and prosperity beyond even the visions of the Fourth of July orator, and we shall see Freedom, while she proudly repairs the ruins of war, as the Italian poet saw her,—

> "Girar la Libertà mirai
> E baciar lieta ogni ruina e dire
> Ruine sì, ma servitù non mai."

January 1864

Harriet Beecher Stowe

The daughter and sister of famous Congregational clergymen, Stowe (1811–1896) caused a sensation in 1852 with the publication of her *Uncle Tom's Cabin, or Life Among the Lowly*, arguably the most popular and influential novel of the 19th century. Although it is widely credited with intensifying the sectional crisis by vivifying the horrors of slavery for a wider public, there is no evidence that Lincoln himself ever read the book. However, in June 1862 he did borrow from the Library of Congress a copy of her 1853 companion volume, *A Key to Uncle Tom's Cabin; Presenting the Original Facts and Documents upon which the Story is Founded*. Several months later Stowe finally met Lincoln at the White House, where, according to Stowe family tradition, he greeted her with the words: "Is this the little woman who made this great war?" Stowe originally wrote this portrait for the *Christian Watchman and Reflector*; it achieved greater circulation when it was reprinted in the magazine *The Living Age*.

Abraham Lincoln

The revolution through which the American nation is passing is not a mere local convulsion. It is a war for a principle which concerns all mankind. It is THE war for the rights of the working classes of mankind, as against the usurpation of privileged aristocracies. You can make nothing else of it. That is the reason why, like a shaft of light in the judgment-day, it has gone through all nations, dividing to the right and the left the multitudes. *For* us and our cause, all the common working classes of Europe—all that toil and sweat and are oppressed. *Against* us, all privileged classes, nobles, princes, bankers, and great manufacturers, and all who live at ease. A silent instinct, piercing to the dividing of soul and spirit, joints and marrow, has gone through the earth, and sent every soul with instinctive certainty where it belongs. The poor laborers of Birmingham and Manchester, the poor silk weavers of Lyons, to whom our conflict has been present starvation and lingering death, have stood bravely *for* us. No sophistries could blind or deceive *them*; they knew that *our* cause was *their* cause, and they have suffered their part heroically, as if fighting by our side, because they knew that our victory was to be their victory. On the other side, all aristocrats and holders of exclusive privileges have felt the instinct of opposition, and the sympathy with a struggling aristocracy, for they, too, feel that our victory will be their doom.

This great contest has visibly been held in the hands of Almighty God, and is a fulfilment of the solemn prophecies with which the Bible is sown thick as stars, that he would spare the soul of the needy, and judge the cause of the poor. It was he who chose the instrument for this work, and he chose him with a visible reference to the rights and interests of the great majority of mankind, for which he stands.

Abraham Lincoln is in the strictest sense *a man of the working classes.* All his advantages and abilities are those of a man of the working classes; all his disadvantages and disabilities are those of a man of the working classes; and his position now at the head of one of the most powerful nations of the earth, is a sign to all who live by labor that their day is coming. Lincoln was born to the inheritance of hard work as truly as the poorest laborer's son that digs in our fields. At seven years of age he was set to work, axe in hand, to clear up a farm in a Western forest. Until he was seventeen his life was that of a simple farm laborer, with only such intervals of schooling as farm laborers get. Probably the school instruction of his whole life would not amount to more than one year. At nineteen he made a trip to New Orleans as a hired hand on a flat boat, and on his return he split the rails for a log cabin and built it, and enclosed ten acres of land with a rail fence of his own handiwork. The next year he hired himself for twelve dollars a month to build a flat boat and take her to New Orleans; and any one who knows what the life of a Mississippi boatman was in those days, must know that it involved every kind of labor. In 1832, in the Black Hawk Indian War, the hardy boatman volunteered to fight for his country, and was unanimously elected a captain, and served with honor for a season in frontier military life. After this, while serving as a postmaster, he began his law studies, borrowing the law books he was too poor to buy, and studying by the light of his evening fire. He acquired a name in the country about as a man of resources and shrewdness; he was one that people looked to for counsel in exigencies, and to whom they were ready to depute almost any enterprise which needed skill and energy. The surveyor of Sangamon County being driven with work, came to him to take the survey of a tract off from his hands. True, he had never studied surveying—but what of that? He accepted the "job," procured a chain, a treatise on surveying, and *did the work*. Do we not see in this a parable of the wider wilderness which in later years he has undertaken to survey and fit for human habitation *without* chart or surveyor's chain?

In 1836 our backwoodsman, flat-boat hand, captain, surveyor, obtained a license to practise law, and, as might be expected, rose rapidly.

His honesty, shrewdness, energy, and keen practical insight into men and things soon made him the most influential man in his State. He became the reputed leader of the Whig party, and canvassed the State as stump speaker in time of Henry Clay, and in 1846 was elected representative to Congress. Here he met the grinding of the great question of the day—the upper and nether millstone of slavery and freedom revolving against each other. Lincoln's whole nature inclined him to be a harmonizer of conflicting parties rather than a committed combatant on either side. He was firmly and from principle an enemy to slavery—but the ground he occupied in Congress was in some respects a middle one between the advance guard of the anti-slavery and the spears of the fire-eaters. He voted with John Quincy Adams for the receipt of anti-slavery petitions; he voted with Giddings for a committee of inquiry into the constitutionality of slavery in the District of Columbia, and the expediency of abolishing slavery in that District; he voted for the various resolutions prohibiting slavery in the territories to be acquired from Mexico, and he voted forty-two times for the Wilmot Proviso. In Jan. 16, 1849, he offered a plan for abolishing slavery in the District of Columbia, by compensation from the national treasury, with the consent of a majority of the citizens. He opposed the annexation of Texas, but voted for the bill to pay the expenses of the war.

But at the time of the repeal of the Missouri Compromise he took the field, heart and soul, against the plot to betray our territories to slavery. It was mainly owing to his exertions that at this critical period a Republican Senator was elected from Illinois, when a Republican Senator in the trembling national scales of the conflict was worth a thousand times his weight in gold.

Little did the Convention that nominated Abraham Lincoln for President know what they were doing. Little did the honest, fatherly, patriotic man, who stood in his simplicity on the platform at Springfield, asking the prayers of his townsmen and receiving their pledges to remember him, foresee how awfully he was to need those prayers, the prayers of all this nation, and the prayers of all the working, suffering common people throughout the world. God's hand was upon him with a visible protection, saving first from the danger of assassination at Baltimore and bringing him safely to our national capital. Then the world has seen and wondered at the greatest sign and marvel of our day, to wit; a plain working man of the people, with no more culture, instruction, or education than any such working man may obtain for himself, called on to conduct the passage of a great people through a crisis involving the destinies of the whole world. The eyes of princes, nobles, aristocrats, of dukes, earls, scholars, statesmen, warriors, all turned on the plain backwoodsman, with his simple sense, his imperturbable simplicity, his determined self-reliance, his impracticable and incorruptible honesty, as he sat amid the war of conflicting elements, with unpretending steadiness, striving to guide the national ship through a channel at whose perils the world's oldest statesmen stood aghast. The brilliant courts of Europe levelled their operaglasses at the phenomenon. Fair ladies saw that he had horny hands and disdained white gloves. Dapper diplomatists were shocked at his system of etiquette; but old statesmen, who knew the terrors of that passage, were wiser than court ladies and dandy diplomatists, and watched him with a fearful curiosity, simply asking, "*Will* that awkward old backwoodsman really get that ship through? If he does, it will be time for us to look about us."

Sooth to say, our own politicians were somewhat shocked with his state-papers at first. Why not let *us* make them a little more conventional, and file them to a classical pattern? "No," was his reply, "I shall write them myself. *The people will understand them*." "But this or that form of expression is not elegant, not classical." "*The people will understand it*," has been his invariable reply. And whatever may be said of his state-papers, as compared with the classic standards, it has been a fact that they have always been wonderfully well understood by the people, and that since the time of Washington, the state-papers of no President have more controlled the popular mind. And one reason for this is, that they have been informal and undiplomatic. They have more resembled a father's talks to his children than a state-paper. And they have had that relish and smack of the soil, that appeal to the simple human heart and head, which is a greater power in writing than the most artful devices of rhetoric. Lincoln might well say with the apostle, "But though I be rude in speech yet not in knowledge, but we have been thoroughly *made manifest among you* in all things." His rejection of what is called fine writing was as deliberate as St. Paul's, and for the same reason—because he felt that he was speaking on a subject which must be made clear to the lowest intellect, though it should fail to captivate the highest. But we say of Lincoln's writing, that for all true, manly purposes of writing, there are passages in his state-papers that could not be better put; they are absolutely perfect. They are brief, condensed, intense, and with a power of insight and expression which make them worthy to be inscribed in letters of gold. Such are some passages of the celebrated Springfield letter, especially that masterly one where he compares the conduct of the patriotic and loyal blacks with that of the treacherous and disloyal whites. No one can read this letter without feeling the influence of a mind both strong and generous.

Lincoln is a strong man, but his strength is of a peculiar kind; it is not aggressive so much as passive, and among passive things, it is like the strength not so much of a stone buttress as of a wire cable. It is strength swaying to every influence, yielding on this side and on that to popular needs, yet tenaciously and inflexibly bound to carry its great end; and probably by no other kind of strength could our national ship have been drawn safely thus far during the tossings and tempests which beset her way.

Surrounded by all sorts of conflicting claims, by traitors, by half-hearted, timid men, by Border States men, and Free States men, by radical Abolitionists and Conservatives, he has listened to all, weighed the words of all, waited, observed, yielded now here and now there, but in the main kept one inflexible, honest purpose, and drawn the national ship through.

In times of our trouble Abraham Lincoln has had his turn of being the best abused man of our nation. Like Moses leading his Israel through the wilderness, he has seen the day when every man seemed ready to stone him, and yet, with simple, wiry, steady perseverance, he has held on, conscious of honest intentions, and looking to God for help. All the nation have felt, in the increasing solemnity of his proclamations and papers, how deep an education was being wrought in his mind by this simple faith in God, the ruler of nations, and this humble willingness to learn the awful lessons of his providence.

We do not mean to give the impression that Lincoln is a religious man in the sense in which that term is popularly applied. We believe he has never made any such profession, but we see evidence that in passing through this dreadful national crisis he has been forced by the very anguish of the struggle to look upward, where any rational creature must look for support. No man in this agony has suffered more and deeper, albeit with a dry, weary, patient pain, that seemed to some like insensibility. "Whichever way it ends," he said to the writer, "I have the impression that *I* sha'n't last long after it's over." After the dreadful repulse of Fredericksburg, his heavy eyes and worn and weary air told how our reverses wore upon him, and yet there was a never-failing fund of patience at bottom that sometimes rose to the surface in some droll, quaint saying, or story, that forced a laugh even from himself.

There have been times with many, of impetuous impatience, when our national ship seemed to lie water-logged and we have called aloud for a deliverer of another fashion,—a brilliant general, a dashing, fearless statesman, a man who could dare and do, who would stake all on a die, and win or lose by a brilliant *coup de main*. It may comfort our minds that since He who ruleth in the armies of nations set no such man to this work, that perhaps He saw in the man whom He did send some peculiar fitness and aptitudes therefor.

Slow and careful in coming to resolutions, willing to talk with every person who has anything to show on any side of a disputed subject, long in weighing and pondering, attached to constitutional limits and time-honored landmarks, Lincoln certainly was the *safest* leader a nation could have at a time when the *habeas corpus* must be suspended, and all the constitutional and minor rights of citizens be thrown into the hands of their military leader. A reckless, bold, theorizing dashing man of genius might have wrecked our Constitution and ended us in a splendid military despotism.

Among the many accusations which in hours of ill-luck have been thrown out upon Lincoln, it is remarkable that he has never been called self-seeking, or selfish. When we were troubled and sat in darkness, and looked doubtfully towards the presidential chair, it was never that we doubted the goodwill of our pilot—only the clearness of his eyesight. But Almighty God has granted to him that clearness of vision which he gives to the true-hearted, and enabled him to set his honest foot in that promised land of freedom which is to be the patrimony of all men, black and white—and from henceforth nations shall rise up to call him blessed.

February 6, 1864

Anonymous

Lincoln's campaign for re-election in the midst of Civil War inspired as much attack as acclaim, particularly over the volatile issue of race. In one notorious example, two Democratic newspapermen anonymously published a pamphlet, *Miscegenation: The Theory of the Blending of the Races*, that, with apparent sincerity, advocated racial equality and intermarriage. They then unsuccessfully sought Lincoln's endorsement for their work in the hope that his approval would mark him as a dangerous "amalgamationist." Another anonymous offering was the satirical pamphlet *Abraham Africanus I: His Secret Life, as revealed under the Mesmeric Influence*, which assailed Lincoln in prose and amateurish verse as a buffoonish knave beholden to Satan. "It is a little singular," Lincoln sadly confided on election day in 1864 to his secretary John Hay, "that I, who am not a vindictive man, should have always been before the people for election in canvasses marked for their bitterness. . . ."

Abraham Africanus I

"**B**ully for you," cried Satan, enraptured, "you are the smartest pupil I ever had! I am afraid people will find you out after a while, though."

"Devil a fear, Old Boy. *As long a I'm called 'Honest Old Abe,' the people will swallow anything. There's nothing like having an honest name. It is a cloak for everything.*"

"True," said Beelzebub. He forbore to say any more. His mind was filled with uneasy suspicions. What if the cute Bram should slip out of his bargain with *him*? "True," he continued, rolling this idea over in his mind; "if I hadn't tacked this name to you, you would have been nowhere to-day. It gave *confidence*, and you've profited well by it. But how about *our* arrangement. You don't expect to argue *me* out of *that*, do you?"

"Come, come, brother," said Bram with an affected air of honest indignation. "You don't suspect my *intentions* do you?"

"Hell is paved with them," said the Father of Lies, sententiously. "I want something more palpable than your assurances, Abe. Suppose we draw up a little memorandum of our agreement?"

So saying, he whipped out a little scroll of parchment, and tapping a hole in Bram's arm before he was sufficiently aware of his intention to prevent it, used his blood for ink. Then scribbing furiously for a few minutes, he covered the scroll with fine writing, and read the contract to his *confrere*:

"'I hereby pledge to elevate Abraham Lincoln to a life Presidency of the United States of America—'"

"Stop, stop!" cried Bram, "you promised a Monarchy, or at least a First Consulship."

"Fool!" said the Devil. "Don't you perceive that if you call yourself a King or First Consul, the whole people will rise upon you?"

"Let them rise," said Bram, "I have my army. Every officer has been selected and appointed with that view. They are all men who believe the government needs to be *strengthened*."

"Your army wouldn't be worth a straw if you proceed so rudely. There are democrats enough in the country to eat up your army."

"But they're not organized," urged Bram, "and what's more, I don't intend to let them organize."

"Very strongly put, brother; but still there's nothing like doing things smoothly. My word for it, the easiest way is the best. You owe all your present success to four things. *First*, My NOMINATION. *Second*, Your sobriquet of 'Honest.' *Third*, Those weak points of the Constitution which a little management converted into flaws, and a little stretching widened into fissures wide enough to drive a train of cars through. 'Military necessity' did the rest. *Fourth*, DOING THINGS QUIETLY. All these things combined have given you what I promised you in our first contract, POWER. In return you brought on a war which has made, taking both belligerents together, something like a million of victims."

"And out of that million," chuckled Abe, "of course, you reaped a plentiful harvest."

"Not so, Bram. I never was more deceived in my life. I GOT

MY SHARE; but the majority of them were poor ignorant fools, infused with a false patriotism. I did well with the Abolitionists, and the men who accepted bounties; but the former were very scarce and the latter were hardly worth picking up. But to our contract. If you're elected for another term, you can easily get a law passed declaring the country in a state of permanent insurrection, and demanding more power to put it down. The first thing will be, a law to make the Presidency perpetual while the war lasts; the next, another making it perpetual during your life. Thus you will have got over the hardest part of it. The rest is easy enough. You can then have it entailed on your posterity, and change the title whenever you please. I should advise you to stick to that of President, though. There's nothing like a mild name. To continue:

"'I hereby pledge to elevate Abraham Lincoln to a life Presidency of the United States of America, and to stand by him and assist him to subvert the liberties of the American people and debauch their civic aspirations; to impose upon them in every imaginable form of low cunning, and cheat them with words of double meaning and with false promises, until by these, and kindred means, that end is accomplished, and his dynasty firmly established.'"

While Satan was writing the contract, Bram held out his arm very patiently by way of inkstand; but now he withdrew it hastily, and looking at his watch, exclaimed:

"All right, my boy, I'll sign that, and then you'll please to consider this interview at an end, for some of my generals have been advancing too quickly, and if I don't relieve them of their commands the war will be over in a jiffy, and good-bye to my plans."

"You forget," said Beelzebub meaningly, and fixed his burning eyes upon Bram's till the latter winced and wiggled as though he was on a toasting fork, "you forget, my dear Bram."

"What?" stammered Bram, fearing he had been detected, yet hoping to escape, "What do I forget?"

"What!" roared the Evil One, "Do you pretend you don't know! you low, cunning, pettifogging, cringing, artful, Illinois stump lawyer! Would you cheat *me*? You know very well *there's no consideration expressed in that deed*, or you wouldn't have been in such a hurry to sign it, and run to look after your major-generals. But come, let us remain friends. I admire you the more for your dishonesty; only you musn't think to 'beat the Devil round a stump.' Honor amongst thieves, you know."

So saying, the worthy pair shook hands and *smiled*. The *elder one* then proceeded to finish the agreement:

"'In consideration whereof my friend promises, (no— pledges,) pledges to render unto me what he possesses (it ain't much, any how,) of a MORTAL SOUL, the same to be MINE for-ever!'

(Signed)   BAAL."
(Signed)   BRAM."

"Now," said Baal, as Old Abe with trembling fingers and face white as a sheet, signed the bond; "now, my dear Abe, if you want any advice, just let me know, for like yourself, I've other matters to attend to."

1864

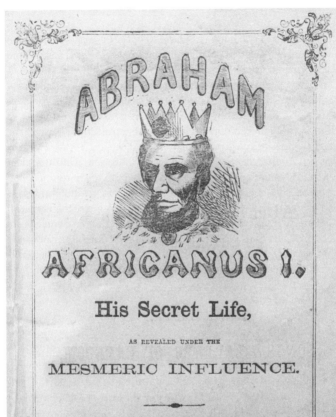

ABRAHAM

AFRICANUS I.

His Secret Life,

AS REVEALED UNDER THE

MESMERIC INFLUENCE.

Mysteries of the White House.

J. F. FEEKS, PUBLISHER,

No. 26 ANN STREET, N. Y.

Title page, *Abraham Africanus I* (1864).
Collection of Frank J. and Virginia Williams.

Petroleum V. Nasby

Like Artemus Ward, humorist David Ross Locke (1833–1888) found a wide and appreciative audience among readers eager to escape from the worry and grief of war. In 1861 Locke, the editor of a Findlay, Ohio, newspaper, encountered a neighborhood drunk circulating a petition demanding the expulsion of the local African-American population. He responded by penning a reply over the signature of an absurd pro-Confederate bigot he named "Petroleum V. Nasby," the first in a series of satiric pieces that were collected as *The Nasby Papers* in 1864. Among them was the following "interview" with President Lincoln. ("Church uv St. ——" is an allusion to the notorious Ohio Copperhead Clement L. Vallandigham.) In a more straightforward essay published in 1886, Locke wrote of his real-life encounters with Lincoln: "He said wonderfully witty things, but never from a desire to be witty. His wit was entirely illustrative. He used it because, and only because, at times he could say more in this way, and better illustrate the idea with which he was pregnant."

Has an Interview with the President

CHURCH UV ST. —— Nov. 1, '63.

I felt it my dooty to visit Washinton. The misarable condishon the Dimocrisy find themselvs into sinse the elecshen, makes it nessary that suthin be did, and therefore I determind to see wat cood be effectid by a persnel interview with the Presdent.

Interdoosin myself, I opened upon him delikitly, thus:

"Linkin," sez I, "ez a Dimocrat, a free-horn Dimocrat, who is prepard to die with neetnis and dispatch, and on short notis, fer the inalienable rite uv free speech—knoin also that you er a goriller, a feendish ape, a thirster after blud, I speck."

"Speek on," sez he.

"I am a Ohio Dimocrat," sez I, "who hez repoodiatid Valandigum."

"Before or sinse the elecshin, did yoo repoodiate him?" sez he.

"Sinse," retortid I.

96

"I thot so," sed he. "I would hev dun it too, hed I bin you," continnered he with a goriller-like grin.

"We air now in favor uv a wiggerus prosecushen uv the war, and we want you to so alter yoor polisy that we kin act with yoo, corjelly," sez I.

"Say on," sez he.

"I will. We don't want yoo to change yoor polisy, materially. We air modrit. Anxshus to support yoo we ask yoo to adopt the follerin trifling changis:

Restoar to us our habis corpusses, as good ez new.

Arrest no moar men, wimmin and children, fer opinyun's saik.

Repele the ojus confisticashen bill, wich irrytaits the Suthern mind and fires the Suthern hart.

Do away with drafts and conskripshens.

Revoak the Emansipashen proclamashen, and give bonds that you'll never ishoo a nother.

Do away with tresury noats and sich, and pay nuthin but gold.

Protect our dawters frum nigger eqwality.

Disarm yoor nigger soljers, and send back the niggers to ther owners to conciliate them.

Offer to assoom the war indetednis uv the South, and plej the Guverment to remoonerate our Suthrin brethren fer the looses they hev sustaned in this onnatral war.

Call a convenshen uv Suthern men and sech gileless North-ern men ez F. Peerce, J. Bookannun, Fernandough Wood and myself, to agree upon the terms uv re-union."

"Is that all," sez the goriller.

"No," sez I promptly. "Ez a garantee uv good faith to us, we shel insist that the best haff uv the orifises be given to Dimocrats who repoodiate Valandigum. Do this, Linkin, and yoo throw lard ile on the trubbled waters. Do this and yoo rally to yoor support thowsends uv noble Dimocrats, who went out uv offis with Bookannon, and hev bin gittin ther whisky on tick ever sinse. We hev maid sakrifises. We hev repoodiatid Valandigum—we care not ef he rots in Canady—we are willin to jine the war party reservin to ourselvs the poor privilidg uv dictatin how and on wat prinsipples it shel be carried on. Linkin! Goriller! Ape! I hev dun."

The President replide that he wood give the matter serious considerashen. He wood menshen the idee uv resinin to Seward, Chais and Blair, and wood addres a serculer to the Postmasters et settry, an and see how menny uv em wood be willin to resine to acommodai Dimocrats. He hed no dout sevral wood do it to-wunst. "Is ther any littel thing I kin do fer you?"

"Nothin pertikler. I wood accept a small Post orifis, if sitooa-tid within ezy range uv a distilry. My politikle daze is well nigh over. Let me but see the old party wunst moar in the assend-ency—let these old eyes onct moar behold the Constooshn ez it is, the Union ez it wuz, and the Nigger ware he ought 2 be, and I will rap the mantel uv privit life arownd me, and go in2 deli-rum tremens happy. I hev no ambishen. I am in the sear and yaller leef. These whitnin lox, them sunken cheak, warn me that age and whisky hev dun ther perfeek work, and that I shell soon go hents. Linkin, scorn not my wurds. I hev sed. Adoo."

So sayin I wavd my hand impressively and walkd away.

PETROLEUM V. NASBY,
Paster uv sed Church, in charge.
1864

Anonymous

Lincoln's resounding re-election victory in November 1864 did little to still the critics at home or abroad. A month later, the influential British magazine *Punch* published this anonymous poem comparing Lincoln to the mythical bird that rose from the ashes. It was accompanied by a woodcut engraving by John Tenniel—most famous for his illustrations for *Alice in Wonderland*—depicting a fierce-looking Lincoln taking flight from a bonfire fueled by burning logs labeled "Commerce," "United States Constitution," "Free Press," "State Rights," "Habeas Corpus," and "Credit."

The Federal Phœnix

When HERODOTUS, surnamed "The Father of History"
    (We are not informed who was History's mother),
Went a travelling to Egypt, that region of mystery,
    Where each step presented some marvel or other,

In a great city there, called (in Greek) Heliopolis,
    The priests put him up to a strange story—rather—
Of a bird, who came up to that priestly metropolis,
    Once in five hundred years, to inter its own father.

When to filial feeling apparently callous,
    Not a plume ruffled (as we should say, not a nair rent),
In a *pot-pourri* made of sweet-spice, myrrh, and aloes,
    He flagrantly, burnt, after burying, his parent.

But POMPONIUS MELA has managed to gather
    Of this curious story a modified version,
In which the bird burns up itself, not its father,
    And soars to new life from its fiery immersion.

This bird has oft figured in emblems and prophecies—
    And though SNYDERS ne'er painted its picture, nor WEENIX
Its portraits on plates of a well-known fire-office is,
    Which, after this bird's name, is christened the Phœnix.

Henceforth a new Phœnix, from o'er the Atlantic,
    Our old fire-office friend from his brass-plate displaces;
With a plumage of greenbacks, all ruffled, and antic
    In OLD ABE's rueful phiz and OLD ABE's shambling graces.

As the bird of Arabia wrought resurrection
    By a flame all whose virtues grew out of what fed it,
So the Federal Phœnix has earned re-election
    By a holocaust huge of rights, commerce, and credit.

December 3, 1864

George Templeton Strong

In New York City, Strong recorded his immediate reactions to Lincoln's assassination in a series of remarkable entries that zigzag between grief and outrage, mourning and the desire for vengeance, reflecting all of the conflicted emotions that overtook the North in the days following the President's murder.

FROM
The Diaries

April 15, SATURDAY. Nine o'clock in the morning. *LINCOLN AND SEWARD ASSASSINATED LAST NIGHT! ! ! !*
The South has nearly filled up the measure of her iniquities at last! Lincoln's death not yet certainly announced, but the one o'clock despatch states that he was then dying. Seward's side room was entered by the same or another assassin, and his throat cut. It is unlikely he will survive, for he was suffering from a broken arm and other injuries, the consequence of a fall, and is advanced in life. Ellie brought this news two hours ago, but I can hardly *take it in* even yet. *Eheu* A. Lincoln!

I have been expecting this. I predicted an attempt would be made on Lincoln's life when he went into Richmond; but just now, after his generous dealings with Lee, I should have said the danger was past. But the ferocious malignity of Southerners is infinite and inexhaustible. I am stunned, as by a fearful personal calamity, though I can see that this thing, occurring just at this time, may be overruled to our great good. Poor Ellie is heartbroken, though never an admirer of Lincoln's. We shall appreciate him at last.

Up with the Black Flag now!

Ten P.M. What a day it has been! Excitement and suspension of business even more general than on the 3rd instant. Tone of feeling very like that of four years ago when the news came of Sumter. This atrocity has invigorated national feeling in the same way, almost in the same degree. People who pitied our misguided brethren yesterday, and thought they had been punished enough already, and hoped there would be a general amnesty, including J. Davis himself, talk approvingly today of vindictive justice and favor the introduction of judges, juries, gaolers, and hangmen among the dramatis personae. Above all, there is a profound, awe-stricken feeling that we are, as it were, in immediate presence of a fearful, gigantic crime, such as has not been committed in our day and can hardly be matched in history.

Faulkner, one of our Kenzua directors, called for me by appointment at half-past nine, and we drove to the foot of Jane Street to inspect apparatus for the reduction of gold ore by amalgamation, which he considers a great improvement on the machinery generally used for that purpose. Returned uptown and saw Bellows to advise about adjournment of our Sanitary Commission meeting next week. Thence to Wall Street. Immense crowd. Bulletins and extras following each other in quick, contradictory succession. Seward and his Fred had died and had not. Booth (one of the assassins, a Marylander, brother of Edwin Booth) had been taken and had not. So it has gone on all day. Tonight the case stands thus:

Abraham Lincoln died at twenty-two minutes after seven this morning. He never regained consciousness after the pistol ball fired at him from behind, over his wife's shoulder, entered his brain. Seward is living and may recover. The gentleman assigned to the duty of murdering him did his butchery badly. The throat is severely lacerated by his knife, but it's believed that no arteries are injured. Fred Seward's situation is less hopeful, his skull being fractured by a bludgeon or sling shot used by the same gentleman. The attendant who was stabbed, is dead. (Is not.)

The temper of the great meeting I found assembled in front of the Custom House (the old Exchange) was grim. A Southerner would compare it with that of the first session of the Jacobins after Marat's death. I thought it healthy and virile. It was the first great patriotic meeting since the war began at which there was no talk of concession and conciliation. It would have endured no such talk. Its sentiment seemed like this: "Now it is plain at last to everybody that there can be no terms with the woman-flogging aristocracy. Grant's generous dealing with Lee was a blunder. The *Tribune's* talk for the last fortnight was folly. Let us henceforth deal with rebels as they deserve. The rose-water treatment does not meet their case." I have heard it said fifty times today: "These madmen have murdered the two best friends they had in the world!" I heard of three or four men in Wall Street and near the Post Office who spoke lightly of the tragedy, and were instantly set upon by the bystanders and pummelled. One of them narrowly escaped death. It was Charles E. Anderson, brother of our friend Professor Henry James Anderson, father of pretty Miss Louisa. Moses H. Grinnell and the police had hard work to save him. I never supposed him a secessionist.

To Trinity Church vestry meeting, specially called, at half-past three at the rebuilt vestry office, corner Fulton and Church. A series of resolutions was read, drawn by the Rector. They were masculine and good, and they were passed *nem. con.*, though Verplanck and Tillou were in their seats—Copperheads both. I looked at the record of our action when Washington died sixty-six years ago. It was a mere resolution that the church and chapels be put in mourning. Our resolutions of today went, naturally, much further. I record to the credit of Gouverneur Ogden, whom I have always held cold-hearted and selfish, that he broke down in trying to read these resolutions, could not get beyond the first sentence, and had to hand them back to the Rector. There was a little diversity of opinion whether we should put our chancel into mourning tomorrow, being Easter Sunday, or postpone it a day longer. We left it to the Rector's discretion. No business was done today. Most shops are closed and draped with black and white muslin. Broadway is clad in "weepers" from Wall Street to Union Square. At 823 with Agnew, Bellows, and Gibbs. George Anthon dined here; with him to Union League Club. Special meeting and dense, asphyxiating crowd. Orations by George Bancroft and by the Rev. (Presbyterian) Thompson of the Tabernacle. Both good; Thompson's very good. "When A. Johnson was sworn in as President today," said the Rev. Thompson, "the Statue of Liberty that surmounts the dome of the Capitol and was put there by Lincoln, looked down on the city and on the nation and said, 'Our Government is unchanged—it has merely passed from the hands of one man into those of another. Let the dead bury their dead. Follow thou Me.'" Burnside tells me this morning that he ranks Johnson very high.

Jeff Davis has at last issued a manifesto. It is from Danville, before Lee's surrender and is full of fight.

April 16. An Easter Sunday unlike any I have seen. Drove downtown very early with Ellie, Johnny, and Temple. Nearly every building in Broadway and in all the side streets, as far as one could see, festooned lavishly with black and white muslin. Columns swathed in the same material. Rosettes pinned to window curtains. Flags at half mast and tied up with crape. I hear that even in second and third class quarters, people who could afford to do no more have generally displayed at least a little twenty-five cent flag with a little scrap of crape annexed. Never was a public mourning more spontaneous and general. It is like what we read of the demonstrations that followed Princess Charlotte's death, but with feelings of just wrath and aspirations for vengeance that had no place there.

Trinity was never filled so full, not even last Tuesday. The crowd packed the aisles tight and even occupied the choir steps and the choir itself nearly to the chancel rails. The outer doors, by the by, were in mourning, and the flag on the spire edged in black pursuant to my suggestion yesterday. Within the church, the symbols of public sorrow properly gave place to those of Easter. When we came to the closing prayers of the litany, Vinton proclaimed, "I bid you all unite with me in prayer for all the bereaved and afflicted families of this land, and especially for that of Abraham Lincoln, late President of the United States, recently destroyed by assassination," and read the proper prayer for those in affliction. He then prefaced the usual prayer for a sick person by a like bidding "for the Secretary of State and the Assistant Secretary of State, now in peril of death from wounds inflicted on them by an assassin." The effect of these formulas introduced into the service was telling. The anthem (Hallelujah Chorus) represented the ecclesiastical aspect of the day and was admirably well done. Vinton's sermon, or rather address, was far the best I have heard him deliver; extemporaneous, as he told us afterwards, when Ellie asked him for a copy. He blended the Easter sentiment with that of public grief most skillfully, or I should rather say by presenting suggestions of deep-lying truths that harmonized them. He brought out clearly the thought that had occurred to me and to many others: Perhaps Lincoln had done his appointed work; his honesty, sagacity, kindliness, and singleness of purpose had united the North and secured the suppression of rebellion. Perhaps the time has come for something beside kindliness, mercy, and forbearance, even for vengeance and judgment. Perhaps the murdered President's magnanimity would have been circumvented and his generosity and goodness abused by rebel subtlety and falsehood to our lasting national injury. Perhaps God's voice in this tragedy is "Well done, good and faithful servant. Thou hast done thy work of mercy. To others is given the duty of vengeance. Thy murder will help teach them that duty. Enter thou, by a painless process of death, into the joy of the Lord."

Southern barbarism has largely promoted our ethical education. What should we have said four years ago of Vinton earnestly enforcing on us the duty of hewing the (Southern) Agag in pieces before the Lord, not from personal animosity, but as a sacred obligation to be neglected only at peril of divine punishment, public and private? The whole service was a new experience to me. Men and women (poor Ellie among them) were sobbing and crying bitterly all around. My own eyes kept filling, and the corners of my mouth would twitch now and then in spite of all I could do.

Tonight Osten-Sacken, little Kate and her papa, George Anthon, and Colonel Howe, with a pocket full of telegrams from Washington. Seward and his son seem doing well. Sorry to say that neither assassin has yet been caught. There are reports that our policy at Richmond is to be changed, that the proposed convocation of Virginia rebels will be dispersed, and that some of them will be held as hostages against further attempts at assassination of presidents and cabinet officers.

There is intense exasperation. I hear of a dozen households whose Celtic handmaidens have been summarily discharged for some talk rejoicing at Abe Lincoln's death. The New York Hotel was protected by policemen last night and today on its proprietor's petition. The President's funeral is to be Thursday next. Gramercy Park House dismissed a batch of waiters today, at Howe's instigation, for blind, foolish, Celtic talk approving Lincoln's murder. Horace Greeley, the advocate of pacification and amnesty, is as unpopular as General Lee. I directed my waiter to stop the *Tribune*. There are hopeful signs that the community may be ready at last for action against its Barlows, LaRocques, Belmonts, and Duncans.

April 17. Very busy in Wall Street, and at two to Columbia College meeting. A little progress made in the ancient undertaking of the "new statutes." Did any one of the pyramids take so much time to build? Also we passed and ordered published a series of resolutions on the assassination. Barnard drew them. They are plain-spoken and radical enough, declaring this atrocity, like the attempted incendiarism of last November and the systematic starvation of 60,000 prisoners of war, due to the brutalizing influences of slavery. They seemed diffuse, and too abundantly peppered with vehemence of adjectives, but it is hard to find words too strong for this case. Betts and Zabriskie recalcitrated, of course; doubted, demurred, and did not like the resolutions a bit. But they passed without a division. Thence to No. 823, making arrangements for the Sanitary Commission session at Washington, for which I expect to leave town tomorrow.

All over the city, people have been at work all day, draping street fronts, so that hardly a building on Wall Street, Broadway, Chambers Street, Bowery, Fourth Avenue is without its symbol of the profound public sorrow. What a place this man, whom his friends have been patronizing for four years as a well-meaning, sagacious, kind-hearted, ignorant, old codger, had won for himself in the hearts of the people! What a place he will fill in history! I foresaw most clearly that he would be ranked high as the Great Emancipator twenty years hence, but I did not suppose his death would instantly reveal—even to Copperhead newspaper editors—the nobleness and the glory of his part in this great contest. It reminds one of the last line of Blanco White's great sonnet, "If Light can thus deceive, wherefore not

Life?" *Death* has suddenly opened the eyes of the people (and I think of the world) to the fact that a hero has been holding high place among them for four years, closely watched and studied, but despised and rejected by a third of this community, and only tolerated by the other two-thirds.

1865

Abraham Lincoln, The Martyr Victorious, print by John Sartain after a design by W. H. Hermans (1865). *Courtesy of the Library of Congress.*

Edward Everett Hale

On the unforgettable Easter that followed Lincoln's death by a single day, most of the ministers throughout the North all but declared the martyred President an American saint—a martyr who, evocatively, had given up his life for the nation's sins on Good Friday. Their sermons defined, and undoubtedly influenced, a radical transfiguration in Lincoln's reputation; overnight the once-controversial politician became a second Washington, a latter-day Moses, an American Christ. The sermon below was preached by Edward Everett Hale (1822–1909), a Unitarian clergyman best known for his riveting 1863 story of treason and patriotism, "The Man Without a Country."

Sermon Preached in Boston

1 CORINTHIANS XV: 57.
Who Giveth us the Victory
Through our Lord Jesus Christ.

The contrasts of Passion Week are those of human triumph, of death in agony, and of Eternal Life.

The week begins with the Sunday of victory,—Palm Sunday, —when the Lord rides in triumph into the city. From day to day the triumph takes different forms, till on Friday the whole changes. His life ends at the hands of treachery and murder. Then comes the last of Jewish Sabbaths,—that Saturday sad beyond words. And then on this first day of the week, He rises: all the chains of earth are broken forever; and, from that moment, man knows he is immortal. Human triumph! Then, death in agony! Then, the unveiling of Eternal Life. These are our contrasts. Hidden in them are our lessons. Never since has the world needed them as we need them this day!

Of their Sunday of triumph we cannot paint the picture, without recalling their year, as it had gone by. These apostles, who could not understand, could feel and wonder. They had walked up and down through the cities of Israel. They had proclaimed the new kingdom. They had named the King. Nay, they had heard him sometimes make fit promise of his empire. He had spoken of it as the one thing certain. He had laid down its constitution and laws. At his word thousands had followed. To his word thousands had listened. At his word, again, the multitudes had melted away. The very voice of God had testified that here was God's beloved Son.

Yet there was, till now, no sign of empire! He would not give a sign. If he fed these thousands, it was that they might leave him. His prophet, John, had been beheaded by a tyrant. His own overtures to the rulers had been rejected with scorn. We can imagine then the darkness which brooded over even the faithful's faith, till the Sunday of victory came. Then, after such anxiety, all seems changed. They have endured to the end. Surely now they are safe. Hosanna! hosanna! Victory! victory! Even the capital has opened its gates to us. Here are coming out its very children, with their palms and their songs. "The Son of David! The Son of David! Hosanna! hosanna! Blessed is he that cometh in the name of the Lord! Hosanna in the highest!" Thus the week begins.

Easy to picture such exultant joy, when seen on a background of a year's defeat, anxiety, long-suffering, and gloom.

Nor, as the week goes by, does their mood change. True, the capital can open its gates but once. There can be but one triumphal entry. When the enemy surrenders Sunday, he cannot surrender again on Monday. But the week seems victory! Speculators and brokers are driven, crestfallen, from the temple. The lovers of the nation's enemies follow them,—the Herodians. The lovers of wealth; they are driven out also, set to scorn,—the Sadducees. The hypocrites who exalt themselves and curse the people, all are rebuked in turn,—the Pharisees. "Lord, what shall be the sign of thy coming?" That question is key-note to the apostles' feeling, when the eve of Friday comes.

And then, victory is changed in a moment into treachery, blood, and death!

Of his feelings we can say nothing but what he tells us. There is no likeness which we can compare to him. But, his enemies:

ah, wicked men and mean men are so common, that we have seen them with these eyes. Whether they deal with the son of God, or whether they work in some mean cabal of their own lust, they are always the same. What the soldiery of Herod could not do; what the officers of Caiaphas could not compass; what Pilate was not mean enough to descend to,—could be wrought out, when that fatal Friday came, by this coward Judas, with his midnight kiss. Of Judas, the world has never known precisely what was his fate, or what his character; whether he were finished villain, or whether he were fanatic fool. Satan chooses such accomplices. Such tool served the purpose of crafty Caiaphas; and, by the work of such tool, even the Lord of Life can be betrayed. They seize him; they lead him out to Calvary; they kill him, the world's best friend; nay, their best friend, if they knew it; the only friend in the Universe of God, who, at that hour, was seeking to save them. So that never were words so terribly true as the words of his prayer,—"they know not what they do." From the terrible retribution which came upon them so soon; the retribution in which women drank the blood of their own infants; in which brothers fought brothers to the death, in the ruins of their own temple,—he whom that day they slew was the only being who could have saved them. And so, praying for them, he died.

And his mother and his well-beloved crept out from their hiding-places, and wept over him! And they laid him in a tomb, wherein never man lay. And his enemies sealed the stone with such cements as man can devise; and set over it such sentry police as Roman wit in arms had trained. And then came the Sabbath,—the Jewish Sabbath, the last day of the week;— saddest of days till then.

"Is this the end?" we can almost hear Nathaniel saying to Philip; "better I had staid brooding under my fig-tree; my poet-dreams, so vague and dim, were yet better than this horrid certainty!" "Is this the end?" might Andrew say to Simon Peter; "better we had swept the lake,—better traded fish in the market-place our lives long, than come to look on such horror!" "Is this the end?" might John, son of Thunder, say to his fierce brother James. "Better had we cast in our lot with Theudas, rushed on the Roman spear and shield, and died in fight like men!" "Is this the end?" might Mary mother, whisper; "better had my child died in his infant innocence, when Herod slew the others in Bethlehem." But no, this is not the end.

"Lo, I am with you always, even unto the end of the world."

"The works that I do, shall he do also; and greater works than these shall he do."

Such is the promise. And when the sad Saturday has at last crept by; and when the light of this darker morning just begins to break; when, on that night, so cold, and black, there just creeps up the ray of promise, lo, it is a blush of hope! The grave cannot hold him. These keepers fall fainting on the ground. This man-sealed rock rolls, tottering, from its bed. And he is risen! as he said.

He was the well beloved Son of God. Yes; and we are all God's children. Children of God's nature,—and therefore immortal, as is he. We are his children. Children? Yes! and therefore he gives to us the victory.

God is with us, and we are with him. Therefore there is no death to us, nor to his purpose failure. It may please him to call away even our Saviour from our sight. But if he goes away, the Holy Spirit comes! It may please him to bring in his kingdom, as Israel has not dreamed. But, none the less certainly, does his kingdom come! It may please him to win that victory by the Saviour's death on Calvary; nay, to give to a dying thief at his Saviour's side the first laurels of triumph. The victory may be won when Stephen faints; when James is beheaded; when Paul and Barnabas are stoned. But none the less is it victory! It is not upon fields of battle only that he asks for his martyrs. At the hands of Herod, dying of lust, he will call away St. James. At the wish of a dancing harlot, will John Baptist give his head. But they are martyrs still! And when their Master dies, because he has given a Judas the access to his person; when, on the morning of this "day of days," he rises; to all such martyrs, nay to all God's martyrs in all time,—to all their brethren—nay, to all his breth-ren, in all time,—God promises, that, while they will and do of his good pleasure, He will give to them the victory!

[The choir then sang the anthem, by Rev. Henry Ware: "Lift your glad voices in triumph on high." After the anthem, Mr. Hale said:]

I cannot think that it is necessary for me to try to illustrate the lesson of scripture. The contrasts which we have been tracing in the history, as we might have traced them last year or any year since that history passed, teach us the lessons of to-day, so that we cannot fail to learn them. We often tell you from the pulpit that there is no experience of your lives, however glad or however painful, however great or however small, for which you do not find fit lesson in these experiences of your Saviour's life. I do not know whether you always believe this. But I am sure you feel it and believe it in the great trial of to-day,—in these terrible contrasts of the week that has gone by. Sunday, our day of triumph: and, Monday, again, we thronged the temple here with our praises. Each day, a new victory; each day a new congratulation; till, when Thursday came,—the fast day of our old Puritan calendar,—we did not know whether fasting belonged to us. Could the children of the bride-chamber fast indeed? Who were we that we should condescend to fasting and humiliation?

My friends! in the few words which I spoke to you on that day,—the last words which I spoke to you before this morning,—I said that Christian humiliation and Christian thanksgiving belonged together. We gave God the glory, which we dared not claim ourselves. "When I am weak, then I am strong." That is the Christian's ejaculation, and on that Thursday of victory and thanksgiving, it was very easy for us to repeat it!

It ought to be as easy to repeat it to-day! Would God it were! Fasting and rejoicing are strangely mingled indeed to-day. The day of a nation's grief is the day of the church's rejoicing. Fittest day of all, indeed, for the day of such grief; for, but for this resurrection, this immortality of which to-day is token and symbol, such grief were intolerable! But for to-day's promise of victory, what should we have worth living for? It is not simply that this day assures us of the immortal life of the good, great man, who, in an instant, puts off this mortal body that he may put on his spiritual body. It is not simply that to-day tells us all is well with him. It is to the country, which he loved and served, that to-day, in its promises, gives a like assurance. That death has no power over the immortal spirit; that is the lesson of to-day. That Jesus Christ gives victory to his flock, in giving them the help, comfort, and blessing of the Most High; that promise is sealed to-day. That the eternal laws of God reign in men's affairs, and that men may trust him if they strive to follow those laws; that is the promise of his victory. That the republic is eternal if it makes itself a part of his kingdom. If its laws conform to his laws, no cerements can bind it, and no tombs can hold it. If it serve God, God gives to it immortality.

I dare not trust myself to speak a word regarding this simple, godly, good, great man, who, in a moment, has been called from the rule over a few cities to be master over many things, in that higher service where he enters into the joy of his Lord. To speak of him I must seek some other hour. Our lesson for to-day is, that the kingdom of God comes, and is eternal. The republic, if in simple faith it strive to make itself a part of that kingdom, lives forever. When we built this church, four years ago, we painted here upon the wall before you the beginning of the angels' song, in the words:

"Glory to God in the highest."

It was in the very outset of war; our own boys were coming home to us bleeding from the field, or were lying dead after the battle. And we stayed our hands at those words. We did not add the other words of the promise. But when last Sunday came, with its glad tidings, when it seemed as if we had endured to the very end, we ventured, in the fulfilment of the glad prophecy, to complete our imperfect inscription, and to add here the rest of the blessed legend:

"And on earth peace, good will toward men."

The martyrdom of Good Friday does not make us veil the motto, though we read it through our tears. Of such martyrs, it is as true as ever, that their blood is the seed of the church. Because they die, the kingdom comes! We do not forego our hope in the promise, "On earth peace, and good will among men." The President may be killed to-morrow, and his successor may be killed to-morrow, and his successor, and his; but the republic lives! While it seeks to do God's will, to will and to do of his good pleasure, He works with it, and gives it immortality. "Fear not little flock, it is your Father's good pleasure to give you the kingdom."

April 16, 1865

Ralph Waldo Emerson

Four days after Lincoln's death, as his body was being borne back to Springfield for burial, mourners gathered at the Unitarian Church in Concord to hear these remarks by Emerson. For an audience that had often found Lincoln lacking in his zeal for liberty, Emerson emphasized the late President's quintessentially American, log cabin to White House life, and accurately predicted that as a symbol of what historian Gabor Boritt has called "the right to rise," Lincoln would "serve his country even more by his death."

Remarks at the Services Held in Concord

We meet under the gloom of a calamity which darkens down over the minds of good men in all civil society, as the fearful tidings travel over sea, over land, from country to country, like the shadow of an uncalculated eclipse over the planet. Old as history is, and manifold as are its tragedies, I doubt if any death has caused so much pain to mankind as this has caused, or will cause, on its announcement; and this, not so much because nations are by modern arts brought so closely together, as because of the mysterious hopes and fears which, in the present day, are connected with the name and institutions of America.

In this country, on Saturday, every one was struck dumb, and saw at first only deep below deep, as he meditated on the ghastly blow. And perhaps, at this hour, when the coffin which contains the dust of the President sets forward on its long march through mourning States, on its way to his home in Illinois, we might well be silent, and suffer the awful voices of the time to thunder to us. Yes, but that first despair was brief: the man was not so to be mourned. He was the most active and hopeful of men; and his work had not perished: but acclamations of praise for the task he had accomplished burst out into a song of triumph, which even tears for his death cannot keep down.

The President stood before us as a man of the people. He was thoroughly American, had never crossed the sea, had never been spoiled by English insularity or French dissipation; a quite native, aboriginal man, as an acorn from the oak; no aping of foreigners, no frivolous accomplishments, Kentuckian born, working on a farm, a flatboatman, a captain in the Black Hawk war, a country lawyer, a representative in the rural Legislature of Illinois;—on such modest foundations the broad structure of his fame was laid. How slowly, and yet by happily prepared steps, he came to his place. All of us remember,—it is only a history of five or six years,—the surprise and the disappointment of the country at his first nomination by the Convention at Chicago. Mr. Seward, then in the culmination of his good fame, was the favorite of the Eastern States. And when the new and comparatively unknown name of Lincoln was announced, (notwithstanding the report of the acclamations of that Convention,) we heard the result coldly and sadly. It seemed too rash, on a purely local reputation, to build so grave a trust in such anxious times; and men naturally talked of the chances in politics as incalculable. But it turned out not to be chance. The profound good opinion which the people of Illinois and of the West had conceived of him, and which they had imparted to their colleagues that they also might justify themselves to their constituents at home, was not rash, though they did not begin to know the riches of his worth.

A plain man of the people, an extraordinary fortune attended him. He offered no shining qualities at the first encounter; he did not offend by superiority. He had a face and manner which disarmed suspicion, which inspired confidence, which confirmed good-will. He was a man without vices. He had a strong sense of duty, which it was very easy for him to obey. Then, he had what farmers call a long head; was excellent in working out the sum for himself; in arguing his case and convincing you fairly and firmly. Then, it turned out that he was a great worker; had prodigious faculty of performance; worked easily. A good worker is so rare; everybody has some disabling quality. In a host of young men that start together and promise so many brilliant leaders for the next age, each fails on trial; one by bad health, one by conceit, or by love of pleasure, or lethargy, or an ugly temper,—each has some disqualifying fault that throws him out of the career. But this man was sound to the core, cheerful, persistent, all right for labor, and liked nothing so well.

Then, he had a vast good-nature, which made him tolerant and accessible to all; fair-minded, leaning to the claim of the petitioner; affable, and not sensible to the affliction which the innumerable visits paid to him when President would have brought to any one else. And how this good-nature became a noble humanity, in many a tragic case which the events of the war brought to him, every one will remember; and with what increasing tenderness he dealt when a whole race was thrown on his compassion. The poor negro said of him, on an impressive occasion, "Massa Linkum am eberywhere."

Then his broad good-humor, running easily into jocular talk, in which he delighted and in which he excelled, was a rich gift to this wise man. It enabled him to keep his secret; to meet every kind of man and every rank in society; to take off the edge of the severest decisions; to mask his own purpose and sound his companion; and to catch with true instinct the temper of every company he addressed. And, more than all, it is to a man of severe labor, in anxious and exhausting crises, the natural restorative, good as sleep, and is the protection of the overdriven brain against rancor and insanity.

He is the author of a multitude of good sayings, so disguised as pleasantries that it is certain they had no reputation at first but as jests; and only later, by the very acceptance and adoption they find in the mouths of millions, turn out to be the wisdom of the hour. I am sure if this man had ruled in a period of less facility of printing, he would have become mythological in a very few years, like Æsop or Pilpay, or one of the Seven Wise Masters, by his fables and proverbs. But the weight and penetration of many passages in his letters, messages and speeches, hidden now by the very closeness of their application to the moment, are destined hereafter to wide fame. What pregnant definitions; what unerring common sense; what foresight; and, on great occasion, what lofty, and more than national, what humane tone! His brief speech at Gettysburg will not easily be surpassed by words on any recorded occasion. This, and one other American speech, that of John Brown to the court that tried him, and a part of Kossuth's speech at Birmingham, can only be compared with each other, and with no fourth.

His occupying the chair of State was a triumph of the good-sense of mankind, and of the public conscience. This middle-class country had got a middle-class President, at last. Yes, in manners and sympathies, but not in powers, for his powers were superior. This man grew according to the need. His mind mastered the problem of the day; and, as the problem grew, so did his comprehension of it. Rarely was man so fitted to the event. In the midst of fears and jealousies, in the Babel of counsels and parties, this man wrought incessantly with all his might and all his honesty, laboring to find what the people wanted, and how to obtain that. It cannot be said there is any exaggeration of his worth. If ever a man was fairly tested, he was. There was no lack of resistance, nor of slander, nor of ridicule. The times have allowed no state secrets; the nation has been in such ferment, such multitudes had to be trusted, that no secret could be kept. Every door was ajar, and we know all that befell.

Then, what an occasion was the whirlwind of the war. Here was place for no holiday magistrate, no fair-weather sailor; the new pilot was hurried to the helm in a tornado. In four years,—four years of battle-days,—his endurance, his fertility of resources, his magnanimity, were sorely tried and never found wanting. There, by his courage, his justice, his even temper, his fertile counsel, his humanity, he stood a heroic figure in the centre of a heroic epoch. He is the true history of the American people in his time. Step by step he walked before them; slow with their slowness, quickening his march by theirs, the true representative of this continent; an entirely public man; father of his country, the pulse of twenty millions throbbing in his heart, the thought of their minds articulated by his tongue.

Adam Smith remarks that the axe, which in Houbraken's portraits of British kings and worthies is engraved under those who have suffered at the block, adds a certain lofty charm to the picture. And who does not see, even in this tragedy so recent, how fast the terror and rain of the massacre are already burning into glory around the victim? Far happier this fate than to have lived to be wished away; to have watched the decay of his own faculties; to have seen,—perhaps even he,—the proverbial ingratitude of statesmen; to have seen mean men preferred. Had he not lived long enough to keep the greatest promise that ever man made to his fellow-men,—the practical abolition of slavery? He had seen Tennessee, Missouri and Maryland emancipate their slaves. He had seen Savannah, Charleston and Richmond surrendered; had seen the main army of the rebellion lay down its arms. He had conquered the public opinion of Canada, England and France. Only Washington can compare with him in fortune.

And what if it should turn out, in the unfolding of the web, that he had reached the term; that this heroic deliverer could no longer serve us; that the rebellion had touched its natural conclusion, and what remained to be done required new and uncommitted hands,—a new spirit born out of the ashes of the war; and that Heaven, wishing to show the world a completed benefactor, shall make him serve his country even more by his death than by his life? Nations, like kings, are not good by facility and complaisance. "The kindness of kings consists in justice and strength." Easy good-nature has been the dangerous foible of the Republic, and it was necessary that its enemies should outrage it, and drive us to unwonted firmness, to secure the salvation of this country in the next ages.

The ancients believed in a serene and beautiful Genius which ruled in the affairs of nations; which, with a slow but stern justice, carried forward the fortunes of certain chosen houses, weeding out single offenders or offending families, and securing at last the firm prosperity of the favorites of Heaven. It was too narrow a view of the Eternal Nemesis. There is a serene Providence which rules the fate of nations, which makes little account of time, little of one generation or race, makes no account of disasters, conquers alike by what is called defeat or by what is called victory, thrusts aside enemy and obstruction, crushes everything immoral as inhuman, and obtains the ultimate triumph of the best race by the sacrifice of everything which resists the moral laws of the world. It makes its own instruments, creates the man for the time, trains him in poverty, inspires his genius, and arms him for his task. It has given every race its own talent, and ordains that only that race which combines perfectly with the virtues of all shall endure.

April 19, 1865

William Cullen Bryant

Since introducing Lincoln at Cooper Union more than five years earlier, Bryant had met him only once more—greeting him, along with other presidential electors from New York City, when Lincoln passed through town again en route to his inauguration in 1861. Bryant and his newspaper remained faithfully pro-Lincoln during the Civil War, and after the assassination he joined the chorus of posthumous praise.

The Death of Lincoln

Oh, slow to smite and swift to spare,
    Gentle and merciful and just!
Who, in the fear of God, didst bear
    The sword of power, a nation's trust!

In sorrow by thy bier we stand,
    Amid the awe that hushes all,
And speak the anguish of a land
    That shook with horror at thy fall.

Thy task is done; the bond are free:
    We bear thee to an honored grave,
Whose proudest monument shall be
    The broken fetters of the slaves.

Pure was thy life; its bloody close
    Hath placed thee with the sons of light,
Among the noble host of those
    Who perished in the cause of Right.

April, 1865.

Henry Ward Beecher

A younger brother of Harriet Beecher Stowe, Henry Ward Beecher (1813–1887) accepted the pulpit of the Plymouth Church in Brooklyn in 1847 and soon became one of the most famous preachers in America. During his trip east in 1860 to speak at Cooper Union, Lincoln heard Beecher preach twice, and reportedly later told another clergyman he believed "there was not upon record, in ancient or modern biography, so productive a mind, as had been exhibited in the career of Henry Ward Beecher." A staunch opponent of slavery, Beecher delivered the oration at the ceremonial re-raising of the American flag over Fort Sumter on April 14, 1865, and was returning home by sea when he learned of Lincoln's murder. He gave this sermon on the second Sunday after the assassination.

Sermon Preached in Brooklyn

"And Moses went up from the plains of Moab, unto the mountain of Nebo, to the top of Pisgah, that is over against Jericho; and the Lord showed him all the land of Gilead, unto Dan, and all Naphtali, and the land of Ephraim, and Manasseh, and all the land of Judah, unto the utmost sea, and the south, and the plain of the valley of Jericho, the city of palm trees, unto Zoor. And the Lord said unto him, this is the land which I swear unto Abraham, unto Isaac, and unto Jacob, saying, I will give it unto thy seed: I have caused thee to see it with thine eyes, but thou shalt not go over thither. So Moses, the servant of the Lord, died there in the land of Moab, according to the word of the Lord."—Deut. xxxiv. 1–5.

There is no historic figure more noble than that of the Jewish lawgiver. After so many thousand years, the figure of Moses is not diminished, but stands up against the background of early days, distinct and individual as if he had lived but yesterday. There is scarcely another event in history more touching than his death. He had borne the great burdens of state for forty years, shaped the Jews to a nation, filled out their civil and religious polity, administered their laws, guided their steps, or dwelt with them in all their journeyings in the wilderness; had mourned in their punishment, kept step with their march, and led them in wars, until the end of their labors drew nigh. The last stage was reached. Jordan only lay between them and the promised land. The promised land!—oh, what yearnings had heaved his breast for that divinely place! He had dreamed of it by night, and mused by day. It was holy and endeared as God's favored spot. It was to be the cradle of an illustrious history. All his long, laborious, and now weary life, he had aimed at this as the consummation of every desire, the reward of every toil and pain. Then came the word of the Lord to him, "Thou mayest not go over. Get thee up into the mountain, look upon it, and die."

From that silent summit, the hoary leader gazed to the north, to the south, to the west, with hungry eyes. The dim outlines rose up. The hazy recesses spoke of quiet valleys between the hills. With eager longing, with sad resignation, he looked upon the promised land. It was now to him a forbidden land. It was a moment's anguish. He forgot all his personal wants, and drank in the vision of his people's home. His work was done. There lay God's promise fulfilled. There was the seat of coming Jerusalem; there the city of Judah's King; the sphere of judges and prophets; the mount of sorrow and salvation; the nest whence were to fly blessings innumerable to all mankind. Joy chased sadness from every feature, and the prophet laid him down and died.

Again a great leader of the people has passed through toil, sorrow, battle, and war, and come near to the promised land of peace, into which he might not pass over. Who shall recount our martyr's sufferings for this people? Since the November of 1860, his horizon has been black with storms. By day and by night, he trod a way of danger and darkness. On his shoulders rested a government dearer to him than his own life. At its integrity millions of men were striking at home. Upon this government foreign eyes lowered. It stood like a lone island in a sea full of storms; and every tide and wave seemed eager to devour it. Upon thousands of hearts great sorrows and anxieties have rested, but not on one such, and in such measure, as upon that simple, truthful, noble soul, our faithful and sainted Lincoln. Never rising to the enthusiasm of more impassioned natures in hours of hope, and never sinking with the mercurial in hours of defeat to the depths of despondency, he held on with immovable patience and fortitude, putting caution against hope, that it might not be premature, and hope against caution, that it might not yield to dread and danger. He wrestled ceaselessly, through four black and dreadful purgatorial years, wherein God was cleansing the sin of his people as by fire.

At last, the watcher beheld the gray dawn for the country. The mountains began to give forth their forms from out the darkness; and the East came rushing toward us with arms full of joy for all our sorrows. Then it was for him to be glad exceedingly, that had sorrowed immeasurably. Peace could bring to no other heart such joy, such rest, such honor, such trust, such gratitude. But he looked upon it as Moses looked upon the promised land. Then the wail of a nation proclaimed that he had gone from among us. Not thine the sorrow, but ours, sainted soul. Thou hast indeed entered the promised land, while we are yet on the march. To us remains the rocking of the deep, the storm upon the land, days of duty and nights of watching; but thou art sphered high above all darkness and fear, beyond all sorrow and weariness. Rest, oh weary heart! Rejoice exceedingly, thou that hast enough suffered! Thou hast beheld Him who invisibly led thee in this great wilderness. Thou standest among the elect. Around thee are the royal men that have ennobled human life in every age. Kingly art thou, with glory on thy brow as a diadem. And joy is upon thee for ever more. Over all this land, over all the little cloud of years that now from thine infinite horizon moves back as a speck, thou art lifted up as high as the star is above the clouds that hide us, but never reach it. In the goodly company of Mount Zion thou shalt find that rest which thou hast sorrowing sought in vain; and thy name, an everlasting name in heaven, shall flourish in fragrance and beauty as long as men shall last upon the earth, or hearts remain, to revere truth, fidelity, and goodness.

Never did two such orbs of experience meet in one hemisphere, as the joy and the sorrow of the same week in this land. The joy was as sudden as if no man had expected it, and as entrancing as if it had fallen a sphere from heaven. It rose up over sobriety, and swept business from its moorings, and ran down through the land in irresistible course. Men embraced each other in brotherhood that were strangers in the flesh. They sang, or prayed, or, deeper yet, many could only think thanksgiving and weep gladness. That peace was sure; that government was firmer than ever; that the land was cleansed of plague; that the ages were opening to our footsteps, and we were to begin a march of blessings; that blood was staunched, and scowling enmities were sinking like storms beneath the horizon; that the dear fatherland, nothing lost, much gained, was to rise up in unexampled honor among the nations of the earth—these thoughts, and that undistinguishable throng of fancies, and hopes, and desires, and yearnings, that filled the soul with tremblings like the heated air of midsummer days—all these kindled up such a surge of joy as no words may describe.

In one hour joy lay without a pulse, without a gleam, or breath. A sorrow came that swept through the land as huge storms sweep through the forest and field, rolling thunder along the sky, disheveling the flowers, daunting every singer in thicket or forest, and pouring blackness and darkness across the land and up the mountains. Did ever so many hearts, in so brief a time, touch two such boundless feelings? It was the uttermost of joy; it was the uttermost of sorrow—noon and midnight, without a space between.

The blow brought not a sharp pang. It was so terrible that at first it stunned sensibility. Citizens were like men awakened at midnight by an earthquake, and bewildered to find everything that they were accustomed to trust wavering and falling. The very earth was no longer solid. The first feeling was the least. Men waited to get straight to feel. They wandered in the streets as if groping after some impending dread, or undeveloped sorrow, or some one to tell them what ailed them. They met each other as if each would ask the other, "Am I awake, or do I dream?" There was a piteous helplessness. Strong men bowed down and wept. Other and common griefs belonged to some one in chief: this belonged to all. It was each and every man's. Every virtuous household in the land felt as if its first-born were gone. Men were bereaved, and walked for days as if a corpse lay unburied in their dwellings. There was nothing else to think of. They could speak of nothing but that; and yet, of that they could speak only falteringly. All business was laid aside. Pleasure forgot to smile. The city for nearly a week ceased to roar. The great Leviathan lay down, and was still. Even avarice stood still, and greed was strangely moved to generous sympathy and universal sorrow. Rear to his name monuments, found charitable institutions, and write his name above their lintels; but no monument will ever equal the universal, spontaneous, and sublime sorrow that in a moment swept down lines and parties, and covered up animosities, and in an hour brought a divided people into unity of grief and indivisible fellowship of anguish.

For myself, I cannot yet command that quietness of spirit needed for a just and temperate delineation of a man whom goodness has made great. Leaving that, if it please God, to some other occasion, I pass to some considerations, aside from the martyr President's character, which may be fit for this hour's instruction.

1. Let us not mourn that his departure was so sudden, nor fill our imagination with horror at its method. Men, long eluding and evading sorrow, when at last they are overtaken by it, seem enchanted, and seek to make their sorrow sorrowful to the very uttermost, and to bring out every drop of suffering which they possibly can. This is not Christian, though it may be natural. When good men pray for deliverance from sudden death, it is only that they may not be plunged without preparation, all disrobed, into the presence of their Judge. When one is ready to depart, suddenness of death is a blessing. It is a painful sight to see a tree overthrown by a tornado, wrenched from its foundations, and broken down like a weed; but it is yet more painful to see a vast and venerable tree lingering with vain strife against decay, which age and infirmity have marked for destruction. The process by which strength wastes, and the mind is obscured, and the tabernacle is taken down, is humiliating and painful; and it is good and grand when a man departs to his rest from out of the midst of duty, full-armed and strong, with pulse beating

time. For such an one to go suddenly, if he be prepared to go, is but to terminate a most noble life in its most noble manner Mark the words of the Master:

"Let your loins be girded about, and your lights burning; and ye yourselves like unto men that wait for their lord, when he will return from the wedding; that when he cometh and knocketh they may open unto him immediately. Blessed are those servants whom the lord when he cometh shall find watching."

Not they that go in a stupor, but they that go with all their powers about them, and wide-awake, to meet their Master, as to a wedding, are blessed. He died watching. He died with his armor on. In the midst of hours of labors, in the very heart of patriotic consultations, just returned from camps and councils, he was stricken down. No fever dried his blood. No slow waste consumed him. All at once, in full strength and manhood, with his girdle tight about him, he departed, and walks with God.

Nor was the manner of his death more shocking, if we divest it of the malignity of the motives which caused it. The mere instrument itself is not one that we should shrink from contemplating. Have not thousands of soldiers fallen on the field of battle by the bullets of the enemy? Is being killed in battle counted to be a dreadful mode of dying? It was as if he had died in battle. Do not all soldiers that must fall ask to depart in the hour of battle and victory? He went in the hour of victory.

There has not been a poor drummer-boy in all this war that has fallen for whom the great heart of Lincoln would not have bled; there has not been one private soldier, without note or name, slain among thousands, and hid in the pit among hundreds without even the memorial of a separate burial, for whom the President would not have wept. He was a man from the common people that never forgot his kind. And now that he who might not bear the march, and toil, and battles with these humble citizens has been called to die by the bullet, as they were, do you not feel that there was a peculiar fitness to his nature and life, that he should in death be joined with them, in a final common experience, to whom he had been joined in all his sympathies.

For myself, when any event is susceptible of a higher and nobler garnishing, I know not what that disposition is that should seek to drag it down to the depths of gloom, and write it all over with the scrawls of horror or fear. I let the light of nobler thoughts fall upon his departure, and bless God that there is some argument of consolation in the matter and manner of his going, as there was in the matter and manner of his staying.

2. This blow was but the expiring rebellion. As a miniature gives all the form and features of its subject, so, epitomized in this foul act, we find the whole nature and disposition of slavery. It begins in a wanton destruction of all human rights, and in a desecration of all the sanctities of heart and home; and it is the universal enemy of mankind, and of God, who made man. It can be maintained only at the sacrifice of every right and moral feeling in its abettors and upholders. I deride the man that points me to any man bred amid slavery, believing in it, and willingly practicing it, and tells me that he is a *man*. I shall find saints in perdition sooner than I shall find true manhood under the influences of so accursed a system as this. It is a two-edged sword, cutting both ways, violently destroying manhood in the oppressed, and insidiously destroying manhood in the oppressor. The problem is solved, the demonstration is completed, in our land. Slavery wastes its victims; and it destroys the masters. It destroys public morality, and the possibility of it. It corrupts manhood in its very centre and elements. Communities in which it exists are not to be trusted. They are rotten. Nor can you find timber grown in this accursed soil of iniquity that is fit to build our ship of state, or lay the foundation of our households. The patriotism that grows up under this blight, when put to proof, is selfish and brittle; and he that leans upon it shall be pierced. The honor that grows up in the midst of slavery is not honor, but a bastard quality that usurps the place of its better, only to disgrace the name of honor. And, as long as there is conscience, or reason, or Christianity, the honor that slavery begets will be a bye-word and a hissing. The whole moral nature of men reared to familiarity and connivance with slavery is death-smitten. The needless rebellion; the treachery of its leaders to oaths and solemn trusts; their violation of the commonest principles of fidelity, sitting in senates, in councils, in places of public confidence, only to betray and to destroy; the long, general, and unparalleled

cruelty to prisoners, without provocation, and utterly without excuse: the unreasoning malignity and fierceness—these all mark the symptoms of that disease of slavery which is a deadly poison to soul and body.

1. I do not say that there are not single natures, here and there, scattered through the vast wilderness which is covered with this poisonous vine, who escape the poison. There are, but they are not to be found among the men that believe in it, and that have been moulded by it. They are the exceptions. Slavery is itself barbarity. That nation which cherishes it is barbarous; and no outward tinsel or glitter can redeem it from the charge of barbarism. And it was fit that its expiring blow should be such as to take away from men the last forbearance, the last pity, and fire the soul with an invincible determination that the breeding-ground of such mischiefs and monsters shall be utterly and forever destroyed.

2. We needed not that he should put on paper that he believed in slavery, who, with treason, with murder, with cruelty infernal, hovered around that majestic man to destroy his life. He was himself but the long sting with which slavery struck at liberty; and he carried the poison that belonged to slavery. And as long as this nation lasts, it will never be forgotten that we have had one martyred President—never! Never, while time lasts, while heaven lasts, while hell rocks and groans, will it be forgotten that slavery, by its minions, slew him, and, in slaying him, made manifest its whole nature and tendency.

3. This blow was aimed at the life of the Government and of the nation. Lincoln was slain; America was meant. The man was cast down; the Government was smitten at. The President was killed: it was national life, breathing freedom, and meaning beneficence, that was sought. He, the man of Illinois, the private man, divested of robes and the insignia of authority, representing nothing but his personal self, might have been hated; but it was not that that ever would have called forth the murderer's blow. It was because he stood in the place of government, representing government, and a government that represented right and liberty, that he was singled out.

This, then, is a crime against universal government. It is not a blow at the foundations of our government, more than at the foundations of the English Government, of the French Government, of every compacted and well-organized government. It was a crime against mankind. The whole world will repudiate and stigmatize it as a deed without a shade of redeeming light. For this was not the oppressed, goaded to extremity, turning on his oppressor. Not the shadow of a cloud, even, has rested on the South, of wrong; and they knew it right well.

In a council held in the City of Charleston, just preceding to the attack on Fort Sumter, two commissioners were appointed to go to Washington; one on the part of the army from Fort Sumter, and one on the part of the Confederates. The lieutenant that was designated to go for us said it seemed to him that it would be of little use for him to go, as his opinion was immovably fixed in favor of maintaining the Government in whose service he was employed. Then Gov. Pickens took him aside, detaining, for an hour and a half, the railroad train that was to convey them on their errand. He opened to him the whole plan and secret of the Southern conspiracy, and said to him, distinctly and repeatedly (for it was needful, he said, to lay aside disguises), that the South had never been wronged, and that all their pretences of grievance in the matter of tariffs, or anything else, were invalid. "But," said he, "we must carry the people with us; and we allege these things, as all statesmen do many things that they do not believe, because they are the only instruments by which the people can be managed." He then and there declared that the two sections of country were so antagonistic in ideas and policies that they could not live together, that it was fore-ordained that Northern and Southern men must keep apart on account of differences in ideas and policies, and that all the pretences of the South about wrongs suffered were but pretences, as they very well knew. This is testimony which was given by one of the leaders in the rebellion, and which will, probably, ere long, be given under hand and seal to the public. So the South has never had wrong visited upon it except by that which was inherent in it.

This was not, then, the avenging hand of one goaded by tyranny. It was not a despot turned on by his victim. It was the venomous hatred of liberty wielded by an avowed advocate of slavery. And, though there may have been cases of murder in which there were shades of palliation, yet this murder was without provocation, without temptation, without reason, sprung from the fury of a heart cankered to all that was just and good, and corrupted by all that was wicked and foul.

4. The blow has signally failed. The cause is not stricken; it is strengthened. This nation has dissolved—but in tears only. It stands four-square, more solid, to-day, than any pyramid in Egypt. This people are neither wasted, nor daunted, nor disordered. Men hate slavery and love liberty with stronger hate and love to-day than ever before. The Government is not weakened, it is made stronger. How naturally and easily were the ranks closed! Another stepped forward, in the hour that the one fell, to take his place and his mantle; and I avow my belief that he will be found a man true to every instinct of liberty; true to the whole trust that is reposed in him; vigilant of the Constitution; careful of the laws; wise for liberty, in that he himself, through his life, has known what it was to suffer from the stings of slavery, and to prize liberty from bitter personal experiences. [Applause.]

Where could the head of government in any monarchy be smitten down by the hand of an assassin, and the funds not quiver nor fall, one-half of one per cent? After a long period of national disturbance, after four years of drastic war, after tremendous drafts on the resources of the country, in the height and top of our burdens, the heart of this people is such that now, when the head of government is stricken down, the public funds do not waver, but stand as the granite ribs in our mountains.

Republican institutions have been vindicated in this experience as they never were before; and the whole history of the last four years, rounded up by this cruel stroke, seems, in the providence of God, to have been clothed, now, with an illustration, with a sympathy, with an aptness, and with a significance, such as we never could have expected nor imagined. God, I think, has said, by the voice of this event, to all nations of the earth, "Republican liberty, based upon true Christianity, is firm as the foundation of the globe." [Applause.]

5. Even he who now sleeps has, by this event, been clothed with new influence. Dead, he speaks to men who now willingly hear what before they refused to listen to. Now his simple and weighty words will be gathered like those of Washington, and your children, and your children's children, shall be taught to ponder the simplicity and deep wisdom of utterances which, in their time, passed, in party heat, as idle words. Men will receive a new impulse of patriotism for his sake, and will guard with zeal the whole country which he loved so well. I swear you, on the altar of his memory, to be more faithful to the country for which he has perished. [Applause.] They will, as they follow his hearse, swear a new hatred to that slavery against which he warred, and which in vanquishing him, has made him a martyr and a conqueror. I swear you, by the memory of this martyr, to hate slavery with an unappeasable hatred. [Applause.] They will admire and imitate the firmness of this man, his inflexible conscience for the right; and yet his gentleness, as tender as a woman's, his moderation of spirit, which not all the heat of party could inflame, nor all the jars and disturbances of this country shake out of its place. I swear you to a emulation of his justice, his moderation, and his mercy.

You I can comfort; but how can I speak to that twilight million to whom his name was as the name of an angel of God? There will be wailing in places which no minister shall be able to reach. When, in hovel and in cot, in wood and in wilderness, in the field throughout the South, the dusky children, who looked upon him as that Moses whom God sent before them to lead them out of the land of bondage, learn that he has fallen, who shall comfort them? O, thou Shepherd of Israel, that didst comfort thy people of old, to thy care we commit the helpless, the long-wronged, and grieved.

And now the martyr is moving in triumphal march, mightier than when alive. The nation rises up at every stage of his coming. Cities and states are his pall-bearers, and the cannon beats the hours with solemn progression. Dead, *dead*, DEAD, he yet speaketh! Is Washington dead? Is Hampden dead? Is David dead? Is any man that ever was fit to live dead? Disenthralled of flesh, and risen in the unobstructed sphere where passion never comes, he begins his illimitable work. His life now is grafted upon the infinite, and will be fruitful as no earthly life can be. Pass on, thou that hast overcome! Your sorrows, oh people, are his peace! Your bells, and bands, and muffled drums, sound triumph in his ear. Wail and weep here; God makes it echo joy and triumph there. Pass on!

Four years ago, oh, Illinois, we took from your midst an untried man, and from among the people. We return him to you a mighty conqueror. Not thine any more, but the nation's; not ours, but the world's. Give him place, oh, ye prairies! In the midst of this great continent his dust shall rest, a sacred treasure to myriads who shall pilgrim to that shrine to kindle anew their zeal and patriotism. Ye winds that move over the mighty places of the West, chant his requiem! Ye people, behold a martyr whose blood, as so many articulate words, pleads for fidelity, for law, for liberty!

April 23, 1865

George Bancroft

Best known for his popular and influential multi-volume work *A History of the United States*, Bancroft (1800–1891) had served as Secretary of the Navy and minister to Great Britain during the Polk administration and backed Stephen A. Douglas in the 1860 presidential election. Bancroft supported the war against secession while initially retaining doubts about Lincoln's leadership. When the slain President's body arrived in New York City for a lavish funeral procession witnessed by hundreds of thousands of mourners, Bancroft was chosen to deliver the principal oration at a huge public rally in Union Square. Unlike many eulogists of the period, Bancroft maintained a secular tone, commending Lincoln for his role in preserving the Union and emancipating the slaves without engaging in sanctification. His oration also recorded some of the passions of the moment: the "state in our vicinity" he reproached for refusing to ratify the abolitionist Thirteenth Amendment is New Jersey, and the unnamed general he criticized is William T. Sherman, who had signed an ill-advised (and quickly repudiated) lenient surrender agreement with Confederate General Joseph Johnston in North Carolina on April 18.

Oration in Union Square, New York City

Our grief and horror at the crime which has clothed the continent in mourning, find no adequate expression in words, and no relief in tears. The President of the United States of America has fallen by the hands of an assassin. Neither the office with which he was invested by the approved choice of a mighty people, nor the most simple-hearted kindliness of nature, could save him from the fiendish passions of relentless fanaticism. The wailings of the millions attend his remains as they are borne in solemn procession over our great rivers, along the seaside, beyond the mountains, across the prairie, to their resting place in the valley of the Mississippi. His funeral knell vibrates through the world, and the friends of freedom of every tongue and in every clime are his mourners.

Too few days have passed away since Abraham Lincoln stood in the flush of vigorous manhood, to permit any attempt at an analysis of his character or an exposition of his career. We find it hard to believe that his large eyes, which in their softness and beauty expressed nothing but benevolence and gentleness, are closed in death; we almost look for the pleasant smile that brought out more vividly the earnest cast of his features, which were serious even to sadness. A few years ago he was a village attorney, engaged in the support of a rising family, unknown to fame, scarcely named beyond his neighborhood; his administration made him the most conspicuous man in his country, and drew on him first the astonished gaze, and then the respect and admiration of the world.

Those who come after us will decide how much of the wonderful results of his public career is due to his own good common sense, his shrewd sagacity, readiness of wit, quick interpretation of the public mind, his rare combination of fixedness and pliancy, his steady tendency of purpose; how much to the American people, who, as he walked with them side by side, inspired him with their own wisdom and energy; and how much to the overruling laws of the moral world, by which the selfishness of evil is made to defeat itself. But after every allowance, it will remain that members of the government which preceded his administration opened the gates to treason, and he closed them; that when he went to Washington the ground on which he trod shook under his feet, and he left the republic on a solid foundation; that traitors had seized public forts and arsenals, and he recovered them for the United States, to whom they belonged; that the capital, which he found the abode of slaves, is now the home only of the free; that the boundless public domain which was grasped at, and, in a great measure, held for the diffusion of slavery, is now irrevocably devoted to freedom; that then men talked a jargon of a balance of power in a republic between slave states and free states, and now the foolish words are blown away forever by the breath of Maryland, Missouri, and Tennessee; that a terrible cloud of political heresy rose from the abyss, threatening to hide the light of the sun, and under its darkness a rebellion was growing into indefinable proportions; now the atmosphere is purer than ever before, and the insurrection is vanishing away; the country is cast into another mould, and the gigantic system of wrong, which had been the work of more than two centuries, is dashed down, we hope forever. And as to himself, personally: he was then scoffed at by the proud as unfit for his station, and now against the usage of later years and in spite of numerous competitors he was the unbiased and the undoubted choice of the American people for a second term of service. Through all the mad business of treason he retained the sweetness of a most placable disposition; and the slaughter of myriads of the best on the battle field, and the more terrible destruction of our men in captivity by the slow torture of exposure and starvation, had never been able to provoke him into harboring one vengeful feeling or one purpose of cruelty.

How shall the nation most completely show its sorrow at Mr. Lincoln's death? How shall it best honor his memory? There can be but one answer. He was struck down when he was highest in its service, and in strict conformity with duty was engaged in carrying out principles affecting its life, its good name, and its relations to the cause of freedom and the progress of mankind. Grief must take the character of action, and breathe itself forth in the assertion of the policy to which he fell a victim. The standard which he held in his hand must be uplifted again higher and more firmly than before, and must be carried on to triumph. Above everything else, his proclamation of the first day of January, 1863, declaring throughout the parts of the country in rebellion, the freedom of all persons who had been held as slaves, must be affirmed and maintained.

Events, as they rolled onward, have removed every doubt of the legality and binding force of that proclamation. The country and the rebel government have each laid claim to the public service of the slave, and yet but one of the two can have a rightful claim to such service. That rightful claim belongs to the United States, because every one born on their soil, with the few exceptions of the children of travellers and transient residents, owes them a primary allegiance. Every one so born has been counted among those represented in Congress; every slave has ever been represented in Congress; imperfectly and wrongly it may be—but still has been counted and represented. The slave born on our soil always owed allegiance to the general government. It may in time past have been a qualified allegiance, manifested through his master, as the allegiance of a ward through its guardian, or of an infant through its parent. But when the master became false to his allegiance, the slave stood face to face with his country; and his allegiance, which may before have been a qualified one, became direct and immediate. His chains fell off, and he rose at once in the presence of the nation, bound, like the rest of us, to its defence. Mr. Lincoln's proclamation did but take notice of the already existing right of the bondman to freedom. The treason of the master made it a public crime for the slave to continue his obedience; the treason of a state set free the collective bondmen of that state.

This doctrine is supported by the analogy of precedents. In the times of feudalism the treason of the lord of the manor deprived him of his serfs; the spurious feudalism that existed among us differs in many respects from the feudalism of the middle ages, but so far the precedent runs parallel with the present case; for treason the master then, for treason the master now, loses his slaves.

In the middle ages the sovereign appointed another lord over the serfs and the land which they cultivated; in our day the sovereign makes them masters of their own persons, lords over themselves.

It has been said that we are at war, and that emancipation is not a belligerent right. The objection disappears before analysis. In a war between independent powers the invading foreigner invites to his standard all who will give him aid, whether bond or free, and he rewards them according to his ability and his pleasure, with gifts or freedom: but when at a peace, he withdraws from the invaded country, he must take his aiders and comforters with him; or if he leaves them behind, where he has no court to enforce his decrees, he can give them no security, unless it be by the stipulations of a treaty. In a civil war it is altogether different. There, when rebellion is crushed, the old government is restored, and its courts resume their jurisdiction. So it is with us; the United States have courts of their own, that must punish the guilt of treason and vindicate the freedom of persons whom the fact of rebellion has set free.

Nor may it be said, that because slavery existed in most of the states when the Union was formed, it cannot rightfully be interfered with now. A change has taken place, such as Madison foresaw, and for which he pointed out the remedy. The constitutions of states had been transformed before the plotters of treason carried them away into rebellion. When the federal Constitution was framed, general emancipation was thought to be near; and everywhere the respective legislatures had authority, in the exercise of their ordinary functions, to do away with slavery. Since that time the attempt has been made in what are called slave states, to render the condition of slavery perpetual; and events have proved with the clearness of demonstration, that a constitution which seeks to continue a caste of hereditary bondmen through endless generations is inconsistent with the existence of republican institutions.

So, then, the new President and the people of the United States must insist that the proclamation of freedom shall stand as a reality. And, moreover, the people must never cease to insist that the Constitution shall be so amended as utterly to prohibit slavery on any part of our soil for evermore.

Alas! that a state in our vicinity should withhold its assent to this last beneficent measure; its refusal was an encouragement to our enemies equal to the gain of a pitched battle; and delays the only hopeful method of pacification. The removal of the cause of the rebellion is not only demanded by justice; it is the policy of mercy, making room for a wider clemency; it is the part of order against a chaos of controversy; its success brings with it true reconcilement, a lasting peace, a continuous growth of confidence through an assimilation of the social condition.

Here is the fitting expression of the mourning of to-day.

And let no lover of his country say that this warning is uncalled for. The cry is delusive that slavery is dead. Even now it is nerving itself for a fresh struggle for continuance. The last winds from the south waft to us the sad intelligence that a man who had surrounded himself with the glory of the most brilliant and most varied achievements, who but a week ago was counted with affectionate pride among the greatest benefactors of his country and the ablest generals of all time, has initiated the exercise of more than the whole power of the Executive, and under the name of peace has, perhaps unconsciously, revived slavery, and given the hope of security and political power to traitors, from the Chesapeake to the Rio Grande. Why could he not remember the dying advice of Washington, never to draw the sword but for self-defence or the rights of his country, and when drawn, never to sheath it till its work should be accomplished? And yet, from this ill-considered act, which the people with one united voice condemn, no great evil will follow save the shadow on his own fame, and that also we hope will pass away. The individual, even in the greatness of military glory, sinks into insignificance before the resistless movements of ideas in the history of man. No one can turn back or stay the march of Providence.

No sentiment of despair may mix with our sorrow. We owe it to the memory of the dead, we owe it to the cause of popular liberty throughout the world, that the sudden crime which has taken the life of the President of the United States shall not produce the least impediment in the smooth course of public affairs. This great city, in the midst of unexampled emblems of deeply-seated grief, has sustained itself with composure and magnanimity. It has nobly done its part in guarding against the derangement of business or the slightest shock to public credit. The enemies of the republic put it to the severest trial; but the voice of faction has not been heard; doubt and despondency have been unknown. In serene majesty the country rises in the beauty and strength and hope of youth, and proves to the world the quiet energy and the durability of institutions growing out of the reason and affections of the people.

Heaven has willed it that the United States shall live. The nations of the earth cannot spare them. All the wornout aristocracies of Europe saw in the spurious feudalism of slaveholding, their strongest outpost, and banded themselves together with the deadly enemies of our national life. If the Old World will discuss the respective advantages of oligarchy or equality; of the union of church and state, or the rightful freedom of religion; of land accessible to the many, or of land monopolized by an ever-decreasing number of the few, the United States must live to control the decision by their quiet and unobtrusive example. It has often and truly been observed, that the trust and affection of the masses gather naturally round an individual; if the inquiry is made, whether the man so trusted and beloved shall elicit from the reason of the people enduring institutions of their own, or shall sequester political power for a superintending dynasty, the United States must live to solve the problem. If a question is raised on the respective merits of Timoleon or Julius Cæsar, of Washington or Napoleon, the United States must be there to call to mind that there were twelve Cæsars, most of them the opprobrium of the human race, and to contrast with them the line of American presidents.

The duty of the hour is incomplete, our mourning is insincere, if, while we express unwavering trust in the great principles that underlie our government, we do not also give our support to the man to whom the people have entrusted its administration.

Andrew Johnson is now, by the Constitution, the president of the United States, and he stands before the world as the most conspicuous representative of the industrial classes. Left an orphan at four years old, poverty and toil were his steps to honor. His youth was not passed in the halls of colleges; nevertheless he has received a thorough political education in statesmanship, in the school of the people and by long experience of public life. A village functionary; member successively of each branch of the Tennessee legislature, hearing with a thrill of joy, the words, "The Union, it must be preserved;" a representative in Congress for successive years; governor of the great state of Tennessee; approved as its governor by re-election; he was at the opening of the rebellion a senator from that state in Congress. Then at the Capitol, when senators, unrebuked by the government, sent word by telegram to seize forts and arsenals, he alone from that southern region told them what the government did not dare to tell them, that they were traitors, and deserved the punishment of treason. Undismayed by a perpetual purpose of public enemies to take his life, bearing up against the still greater trial of the persecution of his wife and children, in due time he went back to his state, determined to restore it to the Union, or die with the American flag for his winding sheet. And now, at the call of the United States, he has returned to Washington as a conqueror, with Tennessee as a free state for his trophy. It remains for him to consummate the vindication of the Union.

To that Union Abraham Lincoln has fallen a martyr. His death, which was meant to sever it beyond repair, binds it more closely and more firmly than ever. The blow aimed at him, was aimed not at the native of Kentucky, not at the citizen of Illinois, but at the man, who, as President, in the executive branch of the government, stood as the representative of every man in the United States. The object of the crime was the life of the whole people; and it wounds the affections of the whole people. From Maine to the southwest boundary on the Pacific, it makes us one. The country may have needed an imperishable grief to touch its inmost feeling. The grave that receives the remains of Lincoln, receives the costly sacrifice to the Union; the monument which will rise over his body will bear witness to the Union; his enduring memory will assist during countless ages to bind the states together, and to incite to the love of our one undivided, indivisible country. Peace to the ashes of our departed friend, the friend of his country and his race. He was happy in his life, for he was the restorer of the republic; he was happy in his death, for his martyrdom will plead for ever for the Union of the states and the freedom of man.

April 25, 1865

Edmund Clarence Stedman

Born in Hartford, Connecticut, Stedman (1833–1908) covered the opening months of the Civil War for the *New York World* before becoming a successful stockbroker and popular figure in New York literary circles. His call for vengeance in response to Lincoln's assassination reflected a popular mood that also found expression in the swift hanging of four of Booth's co-conspirators after their trial before a military commission.

Abraham Lincoln
Assassinated Good Friday, 1865

"Forgive them, for they know not what they do!"
   He said, and so went shriven to his fate,—
Unknowing went, that generous heart and true.
   Even while he spoke the slayer lay in wait,
   And when the morning opened Heaven's gate
There passed the whitest soul a nation knew.
   Henceforth all thoughts of pardon are too late;
They, in whose cause that arm its weapon drew,
   Have murdered Mercy. Now alone shall stand
Blind justice, with the sword unsheathed she wore.
   Hark, from the eastern to the western strand,
The swelling thunder of the people's roar:
   What words they murmur,—Fetter not her hand!
So let it smite, such deeds shall be no more!

April 1865

Tom Taylor

Taylor (1817–1880) was a prolific British playwright probably best remembered as the author of the comedy *Our American Cousin* (1858), which Lincoln was enjoying when John Wilkes Booth shot him at Ford's Theatre on April 14, 1865. Several weeks later Taylor, a staff writer for *Punch*, wrote this poem to express his—and the magazine's —remorse and contrition for years of British hostility toward Lincoln. It was accompanied in *Punch* by an equally gracious engraving by John Tenniel depicting a grieving Britannia sorrowfully paying her respects at Abraham Lincoln's bier. Throughout the war, support for Lincoln in Britain had been largely limited to anti-slavery activists and workingmen's groups; now, in the aftermath of Lincoln's murder and the final triumph of the Union cause, his numerous critics either recanted or fell silent.

Abraham Lincoln
Foully Assassinated April 14, 1865

You lay a wreath on murdered Lincoln's bier,
   You, who with mocking pencil wont to trace
Broad for the self-complacent British sneer
   His length of shambling limb, his furrowed face,

His gaunt, gnarled hands, his unkempt, bristling hair,
   His garb uncouth, his bearing ill at ease;
His lack of all we prize as debonair,
   Of power or will to shine, of art to please.

You, whose smart pen backed up the pencil's laugh,
   Judging each step, as though the way were plain;
Reckless, so it could point its paragraph
   Of chief's perplexity or people's pain.

Beside this corps, that beats for winding sheet
   The Stars and Stripes he lived to rear anew,
Between the mourners at his head and feet,
   Say, scurril-jester, is there room for you?

Yes, he had lived to shame me from my sneer,
   To lame my pencil, and confute my pen—
To make me own this hind of princes peer,
   This rail-splitter a true-born king of men.

My shallow judgment I had learnt to rue,
   Noting how to occasion's height he rose,
How his quaint wit made home-truth seem more true,
   How, iron-like, his temper grew by blows.

How humble yet how hopeful he could be;
   How in good fortune and in ill the same;
Nor bitter in success, nor boastful he,
   Thirsty for gold, nor feverish for fame.

He went about his work—such works as few
   Ever had laid on head and heart and hand—
As one who knows where there's a task to do
   Man's honest will must heaven's good grace command:

Who trusts the strength will with the burden grow,
   That God makes instruments to work his will,
If but that will we can arrive to know,
   Nor tamper with the weights of good and ill.

So he went forth to battle on the side
   That he felt clear was liberty's and right's,
As in his peasant boyhood he had plied
   His warfare with rude nature's thwarting mights—

The uncleared forest, the unbroken soil,
    The iron back, that turns the lumberer's axe;
The rapid, that o'erbears the boatman's toil,
    The prairie, hiding the mazed wanderer's tracks.

The ambushed Indian, and the prowling bear—
    Such were the needs that helped his youth to train:
Rough culture—but such trees large fruit may bear
    If but their stocks be of right girth and grain.

So he grew up, a destined work to do,
    And lived to do it; four long-suffering years'
Ill-fate, ill-feeling, ill-report lived through,
    And then he heard the hisses change to cheers,

The taunts to tribute, the abuse to praise,
    And took both with the same unwavering mood:
Till, as he came on light from darkling days
    And seemed to touch the goal from where he stood,

A felon hand, between the goal and him,
    Reached from behind his back, a trigger prest—
And those perplexed and patient eyes were dim,
    Those gaunt, long-laboring limbs were laid to rest.

The words of mercy were upon his lips,
    Forgiveness in his heart and on his pen,
When this vile murderer brought swift eclipse
    To thoughts of peace on earth, good will to men.

The Old World and the New, from sea to sea,
    Utter one voice of sympathy and shame!
Sore heart, so stopped when it at last beat high,
    Sad life, cut short just as its triumph came.

A deed accurst! Strokes have been struck before
   By the assassin's hand, whereof men doubt
If more of horror or disgrace they bore;
   But thy foul crime, like Cain's, stands darkly out.

Vile hand, that brandest murder on a strife,
   Whate'er its grounds, stoutly and nobly striven;
And with the martyr's crown crownest a life
   With much to praise, little to be forgiven!

May 6, 1865

Henrik Ibsen

The Norwegian-born Ibsen (1828–1906) had not yet written the plays that would define modern drama when he composed this poem in Rome on April 30, 1865. Published in the Copenhagen newspaper *Fædrelandet* (*The Fatherland*) on May 15, Ibsen's verses envision the example of American republicanism as a threat to entrenched European despotism—an idea Lincoln himself had espoused in many of his pre-presidential speeches. The third stanza alludes to the Prussian defeat of Denmark in 1864, the suppression of the 1863 uprising in Poland, and the deadly bombardment of Copenhagen by the British navy in 1807.

Abraham Lincoln's Murder

They fired a shot out there in the West
and the shock throughout Europe rang.
My word! What life all at once expressed
by the whole of the fancy-dress gang!
Old Europe, so ordered, so patently right,
with laws for each rung on the scale,
with honour unblemished, clean and bright,
with proper scorn for all black-not-white,—
you turned quite remarkably pale!

In sealing-wax, eagles and unicorns burn
and all other beasts, no less;
the packet-boat rides on its cable's turn,
despatches, they swarm and they press.
Magnates in cotton, 'gloire's' proud son,
the mob from the land of lies,
they reached for the palmfrond of peace as one,
then sounded that shot from a single gun,
and a man falls, one person dies.

And then you were scared. Had Europe's lead
been followed as fit and right?
A Prussian exploit, a Dybbøl-deed,
the world had all witnessed the sight.
No dog eats dog, and no raven raven;—
remember the Poles and that row?
The English action at Copenhaven?
the war-tomb at Flensborg? and 'Sønderborg' graven?
So why so indignant now?

That crimson rose there, whose flowers shock
and frighten you here at home,
our Europe it was that supplied the stock,
the West its luxurious loam.
You planted as seedling that stem grown so grand
it reddens America's shore,
you tied on his breast, with your own fair hand,
that patent of martyrdom's blood-red band
that Abraham Lincoln wore.

With broken promises, words betrayed
and with treaties mere paperish toil,
with this season's crimes against oaths last year made
you have fertilised history's soil.
Then at peace with your minds you looked to the day
for noblest of harvests to dawn!
Now it's sprouting, your seed. Look—a blazing display!
You're puzzled, confounded, can't think what to say,—
for stilettos have grown as your corn.

Where law is poised on the dagger's edge
and right on the gallow's sill,
the triumph of dawn has surer pledge
than here, where it's words that can kill.
A passion wakens, a judgement keen
that shatters each lair of lies;—

but first must the worm pick the skull quite clean,
and times must first change from what they have been
to their own self-parodies.

A demon's in charge, one of boundless strength.
Just cross him! do try, if you must!
The Aurea Domus crumbled at length
like Nero's colossus to dust.
But first had the crime that was Rome to spread wide
from the pole of the earth to pole,
the tyrant be worshipped and deified,
the Caesars' gold busts range side by side
as gods on the Capitol.

Then all of it crumbled; circus and camp,
temples and columned roof,
store-rooms, arcades pounded small by the stamp
of the buffalo's armoured hoof.
Then men built anew on those old decays
and clean, for a while, was the air.
Now signs suggest there's a second phase;
the pestilence climbs from its waterlogged maze
and hovers now here, now there.

But if we all sink in corruption's lair
don't count on laments from me
over each of the poisonous flowers that flare
and mass on this age's tree.
Just let the worm burrow. The walls won't decay
till all of the skull's picked clean.
Just let the whole system be wrenched away;
the sooner comes vengeance and Judgment Day
on us for the lies we have been!

May 15, 1865

Karl Marx

Marx's public letter to Lincoln's White House successor, Andrew Johnson, was adopted by the General Council of the International on May 9, 1865, and published in the British trade union newspaper *Bee-Hive* on May 20. Its impassioned tribute to Lincoln reflects the importance Marx attributed to the victory of the Union cause. "As the American War of Independence initiated a new era of ascendancy for the middle class," he wrote, "so the American anti-slavery war will do for the working classes."

Address of the International Working Men's Association to President Johnson

Sir:

The demon of the "peculiar institution," for the supremacy of which the South rose in arms, would not allow his worshipers to honorably succumb in the open field. What he had begun in treason, he must needs end in infamy. As Philip II's war for the Inquisition bred a Gérard, thus Jefferson Davis's proslavery war a Booth.

It is not our part to call words of sorrow and horror, while the heart of two worlds heaves with emotion. Even the sycophants who, year after year, and day by day, stick to their Sisyphus work of morally assassinating Abraham Lincoln, and the great Republic he headed, stand now aghast at this universal outburst of popular feeling, and rival with each other to strew rhetorical flowers on his open grave. They have now at last found out that he was a man, neither to be browbeaten by adversity, nor intoxicated by success, inflexibly pressing on to his great goal, never compromising it by blind haste, slowly maturing his steps, never retracing them, carried away by no surge of popular favor, disheartened by no slackening of the popular pulse, tempering stern acts by the gleams of a kind heart, illuminating scenes dark with passion by the smile of humor, doing his titanic work as humbly and homely as Heaven-born rulers do little things with the grandiloquence of pomp and state; in one word, one of the rare men who succeed in becoming great, without ceasing to be good. Such, indeed, was the modesty of this great and good man, that the world only discovered him a hero after he had fallen a martyr.

To be singled out by the side of such a chief, the second victim to the infernal gods of slavery, was an honor due to Mr. Seward. Had he not, at a time of general hesitation, the sagacity to foresee and the manliness to foretell "the irrepressible conflict"? Did he not, in the darkest hours of that conflict, prove true to the Roman duty to never despair of the Republic and its stars? We earnestly hope that he and his son will be restored to health, public activity, and well-deserved honors within much less than "ninety days."

After a tremendous civil war, but which, if we consider its vast dimensions, and its broad scope, and compare it to the Old World's Hundred Years' Wars, and Thirty Years' Wars, and Twenty-three Years' Wars, can hardly be said to have lasted ninety days, yours, sir, has become the task to uproot by the law what has been felled by the sword, to preside over the arduous work of political reconstruction and social regeneration. A profound sense of your great mission will save you from any compromise with stern duties. You will never forget that, to initiate the new era of the emancipation of labor, the American people devolved the responsibilities of leadership upon two men of labor—the one Abraham Lincoln, the other Andrew Johnson.

Signed, on behalf of the International Working Men's Association, London, May 13, 1865, by the Central Council—

Charles Kaub, Edward Coulson, F. Lessner, Carl Pfänder, N. P. Hansen, Karl Schapper, William Dell, George Lochner, George Eccarius, John Osborne, P. Petersen, A. Janks, H. Klimosch, John Weston, H. Bolleter, B. Lucraft, J. Buckley, Peter Fox, N. Salvatella, George Howell, Bordage, A. Valltier, Robert Shaw, J. H. Longmaid, W. Morgan, G. W. Wheeler, J. D. Nieass, W. C. Worley, D. Stainsby, F. de Lassassie, J. Carter; Emile Holtorp, Secretary for Poland; *Karl Marx,* Secretary for Germany; *H. Jung,* Secretary for Switzerland; *E. Dupont,* Secretary for France; *J. Whitlock,* Financial Secretary; *G. Odger,* President; *W. R. Cremer,* Hon. Gen. Secretary.

May 20, 1865

Richard Henry Stoddard

Stoddard (1825–1903) grew up in grinding poverty in Boston and New York City. He began publishing poetry in the 1840s while working as an iron molder, and continued to write after he secured a position as a customs inspector in Manhattan. "An Horatian Ode," his response to the President's death, clearly drew inspiration from the unprecedented outpouring of mourners that massed to see Lincoln's remains as his funeral train moved across the country. The text presented here is taken from the original 1865 pamphlet printing, in which Stoddard's poem is prefaced by a series of passages from *Macbeth*—epigraphs chosen certainly for their grim appropriateness, but possibly also in the awareness that it was Lincoln's favorite Shakespeare play.

Abraham Lincoln: An Horatian Ode

"Confusion now hath made his masterpiece!
 Most sacrilegious murder hath broke ope
 The Lord's anointed temple, and stole thence
 The life o' the building.
*   *   *   *   *   *   *   *   *   *   *   *   *   *   *   *
"Approach the chamber, and destroy your sight
 With a new Gorgon:—Do not bid me speak;
 See, and then speak yourselves.—Awake! awake!
 Ring the alarum-bell:—Murder! and treason!
*   *   *   *   *   *   *   *   *   *   *   *   *   *   *   *
"Shake off this downy sleep, death's counterfeit,
 And look on death itself!—up, up, and see
 The great doom's image!
*   *   *   *   *   *   *   *   *   *   *   *   *   *   *   *
"Our royal master's murdered!
*   *   *   *   *   *   *   *   *   *   *   *   *   *   *   *
"Had I but died an hour before this chance,
 I had lived a blessed time; for from this instant
 There's nothing serious in mortality:
 All is but toys: renown and grace is dead;
 The wine of life is drawn, and the mere lees
 Is left this vault to brag of.

"After life's fitful fever, he sleeps well;
  Treason has done his worst: nor steel, nor poison,
  Malice domestic, foreign levy, nothing,
  Can touch him further."

                                    MACBETH.

Not as when some great Captain falls
In battle, where his Country calls,
      Beyond the struggling lines
      That push his dread designs

To doom, by some stray ball struck dead:
Or, in the last charge, at the head
      Of his determined men,
      Who *must* be victors then!

Nor as when sink the civic Great,
The safer pillars of the State,
      Whose calm, mature, wise words
      Suppress the need of swords!—

With no such tears as o'er were shed
Above the noblest of our Dead
      Do we to-day deplore
      The Man that is no more!

Our sorrow hath a wider scope,
Too strange for fear, too vast for hope,—
      A Wonder, blind and dumb,
      That waits—what is to come!

Not more astounded had we been
If Madness, that dark night, unseen,
      Had in our chambers crept,
      And murdered while we slept!

We woke to find a mourning Earth—
Our Lares shivered on the hearth,—
    The roof-tree fallen,—all
    That could affright, appall!

Such thunderbolts, in other lands,
Have smitten the rod from royal hands,
    But spared, with us, till now,
    Each laurelled Cesar's brow!

No Cesar he, whom we lament,
A Man without a precedent,
    Sent, it would seem, to do
    His work—and perish too!

Not by the weary cares of State,
The endless tasks, which will not wait,
    Which, often done in vain,
    Must yet be done again:

Not in the dark, wild tide of War,
Which rose so high, and rolled so far,
    Sweeping from sea to sea
    In awful anarchy:—

Four fateful years of mortal strife,
Which slowly drained the Nation's life.
    (Yet, for each drop that ran
    There sprang an armed man!)

Not then;—but when by measures meet,—
By victory, and by defeat,—
    By courage, patience, skill,
    The People's fixed *"We will!"*

Had pierced, had crushed Rebellion dead,—
Without a Hand, without a Head:—
 At last, when all was well,
 He fell—O, *how* he fell!

The time,—the place,—the stealing Shape,—
The coward shot,—the swift escape,—
 The wife—the widow's scream,—
 It is a hideous Dream!

A Dream?—what means this pageant, then?
These multitudes of solemn men,
 Who speak not when they meet,
 But throng the silent street?

The flags half-mast, that late so high
Flaunted at each new victory?
 (The stars no brightness shed,
 But bloody looks the red!)

The black festoons that stretch for miles,
And turn the streets to funeral aisles?
 (No house too poor to show
 The Nation's badge of woe!)

The cannon's sudden, sullen boom,—
The bells that toll of death and doom,—
 The rolling of the drums,—
 The dreadful Car that comes?

Cursed be the hand that fired the shot!
The frenzied brain that hatched the plot!
 Thy Country's Father slain
 By thee, thou worse than Cain!

Tyrants have fallen by such as thou,
And Good hath followed—May it now!
    (God lets bad instruments
    Produce the best events.)

But he, the Man we mourn to-day,
No tyrant was: so mild a sway
    In one such weight who bore
    Was never known before!

Cool should he be, of balanced powers,
The Ruler of a Race like ours,
    Impatient, headstrong, wild,—
    The Man to guide the Child!

And this *he* was, who most unfit
(So hard the sense of God to hit!)
    Did seem to fill his Place.
    With such a homely face,—

Such rustic manners,—speech uncouth,—
(That somehow blundered out the Truth!)
    Untried, untrained to bear
    The more than kingly Care?

Ay! And his genius put to scorn
The proudest in the purple born,
    Whose wisdom never grew
    To what, untaught, he knew—

The People, of whom he was one.
No gentleman like Washington,—
    (Whose bones, methinks, make room,
    To have him in their tomb!)

A laboring man, with horny hands,
Who swung the axe, who tilled his lands,
    Who shrank from nothing new,
    But did as poor men do!

One of the People! Born to be
Their curious Epitome;
    To share, yet rise above
    Their shifting hate and love.

Common his mind (it seemed so then),
His thoughts the thoughts of other men:
    Plain were his words, and poor—
    But now they will endure!

No hasty fool, of stubborn will,
But prudent, cautious, pliant, still;
    Who, since his work was good,
    Would do it, as he could.

Doubting, was not ashamed to doubt,
And, lacking prescience, went without:
    Often appeared to halt,
    And was, of course, at fault:

Heard all opinions, nothing loth,
And loving both sides, angered both:
    Was—*not* like Justice, blind,
    But, watchful, clement, kind.

No hero, this, of Roman mould;
Nor like our stately sires of old:
    Perhaps he was not Great—
    But he preserved the State!

O honest face, which all men knew!
O tender heart, but known to few!
    O Wonder of the Age,
    Cut off by tragic Rage!

Peace! Let the long procession come,
For hark!—the mournful, muffled drum—
    The trumpet's wail afar,—
    And see! the awful Car!

Peace! Let the sad procession go,
While cannon boom, and bells toll slow:
    And go thou sacred Car,
    Bearing our Woe afar!

Go, darkly borne, from State to State,
Whose loyal, sorrowing Cities wait
    To honor all they can
    The dust of that Good Man!

Go, grandly borne, with such a train
As greatest kings might die to gain:
    The Just, the Wise, the Brave
    Attend thee to the grave!

And you, the soldiers of our wars,
Bronzed veterans, grim with noble scars,
    Salute him once again,
    Your late Commander—slain!

Yes, let your tears, indignant, fall,
But leave your muskets on the wall:
    Your Country needs you now
    Beside the forge, the plough!

(When Justice shall unsheathe her brand,—
If Mercy may not stay her hand,
    Nor would we have it so—
    She must direct the blow!)

And you, amid the Master-Race,
Who seem so strangely out of place,
    Know ye who cometh? He
    Who hath declared ye Free!

Bow while the Body passes—Nay,
Fall on your knees, and weep, and pray!
    Weep, weep—I would ye might—
    Your poor, black faces white!

And, Children, you must come in bands,
With garlands in your little hands,
    Of blue, and white, and red,
    To strew before the Dead!

So, sweetly, sadly, sternly goes
The Fallen to his last repose;
    Beneath no mighty dome,
    But in his modest Home;

The churchyard where his children rest,
The quiet spot that suits him best:
    There shall his grave be made,
    And there his bones be laid!

And there his countrymen shall come,
With memory proud, with pity dumb,
    And strangers far and near,
    For many and many a year!

For many a year, and many an Age,
While History on her ample page
    The virtues shall enroll
    Of that Paternal Soul!

1865

Julia Ward Howe

Howe (1819–1910) had been the co-editor of the Boston abolitionist newspaper *The Commonwealth* for a decade when she wrote "The Battle-Hymn of the Republic," the poem that became more closely associated with Lincoln than perhaps any other. Yet her inspiration for the famous verses, composed to the music of the song "John Brown's Body" after visiting a Union army encampment near Washington in December 1861, had nothing to do with the President, and its identification with Lincoln came only later. Howe met Lincoln only once, when Senator Charles Sumner and Massachusetts Governor John A. Andrew introduced her to the President at the White House in November 1862. After his assassination she offered this tribute.

———

Crown his blood-stained pillow
    With a victor's palm;
Life's receding billow
    Leaves eternal calm.

At the feet Almighty
    Lay this gift sincere;
Of a purpose weighty,
    And a record clear.

With deliverance freighted
    Was this passive hand,
And this heart, high-fated,
    Would with love command.

Let him rest serenely
    In a Nation's care,
Where her waters queenly
    Make the West most fair.

In the greenest meadow
   That the prairies show,
Let his marble's shadow
   Give all men to know:

"Our First Hero, living,
   Made his country free;
Heed the Second's giving,
   Death for Liberty."

1865

Noah Brooks

Born in Maine, Brooks (1830–1903) first met Lincoln in Illinois during the 1856 election campaign. He moved to California in 1859, then returned east in November 1862 as the Washington correspondent of the pro-administration *Sacramento Daily Union*. During the war Brooks wrote 258 dispatches for the paper (signed "Castine" after his birthplace in Maine) and grew increasingly close to the President. It is likely that if Lincoln had escaped assassination, Brooks would have succeeded John G. Nicolay as the President's private secretary, but instead he was appointed to a position in the San Francisco custom house. He returned to journalism after losing his port job in 1866 when President Andrew Johnson purged the government service of officeholders suspected of having Radical Republican views. In 1888 Brooks published a sympathetic Lincoln biography in which he argued that, contrary to recent assertions that the late President was a free-thinker, Lincoln was a believing Christian who would have formally affiliated himself with a denomination had he survived. Aside from his contemporary dispatches, his most valuable contribution to history may be this brief memoir, written in the months after Lincoln's death when the memory of their acquaintanceship was still fresh.

Personal Recollections of Abraham Lincoln

It is natural that friends should tenderly and frequently talk of the loved and lost, descanting upon their virtues, narrating the little incidents of a life ended, and dwelling with minute particularity upon traits of character which, under other circumstances, might have remained unnoted and be forgotten, but are invested now with a mournful interest which fixes them in the memory. This, and the general desire to know more of the man Abraham Lincoln, is the only excuse offered for the following simple sketch of some parts of the character of our beloved Chief Magistrate, now passed from earth.

All persons agree that the most marked characteristic of Mr.

Lincoln's manners was his simplicity and artlessness; this immediately impressed itself upon the observation of those who met him for the first time, and each successive interview deepened the impression. People seemed delighted to find in the ruler of the nation freedom from pomposity and affectation, mingled with a certain simple dignity which never forsook him. Though oppressed with the weight of responsibility resting upon him as President of the United States, he shrank from assuming any of the honors, or even the titles, of the position. After years of intimate acquaintance with Mr. Lincoln the writer can not now recall a single instance in which he spoke of himself as President, or used that title for himself, except when acting in an official capacity. He always spoke of his position and office vaguely, as "this place," "here," or other modest phrase. Once, speaking of the room in the Capitol used by the Presidents of the United States during the close of a session of Congress, he said, "That room, you know, that they call"—dropping his voice and hesitating—"the President's room." To an intimate friend who addressed him always by his own proper title he said, "Now call me Lincoln, and I'll promise not to tell of the breach of etiquette—if you won't—and I shall have a resting-spell from 'Mister President.'"

With all his simplicity and unacquaintance with courtly manners, his native dignity never forsook him in the presence of critical or polished strangers; but mixed with his angularities and *bonhomie* was something which spoke the fine fibre of the man; and, while his sovereign disregard of courtly conventionalities was somewhat ludicrous, his native sweetness and straightforwardness of manner served to disarm criticism and impress the visitor that he was before a man pure, self-poised, collected, and strong in unconscious strength. Of him an accomplished foreigner, whose knowledge of the courts was more perfect than that of the English language, said, "He seems to me one grand gentilhomme in disguise."

In his eagerness to acquire knowledge of common things he sometimes surprised his distinguished visitors by inquiries about matters that they were supposed to be acquainted with, and those who came to scrutinize went away with a vague sense of having been unconsciously pumped by the man whom they expected to pump. One Sunday evening last winter, while sitting alone with the President, the cards of Professor Agassiz and a friend were sent in. The President had never met Agassiz at that time, I believe, and said, "I would like to talk with that man; he is a good man, I do believe; don't you think so?" But one answer could be returned to the query, and soon after the visitors were shown in, the President first whispering, "Now sit still and see what we can pick up that's new." To my surprise, however, no questions were asked about the Old Silurian, the Glacial Theory, or the Great Snow-storm, but, introductions being over, the President said: "I never knew how to properly pronounce your name; won't you give me a little lesson at that, please?" Then he asked if it were of French or Swiss derivation, to which the Professor replied that it was partly of each. That led to a discussion of different languages, the President speaking of several words in different languages which had the same root as similar words in our own tongue; then he illustrated that by one or two anecdotes, one of which he borrowed from Hood's "Up the Rhine." But he soon returned to his gentle cross-examination of Agassiz, and found out how the Professor studied, how he composed, and how he delivered his lectures; how he found different tastes in his audiences in different portions of the country. When afterward asked why he put such questions to his learned visitor he said, "Why, what we got from him isn't printed in the books; the other things are."

At this interview, it may be remarked in passing, the President said that many years ago, when the custom of lecture-going was more common than since, he was induced to try his hand at composing a literary lecture—something which he thought entirely out of his line. The subject, he said, was not defined, but his purpose was to analyze inventions and discoveries—"to get at the bottom of things"—and to show when, where, how, and why such things were invented or discovered; and, so far as possible, to find where the first mention is made of some of our common things. The Bible, he said, he found to be the richest store-house for such knowledge; and he then gave one or two illustrations, which were new to his hearers. The lecture was never finished, and was left among his loose papers at Springfield when he came to Washington.

The simplicity of manner which shone out in all such interviews as that here noticed was marked in his total lack of consideration of what was due his exalted station. He had an almost morbid dread of what he called "a scene"—that is, a demonstration of applause such as always greeted his appearance in public. The first sign of a cheer sobered him; he appeared sad and oppressed, suspended conversation, and looked out into vacancy; and when it was over resumed the conversation just where it was interrupted, with an obvious feeling of relief. Of the relations of a senator to him he said, "I think that Senator ——'s manner is more cordial to me than before." The truth was that the senator had been looking for a sign of cordiality from his superior, but the President had reversed their relative positions. At another time, speaking of an early acquaintance, who was an applicant for an office which he thought him hardly qualified to fill, the President said, "Well, now, I never thought M—— had any more than average ability when we were young men together; really I did not"—a pause.—"But, then, I suppose he thought just the same about me; he had reason to, and—here I am!"

The simple habits of Mr. Lincoln were so well known that it is a subject for surprise that watchful and malignant treason did not sooner take that precious life which he seemed to hold so lightly. He had an almost morbid dislike for an escort, or guard, and daily exposed himself to the deadly aim of an assassin. One summer morning, passing by the White House at an early hour, I saw the President standing at the gateway, looking anxiously down the street; and, in reply to a salutation, he said, "Good-morning, good-morning! I am looking for a news-boy; when you get to that corner I wish you would start one up this way." There are American citizens who consider such things beneath the dignity of an official in high place.

In reply to the remonstrances of friends, who were afraid of his constant exposure to danger, he had but one answer: "If they kill me, the next man will be just as bad for them; and in a country like this, where our habits are simple, and must be, assassination is always possible, and will come if they are determined upon it." A cavalry guard was once placed at the gates of the White House for a while, and he said, privately, that he "worried until he got rid of it." While the President's family were at their summer-house, near Washington, he rode into town of a morning, or out at night, attended by a mounted escort; but if he returned to town for a while after dark, he rode in unguarded, and often alone, in his open carriage. On more than one occasion the writer has gone through the streets of Washington at a late hour of the night with the President, without escort, or even the company of a servant, walking all of the way, going and returning.

Considering the many open and secret threats to take his life, it is not surprising that Mr. Lincoln had many thoughts about his coming to a sudden and violent end. He once said that he felt the force of the expression, "To take one's life in his hand;" but that he would not like to face death suddenly. He said that he thought himself a great coward physically, and was sure that he should make a poor soldier, for, unless there was something in the excitement of a battle, he was sure that he would drop his gun and run at the first symptom of danger. That was said sportively, and he added, "Moral cowardice is something which I think I never had." Shortly after the presidential election, in 1864, he related an incident which I will try to put upon paper here, as nearly as possible in his own words:

"It was just after my election in 1860, when the news had been coming in thick and fast all day, and there had been a great 'Hurrah, boys!' so that I was well tired out, and went home to rest, throwing myself down on a lounge in my chamber. Opposite where I lay was a bureau, with a swinging-glass upon it"—(and here he got up and placed furniture to illustrate the position)— "and, looking in that glass, I saw myself reflected, nearly at full length; but my face, I noticed, had *two* separate and distinct images, the tip of the nose of one being about three inches from the tip of the other. I was a little bothered, perhaps startled, and got up and looked in the glass, but the illusion vanished. On lying down again I saw it a second time—plainer, if possible, than before; and then I noticed that one of the faces was a little paler, say five shades, than the other. I got up and the thing melted away, and I went off and, in the excitement of the hour, forgot all about it—nearly, but not quite, for the thing would once in a while come up, and give me a little pang, as though something uncomfortable had happened. When I went home I told my wife about it, and a few days after I tried the experiment again, when [with a laugh], sure enough, the thing came again; but I never succeeded in bringing the ghost back after that, though I once tried very industriously to show it to my wife, who was worried about it somewhat. She thought it was 'a sign' that I was to be elected to a second term of office, and that the paleness of one of the faces was an omen that I should not see life through the last term."

The President, with his usual good sense, saw nothing in all this but an optical illusion; though the flavor of superstition which hangs about every man's composition made him wish that he had never seen it. But there are people who will now believe that this odd coincidence was "a warning."

If Mr. Lincoln's critics may be trusted, he had too much goodness of heart to make a good magistrate. Certain it is that his continually-widening charity for all, and softness of heart, pardoned offenders and mitigated punishments when the strict requirements of justice would have dealt more severely with the criminal. It was a standing order of his office that persons on matters involving the issue of life and death should have immediate precedence. Nor was his kindness confined to affairs of state; his servants, and all persons in his personal service, were the objects of his peculiar care and solicitude. They bore no burdens or hardships which he could relieve them of; and if he carried this virtue to an extreme, and carried labors which others should have borne, it was because he thought he could not help it.

He was often waylaid by soldiers importunate to get their back-pay, or a furlough, or a discharge; and if the case was not too complicated, would attend to it then and there. Going out of the main-door of the White House one morning, he met an old lady who was pulling vigorously at the door-bell, and asked her what she wanted. She said that she wanted to see "Abraham the Second." The President, amused, asked who Abraham the First might be, if there was a second? The old lady replied,

"Why, Lor' bless you! we read about the first Abraham in the Bible, and Abraham the Second is our President." She was told that the President was not in his office then, and when she asked where he was, she was told, "Here he is!" Nearly petrified with surprise, the old lady managed to tell her errand, and was told to come next morning at nine o'clock, when she was received and kindly cared for by the President. At another time, hearing of a young man who had determined to enter the navy as a landsman, after three years of service in the army, he said to the writer, "Now do you go over to the Navy Department and mouse out what he is fit for, and he shall have it, if it's to be had, for that's the kind of men I like to hear of." The place was duly "moused out," with the assistance of the kind-hearted Assistant-Secretary of the Navy; and the young officer, who may read these lines on his solitary post off the mouth of the Yazoo River, was appointed upon the recommendation of the President of the United States. Of an application for office by an old friend, not fit for the place he sought, he said, "I had rather resign my place and go away from here than refuse him, if I consulted only my personal feelings; but refuse him I must." And he did.

This same gentleness, mixed with firmness, characterized all of Mr. Lincoln's dealings with public men. Often bitterly assailed and abused, he never appeared to recognize the fact that he had political enemies; and if his attention was called to unkind speeches or remarks, he would turn the conversation of his indignant friends by a judicious story, or the remark, "I guess we won't talk about that now." He has himself put it on record that he never read attacks upon himself, and if they were brought persistently before him he had some ready excuse for their authors. Of a virulent personal attack upon his official conduct he mildly said that it was ill-timed; and of one of his most bitter political enemies he said: "I've been told that insanity is hereditary in his family, and I think we will admit the plea in his case." It was noticeable that Mr. Lincoln's keenest critics and bitter opponents studiously avoided his presence; it seemed as though no man could be familiar with his homely, heart-lighted features, his single-hearted directness and manly kindliness, and remain long an enemy, or be any thing but his friend. It was this warm frankness of Mr. Lincoln's manner that made a hard-headed old "hunker" once leave the hustings where Lincoln was speaking, in 1856, saying, "I won't hear him, for I don't like a man that makes me believe in him in spite of myself."

"Honest Old Abe" has passed into the language of our time and country as a synonym for all that is just and honest in man. Yet thousands of instances, unknown to the world, might be added to those already told of Mr. Lincoln's great and crowning virtue. He disliked innuendoes, concealments, and subterfuges; and no sort of approach at official "jobbing" ever had any encouragement from him. With him the question was not, "Is it convenient? Is it expedient?" but, "Is it right?" He steadily discountenanced all practices of government officers using any part of the public funds for temporary purposes; and he loved to tell of his own experience when he was saved from embarrassment by his rigid adherence to a good rule. He had been postmaster at Salem, Illinois, during Jackson's administration, William T. Barry being then Postmaster-General, and resigning his office, removed to Springfield, having sent a statement of account to the Department at Washington. No notice was taken of his account, which showed a balance due the Government of over one hundred and fifty dollars, until three or four years after, when, Amos Kendall being Postmaster-General, he was presented with a draft for the amount due. Some of Mr. Lincoln's friends, who knew that he was in straitened circumstances then, as he had always been, heard of the draft and offered to help him out with a loan; but he told them not to worry, and producing from his trunk an old pocket, tied up and marked, counted out, in six-pences, shillings, and quarters, the exact sum required of him, in the identical coin received by him while in office years before.

The honesty of Mr. Lincoln appeared to spring from religious convictions; and it was his habit, when conversing of things which most intimately concerned himself, to say that, however he might be misapprehended by men who did not appear to know him, he was glad to know that no thought or intent of his escaped the observation of that Judge by whose final decree he expected to stand or fall in this world and the next. It seemed as though this was his surest refuge at times when he was most misunderstood or misrepresented. There was something touching in his childlike and simple reliance upon Divine aid, especially when in such extremities as he sometimes fell into; then, though prayer and reading of the Scriptures was his constant habit, he more earnestly than ever sought that strength which is promised when mortal help faileth. His address upon the occasion of his re-inauguration has been said to be as truly a religious document as a state-paper; and his acknowledgment of God and His providence and rule are interwoven through all of his later speeches, letters, and messages. Once he said: "I have been driven many times upon my knees by the overwhelming conviction that I had nowhere else to go. My own wisdom and that of all about me seemed insufficient for that day."

Just after the last presidential election he said: "Being only mortal, after all, I should have been a little mortified if I had been beaten in this canvass before the people; but that sting would have been more than compensated by the thought that the people had notified me that all my official responsibilities were soon to be lifted off my back." In reply to the remark that he might remember that in all these cares he was daily remembered by those who prayed, not to be heard of men, as no man had ever before been remembered, he caught at the homely phrase and said: "Yes, I like that phrase, 'not to be heard of men,' and guess it's generally true, as you say; at least I have been told so, and I have been a good deal helped by just that thought." Then he solemnly and slowly added: "I should be the most presumptuous blockhead upon this footstool if I for one day thought that I could discharge the duties which have come upon me since I came into this place without the aid and enlightenment of One who is wiser and stronger than all others."

At another time he said, cheerfully, "I am very sure that if I do not go away from here a wiser man, I shall go away a better man, for having learned here what a very poor sort of a man I am." Afterward, referring to what he called a change of heart, he said that he did not remember any precise time when he passed through any special change of purpose or of heart; but he would say that his own election to office, and the crisis immediately following, influentially determined him in what he called "a process of crystallization," then going on in his mind. Reticent as he was, and shy of discoursing much of his own mental exercises, these few utterances now have a value with those who knew him which his dying words would scarcely have possessed.

No man but Mr. Lincoln ever knew how great was the load of care which he bore, nor the amount of mental labor which he daily accomplished. With the usual perplexities of the office—greatly increased by the unusual multiplication of places in his gift—he carried the burdens of the civil war, which he always called "This great trouble." Though the intellectual man had greatly grown meantime, few persons would recognize the hearty, blithesome, genial, and wiry Abraham Lincoln of earlier days in the sixteenth President of the United States, with his stooping figure, dull eyes, care-worn face, and languid frame. The old, clear laugh never came back; the even temper was sometimes disturbed; and his natural charity for all was often turned into an unwonted suspicion of the motives of men, whose selfishness cost him so much wear of mind. Once he said, "Sitting here, where all the avenues to public patronage seem to come together in a knot, it does seem to me that our people are fast approaching the point where it can be said that seven-eighths of them were trying to find how to live at the expense of the other eighth."

It was this incessant demand upon his time, by men who sought place or endeavored to shape his policy, that broke down his courage and his temper, as well as exhausted his strength. Speaking of the "great flood-gates" which his doors daily opened upon him, he said, "I suppose I ought not to blame the aggregate, for each abstract man or woman thinks his or her case a peculiar one, and must be attended to, though all others be left out; but I can see this thing growing every day." And at another time, speaking of the exhaustive demands upon him, which left him in no condition for more important duties, he said, "I sometimes fancy that every one of the numerous grist ground through here daily, from a Senator seeking a war with France down to a poor woman after a place in the Treasury Department, darted at me with thumb and finger, picked out their especial piece of my vitality, and carried it off. When I get through with such a day's work there is only one word which can express my condition, and that is—*flabbiness*." There are some public men who can now remember, with self-reproaches, having increased with long evening debates that reducing "flabbiness" of the much-enduring President.

Mr. Lincoln visited the Army of the Potomac in the spring of 1863, and, free from the annoyances of office, was considerably refreshed and rested; but even there the mental anxieties which never forsook him seemed to cast him down, at times, with a great weight. We left Washington late in the afternoon, and a snowstorm soon after coming on, the steamer was anchored for the night off Indian Head, on the Maryland shore of the Potomac. The President left the little knot in the cabin, and sitting alone in a corner, seemed absorbed in the saddest reflections for a time; then, beckoning a companion to him, said, "What will you wager that half our iron-clads are at the bottom of Charleston Harbor?" This being the first intimation which the other had had of Dupont's attack, which was then begun, hesitated to reply, when the President added, "The people will expect big things when they hear of this; but it is too late—*too late!*"

During that little voyage the captain of the steamer, a frank, modest old sailor, was so much affected by the care-worn appearance of the President, that he came to the writer and confessed that he had received the same impression of the Chief Magistrate that many had; hearing of his "little stories" and his humor, he had supposed him to have no cares or sadness; but a sight of that anxious and sad face had undeceived him, and he wanted to tell the President how much he had unintentionally wronged him, feeling that he had committed upon him a personal wrong. The captain was duly introduced to the President, who talked with him privately for a space, being touched as well as amused at what he called "Captain M——'s freeing his mind."

The following week, spent in riding about and seeing the army, appeared to revive Mr. Lincoln's spirits and to rest his body. A friend present observed as much to him, and he replied, "Well, yes, I do feel some better, I think; but, somehow, it don't appear to touch the tired spot, which can't be got at." And that, by-the-way, reminded him of a little story of his having once used that word, spot, a great many times in the course of a speech in Congress, years ago, so that some of his fellow-members called him "spot Lincoln," but he believed that the nickname did not stick. Another reminiscence of his early life, which he recalled during the trip, was one concerning his experience in rail-splitting. We were driving through an open clearing, where the Virginia forest had been felled by the soldiers, when Mr. Lincoln observed, looking at the stumps, "That's a good job of felling; they have got some good axemen in this army, I see." The conversation turning upon his knowledge of rail-splitting, he said, "Now let me tell you about that. I am not a bit anxious about my reputation in that line of business; but if there is any thing in this world that I am a judge of, it is of good felling of timber, but I don't remember having worked by myself at splitting rails for one whole day in my life." Upon surprise being expressed that his national reputation as a rail-splitter should have so slight a foundation, he said, "I recollect that, some time during the canvass for the office I now hold, there was a great mass meeting, where I was present, and with a great flourish several rails were brought into the meeting, and being informed where they came from, I was asked to identify them, which I did, with some qualms of conscience, having helped my father to split rails, as at other odd jobs. I said if there were any rails which I had split, I shouldn't wonder if those were the rails." Those who may be disappointed to learn of Mr. Lincoln's limited experience in splitting rails, may be relieved to know that he was evidently proud of his knowledge of the art of cutting timber, and explained minutely how a good job differed from a poor one, giving illustrations from the ugly stumps on either side.

An amusing yet touching instance of the President's preoccupation of mind occurred at one of his levees, when he was shaking hands with a host of visitors, passing him in a continuous stream. An intimate acquaintance received the usual conventional hand-shake and salutation; but, perceiving that he was not recognized, kept his ground, instead of moving on, and spoke again; when the President, roused by a dim consciousness that something unusual had happened, perceived who stood before him, and seizing his friend's hand, shook it again heartily, saying, "How do you do? How do you do? Excuse me for not noticing you at first; the fact is, I was thinking of a man down South." He afterward privately acknowledged that the "man down South" was Sherman, then on his march to the sea.

Mr. Lincoln had not a hopeful temperament, and, though he looked at the bright side of things, was always prepared for disaster and defeat. With his wonderful faculty for discerning results he often saw success where others saw disaster, but oftener perceived a failure when others were elated with victory, or were temporarily deceived by appearances. Of a great cavalry raid, which filled the newspapers with glowing exultation, but failed to cut the communications which it had been designed to destroy, he briefly said: "That was good circus-riding; it will do to fill a column in the newspapers; but I don't see that it has brought any thing else to pass." He often said that the worst feature about newspapers was that they were so sure to be "ahead of the hounds," outrunning events, and exciting expectations which were sure to be disappointed. One of the worst effects of a victory, he said, was to lead people to expect that the war was about over in consequence of it; but he was never weary of commending the patience of the American people, which he thought something matchless and touching. I have seen him shed tears when speaking of the cheerful sacrifice of the light and strength of so many happy homes throughout the land. His own patience was marvelous; and never crushed at defeat or unduly excited by success, his demeanor under both was an example for all men. Once he said the keenest blow of all the war was at an early stage, when the disaster of Ball's Bluff and the death of his beloved Baker smote upon him like a whirlwind from a desert.

It is generally agreed that Mr. Lincoln's slowness was a prominent trait of his character; but it is too early, perhaps, to say how much of our safety and success we owe to his slowness. It may be said, however, that he is to-day admired and beloved as much for what he did not do as for what he did. He was well aware of the popular opinion concerning his slowness, but was only sorry that such a quality of mind should sometimes be coupled with weakness and vacillation. Such an accusation he thought to be unjust. Acknowledging that he was slow in arriving at conclusions, he said that he could not help that; but he believed that when he did arrive at conclusions they were clear and "stuck by." He was a profound believer in his own fixity of purpose, and took pride in saying that his long deliberations made it possible for him to stand by his own acts when they were once resolved upon. It would have been a relief to the country at one time in our history if this trait of the President's character had been better understood. There was no time, probably, during the last administration, when any of the so-called radical measures were in any danger of being qualified or recalled. The simple explanation of the doubt which often hung over his purposes may be found in the fact that it was a habit of his mind to put forward all of the objections of other people and of his own to any given proposition, to see what arguments or counter-statements could be brought against them. While his own mind might be perfectly clear upon the subject, it gave him real pleasure to state objections for others to combat or attempt to set aside.

His practice of being controlled by events is well known. He often said that it was wise to wait for the developments of Providence; and the Scriptural phrase that "the stars in their courses fought against Sisera" to him had a depth of meaning. Then, too, he liked to feel that he was the attorney of the people, not their ruler; and I believe that this idea was generally uppermost in his mind. Speaking of the probability of his second nomination, about two years ago, he said: "If the people think that I have managed their case for them well enough to trust me to carry up to the next term, I am sure that I shall be glad to take it."

He liked to provide for his friends, who were often remembered gratefully for services given him in his early struggles in life. Sometimes he would "break the slate," as he called it, of those who were making up a list of appointments, that he might insert the name of some old acquaintance who had befriended him in days when friends were few. He was not deceived by outside appearances, but took the measure of those he met, and few men were worth any more or any less than the value which Abraham Lincoln set upon them.

Upon being told that a gentleman upon whom he was about to confer a valuable appointment had been bitterly opposed to his renomination, he said: "I suppose that Judge ——, having been disappointed before, did behave pretty ugly; but that wouldn't make him any less fit for this place, and I have a Scriptural authority for appointing him. You recollect that while the Lord on Mount Sinai was getting out a commission for Aaron, that same Aaron was at the foot of the mountain making a false god, a golden calf, for the people to worship; yet Aaron got his commission, you know." At another time, when remonstrated with upon the appointment to place of one of his former opponents, he said: "Nobody will deny that he is a first-rate man for the place, and I am bound to see that his opposition to me personally shall not interfere with my giving the people a good officer."

The world will never hear the last of the "little stories" with which the President garnished or illustrated his conversation and his early stump speeches. He said, however, that as near as he could reckon, about one-sixth of those which were credited to him were old acquaintances; all of the rest were the productions of other and better story-tellers than himself. Said he: "I do generally remember a good story when I hear it, but I never did invent any thing original; I am only a retail dealer." His anecdotes were seldom told for the sake of the telling, but because they fitted in just where they came, and shed a light on the argument that nothing else could. He was not witty, but brimful of humor; and though he was quick to appreciate a good pun, I never knew of his making but one, which was on the Christian name of a friend, to whom he said: "You have yet to be elected to the place I hold; but Noah's *reign* was before Abraham." He thought that the chief characteristic of American humor was its grotesqueness and extravagance; and the story of the man who was so tall that he was "laid out" in a rope-walk, the soprano voice so high that it had to be climbed over by a ladder, and the

Dutchman's expression of "somebody tying his dog loose," all made a permanent lodgment in his mind.

His accuracy and memory were wonderful, and one illustration of the former quality may be given in the remarkable correspondence between the figures of the result of the last presidential election and the actual sum total. The President's figures, collected hastily, and partially based upon his own estimates, made up only four weeks after the election, have been found to be only one hundred and twenty-nine less in their grand total than that made up by Mr. M'Pherson, the Clerk of the House of Representatives, who has compiled a table from the returns furnished him from the official records of all the State capitals in the loyal States.

Latterly Mr. Lincoln's reading was with the humorous writers. He liked to repeat from memory whole chapters from these books; and on such occasions he always preserved his own gravity though his auditors might be convulsed with laughter. He said that he had a dread of people who could not appreciate the fun of such things; and he once instanced a member of his own Cabinet, of whom he quoted the saying of Sydney Smith, "that it required a surgical operation to get a joke into his head." The light trifles spoken of diverted his mind, or, as he said of his theatre-going, gave him refuge from himself and his weariness. But he also was a lover of many philosophical books, and particularly liked Butler's Analogy of Religion, Stuart Mill on Liberty, and he always hoped to get at President Edwards on the Will. These ponderous writers found a queer companionship in the chronicler of the Mackerel Brigade, Parson Nasby, and Private Miles O'Reilly. The Bible was a very familiar study with the President, whole chapters of Isaiah, the New Testament, and the Psalms being fixed in his memory, and he would sometimes correct a misquotation of Scripture, giving generally the chapter and verse where it could be found. He liked the Old Testament best, and dwelt on the simple beauty of the historical books. Once, speaking of his own age and strength, he quoted with admiration that passage, "His eye was not dim, nor his natural force abated." I do not know that he thought then how, like that Moses of old, he was to stand on Pisgah and see a peaceful land which he was not to enter.

Of the poets the President appeared to prefer Hood and Holmes, the mixture and pathos in their writings being attractive to him beyond any thing else which he read. Of the former author he liked best the last part of "Miss Kilmansegg and her Golden Leg," "Faithless Sally Brown," and one or two others not generally so popular as those which are called Hood's best poems. Holmes's "September Gale," "Last Leaf," "Chambered Nautilus," and "Ballad of an Oysterman" were among his very few favorite poems. Longfellow's "Psalm of Life" and "Birds of Killingworth" were the only productions of that author he ever mentioned with praise, the latter of which he picked up somewhere in a newspaper, cut out, and carried in his vest pocket until it was committed to memory. James Russell Lowell he only knew as "Hosea Biglow," every one of whose effusions he knew. He sometimes repeated, word for word, the whole of "John P. Robinson, he," giving the unceasing refrain with great unction and enjoyment. He once said that originality and daring impudence were sublimed in this stanza of Lowell's:

"Ef you take a sword and dror it,
    An' stick a feller creetur thru,
Gov'ment hain't to answer for it,
    God'll send the bill to you."

Mr. Lincoln's love of music was something passionate, but his tastes were simple and uncultivated, his choice being old airs, songs, and ballads, among which the plaintive Scotch songs were best liked. "Annie Laurie," "Mary of Argyle," and especially "Auld Robin Gray," never lost their charm for him; and all songs which had for their theme the rapid flight of time, decay, the recollections of early days, were sure to make a deep impression. The song which he liked best, above all others, was one called "Twenty Years Ago"—a simple air, the words to which are supposed to be uttered by a man who revisits the play-ground of his youth. He greatly desired to find music for his favorite poem, "Oh, why should the spirit of mortal be proud?" and said once, when told that the newspapers had credited him with the authorship of the piece, "I should not care much for the reputation of having written that, but would be glad if I could compose music as fit to convey the sentiment as the words now do."

He wrote slowly, and with the greatest deliberation, and liked to take his time; yet some of his dispatches, written without any corrections, are models of compactness and finish. His private correspondence was extensive, and he preferred writing his letters with his own hand, making copies himself frequently, and filing every thing away in a set of pigeon-holes in his office. When asked why he did not have a letter-book and copying-press, he said, "A letter-book might be easily carried off, but that stock of filed letters would be a back-load." He conscientiously attended to his enormous correspondence, and read every thing that appeared to demand his own attention. He said that he read with great regularity the letters of an old friend who lived on the Pacific coast until he received a letter of *seventy pages* of letter paper, when he broke down, and never read another.

People were sometimes disappointed because he appeared before them with a written speech. The best explanation of that habit of his was his remark to a friend who noticed a roll of manuscript in the hand of the President as he came into the parlor while waiting for the serenade which was given him on the night following his re-election. Said he: "I know what you are thinking about; but there's no clap-trap about me, and I am free to say that in the excitement of the moment I am sure to say something which I am sorry for when I see it in print; so I have it here in black and white, and there are no mistakes made. People attach too much importance to what I say any how." Upon another occasion, hearing that I was in the parlor, he sent for me to come up into the library, where I found him writing on a piece of common stiff box-board with a pencil. Said he, after he had finished, "Here is one speech of mine which has never been printed, and I think it worth printing. Just see what you think." He then read the following, which is copied *verbatim* from the familiar handwriting before me:

"On Thursday of last week two ladies from Tennessee came before the President, asking the release of their husbands, held as prisoners of war at Johnson's Island. They were put off until

Friday, when they came again, and were again put off until Saturday. At each of the interviews one of the ladies urged that her husband was a religious man. On Saturday, when the President ordered the release of the prisoners, he said to this lady: 'You say your husband is a religious man; tell him when you meet him that I say I am not much of a judge of religion, but that, in my opinion, the religion that sets men to rebel and fight against their Government because, as they think, that Government does not sufficiently help *some* men to eat their bread in the sweat of *other* men's faces, is not the sort of religion upon which people can get to heaven.'"

To this the President signed his name at my request, by way of joke, and added for a caption, "The President's Last, Shortest, and Best Speech," under which title it was duly published in one of the Washington newspapers. His Message to the last session of Congress was first written upon the same sort of white pasteboard above referred to, its stiffness enabling him to lay it on his knee as he sat easily in his armchair, writing and erasing as he thought and wrought out his idea.

The already extended limits of this article will not permit any thing more than a mention of many of the traits of Mr. Lincoln's peculiar character, many of which are already widely known by his published writings and speeches, and by the numerous anecdotes which have been narrated by others who have been ready to meet the general desire to know more of the man whose life was so dear to the people. His thoughtfulness for those who bore the brunt of the battles, his harmonious family relations, his absorbing love for his children, his anxiety for the well-being and conduct of the emancipated colored people, his unwavering faith in the hastening doom of human slavery, his affectionate regard for "the simple people," his patience, his endurance, his mental sufferings, and what he did for the Nation and for Humanity and Liberty—these all must be left to the systematic and enduring labors of the historian. Though he is dead, his immortal virtues are the rich possession of the nation; his fame shall grow with our young Republic; and as years roll on brighter lustre will adorn the name of Abraham Lincoln.

July 1865

James Russell Lowell

On July 21, 1865, Harvard held a Commemoration Day to honor its Union veterans and war dead. Lowell, who had lost three nephews in the conflict, was asked to compose and recite an ode for the occasion. Initially blocked, he eventually managed to write the poem in the two days preceding the ceremony. Shortly after Commemoration Day he added a canto about the recently fallen President that may be the most deeply felt of all his writings on Lincoln; it first appeared when the Commemoration Ode was published in the September 1865 *Atlantic Monthly* to wide acclaim.

FROM

Ode Recited at the Harvard Commemoration

VI

Such was he, our Martyr-Chief,
    Whom late the Nation he had led,
    With ashes on her head,
Wept with the passion of an angry grief:
Forgive me, if from present things I turn
To speak what in my heart will beat and burn,
And hang my wreath on his world-honored urn.
      Nature, they say, doth dote,
      And cannot make a man
      Save on some worn-out plan,
      Repeating us by rote:
For him her Old World moulds aside she threw,
    And, choosing sweet clay from the breast
      Of the unexhausted West,
With stuff untainted shaped a hero new,
Wise, steadfast in the strength of God, and true.
    How beautiful to see
Once more a shepherd of mankind indeed,
Who loved his charge, but never loved to lead;
One whose meek flock the people joyed to be,

Not lured by any cheat of birth,
But by his clear-grained human worth,
And brave old wisdom of sincerity!
They knew that outward grace is dust;
They could not choose but trust
In that sure-footed mind's unfaltering skill,
And supple-tempered will
That bent like perfect steel to spring again and thrust.
His was no lonely mountain-peak of mind,
Thrusting to thin air o'er our cloudy bars,
A sea-mark now, now lost in vapors blind;
Broad prairie rather, genial, level-lined,
Fruitful and friendly for all human kind,
Yet also nigh to Heaven and loved of loftiest stars.
Nothing of Europe here,
Or, then, of Europe fronting mornward still,
Ere any names of Serf and Peer
Could Nature's equal scheme deface;
Here was a type of the true elder race,
And one of Plutarch's men talked with us face to face.
I praise him not; it were too late;
And some innative weakness there must be
In him who condescends to victory
Such as the Present gives, and cannot wait,
Safe in himself as in a fate.
So always firmly he:
He knew to bide his time,
And can his fame abide,
Still patient in his simple faith sublime,
Till the wise years decide.
Great captains, with their guns and drums,
Disturb our judgment for the hour,
But at last silence comes;
These all are gone, and, standing like a tower,
Our children shall behold his fame,
The kindly-earnest, brave, foreseeing man,
Sagacious, patient, dreading praise, not blame,
New birth of our new soil, the first American.

1865

Victor Hugo

Hugo (1802–1885) wrote this brief meditation on Lincoln's murder during his long exile (1851–70) from France during the reign of Louis-Napoleon. The great French writer's deep respect for the martyred American President reflected not only Hugo's hatred of slavery, but also his hope that the example of Lincoln's dedicated republicanism might inspire the French to overthrow the Second Empire. Defying official censorship, Hugo led a fundraising campaign that solicited ten-centime contributions to finance a commemorative medal for presentation to Mary Lincoln. Despite government opposition, the organizers enlisted 40,000 donors and succeeded in striking a small bronze, bearing a profile of Lincoln on the obverse and an allegorical tribute to emancipation on the reverse. In a letter to Mary Lincoln accompanying the gift, Hugo and other French liberals declared: "If France had the freedom enjoyed by republican America, not thousands, but millions among us would have been counted as admirers."

Notebook Entry

Two dead men have killed slavery. What John Brown's death had initiated, Lincoln's death brought to completion.

These two murderers, Wyse's in 1859, Booth's in 1865, unintentionally played the role of liberators, the one by setting up the gallows and the other by drawing his dagger. The guiding principle of their act, slavery erect, and, so to speak pilloried between two murders, was thus revealed.

September–October 1865

Herman Melville

A decade after *Moby-Dick* appeared to an indifferent reception, its author sought an appointment as consul to Florence from the new Lincoln administration. Bearing a recommendation from Julius Rockwell, a former Whig congressman from Massachusetts who had helped Lincoln's son Robert enter Harvard, Melville (1819–1891) went to Washington, D.C., shortly after the inauguration and met the President at a White House reception on March 22, 1861. "Old Abe is much better looking than I expected & younger looking," he wrote to his wife. "He shook hands like a good fellow—working hard at it like a man sawing wood at so much per cord." Five days later Lincoln gave the Florence position to another man, and Melville returned to a life of financial worry and publishing failure. When he wrote about the Civil War, he did so in verse, publishing *Battle-Pieces and Aspects of the War* in August 1866. In "The Martyr" Melville warned of the popular passions aroused by Lincoln's murder, although in his note to the poem, also printed below, he expressed relief that his worst fears had not come to pass. A few months after the publication of *Battle-Pieces*, Melville began working as a customs inspector on the Manhattan docks; when he retired two decades later, unsold copies of the collection still sat in the publisher's warehouse.

The Martyr
Indicative of the passion of the people on the 15th of April, 1865.

Good Friday was the day
  Of the prodigy and crime,
When they killed him in his pity,
  When they killed him in his prime
Of clemency and calm—
    When with yearning he was filled
    To redeem the evil-willed,
And, though conqueror, be kind;
  But they killed him in his kindness,
  In their madness and their blindness,
And they killed him from behind.

There is sobbing of the strong,
      And a pall upon the land;
But the People in their weeping
            Bare the iron hand:
Beware the People weeping
      When they bare the iron hand.

He lieth in his blood—
      The father in his face;
They have killed him, the Forgiver—
      The Avenger takes his place,*
The Avenger wisely stern,
      Who in righteousness shall do
      What the heavens call him to,
And the parricides remand;
      For they killed him in his kindness,
      In their madness and their blindness,
And his blood is on their hand.

There is sobbing of the strong,
      And a pall upon the land;
But the People in their weeping
            Bare the iron hand:
Beware the People weeping
      When they bare the iron hand.

*At this period of excitement the thought was by some passionately welcomed that the Presidential successor had been raised up by heaven to wreak vengeance on the South. The idea originated in the remembrance that Andrew Johnson by birth belonged to that class of Southern whites who never cherished love for the dominant one; that he was a citizen of Tennessee, where the contest at times and in places had been close and bitter as a Middle-Age feud; that himself and family had been hardly treated by the Secessionists.

But the expectations built hereon (if, indeed, ever soberly entertained), happily for the country, have not been verified.

Likewise the feeling which would have held the entire South chargeable with the crime of one exceptional assassin, this too has died away with the natural excitement of the hour.

1866

William H. Herndon

Few people knew Lincoln better, or more determinedly sought to shape his image for posterity, than his longtime Springfield law partner. The Kentucky-born Herndon (1818–1891) became the future President's junior partner in 1844, and their association continued until Lincoln's departure for Washington in 1861. (For whatever reason, Herndon received no job offers from the new administration.) After his friend's death, Herndon recoiled from the popular tendency to idealize and mythologize Lincoln, and he resolved to write a biography that would combine his own recollections with "*solid facts & well attested truths*" about Lincoln's early years. In May 1865 he began almost two years of investigative work, interviewing and corresponding with dozens of people who had known Lincoln and his family in Kentucky, Indiana, and Illinois. While conducting his research Herndon also began giving public lectures on Lincoln. The first three, on Lincoln's "Life and Character" and "Patriotism and Statesmanship," aroused little controversy, but the fourth, delivered in Springfield on November 16, 1866, boldly declared that the doomed Ann Rutledge of New Salem, and not Mary Todd, had been the only woman ever to earn Lincoln's love. Mrs. Lincoln was understandably furious; in private letters she called Herndon "a hopeless inebriate" and "a dirty dog," lamenting: "This is the return for all my husband's kindness to this miserable man." Biographers and historians continue to debate the accuracy of Herndon's claims about Ann Rutledge, but it is certain that this widely quoted lecture established one of the most enduring mythic images of Lincoln, that of a heartbroken, melancholic young man haunted by lost love and fated to endure a loveless marriage.

The text presented here follows the original 1866 broadside printing, which used dashes to conceal the identity of Ann Rutledge's fiancé John McNamar (who was referred to by Herndon in his spoken lecture as "the Scotchman"), as well as that of Ann's third suitor, the New Salem storekeeper Samuel Hill. In the passage describing his visit to McNamar's farm in October 1866, Herndon (or his printer) also substituted dashes in several places for words such as "farm."

Abraham Lincoln, Ann Rutledge,
and New Salem: A Lecture

Ladies and Gentlemen:—

I am about to deliver a Lecture tonight on Abraham Lincoln, Miss Ann Rutledge, New Salem, Pioneering, and the Poem commonly called Immortality or "Oh! Why should the spirit of mortal be proud?"

Lincoln loved Ann Rutledge better than his own life; and I shall give the history of the poem so far as to connect it with the two in its own proper place and time.

The facts in relation to Abraham, Ann, and the poem, making a complete history, lie in fragments in the desk at my office, in the bureau drawers at my home, and in my memory—in the memories of men, women and children all over this broad land, and especially in the counties of Menard and Sangamon, covering an area of sixty miles square.

The facts, I say, are fragmentary. They lie floating on the memories of men, women and children in and about New Salem, and in and about this city. This lecture is but a part—a *small* part—of a long, thrilling and eloquent story. I have not here told the whole story; nay, not the half of it; nor can I do so here understandingly, for the want of time. I am forced to keep something back from necessity which shall, in due time, assume a more permanent form. That which is withheld is just as interesting, and more lovely, than I here can tell or relate. Some one has said that "truth is stranger than fiction;" and as it is stranger, so it is sometimes more beautiful and more sad. We see the truth; we feel it; it is present, and we deeply sympathize with it.

All human life is more uncertain, and it may reasonably be thought that the invisible and intangible threads that enwrap and tie up life, may be suddenly snapped, and historic events of great interest and importance to mankind—lost forever. I do not *think*—wishing to arrogate nothing to myself—that any living man or woman so well understands, the many delicate wheels and hidden springs of the story of Lincoln, Miss Rutledge, the Poem, and its relation to the two, in time and place, as I do. My pecuniary condition will not let me rest. Duty to myself, my family, and my clients, holds me sternly to my profession. I cannot drop these duties, spurred on by necessity, as I am, to sit down and at once furnish the long contemplated life of Mr. Lincoln. I am compelled to walk slowly, but what I shall lose in speed I shall gain in volume and certainty of record. To put these fragmentary facts and historic events therefore beyond danger, I consent tonight to speak, write and utter what I know. I have no right to retain facts and events. so important to a good understanding of Mr. Lincoln's life, in my own selfish bosom any longer. I rest under a sacred duty to mankind, to relate the facts and narrate the circumstances that lawfully and truthfully belong to the story. I owe to man the facts and the story which shall soon become, I believe, not through me, as to artistic beauty, one of the world's most classic stories.

You know my Religion, my Philosophy namely: That the highest thought and acts of the human soul in its religious sphere, are to think, love, obey and worship God, by thinking freely, by loving, teaching, doing good to and elevating mankind. My first duty is to God, then to mankind, and then to the individual man or woman. I wish to perform my duty honestly and truthfully. I do not wish to awaken or injure the dead, nor to wound or injure the feelings of any living man or woman. I am glad—nay, happy,—to be able to speak to my own fellow citizens of this city—neighbors, friends, and enemies too, tonight, so near the scene and facts that I am about to relate. Each one of you, every man, woman and child, has the same powers, the same means, opportunities and capacities I have, to hunt up, find and criticise the facts, know them and to verify them, each for himself.

The truth of the story is open to all alike, rich and poor, energetic and lazy. If any man or woman, or child, after hearing this lecture, still doubts what is here told, let him or her come to my office and have all skepticism wiped out at once from his or her mind. There is no doubt about the story; there can be none. I want only truth, and I, in common with all mankind, for all time to come, am deeply interested to have the facts known exactly as they are, truthfully and substantially told.

If I am mistaken substantially in any particular, or in general, expose me by exposing the error. I am willing that my character among you may stand or fall by the substantial truthfulness of this lecture *in every* particular. I want no doubts to hang over the subject, nor shall they so hang if I can avoid it, between the honest gaze of mankind and their search for truth, blurring their mental vision.

Truth in history is my sole and only motive for making this sad story now public for the first time. History is sacred, and should be so held eternally by all men. What would you give for a manly, honest, candid and noble biography of Washington? Let the universal regrets of mankind fix the price and stamp the value.

The facts which I shall relate, including the scenery of New Salem, shall, in my humble judgment, throw a strong foot-light on the path of Abraham Lincoln, from New Salem, through Springfield, to and through Washington, to the grave. They, *to me*, throw their rays all over Mr. Lincoln's thoughts, acts, deeds, and life, privately, domestically, socially, religiously and otherwise. I hope they will *to you*. I dare not keep these facts longer. Men need to read history by a blazing light. This is my apology for the publication of these facts *now*, and I appeal to time for my defense. The world needs but one other set of facts to get the whole, almost the divine light, that illuminates Mr. Lincoln's pathway. The facts are a little older than he was—some a little younger. Will the world dare hear them and defend the man that tells them?

Ladies and gentlemen, friends, enemies, too, give me the good, kind, sad and tender corner of your hearts tonight, not forgetting your heads. Ann Rutledge was a beautiful girl of New Salem *from* 1824 to 1836. She was born in Kentucky, January 7th, 1813. She was a grandchild of the liberty-loving patriotic Rutledges of South Carolina. Her father was born in South Carolina, amid the echoes of the cannon's revolutionary roar. Mr. Lincoln lived in New Salem from 1830 to 1837, and boarded for awhile with Cameron, who was a partner of Mr. Rutledge. Mr. Lincoln soon changed his home. He went and boarded with Mr. James Rutledge about the year 1833 and 1834, and then and there first became well acquainted with Ann Rutledge. He may have known her well before this. I have no space here to give a description of this beautiful, amiable, and lovely girl of nineteen. She was gifted with a good mind. Three good and influential men of the little village of New Salem, simultaneously fell in love with this girl—A. Lincoln, Mr. ——, and Mr. ——. The third man she quickly rejected. He was a gentleman; so was Lincoln; so was Mr. ——. All these men were strong men, men of power, as time demonstrated. Circumstances, fate, Providence, the iron chain of sweeping events, so willed it that this young lady was engaged to Mr. Lincoln and Mr. —— at the same time.

No earthly blame can be attached to the girl, and none to the men in their fidelity and honor to her. It all so happened, or was decided by fate. It shall, in truth, be explained hereafter to the satisfaction of all. It is a sad, thrilling story. The young girl saw her condition. Her word of promise was out to two men at the same time, both of whom she loved, dearly loved. The consciousness of this, and the conflict of duties, love's promises, and womanly engagements, made her think, grow sad, become restless and nervous. She suffered, pined, ate not and slept not. Time and struggle, as supposed and believed by many, caused her to have a raging fever, of which she died on the 25th of August, A. D. 1835. She died on a farm seven miles north, bearing a little west of New Salem, and now lies buried in the Concord graveyard, six miles north, bearing a little west of New Salem, and four miles from Petersburg.

On Sunday, the 14th day of October, A. D. 1866, I went to the well cultured and well stocked farm of Mr. ——. I went with book in hand, in search of *facts*. I have known the gentleman whom I visited, for more than thirty years. He received and welcomed me into his house most cordially, and treated me most hospitably. He acted like a gentleman, and is one. He is the man who knows all the story so far as it relates to ——. He knows it and has ——. He owns the —— on which the young girl died; and if I could risk a rapid and random *opinion*, I should say he purchased the —— in part, if not solely, because of the sad memories that cluster over and around it. The visit and my task were truly delicate. Without holding you longer in uneasy and unnecessary suspense, from what took place then and there, permit me to say, that I asked the gentleman this question: "Did you know Miss Rutledge? If so, where did she die?" He sat by his open window, looking westerly, and pulling me closer to himself, looked through the window and said: "There, by that —" choking up with emotion, pointing his long forefinger, nervous and trembling, towards the spot—"there, by *that* currant bush, she died. The old house in which she and her father died, is gone."

I then, after some delay, asked the further question: "In what month and year did she die?" He replied, "In the month of August, 1835." After further conversation, leaving the sadness to momentarily pass away, I asked this additional question: "Where was she buried?" In reply to which he said, "In Concord burying ground, one mile southeast from this place." "Can you tell me exactly where she lies buried?" I remarked. He said, "No, I cannot. I left the country in 1832 or 1833. My mother soon after died, and she too, was buried in the same little sacred graveyard, and when I returned here in 1835 I could find neither grave. The Berrys, however, may know Ann's."

To Berry's I speedily went, with my friend and guide, James Miles. The time was 11:20 a. m., Sunday, the 14th day of October, A. D. 1866. I found S. C. Berry at the Concord church, a little, white, neat meeting house, that crowns the brow of a small knoll overlooking Concord creek—Berry's creek, southward. S. C. Berry, James Short—the gentleman who purchased in Mr. Lincoln's compass and chain in 1834, under an execution against Lincoln, or Lincoln and Berry, and gratuitously gave them back to Mr. Lincoln—James Miles and myself, were together. We all went into the meadow eastward of the church and sat down in the shade of a walnut tree. I asked Mr. Berry if he knew where Miss Rutledge was buried—the place and exact surroundings? He replied: "I do. The grave of Miss Rutledge lies just north of her brother's, David Rutledge, a young lawyer of great promise, who died in 1842, in his 27th year."

I went from the neat little church to the Concord burying ground, and soon found the grave of Miss Ann Rutledge. The cemetery contains about one acre of ground, and is laid out in a

square. The dead lie in rows, not in squares, as is usual. The
ground, the yard, is beautifully situated on a mound, and lies on
the main road leading from Springfield, in Sangamon County,
to Havana, in Mason County. It is situated—lies on Berry's
creek, and on the left bank or west side. The ground gradually
slopes off east and west, north and south. A ribbon of small timber runs up the creek. It does not here break into groves. The
creek runs northward—i. e., its general course, and runs into
what is called Blue Lake in the Sangamon bottom, and thence
running into the Sangamon river, some three miles distant from
the burying ground. The grounds are otherwise beautifully situated. A thin skirt of timber lies on the east, commencing at the
fence of the cemetery. The ribbon of timber, some fifty yards
wide, hides the sun's early rise. At 9 o'clock the sun pours all his
rays into the cemetery. An extensive prairie lies west, the forest
north, a field on the east, and timber and prairie lie on the south.
In this lovely ground lie the Berrys, the Rutledges, the Clarrys,
the Armstrongs, and the Jones, old and respected citizens, pioneers of an early day.

I write—or rather did write, the original draft of this description in the immediate presence of the ashes of Miss Ann Rutledge, the beautiful and tender dead. "My heart lies buried
here," said Lincoln to a friend. I wrote in the presence of the
spirits of David and Ann Rutledge, remembering the good spirit
of Abraham. I knew the young man as early as 1841, probably
when he had first commenced his profession as lawyer. The village of the dead is a sad, solemn place, and when out in the
country, especially so. Its very presence imposes truth on the
mind of the living writer. Ann Rutledge lies buried north of her
brother, and rests sweetly on his left arm, angels to guard her.
The cemetery is fast filling with the hazel and the dead.

I shall now have to take you back with me some five years or
more. After Mr. Lincoln returned from New Orleans, in 1831,
and after a short visit to his father and mother in Coles County,
in Illinois, who then lived on a farm eight miles south of Charleston, the county seat of Coles County, he returned to New Salem,
twenty miles northwest of Springfield, now the capitol, and the
home of Lincoln in 1860. At that time New Salem and Spring-

field were in one county, the County of Sangamon. Mr. Lincoln first saw New Salem hill on the 18th day of April, 1831, and he *must* have been struck with the beauty of the scene, if not with its grandeur and sublimity.

Objects of beauty, objects of grandeur, objects of sublimity, have a supreme power over the mind, elevating and expanding it, humanizing and educating it. These educate us, and give us an expanded, ever-widening view of nature and of God. It is said that the Alpine heights with their majestic sceneries, make the Swiss a patriotic, liberty-loving people, who have defied Austrian bayonets for ages. It is said that the sacred hills and mountains around Athens, and the great deep blue sea that sweeps around her feet—that is to say, the peninsula's feet—made and fashioned her poets, statesmen and orators. New Salem had and has some power in this way and did have on Mr. Lincoln's mind. I am now necessitated—that *you* may understand much that goes before and comes after—to describe New Salem and her surroundings.

I do this for various reasons in addition to what I specially name, in order to give you a running picture of New Salem— her rivers, peaks, bluffs, and other views. I first knew this hill or bluff as early as 1829. I have seen it in spring time and winter, in summer time and fall. I have seen it in daylight and night time; have seen it when the sward was green, living and vital, and I have seen it wrapt in snow, frost and sleet. I have closely studied it for more than five long years. The town of New Salem lies on the west—the left—bank of the river Sangamon, and is situated on a bluff, which rises above low water mark in the river about 100 feet.

The town is on the road leading from Springfield to Havana —the former in Sangamon County and the latter in Mason County. New Salem hill was once covered with the wild forest— tree—not a very thick heavy timber, rather barren, so called. The forest was cut off to make room for the village, which was laid out in 1828. It became a trading place at that time, and in 1836 contained a population of about 100 souls, living in about 20 houses, some of which cost from $10 to $100—none exceeded the latter sum. The village had one regular, straight street, running east and west, the east end resting on the brow of the hill, overlooking the Sangamon, and the west end abutting against the forest. The village runs along on what is called the backbone of the hill, it sloping on the north and south.

The north branch rises in a meadow or field, about three-fourths of a mile west of New Salem, and sweeps east, cutting a deep channel as it rushes and runs. The branch pours its waters in the Sangamon river about three hundred yards below and north of the village.

The creek on the south—a larger and a longer one than the north branch—by its cuts and deep channels, 80 or 100 feet deep, leaves New Salem on the back of the hill—the very backbone of the ridge. The only and main street was about 70 feet wide, and the backbone of the hill is about 250 feet across—sufficiently wide for a street, with lots 180 feet deep—till it runs back westerly for some distance, growing wider, to the then forest and now meadow or field. The hill on the east end of the street where the river runs, and which the bluffs boldly overlook, rises at some places almost to perpendicular heights. At other places it rises from an angle of 25 to 80 degrees.

There is an old mill at the foot of the bluff, on the Sangamon, driven by water power. The river washes the base of the bluff for about 400 yards, the hill breaking off almost abruptly at the north. The river along this line runs about due north; it strikes the bluff coming around a sudden bend from the south-east, the river being checked and turned by the rocky hill. The milldam running across the Sangamon river just at the mill, checks the rapidity of the water. It was here and on this dam that Mr. Lincoln's flatboat "stuck on the 19th of April, 1831." The dam is about eight feet high, and 220 feet long, and as the old Sangamon rolls her turbid waters over the dam, plunging them into the whirl and eddy beneath, the roar and hiss of waters, like the low, continuous, distant thunder, can be distinctly heard through the whole village, day and night, week day and Sunday, spring and fall, or other high water time. The river, at the base of the bluff, is about 250 feet wide. The mill using up 30 feet, leaving the dam only about 220 feet long. Green's rocky branch, so called, which rises west by a little south of New Salem, sweeps eastwardly and washes the southern line of the base of the hill; it is a narrow, winding stream, whose bottom is covered with pretty little pebbles of all shapes, colors and sizes. Standing on New Salem hill and looking southward some 800 yards across a valley, rises the opposite bank or bluff of the hill, made by the branch or double force of branch and river. The bluff rises to an equal elevation with the Salem hill, if not a little higher. The hills or bluffs are covered with a heavy timber. The creek leaps and pours her waters into the Sangamon just above the milldam, sometimes adding its rapid and clear and clean volume to the pond. On the eastern side of the river, on the right bank of the river, looking east down the village street, running east and west, the range of bluffs rises generally to the level of the surrounding hills. The distance from bluff to bluff, across the river, is about 1,000 yards, possibly 1,500 yards. The general range of the hills on the eastern side of the river is likewise bearded with timber—the wild forest trees—mostly oak, hickory, walnut, ash and elm. The bottom, the rich lowlands that lie between hill and hill, are about 800 yards wide, possibly more, and between peak and peak, hill and hill, through this rich and deep alluvial soil, flint and limestone, chalk and sand, clay and lime, slate and soapstone, animal and vegetable remains, rolls, washes and plays from east to west, from peak to peak, through the ages, the eternal Sangamon, casting and rolling sand and clay, flint and limestone, animal and vegetable *debris*, on either shore as it half omnipotently wills, sometimes kissing the feet of one bluff, and then washing the other. At other times—in spring time or other high water seasons—the river at other places is more than a mile wide, ranging from its head to its mouth. As we look up the river southeast, and follow with our eyes its winding course, beyond bluff rises bluff on bluff, and forest on forest, the first tier of timber giving and presenting to the eye, in the month of October—the time of writing this—a mellow green orange color of various shades, according to distance and the angle of view. The second ribbon of timber, rising over the first and beyond, gives and presents to the eye a more distinct and darker green, tinted with blue—a more uniform color and not so abrupt in its dash, its risings and swells. The third belt of timber, still beyond, rising over the first and second timber, to the eye gives and presents a still deeper and more distinct blue, wrapt in mist generated in the distance, as it rises and recedes in the infinite east, leaving a clear, sharp outline, less abrupt and more uniform than either of the closer ones, slightly undulating, out against the clear, clean blue eastern sky, measuring and fixing beyond doubt the earth's general level and its rotundity here. Down the river, a little east, is the same general view, though not so beautiful, not so grand, because less distinct and prominent to the eye. About two miles north, in a beautiful valley, nestles snugly the handsome town of Petersburg, which Lincoln surveyed and laid out in 1836, and which is now the county seat of Menard County, with a population of about 1,500 souls. About three-fourths of a mile below New Salem, at the foot of the main bluff, and in a hollow between two lateral bluffs, stands the house of Bolin Green, now uninhabited. It is a log-house, weather-boarded; and about the same distance north from Bolin Green's house, *now* at the foot of the bluff, stands the building, the house and home once of Bennett Able. When the proper time comes I shall have to tell of another quite romantic love story that happened at this house.

These descriptions mean something, and in our historic evolution you will perceive the absolute necessity of them; then you will thank me, not before, possibly. New Salem, Petersburg, Green's and Able's houses, all lie on the western bank of the river, namely on the left-hand shore. These bluffs, houses, and general scenery give a beautiful appearance to the eye. I cannot truthfully say they rise to the grand, yet they are most beautiful indeed.

When I wrote the original of this on my knee, I was on the hill and bluff, the sun was just climbing upward out of the forest in the east, hanging over the timber like a fire-wheel, climbing and rolling up the deep unmeasured immensities above me. The morning, the 15th day of October, 1866, was misty, cloudy, foggy and cold. The orb of day soon dissipated and scattered mist and fog, cloud and cold. The Circuit Court of Menard County had adjourned and my business was finished, and I was free, at least for *one* day. I sat down to write amid the ruins of

New Salem. Only one lone and solitary log hut was in view—all that remains of New Salem; it is one-story high, had two doors, two chimneys, two rooms, fronts north, and is a log house, weather-boarded with plank. Abraham has been in it possibly a hundred times.

The logs are hewed a little, simply faced. The chimneys are one at the east end and the other at the west end of the house. On the south of the house stands now a smoke house of plank, a seemingly newer erection. My guide, a new man, sat at my right hand, my feet in the ruins of the town, and close to me, and a little southwest, rang and rolled out and tinkled the ring of a lone cow bell, rattling, tapping and sounding here and there, as the cow browsed along the hills. The roll and roar of the Sangamon is distinctly heard eastward, as the waters curl and leap over the dam and plunge into the stream beneath. Lincoln has heard it often, and though he is gone, it rolls and roars on, and will for ages yet to come. All human life is transient, Nature permanent. Life is but for an instant, Nature is eternal. Why burn the short span of our human life by undue use and haste.

As I sat on the verge of the town, in the presence of its ruins, I called to mind the street running east and west through the village, the river eastward, Green's rocky branch, with its hills, southward; Clarry's Grove westerly about three miles; Petersburg northward and Springfield southeast, and now I cannot exclude from my memory or imagination, the forms, faces, voices, and features of those I once knew so well. In my imagination, the little village perched on the hill is astir with the hum of busy men, and the sharp, quick buzz of women; and from the country come men and women afoot or on horseback, to see and to be seen; to hear and to be heard; to barter and exchange what they have with the merchant and laborer. There are Jack Armstrong, and Wm. Green, Kelso and *Jason Duncan*, Alley and Cameron, Hill and McNamara, Herndons and Rutledges, Warburton and Sincho, Bale and Ellis, Abraham and Ann.

Oh! what a history. Here it was that the bold, rattling and brave roysterer met and greeted roysterer; bumper rang to bumper, and strong friend met friend and fought friend, for friendship's sake. Here it was that all strangers, every new comer, was initiated quickly, sharply and rudely, into the lights and mysteries of western civilization. The stranger was compelled, if he assumed the appearance of a man, to walk through the strength and courage of naturally great men.

They were men of no college culture, but they had their many and broad, well tested experiences, good sense and sound judgment, and if the stranger bore well his part, acted well, he at once became, thenceforward, a brother of the clan forever. But if—but if he failed, he quickly, amid their mocking jeers, sank out of sight to rise no more; or existed as an enemy stranger, to be killed anywhere at first sight by any of the clan, and to be forever damned to the eternity of their unending scorn, or scorched in the social hell forevermore. This is no fancy picture. It existed as I have told it, and Lincoln had to pass it. He did it nobly and well, and thenceforward held unlimited sway over the clan. Lincoln did it by calm, cool courage and physical strength. He said to the clan one day—"If you want and *must* have a fight, prepare." The word prepare, with the courage and body behind it, settled the affair. The clan had seen him, strapped, lift in a box in the old mill, a thousand pounds.

They knew his courage well, and the word *prepare*, settled all. Here it was that manly honesty with womanly tenderness, valor, strength, and great natural capacity, went hand in hand, however absurd it may appear to the world. I affirm the truth of this here and now. Such a people the world never sees but once, and such people! I knew them all; have been with them all; and respect them all. A man with vastly greater powers than I possess might well quail from the task of writing the history of the men and times of New Salem. This is the ground on which Lincoln walked, and sported, joked and laughed, loved and despaired, read law, studied surveying and grammar, read for the first time Shakespeare and Burns, and here it was that his reason once bent to its burdens. And oh! how sad and solemn are New Salem's memories to me. The spirit of the place to me is lonely and yet sweet. It presides over the soul gently, tenderly, yet sadly. It does not down. It does not crush. It entices and enwraps. May the spirits of the loved and loving dead here meet and embrace, as they were denied them on earth. A friend of mine, who knew Mr. Lincoln as well as I did, and whose judgment I always respect, profoundly so, said that if Mr. Lincoln had married Ann Rutledge, the sweet, tender and loving girl, he would have gravitated insensibly into a purely domestic man; that locality, home, and domesticity, were the tendencies of Mr. Lincoln; that the love and death of the girl shattered Lincoln's purposes and tendencies; that he threw off this infinite grief and sorrow to the man, and leaped wildly into the political arena as a refuge from his despair. Another gentleman agrees with this, and affirms that Lincoln needed a whip and spur to rouse him to deeds of fame. I give no opinion now for want of space. The affirmation or denial needs argument to my mind.

As I clambered from bluff to bluff, crossing streams and hollows, which ran into the creek, flowing thence into the river, I tread on and pass the wild mistletoe, so called, green, living moss, clinging to rock and sandy, cold, shaded, damp clay. The ferns and low creeping vines cover the hillsides here. While I was taking the notes of this lecture on the spot, I sat in the infinite past, ages, where they have written their origin, creation, their growth, their development, death and decay, on the coal and rock records of Nature, that lay at my feet and rose above my head. The blue sky above me, however, refuses to vegetable and to man her clear, clean blue leaves, whereon to record their creation, growth, death and decay. One as he sits in the present, on the past, cannot avoid thinking and speculating on the immense, endless, boundless, infinite future, in *this* world and *that* to come. The day on which I took my notes was the 15th day of October, A. D. 1866. The frost had scorched the leaves of the forest, and they hung dry, curled and quivering in the winds, as they sighed and moaned. Death rides everywhere, but life has begun everywhere before death comes.

Death is a natural condition of life and life a condition of death. Which is the normal one? Are death and life normal? As I wander up Green's rocky creek, say one mile from its mouth, I cross the stream and climb along the northern face of the hill, where the sun seldom, if ever, warms the sod.

The rolling brook has, here and there, beds or groups of

long, green, waving moss, that waves from bank to bank, not upward and downward from bottom to top. This moss, called here deer moss, is from three to six feet long, is vital, living and a beautiful pale green. Lichen clings to the rocks, and the short green forest moss grows luxuriantly here; and as it seems to me ages on long ages ago, as the frozen waters swept and rushed southward from their icy homes, on the Laurentian hills, with huge rocks, called boulders, in their frozen arms, they threw them at the northern face of the hill, and piled them at random here and there. These rocks rest or stand imbedded in the hill, south of New Salem, at every elevation on its sides, and in every angle of its face. One of these boulders seems as if it came from some fiery pool, and not from the northern pole. It has the looks, and smell, and feel of fire on it. On the southern face of another hill, across the branch, not far from where I stood at the rock just described, I heard the rock quarrier's iron rod ring out steel-like, as it bit and bored its way through the thick limestone ledges, rock on rock, sounding through valley and over hill. Here are lime-burners' kilns, and coal diggers' shafts, horizontal, going under the hill, or perpendicular, eighty feet or more, to reach the third great stratum of Illinois coal, deposited here millions of years now gone by.

I returned to New Salem hill again and now, as I intently gaze over the whole field and scene, to my left, a little to the northeast, lies beautifully what is called Baker's prairie, about one mile off, stretching out eastward two and one-half miles long, by one and one-quarter miles wide. The prairie on the east side of the river, and the bottom land on the west side of the river, seem to me to be halves of a common lake through which the Sangamon river originally cut and burst. The bottom on the west side of the river, just north of Salem, is three-fourths of a mile wide, by one and a half miles long. The prairie on the east side contains probably fifteen hundred acres of rich—the very richest alluvial soil, and the bottom on the west side contains about eight hundred acres of the same kind of sod and soil.

The whole supposed lake, the eastern and the western side of the rolling river, is surrounded by hill and bluff, that rise to an equal elevation with the Salem hill. The Sangamon river runs into the lake at the south, and runs out at the north. These hills, bluffs, and peaks surrounded this lake before the great sea—long, long before the great sea of waters passed off southward, between Missouri and Kentucky, roaring into the great gulf below.

These hills are bearded with heavy forest trees. Now, all over these hills and valleys are, here and there, neat little frame houses, and large, rich, and beautiful fields, clothed in green meadows and yellow, ripened corn. Barns, orchards, and wheat stacks dot the plain, where once probably floated the shark or other monster of the deep, or browsed the mastodon and other beasts. In the spring and summer all the lands are covered with rich meadows, wheat, oat and barley fields, over whose surface floats the clouds, chasing clouds, casting their shadows of various shapes and sizes on the ground, covered with grass and grain; and as the wings of the wind gently move over the plains and fields, varied shades and colors, deep green, pale green, ripening into straw, salmon, dark straw and bright, in long, wide, wild waves, chase and follow each other as wave runs on and rolls after wave, in the ocean's sport and play. Do not forget, never forget, that Lincoln gazed on these scenes, which aided to educate him. Never forget this for one moment. Did he love the beautiful and grand? If he did those faculties were developed here. Remember it was amid these scenes he loved and despaired, and—but I must pass on.

While on my winding way, at my right hand and on my left, in front of me and beneath my feet, I saw and was met and greeted by the wild aster—blue, purple and white—whose blossoms stand trembling on their wiry stem in the wind. The blue lobelia, the morning and evening primroses, the shrubby acacia, growing ten inches high, filled with yellow blooms, and the tall, huge mullen, whose single shaft runs up from three to six feet high, and whose broad, hairy, or velvety leaves lie broad and flat on the ground—the very emblem of desolation—were scattered here and there. Other flowers were here.

In the early spring, in the first days of March, on the southern slope or face of the New Salem hill, comes first in the floral train, the blue and purple johnny, with which all western children, in their tender youth, fight rooster in the early spring. Soon follows the hardy, perennial mountain phlox, on the eastern side of the hill, where the sun first strikes it square in the face, an evergreen in winter, sending up in early spring from a common crown, ten or twenty stalks with many flowers on their slender stems, and on whose heads come and go many peach-colored blossoms with five petals, blooming from March to May. These grow about six inches high. Then follows, on the southern slope of the hill, the purple phlox, called the wild sweet-william, growing about ten inches high, and blooming from April to June. They too are hardy and perennial—they may almost be called perpetual bloomers, taking all localities and situations into account. At last, according to moisture, light and heat, they girdle the hill on three sides—south, east and north, and finally running back through the woods, to and through the prairies westerly. The blue bell comes with its hundreds tubular, purple flowers, flaring at the mouth, bending in beauty and humility to the ground. The meadow lily is here, with its from two to four orange-colored flowers. The lady slipper, called the whippoor-will shoe by some, and the asclepias, red and orange, are here. The Judas tree, called the red-bud, colors in spring the forest's view. The may-apple and the wild dielytra, the wild hyacinth, the wild pansy, and the butter cup, among other fibrous, tuberous, and bulbous rooted flowers, hardy and perennial, are likewise here, growing in patches or groups. The wild scarlet honeysuckle, and the sweet-scented clematis, throw their tendrils from limb to limb of hazel and haw, and climb up high towards the sun, adding their beauty to the scene.

The bignonia climbs the elm of the valley, and the maple of the bottom; and in and during the year, each of the flowers named here comes and blooms, seeds and dies, according to its floral season. The wild, fiery scarlet Indian pink is scattered broadcast over the hill, and we must not forget the haw, the crab apple and the plum, whose united fragrance of a dewy morning or evening, cannot be excelled in the floral world. The bushy dwarf and running wild rose squats or climbs all over and around the place. All, all these flowers come, bloom, have their passions, form and bear their seeds, and perish; and yet come again, making the ages one grand floral procession; and yet, and *yet* how few, oh! how few men and women ever look upon and study these beauties of valley and hill.

The fruit of this and the neighboring hills, woods, valleys and forests, is the blackberry, the raspberry and the dewberry, the red and black haw, the crab-apple, the plum, strawberry, the cherry, the hackberry, and the paw-paw. Here are the walnut, the hickory nut—black and white, hard shell and soft shell—the acorn in variety, and the grape, summer and fall, small and fox, sweet and sour.

The birds that come, sing, mate, raise their young, and go or stay, are the eternal, universal and uneasy jay, the wood cock, the wood pecker, the robin and the dove, the duck and wild pigeon, the quail and the wild goose, the prairie hen and turkey, the martin and bee bird, the raven and the crow, the owl and whipporwill, birds of night, the wren and swallow, the cat bird and thrush, the snow bird and snipe, the king fisher, the oriole, the humming bird, and above all and over all, floats high, the gray or bold bald eagle.

The timber and forest trees on the high and back grounds, are the oak in variety, the hickory in variety, sugar tree, walnut, ash, cherry and elm. The timber in the bottom is mostly elm, buckeye, sycamore, cottonwood, maple and the huge oak. I do not name all the trees, only some of the leading ones. The river's edges are lined and filled and fringed with the climbers, and the willows that grow running and wild over its waters.

The river and creeks give abundance of fish, such as the pike and cat, salmon and sucker, bass and buffalo, perch and red-horse, gar and sturgeon. The forests are full of game, such as deer, turkey, squirrel, quail, coon and o'possum, mink, muskrat and rabbit.

Probably, I had better say the forest *was* once full of game, and the river full of fish. The game and fish are fast going. Game once served for sport, fun, chase and food, for cheer and life; and if the western eye could see its game, and his fore-finger, educated to *the feel*, could but softly touch the well set hair trigger of his own long, close shooting and trusty gun, away goes as quick as lightning, the fast, hissing, leaden bullet, and down drops life in man and woman. Such were our people, and here they lived, loved, bore and died.

On the opposite side of the river, eastward, across the river from New Salem, on the bluffs, mounds and peaks, may be found by thousands, the dead of the Silurian period of the world, millions of years gone by. We find the periwinkle, the bivalve, and other such shells in abundance, with other higher animal remains. The sand bars on the river's edge and in the river, present and give up to man the dead of all past time; and all around, all beneath, and above are life and death, and all is the past, the present, and the future, meeting, mingling, mixing and sinking into one—God, who is all.

There have been four distinct and separate waves—classes of men, who have followed each other on the soil we now daily tread. The first is the Indian. The second is the bee and beaver hunter, the embodied spirit of western and southwestern pioneering; they roam with the first class, nomads, wandering Gipsies of the forests and the plains. The third class, with sub-classes and varieties, is composed of three distinct varieties of man, coming as a triple wave. The first is the religious man, the John the Baptist, preaching in the wilderness; the second is the honest, hardy, thrifty, active and economical farmer, and the third is composed of the wild, hardy, honest, genial and social man—a mixture of the gentleman, the rowdy, the roysterer; they are a wild, rattling, brave, social and hospitable class of men; they have no economy, caring only for the hour, and yet thousands of them grow rich; they give tone and cast and character to the neighborhood in spite of all that can be said or done; they are strong, shrewd, clever fellows; it is impossible to outwit or whip them. The fourth class, with sub-classes and varieties, have come among us seeking fortune, position, character, power, fame, having ideas, philosophy, gearing the forces of nature for human uses, wants and purposes. They come from the East, from the Middle States, from the South; they come from every quarter of the globe, full grown men. Here are the English and the German, the Scotch and the Irish, the French and the Scandinavian, the Italian, the Portuguese, the Spaniard, Jew and Gentile; and *here* and *there* and *everywhere* is the universal, the eternal, indomitable and inevitable "Yankee," victorious over all, and I as a "Sucker," say welcome all. All, all, however, have their divine purposes in the high, deep, broad and wide extended, the sublime economy of God.

I am necessitated, as it were in self-defense, to speak some words of the second and the third class, with sub-classes and varieties. The fourth class needs none.

The original western and southwestern pioneer—the type of him is at times a somewhat open, candid, sincere, energetic, spontaneous, trusting, tolerant, brave and generous man. He is hospitable in his tent, thoroughly acquainted with the stars in the heavens, by which he travels, more or less; he is acquainted with all the dangers of his route—horse flesh and human flesh. He trusts to his own native sagacity—a keen shrewdness, and his physical power—his gun and dog alone. The original man is a long, tall, lean, lank man; he is a cadaverous, sallow, sunburnt, shaggy haired man; his face is very sharp and exceedingly angular; his nose is long, pointed, and keen, Roman or Greek as it may be; his eyes are small, gray or black, and sunken, are keen, sharp and inquisitive, piercing, as if looking through the object seen, and to the very background of things; he is sinewy and tough, calm or uneasy, according to circumstances; he is all bone and sinew, scarcely any muscle; is wise and endless in determinations—obstinate. He wears a short linsey-woolsy hunting shirt, or one made of soft buck or doe skin, fringed with the same; it is buckled tightly about his body. His moccasins are made of the very best heavy buck. His trusty and true rifle is on his shoulder, or stands by his side, his chin gracefully resting on his hand, which covers the muzzle of the gun. The gaunt, strong, hungry cur, crossed with the bull dog, and his hound, lie crouched at his feet, their noses resting on and between their forepaws, thrown straight out in front, ready to bound, sieze, master and defend. The lean, short, compact, tough and hardy, crop eared, shaved mane and bob-tailed pony browses around, living where the hare, the deer, mule or hardy mountain goat can live. It makes no difference where night or storm overtakes him, his wife and children sleep well and sound, knowing that the husband, the father, protector and defender is safe from all harm.

He sleeps on his rifle for pillow, his right hand *awake* on the long, sharp, keen hunting knife in the girdle, carved over and over with game and deer. The will in the hand is *awake*. Such is the conscious will on the nerve and muscle of the hand, amid danger of a night, placed there to keep watch and ward while the general soul is asleep, that it springs to defense long before the mind is fully conscious of the facts. How grand and mysterious is mind! The family makes no wild outcry—"He's shot or lost!" This man, his trusty long rifle, his two dogs—one to fight and one to scent and trail—the long, sharp and keen butcher knife, that never holds fire or flashes in the pan, are equal to all emergencies. As for himself, his snores on the grass, or brush-pile, cut to make his bed, testify to the soul's conscious security. Whether in a hollow tree or log, or under and beneath the river's bank for shelter—screen or fort—in night or daytime, his heart beats calm; he is a fatalist, and says, "What is to be, will be." He never tires, is quick and shrewd, is physically powerful, is cunning, suspicious, brave and cautious alternately or all combined, according to necessity. He is swifter than the Indian, is stronger, is as long-winded, and has more brains. This man is bee hunter, or trapper, or Indian fighter. He is shy, nervous, uneasy, and quite fidgety in the villages where he goes twice a year to exchange his furs for whisky, tobacco, powder, flints and lead. He dreads, does not scorn, our civilization. Overtake the man, catch him, and try to hold a conversation with him, if you can. His eye and imagination are on the chase in the forest when you think you are attracting his simple mind. He is restless in eye and motion about towns and villages; his muscles and nerves dance an uneasy, rapid, jerking dance when in presence of our civilization. He is suspicious here, and dangerous from his ignorance of the social world. This man is a man of acts and deeds, not speech; he is at times stern, silent, secretive and somewhat uncommunicable. His words are words of one syllable, sharp nouns and active verbs mostly. He scarcely ever uses adjectives, and always replies to questions asked him—"Yes," "No," "I will," "I wont." Ask him where he is from, and his answer is— "Blue Ridge," "Cumberland," "Bear Creek." Ask him where he kills his game, or gets his furs, and his answer ever is—"Illinois," "Sangamon," "Salt Creek." Ask him where he is going—"Plains," "Forests," "Home," is his unvarying answer. See him in the wilds, as I have seen him, strike up with his left hand's forefinger the loose rim of his old home-made wool or other hat, that hangs like a rag over his eyes, impeding his sight and perfect vision, peering keenly into the distance for fur or game, Indian or deer. See him look and gaze and determine what the thing seen is—see him at that instant stop and crouch and crawl toward the object like a wild hungry tiger, measuring the distances between twig and weed with his beard, so as to throw no shadow of sensation on the distant eye of foe or game—the thing to be crept on and inevitably killed. See him watch even the grass and brush beneath his feet, as he moves and treads, that no rustle, or crack or snap, shall be made by which the ear of foe or game shall be made aware of his danger. See him carefully wipe off and raise his long and trusty gun to shoulder and cheek—see him throw his eye lockward and along the barrel—watch him, see the first upcoil of smoke, before the crack and ring and roll and roar comes. The bullet has already quickly done its work of death. Caution makes this man stand still and reload before moving a foot. Then he eyes the dead keenly. "There's danger in the apparent dead," he whispers to himself, cocks his gun and walks, keeping his finger on the trigger.

The third class I am about to describe—the brave, rollicking roysterer—is still among us, though tamed by age into a moral man. He is large, bony, muscular, strong almost as an ox. He is strongly physically developed. He is naturally strong minded, naturally gifted, brave, daring to a fault. He is a hardy, rough and tumble man. He has a strong, quick sagacity, fine intuitions, with great, good common sense. He is hard to cheat, hard to whip and still harder to fool. These people are extremely sociable and good natured—too much so for their own good, as a general rule. They are efficient, ready, practical men, and are always ready for any revolution. I wish, I am anxious, to defend these men, as well as the God-given spirit of pioneering. One of the writers on Mr. Lincoln's life says, speaking of Thomas Lincoln, "When inefficient men become very uncomfortable they are quite likely to try emigration as a remedy. A good deal of what is called the pioneer spirit *is simply the spirit of shiftless discontent*." But more of this hereafter, not now and just here.

These men, especially about New Salem, could shave a horse's mane and tail, paint, disfigure and offer him for sale to the owner in the very act of inquiring for his own horse, that knew his master, but his master recognizing him not. They could hoop up in a hogshead a drunken man, they being themselves drunk, put in and nail down the head, and roll the man down New Salem hill a hundred feet or more. They could run down a lean, hungry wild pig, catch it, heat a tin-plate stove furnace hot, and putting in the pig, could cook it, they dancing the while a merry jig. They could, they did, these very things occasionally, yet they could clear and clean a forest of Indians and wolves in a short time; they could shave off a forest as clean and clear as a man's beard close cut to his face; they could trench a pond, ditch a bog or lake, erect a log house, pray and fight, make a village or create a state. They would do all for sport or fun, or from necessity—do it for a neighbor—and they could do the reverse of all this for pure and perfectly unalloyed deviltry's sake. They attended church, heard the sermon, wept and prayed, shouted, got up and fought an hour, and then went back to pray, just as the spirit moved them. These men—I am speaking generally—were always true to women—their fast and tried friends, protectors and defenders. There are scarcely any such on the globe for this virtue. They were one thing or the other—praying or fighting, creating or destroying, shooting Indians or getting shot by whisky, just as they willed. Though these men were rude and rough, though life's forces ran over the edge of its bowl, foaming and sparkling in pure and perfect deviltry for deviltry's sake, yet place before them a poor weak man, who needed their aid, a sick man, a man of misfortune, a lame man, a woman, a widow, a child, an orphaned little one, then these men melted up into sympathy and charity at once, quick as a flash, and gave all they had, and willingly and honestly toiled or played cards for more. If a minister of religion preached the devil and his fire, they would cry out "to your rifles, oh boys, and let's clean out the devil, with his fire and all, they are enemies to mankind." If the good minister preached Jesus and him crucified, with his precious blood trickling down the spear and cross, they would melt into honest prayer, praying honestly, and with deep, deep *feeling* and humility, saying aloud, "would to God we had been there with our good trusty rifles amid those murderous Jews." I wish to quote the author's sentence again, it reads—"When *inefficient* men become very uncomfortable, they are quite likely to try emigration as a remedy. A good deal of what is called the pioneer spirit is *simply the spirit of shiftless discontent.*" Here are two distinct allegations or assertions, rather charges: 1st, that *inefficient* men, through the spirit of discontent at home, emigrate as a remedy for that uncomfortableness; and 2nd, that a good deal of the spirit of pioneering *comes from the spirit of shiftless discontent*. I wish to say a few words on this sentence, and first as to fact, and secondly, as to principal. It is not, I hope, necessary for me to defend the particular man spoken of—Thomas Lincoln— the father of President Lincoln. It is not necessary that I should flatter the pioneer to defend him, yet I feel that other men and women in New England, possibly in Europe, may be grossly misled by such an assertion, such an idea, as is contained in this sentence. It is admitted by me that man's condition at home sometimes is exceedingly uncomfortable. To throw off that condition of uncomfortableness is the sole, only and eternal motive that prompts and drives men and women to pioneering. Men of capacity, integrity and energy—for such are the generality of pioneers in the west—emigrate to this new land from their own homes, not because they are inefficient men, men unable to grapple with the home condition, but rather *because they refuse to submit to the bad conditions at home*. Their manly souls and indomitable spirits rise up against the cold, frigid, despotic caste crystallizations at home—a glorious rebellion for the freedom of man. All men emigrate from their homes to new lands in hope of bettering their human conditions, which at home are sometimes chafingly uncomfortable. The spirit of pioneering is not a spirit of *shiftless discontent*, nor any part of it, but is the creating spirit, a grand desire, wish and will to rise up in the scale of being; it has moved mankind—each man and woman and placed them on the globe, with genius in their heads, and hope and faith in their souls. God's intentions, purposes and laws, as written on the human soul, forever interpret themselves thus: "My child, my good children, man, woman and child, each and all—hope, struggle, I am with you and will forever be, go on, go upward, go westward, go heavenward, on and on forever." Good men and women do not, from the spirit of shiftless discontent, quit the sacred ashes of the dead loved ones, and wildly rush into a cold, damp, uncleared, gloomy, unsettled, wild wilderness, where they know they *must struggle* with disease, poverty, nature, the wild wolf and wilder men, and the untamed and ungeared elements of nature, that sweep everywhere unconfined. They do not go for game, nor sport, nor daring adventure with wild beast, nor daring sport with wilder men. They go or come at God's command—"Children, my good children, one and all, man, woman and child, all, all—hope, struggle, to better your condition—onward, forestward, upward—and on and on forever, or miserably perish, and quit the globe to be repeopled by better beings."

Men, tender and lovely women, do not quit their homes, where are comforts, luxuries, arts, science, general knowledge and ease, amid the civilized and civilizing influences at home, to go westward from a *spirit of shiftless discontent*. What! are these brave men and women all through the west, and such as these the world over, inefficient men, inactive consumers, unenergetic, insufficients, lazy and do-nothing people, bursting westward from the spirit of shiftless discontent, where they involuntarily clap their hands to their heads and spasmodically feel for their crowns, in order to preserve their scalps, as the quick flash and fire-steel gleam of the Indian's knife glints and glistens against the western sky! What! Are Grant and Jackson, Douglas and Benton, Clay and *Lincoln, inefficient men, coming west from the spirit of shiftless discontent*? Is fire efficiently hot? Is lightning efficiently active? Is nature efficiently creative, massing and rolling up all these visible worlds to heat and light and life, and holding them suspended there by God's will—called by men gravity—for a human idea's sake? If these things are so, then these men and women whom I have described, *the pioneers*, with their brave hearts and their defiant and enduring souls, are and were efficient men and women—efficiently warm, for they consumed and burnt the forest and cleared and cleaned it. They had and have energy and creative activity, with capacity, honesty and valor. They created states and hold them to the Union, to liberty and to justice. They and their children after them can and do point with the highest pride and confidence to the deep, broad-laid, tolerant, generous, magnanimous foundations of these mighty several western states, whereon our liberty and civilization so proudly and firmly stand, that they, the pioneer, in the spirit of pioneering embodied in them, made and created, and hold up to light and heat and life, suspended there rolling, by the electro-magnetic power of the intelligent popular will.

My defense has ended. The wild animals that preceded the Indians are gone, the Indian treading closely on their heels. The red man has gone. The pioneer, the type of him, is gone, gone with the Indian, the bear, and the beaver, the buffalo and deer. They all go with the same general wave, and are thrown high on the beach of the wilderness, by the deep, wide sea of our civilization. He that tramped on the heels of the red man, with his wife and children, pony and dog, are gone, leaving no trace behind. He is the master of the bee and the beaver, the Indian and the bear, the wolf and buffalo. He and they are gone, never to return. God speed them on their way, their journey and destiny. As path makers, blazers, mappers, as fighters and destructive, they have had, and have their uses and purposes in the divine plan. Such are succeeded by the Armstrongs, the Clarrys, the Rutledges, the Greens, Spears, and Lincolns, who too have their uses and purposes in the great Idea, and are succeeded by others, now among us, who are forces in the same universal plan. And let us not complain, for the great Planner knows and has decreed what is best and wisest in his grand and sublime economics. The animal is gone; the Indian is gone. The trapper, bee and beaver hunter is gone—all are gone. A few of the third class still remain among us, standing or leaning like grand, gray, old towers, with lights on their brow, quietly inclining, leaning, almost dipping in the deep, the unknown, the unknowable and unfathomable deeps of the future, that roll through all time and space, and last up against the Throne. They did not come here from *the spirit of shiftless discontent*, nor shall they take up their soul's greatest pioneering march on to God, through the cowardly *spirit* of *shiftless* discontent. They are fast going, one by one. Respect them while living, reverence them when dead, and tread lightly on their sacred dust, ye all. The children of such may be trusted to preserve and hand down to all future time what they created, wrought and planted in the forest. The fourth class is ready to clasp hands with the third, taking an oath of fidelity to Liberty, sacred as heaven. We thus come and go, and in the coming and going we have shaded—risen up, progressed—during these various and varied waves of immigration, with their respective civilizations, through force, cunning and the rifle, to the dollars, the steam engine, and the Idea. We have moved from wolf to mind. We have grown outward, upward, higher and better, living generally in more virtue, less vice, longer and more civilized, freer and purer, and thus man ever mounts upward. So are the records of all time.

Abraham Lincoln loved Ann Rutledge with all his soul, mind and strength. She loved him as dearly, tenderly and affectionately. They seemed made in heaven for each other, though opposite in many things. As before remarked, she was accidentally, innocently and honestly engaged to A. Lincoln and Mr. —— at one and the same time. It is said and thought that the young lady was conditionally promised to Mr. Lincoln, to be consummated upon a release from her first engagement with Mr. ——. The primary causes, facts and conditions which led to this complication shall be related to you at another time and place. There is no dishonor in it to any of the three. In her conflicts of honor, duty, love, promises, and womanly engagements—she was taken sick. She struggled, regretted, grieved, became nervous. She ate not, slept not, was taken sick of brain fever, became emaciated, and was fast sinking in the grave. Lincoln wished to see her. She silently prayed *to see him*. The friends of both parties at first refused the wish and prayer of both, still the wishes and prayers of both prevailed. Mr. Lincoln did go to see her about the 10th day of August, A. D. 1835. The meeting was quite as much as either could bear, and more than Lincoln, with all his coolness and philosophy, could endure. The voice, the face, the features of her; the love, sympathy and interview fastened themselves on his heart and soul forever. Heaven only knows what was said by the two. God only knows what was thought. Dr. Jason Duncan, of New Salem, about September, A. D. 1833, had shown and placed in Mr. Lincoln's hands the poem called in short, now, "Immortality," or properly, "Oh, Why Should the Spirit of Mortal be Proud?" Remember, Miss Rutledge died on the 25th of August, A. D. 1835, and was buried in the Concord cemetery, six miles north, bearing a little west, of New Salem, as stated before. Mr. Lincoln has stated that his heart, sad and broken, was buried there. He said in addition, to the same friend, "I cannot endure the thought that the sleet and storm, frost and snow of heaven should beat on her grave." He *never* addressed another woman, in my opinion, "yours affectionately;" and generally and characteristically abstained from the use of the word "love." That word cannot be found more than a half dozen times, if that often, in all his letters and speeches, since that time. I have seen some of his letters to other ladies, but he never says "love." He never ended his letters with "yours affectionately," but signed his name, "your friend, A. Lincoln." Abraham Lincoln was, by nature, more or less, in tendency, abstracted—had the power of continuous concentrated thought. It may be, as alleged, that he was a warm, ardent and more or less impulsive man, before 1834, and of which I give no opinion. He never did care for food—eating mechanically. He sorrowed and grieved, rambled over the hills and through the forests, day and night. He suffered and bore it for a while like a great man—a philosopher. He slept not, he ate not, joyed not. This he did until his body became emaciated and weak, and gave way. His mind wandered from its throne. In his imagination he muttered words to her he loved. His mind, his reason, somewhat dethroned, walked out of itself along the uncolumned air, and kissed and embraced the shadows and illusions of the heated brain. Love, future happiness, death, sorrow, grief, and pure and perfect despair, the want of sleep, the want of food, a cracked and aching heart, over and intense thought, soon worked a partial wreck of body and mind.

It has been said that Mr. Lincoln became and was totally insane at that time and place. This is not exactly the truth. The dethronement of his reason was only partial, and could alone be detected by his closest friends, and sharpest observers, through the abruptness of his sentences and the sharp contrasts of his ideas and language. To give you a fair idea, an exact one of his then true mental state and condition imagine Mr. Lincoln situated as I have attempted to describe. Mr. Lincoln had a strong mind, a clear and distinct one. His style and mode of expression in 1835, were entirely different from what they were from 1853 to 1864. He had more, much more, emotion, fancy and imagination, in 1835, when he was 26 years of age, than he had in 1853 to 1864 when he was 47 to 55 years of age. He grew stronger as he grew older.

Did this dread calamity, of which I have spoken, crush him and thus modify, if it did not change his nature? It must be expected that his expressions would follow truly his own rational thoughts in part only, not wholly so in logic, at least. His utterances and expressions would be necessarily disconnected and sharply contrasted. It is said, and I believe it, that he lost his logical faculty—power over cause and effect, and their legitimate relation—through the momentary loss of memory alone. Imagine him racked in heart and body, in mind and soul, not forgetting the immediate and proximate cause of his condition. He must naturally and necessarily speak and utter what is in his own mind; sharply and incoherently, sadly and wildly. Hear him: "What a time for joy today in town; the men and women looked so happy all through the village. Ah! me. No. Not today; its night. There's a trick in it, and where's the fallacy? Does nature deal unjustly? I thought not. I'll see and tell myself. 'Tis a rude wind that blows no man joy. Where am I? What strange woods are these. It seems that I've run my compass and dragged my chains along this path. Why, wherefore is all this? These hills I've never seen before, and the wild valleys at my feet now have no more familiar face for me. What? 'Tis strange. How is it? What's that? These hands I think I've seen before, and yet I know them not. The clouds are cold, and where's fire? There it is! No, 'tis not. How goes it out? Who cheats me? and for what?

I am sad; and thou sweet bird of night, sing on thy tune of whippor-will; ah! who's that? 'Tis her I love. This path and hill I know; yet 'tis strange, strange, uncommon strange. I know it here and there, in spots. Why, wherefore is this? Who am I and what, 'mid nature's profoundest uncertainties, that come and go like chance, whither, no one knows. There, the cocks crow. Did I not read—but, stay, did I not read law beneath the shade of this tree, grinding 'round the sun? I love her. Oh! immensities above me, below me, and around me.

"The dogs, the very dogs bark at me. These limbs and legs, feet and hands, are mine; yet 'tis strange! and ah! thou mysterious state of things. Isn't fate, chance, Providence, God—that so unwinds the world's and all their life? Grief! What's that? I'm tired and weary. The clothes I've got on and wear, I know are mine, and yet they seem not to be. Ah! dead and gone from me thou sweet one; and shall this aching, crushed heart of mine never die and feel the pangs of nature never more. This old mill I've seen before, and often heard it grind. The waters in the pond are filled with shining, floating stars. Why don't they go out and sink in water ten feet deep, or more? It's curious, curious strange wondrous strange. Why, wherefore is that? Some trick deludes me. I'll search and tell myself. Ah! dead and gone, thou sweet one; dead and buried forever, forever—more, in the grave. Mortal man! so it is, and must be. Our hopes forever blast and wither in their tender growth. What is hope? What is death? What is forever, evermore, forevermore? Come gentle winds and cool my aching head; or, thou hanging thunderbolt, swiftly strike and scorch me. What's that in the mill pond, going splash, splash? 'Twas a fish, I guess. Let's go and feed it, and make it joy, and be happy. I love her, and shall marry her on tomorrow's eve. So soul be content, and endless joy shall come. Heart of mine be still, for remember sweet tomorrow eve. Oh! thou calmest, most boisterous profoundest uncertainties of things, hold off, or take another path not coming here. What! did I dream? Think; what did I say? It cannot be. No, it cannot be. She's dead and gone— gone forever. Fare thee well, sweet girl! We'll meet again."

I am not now discussing the complicated causes of insanity in a scientific method. I am not able to do so. I am giving you a probable example of what Lincoln was in September A. D. 1834. I give you the broad facts. I shall not, now and here, enter into a scientific disquisition on lunacy—what are illusions, or delusions; nor other false appearances in the mind of the insane; nor whether these illusions, delusions, or other false appearances in a fevered, wrecked brain are *caused* objectively from or through irregular and feverish sensations; nor subjectively by the same; nor whether they come from perceptions distorted nor from memory or imagination, abnormally developed; nor from all combined. One thing ought to be certain: namely, that the mind cannot *create* normally, regularly, in a wrecked and shattered condition. *Creation, through mental energy, is the law of the mind;* and when it cannot create lawfully, regularly, through normal mental energy in activity, it cannot create according to its law. This is the great law of the mind. *Creations* are distortions when the mind is diseased. Mental creations lift us heavenward, in proportion to the number of such creations. Who shall promulgate this great law and teach it?

The friends of Mr. Lincoln—men, women and children—begged him to quit his home and place of business. They coaxed and threatened him by turns in order to get him to quit the places and scenes of his sorrows and griefs. His women friends tried their arts on him. Men begged and held out strong inducements to go into the country. The boys and girls of the town and neighborhood aided and assisted the older people all they could. All tricks were detected by the man the whole people so dearly loved. Bolin Green and some of his and Lincoln's special friends at last tried their powers. They succeeded in throwing Lincoln off his guard by robbing him of his suspicions. Mr. Lincoln, in September, went down to Bolin Green's in consequence of the pressure thrown on him and around him, and in the space of a week or ten days, by Bolin's humor, generosity and hospitality, his care and kindness, aided by the womanly sympathy, gentleness and tenderness of his wife, Lincoln soon rose up, a man once more. He was visited daily by men, women, boys and girls, whose conversation, stories, jokes, witticisms, fun and sport, soon roused up the man, thus enabling him to momentarily throw off sorrow, sadness, grief, pain and anxiety. They walked over the hills with him, danced for him, read for him, laughed for him, and amused him in a thousand ways. He evidently enjoyed all as man scarcely ever enjoyed two weeks before, nor since. He got well and bade adieu, for a short season, to Bolin's kind roof and generous hospitality. Mrs. Bolin Green still lives, God bless her; she survives her own husband, and their ward and guest. Mr. Lincoln went back to New Salem, as thought, a changed, a radically changed man. He went to New Salem about the last of September, A. D. 1835. He now once more picked up, took up, and read, and re-read the poem called "Immortality;" or, "Oh, Why Should the Spirit of Mortal Be Proud?" He saw new beauties in it. He seized it, and it seized him—a mutual seizure and arrest. He learned, learned it by heart, committed it to memory, and repeated it over and over to his friends.

Such is the true history of things—such are New Salem and surrounding country—such are her hills, and bluffs, and valleys. Such are her geology and her general past—such is her floral world—such are her fruits, trees and plants, birds, fish and game—and such were and are her people. Such is New Salem—such was she in the past—such is she now. So is she in the spring-time, in the summer-time, fall and winter-time. So she is in daylight, and darkness, beneath sun, moon, and stars. So is her rise—her growth—her fall and ruin, death and decay. Such is man. It was here Abraham Lincoln first came to himself, after so great grief. It was here, amid these hills and peaks, bluffs and valleys, creeks and paths, branches and rivulets, he moved among men and women, walked and roamed sadly, gloomily, frantically, despairingly, almost insanely. He thought and reflected on man and women, the transient and permanent,—love, duty, nature, destiny, the past, present, and the future—of God. It was here he walked in daylight—at night time—under the forest trees and beneath the moon's pale, sad glance, contemplating all human life, its laws and springs, its mysterious ways and ends, his own insignificance, the utter insignificance of all men and things, the follies, foibles, ambitions and corruptions, as compared with nature, laws and principles, all embodied in the permanent, and it in the never-beginning and never-ending, absolute, unconditioned and illimitable. It was about the 20th day of October, A. D. 1835, that Abraham Lincoln, as he wandered and wended his sad and melancholy way over hill and dale, gloomily burst forth—

Oh! why should the spirit of mortal be proud?—
Like a swift-fleeing meteor, a fast-flying cloud,
A flash of the lightning, a break of the wave,
He passeth from life to his rest in the grave.

The leaves of the oak and the willow shall fade,
Be scattered around and together be laid;
And the young and the old, and the low and the high,
Shall moulder to dust and together shall lie.

The infant, a mother attended and loved:
The mother, that infant's affection who proved;
The husband, that mother and infant who blest,—
Each, all, are away to their dwellings of rest.

The maid on whose cheek, on whose brow, in whose eye,
Shone beauty and pleasure—her triumphs are by.
And the memory of those who loved her and praised,
Are alike from the minds of the living erased.

The hand of the king, that the sceptre hath borne,
The brow of the priest, that the mitre hath worn,
The eye of the sage and the heart of the brave,
Are hidden and lost in the depths of the grave.

The peasant, whose lot was to sow and to reap,
The herdsman, who climbed with his goats up the steep,
The beggar who wandered in search of his bread,
Have faded away like the grass that we tread.

The saint, who enjoyed the communion of heaven,
The sinner, who dared to remain unforgiven,
The wise and the foolish, the guilty and just,
Have quietly mingled their bones in the dust.

So the multitude goes—like the flower of the weed,
That withers away to let others succeed;
So the multitude comes—even those we behold,
To repeat every tale that has often been told;

For we are the same our fathers have been;
We see the same sights our fathers have seen;
We drink the same stream, we view the same sun,
And run the same course our fathers have run.

The thoughts we are thinking, our fathers would think;
From the death we are shrinking, our fathers would shrink;
To the life we are clinging, they also would cling—
But it speeds from us all, like a bird on the wing.

They loved—but the story we cannot unfold:
They scorned but the heart of the haughty is cold;
They grieved—but no wail from their slumber will come;
They joyed—but the tongue of their gladness is dumb.

They died—ay, they died—we things that are now,
That walk on the turf that lies over their brow,
And make in their dwellings a transient abode,
Meet the things that they met on their pilgrimage road.

Yea! hope and despondency, pleasure and pain,
Are mingled together in sunshine and rain;
And the smile and the tear, the song and the dirge,
Still follow each other, like surge upon surge.

'Tis the wink of an eye—'tis the draught of a breath,
From the blossom of health to the paleness of death;
From the gilded saloon to the bier and the shroud:—
Oh! why should the spirit of mortal be proud?

November 1866

Frederick Douglass

By the time of Lincoln's inauguration Douglass (1818–1895), a self-educated former slave, had become the most famous black abolitionist in America. Although he had written favorably about Lincoln during the election campaign, Douglass harshly criticized the new President for his attempts to conciliate the South and willingness to enforce the Fugitive Slave Law, and in the early stages of the war he judged Lincoln to be inexcusably tardy in freeing the slaves. Once Lincoln issued the Emancipation Proclamation, and especially after they began discussing policy together in several unprecedented White House meetings, Douglass radically altered his views and publicly praised Lincoln before and after the assassination. Eleven years after the President's death, Douglass delivered the oration at the dedication in Washington of the Freedmen's Monument to Abraham Lincoln. Funded entirely by contributions from African Americans, Thomas Ball's statue group depicted a freed slave kneeling before Lincoln—or perhaps rising symbolically from his bondage—a design Douglass disapproved of, believing "a more manly attitude would have been indicative of freedom." In front of an audience that included much of official Washington, Douglass declared that Lincoln had been "preeminently the white man's President, entirely devoted to the welfare of white men," and that blacks were "at best only his step-children." No speech on Lincoln and race, before or since, has been as provocative, proved as influential, or arguably has been as insightful, as the one printed below.

Oration in Memory of Abraham Lincoln
Washington, D.C.

Friends and Fellow Citizens: I warmly congratulate you upon the highly interesting object which has caused you to assemble in such numbers and spirit as you have today. This occasion is in some respects remarkable. Wise and thoughtful men of our race, who shall come after us, and study the lessons of our history in the United States, who shall survey the long and dreary space over which we have traveled, who shall count the links in the great chain of events by which we have reached our present position, will make a note of this occasion—they will think of it, and with a sense of manly pride and complacency. I congratulate you also upon the very favorable circumstances in which we meet to-day. They are high, inspiring and uncommon. They lend grace, glory and significance to the object for which we have met. Nowhere else in this great country, with its uncounted towns and cities, uncounted wealth, and immeasurable territory extending from sea to sea, could conditions be found more favorable to the success of this occasion than here. We stand to-day at the national centre to perform something like a national act, an act which is to go into history, and we are here where every pulsation of the national heart can be heard, felt and reciprocated.

A thousand wires, fed with thought and winged with lightning, put us in instantaneous communication with the loyal and true men all over this country. Few facts could better illustrate the vast and wonderful change which has taken place in our condition as a people, than the fact of our assembling here for the purpose we have to-day. Harmless, beautiful, proper and praiseworthy as this demonstration is, I cannot forget that no such demonstration would have been tolerated here twenty years ago. The spirit of slavery and barbarism, which still lingers to blight and destroy in some dark and distant parts of our country, would have made our assembling here to-day the signal and excuse for opening upon us all the flood-gates of wrath and violence. That we are here in peace to-day is a compliment and credit to American civilization, and a prophecy of still greater national enlightenment and progress in the future. I refer to the past not in malice, for this is no day for malice, but simply to place more distinctly in front the gratifying and glorious change which has come both to our white fellow-citizens and ourselves, and to congratulate all upon the contrast between now and then, the new dispensation of freedom with its thousand blessings to both races, and the old dispensation of slavery with its ten thousand evils to both races—white and black. In view then, of the past, the present and the future, with the long and dark history of our bondage behind us, and with liberty, progress and enlightenment before us, I again congratulate you upon this auspicious day and hour.

Friends and fellow-citizens: The story of our presence here is soon and easily told. We are here in the District of Columbia; here in the city of Washington, the most luminous point of American territory—a city recently transformed and made beautiful in its body and in its spirit; we are here, in the place where the ablest and best men of the country are sent to devise the policy, enact the laws and shape the destiny of the Republic; we are here, with the stately pillars and majestic dome of the Capitol of the nation looking down upon us; we are here, with the broad earth freshly adorned with the foliage and flowers of spring for our church, and all races, colors and conditions of men for our congregation; in a word, we are here to express, as best we may, by appropriate forms and ceremonies, our grateful sense of the vast, high and pre-eminent services rendered to ourselves, to our race, to our country and to the whole world by Abraham Lincoln.

The sentiment that brings us here to-day is one of the noblest that can stir and thrill the human heart. It has crowned and made glorious the high places of all civilized nations, with the grandest and most enduring works of art, designed to illustrate characters and perpetuate the memories of great public men. It is the sentiment which from year to year adorns with fragrant and beautiful flowers the graves of our loyal, brave, and patriotic soldiers who fell in defense of the Union and liberty. It is the sentiment of gratitude and appreciation, which often, in the presence of many who hear me, has filled yonder heights of Arlington with the eloquence of eulogy and the sublime enthusiasm of poetry and song; a sentiment which can never die while the Republic lives. For the first time in the history of our people, and in the history of the whole American people, we join in this high worship and march conspicuously in the line of this time-honored custom. First things are always interesting, and this is one of our first things. It is the first time that, in this form and manner, we have sought to do honor to any American great man, however deserving and illustrious. I commend the fact to notice. Let it be told in every part of the Republic; let men of all parties and opinions hear it; let those who despise us, not less than those who respect us, know that now and here, in the spirit of liberty, loyalty, and gratitude, let it be known everywhere and by everybody who takes an interest in human progress and in the amelioration of the condition of mankind, that in the presence and with the approval of the members of the American House of Representatives, reflecting the general sentiment of the country; that in the presence of that august body, the American Senate, representing the highest intelligence and the calmest judgment of the country; in presence of the Supreme Court and Chief Justice of the United States, to whose decisions we all patriotically bow; in the presence and under the steady eye of the honored and trusted President of the United States, we, the colored people, newly emancipated and rejoicing in our blood-bought freedom, near the close of the first century in the life of this Republic, have now and here unveiled, set apart, and dedicated a monument of enduring granite and bronze, in every line, feature, and figure of which the men of this generation may read —and those of after-coming generations may read—something of the exalted character and great works of Abraham Lincoln, the first martyr President of the United States.

Fellow citizens: In what we have said and done to-day, and in what we may say and do hereafter, we disclaim everything like arrogance and assumption. We claim for ourselves no superior devotion to the character, history and memory of the illustrious name whose monument we have here dedicated to-day. We fully comprehend the relation of Abraham Lincoln, both to ourselves and the white people of the United States. Truth is proper and beautiful at all times and in all places, and it is never more proper and beautiful in any case than when speaking of a great public man whose example is likely to be commended for honor and imitation long after his departure to the solemn shades, the silent continents of eternity. It must be admitted, truth compels me to admit even here in the presence of the monument we have erected to his memory, Abraham Lincoln was not, in the fullest sense of the word, either our man or our model. In his interests, in his associations, in his habits of thought, and in his prejudices, he was a white man. He was preeminently the white man's President, entirely devoted to the welfare of white men. He was ready and willing at any time during the last years of his administration to deny, postpone and sacrifice the rights of humanity in the colored people, to promote the welfare of the white people of his country. In all his education and feelings he was an American of the Americans.

He came into the Presidential chair upon one principle alone, namely, opposition to the extension of slavery. His arguments in furtherance of this policy had their motive and mainspring in his patriotic devotion to the interest of his own race. To protect, defend and perpetuate slavery in the States where it existed, Abraham Lincoln was not less ready than any other President to draw the sword of the nation. He was ready to execute all the supposed constitutional guarantees of the Constitution in favor of the slave system anywhere inside the Slave States. He was willing to pursue, recapture, and send back the fugitive slave to his master, and to suppress a slave rising for liberty, though his guilty masters were already in arms against the Government. The race to which we belong were not the special objects of his consideration. Knowing this, I concede to you, my white fellow-citizens, a pre-eminence in this worship at once full and supreme. First, midst and last you and yours were the object of his deepest affection and his most earnest solicitude.

You are the children of Abraham Lincoln. We are at best only his step-children, children by adoption, children by force of circumstances and necessity. To you it especially belongs to sound his praises, to preserve and perpetuate his memory, to multiply his statues, to hang his pictures on your walls, and commend his example, for to you he was a great and glorious friend and benefactor. Instead of supplanting you at this altar we would exhort you to build high his monuments; let them be of the most costly material, of the most costly workmanship; let their forms be symmetrical, beautiful and perfect; let their bases be upon solid rocks, and their summits lean against the unchanging blue overhanging sky, and let them endure forever! But while in the abundance of your wealth and in the fullness of your just and patriotic devotion you do all this, we entreat you to despise not the humble offering we this day unveil to view: for while Abraham Lincoln saved for you a country, he delivered us from a bondage, according to Jefferson, one hour of which was worse than ages of the oppression your fathers rose in rebellion to oppose.

Fellow-citizens: Ours is a new-born zeal and devotion, a thing of the hour. The name of Abraham Lincoln was near and dear to our hearts in the darkest and most perilous hours of the Republic. We were no more ashamed of him when shrouded in clouds of darkness, of doubt and defeat than when crowned with victory, honor and glory. Our faith in him was often taxed and strained to the uttermost, but it never failed. When he tarried long in the mountain; when he strangely told us that we were the cause of the war; when he still more strangely told us to leave the land in which we were born; when he refused to employ our arms in defense of the Union; when, after accepting our services as colored soldiers, he refused to retaliate when we were murdered as colored prisoners; when he told us he would save the Union if he could with slavery; when he revoked the proclamation of emancipation of General Frémont; when he refused to remove the commander of the Army of the Potomac, who was more zealous in his efforts to protect slavery than suppress rebellion; when we saw this, and more, we were at times stunned, grieved and greatly bewildered; but our hearts believed while they ached and bled. Nor was this, even at that time, a blind and unreasoning superstition. Despite the mist and haze that surrounded him; despite the tumult, the hurry and confusion of the hour, we were able to take a comprehensive view of Abraham Lincoln, and to make reasonable allowance for the circumstances of his position. We saw him, measured him, and estimated him; not by stray utterances to injudicious and tedious delegations, who often tried his patience; not by isolated facts torn from their connection; not by any partial and imperfect glimpses, caught at inopportune moments; but by a broad survey, in the light of the stern logic of great events—and in view of that divinity which shapes our ends, rough hew them as we will, we came to the conclusion that the hour and the man of our redemption had met in the person of Abraham Lincoln. It mattered little to us what language he might employ upon special occasions; it mattered little to us, when we fully knew him, whether he was swift or slow in his movements; it was enough for us that Abraham Lincoln was at the head of a great movement, and was in living and earnest sympathy with that movement; which, in the nature of things, must go on till slavery should be utterly and forever abolished in the United States. When, therefore, it shall be asked what we have to do with the memory of Abraham Lincoln, or what Abraham Lincoln had to do with us, the answer is ready, full and complete. Though he loved Caesar less than Rome, though the Union was more to him than our freedom or our future, under his wise and beneficent rule we saw ourselves gradually lifted from the depths of slavery to the heights of liberty and manhood; under his wise and beneficent rule, and by measures approved and vigorously pressed by him, we saw that the handwriting of ages, in the form of prejudice and proscription, was rapidly fading away from the face of our whole country; under his rule, and in due time, about as soon after all as the country could tolerate the strange spectacle, we saw our brave sons and brothers laying off the rags of bondage, and being clothed all over in the blue uniforms of the soldiers of the United States; under his rule we saw two hundred thousand of our dark and dusky people responding to the call of Abraham Lincoln, and, with muskets on their shoulders and eagles on their buttons, timing their high footsteps to liberty and union under the national flag; under his rule we saw the independence of the black Republic of Hayti, the special object of slaveholding aversion and horror fully recognized, and her minister, a colored gentleman, duly received here in the city of Washington; under his rule we saw the internal slave trade which so long disgraced the nation abolished, and slavery abolished in the District of Columbia; under his rule we saw for the first time the law enforced against the foreign slave trade and the first slave-trader hanged, like any other pirate or murderer; under his rule and his inspiration we saw the Confederate States, based upon the idea that our race must be slaves, and slaves forever, battered to pieces and scattered to the four winds; under his rule, and in the fullness of time, we saw Abraham Lincoln, after giving the slaveholders three months of grace in which to save their hateful slave system, penning the immortal paper which, though special in its language, was general in its principles and effect, making slavery forever impossible in the United States. Though we waited long, we saw all this and more.

Can any colored man, or any white man friendly to the freedom of all men, ever forget the night which followed the first day of January, 1863? When the world was to see if Abraham Lincoln would prove to be as good as his word? I shall never forget that memorable night, when in a distant city I waited and watched at a public meeting, with three thousand others not less anxious than myself, for the word of deliverance which we have heard read to-day. Nor shall I ever forget the outburst of joy and thanksgiving that rent the air when the lightning brought to us the emancipation. In that happy hour we forgot all delay, and forgot all tardiness, forgot that the President had bribed the rebels to lay down their arms by a promise to withhold the bolt which would smite the slave system with destruction; and we were thenceforward willing to allow the President all the latitude of time, phraseology, and every honorable device that statesmanship might require for the achievement of a great and beneficent measure of liberty and progress.

Fellow-citizens, there is little necessity on this occasion to speak at length and critically of this great and good man, and of his high mission in the world. That ground has been fully occupied and completely covered both here and elsewhere. The whole field of fact and fancy has been gleaned and garnered. Any man can say things that are true of Abraham Lincoln, but no man can say anything new of Abraham Lincoln. His personal traits and public acts are better known to the American people than are those of any other man of his age. He was a mystery to no man who saw him and heard him. Though high in position, the humblest could approach him and feel at home in his presence. Though deep, he was transparent; though strong, he was gentle; though decided and pronounced in his convictions, he was tolerant towards those who differed from him, and patient under reproaches.

Even those who only knew him through his public utterances

obtained a tolerably clear idea of his character and his personality. The image of the man went out with his words, and those who read him knew him. I have said that President Lincoln was a white man, and shared the prejudices common to his countrymen towards the colored race. Looking back to his times and to the condition of the country, this unfriendly feeling on his part may safely be set down as one element of his wonderful success in organizing the loyal American people for the tremendous conflict before them, and bringing them safely through that conflict. His great mission was to accomplish two things; first, to save his country from dismemberment and ruin, and second, to free his country from the great crime of slavery. To do one or the other, or both, he must have the earnest sympathy and the powerful cooperation of his loyal fellow-countrymen. Without this primary and essential condition to success, his efforts must have been vain and utterly fruitless. Had he put the abolition of slavery before the salvation of the Union, he would have inevitably driven from him a powerful class of the American people, and rendered resistance to rebellion impossible. Viewed from the genuine abolition ground, Mr. Lincoln seemed tardy, cold, dull, and indifferent: but measuring him by the sentiment of his country, a sentiment he was bound as a statesman to consult, he was swift, zealous, radical, and determined. Though Mr. Lincoln shared the prejudices of his white fellow-countrymen against the negro, it is hardly necessary to say that in his heart of hearts he loathed and hated slavery. He was willing while the South was loyal that it should have its pound of flesh, because he thought it was so nominated in the bond, but further than this no earthly power could make him go.

Fellow-citizens, whatever else in this world may be partial, unjust and uncertain, *time! time!* is impartial, just and certain in its actions. In the realm of mind, as well as in the realm of matter, it is a great worker, and often works wonders. The honest and comprehensive statesman, clearly discerning the needs of his country, and earnestly endeavoring to do his whole duty, though covered and blistered with reproaches, may safely leave his course to the silent judgment of time. Few great public men have ever been the victims of fiercer denunciation than Abraham Lincoln was during his administration. He was often wounded in the house of his friends. Reproaches came thick and fast upon him from within and from without, and from opposite quarters. He was assailed by abolitionists; he was assailed by slaveholders; he was assailed by men who were for peace at any price; he was assailed by those who were for a more vigorous prosecution of the war; he was assailed for not making the war an abolition war; and he was most bitterly assailed for making the war an abolition war.

But now behold the change; the judgment of the present hour is, that taking him for all in all, measuring the tremendous magnitude of the work before him, considering the necessary means to ends, and surveying the end from the beginning, infinite wisdom has seldom sent any man into the world better fitted for his mission than was Abraham Lincoln. His birth, his training, and his natural endowments, both mental and physical, were strongly in his favor. Born and reared among the lowly, a stranger to wealth and luxury, compelled to grapple single-handed with the flintiest hardships from tender youth to sturdy manhood, he grew strong in the manly and heroic qualities demanded by the great mission to which he was called by the votes of his countrymen. The hard condition of his early life, which would have depressed and broken down weaker men, only gave greater life, vigor and buoyancy to the heroic spirit of Abraham Lincoln. He was ready for any kind and any quality of work. What other young men dreaded in the shape of toil, he took hold of with the utmost cheerfulness.

> A spade, a rake, a hoe,
>   A pick-axe or a bill;
> A hook to reap, a scythe to mow,
>   A flail, or what you will.

All day long he could split heavy rails in the woods, and half the night long he could study his English grammar by the uncertain flare and glare of the light made by a pine knot. He was at home on the land with his axe, with his maul, with gluts and his wedges; and he was equally at home on water, with his oars, with his poles, with his planks and with his boathooks. And whether in his flatboat on the Mississippi river, or at the fireside of his frontier cabin, he was a man of work. A son of toil himself he was linked in brotherly sympathy with the sons of toil in every loyal part of the Republic. This very fact gave him tremendous power with the American people, and materially contributed not only to selecting him to the Presidency, but in sustaining his administration of the Government.

Upon his inauguration as President of the United States, an office even where assumed under the most favorable conditions, it is fitted to tax and strain the largest abilities, Abraham Lincoln was met by a tremendous pressure. He was called upon not merely to administer the Government, but to decide, in the face of terrible odds, the fate of the Republic. A formidable rebellion rose in his path before him; the Union was already practically dissolved. His country was torn and rent asunder at the centre. Hostile enemies were already organized against the Republic, armed with the munitions of war which the Republic had provided for its own defense. The tremendous question for him to decide was whether his country should survive the crisis and flourish or be dismembered and perish. His predecessor in office had already decided the question in favor of national dismemberment, by denying it the right of self-defense and self-preservation.

Happily for the country, happily for you and for me, the judgment of James Buchanan, the patrician, was not the judgment of Abraham Lincoln, the plebeian. He brought his strong common sense, sharpened in the school of adversity, to bear upon the question. He did not hesitate, he did not doubt, he did not falter, but at once resolved at whatever peril, at whatever cost, the union of the States should be preserved. A patriot himself, his faith was firm and unwavering in the patriotism of his countrymen. Timid men said before Mr. Lincoln's inauguration that we had seen the last President of the United States. A voice in influential quarters said let the Union slide. Some said that a Union maintained by the sword was worthless. Others said a rebellion of 8,000,000 cannot be suppressed. But in the midst of all this tumult and timidity, and against all this Abraham Lincoln was clear in his duty and had an oath in heaven. He calmly and bravely heard the voice of doubt and fear all around him, but he had an oath in heaven, and there was not power enough on the earth to make this honest boatman, backwoodsman and broad-handed splitter of rails evade or violate that sacred oath. He had not been schooled in the ethics of slavery; his plain life favored his love of truth. He had not been taught that treason and perjury were the proofs of honor and honesty. His moral training was against his saying one thing when he meant another. The trust which Abraham Lincoln had of himself and in the people was surprising and grand, but it was also enlightened and well founded. He knew the American people better than they knew themselves, and his truth was based upon his knowledge.

Had Abraham Lincoln died from any of the numerous ills to which flesh is heir; had he reached that good old age of which his vigorous constitution and his temperate habits gave promise; had he been permitted to see the end of his great work; had the solemn curtain of death come down but gradually, we should still have been smitten with a heavy grief and treasured his name lovingly. But dying as he did die, by the red hand of violence; killed, assassinated, taken off without warning, not because of personal hate, for no man who knew Abraham Lincoln could hate him, but because of his fidelity to Union and liberty, he is doubly dear to us, and will be precious forever.

Fellow-citizens, I end as I began, with congratulations. We have done a good work for our race to-day. In doing honor to the memory of our friend and liberator we have been doing highest honor to ourselves and those who come after us. We have been fastening ourselves to a name and fame imperishable and immortal. We have also been defending ourselves from a blighting slander. When now it shall be said that the colored man is soulless; that he has no appreciation of benefits or benefactors; when the foul reproach of ingratitude is hurled at us, and it is attempted to scourge us beyond the range of human brotherhood, we may calmly point to the monument we have this day erected to the memory of Abraham Lincoln.

April 14, 1876

Freedmen's Monument to Abraham Lincoln, Washington, D.C., sculpture group by Thomas Ball (1876). *Collection of Harold Holzer.*

John Greenleaf Whittier

Whittier (1807–1892) helped found the anti-slavery Liberty party in 1840, supported Republican candidate John C. Frémont in the 1856 presidential election, and served as a presidential elector in 1860, casting his ballot for Lincoln in the electoral college after the Republicans carried New Hampshire. Yet it was not until 1879 that one of New England's greatest poets wrote his first verse about Lincoln. The occasion was the unveiling in Park Square, Boston, of a replica of the Thomas Ball statue, depicting Lincoln freeing a kneeling slave, that Frederick Douglass had helped dedicate in Washington three years earlier. Whittier himself did not read his composition at the Faneuil Hall ceremony that followed the unveiling, an honor that was bestowed on Andrew Chamberlain, an African-American schoolboy. Today, the Ball statues in Washington and Boston are often seen as racially insensitive embarrassments, though they—and the literature they inspired—represent an era in which the celebration of emancipation was still an essential part of the mainstream remembrance of Lincoln.

The Emancipation Group
Boston, 1879

Amidst thy sacred effigies
   Of old renown give place,
O city, Freedom-loved! to his
   Whose hand unchained a race.

Take the worn frame, that rested not
   Save in a martyr's grave—
The care-lined face, that none forgot,
   Bent to the kneeling slave.

Let man be free! The mighty word
   He spake was not his own;
An impulse from the Highest stirred
   These chiselled lips alone.

The cloudy sign, the fiery guide,
    Along his pathway ran,
And Nature, through his voice, denied
    The ownership of man.

We rest in peace where these sad eyes
    Saw peril, strife, and pain;
His was the nation's sacrifice,
    And ours the priceless gain.

O symbol of God's will on earth
    As it is done above!
Bear witness to the cost and worth
    Of justice and of love.

Stand in thy place and testify
    To coming ages long,
That truth is stronger than a lie,
    And righteousness than wrong.

                                    1879

Richard Henry Stoddard

Stoddard's continuing fascination with Lincoln was expressed in this tribute, published 15 years after the assassination. It appeared in an election year in which James A. Garfield, a Union Civil War hero, became the third consecutive Republican president elected since Lincoln's death.

Abraham Lincoln

This man whose homely face you look upon,
Was one of Nature's masterful, great men;
Born with strong arms, that unfought battles won;
Direct of speech, and cunning with the pen.
Chosen for large designs, he had the art
Of winning with his humor, and he went
Straight to his mark, which was the human heart;
Wise, too, for what he could not break he bent.
Upon his back a more than Atlas-load,
The burden of the Commonwealth, was laid;
He stooped, and rose up to it, though the road
Shot suddenly downwards, not a whit dismayed.
   Hold, warriors, councilors, kings! All now give place
   To this dear benefactor of the Race.

1880

Walt Whitman

Few writers of the 19th century dwelled as passionately or creatively on the subject of Lincoln as Whitman (1819–1892), who created a new American style in poetry as surely as the 16th President forged a revolutionary native idiom in oratory. Scholars—most recently the modern poet and biographer Daniel Mark Epstein—have debated for years whether Lincoln found creative inspiration in, or even read, Whitman's 1855 collection *Leaves of Grass*. But Whitman surely found inspiration in Lincoln, seeing him for the first time when the President-elect arrived in politically unfriendly New York City en route to his inauguration in 1861 and observing him repeatedly in Washington during the war, when the poet toiled as a nurse for wounded soldiers. He responded to Lincoln's death with this quartet of poetic tributes, ranging from the complex and elegiac "Lilacs" to the more conventional and hugely popular "O Captain! My Captain!" Originally published between 1865 and 1871, the four poems are presented here in the order in which Whitman arranged them in the 1881 edition of *Leaves of Grass*.

FROM
Leaves of Grass

When Lilacs Last in the Dooryard Bloom'd

1

When lilacs last in the dooryard bloom'd,
And the great star early droop'd in the western sky in the night,
I mourn'd, and yet shall mourn with ever-returning spring.

Ever-returning spring, trinity sure to me you bring,
Lilac blooming perennial and drooping star in the west,
And thought of him I love.

2

O powerful western fallen star!
O shades of night—O moody, tearful night!
O great star disappear'd—O the black murk that hides the star!

O cruel hands that hold me powerless—O helpless soul of me!
O harsh surrounding cloud that will not free my soul.

3

In the dooryard fronting an old farm-house near the
    white-wash'd palings,
Stands the lilac-bush tall-growing with heart-shaped leaves of
    rich green,
With many a pointed blossom rising delicate, with the
    perfume strong I love,
With every leaf a miracle—and from this bush in the
    dooryard,
With delicate-color'd blossoms and heart-shaped leaves of
    rich green,
A sprig with its flower I break.

4

In the swamp in secluded recesses,
A shy and hidden bird is warbling a song.

Solitary the thrush,
The hermit withdrawn to himself, avoiding the settlements,
Sings by himself a song.
Song of the bleeding throat,
Death's outlet song of life, (for well dear brother I know,
If thou wast not granted to sing thou would'st surely die.)

5

Over the breast of the spring, the land, amid cities,
Amid lanes and through old woods, where lately the violets
    peep'd from the ground, spotting the gray debris,
Amid the grass in the fields each side of the lanes, passing the
    endless grass,
Passing the yellow-spear'd wheat, every grain from its shroud
    in the dark-brown fields uprisen,
Passing the apple-tree blows of white and pink in the
    orchards,
Carrying a corpse to where it shall rest in the grave,
Night and day journeys a coffin.

6

Coffin that passes through lanes and streets,
Through day and night with the great cloud darkening the
      land,
With the pomp of the inloop'd flags with the cities draped in
      black,
With the show of the States themselves as of crape-veil'd
      women standing,
With processions long and winding and the flambeaus of the
      night,
With the countless torches lit, with the silent sea of faces and
      the unbared heads,
With the waiting depot, the arriving coffin, and the sombre
      faces,
With dirges through the night, with the thousand voices
      rising strong and solemn,
With all the mournful voices of the dirges pour'd around the
      coffin,
The dim-lit churches and the shuddering organs—where
      amid these you journey,
With the tolling tolling bells' perpetual clang,
Here, coffin that slowly passes,
I give you my sprig of lilac.

7

(Nor for you, for one alone,
Blossoms and branches green to coffins all I bring,
For fresh as the morning, thus would I chant a song for you
      O sane and sacred death.

All over bouquets of roses,
O death, I cover you over with roses and early lilies,
But mostly and now the lilac that blooms the first,
Copious I break, I break the sprigs from the bushes,
With loaded arms I come, pouring for you,
For you and the coffins all of you O death.)

8

O western orb sailing the heaven,
Now I know what you must have meant as a month since I
        walk'd,
As I walk'd in silence the transparent shadowy night,
As I saw you had something to tell as you bent to me night
        after night,
As you droop'd from the sky low down as if to my side,
        (while the other stars all look'd on,)
As we wander'd together the solemn night, (for something I
        know not what kept me from sleep,)
As the night advanced, and I saw on the rim of the west how
        full you were of woe,
As I stood on the rising ground in the breeze in the cool
        transparent night,
As I watch'd where you pass'd and was lost in the netherward
        black of the night,
As my soul in its trouble dissatisfied sank, as where you sad
        orb,
Concluded, dropt in the night, and was gone.

9

Sing on there in the swamp,
O singer bashful and tender, I hear your notes, I hear your call,
I hear, I come presently, I understand you,
But a moment I linger, for the lustrous star has detain'd me,
The star my departing comrade holds and detains me.

10

O how shall I warble myself for the dead one there I loved?
And how shall I deck my song for the large sweet soul that
        has gone?
And what shall my perfume be for the grave of him I love?

Sea-winds blown from east and west,
Blown from the Eastern sea and blown from the Western sea,
        till there on the prairies meeting,
These and with these and the breath of my chant,
I'll perfume the grave of him I love.

11

O what shall I hang on the chamber walls?
And what shall the pictures be that I hang on the walls,
To adorn the burial-house of him I love?

Pictures of growing spring and farms and homes,
With the Fourth-month eve at sundown, and the gray smoke
        lucid and bright,
With floods of the yellow gold of the gorgeous, indolent,
        sinking sun, burning, expanding the air,
With the fresh sweet herbage under foot, and the pale green
        leaves of the trees prolific,
In the distance the flowing glaze, the breast of the river, with
        a wind-dapple here and there,
With ranging hills on the banks, with many a line against the
        sky, and shadows,
And the city at hand with dwellings so dense, and stacks of
        chimneys,
And all the scenes of life and the workshops, and the
        workmen homeward returning.

12

Lo, body and soul—this land,
My own Manhattan with spires, and the sparkling and
        hurrying tides, and the ships,
The varied and ample land, the South and the North in the
        light, Ohio's shores and flashing Missouri,
And ever the far-spreading prairies cover'd with grass and
        corn.

Lo, the most excellent sun so calm and haughty,
The violet and purple morn with just-felt breezes,
The gentle soft-born measureless light,
The miracle spreading bathing all, the fulfill'd noon,
The coming eve delicious, the welcome night and the stars,
Over my cities shining all, enveloping man and land.

13

Sing on, sing on you gray-brown bird,
Sing from the swamps, the recesses, pour your chant from the
        bushes,
Limitless out of the dusk, out of the cedars and pines.

Sing on dearest brother, warble your reedy song,
Loud human song, with voice of uttermost woe.

O liquid and free and tender!
O wild and loose to my soul—O wondrous singer!
You only I hear—yet the star holds me, (but will soon depart,)
Yet the lilac with mastering odor holds me.

14

Now while I sat in the day and look'd forth,
In the close of the day with its light and the fields of spring,
        and the farmers preparing their crops,
In the large unconscious scenery of my land with its lakes and
        forests,
In the heavenly aerial beauty, (after the perturb'd winds and
        the storms,)
Under the arching heavens of the afternoon swift passing,
        and the voices of children and women,
The many-moving sea-tides, and I saw the ships how they
        sail'd,
And the summer approaching with richness, and the fields all
        busy with labor,
And the infinite separate houses, how they all went on, each
        with its meals and minutia of daily usages,
And the streets how their throbbings throbb'd, and the cities
        pent—lo, then and there,
Falling upon them all and among them all, enveloping me
        with the rest,
Appear'd the cloud, appear'd the long black trail,
And I knew death, its thought, and the sacred knowledge of
        death.

Then with the knowledge of death as walking one side of me,
And the thought of death close-walking the other side of me,
And I in the middle as with companions, and as holding the
    hands of companions,
I fled forth to the hiding receiving night that talks not,
Down to the shores of the water, the path by the swamp in
    the dimness,
To the solemn shadowy cedars and ghostly pines so still.

And the singer so shy to the rest receiv'd me,
The gray-brown bird I know receiv'd us comrades three,
And he sang the carol of death, and a verse for him I love.

From deep secluded recesses,
From the fragrant cedars and the ghostly pines so still,
Came the carol of the bird.

And the charm of the carol rapt me,
As I held as if by their hands my comrades in the night,
And the voice of my spirit tallied the song of the bird.

Come lovely and soothing death,
Undulate round the world, serenely arriving, arriving,
In the day, in the night, to all, to each,
Sooner or later delicate death.

Prais'd be the fathomless universe,
For life and joy, and for objects and knowledge curious,
And for love, sweet love—but praise! praise! praise!
For the sure-enwinding arms of cool-enfolding death.

Dark mother always gliding near with soft feet,
Have none chanted for thee a chant of fullest welcome?
Then I chant it for thee, I glorify thee above all,
I bring thee a song that when thou must indeed come, come
    unfalteringly.

Approach strong deliveress,
When it is so, when thou hast taken them I joyously sing the dead,
Lost in the loving floating ocean of thee,
Laved in the flood of thy bliss O death.

From me to thee glad serenades,
Dances for thee I propose saluting thee, adornments and feastings
        for thee,
And the sights of the open landscape and the high-spread sky are
        fitting,
And life and the fields, and the huge and thoughtful night.

The night in silence under many a star,
The ocean shore and the husky whispering wave whose voice I know,
And the soul turning to thee O vast and well-veil'd death,
And the body gratefully nestling close to thee.

Over the tree-tops I float thee a song,
Over the rising and sinking waves, over the myriad fields and the
        prairies wide,
Over the dense-pack'd cities all and the teeming wharves and ways,
I float this carol with joy, with joy to thee O death.

15

To the tally of my soul,
Loud and strong kept up the gray-brown bird,
With pure deliberate notes spreading filling the night.

Loud in the pines and cedars dim,
Clear in the freshness moist and the swamp-perfume,
And I with my comrades there in the night.

While my sight that was bound in my eyes unclosed,
As to long panoramas of visions.

And I saw askant the armies,
I saw as in noiseless dreams hundreds of battle-flags,

Borne through the smoke of the battles and pierc'd with
  missiles I saw them,
And carried hither and yon through the smoke, and torn and
  bloody,
And at last but a few shreds left on the staffs, (and all in
  silence,)
And the staffs all splinter'd and broken.

I saw battle-corpses, myriads of them,
And the white skeletons of young men, I saw them,
I saw the debris and debris of all the slain soldiers of the war,
But I saw they were not as was thought,
They themselves were fully at rest, they suffer'd not,
The living remain'd and suffer'd, the mother suffer'd,
And the wife and the child and the musing comrade suffer'd,
And the armies that remain'd suffer'd.

16

Passing the visions, passing the night,
Passing, unloosing the hold of my comrades' hands,
Passing the song of the hermit bird and the tallying song of
  my soul,
Victorious song, death's outlet song, yet varying ever-altering
  song,
As low and wailing, yet clear the notes, rising and falling,
  flooding the night,
Sadly sinking and fainting, as warning and warning, and yet
  again bursting with joy,
Covering the earth and filling the spread of the heaven,
As that powerful psalm in the night I heard from recesses,
Passing, I leave thee lilac with heart-shaped leaves,
I leave thee there in the door-yard, blooming, returning with
  spring.

I cease from my song for thee,
From my gaze on thee in the west, fronting the west,
  communing with thee,
O comrade lustrous with silver face in the night.

Yet each to keep and all, retrievements out of the night,
The song, the wondrous chant of the gray-brown bird,
And the tallying chant, the echo arous'd in my soul,
With the lustrous and drooping star with the countenance
    full of woe,
With the holders holding my hand nearing the call of the bird,
Comrades mine and I in the midst, and their memory ever to
    keep, for the dead I loved so well,
For the sweetest, wisest soul of all my days and lands—and
    this for his dear sake,
Lilac and star and bird twined with the chant of my soul,
There in the fragrant pines and the cedars dusk and dim.

O Captain! My Captain!

O Captain! my Captain! our fearful trip is done,
The ship has weather'd every rack, the prize we sought is won,
The port is near, the bells I hear, the people all exulting,
While follow eyes the steady keel, the vessel grim and daring;
        But O heart! heart! heart!
            O the bleeding drops of red,
                Where on the deck my Captain lies,
                    Fallen cold and dead.

O Captain! my Captain! rise up and hear the bells;
Rise up—for you the flag is flung—for you the bugle trills,
For you bouquets and ribbon'd wreaths—for you the shores
    a-crowding,
For you they call, the swaying mass, their eager faces turning;
        Here Captain! dear father!
            This arm beneath your head!
                It is some dream that on the deck,
                    You've fallen cold and dead.

My Captain does not answer, his lips are pale and still,
My father does not feel my arm, he has no pulse nor will,

The ship is anchor'd safe and sound, its voyage closed and
        done,
From fearful trip the victor ship comes in with object won;
        Exult O shores, and ring O bells!
            But I with mournful tread,
                Walk the deck my Captain lies,
                    Fallen cold and dead.

Hush'd Be the Camps To-day
(May, 1865.)

Hush'd be the camps to-day,
And soldiers let us drape our war-worn weapons,
And each with musing soul retire to celebrate,
Our dear commander's death.

No more for him life's stormy conflicts,
Nor victory, nor defeat—no more time's dark events,
Charging like ceaseless clouds across the sky.

But sing poet in our name,
Sing of the love we bore him—because you, dweller in camps,
        know it truly.

As they invault the coffin there,
Sing—as they close the doors of earth upon him—one verse,
For the heavy hearts of soldiers.

This Dust Was Once the Man

This dust was once the man,
Gentle, plain, just and resolute, under whose cautious hand,
Against the foulest crime in history known in any land or age,
Was saved the Union of these States.

                                                1881

Walt Whitman

Although Whitman almost certainly only imagined Lincoln acknowledging the poet's occasional sightings of him on the streets of Washington, it is clear from his recollections that he treasured such "encounters" and experienced a genuine thrill in Lincoln's presence. In prose as well as verse, Whitman remembered and celebrated Lincoln as the supreme embodiment of American democracy and "Nationality." The first selection printed here dates from the summer of 1863, while the last presents the text of a lecture Whitman delivered on three occasions between 1879 and 1881.

FROM
Specimen Days & Collect

Abraham Lincoln

August 12th.—I see the President almost every day, as I happen to live where he passes to or from his lodgings out of town. He never sleeps at the White House during the hot season, but has quarters at a healthy location some three miles north of the city, the Soldiers' home, a United States military establishment. I saw him this morning about $8\frac{1}{2}$ coming in to business, riding on Vermont avenue, near L street. He always has a company of twenty-five or thirty cavalry, with sabres drawn and held upright over their shoulders. They say this guard was against his personal wish, but he let his counselors have their way. The party makes no great show in uniform or horses. Mr. Lincoln on the saddle generally rides a good-sized, easy-going gray horse, is dress'd in plain black, somewhat rusty and dusty, wears a black stiff hat, and looks about as ordinary in attire, &c., as the commonest man. A lieutenant, with yellow straps, rides at his left, and following behind, two by two, come the cavalry men, in their yellow-striped jackets. They are generally going at a slow trot, as that is the pace set them by the one they wait upon. The sabres and accoutrements clank, and the entirely unornamental *cortège* as it trots towards Lafayette square arouses

no sensation, only some curious stranger stops and gazes. I see
very plainly ABRAHAM LINCOLN's dark brown face, with the deep-
cut lines, the eyes, always to me with a deep latent sadness in the
expression. We have got so that we exchange bows, and very
cordial ones. Sometimes the President goes and comes in an
open barouche. The cavalry always accompany him, with drawn
sabres. Often I notice as he goes out evenings—and sometimes
in the morning, when he returns early—he turns off and halts at
the large and handsome residence of the Secretary of War, on K
street, and holds conference there. If in his barouche, I can see
from my window he does not alight, but sits in his vehicle, and
Mr. Stanton comes out to attend him. Sometimes one of his
sons, a boy of ten or twelve, accompanies him, riding at his right
on a pony. Earlier in the summer I occasionally saw the President and his wife, toward the latter part of the afternoon, out in
a barouche, on a pleasure ride through the city. Mrs. Lincoln
was dress'd in complete black, with a long crape veil. The equi-
page is of the plainest kind, only two horses, and they nothing
extra. They pass'd me once very close, and I saw the President
in the face fully, as they were moving slowly, and his look,
though abstracted, happened to be directed steadily in my eye.
He bow'd and smiled, but far beneath his smile I noticed well
the expression I have alluded to. None of the artists or pictures
has caught the deep, though subtle and indirect expression of
this man's face. There is something else there. One of the great
portrait painters of two or three centuries ago is needed.

Death of President Lincoln

April 16, '65.—I find in my notes of the time, this passage on
the death of Abraham Lincoln: He leaves for America's history and biography, so far, not only its most dramatic reminiscence
—he leaves, in my opinion, the greatest, best, most characteristic, artistic, moral personality. Not but that he had faults, and
show'd them in the Presidency; but honesty, goodness, shrewdness, conscience, and (a new virtue, unknown to other lands, and

hardly yet really known here, but the foundation and tie of all, as the future will grandly develop,) UNIONISM, in its truest and amplest sense, form'd the hard-pan of his character. These he seal'd with his life. The tragic splendor of his death, purging, illuminating all, throws round his form, his head, an aureole that will remain and will grow brighter through time, while history lives, and love of country lasts. By many has this Union been help'd; but if one name, one man, must be pick'd out, he, most of all, is the conservator of it, to the future. He was assassinated—but the Union is not assassinated—*ça ira!* One falls, and another falls. The soldier drops, sinks like a wave—but the ranks of the ocean eternally press on. Death does its work, obliterates a hundred, a thousand—President, general, captain, private—but the Nation is immortal.

No Good Portrait of Lincoln

Probably the reader has seen physiognomies (often old farmers, sea-captains, and such) that, behind their homeliness, or even ugliness, held superior points so subtle, yet so palpable, making the real life of their faces almost as impossible to depict as a wild perfume or fruit-taste, or a passionate tone of the living voice—and such was Lincoln's face, the peculiar color, the lines of it, the eyes, mouth, expression. Of technical beauty it had nothing—but to the eye of a great artist it furnished a rare study, a feast and fascination. The current portraits are all failures—most of them caricatures.

Death of Abraham Lincoln
Lecture deliver'd in New York, April 14, 1879—
in Philadelphia, '80—in Boston, '81.

How often since that dark and dripping Saturday—that chilly April day, now fifteen years bygone—my heart has entertain'd the dream, the wish, to give of Abraham Lincoln's death, its own special thought and memorial. Yet now the sought-for opportunity offers, I find my notes incompetent, (why, for truly profound themes, is statement so idle? why does the right phrase never offer?) and the fit tribute I dream'd of, waits unprepared as ever. My talk here indeed is less because of itself or anything in it, and nearly altogether because I feel a desire, apart from any talk, to specify the day, the martyrdom. It is for this, my friends, I have call'd you together. Oft as the rolling years bring back this hour, let it again, however briefly, be dwelt upon. For my own part, I hope and desire, till my own dying day, whenever the 14th or 15th of April comes, to annually gather a few friends, and hold its tragic reminiscence. No narrow or sectional reminiscence. It belongs to these States in their entirety—not the North only, but the South—perhaps belongs most tenderly and devoutly to the South, of all; for there, really, this man's birth-stock. There and thence his antecedent stamp. Why should I not say that thence his manliest traits—his universality—his canny, easy ways and words upon the surface —his inflexible determination and courage at heart? Have you never realized it, my friends, that Lincoln, though grafted on the West, is essentially, in personnel and character, a Southern contribution?

And though by no means proposing to resume the Secession war to-night, I would briefly remind you of the public conditions preceding that contest. For twenty years, and especially during the four or five before the war actually began, the aspect of affairs in the United States, though without the flash of military excitement, presents more than the survey of a battle, or any extended campaign, or series, even of Nature's convulsions. The hot passions of the South—the strange mixture at the North of inertia, incredulity, and conscious power—the incendiarism of the abolitionists—the rascality and *grip* of the politicians, unparallel'd in any land, any age. To these I must not omit adding the honesty of the essential bulk of the people everywhere—yet with all the seething fury and contradiction of their natures more arous'd than the Atlantic's waves in wildest equinox. In politics, what can be more ominous, (though generally unappreciated then)—what more significant than the Presidentiads

of Fillmore and Buchanan? proving conclusively that the weakness and wickedness of elected rulers are just as likely to afflict
us here, as in the countries of the Old World, under their mon-
archies, emperors, and aristocracies. In that Old World were
everywhere heard underground rumblings, that died out, only
to again surely return. While in America the volcano, though
civic yet, continued to grow more and more convulsive—more
and more stormy and threatening.

In the height of all this excitement and chaos, hovering on
the edge at first, and then merged in its very midst, and destined
to play a leading part, appears a strange and awkward figure. I
shall not easily forget the first time I ever saw Abraham Lincoln.
It must have been about the 18th or 19th of February, 1861. It
was rather a pleasant afternoon, in New York city, as he arrived
there from the West, to remain a few hours, and then pass on to
Washington, to prepare for his inauguration. I saw him in Broadway, near the site of the present Post-office. He came down, I
think from Canal street, to stop at the Astor House. The broad
spaces, sidewalks, and street in the neighborhood, and for some
distance, were crowded with solid masses of people, many thousands. The omnibuses and other vehicles had all been turn'd
off, leaving an unusual hush in that busy part of the city. Presently two or three shabby hack barouches made their way with
some difficulty through the crowd, and drew up at the Astor
House entrance. A tall figure step'd out of the centre of these
barouches, paus'd leisurely on the sidewalk, look'd up at the
granite walls and looming architecture of the grand old hotel—
then, after a relieving stretch of arms and legs, turn'd round for
over a minute to slowly and good-humoredly scan the appearance of the vast and silent crowds. There were no speeches—no
compliments—no welcome—as far as I could hear, not a word
said. Still much anxiety was conceal'd in that quiet. Cautious
persons had fear'd some mark'd insult or indignity to the
President-elect—for he possess'd no personal popularity at all
in New York city, and very little political. But it was evidently
tacitly agreed that if the few political supporters of Mr. Lincoln
present would entirely abstain from any demonstration on their
side, the immense majority, who were any thing but supporters,

would abstain on their side also. The result was a sulky, unbroken silence, such as certainly never before characterized so great a New York crowd.

Almost in the same neighborhood I distinctly remember'd seeing Lafayette on his visit to America in 1825. I had also personally seen and heard, various years afterward, how Andrew Jackson, Clay, Webster, Hungarian Kossuth, Filibuster Walker, the Prince of Wales on his visit, and other celebres, native and foreign, had been welcom'd there—all that indescribable human roar and magnetism, unlike any other sound in the universe—the glad exulting thunder-shouts of countless unloos'd throats of men! But on this occasion, not a voice—not a sound. From the top of an omnibus, (driven up one side, close by, and block'd by the curbstone and the crowds,) I had, I say, a capital view of it all, and especially of Mr. Lincoln, his look and gait—his perfect composure and coolness—his unusual and uncouth height, his dress of complete black, stovepipe hat push'd back on the head, dark-brown complexion, seam'd and wrinkled yet canny-looking face, black, bushy head of hair, disproportionately long neck, and his hands held behind as he stood observing the people. He look'd with curiosity upon that immense sea of faces, and the sea of faces return'd the look with similar curiosity. In both there was a dash of comedy, almost farce, such as Shakspere puts in his blackest tragedies. The crowd that hemm'd around consisted I should think of thirty to forty thousand men, not a single one his personal friend—while I have no doubt, (so frenzied were the ferments of the time,) many an assassin's knife and pistol lurk'd in hip or breast-pocket there, ready, soon as break and riot came.

But no break or riot came. The tall figure gave another relieving stretch or two of arms and legs; then with moderate pace, and accompanied by a few unknown looking persons, ascended the portico-steps of the Astor House, disappear'd through its broad entrance—and the dumb-show ended.

I saw Abraham Lincoln often the four years following that date. He changed rapidly and much during his Presidency—but this scene, and him in it, are indelibly stamped upon my recollection. As I sat on the top of my omnibus, and had a good view of him, the thought, dim and inchoate then, has since come out clear enough, that four sorts of genius, four mighty and primal hands, will be needed to the complete limning of this man's future portrait—the eyes and brains and finger-touch of Plutarch and Eschylus and Michel Angelo, assisted by Rabelais.

And now—(Mr. Lincoln passing on from this scene to Washington, where he was inaugurated, amid armed cavalry, and sharpshooters at every point—the first instance of the kind in our history—and I hope it will be the last)—now the rapid succession of well-known events, (too well known—I believe, these days, we almost hate to hear them mention'd)—the national flag fired on at Sumter—the uprising of the North, in paroxysms of astonishment and rage—the chaos of divided councils—the call for troops—the first Bull Run—the stunning cast-down, shock, and dismay of the North—and so in full flood the Secession war. Four years of lurid, bleeding, murky, murderous war. Who paint those years, with all their scenes?—the hard-fought engagements—the defeats, plans, failures—the gloomy hours, days, when our Nationality seem'd hung in pall of doubt, perhaps death—the Mephistophelean sneers of foreign lands and attachés—the dreaded Scylla of European interference, and the Charybdis of the tremendously dangerous latent strata of secession sympathizers throughout the free States, (far more numerous than is supposed)—the long marches in summer—the hot sweat, and many a sunstroke, as on the rush to Gettysburg in '63—the night battles in the woods, as under Hooker at Chancellorsville—the camps in winter—the military prisons—the hospitals—(alas! alas! the hospitals.)

The Secession war? Nay, let me call it the Union war. Though whatever call'd, it is even yet too near us—too vast and too closely overshadowing—its branches unform'd yet, (but certain,) shooting too far into the future—and the most indicative and mightiest of them yet ungrown. A great literature will yet arise out of the era of those four years, those scenes—era compressing centuries of native passion, first-class pictures, tempests of life and death—an inexhaustible mine for the histories, drama, romance, and even philosophy, of peoples to come—indeed the verteber of poetry and art, (of personal character too,) for all future America—far more grand, in my opinion, to the hands capable of it, than Homer's siege of Troy, or the French wars to Shakspere.

But I must leave these speculations, and come to the theme I have assign'd and limited myself to. Of the actual murder of President Lincoln, though so much has been written, probably the facts are yet very indefinite in most persons' minds. I read from my memoranda, written at the time, and revised frequently and finally since.

The day, April 14, 1865, seems to have been a pleasant one throughout the whole land—the moral atmosphere pleasant too—the long storm, so dark, so fratricidal, full of blood and doubt and gloom, over and ended at last by the sun-rise of such an absolute National victory, and utter break-down of Secessionism—we almost doubted our own senses! Lee had capitulated beneath the apple-tree of Appomattox. The other armies, the flanges of the revolt, swiftly follow'd. And could it really be, then? Out of all the affairs of this world of woe and failure and disorder, was there really come the confirm'd, unerring sign of plan, like a shaft of pure light—of rightful rule—of God? So the day, as I say, was propitious. Early herbage, early flowers, were out. (I remember where I was stopping at the time, the season being advanced, there were many lilacs in full bloom. By one of those caprices that enter and give tinge to events without being at all a part of them, I find myself always reminded of the great tragedy of that day by the sight and odor of these blossoms. It never fails.)

But I must not dwell on accessories. The deed hastens. The popular afternoon paper of Washington, the little "Evening Star," had spatter'd all over its third page, divided among the advertisements in a sensational manner, in a hundred different places, *The President and his Lady will be at the Theatre this evening.* . . . (Lincoln was fond of the theatre. I have myself seen him there several times. I remember thinking how funny it was that he, in some respects the leading actor in the stormiest drama known to real history's stage through centuries, should sit there and be so completely interested and absorb'd in those human jack-straws, moving about with their silly little gestures, foreign spirit, and flatulent text.)

On this occasion the theatre was crowded, many ladies in rich and gay costumes, officers in their uniforms, many well-known citizens, young folks, the usual clusters of gas-lights, the usual magnetism of so many people, cheerful, with perfumes, music of violins and flutes—(and over all, and saturating all, that vast, vague wonder, *Victory*, the nation's victory, the triumph of the Union, filling the air, the thought, the sense, with exhilaration more than all music and perfumes.)

The President came betimes, and, with his wife, witness'd the play from the large stage-boxes of the second tier, two thrown into one, and profusely draped with the national flag. The acts and scenes of the piece—one of those singularly written compositions which have at least the merit of giving entire relief to an audience engaged in mental action or business excitements and cares during the day, as it makes not the slightest call on either the moral, emotional, esthetic, or spiritual nature—a piece, ("Our American Cousin,") in which, among other characters, so call'd, a Yankee, certainly such a one as was never seen, or the least like it ever seen, in North America, is introduced in England, with a varied fol-de-rol of talk, plot, scenery, and such phantasmagoria as goes to make up a modern popular drama—had progress'd through perhaps a couple of its acts, when in the midst of this comedy, or non-such, or whatever it is to be call'd, and to offset it, or finish it out, as if in Nature's and the great Muse's mockery of those poor mimes, came interpolated that scene, not really or exactly to be described at all, (for on the many hundreds who were there it seems to this hour to have left a passing blur, a dream, a blotch)—and yet partially to be described as I now proceed to give it. There is a scene in the play representing a modern parlor, in which two unprecedented English ladies are inform'd by the impossible Yankee that he is not a man of fortune, and therefore undesirable for marriage-catching purposes; after which, the comments being finish'd, the dramatic trio make exit, leaving the stage clear for a moment. At this period came the murder of Abraham Lincoln.

Great as all its manifold train, circling round it, and stretching into the future for many a century, in the politics, history, art, &c., of the New World, in point of fact the main thing, the actual murder, transpired with the quiet and simplicity of any commonest occurrence—the bursting of a bud or pod in the growth of vegetation, for instance. Through the general hum following the stage pause, with the change of positions, came the muffled sound of a pistol-shot, which not one-hundredth part of the audience heard at the time—and yet a moment's hush —somehow, surely, a vague startled thrill—and then, through the ornamented, draperied, starr'd and striped spaceway of the President's box, a sudden figure, a man, raises himself with hands and feet, stands a moment on the railing, leaps below to the stage, (a distance of perhaps fourteen or fifteen feet,) falls out of position, catching his boot-heel in the copious drapery, (the American flag,) falls on one knee, quickly recovers himself, rises as if nothing had happen'd, (he really sprains his ankle, but unfelt then)—and so the figure, Booth, the murderer, dress'd in plain black broadcloth, bare-headed, with full, glossy, raven hair, and his eyes like some mad animal's flashing with light and resolution, yet with a certain strange calmness, holds aloft in one hand a large knife—walks along not much back from the footlights—turns fully toward the audience his face of statuesque beauty, lit by those basilisk eyes, flashing with desperation, perhaps insanity—launches out in a firm and steady voice the words *Sic semper tyrannis*—and then walks with neither slow nor very rapid pace diagonally across to the back of the stage, and disappears. (Had not all this terrible scene—making the mimic ones preposterous—had it not all been rehears'd, in blank, by Booth, beforehand?)

A moment's hush—a scream—the cry of *murder*—Mrs. Lincoln leaning out of the box, with ashy cheeks and lips, with involuntary cry, pointing to the retreating figure, *He has kill'd the President*. And still a moment's strange, incredulous suspense— and then the deluge!—then that mixture of horror, noises, uncertainty—(the sound, somewhere back, of a horse's hoofs clattering with speed)—the people burst through chairs and railings, and break them up—there is inextricable confusion and

terror—women faint—quite feeble persons fall, and are tram-
pled on—many cries of agony are heard—the broad stage suddenly fills to suffocation with a dense and motley crowd, like
some horrible carnival—the audience rush generally upon it, at
least the strong men do—the actors and actresses are all there in
their play-costumes and painted faces, with mortal fright showing
through the rouge—the screams and calls, confused talk—
redoubled, trebled—two or three manage to pass up water from
the stage to the President's box—others try to clamber up—
&c., &c.

In the midst of all this, the soldiers of the President's guard,
with others, suddenly drawn to the scene, burst in—(some two
hundred altogether)—they storm the house, through all the tiers,
especially the upper ones, inflamed with fury, literally charging
the audience with fix'd bayonets, muskets and pistols, shouting
Clear out! clear out! you sons of—— . . . . . Such the wild scene,
or a suggestion of it rather, inside the play-house that night.

Outside, too, in the atmosphere of shock and craze, crowds
of people, fill'd with frenzy, ready to seize any outlet for it, come
near committing murder several times on innocent individuals.
One such case was especially exciting. The infuriated crowd,
through some chance, got started against one man, either for
words he utter'd, or perhaps without any cause at all, and were
proceeding at once to actually hang him on a neighboring lamp-
post, when he was rescued by a few heroic policemen, who
placed him in their midst, and fought their way slowly and amid
great peril toward the station house. It was a fitting episode of
the whole affair. The crowd rushing and eddying to and fro—
the night, the yells, the pale faces, many frighten'd people trying
in vain to extricate themselves—the attack'd man, not yet freed
from the jaws of death, looking like a corpse—the silent, resolute, half-dozen policemen, with no weapons but their little
clubs, yet stern and steady through all those eddying swarms—
made a fitting side-scene to the grand tragedy of the murder.
They gain'd the station house with the protected man, whom
they placed in security for the night, and discharged him in the
morning.

And in the midst of that pandemonium, infuriated soldiers,

the audience and the crowd, the stage, and all its actors and actresses, its paint-pots, spangles, and gas-lights—the life blood from those veins, the best and sweetest of the land, drips slowly down, and death's ooze already begins its little bubbles on the lips.

Thus the visible incidents and surroundings of Abraham Lincoln's murder, as they really occur'd. Thus ended the attempted secession of these States; thus the four years' war. But the main things come subtly and invisibly afterward, perhaps long afterward—neither military, political, nor (great as those are,) historical. I say, certain secondary and indirect results, out of the tragedy of this death, are, in my opinion, greatest. Not the event of the murder itself. Not that Mr. Lincoln strings the principal points and personages of the period, like beads, upon the single string of his career. Not that his idiosyncrasy, in its sudden appearance and disappearance, stamps this Republic with a stamp more mark'd and enduring than any yet given by any one man—(more even than Washington's;)—but, join'd with these, the immeasurable value and meaning of that whole tragedy lies, to me, in senses finally dearest to a nation, (and here all our own)—the imaginative and artistic senses—the literary and dramatic ones. Not in any common or low meaning of those terms, but a meaning precious to the race, and to every age. A long and varied series of contradictory events arrives at last at its highest poetic, single, central, pictorial denouement. The whole involved, baffling, multiform whirl of the secession period comes to a head, and is gather'd in one brief flash of lightning-illumination—one simple, fierce deed. Its sharp culmination, and as it were solution, of so many bloody and angry problems, illustrates those climax-moments on the stage of universal Time, where the historic Muse at one entrance, and the tragic Muse at the other, suddenly ringing down the curtain, close an immense act in the long drama of creative thought, and give it radiation, tableau, stranger than fiction. Fit radiation—fit close! How the imagination—how the student loves these things! America, too, is to have them. For not in all great deaths, nor far or near—not Cæsar in the Roman senate-house, or Napoleon passing away in the wild night-storm at St. Helena—not Paleologus, falling, desperately fighting, piled over dozens deep with Grecian corpses—not calm old Socrates, drinking the hemlock—outvies that terminus of the secession war, in one man's life, here in our midst, in our own time—that seal of the emancipation of three million slaves—that parturition and delivery of our at last really free Republic, born again, henceforth to commence its career of genuine homogeneous Union, compact, consistent with itself.

Nor will ever future American Patriots and Unionists, indifferently over the whole land, or North or South, find a better moral to their lesson. The final use of the greatest men of a Nation is, after all, not with reference to their deeds in themselves, or their direct bearing on their times or lands. The final use of a heroic-eminent life—especially of a heroic-eminent death—is its indirect filtering into the nation and the race, and to give, often at many removes, but unerringly, age after age, color and fibre to the personalism of the youth and maturity of that age, and of mankind. Then there is a cement to the whole people, subtler, more underlying, than any thing in written constitution, or courts or armies—namely, the cement of a death identified thoroughly with that people, at its head, and for its sake. Strange, (is it not?) that battles, martyrs, agonies, blood, even assassination, should so condense—perhaps only really, lastingly condense —a Nationality.

I repeat it—the grand deaths of the race—the dramatic deaths of every nationality—are its most important inheritance-value— in some respects beyond its literature and art—(as the hero is beyond his finest portrait, and the battle itself beyond its choicest song or epic.) Is not here indeed the point underlying all tragedy? the famous pieces of the Grecian masters—and all masters? Why, if the old Greeks had had this man, what trilogies of plays—what epics—would have been made out of him! How the rhapsodes would have recited him! How quickly that quaint tall form would have enter'd into the region where men vitalize gods, and gods divinify men! But Lincoln, his times, his death—great as any, any age—belong altogether to our own, and are autochthonic. (Sometimes indeed I think our American days, our own stage—the actors we know and have shaken hands, or talk'd with—more fateful than any thing in Eschylus—more heroic than the fighters around Troy—afford kings of men for our Democracy prouder than Agamemnon—models of character cute and hardy as Ulysses—deaths more pitiful than Priam's.)

When, centuries hence, (as it must, in my opinion, be centuries hence before the life of these States, or of Democracy, can be really written and illustrated,) the leading historians and dramatists seek for some personage, some special event, incisive enough to mark with deepest cut, and mnemonize, this turbulent Nineteenth century of ours, (not only these States, but all over the political and social world)—something, perhaps, to close that gorgeous procession of European feudalism, with all its pomp and caste-prejudices, (of whose long train we in America are yet so inextricably the heirs)—something to identify with terrible identification, by far the greatest revolutionary step in the history of the United States, (perhaps the greatest of the world, our century)—the absolute extirpation and erasure of slavery from the States—those historians will seek in vain for any point to serve more thoroughly their purpose, than Abraham Lincoln's death.

Dear to the Muse—thrice dear to Nationality—to the whole human race—precious to this Union—precious to Democracy —unspeakably and forever precious—their first great Martyr Chief.

1882

Edmund Clarence Stedman

From the beginning of his career, Lincoln attracted nearly as much notice for his physical strength and imposing height as he did for his words and ideas. Lincoln himself well understood the importance of image-making—particularly since he was far from conventionally handsome—and cooperated with photographers, artists, and sculptors to capture and disseminate his unusual but commanding face and figure. The results sometimes proved powerful enough to inspire celebratory poetry of its own, including this ode to the plaster cast of Lincoln's hand. The cast (see page 283) was made by the sculptor Leonard Wells Volk in Springfield two days after Lincoln won the Republican presidential nomination in May 1860, and it was later widely reproduced as a keepsake for generations of admirers. (Ironically, Volk was married to a cousin of Lincoln's archrival, Stephen A. Douglas.) While many observers, including Stedman, have associated the size and shape of Lincoln's hand purely with the hard manual labor he performed in his youth, at the time of the casting Lincoln's right hand was swollen from shaking hands with the many well-wishers who had come to congratulate him on his recent nomination.

The Hand of Lincoln

Look on this cast, and know the hand
　　That bore a nation in its hold:
From this mute witness understand
　　What Lincoln was,—how large of mould

The man who sped the woodman's team,
　　And deepest sunk the ploughman's share,
And pushed the laden raft astream,
　　Of fate before him unaware.

This was the hand that knew to swing
  The axe—since thus would Freedom train
Her son—and made the forest ring,
  And drove the wedge, and toiled amain.

Firm hand, that loftier office took,
  A conscious leader's will obeyed,
And, when men sought his word and look,
  With steadfast might the gathering swayed.

No courtier's, toying with a sword,
  Nor minstrel's, laid across a lute;
A chief's, uplifted to the Lord
  When all the kings of earth were mute!

The hand of Anak, sinewed strong,
  The fingers that on greatness clutch;
Yet, lo! the marks their lines along
  Of one who strove and suffered much.

For here in knotted cord and vein
  I trace the varying chart of years;
I know the troubled heart, the strain,
  The weight of Atlas—and the tears.

Again I see the patient brow
  That palm erewhile was wont to press;
And now 't is furrowed deep, and now
  Made smooth with hope and tenderness.

For something of a formless grace
  This moulded outline plays about;
A pitying flame, beyond our trace,
  Breathes like a spirit, in and out,—

The love that cast an aureole
  Round one who, longer to endure,
Called mirth to ease his ceaseless dole,
  Yet kept his nobler purpose sure.

Lo, as I gaze, the statured man,
  Built up from yon large hand, appears:
A type that Nature wills to plan
  But once in all a people's years.

What better than this voiceless cast
  To tell of such a one as he,
Since through its living semblance passed
  The thought that bade a race be free!

1883

Ulysses S. Grant

Lincoln's most celebrated—and most successful—general began the Civil War as a civilian storekeeper in Galena, Illinois. Three years later, Grant (1822–1885) met Lincoln for the first time when he traveled to the capital in March 1864 to assume command of all the Union armies. By then he had been approached more than once about challenging Lincoln for the presidency. Grant responded by disavowing any interest in political office, and he passed over the subject when he wrote his *Personal Memoirs* in 1885 while dying of cancer. Nor did he explore the question of what might have happened if he had, as originally planned, accompanied the President and the First Lady to Ford's Theatre on the night of April 14, 1865. Instead he recalled, in his characteristically unadorned and straightforward style, several of his personal encounters with Lincoln, while offering a sincere appraisal of his generous leadership.

FROM
Personal Memoirs of U. S. Grant

Although hailing from Illinois myself, the State of the President, I never met Mr. Lincoln until called to the capital to receive my commission as lieutenant-general. I knew him, however, very well and favorably from the accounts given by officers under me at the West who had known him all their lives. I had also read the remarkable series of debates between Lincoln and Douglas a few years before, when they were rival candidates for the United States Senate. I was then a resident of Missouri, and by no means a "Lincoln man" in that contest; but I recognized then his great ability.

In my first interview with Mr. Lincoln alone he stated to me that he had never professed to be a military man or to know how campaigns should be conducted, and never wanted to interfere in them: but that procrastination on the part of commanders, and the pressure from the people at the North and Congress, *which was always with him*, forced him into issuing his series of

"Military Orders"—one, two, three, etc. He did not know but they were all wrong, and did know that some of them were. All he wanted or had ever wanted was some one who would take the responsibility and act, and call on him for all the assistance needed, pledging himself to use all the power of the government in rendering such assistance. Assuring him that I would do the best I could with the means at hand, and avoid as far as possible annoying him or the War Department, our first interview ended.

The Secretary of War I had met once before only, but felt that I knew him better.

While commanding in West Tennessee we had occasionally held conversations over the wires, at night, when they were not being otherwise used. He and General Halleck both cautioned me against giving the President my plans of campaign, saying that he was so kind-hearted, so averse to refusing anything asked of him, that some friend would be sure to get from him all he knew. I should have said that in our interview the President told me he did not want to know what I proposed to do. But he submitted a plan of campaign of his own which he wanted me to hear and then do as I pleased about. He brought out a map of Virginia on which he had evidently marked every position occupied by the Federal and Confederate armies up to that time. He pointed out on the map two streams which empty into the Potomac, and suggested that the army might be moved on boats and landed between the mouths of these streams. We would then have the Potomac to bring our supplies, and the tributaries would protect our flanks while we moved out. I listened respectfully, but did not suggest that the same streams would protect Lee's flanks while he was shutting us up.

I did not communicate my plans to the President, nor did I to the Secretary of War or to General Halleck.

———

On this same visit to Washington I had my last interview with the President before reaching the James River. He had of course become acquainted with the fact that a general movement had been ordered all along the line, and seemed to think it a new feature in war. I explained to him that it was necessary to have a great number of troops to guard and hold the territory we had captured, and to prevent incursions into the Northern States. These troops could perform this service just as well by advancing as by remaining still; and by advancing they would compel the enemy to keep detachments to hold them back, or else lay his own territory open to invasion. His answer was: "Oh, yes! I see that. As we say out West, if a man can't skin he must hold a leg while somebody else does."

———

On the last of January, 1865, peace commissioners from the so-called Confederate States presented themselves on our lines around Petersburg, and were immediately conducted to my headquarters at City Point. They proved to be Alexander H. Stephens, Vice-President of the Confederacy, Judge Campbell, Assistant-Secretary of War, and R. M. T. Hunter, formerly United States Senator and then a member of the Confederate Senate.

It was about dark when they reached my headquarters, and I at once conducted them to the steamer *Mary Martin*, a Hudson River boat which was very comfortably fitted up for the use of passengers. I at once communicated by telegraph with Washington and informed the Secretary of War and the President of the arrival of these commissioners and that their object was to negotiate terms of peace between the United States and, as they termed it, the Confederate Government. I was instructed to retain them at City Point, until the President, or some one whom he would designate, should come to meet them. They remained several days as guests on board the boat. I saw them quite frequently, though I have no recollection of having had any conversation whatever with them on the subject of their mission. It was something I had nothing to do with, and I therefore did not wish to express any views on the subject. For my own part I never had admitted, and never was ready to admit, that they were the representatives of a *government*. There had been too great a waste of blood and treasure to concede anything of the kind. As long as they remained there, however, our relations were pleasant and I found them all very agreeable gentlemen. I directed the captain to furnish them with the best the boat afforded, and to administer to their comfort in every way possible. No guard was placed over them and no restriction was put upon their movements; nor was there any pledge asked that they would not abuse the privileges extended to them. They were permitted to leave the boat when they felt like it, and did so, coming up on the bank and visiting me at my headquarters.

I had never met either of these gentlemen before the war, but knew them well by reputation and through their public services, and I had been a particular admirer of Mr. Stephens. I had always supposed that he was a very small man, but when I saw him in the dusk of the evening I was very much surprised to find so large a man as he seemed to be. When he got down on to the boat I found that he was wearing a coarse gray woollen overcoat, a manufacture that had been introduced into the South during the rebellion. The cloth was thicker than anything of the kind I had ever seen, even in Canada. The overcoat extended nearly to his feet, and was so large that it gave him the appearance of being an average-sized man. He took this off when he reached the cabin of the boat, and I was struck with the apparent change in size, in the coat and out of it.

After a few days, about the 2d of February, I received a dispatch from Washington, directing me to send the commissioners to Hampton Roads to meet the President and a member of the cabinet. Mr. Lincoln met them there and had an interview of short duration. It was not a great while after they met that the President visited me at City Point. He spoke of his having met the commissioners, and said he had told them that there would be no use in entering into any negotiations unless they would recognize, first: that the Union as a whole must be forever preserved, and second: that slavery must be abolished. If they were willing to concede these two points, then he was ready to enter into negotiations and was almost willing to hand them a blank sheet of paper with his signature attached for them to fill in the terms upon which they were willing to live with us in the Union and be one people. He always showed a generous and kindly spirit toward the Southern people, and I never heard him abuse an enemy. Some of the cruel things said about President Lincoln, particularly in the North, used to pierce him to the heart; but never in my presence did he evince a revengeful disposition —and I saw a great deal of him at City Point, for he seemed glad to get away from the cares and anxieties of the capital.

Right here I might relate an anecdote of Mr. Lincoln. It was on the occasion of his visit to me just after he had talked with the peace commissioners at Hampton Roads. After a little conversation, he asked me if I had seen that overcoat of Stephens's. I replied that I had. "Well," said he, "did you see him take it off?" I said yes. "Well," said he, "didn't you think it was the biggest shuck and the littlest ear that ever you did see?" Long afterwards I told this story to the Confederate General J. B. Gordon, at the time a member of the Senate. He repeated it to Stephens, and, as I heard afterwards, Stephens laughed immoderately at the simile of Mr. Lincoln.

———

Wilson's raid resulted in the capture of the fugitive president of the defunct confederacy before he got out of the country. This occurred at Irwinsville, Georgia, on the 11th of May. For myself, and I believe Mr. Lincoln shared the feeling, I would have been very glad to have seen Mr. Davis succeed in escaping, but for one reason: I feared that if not captured, he might get into the trans-Mississippi region and there set up a more contracted confederacy. The young men now out of homes and out of employment might have rallied under his standard and protracted the war yet another year. The Northern people were tired of the war, they were tired of piling up a debt which would be a further mortgage upon their homes.

Mr. Lincoln, I believe, wanted Mr. Davis to escape, because he did not wish to deal with the matter of his punishment. He knew there would be people clamoring for the punishment of the ex-Confederate president, for high treason. He thought blood enough had already been spilled to atone for our wickedness as a nation. At all events he did not wish to be the judge to decide whether more should be shed or not. But his own life was sacrificed at the hands of an assassin before the ex-president of the Confederacy was a prisoner in the hands of the government which he had lent all his talent and all his energies to destroy.

All things are said to be wisely directed, and for the best interest of all concerned. This reflection does not, however, abate in the slightest our sense of bereavement in the untimely loss of so good and great a man as Abraham Lincoln.

He would have proven the best friend the South could have had, and saved much of the wrangling and bitterness of feeling brought out by reconstruction under a President who at first wished to revenge himself upon Southern men of better social standing than himself, but who still sought their recognition, and in a short time conceived the idea and advanced the proposition to become their Moses to lead them triumphantly out of all their difficulties.

———

I remember one little incident which I will relate as an anecdote characteristic of Mr. Lincoln. It occurred a day after I reached Washington, and about the time General Meade reached Burkesville with the army. Governor Smith of Virginia had left Richmond with the Confederate States government, and had gone to Danville. Supposing I was necessarily with the army at Burkesville, he addressed a letter to me there informing me that, as governor of the Commonwealth of the State of Virginia, he had temporarily removed the State capital from Richmond to Danville, and asking if he would be permitted to perform the functions of his office there without molestation by the Federal authorities. I give this letter, only in substance. He also inquired of me whether in case he was not allowed to perform the duties of his office, he with a few others might not be permitted to leave the country and go abroad without interference. General Meade being informed that a flag of truce was outside his pickets with a letter to me, at once sent out and had the letter brought in without informing the officer who brought it that I was not present. He read the letter and telegraphed me its contents. Meeting Mr. Lincoln shortly after receiving this dispatch, I repeated its contents to him. Mr. Lincoln, supposing I was asking for instructions, said, in reply to that part of Governor Smith's letter which inquired whether he with a few friends would be permitted to leave the country unmolested, that his position was like that of a certain Irishman (giving the name) he knew in Springfield who was very popular with the people, a man of considerable promise, and very much liked. Unfortunately he had acquired the habit of drinking, and his friends could see that the habit was growing on him. These friends determined to make an effort to save him, and to do this they drew up a pledge to abstain from all alcoholic drinks. They asked Pat to join them in signing the pledge, and he consented. He had been so long out of the habit of using plain water as a beverage that he resorted to soda-water as a substitute. After a few days this began to grow distasteful to him. So holding the glass behind him, he said: "Doctor, couldn't you drop a bit of brandy in that unbeknownst to myself."

I do not remember what the instructions were the President gave me, but I know that Governor Smith was not permitted to perform the duties of his office. I also know that if Mr. Lincoln had been spared, there would have been no efforts made to prevent any one from leaving the country who desired to do so. He would have been equally willing to permit the return of the same expatriated citizens after they had time to repent of their choice.

———

It may not be out of place to again allude to President Lincoln and the Secretary of War, Mr. Stanton, who were the great conspicuous figures in the executive branch of the government. There is no great difference of opinion now, in the public mind, as to the characteristics of the President. With Mr. Stanton the case is different. They were the very opposite of each other in almost every particular, except that each possessed great ability. Mr. Lincoln gained influence over men by making them feel that it was a pleasure to serve him. He preferred yielding his own wish to gratify others, rather than to insist upon having his own way. It distressed him to disappoint others. In matters of public duty, however, he had what he wished, but in the least offensive way. Mr. Stanton never questioned his own authority to command, unless resisted. He cared nothing for the feeling of others. In fact it seemed to be pleasanter to him to disappoint than to gratify. He felt no hesitation in assuming the functions of the executive, or in acting without advising with him. If his act was not sustained, he would change it—if he saw the matter would be followed up until he did so.

It was generally supposed that these two officials formed the complement of each other. The Secretary was required to prevent the President's being imposed upon. The President was required in the more responsible place of seeing that injustice was not done to others. I do not know that this view of these two men is still entertained by the majority of the people. It is not a correct view, however, in my estimation. Mr. Lincoln did not require a guardian to aid him in the fulfilment of a public trust.

Mr. Lincoln was not timid, and he was willing to trust his generals in making and executing their plans. The Secretary was very timid, and it was impossible for him to avoid interfering with the armies covering the capital when it was sought to defend it by an offensive movement against the army guarding the Confederate capital. He could see our weakness, but he could not see that the enemy was in danger. The enemy would not have been in danger if Mr. Stanton had been in the field. These characteristics of the two officials were clearly shown shortly after Early came so near getting into the capital.

1886

Frederick Douglass

A decade after Douglass gave his oration at the dedication of the Freedmen's Memorial, this piece was published in *Reminiscences of Abraham Lincoln by Distinguished Men of His Time*, a collection edited by Allen Thorndike Rice of the *North American Review*. Its wholly sympathetic portrait of the late President is similar to the one presented by Douglass in his 1881 autobiography *Life and Times*, in which he described Lincoln as "not only a great President, but a GREAT MAN," while also including his critical 1876 oration in an appendix. As the Republicans continued their retreat from Reconstruction, Douglass and other African Americans increasingly found that their fealty to the party, and to the memory of its greatest leader and symbol, brought them less than they hoped for.

FROM
Reminiscences of Abraham Lincoln by Distinguished Men of His Time

I do not know more about Mr. Lincoln than is known by countless thousands of Americans who have met the man. But I am quite willing to give my recollections of him and the impressions made by him upon my mind as to his character.

My first interview with him was in the summer of 1863, soon after the Confederate States had declared their purpose to treat colored soldiers as insurgents, and their purpose not to treat any such soldiers as prisoners of war subject to exchange like other soldiers. My visit to Mr. Lincoln was in reference to this threat of the Confederate States. I was at the time engaged in raising colored troops, and I desired some assurances from President Lincoln that such troops should be treated as soldiers of the United States, and when taken prisoners exchanged like other soldiers; that when any of them were hanged or enslaved the President should retaliate. I was introduced to Mr. Lincoln on this occasion by Senator Pomeroy, of Kansas; I met him at the Executive Mansion.

I was somewhat troubled with the thought of meeting one so august and high in authority, especially as I had never been in the White House before, and had never spoken to a President of the United States before. But my embarrassment soon vanished when I met the face of Mr. Lincoln. When I entered he was seated in a low chair, surrounded by a multitude of books and papers, his feet and legs were extended in front of his chair. On my approach he slowly drew his feet in from the different parts of the room into which they had strayed, and he began to rise, and continued to rise until he looked down upon me, and extended his hand and gave me a welcome. I began, with some hesitation, to tell him who I was and what I had been doing, but he soon stopped me, saying in a sharp, cordial voice:

"You need not tell me who you are, Mr. Douglass, I know who you are. Mr. Seward has told me all about you."

He then invited me to take a seat beside him. Not wishing to occupy his time and attention, seeing that he was busy, I stated to him the object of my call at once. I said:

"Mr. Lincoln, I am recruiting colored troops. I have assisted in fitting up two regiments in Massachusetts, and am now at work in the same way in Pennsylvania, and have come to say this to you, sir, if you wish to make this branch of the service successful you must do four things:

"First—You must give colored soldiers the same pay that you give white soldiers.

"Second—You must compel the Confederate States to treat colored soldiers, when taken prisoners, as prisoners of war.

"Third—When any colored man or soldier performs brave, meritorious exploits in the field, you must enable me to say to those that I recruit that they will be promoted for such service, precisely as white men are promoted for similar service.

"Fourth—In case any colored soldiers are murdered in cold blood and taken prisoners, you should retaliate in kind."

To this little speech Mr. Lincoln listened with earnest attention and with very apparent sympathy, and replied to each point in his own peculiar, forcible way. First he spoke of the opposition generally to employing negroes as soldiers at all, of the prejudice against the race, and of the advantage to colored people that would result from their being employed as soldiers in defense of their country. He regarded such an employment as an experiment, and spoke of the advantage it would be to the colored race if the experiment should succeed. He said that he had difficulty in getting colored men into the United States uniform; that when the purpose was fixed to employ them as soldiers, several different uniforms were proposed for them, and that it was something gained when it was finally determined to clothe them like other soldiers.

Now, as to the pay, we had to make some concession to prejudice. There were threats that if we made soldiers of them at all white men would not enlist, would not fight beside them. Besides, it was not believed that a negro could make a good soldier, as good a soldier as a white man, and hence it was thought that he should not have the same pay as a white man. But said he,

"I assure you, Mr. Douglass, that in the end they shall have the same pay as white soldiers."

As to the exchange and general treatment of colored soldiers when taken prisoners of war, he should insist to their being entitled to all privileges of such prisoners. Mr. Lincoln admitted the justice of my demand for the promotion of colored soldiers for good conduct in the field, but on the matter of retaliation he differed from me entirely. I shall never forget the benignant expression of his face, the tearful look of his eye and the quiver in his voice, when he deprecated a resort to retaliatory measures.

"Once begun," said he, "I do not know where such a measure would stop."

He said he could not take men out and kill them in cold blood for what was done by others. If he could get hold of the persons who were guilty of killing the colored prisoners in cold blood, the case would be different, but he could not kill the innocent for the guilty.

Before leaving Mr. Lincoln, Senator Pomeroy said:

"Mr. President, Mr. Stanton is going to make Douglass Adjutant-General to General Thomas, and is going to send him down the Mississippi to recruit."

Mr. Lincoln said in answer to this:

"I will sign any commission that Mr. Stanton will give Mr. Douglass."

At this point we parted.

I met Mr. Lincoln several times after this interview.

I was once invited by him to take tea with him at the Soldiers' Home. On one occasion, while visiting him at the White House, he showed me a letter he was writing to Horace Greeley in reply to some of Greeley's criticisms against protracting the war. He seemed to feel very keenly the reproaches heaped upon him for not bringing the war to a speedy conclusion; said he was charged with making it an Abolition war instead of a war for the Union, and expressed his desire to end the war as soon as possible. While I was talking with him Governor Buckingham sent in his card, and I was amused by his telling the messenger, as well as by the way he expressed it, to "tell Governor Buckingham to wait, I want to have a long talk with my friend Douglass."

He used those words. I said: "Mr. Lincoln, I will retire." "Oh, no, no, you shall not, I want Governor Buckingham to wait," and he did wait for at least a half hour. When he came in I was introduced by Mr. Lincoln to Governor Buckingham, and the Governor did not seem to take it amiss at all that he had been required to wait.

I was present at the inauguration of Mr. Lincoln, the 4th of March, 1865. I felt then that there was murder in the air, and I kept close to his carriage on the way to the Capitol, for I felt that I might see him fall that day. It was a vague presentiment.

At that time the Confederate cause was on its last legs, as it were, and there was deep feeling. I could feel it in the atmosphere here. I did not know exactly what it was, but I just felt as if he might be shot on his way to the Capitol. I cannot refer to any incident, in fact, to any expression that I heard, it was simply a presentiment that Lincoln might fall that day. I got right in front of the east portico of the Capitol, listened to his inaugural address, and witnessed his being sworn in by Chief Justice Chase. When he came on the steps he was accompanied by Vice-President Johnson. In looking out in the crowd he saw me standing near by, and I could see he was pointing me out to

Andrew Johnson. Mr. Johnson, without knowing perhaps that I saw the movement, looked quite annoyed that his attention should be called in that direction. So I got a peep into his soul. As soon as he saw me looking at him, suddenly he assumed rather an amicable expression of countenance. I felt that, whatever else the man might be, he was no friend to my people.

I heard Mr. Lincoln deliver this wonderful address. It was very short; but he answered all the objections raised to his prolonging the war in one sentence—it was a remarkable sentence.

"Fondly do we hope, profoundly do we pray, that this mighty scourge of war shall soon pass away, yet if God wills it continue until all the wealth piled up by two hundred years of bondage shall have been wasted, and each drop of blood drawn by the lash shall have been paid for by one drawn by the sword, we must still say, as was said three thousand years ago, the judgments of the Lord are true and righteous altogether."

For the first time in my life, and I suppose the first time in any colored man's life, I attended the reception of President Lincoln on the evening of the inauguration. As I approached the door I was seized by two policemen and forbidden to enter. I said to them that they were mistaken entirely in what they were doing, that if Mr. Lincoln knew that I was at the door he would order my admission, and I bolted in by them. On the inside I was taken charge of by two other policemen, to be conducted as I supposed to the President, but instead of that they were conducting me out the window on a plank.

"Oh," said I, "this will not do, gentlemen," and as a gentleman was passing in I said to him, "Just say to Mr. Lincoln that Fred. Douglass is at the door."

He rushed in to President Lincoln, and almost in less than a half a minute I was invited into the East Room of the White House. A perfect sea of beauty and elegance, too, it was. The ladies were in very fine attire, and Mrs. Lincoln was standing there. I could not have been more than ten feet from him when Mr. Lincoln saw me; his countenance lighted up, and he said in a voice which was heard all around: "Here comes my friend Douglass." As I approached him he reached out his hand, gave me a cordial shake, and said: "Douglass, I saw you in the crowd to-day listening to my inaugural address. There is no man's opinion that I value more than yours: what do you think of it?" I said: "Mr. Lincoln, I cannot stop here to talk with you, as there are thousands waiting to shake you by the hand;" but he said again: "What did you think of it?" I said: "Mr. Lincoln, it was a sacred effort," and then I walked off. "I am glad you liked it," he said. That was the last time I saw him to speak with him.

In all my interviews with Mr. Lincoln I was impressed with his entire freedom from popular prejudice against the colored race. He was the first great man that I talked with in the United States freely, who in no single instance reminded me of the difference between himself and myself, of the difference of color, and I thought that all the more remarkable because he came from a State where there were black laws. I account partially for his kindness to me because of the similarity with which I had fought my way up, we both starting at the lowest round of the ladder. I must say this for Mr. Lincoln, that whenever I met him he was in a very serious mood. I heard of those stories he used to tell, but he never told me a story. I remember of one of Mr. Lincoln's stories being told me by General Grant. I had called on him, and he said: "Douglass, stay here, I want to tell you about a little incident. When I came to Washington first, one of the first things that Lincoln said to me was, 'Grant, have you ever read the book by Orpheus C. Kerr?' 'Well, no, I never did,' said I. Mr. Lincoln said: 'You ought to read it, it is a very interesting book. I have had a good deal of satisfaction reading that book. There is one poem there that describes a meeting of the animals. The substance of it being that the animals and a dragon, or some dreadful thing, was near by and had to be conquered, and it was a question as to who would undertake the job. By and by a monkey stepped forward and proposed to do the work up. The monkey said he thought he could do it if he could get an inch or two more put on his tail. The assemblage voted him a few inches more to his tail, and he went out and tried his hand. He was unsuccessful and returned, stating that he wanted a few more inches put on his tail. The request was granted, and he went again. His second effort was a failure. He asked that more inches be put on his tail and he would try a third time.' At last," said General Grant, "it got through my head what Lincoln was aiming at, as applying to my wanting more men, and finally I said: 'Mr. Lincoln, I don't want any more inches put on my tail.'" It was a hit at McClellan, and General Grant told me the story with a good deal of gusto. I got the book afterward and read the lines of Orpheus C. Kerr.

There was one thing concerning Lincoln that I was impressed with, and that was that a statement of his was an argument more convincing than any amount of logic. He had a happy faculty of stating a proposition, of stating it so that it needed no argument. It was a rough kind of reasoning, but it went right to the point. Then, too, there was another feeling that I had with reference to him, and that was that while I felt in his presence I was in the presence of a very great man, as great as the greatest, I felt as though I could go and put my hand on him if I wanted to, to put my hand on his shoulder. Of course I did not do it, but I felt that I could. I felt as though I was in the presence of a big brother, and that there was safety in his atmosphere.

It was often said during the war that Mrs. Lincoln did not sympathize fully with her husband in his anti-slavery feeling, but I never believed this concerning her, and have good reason for being confirmed in my impression of her by the fact that, when Mr. Lincoln died and she was about leaving the White House, she selected his favorite walking cane and said: "I know of no one that would appreciate this more than Fred. Douglass." She sent it to me at Rochester, and I have it in my house to-day, and expect to keep it there as long as I live.

1886

Richard Watson Gilder

In the last decades of the 19th century, Gilder (1844–1909) became one of the best-known poets and editors of his time, a literary eminence (and nearly a namesake) for the Gilded Age. As the editor of *The Century Magazine* from 1881 until his death, Gilder published the popular series "Battles and Leaders of the Civil War" and paid John G. Nicolay and John Hay, Lincoln's former White House secretaries, $50,000 for the rights to run 40 excerpts from their *Abraham Lincoln: A History* over four years beginning in 1886. That same year, Gilder was moved to explore the Lincoln image himself in a poem inspired by the life mask Leonard Wells Volk cast of the future president in 1860. In the summer of 1888 Gilder attended a reunion ceremony held on the Gettysburg battlefield and recited the second poem printed here, a tribute to the "majestic ghost" of Lincoln that praised the courage shown by the soldiers on both sides of the conflict—an example of the growing tendency to invoke the President's memory in the cause of sectional reconciliation.

On the Life-Mask of Abraham Lincoln

This bronze doth keep the very form and mold
   Of our great martyr's face. Yes, this is he:
   That brow all wisdom, all benignity;
   That human, humorous mouth; those cheeks that hold
Like some harsh landscape all the summer's gold;
   That spirit fit for sorrow, as the sea
   For storms to beat on; the lone agony
   Those silent, patient lips too well foretold.
Yes, this is he who ruled a world of men
   As might some prophet of the elder day—
   Brooding above the tempest and the fray
With deep-eyed thought and more than mortal ken.
   A power was his beyond the touch of art
   Or armed strength—his pure and mighty heart.

1886

To the Spirit of Abraham Lincoln
(*Reunion at Gettysburg Twenty-Five Years
After the Battle*)

Shade of our greatest, O look down to-day!
    Here the long, dread midsummer battle roared,
    And brother in brother plunged the accursèd sword;—
    Here foe meets foe once more in proud array,
Yet not as once to harry and to slay,
    But to strike hands, and with sublime accord
    Weep tears heroic for the souls that soared
    Quick from earth's carnage to the starry way.
Each fought for what he deemed the people's good,
    And proved his bravery by his offered life,
    And sealed his honor with his outpoured blood;
But the Eternal did direct the strife,
    And on this sacred field one patriot host
    Now calls thee father—dear, majestic ghost!

                                                        1888

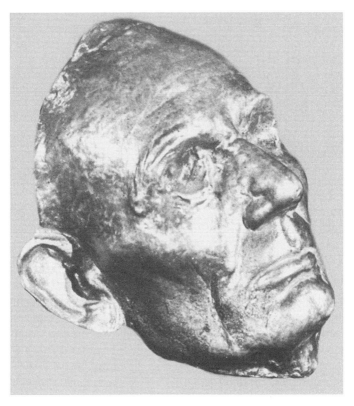

Bronze cast from the plaster life mask of Abraham Lincoln made by Leonard Wells Volk in 1860. *Courtesy of the Abraham Lincoln Presidential Library and Museum.*

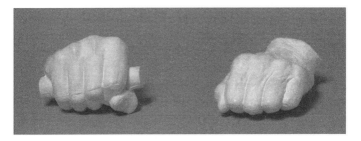

Plaster casts of Lincoln's hands, from the original casts made by Leonard Wells Volk in 1860. *Courtesy of the National Portrait Gallery, Smithsonian Institution.*

Walt Whitman

Whitman originally wrote this piece for the 1886 collection *Reminis-cences of Abraham Lincoln by Distinguished Men of His Time*, then re-vised it slightly for publication in his 1888 prose volume *November Boughs*.

FROM

November Boughs

Abraham Lincoln

Glad am I to give—were anything better lacking—even the most brief and shorn testimony of Abraham Lincoln. Everything I heard about him authentically, and every time I saw him (and it was my fortune through 1862 to '65 to see, or pass a word with, or watch him, personally, perhaps twenty or thirty times,) added to and anneal'd my respect and love at the moment. And as I dwell on what I myself heard or saw of the mighty Westerner, and blend it with the history and literature of my age, and of what I can get of all ages, and conclude it with his death, it seems like some tragic play, superior to all else I know—vaster and fiercer and more convulsionary, for this America of ours, than Eschylus or Shakspere ever drew for Athens or for England. And then the Moral permeating, underlying all! the Lesson that none so remote—none so illiterate—no age, no class—but may directly or indirectly read!

Abraham Lincoln's was really one of those characters, the best of which is the result of long trains of cause and effect—needing a certain spaciousness of time, and perhaps even remote-ness, to properly enclose them—having unequal'd influence on the shaping of this Republic (and therefore the world) as to-day, and then far more important in the future. Thus the time has by no means yet come for a thorough measurement of him. Never-theless, we who live in his era—who have seen him, and heard him, face to face, and are in the midst of, or just parting from, the strong and strange events which he and we have had to do with—can in some respects bear valuable, perhaps indispensable testimony concerning him.

I should first like to give a very fair and characteristic like ness of Lincoln, as I saw him and watch'd him one afternoon in Washington, for nearly half an hour, not long before his death. It was as he stood on the balcony of the National Hotel, Pennsylvania Avenue, making a short speech to the crowd in front, on the occasion either of a set of new colors presented to a famous Illinois regiment, or of the daring capture, by the Western men, of some flags from "the enemy," (which latter phrase, by the by, was not used by him at all in his remarks.) How the picture happen'd to be made I do not know, but I bought it a few days afterward in Washington, and it was endors'd by every one to whom I show'd it. Though hundreds of portraits have been made, by painters and photographers, (many to pass on, by copies, to future times,) I have never seen one yet that in my opinion deserv'd to be called a perfectly *good likeness*; nor do I believe there is really such a one in existence. May I not say too, that, as there is no entirely competent and emblematic likeness of Abraham Lincoln in picture or statue, there is not—perhaps cannot be—any fully appropriate literary statement or summing-up of him yet in existence?

The best way to estimate the value of Lincoln is to think what the condition of America would be to-day, if he had never lived—never been President. His nomination and first election were mainly accidents, experiments. Severely view'd, one cannot think very much of American Political Parties, from the beginning, after the Revolutionary War, down to the present time. Doubtless, while they have had their uses—have been and are "the grass on which the cow feeds"—and indispensable economies of growth—it is undeniable that under flippant names they have merely identified temporary passions, or freaks, or sometimes prejudice, ignorance, or hatred. The only thing like a great and worthy idea vitalizing a party, and making it heroic, was the enthusiasm in '64 for re-electing Abraham Lincoln, and the reason behind that enthusiasm.

How does this man compare with the acknowledg'd "Father

of his country?" Washington was model'd on the best Saxon, and Franklin—of the age of the Stuarts (rooted in the Elizabethan period)—was essentially a noble Englishman, and just the kind needed for the occasions and the times of 1776–'83. Lincoln, underneath his practicality, was far less European, was quite thoroughly Western, original, essentially non-conventional, and had a certain sort of out-door or prairie stamp. One of the best of the late commentators on Shakspere, (Professor Dowden,) makes the height and aggregate of his quality as a poet to be, that he thoroughly blended the ideal with the practical or realistic. If this be so, I should say that what Shakspere did in poetic expression, Abraham Lincoln essentially did in his personal and official life. I should say the invisible foundations and vertebra of his character, more than any man's in history, were mystical, abstract, moral and spiritual—while upon all of them was built, and out of all of them radiated, under the control of the average of circumstances, what the vulgar call *horse-sense*, and a life often bent by temporary but most urgent materialistic and political reasons.

He seems to have been a man of indomitable firmness (even obstinacy) on rare occasions, involving great points; but he was generally very easy, flexible, tolerant, almost slouchy, respecting minor matters. I note that even those reports and anecdotes intended to level him down, all leave the tinge of a favorable impression of him. As to his religious nature, it seems to me to have certainly been of the amplest, deepest-rooted, loftiest kind.

Already a new generation begins to tread the stage, since the persons and events of the Secession War. I have more than once fancied to myself the time when the present century has closed, and a new one open'd, and the men and deeds of that contest have become somewhat vague and mythical—fancied perhaps in some great Western city, or group collected together, or public festival, where the days of old, of 1863 and '4 and '5 are discuss'd—some ancient soldier sitting in the background as the talk goes on, and betraying himself by his emotion and moist eyes—like the journeying Ithacan at the banquet of King Alcinoüs, when the bard sings the contending warriors and their battles on the plains of Troy:

“So from the sluices of Ulysses' eyes
 Fast fell the tears, and sighs succeeded sighs.”

I have fancied, I say, some such venerable relic of this time of ours, preserv'd to the next or still the next generation of America. I have fancied, on such occasion, the young men gathering around; the awe, the eager questions: “What! have you seen Abraham Lincoln—and heard him speak—and touch'd his hand? Have you, with your own eyes, look'd on Grant, and Lee, and Sherman?”

Dear to Democracy, to the very last! And among the paradoxes generated by America, not the least curious was that spectacle of all the kings and queens and emperors of the earth, many from remote distances, sending tributes of condolence and sorrow in memory of one rais'd through the commonest average of life—a rail-splitter and flat-boatman!

Consider'd from contemporary points of view—who knows what the future may decide?—and from the points of view of current Democracy and The Union, (the only thing like passion or infatuation in the man was the passion for the Union of These States,) Abraham Lincoln seems to me the grandest figure yet, on all the crowded canvas of the Nineteenth Century.

1888

William H. Herndon & Jesse W. Weik

After his plans to write a Lincoln biography faltered in the late 1860s, Herndon sold copies of his Lincoln research materials to Ward Hill Lamon, a lawyer who had known Lincoln both in Illinois and in the White House. It was used by Lamon and his ghostwriter Chauncey Black in an 1872 biography that aroused controversy by its depiction of the future President's religious "infidelity" as a young man. When Herndon weighed in by delivering a lecture, "Lincoln's Religion," in which he denied that his former partner had been a Christian believer, he was denounced by the *New York Herald* as "Judas in Springfield" and drawn into a bitter public dispute with Mary Todd Lincoln. Herndon's biographical project languished for another decade until he met Jesse W. Weik (1857–1930), a young writer from Indiana. Working from materials provided by Herndon, Weik shaped and wrote *Herndon's Lincoln: The True Story of a Great Life*, which appeared under both their names in 1889. While scholars continue to debate the reliability of some of Herndon's claims, and question his bias against Mary Todd Lincoln (he once privately called her "the female wild cat of the age"), no other author has ever offered more acute first-hand observations of Lincoln's Springfield years, or written more persuasively about his ambition and devotion to reason and logic. The excerpt presented here vividly describes how Lincoln and Stephen A. Douglas squared off against each other in the 1858 Senate contest.

FROM

Herndon's Lincoln:
The True Story of a Great Life

History furnishes few characters whose lives and careers were so nearly parallel as those of Lincoln and Douglas. They met for the first time at the Legislature in Vandalia in 1834, where Lincoln was a member of the House of Representatives and Douglas was in the lobby. The next year Douglas was also a member. In 1839 both were admitted to practice in the Supreme

Court of Illinois on the same day.* In 1841 both courted the same young lady. In 1846 both represented Illinois in Congress at Washington, the one in the upper and the other in the lower House. In 1858 they were opposing candidates for United States Senator; and finally, to complete the remarkable counterpart, both were candidates for the Presidency in 1860. While it is true that their ambitions ran in parallel lines, yet they were exceedingly unlike in all other particulars. Douglas was short,—something over five feet high,—heavy set, with a large head, broad shoulders, deep chest, and striking features. He was polite and affable, but fearless. He had that unique trait, magnetism, fully developed in his nature, and that attracted a host of friends and readily made him a popular idol. He had had extensive experience in debate, and had been trained by contact for years with the great minds and orators in Congress. He was full of political history, well informed on general topics, eloquent almost to the point of brilliancy, self-confident to the point of arrogance, and a dangerous competitor in every respect. What he lacked in ingenuity he made up in strategy, and if in debate he could not tear down the structure of his opponent's argument by a direct and violent attack, he was by no means reluctant to resort to a strained restatement of the latter's position or to the extravagance of ridicule. Lincoln knew his man thoroughly and well.[†] He had often met Douglas on the stump; was familiar with his tactics, and though fully aware of his "want of

---

*December 3d.

[†]An erroneous impression has grown up in recent years concerning Douglas's ability and standing as a lawyer. One of the latest biographies of Lincoln credits him with many of the artifices of the "shyster." This is not only unfair, but decidedly untrue. I always found Douglas at the bar to be a broad, fair, and liberal-minded man. Although not a thorough student of the law his large fund of good common-sense kept him in the front rank. He was equally generous and courteous, and he never stooped to gain a case. I know that Lincoln entertained the same view of him. It was only in politics that Douglas demonstrated any want of inflexibility and rectitude, and then only did Lincoln manifest a lack of faith in his morals.

fixed political morals," was not averse to measuring swords with the elastic and flexible "Little Giant."

Lincoln himself was constructed on an entirely different foundation. His base was plain common-sense, direct statement, and the inflexibility of logic. In physical make-up he was cold—at least not magnetic—and made no effort to dazzle people by his bearing. He cared nothing for a following, and though he had often before struggled for a political prize, yet in his efforts he never had strained his well-known spirit of fairness or open love of the truth. He analyzed everything, laid every statement bare, and by dint of his broad reasoning powers and manliness of admission inspired his hearers with deep conviction of his earnestness and honesty. Douglas may have electrified the crowds with his eloquence or charmed them with his majestic bearing and dexterity in debate, but as each man, after the meetings were over and the applause had died away, went to his home, his head rang with Lincoln's logic and appeal to manhood.

A brief description of Mr. Lincoln's appearance on the stump and of his manner when speaking may not be without interest. When standing erect he was six feet four inches high. He was lean in flesh and ungainly in figure. Aside from the sad, pained look due to habitual melancholy, his face had no characteristic or fixed expression. He was thin through the chest, and hence slightly stoop-shouldered. When he arose to address courts, juries, or crowds of people, his body inclined forward to a slight degree. At first he was very awkward, and it seemed a real labor to adjust himself to his surroundings. He struggled for a time under a feeling of apparent diffidence and sensitiveness, and these only added to his awkwardness. I have often seen and sympathized with Mr. Lincoln during these moments. When he began speaking, his voice was shrill, piping, and unpleasant. His manner, his attitude, his dark, yellow face, wrinkled and dry, his oddity of pose, his diffident movements—everything seemed to be against him, but only for a short time. After having arisen, he generally placed his hands behind him, the back of his left hand in the palm of his right, the thumb and fingers of his right hand clasped around the left arm at the wrist. For a few moments he played the combination of awkwardness, sensitiveness, and diffidence. As he proceeded he became somewhat animated, and to keep in harmony with his growing warmth his hands relaxed their grasp and fell to his side. Presently he clasped them in front of him, interlocking his fingers, one thumb meanwhile chasing another. His speech now requiring more emphatic utterance, his fingers unlocked and his hands fell apart. His left arm was thrown behind, the back of his hand resting against his body, his right hand seeking his side. By this time he had gained sufficient composure, and his real speech began. He did not gesticulate as much with his hands as with his head. He used the latter frequently, throwing it with vim this way and that. This movement was a significant one when he sought to enforce his statement. It sometimes came with a quick jerk, as if throwing off electric sparks into combustible material. He never sawed the air nor rent space into tatters and rags as some orators do. He never acted for stage effect. He was cool, considerate, reflective —in time self-possessed and self-reliant. His style was clear, terse, and compact. In argument he was logical, demonstrative, and fair. He was careless of his dress, and his clothes, instead of fitting neatly as did the garments of Douglas on the latter's well-rounded form, hung loosely on his giant frame. As he moved along in his speech he became freer and less uneasy in his movements; to that extent he was graceful. He had a perfect naturalness, a strong individuality; and to that extent he was dignified. He despised glitter, show, set forms, and shams. He spoke with effectiveness and to move the judgment as well as the emotions of men. There was a world of meaning and emphasis in the long, bony finger of his right hand as he dotted the ideas on the minds of his hearers. Sometimes, to express joy or pleasure, he would raise both hands at an angle of about fifty degrees, the palms upward, as if desirous of embracing the spirit of that which he loved. If the sentiment was one of detestation— denunciation of slavery, for example—both arms, thrown upward and fists clenched, swept through the air, and he expressed an execration that was truly sublime. This was one of his most effective gestures, and signified most vividly a fixed determination to drag down the object of his hatred and trample it in the dust. He always stood squarely on his feet, toe even with toe;

that is, he never put one foot before the other. He neither touched nor leaned on anything for support. He made but few changes in his positions and attitudes. He never ranted, never walked backward and forward on the platform. To ease his arms he frequently caught hold, with his left hand, of the lapel of his coat, keeping his thumb upright and leaving his right hand free to gesticulate. The designer of the monument recently erected in Chicago has happily caught him in just this attitude. As he proceeded with his speech the exercise of his vocal organs altered somewhat the tone of his voice. It lost in a measure its former acute and shrilling pitch, and mellowed into a more harmonious and pleasant sound. His form expanded, and, notwithstanding the sunken breast, he rose up a splendid and imposing figure. In his defence of the Declaration of Independence—his greatest inspiration—he was "tremendous in the directness of his utterances; he rose to impassioned eloquence, unsurpassed by Patrick Henry, Mirabeau, or Vergniaud, as his soul was inspired with the thought of human right and Divine justice."* His little gray eyes flashed in a face aglow with the fire of his profound thoughts; and his uneasy movements and diffident manner sunk themselves beneath the wave of righteous indignation that came sweeping over him. Such was Lincoln the orator.

We can somewhat appreciate the feeling with which Douglas, aggressive and fearless though he was, welcomed a contest with such a man as Lincoln. Four years before, in a joint debate with him, he had asked for a cessation of forensic hostilities, conceding that his opponent of rail-splitting fame had given him "more trouble than all the United States Senate together." Now he was brought face to face with him again.†

It is unnecessary and not in keeping with the purpose of this work to reproduce here the speeches made by either Lincoln or Douglas in their justly renowned debate. Briefly stated, Lin-

---

*Horace White, who was present and reported the speech for his paper, the Chicago *Tribune*, Letter, June 9, 1865, MS.

†"Douglas and I, for the first time this canvass, crossed swords here yesterday. The fire flew some, and I am glad to know I am yet alive."— Lincoln to J. O. Cunningham, Ottawa, Ill., August 22, 1858, MS.

coln's position was announced in his opening speech at Spring-field: "'A house divided against itself cannot stand,' I believe this Government cannot endure permanently half slave and half free. I do not expect the Union to be dissolved, I do not expect the house to fall—but I do expect it will cease to be divided. It will become all the one thing or the other. Either the opponents of slavery will arrest the further spread of it and place it where the public mind shall rest in the belief that it is in the course of ul-timate extinction; or its advocates will push it forward till it becomes alike lawful in all the states, old as well as new, North as well as South." The position of Douglas on the question of slavery was one of indifference. He advocated with all his power the doctrine of "Popular Sovereignty," a proposition, as quaintly put by Lincoln, which meant that, "if one man chooses to en-slave another, no third man has a right to object." At the last joint discussion in Alton, Lincoln, after reflecting on the patri-otism of any man who was so indifferent to the wrong of slavery that he cared not whether it was voted up or down, closed his speech with this stirring summary: "That [slavery] is the real issue. That is the issue that will continue in this country when these poor tongues of Judge Douglas and myself shall be silent. It is the eternal struggle between these two principles—right and wrong—throughout the world. They are the two principles that have stood face to face from the beginning of time, and will ever continue to struggle. The one is the common right of humanity, and the other the divine right of kings. It is the same principle, in whatever shape it develops itself. It is the same spirit that says: 'You work and toil and earn bread, and I eat it.' No matter in what shape it comes, whether from the mouth of a king who seeks to bestride the people of his own nation and live by the fruit of their labor, or from one race of men as an apology for enslaving another race, it is the same tyrannical principle."

It is unnecessary, I presume, to insert here the seven questions which Douglas propounded to Lincoln at their first meeting at Ottawa, nor the historic four which Lincoln asked at Freeport. It only remains to say that in answering Lincoln at Freeport, Douglas accomplished his own political downfall. He was swept entirely away from his former foundation, and even the glory of a subsequent election to the Senate never restored him to it.

During the canvass Mr. Lincoln, in addition to the seven meetings with Douglas, filled thirty-one appointments made by the State Central Committee, besides speaking at many other times and places not previously advertised. In his trips to and fro over the State, between meetings, he would stop at Springfield sometimes, to consult with his friends or to post himself up on questions that occurred during the canvass. He kept me busy hunting up old speeches and gathering facts and statistics at the State library. I made liberal clippings bearing in any way on the questions of the hour from every newspaper I happened to see, and kept him supplied with them; and on one or two occasions, in answer to letters and telegrams, I sent books forward to him. He had a little leather bound book, fastened in front with a clasp, in which he and I both kept inserting newspaper slips and newspaper comments until the canvass opened. In arranging for the joint meetings and managing the crowds Douglas enjoyed one great advantage. He had been United States Senator for several years, and had influential friends holding comfortable government offices all over the State. These men were on hand at every meeting, losing no opportunity to applaud lustily all the points Douglas made and to lionize him in every conceivable way. The ingeniously contrived display of their enthusiasm had a marked effect on certain crowds—a fact of which Lincoln frequently complained to his friends. One who accompanied him during the canvass* relates this: "Lincoln and I were at the Centralia agricultural fair the day after the debate at Jonesboro. Night came on and we were tired, having been on the fair grounds all day. We were to go north on the Illinois Central railroad. The train was due at midnight, and the depot was full of people. I managed to get a chair for Lincoln in the office of the superintendent of the railroad, but small politicians would intrude so that he could scarcely get a moment's sleep. The train came and was filled instantly. I got a seat near the door for Lincoln and myself. He was worn out, and had to meet Douglas the

*Henry C. Whitney, MS., July 21, 1865.

next day at Charleston. An empty car, called a saloon car, was hitched on to the rear of the train and locked up. I asked the conductor, who knew Lincoln and myself well,—we were both attorneys of the road,—if Lincoln could not ride in that car; that he was exhausted and needed rest; but the conductor refused. I afterwards got him in by a stratagem. At the same time George B. McClellan in person was taking Douglas around in a special car and special train; and that was the unjust treatment Lincoln got from the Illinois Central railroad. Every interest of that road and every employee was against Lincoln and for Douglas."

The heat and dust and bonfires of the campaign at last came to an end. The election took place on the second of November, and while Lincoln received of the popular vote a majority of over four thousand, yet the returns from the legislative districts foreshadowed his defeat. In fact, when the Senatorial election took place in the Legislature, Douglas received fifty-four and Lincoln forty-six votes—one of the results of the lamentable apportionment law then in operation.*

---

*Horace Greeley was one of the most vigilant men during the debate. He wrote to Lincoln and me many letters which I still retain. In a letter to me during the campaign, October 6, he says with reference to Douglas: "In his present position I could not of course support him, but he need not have been in this position had the Republicans of Illinois been as wise and far-seeing as they are earnest and true. . . . but seeing things are as they are, I do not wish to be quoted as authority for making trouble and division among our fiends." Soon after hearing of the result of November election he again writes: "I advise you privately that Mr. Douglas would be the strongest candidate that the Democratic party could present for President; but they will not present him. The old leaders wouldn't endorse it. As he is doomed to be slaughtered at Charleston it is good policy to fatten him meantime. He will cut up the better at killing time." An inquiry for his preference as to Presidential timber elicited this response, December 4th. "As to President, my present judgment is Edward Bates, with John M. Read for Vice; but I am willing to go anything that looks strong. I don't wish to load the team heavier than it will pull through. As to Douglas, he is like the man's boy who (he said) 'didn't weigh so much as he expected, and he always knew he wouldn't.' I never thought him very sound coin; but I didn't think it best to beat him on the back of his anti-Lecompton fight and I am still of that opinion."

The letters of Lincoln at this period are the best evidence of his feelings now obtainable, and of how he accepted his defeat. To Henry Asbury, a friend who had written him a cheerful letter admonishing him not to give up the battle, he responded:

"Springfield, November 19, 1858.

"Mr. Henry Asbury,

"My Dear Sir:—Yours of the 13th was received some days ago. The fight must go on. The cause of civil liberty must not be surrendered at the end of one or even one hundred defeats. Douglas had the ingenuity to be supported in the late contest both as the best means to break down and to uphold the slave interest. No ingenuity can keep these antagonistic elements in harmony long. Another explosion will soon come.

"Yours truly,

"A. Lincoln."

To another friend* on the same day he writes: "I am glad I made the late race. It gave me a hearing on the great and durable questions of the age which I could have had in no other way; and though I now sink out of view and shall be forgotten, I believe I have made some marks which will tell for the cause of liberty long after I am gone."

*Dr. Henry.

1889

John G. Nicolay & John Hay

After his nomination in May 1860 Lincoln hired John G. Nicolay (1832–1901) as his private secretary. Nicolay, born in Germany, was a self-educated orphan who had worked for the *Pike County Free Press* in western Illinois before becoming a government clerk in Springfield. Following his election in November, Lincoln chose John Hay (1838–1905), a Brown graduate and nephew of one of his legal colleagues, to assist Nicolay. The two young men journeyed with Lincoln in 1861 to Washington, where they worked and lived with the President in the Executive Mansion for the next four years, serving as his principal secretaries and, aside from clerks lent to the White House by other federal departments, constituting his entire presidential staff. Following the assassination Nicolay and Hay served as diplomats in Europe for several years, then returned to the United States and began working on a monumental biography of Lincoln authorized by Robert Lincoln, who granted them exclusive access to his father's papers. The resulting ten-volume work, *Abraham Lincoln: A History*, was published in 1890. Nicolay and Hay also edited what remained the standard edition of Lincoln's works until the 1950s, and Hay went on to serve as Secretary of State (1898–1905) in the administrations of William McKinley and Theodore Roosevelt. More of an official history of the Lincoln administration than a biography (Lincoln's entire life up to his election in 1860 is covered in the first two volumes), and undoubtedly the work of "Lincoln men all the way through," the Nicolay-Hay volumes remain an incomparable source of information about the inner workings of the Civil War White House. The two authors fashion a convincing portrait of a wise statesman, and increasingly canny executive and commander-in-chief, successfully meeting a series of unprecedented challenges. In this famous section they vividly describe how the President waited in April 1861 for Union troops to arrive in the imperiled national capital.

Abraham Lincoln: A History

The two Sunday interviews of the Mayor of Baltimore with President Lincoln, and the resulting arrangement that troops should hereafter come by the Annapolis route, have been detailed. The telegraph, in the mean time, was still working, though with delays and interruptions. As an offset to the disagreeable necessity of ordering the Pennsylvania troops back from Cockeysville, the cheering news of Butler's arrival at Annapolis had come directly to hand. That same Sunday afternoon President Lincoln and his Cabinet met at the Navy Department, where they might deliberate in greater seclusion, and the culminating dangers to the Government underwent scrutinizing inquiry and anxious comment.

The events of Friday, Saturday, and Sunday, as developed by the military reports and the conferences with the Baltimore committees, exhibited a degree of real peril such as had not menaced the capital since the British invasion in 1814. Virginia was in arms on one side, Maryland on the other; the railroad was broken; the Potomac was probably blockaded; a touch would sever the telegraph. Of this occasion the President afterwards said: "It became necessary for me to choose whether, using only the existing means, agencies, and processes which Congress had provided, I should let the Government at once fall into ruin, or whether, availing myself of the broader powers conferred by the Constitution in cases of insurrection, I would make an effort to save it, with all its blessings, for the present age and for posterity."

Lincoln, Special Message, "Globe," May 27, 1862, p. 2383.

Surveying the emergency in its remote as well as present aspects, and assuming without hesitation the responsibilities which existing laws did not authorize, but which the needs of the hour imperatively demanded, Lincoln made a series of orders designed to meet, as well as might be, the new crisis in public affairs. A convoy was ordered out to guard the California steamers bringing heavy shipments of gold; fifteen merchant steamers were ordered to be purchased or chartered, and armed at the navy yards of Boston, New York, and Philadelphia for coast protection and blockade service; two million dollars were placed in the hands of three eminent citizens of New York, John A. Dix, George Opdyke, and Richard M. Blatchford, to be in their judgment disbursed for the public defense; another commission of leading citizens of New York, George D. Morgan, William M. Evarts, Richard M. Blatchford, and Moses H. Grinnell, in connection with Governor Edwin D. Morgan, was empowered to exercise practically the full authority of the War and Navy Departments in organizing troops and forwarding supplies; two of the ablest naval officers were authorized each to arm two additional merchant vessels to cruise in the Potomac River and Chesapeake Bay; and sundry minor measures and precautions were taken. Before these various orders could even be prepared for transmittal, the crowning embarrassment had come upon the Government. On that Sunday night (April 21) the telegraph operator at Baltimore reported that the insurrectionary authorities had taken possession of his office; to which the Washington telegraph superintendent laconically added, "Of course this stops all."

So the prospect closed on Sunday night. Monday forenoon brought rather an exaggeration of the symptoms of danger. Governor Hicks, influenced by his secession surroundings at Annapolis, neither having consented to Butler's landing nor yet having dissuaded him from that purpose, turned his appeals to the President. "I feel it my duty," he wrote, "most respectfully to advise you that no more troops be ordered or allowed to pass through Maryland, and that the troops now off Annapolis be sent elsewhere; and I most respectfully urge that a truce be offered by you, so that the effusion of blood may be prevented. I respectfully suggest that Lord Lyons be requested to act as mediator between the contending parties of our country." The suggestion was not only absurd in itself, but it awakened painful apprehension lest his hitherto friendly disposition might suddenly change to active hostility. This was a result to be avoided; for, even in his present neutral mood, he was still an effective breakwater against those who were striving day and night to force Maryland into some official act of insurrection. Mr. Seward therefore

Hicks to Lincoln, Apl. 22, 1861. W. R. Vol. II., pp. 588, 589.

wrote the Governor a very kindly and yet dignified rebuke, reminding him of the days "when a general of the American Union with forces designed for the defense of its capital was not unwelcome anywhere in the State of Maryland, and certainly not at Annapolis"; and suggesting at its close "that no domestic contention whatever that may arise among the parties of this Republic ought in any case to be referred to any foreign arbitrament, least of all to the arbitrament of an European monarchy."

Seward to Hicks, Apl. 22, 1861. Moore, "Rebellion Record," Vol. I. Documents, p. 133.

Meanwhile another Baltimore committee found its way to the President—this time from one of the religious bodies of that city, with a Baptist clergyman as its spokesman, who bluntly proposed that Mr. Lincoln should "recognize the independence of the Southern States." Though such audacity greatly taxed his patience, he kept his temper, and replied that neither the President nor Congress possessed the power or authority to do this; and to the further request that no more troops be sent through Maryland, he answered in substance:

You, gentlemen, come here to me and ask for peace on any terms, and yet have no word of condemnation for those who are making war on us. You express great horror of bloodshed, and yet would not lay a straw in the way of those who are organizing in Virginia and elsewhere to capture this city. The rebels attack Fort Sumter, and your citizens attack troops sent to the defense of the Government, and the lives and property in Washington, and yet you would have me break my oath and surrender the Government without a blow. There is no Washington in that—no Jackson in that—there is no manhood or honor in that. I have no desire to invade the South; but I must have troops to defend this capital. Geographically it lies surrounded by the soil of Maryland; and mathematically the necessity exists that they should come over her territory. Our men are not moles, and can't dig under the earth; they are not birds, and can't fly through the air. There is no way but to march across, and that they must do. But in doing this, there is no need of collision. Keep your rowdies in Baltimore, and there will be no bloodshed. Go home and tell your people that if they will not attack us, we will not attack them; but if they do attack us, we will return it, and that severely.

Washington now began to take on some of the aspects of a siege. The large stores of flour and grain at the Georgetown mills, and even that already loaded for shipment on schooners, were seized, and long trains of carts were engaged in removing it to safer storage in the public buildings. Prices of provisions were rising. The little passenger steamers plying on the Potomac were taken possession of by the military officers to be used for guard and picket duty on the river. The doors, windows, and stairways of the public buildings were protected by barricades, and the approaches to them guarded by sentinels. All travel and nearly all business came to a standstill, and theaters and places of amusement were closed.

With the first notice of the burning of the railroad bridges, the strangers, visitors, and transient sojourners in the city became possessed of an uncontrollable desire to get away. So long as the trains ran to Baltimore, they proceeded to that point; from there they sought to escape northward by whatever chances of transportation offered themselves. By some of these fugitives the Government had taken the precaution to send duplicates of important orders and dispatches to Northern cities. This *sauve qui peut* quickly denuded Washington of its redundant population. While the Unionist non-combatants were flying northward, the secessionists were making quite as hurried an escape to the South; for it was strongly rumored that the Government intended to impress the whole male population of Washington into military service for the defense of the city.

One incidental benefit grew out of the panic—the Government was quickly relieved of its treasonable servants. Some hundreds of clerks resigned out of the various departments on this Monday, April 22, and the impending danger not only brought these to final decision, but also many officers of high grades and important functions. Commodore Franklin Buchanan, in charge of the Washington navy yard, together with nearly all his subordinate officers, suddenly discovered their unwillingness longer to keep their oaths and serve the United States; and that night this invaluable navy depot, with all its vast stores of material, its immense workshops and priceless machinery, was intrusted solely to the loyalty and watchfulness of Commander John A. Dahlgren and a little handful of marines, scarcely enough in number to have baffled half a dozen adroit incendiaries, or to ascertain the street gossip outside the walls of the establishment.*

Among the scores of army and navy resignations reported the same day was that of Captain John B. Magruder, 1st Artillery, then in command of a light battery on which General Scott had placed special reliance for the defense of Washington. No single case of defection gave Lincoln such astonishment and pain as this one. "Only three days ago," he said, when the fact was made known to him, "Magruder came voluntarily to me in this room, and with his own lips and in my presence repeated over and over again his asseverations and protestations of loyalty and fidelity." J. H., Diary. MS.

It was not merely the loss of an officer, valuable and necessary though he might be in the emergency, but the significance of this crowning act of perfidy which troubled the President, and to the suggestiveness of which he could not close his eyes. Was there not only no patriotism left, but was all sense of personal obligation, of everyday honesty, and of manliness of character gone also? Was everything crumbling at his touch? In whom should he place confidence? To whom should he give orders, if clerks, and captains, and commodores, and quartermaster-generals, and governors of States, and justices of the Supreme Court proved false in the moment of need? If men of the character and rank of the Magruders, the Buchanans, the

*"Mem. for the War Department. The *Anacostia*, a small Potomac steamer, anchored off Giesboro' Point, and after remaining a short time returned down the river. The *Harriet Lane*, supposed revenue cutter, is now off the Arsenal and has been there a short time. I have not been able to communicate with her. I should wish to have a company of Massachusetts or United States troops in the yard at night if they can be spared.—JOHN A. DAHLGREN, Acting Commandant, 22d April." MS.

McCauleys, the Lees, the Johnstons, the Coopers, the Camp-
bells were giving way, where might he not fear treachery? There
was certainly no danger that all the officers of the Government
would thus prove recreant; but might not the failure of a single
one bearing an important trust cause a vital and irreparable
disaster?

The perplexities and uncertainties of the hour are set forth
with frank brevity by General Scott, in the report which was
sent to the President that night of Monday, April 22:

> I have but little that is certain to report, viz.: *First*, That
> there are three or four steamers off Annapolis, with volun-
> teers for Washington; *Second*, That their landing will be op-
> posed by the citizens, reënforced from Baltimore; *Third*, That
> the landing may be effected nevertheless by good manage-
> ment; and *Fourth*, That the rails on the Annapolis road
> (twenty miles) have been taken up. Several efforts to com-
> municate with those troops to-day have failed; but three
> other detached persons are repeating the attempt, and one or
> more of them will, I think, succeed. Once ashore, the regi-
> ments (if but two, and there are probably more) would have
> no difficulty in reaching Washington on foot, other than the
> want of wagons to transport camp equipage; and the quarter-
> master that I have sent there (I do not know that he has ar-
> rived) has orders to hire wagons if he can, and if not, to im-
> press, etc. Of rumors, the following are probable, viz.: *First*,
> That from 1500 to 2000 troops are at the White House (four
> miles below Mount Vernon, a narrow point in the Potomac)
> engaged in erecting a battery; *Second*, That an equal force is
> collected or in progress of assemblage on the two sides of the
> river to attack Fort Washington; and *Third*, That extra cars
> went up yesterday to bring down from Harper's Ferry about
> 2000 other troops to join in a general attack on this capital
> —that is, on many of its fronts at once. I feel confident that
> with our present forces we can defend the Capitol,
> the Arsenal, and all the executive buildings (seven)   MS.
> against 10,000 troops not better than our district
> volunteers.

Tuesday morning came, but no news from Annapolis, no volunteers up the Potomac. It was Cabinet day; and about noon, after the President and his councilors were assembled, messengers announced the arrival of two steamers at the navy yard. There was a momentary hope that these might be the long-expected ships from New York; but inquiries proved them to be the *Pawnee* and a transport on their return from the expedition to Norfolk. The worst apprehensions concerning that important post were soon realized—it was irretrievably lost. The only bit of comfort to be derived from the affair was that the vessels brought back a number of marines and sailors, who would now add a little fraction of strength to the defense of the capital. The officers of the expedition were soon before the President and Cabinet, and related circumstantially the tale of disaster and destruction which the treachery of a few officers and the credulity of the commandant had rendered unavoidable.

The Gosport navy yard, at Norfolk, Virginia, was of such value and importance that its safety, from the very beginning of Mr. Lincoln's Administration, had neither been overlooked nor neglected. But, like every other exposed or threatened point,—like Sumter, Pickens, Tortugas, Key West, Fort Monroe, Baltimore, Harper's Ferry, and Washington itself,—its fate was involved in the want of an army and navy of adequate strength. The day the President resolved on the Sumter expedition, 250 seamen had been ordered from Brooklyn to Norfolk to render Gosport more safe. Instead of going there, it was thought necessary to change their destination to Sumter and Pickens. And so, though the danger to Gosport was not lost sight of, the reënforcements to ward it off were never available.

The officers of the navy yard were outwardly loyal; the commandant had grown gray in the service of his country, and enjoyed the full confidence of his equals and superiors. It was known that the secessionists had designs upon the post; but it was believed that the watchfulness which had been ordered and the measures of precaution which had been arranged under the special supervision of two trusted officers of the Navy Department, who were carrying out the personal instructions of Secretary Welles, would meet the danger. At a critical moment, Commandant Charles S. McCauley committed a fatal mistake. The subordinate officers of the yard, professing loyalty, practiced treason, and lured him into their designs.

Several valuable vessels lay at the navy yard. To secure them eventually for Virginia, Governor Letcher had, among his first acts of hostility, attempted to obstruct the channel from Norfolk to Fort Monroe by means of sunken vessels. But the effort failed; the passage still remained practicable. Ascertaining this, Commodore James Alden and Chief Engineer Benjamin F. Isherwood, specially sent for the task by Secretary Welles, had, with the help of the commandant of the yard, prepared the best ships—the *Merrimac*, the *Germantown*, the *Plymouth*, and the *Dolphin*—for quick removal to Fort Monroe. The engines of the *Merrimac* were put in order, the fires under her boilers were lighted, the moment of her departure had been announced, when suddenly a change came over the spirit of Commandant McCauley. Virginia passed her ordinance of secession; the traitorous officers of the navy yard were about to throw off their mask and desert their flag; and, as a parting stroke of intrigue, they persuaded the commandant that he must retain the *Merrimac* for the security of the yard. Yielding to this treacherous advice, he countermanded her permission to depart and ordered her fires to be put out. Thus baffled, Isherwood and Alden hastened back to Washington to obtain the superior orders of the Secretary over this most unexpected and astounding action.

They reached Washington on this errand respectively on the 18th and 19th of April, just at the culminating point of insurrection and danger. Hasty consultations were held and energetic orders were issued. The *Pawnee*, just returned from her Sumter cruise, was again coaled, supplied, and fitted out—processes consuming precious hours, but which could not be omitted. On the evening of April 19 she steamed down the Potomac under command of Commodore Hiram Paulding, with discretionary orders to defend or to destroy. Next evening, April 20, having landed at Fort Monroe and taken on board three to five hundred men of the Third Massachusetts, only that morning arrived from Boston, and who embarked without a single ration, the *Pawnee* proceeded to Norfolk, passing without difficulty through the seven sunken hulks in the Elizabeth River. But Commodore Paulding was too late. The commandant, once more successfully plied with insidious advice, had yielded to the second suggestion of his juniors, and had scuttled the removable ships—ostensibly to prevent their being seized and used by the rebels. As they were slowly sinking, no effort to remove them could succeed, and no resource was left but to destroy everything so far as could be done. Accordingly, there being bright moonlight, the greater part of Saturday night was devoted to the work of destruction. Several parties were detailed to fire the ships and the buildings and to lay a mine to blow up the dry-dock, and the sky was soon lighted by an immense conflagration.

Yet, with all this effort, the sacrifice was left incomplete. Not more than half the buildings were consumed. The workshops, with their valuable machinery, escaped. The 1500 to 2000 heavy cannon in the yard could neither be removed nor rendered unserviceable. Some unforeseen accident finally prevented the explosion of the dry-dock. Of the seven ships burned to the water's edge, the hull of the *Merrimac* was soon afterwards raised, and in the course of events changed by the rebels into the iron-clad *Merrimac*, or, as they named her, the *Virginia*. At five o'clock on Sunday morning the *Pawnee* considered her work finished, and steamed away from Gosport, followed by the sailing-ship *Cumberland*.

No point of peril had been so clearly foreseen, and apparently so securely guarded against, as the loss of the three or four valuable ships at Norfolk; and yet, in spite of foresight and precaution, they had gone to worse than ruin through the same train of circumstances which had lost Sumter and permitted the organization of the Montgomery rebellion. The loss of ships and guns was, however, not all; behind these was the damaging moral effect upon the Union cause and feeling.

For four consecutive days each day had brought a great disaster—Virginia's secession on the 17th; the burning of Harper's Ferry on the 18th; the Baltimore riot and destruction of railroad bridges on the 19th; the abandonment and destruction of the great navy yard and its ships on the night of the 20th. This began to look like an irresistible current of fate. No popular sentiment could long stem such a tide of misfortune. The rebels of Virginia, Maryland, and especially of Washington began to feel that Providence wrought in their behalf, and that their conspiracy was already crowned with success. Evidently with such a feeling, on this same Tuesday, Associate Justice John A. Campbell, still a member of the Supreme Court and under oath to support the Constitution of the United States, again sent a letter of aid and comfort to Jefferson Davis. He wrote:

> Maryland is the object of chief anxiety with the North and the Administration. Their fondest hope will be to command the Chesapeake and relieve this capital. Their pride and their fanaticism would be sadly depressed by a contrary issue. This will be the great point of contest in all negotiations. . . . I incline to think that they are prepared to abandon the south of the Potomac. But not beyond. Maryland is weak. She has no military men of talents, and I did hear that Colonel Huger was offered command and declined it—however, his resignation had not been accepted. Huger is plainly not competent for such a purpose. Lee is in Virginia. Think of the condition of Baltimore and provide for it, for there is the place of danger. The events at Baltimore have placed a new aspect upon everything to the North. There is a perfect storm there. While it has to be met, no unnecessary addition should be made to increase it.
>
> Campbell to Davis, Apl. 23, 1861. MS.

Another night of feverish public unrest, another day of anxiety to the President—Wednesday, April 24. There was indeed no attack on the city; but, on the other hand, no arrival of troops to place its security beyond doubt. Repetition of routine duties; repetition of unsubstantial rumors; long faces in the streets; a holiday quiet over the city; closed shutters and locked doors of business houses; the occasional clatter of a squad of cavalry from point to point; sentinels about the departments; sentinels about the Executive Mansion; Willard's Hotel, which a week before was swarming with busy crowds, now deserted as if smitten by a plague, with only furtive servants to wake echoes along the vacant corridors—an oppressive contrast to the throng of fashion and beauty which had so lately made it a scene of festivity from midday to midnight.

Ever since the telegraph stopped on Sunday night, the Washington operators had been listening for the ticking of their instruments, and had occasionally caught fugitive dispatches passing between Maryland secessionists, which were for the greater part immediately known to be untrustworthy; for General Scott kept up a series of military scouts along the Baltimore railroad as far as Annapolis Junction, twenty miles from Washington, from which point a branch railroad ran at a right angle to the former, twenty miles to Annapolis, on Chesapeake Bay. The general dared not risk a detachment permanently to hold the junction; no considerable secession force had been encountered, and the railroad was yet safe. But it was known, or at least strongly probable, that the volunteers from the North had been at Annapolis since Sunday morning. Why did they not land? Why did they not advance? The Annapolis road was known to be damaged; but could they not march twenty miles?

The previous day (April 23) had, by some lucky chance, brought a New York mail three days old. The newspapers in it contained breezy premonitions of the Northern storm— Anderson's enthusiastic reception; the departure of the Seventh New York regiment; the sailing of Governor Sprague with his Rhode Islanders; the monster meeting in Union Square, with the outpouring of half a million of people in processions and listening to speeches from half a dozen different stands; the energetic measures of the New York Common Council; the formation of the Union Defense Committee; whole columns of orders and proclamations; the flag-raisings; the enlistments; the chartering and freighting of ships; and from all quarters news of the wild, jubilant uprising of the whole immense population of the free States. All this was gratifying, pride-kindling, reassuring; and yet, read and re-read with avidity in Washington that day, it would always bring after it the galling reflection that all this magnificent outburst of patriotism was paralyzed by the obstacle of a twenty miles' march between Annapolis and the junction. Had the men of the North no legs?

Lincoln, by nature and habit so calm, so equable, so undemonstrative, nevertheless passed this period of interrupted communication and isolation from the North in a state of nervous tension which put all his great powers of mental and physical endurance to their severest trial. General Scott's reports, though invariably expressing his confidence in successful defense, frankly admitted the evident danger; and the President, with his acuteness of observation and his rapidity and correctness of inference, lost no single one of the external indications of doubt and apprehension. Day after day prediction failed and hope was deferred; troops did not come, ships did not arrive, railroads remained broken, messengers failed to reach their destination. That fact itself demonstrated that he was environed by the unknown—and that whether a Union or a Secession army would first reach the capital was at best an uncertainty.

To a coarse or vulgar nature such a situation would have brought only one of two feelings—either overpowering personal fear, or overweening bravado. But Lincoln, almost a giant in physical stature and strength, combined in his intellectual nature a masculine courage and power of logic with an ideal sensitiveness of conscience and a sentimental tenderness as delicate as a woman's. This Presidential trust which he had assumed was to him not a mere regalia of rank and honor. Its terrible duties and responsibilities seemed rather a coat of steel armor, heavy to bear, and cutting remorselessly into the quick flesh. That one of the successors of Washington should find himself even to this degree in the hands of his enemies was personally humiliating; but that the majesty of a great nation should be thus insulted and its visible symbols of authority be placed in jeopardy; above all, that the hitherto glorious example of the republic to other nations should stand in this peril of surprise and possible sudden collapse, the Constitution be scoffed, and human freedom become a by-word and reproach—this must have begot in him an anxiety approaching torture.

In the eyes of his countrymen and of the world he was holding the scales of national destiny; he alone knew that for the moment the forces which made the beam vibrate with such uncertainty were beyond his control. In others' society he gave no sign of these inner emotions. But once, on the afternoon of the

23d, the business of the day being over, the Executive office deserted, after walking the floor alone in silent thought for nearly half an hour, he stopped and gazed long and wistfully out of the window down the Potomac in the direction of the expected ships; and, unconscious of other presence in the room, at length broke out with irrepressible anguish in the repeated exclamation, "Why don't they come! Why don't they come!"

One additional manifestation of this bitterness of soul occurred on the day following, though in a more subdued manner. The wounded soldiers of the Sixth Massachusetts, including several officers, came to pay a visit to the President. They were a little shy when they entered the room—having the traditional New England awe of authorities and rulers. Lincoln received them with sympathetic kindness which put them at ease after the interchange of the first greetings. His words of sincere thanks for their patriotism and their suffering, his warm praise of their courage, his hearty recognition of their great service to the public, and his earnestly expressed confidence in their further devotion, quickly won their trust. He spoke to them of the position and prospect of the city, contrasting their prompt arrival with the unexplained delay which seemed to have befallen the regiments supposed to be somewhere on their way from the various States. Pursuing this theme, he finally fell into a tone of irony to which only intense feeling ever drove him. "I begin to believe," said he, "that there is no North. The Seventh regiment is a myth. Rhode Island is another. You are the only real thing." There are few parchment brevets as precious as such   J. H., a compliment, at such a time, from such a man.   Diary. MS.

                                                            1890

William O. Stoddard

Born in upstate New York, Stoddard (1835–1925) became co-editor of the *Central Illinois Gazette* in 1858. He liked to boast that he was the first newspaperman to endorse Abraham Lincoln for president, a claim he made often in his numerous writings about Lincoln. Initially hired to sign land patents in the Interior Department, Stoddard became the so-called "third secretary" at the White House in mid-1861, taking charge of the incoming correspondence, which sometimes approached an overwhelming 500 letters and parcels daily. He held the position until 1864, when Lincoln appointed him U.S. marshal for eastern Arkansas, and he also contributed more than 100 dispatches (signed "Illinois") to the *New York Examiner* while working at the White House. After the war Stoddard published more than 100 books, including 76 written for boys; his works on Lincoln include an 1884 biography and the 1890 memoir *Inside the White House in War Times*, whose opening chapters examine Lincoln's grueling daily routine—replete with lines of visitors, lax security, bustling family activities, and voluminous paperwork.

FROM

Inside the White House in War Times

CHAPTER I

Opening the Door

BEFORE me on the table lies a small brass latch-key. It has a worn-out look, as if it had served its time and had been honorably discharged, but if it had a tongue few other keys could tell so notable a history. During the administrations of seventeen successive Presidents of the United States, it opened the front door of the Executive Mansion at Washington. The lock it belonged to was put on when that house was built, and was replaced by a new one in the time of President Grant. In my own mind and memory, this key is associated with the years which I spent in and about the White House; the years of Lincoln's administration; the days of the Civil War; the terrible furnace time, during which, as it then and ever since has seemed to me, the old nation melted away and a new nation was moulded.

This is the year 1861, and although it is so early in the spring the weather is warm. Suppose we stroll toward the White House.

The short, thin, smiling, humorous-looking elderly Irishman in the doorway is Old Edward, the all but historic doorkeeper, who has been so great a favorite through so many administrations. He is as well liked by his seventh President as he was by even General Taylor. There is no end of quiet fun in him as well as intelligence, and his other name is Fidelity. He is said to have been the first man met in the White House by Mr. Lincoln who succeeded in making him laugh.

"Mr. Secretary"—and he is holding out something upon the palm of his open hand—"I've been getting some new latch-keys for the young gentlemen. I don't know what's become of the keys we had. Maybe they've gone South and mean to come back, some day, and open the door."

Two of the keys are bright and new, but one is old and tarnished.

"There's one for Mr. Nicolay, and one for Mr. Hay, and one for yourself. That's the old one, that belonged to the lock when it was put on."

"That's the key I want, Edward. Give Nicolay and Hay the new ones."

"It's like meself—it can open the door as well as ever it could," laughs Old Edward.

We have the key, therefore, and we can go into and out of the house as we please.

Americans are sufficiently familiar with the external appearance of this simple white oblong structure, built upon this low rise of ground sloping to the Potomac. Yonder, westward, are the dingy old War and Navy buildings. Eastward is the Treasury, half built, part old, part new, and beyond it lies most of the city, and just one mile distant, in that direction, is the Capitol. This pillared portico and covered carriageway, on the north front of the house is where Lincoln will stand in a few days to review the first troops that are coming from the North. The secessionists hold Baltimore and claim Maryland, and Washington City is in a besieged condition. Its communications with the rest of the world are almost cut off, and there is no use in saying how easily it might be captured by a small body of daring men—Ethan Allens of the Confederacy.

A sort of uncanny glamour seems to have been settling upon the city, week after week. It has grown under the shadow of the tremendous events which are to come. It will remain long, and it will not entirely depart until the end of Andrew Johnson's term. It is a strange and shuddering kind of thing, and its central, darkest, most bewildering witchcraft works around this Executive Mansion.

The stones of the pavement of this portico are foot-worn into furrows, and every furrow is a kind of historical wrinkle. There! When you try it, the door opens to this key, now, in these early days of the Civil War, as it may have opened to it in the hands of Thomas Jefferson or Andrew Jackson.

Within the doorway there is a mere coop of a lobby, and beyond that is an ample vestibule. This is where they sometimes set up the racks for hats and coats on grand reception evenings. All along through March, after the inauguration, this was one of the most anxious places on the face of the earth, but it was not at all on account of the Rebellion. Men gathered in groups up and down the walks, outside, and filled the portico, and there was anxiety out there; but in here there was more of it, for the crowd was denser. They were all patriots and they loved their country and they were willing to serve it, here or at their homes, and they were all anxious to see the President.

This door, to the left, leads into a broad entryway. That flight of stairs goes up to the business part of the house. That is the door of the great East Room, the White House drawing-room. There, at the heel of the stairway, is the place for the Marine Band to sit and make music on reception evenings, but no band could have found any footing there during that first rush of office-seekers. The greater part of each day the East Room itself was thronged. The first men who volunteered for the defense of any part of Washington were a full battalion of these very patriots who crowded the White House. They bravely proposed to have guns furnished them and to bivouac in the East Room on the floor all night, so they would be here in the morning, first thing, ahead of anybody else, with their muskets stacked around them, and with better chances for interviews with Lincoln. Those were exciting days when, for hours and hours, the anterooms and halls upstairs were so full that they would hold no more, and when this broad staircase itself was also packed and jammed, stair by stair, from top to bottom, so that you could hardly squeeze your way up or down. It was all cut short by one of Lincoln's decrees. He decided not to interfere with his Cabinet officers in the selection of their clerks and other subordinates. As he expressed it, he "ceased to have any influence with this Administration" in the matter of appointments to minor offices.

The East Room has a faded, worn, untidy look, in spite of its frescoing and its glittering chandeliers. Its paint and furniture require renewal; but so does almost everything else about the house, within and without. Westward from the East Room, facing south, are the three reception rooms—the Blue Room, another, and the Red Room. The latter is the special private and public reception-room of the lady of the White House. Between these and the vestibule runs a broad hall, from the East Room to the entrance of the State Dining-room. The remainder of this floor, westward, belongs to family uses, and beyond all, without, is the conservatory, a respectable affair, and containing many rare and valuable plants.

The anxious throng of office-seekers long since dwindled from a river into a brook of manageable size. There is nobody at all here this morning, and we will go upstairs. At the head of them is a spacious entryway, and as we stand here, looking southward, to the right of us are apartments which are used as sleeping-rooms, but which, hereafter, will be turned into offices.

This fine broad hall that we next walk into runs the entire length of the building, east and west. Yonder, across the hall, is a large room which serves as a citadel and place of refuge for Presidents to retreat into when they are too severely pressed in their own business office adjoining, on the east. Beyond that, in the southeastern corner of the house, is the private secretary's

office, occupied now by Mr. Nicolay and his immediate assistant, Mr. Hay. This large chamber on the north side of the hall
is their sleeping-room. The northeastern room, next to it, a
narrow room, corresponding to Mr. Nicolay's office on the
other side of the hall, contains three desks. The two upright,
antiquated, mahogany structures in the further corners belong
to Mr. Hay. This heavy-looking table-desk of drawers, green-
clothed and curiously littered, out here in front of the door,
with its left elbow toward the fireplace, is to be yours through
several years to come. It is, in some respects, a kind of breakwater, and the duties attached to it will be almost entirely separated from those performed by the other private secretaries.

We have a good reason for visiting the White House so very
early, before the beginning of its official business hours.

It is the morning of the 12th of April, 1861, and at no previous date has the cloud hung so low above the White House, nor
has the air here and throughout the country been so painfully
dense with doubt and suspense, and with the dread of that which
must surely come. The Civil War really began long ago, but it
has not yet been wise for the President to say as much, nor to
ask for troops to carry it on with. Leaving the northeast room,
and walking westward along the hall, it seems a gloomy, shadowy, chilly corridor, and not a living soul is to be seen in it. The
hall is severed here, near the head of the stairs, by folding doors,
but they are wide open. Beyond, to the left, in the middle, is the
very pleasant library, and adjoining it is the chamber in which
Mr. Lincoln will one day lie, sick with the varioloid. Then come
other folding doors, and behind them are the rooms of the
family.

A remarkably tall and forward-bending form is coming
through the further folding doors, leaving them carelessly open
behind him. He is walking slowly, heavily, like a man in a dream.
His strongly marked features have a drawn look, there are dark
circles under his deep-set eyes, and these seem to be gazing at
something far away, or into the future.

The President knows, as only a few others know, that the
bombardment of Fort Sumter, in the harbor of the city of Charleston, S.C., has probably, has almost certainly, begun already,

although positive official information of the fact cannot arrive until tomorrow.

We ourselves have no idea that all his soul is listening for the Sumter gun, while all his mind is busy with its consequences.

"Good morning, Mr. Lincoln."

For a moment he stands still, looking down into your face, but the far-away expression of his own does not change. He may be looking, prophetically, at future battlefields, and hearing the roar of other cannon than those in Charleston harbor, but you do not understand, and you exclaim, in astonishment:

"Why, Mr. Lincoln! you don't seem to know me!"

"Oh, yes, I do," he responds, wearily. "What is it?"

"I wish to ask a favor."

His lips contract as he asks, half petulantly,

"Well, well—what is it?"

Every man, almost, that he is meeting, every day and all day long, is saying about the same thing.

"It's just this, Mr. Lincoln: I believe there is going to be fighting, pretty soon, right here, and I don't feel like sitting at a desk in the Patent Office, or here, either, while any fight is going on. I've been serving with a company already, and if it's ordered on duty I want to go with it——"

"Well, well," he interrupts, but with a quickly brightening face, "why don't you go?"

"Why, Mr. Lincoln, only a few days ago I took a pretty big oath to obey your orders, and now I'm likely to be asked to take another to obey somebody else. I don't see how I can manage them both without your permission. I may be ordered to service outside of the District of Columbia——"

He is all but smiling as he cuts the explanation short with:

"Go ahead! Go ahead! Swear in! Go wherever you are ordered to go."

"That's all I want, Mr. Lincoln."

You have turned away, but he has called you back, and he says to you, earnestly,

"Young man, go just where you're ordered. Do your duty. You won't lose anything by this!"

A memorable morning interview with Lincoln is over, but it

will seem, at a later day, listening back through the years, as if the roar of the "Sumter gun" broke through the brooding, ominous silence almost instantly. You will know, however, that the news did not reach Washington until the next day, the 13th; that the proclamation calling for troops went out on Sunday, the 14th; and that while the country was reading it in the papers of Monday morning, the 15th, the first company of volunteers that was mustered in, "Company A, Third Battalion," was drawn up in front of the War Office to be sworn, and that you became a three-months' volunteer private soldier by special permission of the President.

There is an accumulated heap of land patents, waiting the pen of a secretary to sign patents for land. They are old affairs, and not many new ones are making out now, and your entire work is soon to be transferred from your snug office in the Interior Department building to the former table-desk in the northeast room.

The duties of a private in Company A are severe, but furloughs of a few hours' each can be had, now and then, to sign important papers or to make flying visits to the White House. Going or coming, or in camp, or on guard duty, you are more and more convinced that all the young women of Washington, and some that are older, know more or less how to play the piano. The tone of the piano-playing part of Washington society, moreover, is in romantic sympathy with "the sunny South," and there is a perpetual tinkle of the favorite secession airs pouring through the windows, which they leave open for the benefit of any Northern vandals who may happen to pass within hearing.

The first favorite of all is "Dixie's Land," and its music has sounded almost day and night until it has taken on a weird, spell-like influence, and it seems a part and a voice of this horrible glamour that sweeps in upon the souls and hearts of men. It fairly makes one shudder to have that tune spring out upon him when he least expects it. A little behind "Dixie," in persistency of repetition, are the "Bonnie Blue Flag," and "Maryland, my Maryland."

The Pennsylvania Fifth has arrived, but it came without any muskets, and it brought no music. The New York Seventh is here, and the Massachusetts Eighth, and the blockade of Washington is broken through. Splendid bands, fine music, a magnificent river of steel points glittering down the avenue, but the bands play only commonplace national music, and the like. Company A is too busy to more than know that relief has come, although it met the Seventh at Annapolis Junction; but to-day the New York Twelfth has arrived, and is forming at the railway depot near the Capitol, and the orders you are obeying will take you with them.

Full company front, in excellent drill, perfect equipment, bayonets glittering, flags flying, and a brass band that makes a rank all the way across the avenue. The drums beat, and your heart beats for a moment as the gallant boys step off. What's that?

"I wish I was in Dixie! Look away!"

Hurrah! They are playing as if for a wager, and the cheering along the thronged sidewalks answers uproariously. Suddenly, as if a counter spell had been uttered, the weird and mocking power has passed away from the boding melody, and yet, somehow, it will never sound to you like any other tune.

We are half-way down the avenue, keeping step with the Twelfth. There is again only a roll of drums for a moment, and then that blessed band puts all its musical energies into the "Bonnie Blue Flag," past square after square. On sweeps the splendid regiment until it wheels around the Treasury corner to the front of the Executive Mansion, and pours through the wide gateway to pass in review before the waiting President. Again the music changes, and the serried ranks swing forward to the noble cadences of "Maryland, my Maryland," for Baltimore has been occupied by General Butler and his men, and the National Government can safely call the old State "mine."

The young women of Washington City cease playing "Dixie." They shut their windows and mournfully declare that the Yankees have stolen even the national music of the South. Northern or Southern, we are none of us altogether sane in these feverish, bewildered, half-delirious days, but cannot a fever be cured without bleeding the patient?

There are sanguine people who express that kind of hope in

spite of all that has been done, including the Sumter affair, but the State of Virginia is to take an important vote on the 23d of May, and at sunset of that day it will be known whether or not the Old Dominion is to join the Confederacy. Can anybody know beforehand the result of a State election? Perhaps not; but the President is so sure in his own mind that Virginia will adopt the Ordinance of Secession that he has ordered the Union forces to be ready to cross the Potomac at sunset of May 23, this very week upon which we are entering.

Nothing, however, could be more peaceful than is the White House as we enter it this Sunday morning. The President and Mrs. Lincoln are beginning with an effort to keep Sunday, and they have gone to church. They try to be private citizens once a week, but the circumstances are against them. Robert is away at college. The children are in the other part of the house. The two private secretaries may be at church for all we know—they are not in their office. The doors of the rooms are all wide open.

"Hullo, Ellsworth, are you here?"

"Yes, I'm all the President there is on hand this morning. I got away from camp to run over and see him and the boys."

He is a brilliant young fellow, and you like him, and you have an idea that if a war is to come he will play a prominent part in it. He is brimming, running over with health, high spirits, ambition, hope, and all the exuberant life of a rarely vigorous nature. You have been drilling hard as a soldier since a fortnight or so before you were sworn in, and he has picked up a carbine that was leaning against the wall. Put him through the manual of arms, for he has the name of being the most perfect master of it in the army. How like a piece of human mechanism are all his clock-work movements! There! He was standing too near the south window, and the order which brought the butt of that piece against his shoulder sent the muzzle of it through a pane of glass. So much for your defective tactics, and this war is to be a record of badly directed forces. You and he are boys, and when the private secretaries come in, for they too are boys, you can tell them that some assassin, lurking in the shrubbery down yonder, must have mistaken Colonel Ellsworth for the President. His bullet missed its mark, but it ruined the pane of glass. It is but a passing jest, but it illustrates the strong hold which the idea of probable assassination has already taken upon the minds of men.

Has a whole week passed since then? Yes; and here we are, in the same room, standing by the same window. Virginia has been invaded, and on the night in which Ellsworth was slain you were with Company A, and it was given by General Stone the honor of being the first to cross the bridge. The Twelfth New York came next, and now, indeed, they are in Dixie.

"Yes, General Leavenworth, last Sunday morning Ellsworth was here, about this time, and he stood exactly where you are standing. Do you see that?"

The marks of the glazier's fingers on the new glass illustrate the story, but the bright and gay young soldier has fallen on the very threshold of the war in which he hoped to be a leader. The river, down there, at which he and you were looking, has become the northern boundary line of the Confederacy. This White House itself has become the headquarters of a frontier post as well as of the armies of the Republic. The heights, yonder, on the south bank of the Potomac, are within the enemy's country. A Confederate flag floated upon Arlington House last Sunday, but it is not there now, and one reason why the heights were so promptly occupied and fortified by the national troops was that a battery planted upon them could have pitched its shot and shell through the windows of the White House, or into the halls and chambers of the Capitol.

CHAPTER II

Persons and Papers

THIS large south-fronting room has been the business office of all the Presidents who have lived in this house. In one sense it is the nerve-centre of the Republic. It is a wonderful historic cavern to move about in. The hearts and brains of a great people are somehow in connection with it, and they send to this chamber their blind impulses, their thrills of hope, their faintnesses of disappointment, their shivers of fear, and even their sinking of despair.

Mr. Lincoln will be here in a few minutes. He was always an early riser, and it is a good habit for him to have in these over-worked times. He is apt to come striding along the hall at farm hours, as if he were in haste to get here and finish something left over from last evening, or attend to some crisis which came in the night, before the daily procession of visitors can set in.

That long table in the middle of the room is the board around which the Cabinet sits in council, and they are gathered there frequently, nowadays. How they appear when they are gathered will be very well imagined by future generations after looking at Carpenter's picture of the first reading of the Emancipation Proclamation, which is to be painted a few years hence and hung upon a wall of the Capitol. In that picture, however, without purpose of the painter, Mr. Montgomery Blair, the Postmaster-General, will be made to stand upon the square yard of carpet he occupied when he and the President took leave of each other, coldly, formally, without any hand-shaking, the day he ceased to be a member of the Cabinet.

These meetings are wonderfully secret affairs. Only a private secretary may enter the room to so much as bring in a paper. No breath of any "Cabinet secret" will ever transpire, so faithfully is the seal of this room guarded.

There is hardly an ornamental or a superfluous article of furniture in the room. This second-hand mahogany upright desk, from some old furniture auction—or that is what it looks like—here by the middle window, is Mr. Lincoln's working-desk. This is the place where he is expected to perform his political and military miracles. Matters of all kinds are put into shape here for after-consideration by the Cabinet, when they assemble around the long table to be informed why they were sent for. It is not often, however, that a paper or plan prepared by Mr. Lincoln is much changed in its appearance at the end of a meeting.

The opposite rule prevails at the Capitol, for Congress is all the while in a bubble and boil over business which goes to it from this desk. It is their privilege to cut and slash, very much as Tad and Willie are cutting and slashing something or other, on the floor, under and behind and all around this Republican throne. There is nothing on the desk but a few bundles of papers and an outspread map. It is a map of part of the regions which are beginning to be overrun with armies, and now that the President has come in and has dropped into his chair, his forehead wrinkles more deeply than usual as he leans forward. No doubt he knows what he means when he removes a red-headed pin on the map from the junction of the Ohio and Mississippi, at Cairo, and sticks it in again, further down the river. Next goes a black-headed pin away over into Missouri, and it may be that he is thinking of Frémont; but nobody can guess why the blue-headed pin is transferred from Cincinnati down into the heart of Kentucky. It is a way he has of studying the movements of the forces on both sides, and a lot of fresh telegraphic dispatches has just been brought in from the War Office and put down upon the Cabinet table.

There must be something in them, by the brightened look on the President's face as he reads them and puts them down.

What a yell! But it comes from the forces belonging to quite another seat of war. Tad has been trying to make a war-map of Willie, and there are rapid movements in consequence on both sides. Peace is obtained by sending them to their mother, at the other end of the building, but the President does not return to his desk. He is studying one of the maps he has pulled down from the spring-roller above the lounge on the eastern side of the room. It is an outline map of West Virginia and the mountain ranges, and it is likely that something important is going on there.

In the northwestern corner of the room there are standing racks, with many map-rollers, and there are folios of maps on the floor and leaning against the walls. The area of this war, by land and sea, is widening, but the operations at all points are watched and studied, and in their general outline are governed from, and are continually reported to, this central heart and brain room in this civil and military headquarters of the nation.

Hunting for generals? That is it exactly. The President is

collecting and equipping armies, and he is compelled to direct them, more or less, during the processes of creation, but he is all the while searching for men who can take that responsibility off his hands. The men who are willing to take it are hunting him, too, and he could make up a regiment out of the applicants for stars.

The stack of papers on the Cabinet table, when we were in that room, related entirely to brigadier appointments. So do all these rubber-banded bundles in this deep drawer and in that. They gather day by day, and each batch must have a written digest made of its character. It is hard to digest some of them. Men ask authority to lead brigades, who cannot place a company in line, or put an awkward squad through the manual of arms.

There is a world of mournful fun in some of these brigadier papers, and Mr. Lincoln now and then succeeds in laughing over them, as well as in losing his temper.

What is in that other cram-full drawer? Post chaplains, and their papers also require much digestion. The President has an idea that most of the men who are anxious for the rank and pay of religious majors, without the toil and exposure and peril of keeping company with a regiment in the field, are what he calls "loose-footed ministers," and he does not take to them kindly.

Here is our special work coming in. The big sack that Louis, the President's messenger, is perspiring under, contains the morning's mail. What a pile it makes, as he pours it out upon the table! Why, no, it is no larger than usual. Heaps of newspapers? Yes, and no. We have to buy the newspapers we really need and read, like other people, but a host of journals, all over the country, supply the White House gratis. Open them if you wish to learn how the course of human events, and of the President in particular, is really influenced. How very many of these sagacious editors have blue-and-redded their favorite editorials, and have underscored their most stinging paragraphs!

That is because they fear lest Mr. Lincoln may otherwise fail to be duly impressed. He might even not see the points! His first complete failure was an attempt he made to watch the course of public opinion as expressed by the great dailies East and West. After he gave up reading them, he had a daily brief made for him to look at, but at the end of a fortnight he had not once found time to glance at it, and we gave it up.

Besides all other difficulties, the editors are dancing around the situation in such a manner that no man can follow them without getting too dizzy for regular work.

Put aside the journals now, and take up the kind of written papers which come through the post in bundles and bales, mostly sealed a great deal. Do you see what they are? That pile is of applications for appointments to offices of every name and grade, all over the land. They must be examined with care, and some of them must be briefed before they are referred to the departments and bureaus with which the offices asked for are connected. We will not show any of them to Mr. Lincoln at present.

That other pile contains matter that belongs here. They are "pardon papers," and this desk has the custody of them, but their proper place, one would think, is in the War Office. That is where they all must go, after a while; but the President wishes them where he can lay his hands upon them, and every batch of papers and petitions must be in order for him when he calls for it. He will surely do so when some more or less mournful delegation comes to see him about it. He is downright sure to pardon any case that he can find a fair excuse for pardoning, and some people think he carries his mercy too far. There was a vast amount of probable pardon, for instance, in a bale of papers which should have been here day before yesterday. It came from a guerrilla-stricken district in the West, for the pardon of the worst guerrilla in it, and the petitions were largely and eminently and influentially signed. There came up to the President's office in great haste a large and eminent and influential delegation, and the papers were sent for. Somehow or other they were not here. They may have been at the War Office, but the people there denied it. They may have been somewhere else, but the people there denied it, and the delegation had to go away, and the application still hangs fire.

"What did you say? A telegram from——? You don't tell me! Has that man been actually hung? It's a pity about his papers! Seems to me—well, yes, I remember now. I know where——"

"Well, if I did, I guess I wouldn't; not now; but if they're ever called for again, and they won't be, they ought to be where they can be found."

"Certainly, certainly. But it's just as well that one murderer has escaped being pardoned by Abraham Lincoln. Narrow escape, too! The merest piece of luck in all the world!"

There is no sameness in the sizes of the White House mails. Some days there will be less than 200 separate lots, large and small. Some days there will be over 300. Anyhow, every envelope must be opened and its contents duly examined.

Are they all read? Not exactly, with a big wicker waste-basket on either side of this chair. A good half of each mail belongs in them, as fast as you can find it out. The other half calls for more or less respectful treatment, but generally for judicious distribution among the departments, with or without favorable remarks indorsed upon it.

It is lightning work, necessarily, but have you noticed this fine-looking, well-dressed, elderly gentleman, who is sitting in the chair by the mantel? He has been watching, with increasing feverishness, the swift processes which dispose of the President's mail. He has narrowly noted the destructions and the references, and not while he has sat there has a solitary letter been discovered of the kind which seems to require the personal inspection and decision of Mr. Lincoln. It is not often that a mail, morning or evening, brings more than two or three envelopes of that kind. Upon all others the President's judgment is passed as nearly as his proxy can imagine it, and, at all events, the verdict is absolute and final.

The elderly gentleman looks as if he might be a judge, or a college president, or even a Governor, at home, but he is not at home now. The chances are two to one that he has at some time written letters to Mr. Lincoln, and now he is here, and he has sent in his card and he is waiting for an interview. His face is waxing very red and he squirms upon his chair, but we will not let him know we are watching him, and we will put aside that little heap of opened letters by themselves.

The explosion is coming! He actually stamps with anger as he exclaims:

"Is that the way you treat the President's mail? Mr. Lincoln does not know this! What would the people say if they knew that their communications to their Chief Magistrate are dealt with in this shameful manner? Thrown into the waste-basket! What does Lincoln mean? Putting such an awful responsibility into the hands of a mere boy! A boy!"

It is a storm of hot and fiery indignation, but it pauses for breath, and you can hand him the selected lot of opened letters at your elbow.

"Please read those, sir, and give me your own opinion of them. I may be right about them. Do you really think, now, that the President of the United States ought to turn from the affairs of the nation to put in his time on that sort of thing?"

He has them and he is reading, and his fiery face is getting redder yet as he goes along. Now he has struck something that makes him go the other way, and he is positively white with wrath. It was almost too mischievous to give him that horrible selection.

The letters in the hands of that dignified but angry critic tell stories of partisan bitterness and personal hatred; of the most venomous malice, seeking to shoot with poisoned arrows of abuse; of low, slanderous meannesses; of the coarsest, foulest vulgarity to which beastly men can sink; of the wildest, the fiercest and the most obscene ravings of utter insanity; and the elderly gentleman throws them upon the table and sinks back in his chair, for a moment almost speechless with shame and indignation. He has found his breath:

"You are right, young man! You are right! He ought not to see a line of that stuff! Burn it, sir! Burn it! What devils there are!"

He is pacing hotly up and down the room, but the messenger has come to summon him to an interview with the President, and he probably will not complain of what he saw doing here.

Nevertheless, this mail has not contained a larger percentage than usual of the evidence that when any man goes clean crazy in these war-days he at once sits down and pens an epistle to the President. That close-lined, four-page letter, written in red, which professes to be blood, comes every day, and is always signed "The Angel Gabriel," but the contents are the reverse of angelic. This long, elaborate, remarkably well-written, seemingly wise and sound volume of advice concerning the policy to be pursued by the Administration is a curiosity. It is calm, sane, dignified, but it professes to be signed, through a medium, by the spirits of nearly a score of old worthies of the Republic. There are the familiar signatures of George Washington, John Hancock, Benjamin Franklin, Thomas Jefferson, John Adams, and so on to the end of the list, all as perfectly made as they themselves could write them, or as the most expert living forger could imitate them, using the same pen for all. Keep that document and show it to the President some day.

There is all the while a host of letters that are altogether sane, but which give a curious presentation of the fact that the average American, male or female, knows almost nothing about the machinery of the National Government. Simple-minded people send their business to Father Abraham, no matter what it is, and it is the business of this desk to not neglect what they send. There may even be written upon their papers endorsements asking for prompt and favorable consideration, if there is a sufficient assurance that Lincoln would have done so, had he seen them before transmitting them to their proper bureau in one or other of the departments. At some later day, some gratified citizen may tell an admiring neighbor:

"Tell ye haow I did it. I jest cut the red tape and dodged the loryers and writ to Linken, and he searched the matter up and had it 'tended to. He's a good man, he is!"

There is about as large a throng of writers who are ready to offer advice and even instruction upon the management of the war. It is marvelous how they can, theoretically, swing troops back and forth about the country. It is plain that they all have played the game of checkers, and have learned how to "jump" the Confederate forces and forts with their men.

The assassination idea has taken possession of so many minds that not many days go by without the coming of some kind of epistolary threat or warning.

There is no end to the mere fault-finding, nor to the suggestions of plans of campaigns and of proposed improvements in management. Here is one now, just opened. It is from a man in

Tolono, Ill., and he proposes to open the Confederate blockade of the Potomac from Washington down to Fortress Monroe. He says he has invented a cross-eyed gun, with two barrels, set at an angle so as to shoot in both directions; and he proposes to raise a regiment of cross-eyed men to use the new weapons.

"I know enough of cross-eyed men to fill up the regiment, and, by thunder! Mr. Lincoln, I'm cross-eyed enough to be colonel of it. We could march down the river and clean out both banks at once."

We will take that letter across the hall.

"How do you think it would work, Mr. Lincoln?"

"Well, I don't know but what there's about as much in it as there is in some of the other plans they want me to take."

He got a laugh out of it, anyhow, and that is something.

Written acknowledgments of the receipt and disposal of papers are frequently necessary, and it is well that you have the right to frank letters through the mails, for you never could get the President to spend time in franking.

The sack that Louis brings from the post-office is not so large as it would have to be but for the fact that no subordinate military or naval officer communicates directly with the commander-in-chief, the President. The latter may follow the armies as closely as he pleases upon his maps, but the men who make the movements do not report to him, and he does not meddle with the details of their work.

Mrs. Lincoln receives many letters. There lies her mail, ready to be taken to her.

"Somebody has been opening those letters."

Is it possible that such a blunder could have been made? Well, the only thing to be done is to go and see her at once. Take them along, and ask her to meet you in the Red Room.

Mrs. Lincoln is a pleasant-looking woman, and she is in fine health and spirits this morning.

"You sent word that you had a complaint to make to me. What is it?"

"This rascally paper-folder, Mrs. Lincoln. A lot of your letters—here they are—were lying on their faces on my table, and he got at them and opened every one of them. I caught him and choked him off before he had time to read them, but I'd like to know what I am to do about him?"

She does not seem to be at all angry with your long slip of polished ivory.

"Oh, dear me! Is that all? I wish you would open and read every letter that comes. You know my sister's handwriting?"

"Perfectly. That and that are from her."

"Read them, too, if you have any doubt. Don't let a thing come to me that you've not first read yourself, and that you are not sure I would wish to see. I do not wish to open a letter, nor even a parcel, of any kind, until after you have examined it. Never!"

She is suddenly called away, and you have no full explanation until you have carried that correspondence upstairs again.

The President's wife is venomously accused of being at heart a traitor, and of being in communication with the Confederate authorities, to whom, it is said, she sends information as to the plans of Union generals, as these are minutely confided to her by Mr. Lincoln. The newspapers, some of them, assert it openly, and their editors refuse to believe that she is intensely patriotic, and utterly devoted to her husband. She may be thinking of that——

Read! Read! You know now why she wishes you to inspect her letters. The insane, the depraved and the fiendish have by no means restricted themselves to the President in their infamous penmanship. His vilest foes are willing to vent their infernal malice upon his unoffending wife, but from this day forward they will but send their missives to the waste-basket and the fire. That is where some of the writers are going, too.

1890

Carl Schurz

As a university student Schurz (1829–1906) participated in the 1848 Revolution in Germany, then fled to Switzerland. Immigrating to the United States in 1852, he settled in Wisconsin and began campaigning for Republican candidates among both English- and German-speaking voters. An early and ardent supporter of Lincoln's presidential candidacy in 1860, he urged the President-elect not to make concessions to the South once the secession crisis began. After serving as minister to Spain in 1861, Schurz joined the Union Army the following year and commanded divisions at Second Bull Run, Chancellorsville, Gettysburg, and Chattanooga, ending his sometimes checkered military career as a major general. He later served as a Republican senator from Missouri (1869–75) and as Secretary of the Interior (1877–81) and became a leading advocate for civil service reform. His extended essay on Lincoln, excerpted below, was originally written for *Atlantic Monthly* in response to the Nicolay-Hay biography and was published as a book in 1891; it was later included as an introductory essay in the 1905 multi-volume edition of Lincoln's works edited by Arthur Brooks Lapsley.

FROM

Abraham Lincoln: An Essay

No American can study the character and career of Abraham Lincoln without being carried away by sentimental emotions. We are always inclined to idealize that which we love,—a state of mind very unfavorable to the exercise of sober critical judgment. It is therefore not surprising that most of those who have written or spoken on that extraordinary man, even while conscientiously endeavoring to draw a life-like portraiture of his being, and to form a just estimate of his public conduct, should have drifted into more or less indiscriminating eulogy, painting his great features in the most glowing colors, and covering with tender shadings whatever might look like a blemish.

But his standing before posterity will not be exalted by mere praise of his virtues and abilities, nor by any concealment of his limitations and faults. The stature of the great man, one of whose peculiar charms consisted in his being so unlike all other great men, will rather lose than gain by the idealization which so easily runs into the commonplace. For it was distinctly the weird mixture of qualities and forces in him, of the lofty with the common, the ideal with the uncouth, of that which he had become with that which he had not ceased to be, that made him so fascinating a character among his fellow-men, gave him his singular power over their minds and hearts, and fitted him to be the greatest leader in the greatest crisis of our national life.

His was indeed a marvelous growth. The statesman or the military hero born and reared in a log cabin is a familiar figure in American history; but we may search in vain among our celebrities for one whose origin and early life equaled Abraham Lincoln's in wretchedness. He first saw the light in a miserable hovel in Kentucky, on a farm consisting of a few barren acres in a dreary neighborhood; his father a typical "poor Southern white," shiftless and improvident, without ambition for himself or his children, constantly looking for a new piece of land on which he might make a living without much work; his mother, in her youth handsome and bright, grown prematurely coarse in feature and soured in mind by daily toil and care; the whole household squalid, cheerless, and utterly void of elevating inspirations. Only when the family had "moved" into the malarious backwoods of Indiana, the mother had died, and a stepmother, a woman of thrift and energy, had taken charge of the children, the shaggy-headed, ragged, barefooted, forlorn boy, then seven years old, "began to feel like a human being." Hard work was his early lot. When a mere boy he had to help in supporting the family, either on his father's clearing, or hired out to other farmers to plough, or dig ditches, or chop wood, or drive ox teams; occasionally also to "tend the baby," when the farmer's wife was otherwise engaged. He could regard it as an advancement to a higher sphere of activity when he obtained work in a "crossroads store," where he amused the customers by his talk over the counter; for he soon distinguished himself among the backwoods folk as one who had something to say worth listening to.

To win that distinction, he had to draw mainly upon his wits; for, while his thirst for knowledge was great, his opportunities for satisfying that thirst were wofully slender.

In the log school-house, which he could visit but little, he was taught only reading, writing, and elementary arithmetic. Among the people of the settlement, bush farmers and small tradesmen, he found none of uncommon intelligence or education; but some of them had a few books, which he borrowed eagerly. Thus he read and re-read Æsop's Fables, learning to tell stories with a point and to argue by parables; he read Robinson Crusoe, The Pilgrim's Progress, a short history of the United States, and Weems' Life of Washington. To the town constable's he went to read the Revised Statutes of Indiana. Every printed page that fell into his hands he would greedily devour, and his family and friends watched him with wonder, as the uncouth boy, after his daily work, crouched in a corner of the log cabin or outside under a tree, absorbed in a book while munching his supper of corn bread. In this manner he began to gather some knowledge, and sometimes he would astonish the girls with such startling remarks as that the earth was moving around the sun, and not the sun around the earth, and they marveled where "Abe" could have got such queer notions. Soon he also felt the impulse to write; not only making extracts from books he wished to remember, but also composing little essays of his own. First he sketched these with charcoal on a wooden shovel scraped white with a drawing-knife, or on basswood shingles. Then he transferred them to paper, which was a scarce commodity in the Lincoln household; taking care to cut his expressions close, so that they might not cover too much space,— a style-forming method greatly to be commended. Seeing boys put a burning coal on the back of a wood turtle, he was moved to write on cruelty to animals. Seeing men intoxicated with whiskey, he wrote on temperance. In verse-making, too, he tried himself, and in satire on persons offensive to him or others,— satire the rustic wit of which was not always fit for ears polite. Also political thoughts he put upon paper, and some of his pieces were even deemed good enough for publication in the county weekly.

Thus he won a neighborhood reputation as a clever young man, which he increased by his performances as a speaker, not seldom drawing upon himself the dissatisfaction of his employers by mounting a stump in the field, and keeping the farm hands from their work by little speeches in a jocose and sometimes also a serious vein. At the rude social frolics of the settlement he became an important person, telling funny stories, mimicking the itinerant preachers who had happened to pass by, and making his mark at wrestling matches, too; for at the age of seventeen he had attained his full height, six feet four inches in his stockings, if he had any, and a terribly muscular clodhopper he was. But he was known never to use his extraordinary strength to the injury or humiliation of others; rather to do them a kindly turn, or to enforce justice and fair dealing between them. All this made him a favorite in backwoods society, although in some things he appeared a little odd to his friends. Far more than any of them, he was given not only to reading, but to fits of abstraction, to quiet musing with himself, and also to strange spells of melancholy, from which he often would pass in a moment to rollicking outbursts of droll humor. But on the whole he was one of the people among whom he lived; in appearance perhaps even a little more uncouth than most of them,—a very tall, rawboned youth, with large features, dark, shriveled skin, and rebellious hair; his arms and legs long, out of proportion; clad in deerskin trousers, which from frequent exposure to the rain had shrunk so as to sit tightly on his limbs, leaving several inches of bluish shin exposed between their lower end and the heavy tan-colored shoes; the nether garment held usually by only one suspender, that was strung over a coarse home-made shirt; the head covered in winter with a coonskin cap, in summer with a rough straw hat of uncertain shape, without a band.

It is doubtful whether he felt himself much superior to his surroundings, although he confessed to a yearning for some knowledge of the world outside of the circle in which he lived. This wish was gratified; but how? At the age of nineteen he went down the Mississippi to New Orleans as a flatboat hand, temporarily joining a trade many members of which at that time still

took pride in being called "half horse and half alligator." After
his return he worked and lived in the old way until the spring of
1830, when his father "moved again," this time to Illinois; and
on the journey of fifteen days "Abe" had to drive the ox wagon
which carried the household goods. Another log cabin was built,
and then, fencing a field, Abraham Lincoln split those historic
rails which were destined to play so picturesque a part in the
presidential campaign twenty-eight years later.

Having come of age, Lincoln left the family, and "struck out
for himself." He had to "take jobs whenever he could get them."
The first of these carried him again as a flatboat hand to New
Orleans. There something happened that made a lasting impression upon his soul: he witnessed a slave auction. "His heart
bled," wrote one of his companions; "said nothing much; was
silent; looked bad. I can say, knowing it, that it was on this trip
that he formed his opinion on slavery. It run its iron in him then
and there, May, 1831. I have heard him say so often." Then he
lived several years at New Salem, in Illinois, a small mushroom
village, with a mill, some "stores" and whiskey shops, that rose
quickly, and soon disappeared again. It was a desolate, disjointed,
half-working and half-loitering life, without any other aim than
to gain food and shelter from day to day. He served as pilot
on a steamboat trip, then as clerk in a store and a mill; business
failing, he was adrift for some time. Being compelled to measure his strength with the chief bully of the neighborhood, and
overcoming him, he became a noted person in that muscular
community, and won the esteem and friendship of the ruling
gang of ruffians to such a degree that, when the Black Hawk war
broke out, they elected him, a young man of twenty-three, captain of a volunteer company, composed mainly of roughs of
their kind. He took the field, and his most noteworthy deed of
valor consisted, not in killing an Indian, but in protecting against
his own men, at the peril of his own life, the life of an old savage
who had strayed into his camp.

The Black Hawk war over, he turned to politics. The step
from the captaincy of a volunteer company to a candidacy for a
seat in the legislature seemed a natural one. But his popularity,
although great in New Salem, had not spread far enough over

the district, and he was defeated. Then the wretched hand-to-mouth struggle began again. He "set up in store-business" with a dissolute partner, who drank whiskey while Lincoln was reading books. The result was a disastrous failure and a load of debt. Thereupon he became a deputy surveyor, and was appointed postmaster of New Salem, the business of the post office being so small that he could carry the incoming and outgoing mail in his hat. All this could not lift him from poverty, and his surveying instruments and horse and saddle were sold by the sheriff for debt.

But while all this misery was upon him his ambition rose to higher aims. He walked many miles to borrow from a schoolmaster a grammar with which to improve his language. A lawyer lent him a copy of Blackstone, and he began to study law. People would look wonderingly at the grotesque figure lying in the grass, "with his feet up a tree," or sitting on a fence, as, absorbed in a book, he learned to construct correct sentences and made himself a jurist. At once he gained a little practice, pettifogging before a justice of the peace for friends, without expecting a fee. Judicial functions, too, were thrust upon him, but only at horse-races or wrestling matches, where his acknowledged honesty and fairness gave his verdicts undisputed authority. His popularity grew apace, and soon he could be a candidate for the legislature again. Although he called himself a Whig, an ardent admirer of Henry Clay, his clever stump speeches won him the election in the strongly Democratic district. Then for the first time, perhaps, he thought seriously of his outward appearance. So far he had been content with a garb of "Kentucky jeans," not seldom ragged, usually patched, and always shabby. Now he borrowed some money from a friend to buy a new suit of clothes—"store clothes"—fit for a Sangamon County statesman; and thus adorned he set out for the state capital, Vandalia, to take his seat among the lawmakers.

His legislative career, which stretched over several sessions, for he was thrice re-elected, in 1836, 1838, and 1840, was not remarkably brilliant. He did, indeed, not lack ambition. He dreamed even of making himself "the De Witt Clinton of Illinois," and he actually distinguished himself by zealous and effective work in those "log-rolling" operations by which the young State received "a general system of internal improvements" in the shape of railroads, canals, and banks,—a reckless policy, burdening the State with debt, and producing the usual crop of political demoralization, but a policy characteristic of the time and the impatiently enterprising spirit of the Western people. Lincoln, no doubt with the best intentions, but with little knowledge of the subject, simply followed the popular current. The achievement in which, perhaps, he gloried most was the removal of the state government from Vandalia to Springfield; one of those triumphs of political management which are apt to be the pride of the small politician's statesmanship. One thing, however, he did in which his true nature asserted itself, and which gave distinct promise of the future pursuit of high aims. Against an overwhelming preponderance of sentiment in the legislature, followed by only one other member, he recorded his protest against a proslavery resolution,—that protest declaring "the institution of slavery to be founded on both injustice and bad policy." This was not only the irrepressible voice of his conscience; it was true moral valor, too; for at that time, in many parts of the West, an abolitionist was regarded as little better than a horse-thief, and even "Abe Lincoln" would hardly have been forgiven his anti-slavery principles, had he not been known as such an "uncommon good fellow." But here, in obedience to the great conviction of his life, he manifested his courage to stand alone,—that courage which is the first requisite of leadership in a great cause.

Together with his reputation and influence as a politician grew his law practice, especially after he had removed from New Salem to Springfield, and associated himself with a practitioner of good standing. He had now at last won a fixed position in society. He became a successful lawyer, less, indeed, by his learning as a jurist than by his effectiveness as an advocate and by the striking uprightness of his character; and it may truly be said that his vivid sense of truth and justice had much to do with his effectiveness as an advocate. He would refuse to act as the attorney even of personal friends when he saw the right on the other side. He would abandon cases, even during trial, when the testimony convinced him that his client was in the wrong. He would dissuade those who sought his service from pursuing an obtainable advantage when their claims seemed to him unfair. Presenting his very first case in the United States Circuit Court, the only question being one of authority, he declared that, upon careful examination, he found all the authorities on the other side, and none on his. Persons accused of crime, when he thought them guilty, he would not defend at all, or, attempting their defense, he was unable to put forth his powers. One notable exception is on record, when his personal sympathies had been strongly aroused. But when he felt himself to be the protector of innocence, the defender of justice, or the prosecutor of wrong, he frequently disclosed such unexpected resources of reasoning, such depth of feeling, and rose to such fervor of appeal as to astonish and overwhelm his hearers, and make him fairly irresistible. Even an ordinary law argument, coming from him, seldom failed to produce the impression that he was profoundly convinced of the soundness of his position. It is not surprising that the mere appearance of so conscientious an attorney in any case should have carried, not only to juries, but even to judges, almost a presumption of right on his side, and that the people began to call him, sincerely meaning it, "honest Abe Lincoln."

In the mean time he had private sorrows and trials of a painfully afflicting nature. He had loved and been loved by a fair and estimable girl, Ann Rutledge, who died in the flower of her youth and beauty, and he mourned her loss with such intensity of grief that his friends feared for his reason. Recovering from his morbid depression, he bestowed what he thought a new affection upon another lady, who refused him. And finally, moderately prosperous in his worldly affairs, and having prospects of political distinction before him, he paid his addresses to Mary Todd, of Kentucky, and was accepted. But then tormenting doubts of the genuineness of his own affection for her, of the compatibility of their characters, and of their future happiness came upon him. His distress was so great that he felt himself in danger of suicide, and feared to carry a pocket-knife with him; and he gave mortal offense to his bride by not appearing on the appointed wedding day. Now the torturing consciousness of the wrong he had done her grew unendurable. He won back her affection, ended the agony by marrying her, and became a faithful and patient husband and a good father. But it was no secret to those who knew the family well, that his domestic life was full of trials. The erratic temper of his wife not seldom put the gentleness of his nature to the severest tests; and these troubles and struggles, which accompanied him through all the vicissitudes of his life from the modest home in Springfield to the White House at Washington, adding untold private heartburnings to his public cares, and sometimes precipitating upon him incredible embarrassments in the discharge of his public duties, form one of the most pathetic features of his career.

He continued to "ride the circuit," read books while traveling in his buggy, told funny stories to his fellow-lawyers in the tavern, chatted familiarly with his neighbors around the stove in the store and at the post-office, had his hours of melancholy brooding as of old, and became more and more widely known and trusted and beloved among the people of his State for his ability as a lawyer and politician, for the uprightness of his character and the ever-flowing spring of sympathetic kindness in his heart. His main ambition was confessedly that of political distinction; but hardly any one would at that time have seen in him the man destined to lead the nation through the greatest crisis of the century.

His time had not yet come when, in 1846, he was elected to Congress. In a clever speech in the House of Representatives, he denounced President Polk for having unjustly forced war upon Mexico, and he amused the Committee of the Whole by a witty attack upon General Cass. More important was the expression he gave to his anti-slavery impulses by offering a bill looking to the emancipation of the slaves in the District of Columbia, and by his repeated votes for the famous Wilmot Proviso, intended to exclude slavery from the Territories acquired from Mexico. But when, at the expiration of his term, in March, 1849, he left his seat, he gloomily despaired of ever seeing the day when the cause nearest to his heart would be rightly grasped by the people, and when he would be able to render any service to his country in solving the great problem. Nor had his career as a member of

Congress in any sense been such as to gratify his ambition. Indeed, if he ever had any belief in a great destiny for himself, it must have been weak at that period; for he actually sought to obtain from the new Whig President, General Taylor, the place of Commissioner of the General Land Office, willing to bury himself in one of the administrative bureaus of the government. Fortunately for the country, he failed; and no less fortunately, when, later, the territorial governorship of Oregon was offered to him, Mrs. Lincoln's protest induced him to decline it. Returning to Springfield, he gave himself with renewed zest to his law practice, acquiesced in the Compromise of 1850 with reluctance and a mental reservation, supported in the presidential campaign of 1852 the Whig candidate in some spiritless speeches, and took but a languid interest in the politics of the day. But just then his time was drawing near.

The peace promised, and apparently inaugurated, by the Compromise of 1850 was rudely broken by the introduction of the Kansas-Nebraska bill in 1854. The repeal of the Missouri Compromise, opening the Territories of the United States, the heritage of coming generations, to the invasion of slavery, suddenly revealed the whole significance of the slavery question to the people of the free States, and thrust itself into the politics of the country as the paramount issue. Something like an electric shock flashed through the North. Men who but a short time before had been absorbed by their business pursuits, and deprecated all political agitation, were startled out of their security by a sudden alarm, and excitedly took sides. That restless trouble of conscience about slavery, which even in times of apparent repose had secretly disturbed the souls of Northern people, broke forth in an utterance louder than ever. The bonds of accustomed party allegiance gave way. Anti-slavery Democrats and anti-slavery Whigs felt themselves drawn together by a common overpowering sentiment, and soon they began to rally in a new organization. The Republican party sprang into being to meet the overruling call of the hour. Then Abraham Lincoln's time was come. He rapidly advanced to a position of conspicuous championship in the struggle. This, however, was not owing to his virtues and abilities alone. Indeed, the slavery question stirred his soul in its profoundest depths; it was, as one of his intimate friends said, "the only one on which he would become excited;" it called forth all his faculties and energies. Yet there were many others who, having long and arduously fought the anti-slavery battle in the popular assembly, or in the press, or in the halls of Congress, far surpassed him in prestige, and compared with whom he was still an obscure and untried man. His reputation, although highly honorable and well earned, had so far been essentially local. As a stump-speaker in Whig canvasses outside of his State he had attracted comparatively little attention; but in Illinois he had been recognized as one of the foremost men of the Whig party. Among the opponents of the Nebraska bill he occupied in his State so important a position, that in 1854 he was the choice of a large majority of the "Anti-Nebraska men" in the legislature for a seat in the Senate of the United States which then became vacant; and when he, an old Whig, could not obtain the votes of the Anti-Nebraska Democrats necessary to make a majority, he generously urged his friends to transfer their votes to Lyman Trumbull, who was then elected. Two years later, in the first national convention of the Republican party, the delegation from Illinois brought him forward as a candidate for the vice-presidency, and he received respectable support. Still, the name of Abraham Lincoln was not widely known beyond the boundaries of his own State. But now it was this local prominence in Illinois that put him in a position of peculiar advantage on the battlefield of national politics. In the assault on the Missouri Compromise which broke down all legal barriers to the spread of slavery, Stephen Arnold Douglas was the ostensible leader and central figure; and Douglas was a Senator from Illinois, Lincoln's State. Douglas's national theatre of action was the Senate, but in his constituency in Illinois were the roots of his official position and power. What he did in the Senate he had to justify before the people of Illinois, in order to maintain himself in place; and in Illinois all eyes turned to Lincoln as Douglas's natural antagonist.

As very young men they had come to Illinois, Lincoln from Indiana, Douglas from Vermont, and had grown up together in public life, Douglas as a Democrat, Lincoln as a Whig. They had met first in Vandalia, in 1834, when Lincoln was in the legislature and Douglas in the lobby; and again in 1836, both as members of the legislature. Douglas, a very able politician, of the agile, combative, audacious, "pushing" sort, rose in political distinction with remarkable rapidity. In quick succession he became a member of the legislature, a State's attorney, secretary of state, a judge on the supreme bench of Illinois, three times a Representative in Congress, and a Senator of the United States when only thirty-nine years old. In the national Democratic convention of 1852, he appeared even as an aspirant to the nomination for the presidency, as the favorite of "young America," and received a respectable vote. He had far outstripped Lincoln in what is commonly called political success and in reputation. But it had frequently happened that in political campaigns Lincoln felt himself impelled, or was selected by his Whig friends, to answer Douglas's speeches; and thus the two were looked upon, in a large part of the State at least, as the representative combatants of their respective parties in the debates before popular meetings. As soon, therefore, as, after the passage of his Kansas-Nebraska bill, Douglas returned to Illinois to defend his cause before his constituents, Lincoln, obeying not only his own impulse, but also general expectation, stepped forward as his principal opponent. Thus the struggle about the principles involved in the Kansas-Nebraska bill, or, in a broader sense, the struggle between freedom and slavery, assumed in Illinois the outward form of a personal contest between Lincoln and Douglas; and, as it continued and became more animated, that personal contest in Illinois was watched with constantly increasing interest by the whole country. When, in 1858, Douglas's senatorial term being about to expire, Lincoln was formally designated by the Republican convention of Illinois as their candidate for the Senate, to take Douglas's place, and the two contestants agreed to debate the questions at issue face to face in a series of public meetings, the eyes of the whole American people were turned eagerly to that one point; and the spectacle reminded one of those lays of ancient times telling of two armies, in battle array, standing still to see their two principal champions fight out the contested cause between the lines in single combat.

Lincoln had then reached the full maturity of his powers. His equipment as a statesman did not embrace a comprehensive knowledge of public affairs. What he had studied he had indeed made his own, with the eager craving and that zealous tenacity characteristic of superior minds learning under difficulties. But his narrow opportunities and the unsteady life he had led during his younger years had not permitted the accumulation of large stores in his mind. It is true, in political campaigns he had occasionally spoken on the ostensible issues between the Whigs and the Democrats, the tariff, internal improvements, banks, and so on, but only in a perfunctory manner. Had he ever given much serious thought and study to these subjects, it is safe to assume that a mind so prolific of original conceits as his would certainly have produced some utterance upon them worth remembering. His soul had evidently never been deeply stirred by such topics. But when his moral nature was aroused, his brain developed an untiring activity until it had mastered all the knowledge within reach. As soon as the repeal of the Missouri Compromise had thrust the slavery question into politics as the paramount issue, Lincoln plunged into an arduous study of all its legal, historical, and moral aspects, and then his mind became a complete arsenal of argument. His rich natural gifts, trained by long and varied practice, had made him an orator of rare persuasiveness. In his immature days, he had pleased himself for a short period with that inflated, high-flown style which, among the uncultivated, passes for "beautiful speaking." His inborn truthfulness and his artistic instinct soon overcame that aberration, and revealed to him the noble beauty and strength of simplicity. He possessed an uncommon power of clear and compact statement, which might have reminded those who knew the story of his early youth, of the efforts of the poor boy, when he copied his compositions from the scraped wooden shovel, carefully to trim his expressions in order to save paper. His language had the energy of honest directness, and he was a master of logical lucidity. He loved to point and enliven his reasoning by humorous illustrations, usually anecdotes of Western life, of which he had an inexhaustible store at his command. These anecdotes had not seldom a flavor of rustic robustness about them, but he used them with great effect, while amusing the audience, to give life to an abstraction, to explode an absurdity, to clinch an argument, to drive home an admonition. The natural kindliness of his tone, softening prejudice and disarming partisan rancor, would often open to his reasoning a way into minds most unwilling to receive it.

Yet his greatest power consisted in the charm of his individuality. That charm did not, in the ordinary way, appeal to the ear or to the eye. His voice was not melodious; rather shrill and piercing, especially when it rose to its high treble in moments of great animation. His figure was unhandsome, and the action of his unwieldy limbs awkward. He commanded none of the outward graces of oratory as they are commonly understood. His charm was of a different kind. It flowed from the rare depth and genuineness of his convictions and his sympathetic feelings. Sympathy was the strongest element in his nature. One of his biographers, who knew him before he became President, says: "Lincoln's compassion might be stirred deeply by an object present, but never by an object absent and unseen. In the former case he would most likely extend relief, with little inquiry into the merits of the case, because, as he expressed it himself, it 'took a pain out of his own heart.'" Only half of this is correct. It is certainly true that he could not witness any individual distress or oppression, or any kind of suffering, without feeling a pang of pain himself, and that by relieving as much as he could the suffering of others he put an end to his own. This compassionate impulse to help he felt not only for human beings, but for every living creature. As in his boyhood he angrily reproved the boys who tormented a wood turtle by putting a burning coal on its back, so, we are told, he would, when a mature man, on a journey, dismount from his buggy and wade waist-deep in mire to rescue a pig struggling in a swamp. Indeed, appeals to his compassion were so irresistible to him, and he felt it so difficult to refuse anything when his refusal could give pain, that he himself sometimes spoke of his inability to say "no" as a positive weakness. But that certainly does not prove that his compassionate feeling was confined to individual cases of suffering witnessed with his own eyes. As the boy was moved by the aspect of the tortured wood turtle to compose an essay against cruelty to animals in general, so the aspect of other cases of suffering and wrong wrought up his moral nature, and set his mind to work against cruelty, injustice, and oppression in general.

As his sympathy went forth to others, it attracted others to him. Especially those whom he called the "plain people" felt themselves drawn to him by the instinctive feeling that he understood, esteemed, and appreciated them. He had grown up among the poor, the lowly, the ignorant. He never ceased to remember the good souls he had met among them, and the many kindnesses they had done him. Although in his mental development he had risen far above them, he never looked down upon them. How they felt and how they reasoned he knew, for so he had once felt and reasoned himself. How they could be moved he knew, for so he had once been moved himself and practiced moving others. His mind was much larger than theirs, but it thoroughly comprehended theirs; and while he thought much farther than they, their thoughts were ever present to him. Nor had the visible distance between them grown as wide as his rise in the world would seem to have warranted. Much of his backwoods speech and manners still clung to him. Although he had become "Mr. Lincoln" to his later acquaintances, he was still "Abe" to the "Nats" and "Billys" and "Daves" of his youth; and their familiarity neither appeared unnatural to them, nor was it in the least awkward to him. He still told and enjoyed stories similar to those he had told and enjoyed in the Indiana settlement and at New Salem. His wants remained as modest as they had ever been; his domestic habits had by no means completely accommodated themselves to those of his more highborn wife; and though the "Kentucky jeans" apparel had long been dropped, his clothes of better material and better make would sit ill sorted on his gigantic limbs. His cotton umbrella, without a handle, and tied together with a coarse string to keep it from flapping, which he carried on his circuit rides, is said to be remembered still by some of his surviving neighbors. This rusticity of habit was utterly free from that affected contempt of refinement and comfort which self-made men sometimes carry into their more affluent circumstances. To Abraham Lincoln it was entirely natural, and all those who came into contact with him knew it to be so. In his ways of thinking and feeling he had become a gentleman in the highest sense, but the refining process had polished but little the outward form. The plain people, therefore, still considered "honest Abe Lincoln" one of themselves; and when they felt, which they no doubt frequently did, that his thoughts and aspirations moved in a sphere above their own, they were all the more proud of him, without any diminution of fellow-feeling. It was this relation of mutual sympathy and understanding between Lincoln and the plain people that gave him his peculiar power as a public man, and singularly fitted him, as we shall see, for that leadership which was preëminently required in the great crisis then coming on,—the leadership which indeed thinks and moves ahead of the masses, but always remains within sight and sympathetic touch of them.

1891

Bram Stoker

Best known for his classic horror novel *Dracula* (1897), the Irish writer Bram Stoker (1842–1912) traveled extensively throughout the United States as the manager of the renowned English actor Henry Irving. An admirer of Walt Whitman, Stoker met the American poet in 1884, and it is likely that the example of Whitman's lecture on Lincoln (see pages 251–62 in this volume) inspired Stoker to compose his own lecture on the same subject. Stoker first gave his Lincoln lecture while touring the United States in 1886–87 and continued to deliver it in Britain until 1893. His respect and admiration for Lincoln also moved him to purchase new versions, made by Augustus Saint-Gaudens, of the life casts Leonard Wells Volk made of Lincoln's face and hands in 1860.

FROM
Lecture on Abraham Lincoln

Live embodiment of the Northern idea was wanted, some great personality, some living type of the dominant spirit of free America, some one great enough to hold the will and imagination of the people from the Lake border down South to Mason and Dixon Line and from the Atlantic seashore westward to where the tracks of civilisation were already becoming lost in the vastness of the Rocky Mountains; and wise enough to steer the ship of the Republic through the troubled waters full of unknown peril which lay ahead.

The whole country was a seething cauldron of politics. On every side lay danger. Great forces were gathering for contests to the death; and to every true American was borne the conviction that their political system was to be tested in the arena of the world.

And now the hour had come for the final struggle of the world between slavery and freedom. It came attended with the most profound complications. Most especially embarrassing to all who wished to save the free institutions which had grown up with the growth of the Republic.

The hour had come, and with it, as ever happens in the history of God's providence, came the man—Abraham Lincoln.

Let me describe him. He was of lofty stature, six feet four he stood in his stockings: was loosely and lankily built, of gaunt and sinewy frame of odd quaint ungainliness but possessed of enormous strength with muscles of iron and nerves of steel.

His face was a dark brownish colour partially from constant exposure to weather. His hair was black, his eyes were grey. He had a coarse mouth with large yellow teeth. A story was told by him of himself:

'In the days when I used to be "on the circuit" I was accosted in the cars by a stranger who said: "Excuse me, sir, but I have an article in my possession which belongs to you". "How is that?" I asked considerably astonished. The stranger took a jack-knife from his pocket. "This knife", he said, "was placed in my hands several years ago, with the injunction that I was to keep it until I found the ugliest man on earth. I have carried it from that time to this and now, thank heavens, I need search no more. My task is done"'.

A man who knew him and often heard him speak described him thus to me:

'He was the ugliest man I ever saw, but when he began to speak his face became transformed and what a face it was then, it seemed somehow lit from within, as if his very soul was shining through. In such moments he seemed inspired and looked almost beautiful in his strength'.

Lincoln had feet of enormous size, uncommon even in a region where bare feet or moccasins were the ordinary wear for some generations of pioneers.

He had great gifts of voice and speech. He could address twenty thousand persons and be heard by them. He was manifestly a man of the people, born of the wilderness, self taught from the days when he followed the plough, pulled fodder or split rails. A quaint, gaunt uncouth man, with no line of beauty in face or figure, in action or movement, and with a hand such as had no fellow save its own. A mighty hand that those who saw it could never mistake or forget. Truly a mighty hand, and by every law of symbolism it should be so, for the Almighty had fashioned it for great work;—it held in its hollow the destiny of a nation and the freedom of a race.

No promising figure this for heroism. A plain simple man who had taken life as he had found it and made it; and yet a suitable instrument for the working out of a great democratic idea. It was meet that in the time of the Nation's peril, when dismemberment threatened her and when anarchy and slavery combined to crush her aspirations, this type of her working people, this embodiment of her prosaic life should appear as the genius of her safety.

————

Such was the end of that life of patient, worthy toil, the end of those long weary years of patriotic devotion.

It may have been through some occult force or power that he saw that warning dream. Such things have been told of other men before him and shall be told of others still again whilst the world of shadows lies before and behind us as we walk the path of mortality. We pass in light but a little space from gloom to gloom and those only who look out from the farthest darkness knew whence the power and the mystery come and whither they go. It was surely a worthy sign and a fitting one that was given to the Martyr on the last night. The ship that sailed so swiftly before his sleeping eyes was perchance the archetype of that ship of State which had been steered by his Master hand, past all dangers, safe into its haven of peace.

And then he found the dreamland itself, and he knew the mystery of that sailing ship, and of all the ships that sailed, of the thunder of guns and the tramp of marching men, of the inspiration of the battle-flags and the shout of an enfranchised race.

For so this hero when his work was done, through the white clouds of patriot glory passed upward to his place at the table of the Gods.

———

Not long before his death Walt Whitman said to me:

'No man knows—no one in the future can ever know Abraham Lincoln. He was much greater—so much vaster even than his surroundings.—What is not known of him is so much more than what is, that the true man can never be known on earth'.

This we do know, that from the cradle to the grave, from that frontier cabin amid the wilderness where he first saw light, on to his throne in the hearts of a mighty Nation, and still to the victories of a hero and the death of a martyr, in the darkest hour of personal sorrow and National disaster, in the bold assertion of his Country's right to a high place amongst the Nations of the World, even in the wildest flush of victory when bell and bugle and cannon filled the air with clang and trill and roll of triumph from Eastern to Western sea, *no* voice was ever raised against the purity of his purpose, against his integrity, his honour or his truth.

If ever a man of the sons of men walked straight on his path in honourable, laborious worthy course, that man was Abraham Lincoln.

We look now from historic distance and can see with impartial eyes that every step which he ever took was consistent with every other which he had taken on his destined course. There was a distinct guiding purpose in his life from which his every action sprang. Every height which he won, every power which he achieved, every honour accorded to him was in distinct logical and dramatic sequence with his own efforts to an noble end.

It would be vain to try to tell of the grief of the Nation at his death. In his life he had taught nearly every lesson which it is given man to teach, of patience, of work, of purpose, of boldness, of courage, of honesty, of faith, of pity, of love; and his death was a worthy crown.

'Dulce est patria Mori', says the old Roman. After years of agony of anxiety to rest in such an honoured grave was sweet.

There was one lesson left to teach; but the cup of his glory was full and such was not for him, to go from his high place as the chief of a Nation back to his old simple life again, and, so, to teach to the ages the mighty lesson that in true democracy 'the readiness is all'.

Perhaps it was that his death had another lesson still and a sterner one, that he who would lift, howsoever worthily, the sceptre of Man's dominion over Man should know the many cares and perils of its sway, as it is wise in the economy of things that childhood should, now and again, stand face to face with the Mystery of the Open Grave.

1893

Ida M. Tarbell

The author of the famous 1904 muckraking exposé *The History of the Standard Oil Company*, Tarbell (1857–1944) recalled in her autobiography how her mother sobbed at the news of Lincoln's murder. "From that time on," she wrote, Lincoln's name "spelt tragedy and mystery." Tarbell began researching his life in 1895 for *McClure's Magazine*, and succeeded in uncovering numerous new documents, including speeches, letters, newspaper reports, and several previously unknown photographs. Her discoveries doubled *McClure's* circulation when the magazine began publishing her articles, which she expanded into a bestselling two-volume book published in 1900. As historian Mark E. Neely Jr. has observed, Tarbell's work countered an argument advanced by many of Lincoln's contemporaries—that he triumphed *despite* his backwoods origins—by stressing how the frontier helped fashion his character. Tarbell later wrote a popular series of fictional "Billy Brown" stories about Lincoln, a biography for Boy Scouts, and a book extolling Lincoln's pioneer ancestors. Historian Merrill Peterson aptly called Tarbell—whose middle name was Minerva—the "goddess of Lincolniana."

FROM

The Life of Abraham Lincoln

CHAPTER XV

LINCOLN ON THE CIRCUIT—HIS HUMOR AND PERSUASIVENESS—HIS MANNER
OF PREPARING CASES, EXAMINING WITNESSES, AND ADDRESSING JURIES

When in 1849 Lincoln decided to abandon politics finally and to devote himself to the law, he had been practising for thirteen years. In spite of the many interruptions electioneering and office-holding had caused he was well-established. Rejoining his partner Herndon—the firm of Lincoln and Herndon had been only a name during Lincoln's term in Washington —he took up the law with a singleness of purpose which had never before characterized his practice.

Lincoln's headquarters were in Springfield, but his practice was itinerant. The arrangements for the administration of justice in Illinois in the early days were suited to the conditions of the country, the State being divided into judicial circuits including more or less territory according to the population. To each circuit a judge was appointed, who each spring and fall travelled from county-seat to county-seat to hold court. With the judge travelled a certain number of the best-known lawyers of the district. Each lawyer had, of course, a permanent office in one of the county-seats, and often at several of the others he had partners, usually young men of little experience, for whom he acted as counsel in special cases. This peripatetic court prevailed in Illinois until the beginning of the fifties; but for many years after, when the towns had grown so large that a clever lawyer might have enough to do in his own county, a few lawyers, Lincoln among them, who from long association felt that the circuit was their natural habitat refused to leave it.

The circuit which Lincoln travelled was known as the "Eighth Judicial Circuit." It included fifteen counties in 1845, though the territory has since been divided into more. It was about one hundred and fifty miles long by as many broad. There were no railroads in the Eighth Circuit until about 1854, and the court travelled on horseback or in carriages. Lincoln had no horse in the early days of his practice. It was his habit then to borrow one, or to join a company of a half dozen or more in hiring a "three-seated spring wagon." Later he owned a turn-out of his own, which figures in nearly all the traditions of the Eighth Circuit; the horse being described as "poky" and the buggy as "rattling."

There was much that was irritating and uncomfortable in the circuit-riding of the Illinois court, but there was more which was amusing to a temperament like Lincoln's. The freedom, the long days in the open air, the unexpected if trivial adventures, the meeting with wayfarers and settlers—all was an entertainment to him. He found humor and human interest on the route where his companions saw nothing but commonplaces. "He saw the ludicrous in an assemblage of fowls," says H. C. Whitney, one of his fellow-itinerants, "in a man spading his garden, in a clothes-line full of clothes, in a group of boys, in a lot of pigs rooting at a mill door, in a mother duck teaching her brood to

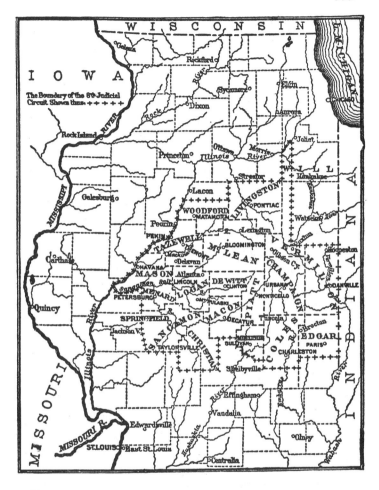

FACSIMILE OF MAP OF CIRCUIT WHICH LINCOLN TRAVELLED IN PRACTISING LAW.

swim—in everything and anything." The sympathetic observations of these long rides furnished humorous settings for some of his best stories. If frequently on these trips he fell into sombre reveries and rode with head bent, ignoring his companions, generally he took part in all the frolicking which went on, joining in practical jokes, singing noisily with the rest, sometimes even playing a Jew's-harp.

When the county-seat was reached, the bench and bar quickly settled themselves in the town tavern. It was usually a large two-story house with big rooms and long verandas. There was little exclusiveness possible in these hostelries. Ordinarily judge and lawyer slept two in a bed, and three or four beds in a room. They ate at the common table with jurors, witnesses, prisoners out on bail, travelling peddlers, teamsters, and laborers. The only attempt at classification on the landlord's part was seating the lawyers in a group at the head of the table. Most of them accepted this distinction complacently. Lincoln, however, seemed to be indifferent to it. One day, when he had come in and seated himself at the foot with the "fourth estate," the landlord called to him, "You're in the wrong place, Mr. Lincoln; come up here."

"Have you anything better to eat up there, Joe?" he inquired quizzically; "if not, I'll stay here."

The accommodations of the taverns were often unsatisfactory —the food poorly cooked, the beds hard. Lincoln accepted everything with uncomplaining good nature, though his companions habitually growled at the hardships of the life. It was not only repugnance to criticism which might hurt others, it was the indifference of one whose thoughts were always busy with problems apart from physical comfort, who had little notion of the so-called, " refinements of life," and almost no sense of luxury and ease.

The judge naturally was the leading character in these nomadic groups. He received all the special consideration the democratic spirit of the inhabitants bestowed on any one, and controlled his privacy and his time to a degree. Judge David Davis, who from 1848 presided over the Eighth Circuit as long as Mr. Lincoln travelled it, was a man of unusual force of character, of large learning, quick impulses, and strong prejudices. Lincoln was from the beginning of their association a favorite with Judge Davis. Unless he joined the circle which the judge formed in his room after supper, his honor was impatient and distraught, interrupting the conversation constantly by demanding: "Where's Lincoln?" "Why don't Lincoln come?" And when Lincoln did come, the judge would draw out story after story, quieting everybody who interrupted with an impatient,

"Mr. Lincoln's talking." If anyone came to the door to see the host in the midst of one of Lincoln's stories he would send a lawyer into the hall to see what was wanted, and, as soon as the door closed, order Lincoln to "go ahead."

The appearance of the court in a town was invariably a stimulus to its social life. In all of the county-seats there were a few fine homes of which the dignity, spaciousness, and elegance still impress the traveller through Illinois. The hospitality of these houses was generous. Dinners, receptions, and suppers followed one another as soon as the court began. Lincoln was a favorite figure at all these gatherings.

His favorite field, however, was the court. The court-houses of Illinois in which he practised were not log houses, as has been frequently taken for granted. "It is not probable," says a leading member of the Illinois bar, "Mr. Lincoln ever saw a log court-house in central Illinois, where he practised law, unless he saw one at Decatur, in Macon County. In a conversation between three members of the Supreme Court of Illinois, all of whom had been born in this State and had lived in it all their lives, and who were certainly familiar with the central portions of the State, all declared they had never seen a log court-house in the State."

The court-houses in which Lincoln practised were stiff, old-fashioned wood or brick structures, usually capped by cupola or tower, and fronted by verandas with huge Doric or Ionic pillars. They were finished inside in the most uncompromising style—hard white walls, unpainted woodwork, pine floors, wooden benches. Usually they were heated by huge Franklin stoves, with yards of stove-pipe running wildly through the air, searching for an exit, and threatening momentarily to unjoint and tumble in sections. Few of the lawyers had offices in the town; and a corner of the court-room, the shade of a tree in the court-yard, a sunny side of a building, were where they met their clients and transacted business.

In the courts themselves there was a certain indifference to formality engendered by the primitive surroundings, which, however, the judges never allowed to interfere with the seriousness of the work. Lincoln habitually, when not busy, whispered stories to his neighbors, frequently to the annoyance of Judge

Davis. If Lincoln persisted too long, the judge would rap on the chair and exclaim: "Come, come, Mr. Lincoln, I can't stand this! There is no use trying to carry on two courts; I must adjourn mine or you yours, and I think you will have to be the one." As soon as the group had scattered, the judge would call one of the men to him and ask: "What was that Lincoln was telling?"

"I was never fined but once for contempt of court," says one of the clerks of the court in Lincoln's day. "Davis fined me five dollars. Mr. Lincoln had just come in, and leaning over my desk had told me a story so irresistibly funny that I broke out into a loud laugh. The judge called me to order in haste, saying, 'This must be stopped. Mr. Lincoln, you are constantly disturbing this court with your stories.' Then to me, 'You may fine yourself five dollars for your disturbance.' I apologized, but told the judge that the story was worth the money. In a few minutes the judge called me to him. 'What was the story Lincoln told you?' he asked. I told him, and he laughed aloud in spite of himself. 'Remit your fine,' he ordered."

The partiality of Judge Davis for Lincoln was shared by the members of the court generally. The unaffected friendliness and helpfulness of his nature had more to do with this than his wit and cleverness. If there was a new clerk in court, a stranger unused to the ways of the place, Lincoln was the first—sometimes the only one—to shake hands with him and congratulate him on his election.

"No lawyer on the circuit was more unassuming than was Mr. Lincoln," says one who practised with him. "He arrogated to himself no superiority over anyone—not even the most obscure member of the bar. He treated everyone with that simplicity and kindness that friendly neighbors manifest in their relations with one another. He was remarkably gentle with young lawyers becoming permanent residents at the several county-seats in the circuit where he had practised for so many years. . . . The result was, he became the much-beloved senior member of the bar. No young lawyer ever practised in the courts with Mr. Lincoln who did not in all his after life have a regard for him akin to personal affection."

"I remember with what confidence I always went to him,"

says Judge Lawrence Welden, who first knew Lincoln at the bar in 1854, "because I was certain he knew all about the matter and would most cheerfully help me. I can see him now, through the decaying memories of thirty years, standing in the corner of the old court-room; and as I approached him with a paper I did not understand, he said, 'Wait until I fix this plug of my "gallis" and I will pitch into that like a dog at a root.' While speaking he was busily engaged in trying to connect his suspenders with his pants by making a plug perform the function of a button."

If for any reason Lincoln was absent from court, he was missed perhaps as no other man on the Eighth Circuit would have been, and his return greeted joyously. He was not less happy himself to rejoin his friends. "Ain't you glad I've come?" he would call out, as he came up to shake hands.

The cases which fell to Lincoln on the Eighth Circuit were of the sort common to a new country. Litigation over bordering lines and deeds, over damages by wandering cattle, over broils at country festivities. Few of the cases were of large importance. When a client came to Lincoln his first effort was to arrange matters, if possible, and to avoid a suit. In a few notes for a law lecture prepared about 1850, he says:

> "Discourage litigation. Persuade your neighbors to compromise whenever you can. Point out to them how the nominal winner is often a real loser—in fees, expenses, and waste of time. As a peacemaker the lawyer has a superior opportunity of being a good man. There will still be business enough.
>
> "Never stir up litigation. A worse man can scarcely be found than one who does this. Who can be more nearly a fiend than he who habitually overhauls the register of deeds in search of defects in titles, whereon to stir up strife, and put money in his pocket? A moral tone ought to be infused into the profession which should drive such men out of it."

He carried out this in his practice. "Who was your guardian?" he asked a young man who came to him to complain that a part of the property left him had been withheld. "Enoch Kingsbury," replied the young man.

"I know Mr. Kingsbury," said Lincoln, "and he is not the man to have cheated you out of a cent, and I can't take the case, and advise you to drop the subject." And it was dropped.

"We shall not take your case," he said to a man who had shown that by a legal technicality he could win property worth six hundred dollars. "You must remember that some things legally right are not morally right. We shall not take your case, but will give you a little advice for which we will charge you nothing. You seem to be a sprightly, energetic man; we would advise you to try your hand at making six hundred dollars in some other way."

Where he saw injustice he was quick to offer his services to the wronged party. A pleasant example of this is related by Joseph Jefferson in his "Autobiography." In 1839, Jefferson, then a lad of ten years, travelled through Illinois with his father's theatrical company. After playing at Chicago, Quincy, Peoria and Pekin, the company went in the fall to Springfield, where the sight of the legislature tempted the elder Jefferson and his partner to remain throughout the season. But there was no theatre. Not to be daunted they built one. But hardly had they completed it before a religious revival broke out in the town, and the church people turned all their influence against the theatre. So effectually did they work that a law was passed by the municipality imposing a license which was practically prohibitory. "In the midst of our trouble," says Jefferson, "a young lawyer called on the managers. He had heard of the injustice, and offered, if they would place the matter in his hands, to have the license taken off, declaring that he only desired to see fair play, and he would accept no fee whether he failed or succeeded. The young lawyer began his harangue. He handled the subject with tact, skill, and humor, tracing the history of the drama from the time when Thespis acted in a cart to the stage of to-day. He illustrated his speech with a number of anecdotes, and kept the council in a roar of laughter. His good humor prevailed, and the exorbitant tax was taken off." The "young lawyer" was Lincoln.

Having accepted a case, Lincoln's first object seemed to be to reduce it to its simplest elements. "If I can clean this case of technicalities, and get it properly swung to the jury, I'll win it," he told his partner Herndon one day. He began by getting at what seemed to him the pivot on which it rested. Sure of that, he cared little for anything else. He trusted very little to books; a great deal to common sense and his ideas of right and wrong.

"In the make of his character Mr. Lincoln had many elements essential to the successful circuit lawyer," says one of his fellow-practitioners. "He knew much of the law as written in the books, and had that knowledge ready for use at all times. That was a valuable possession in the absence of law books, where none were obtainable on the circuit. But he had more than a knowledge of the law. He knew right and justice, and knew how to make their application to the affairs of every-day life. That was an element in his character that gave him power to prevail with the jury when arguing a case before them. Few lawyers ever had the influence with a jury that Mr. Lincoln had."

When a case was clear to him and he was satisfied of its justice, he trusted to taking advantage of the developments of the trial to win. For this reason he made few notes beforehand, rarely writing out his plan of argument. Those he left are amusingly brief; for instance, the notes made for a suit he had brought

FACSIMILE OF A LINCOLN MEMORANDUM.
FROM THE LINCOLN COLLECTION IN THE LAW OFFICES OF MESSRS. VANUXEM & POTTER, OF PHILADELPHIA. THIS CHARACTERISTIC MEMORANDUM WAS FOUNDED BY MESSRS. HERNDON & WEIK IN LOOKING OVER THE PAPERS IN LINCOLN'S LAW OFFICE. IT WAS THE LABEL TO A PACKAGE OF LETTERS, PAMPHLETS, AND NEWSPAPERS WHICH HE HAD TIED TOGETHER AND MARKED.

against a pension agent who had withheld as fee half of the pension he had obtained for the aged widow of a Revolutionary soldier. Lincoln was deeply indignant at the agent, and had resolved to win his suit. He read up the Revolutionary war afresh, and when he came to address the jury drew a harrowing picture of the private soldier's sufferings and of the trials of his separation from his wife. The notes for this argument ran as follows:

"No contract—Not professional services. Unreasonable charge,—Money retained by Def't not given by Pl'ff.—Revolutionary War.—Soldier's bleeding feet.—Pl'ff's husband.— Soldier leaving home for army—*Skin def't.*—Close."

Lincoln's reason for not taking notes, as he told it to H. W. Beckwith, when a student in the Danville office of Lincoln and Lamon, was: "Notes are a bother, taking time to make, and more to hunt them up afterwards; lawyers who do so soon get the habit of referring to them so much that it confuses and tires the jury." "He relied on his well-trained memory," says Mr. Beckwith, "that recorded and indexed every passing detail. And by his skilful questions, a joke, or pat retort as the trial progressed, he steered his jury from the bayous and eddies of side issues and kept them clear of the snags and sandbars, if any were put in the real channel of his case."

Much of his strength lay in his skill in examining witnesses. "He had a most remarkable talent for examining witnesses," says an intimate associate; "with him it was a rare gift. It was a power to compel a witness to disclose the whole truth. Even a witness at first unfriendly, under his kindly treatment would finally become friendly, and would wish to tell nothing he could honestly avoid against him, if he could state nothing for him."

He could not endure an unfair use of testimony or the misrepresentation of his own position. "In the Harrison murder case," says Mr. T. W. S. Kidd of Springfield, a crier of the court in Lincoln's day, "the prosecuting attorney stated that such a witness made a certain statement, when Mr. Lincoln rose and made such a plaintive appeal to the attorney to correct the statement, that the attorney actually made the *amende honorable*, and afterwards remarked to a brother lawyer that he could deny his own child's appeal as quickly as he could Mr. Lincoln's."

Sometimes under provocation he became violently angry. In the murder case referred to above, the judge ruled contrary to his expectations, and, as Mr. Lincoln said, contrary to the decision of the Supreme Court in a similar case. "Both Mr. Lincoln and Judge Logan, who was with him in the case," says Mr. Kidd, "rose to their feet quick as thought. I do think he was the most unearthly looking man I had ever seen. He roared like a lion suddenly aroused from his lair, and said and did more in ten minutes than I ever heard him say or saw him do before in an hour."

He depended a great deal upon his stories in pleading, using them as illustrations which demonstrated the case more conclusively than argument could have done. Judge H. W. Beckwith of Danville, Illinois, in his "Personal Recollections of Lincoln," tells a story which is a good example of Lincoln's way of condensing the law and the facts of an issue in a story.

"A man, by vile words, first provoked and then made a bodily attack upon another. The latter in defending himself gave the other much the worst of the encounter. The aggressor, to get even, had the one who thrashed him tried in our circuit court upon a charge of an assault and battery. Mr. Lincoln defended, and told the jury that his client was in the fix of a man who, in going along the highway with a pitchfork on his shoulder, was attacked by a fierce dog that ran out at him from a farmer's door-yard. In parrying off the brute with the fork its prongs stuck into the brute and killed him.

"'What made you kill my dog?' said the farmer.

"'What made him try to bite me?'

"'But why did you not go at him with the other end of the pitchfork?'

"'Why did he not come after me with his other end?' At this Mr. Lincoln whirled about in his long arms an imaginary dog and pushed its tail end toward the jury. This was the defensive plea of '*son assault demesne*'—loosely, that 'the other fellow brought on the fight,'—quickly told, and in a way the dullest mind would grasp and retain."

Mr. T. W. S. Kidd says that he once heard a lawyer opposed to Lincoln trying to convince a jury that precedent was superior to law, and that custom made things legal in all cases. When Lincoln arose to answer him he told the jury he would argue his case in the same way. Said he: "Old 'Squire Bagly, from Menard, came into my office and said, 'Lincoln, I want your advice as a lawyer. Has a man what's been elected justice of the peace a right to issue a marriage license?' I told him he had not; when the old 'squire threw himself back in his chair very indignantly, and said: 'Lincoln, I thought you was a lawyer. Now Bob Thomas and me had a bet on this thing, and we agreed to let you decide; but if this is your opinion I don't want it, for I know a thunderin' sight better, for I have been 'squire now eight years and have done it all the time.'"

His manner of telling stories was most effective. "When he chose to do so," writes Judge Scott, "he could place the opposite party, and his counsel too, for that matter, in a most ridiculous attitude by relating in his inimitable way a pertinent story. That often gave him a great advantage with the jury. A young lawyer had brought an action in trespass to recover damages done to his client's growing crops by defendant's hogs. The right of action under the law of Illinois, as it was then, depended on the fact whether plaintiff's fence was sufficient to turn ordinary stock. There was some little conflict in the evidence on that question; but the weight of the testimony was decidedly in favor of plaintiff, and sustained beyond all doubt his cause of action. Mr. Lincoln appeared for defendant. There was no controversy as to the damage done by defendant's stock. The only thing in the case that could possibly admit of any discussion was the condition of plaintiff's fence; and as the testimony on that question seemed to be in favor of plaintiff, and as the sum involved was little in amount, Mr. Lincoln did not deem it necessary to argue the case seriously, but by way of saying something in behalf of his client he told a little story about a *fence* that was so *crooked* that when a hog went through an opening in it, invariably it came out on the same side from whence it started. His description of the confused look of the hog after several times going through the fence and still finding itself on the side from which it had started, was a humorous specimen of the best story-telling. The effect was to make plaintiff's case appear ridiculous; and while Mr. Lincoln did not attempt to apply the story to the case, the jury seemed to think it had some kind of application to the fence in controversy—otherwise he would not have told it—and shortly returned a verdict for the defendant."

Those unfamiliar with his methods frequently took his stories as an effort to wring a laugh from the jury. A lawyer, a stranger to Mr. Lincoln, once expressed to General Linder the opinion that this practice of Lincoln was a waste of time. "Don't lay that flattering unction to your soul," Linder answered; "Lincoln is like Tansey's horse, he 'breaks to win.'"

But it was not his stories, it was his clearness which was his strongest point. He meant that the jury should see that he was right. For this reason he never used a word which the dullest juryman could not understand. Rarely, if ever, did a Latin term creep into his arguments. A lawyer quoting a legal maxim one day in court, turned to Lincoln, and said: "That is so, is it not, Mr. Lincoln?"

"If that's Latin," Lincoln replied, "you had better call another witness."

His illustrations were almost always of the homeliest kind. He did not care to "go among the ancients for figures," he said.

"Much of the force of his argument," writes Judge Scott, "lay in his logical statement of the facts of a case. When he had in that way secured a clear understanding of the facts, the jury and the court would seem naturally to follow him in his conclusions as to the law of the case. His simple and natural presentation of the facts seemed to give the impression that the jury were themselves making the statement. He had the happy and unusual faculty of making the jury believe *they*—and not *he*—were trying the case. Mr. Lincoln kept himself in the background, and apparently assumed nothing more than to be an *assistant* counsel to the court or the jury, on whom the primary responsibility for the final decision of the case in fact rested."

He rarely consulted books during a trial, lest he lose the attention of the jury, and if obliged to, translated their statements into the simplest terms. In his desire to keep his case clear he rarely argued points which seemed to him unessential. "In law it is good policy never to plead what you need not, lest you oblige yourself to prove what you can not," he wrote. He would thus give away point after point with an indifferent "I reckon that's so," until the point which he considered pivotal was reached, and there he hung.

"In making a speech," says Mr. John Hill, "Mr. Lincoln was

the plainest man I ever heard. He was not a speaker but a talker. He talked to jurors and to political gatherings plain, sensible, candid talk, almost as in conversation, no effort whatever in oratory. But his talking had wonderful effect. Honesty, candor, fairness, everything that was convincing, was in his manner and expressions."

This candor of which Mr. Hill speaks characterized his entire conduct of a trial. "It is well understood by the profession," says General Mason Brayman, "that lawyers do not read authorities favoring the opposing side. I once heard Mr. Lincoln, in the supreme court of Illinois, reading from a reported case some strong points in favor of his argument. Reading a little too far, and before becoming aware of it, he plunged into an authority against himself. Pausing a moment, he drew up his shoulders in a comical way, and half laughing, went on, 'There, there, may it please the court, I reckon I've scratched up a snake. But, as I'm in for it, I guess I'll read it through.' Then, in his most ingenious and matchless manner, he went on with his argument, and won his case, convincing the court that it was not much of a snake after all."

1900

Winston Churchill

No relation to the British statesman, the American novelist Winston Churchill (1871–1947) achieved popular success with a series of predictable but appealing historical romances, including *Richard Carvel* (1899) and *The Crossing* (1904), set in the Revolution, and *Coniston* (1906), a story of New England politics during the mid-19th century. His most famous work, *The Crisis* (1901), examined the Civil War's impact on the citizens of the bitterly divided border state metropolis of St. Louis (Churchill's native city), and it is the first American novel in which Lincoln plays a prominent role. First seen debating Stephen A. Douglas at Freeport during the 1858 Senate race, Lincoln is later portrayed as a compassionate wartime leader. In the chapter printed here, he helps bring about the symbolic reconciliation of the Confederate heroine with her Unionist lover, while assuring her, and the book's readers, that "I have not suffered by the South, I have suffered *with* the South." In turn, the previously hostile Virginia Carvel sees the President standing "bent and sorrowful, and it was as if a light had fallen on him."

FROM

The Crisis

CHAPTER XV

THE MAN OF SORROWS

The train was late—very late. It was Virginia who first caught sight of the new dome of the Capitol through the slanting rain, but she merely pressed her lips together and said nothing. In the dingy brick station of the Baltimore and Ohio Railroad more than one person paused to look after them, and a kind-hearted lady who had been in the car kissed the girl good-bye.

"You think that you can find your uncle's house, my dear?" she asked, glancing at Virginia with concern. Through all of that long journey she had worn a look apart. "Do you think you can find your uncle's house?"

Virginia started. And then she smiled as she looked at the honest, alert, and squarely built gentleman beside her.

"Captain Brent can, Mrs. Ware," she said. "He can find anything."

Whereupon the kind lady gave the Captain her hand.

"You look as if you could, Captain," said she. "Remember, if General Carvel is out of town, you promised to bring her to me."

"Yes, ma'am," said Captain Lige, "and so I *shall*."

"Kerridge, kerridge! Right dis-a-way! No sah, dat ain't de kerridge you wants. Dat's it, lady, you'se lookin' at it. Kerridge, kerridge, kerridge!"

Virginia tried bravely to smile, but she was very near to tears as she stood on the uneven pavement and looked at the scrawny horses standing patiently in the steady downpour. All sorts of people were coming and going,—army officers and navy officers and citizens of states and territories, driving up and driving away.

And this was Washington!

She was thinking then of the multitude who came here with aching hearts,—with heavier hearts than was hers that day. How many of the throng hurrying by would not flee, if they could, back to the peaceful homes they had left? But perhaps those homes were gone now. Destroyed, like her own, by the war. Women with children at their breasts, and mothers bowed with sorrow, had sought this city in their agony. Young men and old had come hither, striving to keep back the thoughts of dear ones left behind, whom they might never see again. And by the thousands and tens of thousands they had passed from here to the places of blood beyond.

"Kerridge, sah! Kerridge!"

"Do you know where General Daniel Carvel lives?"

"Yes, sah, reckon I does. I Street, sah. Jump right in, sah."

Virginia sank back on the stuffy cushions of the rattle-trap, and then sat upright again and stared out of the window at the dismal scene. They were splashing through a sea of mud. Ever since they had left St. Louis, Captain Lige had done his best to cheer her, and he did not intend to desist now.

"This beats all," he cried. "So this is Washington! Why, it

don't compare to St. Louis, except we haven't got the White House and the Capitol. Jinny, it would take a scow to get across the street, and we don't have ramshackly stores and nigger cabins bang up against fine houses like that. This is ragged. That's what it is, *ragged*. We don't have any dirty pickaninnies dodging among the horses in our residence streets. I declare, Jinny, if those aren't *pigs*!"

Virginia laughed. She could not help it.

"Poor Lige!" she said, "I hope Uncle Daniel has some breakfast for you. You've had a good deal to put up with on this trip."

"Lordy, Jinny," said the Captain, "I'd put up with a good deal more than this for the sake of going anywhere with you."

"Even to such a doleful place as this?" she sighed.

"This is all right, if the sun'll only come out and dry things up and let us see the green on those trees," he said. "Lordy, how I do love to see the spring green in the sunlight!"

She put out her hand over his.

"Lige," she said, "you know you're just trying to keep up my spirits. You've been doing that ever since we left home."

"No such thing," he replied with vehemence. "There's nothing for you to be cast down about."

"Oh, but there is!" she cried. "Suppose I can't make your Black Republican President pardon Clarence!"

"Pooh!" said the Captain, squeezing her hand and trying to appear unconcerned. "Your Uncle Daniel knows Mr. Lincoln. He'll have that arranged."

Just then the rattletrap pulled up at the sidewalk, the wheels of the near side in four inches of mud, and the Captain leaped out and spread the umbrella. They were in front of a rather imposing house of brick, flanked on one side by a house just like it, and on the other by a series of dreary vacant lots where the rain had collected in pools. They climbed the steps and rang the bell. In due time the door was opened by a smiling yellow butler in black.

"Does General Carvel live here?"

"Yas, miss. But he ain't to home now. Done gone to New York."

"Oh," faltered Virginia. "Didn't he get my telegram day before yesterday? I sent it to the War Department."

"He's done gone since Saturday, miss." And then, evidently impressed by the young lady's looks, he added hospitably, "Kin I do anything fo' you, miss?"

"I'm his niece, Miss Virginia Carvel, and this is Captain Brent."

The yellow butler's face lighted up.

"Come right in, Miss Jinny. Done heard de General speak of you often—yas'm. De General'll be to home dis a'ternoon, suah. 'Twill do him good ter see you, Miss Jinny. He's been mighty lonesome. Walk right in, Cap'n, and make yo'selves at home. Lizbeth—Lizbeth!" A yellow maid came running down the stairs. "Heah's Miss Jinny?"

"Lan' of goodness!" cried Lizbeth. "I knows Miss Jinny. Done seed her at Calve't House. How *is* you, Miss Jinny?"

"Very well, Lizbeth," said Virginia, listlessly sitting down on the hall sofa. "Can you give us some breakfast?"

"Yas'm," said Lizbeth, "jes' reckon we kin." She ushered them into a walnut dining room, big and high and sombre, with plush-bottomed chairs placed about—walnut also; for that was the fashion in those days. But the Captain had no sooner seated himself than he shot up again and started out.

"Where are you going, Lige?"

"To pay off the carriage driver," he said.

"Let him wait," said Virginia. "I'm going to the White House in a little while."

"What—what for?" he gasped.

"To see your Black Republican President," she replied, with alarming calmness.

Now, Jinny," he cried, in excited appeal, "don't go doin' any such fool trick as that. Your Uncle Dan'l will be here this afternoon. *He* knows the President. And then the thing'll be fixed all right, and no *mistake*."

Her reply was in the same tone—almost a monotone—which she had used for three days. It made the Captain very uneasy, for he knew when she spoke in that way that her will was in it.

"And to lose that time," she answered, "may be to have him shot."

"But you can't get to the President without credentials," he objected.

"What!" she flashed, "hasn't any one a right to see the President? You mean to say that he will not see a woman in trouble? Then all these pretty stories I hear of him are false. They are made up by the Yankees."

Poor Captain Lige! He had some notion of the multitude of calls upon Mr. Lincoln, especially at that time. But he could not, he dared not, remind her of the principal reason for this,—Lee's surrender and the approaching end of the war. And then the Captain had never seen Mr. Lincoln. In the distant valley of the Mississippi he had only heard of the President very conflicting things. He had heard him criticised and reviled and praised, just as is every man who goes to the White House, be he saint or sinner. And, during an administration, no man at a distance may come at a President's true character and worth. The Captain had seen Lincoln caricatured vilely. And again he had read and heard the pleasant anecdotes of which Virginia had spoken, until he did not know what to believe.

As for Virginia, he knew her partisanship to, and undying love for, the South; he knew the class prejudice which was bound to assert itself, and he had seen enough in the girl's demeanour to fear that she was going to demand rather than implore. She did not come of a race that was wont to bend the knee.

"Well, well," he said despairingly, "you must eat some breakfast first, Jinny."

She waited with an ominous calmness until it was brought in, and then she took a part of a roll and some coffee.

"This won't do," exclaimed the Captain. "Why, why, that won't get you halfway to Mr. Lincoln."

She shook her head half smiling.

"You must eat enough, Lige," she said.

He was finished in an incredibly short time, and amid the protestations of Lizbeth and the yellow butler they got into the carriage again, and splashed and rattled toward the White House. Once Virginia glanced out, and catching sight of the bedraggled flags on the houses in honour of Lee's surrender, a look of pain crossed her face. The Captain could not repress a note of warning.

"Jinny," said he, "I have an idea that you'll find the President a good deal of a *man*. Now if you're allowed to see him, don't get him *mad*, Jinny, whatever you do."

Virginia stared straight ahead.

"If he is something of a man, Lige, he will not lose his temper with a woman."

Captain Lige subsided. And just then they came in sight of the house of the Presidents, with its beautiful portico and its broad wings. And they turned in under the dripping trees of the grounds. A carriage with a black coachman and footman was ahead of them, and they saw two stately gentlemen descend from it and pass the guard at the door. Then their turn came. The Captain helped her out in his best manner, and gave some money to the driver.

"I reckon he needn't wait for us this time, Jinny," said he.

She shook her head and went in, he following, and they were directed to the anteroom of the President's office on the second floor. There were many people in the corridors, and one or two young officers in blue who stared at her. She passed them with her head high.

But her spirits sank when they came to the anteroom.

It was full of all sorts of people. Politicians, both prosperous and seedy, full faced and keen faced, seeking office; women, officers, and a one-armed soldier sitting in the corner. He was among the men who offered Virginia their seats, and the only one whom she thanked. But she walked directly to the door-keeper at the end of the room. Captain Lige was beside her.

"Can we see the President?" he asked.

"Have you got an appointment?" said the old man.

"No."

"Then you'll have to wait your turn, sir," he said, shaking his head and looking at Virginia. And he added: "It's slow work waiting your turn, there's so many governors and generals and senators, although the session's over. It's a busy time, miss."

Virginia went very close to him.

"Oh, can't you do something?" she said. And added, with an inspiration, "I *must* see him. It's a matter of life and death."

She saw instantly, with a woman's instinct, that her words had had their effect. The old man glanced at her again, as if demurring.

"You're sure, miss, it's life and death?" he said.

"Oh, why should I say so if it were not?" she cried.

"The orders are very strict," he said. "But the President told me to give precedence to cases when a life is in question. Just you wait a minute, miss, until Governor Doddridge comes out, and I'll see what I can do for you. Give me your name, please, miss."

She remained standing where she was. In a little while the heavy door opened, and a portly, rubicund man came out with a smile on his face. He broke into a laugh, when halfway across the room, as if the memory of what he had heard were too much for his gravity. The doorkeeper slipped into the room, and there was a silent, anxious interval. Then he came out again.

"The President will see you, miss."

Captain Lige started forward with her, but she restrained him.

"Wait for me here, Lige," she said.

She swept in alone, and the door closed softly after her. The room was a big one, and there were maps on the table, with pins sticking in them. She saw that much, and then—!

Could this fantastically tall, stooping figure before her be that of the President of the United States? She stopped, as from the shock he gave her. The lean, yellow face with the mask-like lines all up and down, the unkempt, tousled hair, the beard—why, he was a hundred times more ridiculous than his caricatures. He might have stood for many of the poor white trash farmers she had seen in Kentucky—save for the long black coat.

"Is—is this Mr. Lincoln?" she asked, her breath taken away.

He bowed and smiled down at her. Somehow that smile changed his face a little.

"I guess I'll have to own up," he answered.

"My name is Virginia Carvel," she said. "I have come all the way from St. Louis to see you."

"Miss Carvel," said the President, looking at her intently, "I have rarely been so flattered in my life. I—I hope I have not disappointed you."

Virginia was justly angry.

"Oh, you haven't," she cried, her eyes flashing, "because I am what you would call a Rebel."

The mirth in the dark corners of his eyes disturbed her more and more. And then she saw that the President was laughing.

"And have you a better name for it, Miss Carvel?" he asked. "Because I am searching for a better name—just now."

She was silent—sternly silent. And she tapped her foot on the carpet. What manner of man was this?

"Won't you sit down?" said the President, kindly. "You must be tired after your journey." And he put forth a chair.

"No, thank you," said Virginia; "I think that I can say what I have come to say better standing."

"Well," said Mr. Lincoln, "that's not strange. I'm that way, too. The words seem to come out better. That reminds me of a story they tell about General Buck Tanner. Ever heard of Buck, Miss Carvel? No? Well, Buck was a character. He got his title in the Mormon war. One day the boys asked him over to the square to make a speech. The General was a little uneasy.

"'I'm all right when I get standing up, Liza,' he said to his wife. 'Then the words come right along. Only trouble is they come too cussed fast. How'm I going to stop 'em when I want to?'

"'Well, I du declare, Buck,' said she, 'I gave you credit for some sense. All you've got to do is to set down. That'll end it, I reckon.'

"So the General went over to the square and talked for about an hour and a half, and then a Chicago man shouted to him to dry up. The General looked pained.

"'Boys,' said he, 'it's jest every bit as bad for me as it is for you. You'll have to hand up a chair, boys, because I'm never going to get shet of this goldarned speech any other way.'"

Mr. Lincoln had told this so comically that Virginia was forced to laugh, and she immediately hated herself. A man who could joke at such a time certainly could not feel the cares and responsibilities of his office. He should have been a comedian.

And yet this was the President who had conducted the war, whose Generals had conquered the Confederacy. And she was come to ask him a favour.

Virginia swallowed her pride.

"Mr. Lincoln," she began, "I have come to talk to you about my cousin, Colonel Clarence Colfax."

"I shall be happy to talk to you about your cousin, Colonel Colfax, Miss Carvel. Is he your third or fourth cousin?"

"He is my first cousin," she retorted.

"Is he in the city?" asked Mr. Lincoln, innocently. "Why didn't he come with you?"

"Oh, haven't you heard?" she cried. "He is Clarence Colfax, of St. Louis, now a Colonel in the army of the Confederate States."

"Which army?" asked Mr. Lincoln.

Virginia tossed her head in exasperation.

"In General Joseph Johnston's army," she replied, trying to be patient. "But now," she gulped, "now he has been arrested as a spy by General Sherman's army."

"That's too bad," answered Mr. Lincoln.

"And—and they are going to shoot him."

"That's worse," said Mr. Lincoln, gravely. "But I expect he deserves it."

"Oh, no, he doesn't," she cried. "You don't know how brave he is! He floated down the Mississippi on a log, out of Vicksburg, and brought back thousands and thousands of percussion caps. He rowed across the river when the Yankee fleet was going down, and set fire to De Soto so that they could see to shoot."

"Well," said Mr. Lincoln, "that's a good starter."

Then he looked thoughtful.

"Miss Carvel," said he, "that argument reminds me of a story about a man I used to know in the old days in Illinois. His name was McNeil, and he was a lawyer. One day he was defending a prisoner for assault and battery before Judge Drake.

"'Judge,' says McNeil, 'you oughtn't to lock this man up. It was a fair fight, and he's the best man in the state in a fair fight. And, what's more, he's never been licked in a fair fight in his life.'"

"'And if your honour does lock me up,' the prisoner put in, 'I'll give your honour a thunderin' big lickin' when I get out.'"

"The Judge took off his coat.

"'Gentlemen,' said he, 'it's a powerful queer argument, but the Court will admit it on its merits. The prisoner will please to step out on the grass.'"

This time Virginia contrived merely to smile. She was striving against something, she knew not what. Her breath was coming deeply, and she was dangerously near to tears. Why? She could not tell. She had come into this man's presence despising herself for having to ask him a favour. The sight of his face she had ridiculed. Now she could not look into it without an odd sensation. What was in it? Sorrow? Yes, that was nearest it.

What had the man done? Told her a few funny stories—given quizzical answers to some of her questions. Quizzical, yes; but she could not be sure then there was not wisdom in them, and that humiliated her. She had never conceived of such a man. And, be it added gratuitously, Virginia deemed herself something of an adept in dealing with men.

"And now," said Mr. Lincoln, "to continue for the defence, I believe that Colonel Colfax first distinguished himself at the time of Camp Jackson, when of all the prisoners he refused to accept a parole."

Startled, she looked up at him swiftly and then down again. "Yes," she answered, "yes. But oh, Mr. Lincoln, please don't hold that against him."

If she could only have seen his face then. But her lashes were dropped.

"My dear young lady," replied the President, "I honour him for it. I was merely elaborating the argument which you have begun. On the other hand, it is a pity that he should have taken off that uniform which he adorned, and attempted to enter General Sherman's lines as a civilian,—as a spy."

He had spoken these last words very gently, but she was too excited to heed his gentleness. She drew herself up, a gleam in her eyes like the crest of a blue wave in a storm.

"A spy!" she cried; "it takes more courage to be a spy than anything else in war. Then he will be shot. You are not content in the North with what you have gained. You are not content with depriving us of our rights, and our fortunes, with forcing us back to an allegiance we despise. You are not content with humiliating our Generals and putting innocent men in prisons. But now I suppose you will shoot us all. And all this mercy that I have heard about means nothing—nothing—"

Why did she falter and stop?

"Miss Carvel," said the President, "I am afraid from what I have heard just now, that it means nothing."

Oh, the sadness of that voice,—the ineffable sadness,—the sadness, and the woe of a great nation! And the sorrow in those eyes, the sorrow of a heavy cross borne meekly,—how heavy none will ever know. The pain of a crown of thorns worn for a world that did not understand.

No wonder Virginia faltered and was silent. She looked at Abraham Lincoln standing there, bent and sorrowful, and it was as if a light had fallen upon him. But strangest of all in that strange moment was that she felt his strength. It was the same strength she had felt in Stephen Brice. This was the thought that came to her.

Slowly she walked to the window and looked out across the green grounds where the wind was shaking the wet trees, past the unfinished monument to the Father of her country, and across the broad Potomac to Alexandria in the hazy distance. The rain beat upon the panes, and then she knew that she was crying softly to herself. She had met a force that she could not conquer, she had looked upon a sorrow that she could not fathom, albeit she had known sorrow.

Presently she felt him near. She turned and looked through her tears at his face that was all compassion. And now she was unashamed. He had placed a chair behind her.

"Sit down, Virginia," he said. Even the name fell from him naturally.

She obeyed him then like a child. He remained standing.

"Tell me about your cousin," he said; "are you going to marry him?"

She hung an instant on her answer. Would that save Clarence? But in that moment she could not have spoken anything but the truth to save her soul.

"No, Mr. Lincoln," she said; "I was—but I did not love him. I—I think that was one reason why he was so reckless."

Mr. Lincoln smiled.

"The officer who happened to see Colonel Colfax captured is now in Washington. When your name was given to me, I sent for him. Perhaps he is in the anteroom now. I should like to tell you, first of all, that this officer defended your cousin and asked me to pardon him."

"He defended him! He asked you to pardon him! Who is he?" she exclaimed.

Again Mr. Lincoln smiled. He strode to the bell-cord, and spoke a few words to the usher who answered his ring. The usher went out. Then the door opened, and a young officer, spare, erect, came quickly into the room, and bowed respectfully to the President. But Mr. Lincoln's eyes were not on him. They were on the girl. He saw her head lifted, timidly. He saw her lips part and the colour come flooding into her face. But she did not rise.

The President sighed. But the light in her eyes was reflected in his own. It has been truly said that Abraham Lincoln knew the human heart.

The officer still stood facing the President, the girl staring at his profile. The door closed behind him.

"Major Brice," said Mr. Lincoln, "when you asked me to pardon Colonel Colfax, I believe that you told me he was inside his own skirmish lines when he was captured."

"Yes, sir, he was."

Suddenly Stephen turned, as if impelled by the President's gaze, and so his eyes met Virginia's. He forgot time and place,— for the while even this man whom he revered above all men. He saw her hand tighten on the arm of her chair. He took a step toward her, and stopped. Mr. Lincoln was speaking again.

"He put in a plea, a lawyer's plea, wholly unworthy of him, Miss Virginia. He asked me to let your cousin off on a technicality. What do you think of that?"

"Oh!" said Virginia. Just the exclamation escaped her—nothing more. The crimson that had betrayed her deepened on her cheeks. Slowly the eyes she had yielded to Stephen came back again and rested on the President. And now her wonder was that an ugly man could be so beautiful.

"I wish it understood, Mr. Lawyer," the President continued, "that I am not letting off Colonel Colfax on a technicality. I am sparing his life," he said slowly, "because the time for which we have been waiting and longing for four years is now at hand—the time to be merciful. Let us all thank God for it."

Virginia had risen now. She crossed the room, her head lifted, her heart lifted, to where this man of sorrows stood smiling down at her.

"Mr. Lincoln," she faltered, "I did not know you when I came here. I should have known you, for I had heard him—I had heard Major Brice praise you. Oh," she cried, "how I wish that every man and woman and child in the South might come here and see you as I have seen you to-day. I think—I think that some of their bitterness might be taken away."

Abraham Lincoln laid his hands upon the girl. And Stephen, watching, knew that he was looking upon a benediction.

"Virginia," said Mr. Lincoln, "I have not suffered by the South, I have suffered *with* the South. Your sorrow has been my sorrow, and your pain has been my pain. What you have lost, I have lost. And what you have gained," he added sublimely, "I have gained."

He led her gently to the window. The clouds were flying before the wind, and a patch of blue sky shone above the Potomac. With his long arm he pointed across the river to the south-east, and as if by a miracle a shaft of sunlight fell on the white houses of Alexandria.

"In the first days of the war," he said, "a flag flew there in sight of the place where George Washington lived and died. I used to watch that flag, and thank God that Washington had not lived to see it. And sometimes,—sometimes I wondered if God had allowed it to be put in irony just there." His voice seemed to catch. "That was wrong," he continued. "I should have known that this was our punishment—that the sight of it was my punishment. Before we could become the great nation He has destined us to be, our sins must be wiped out in blood. You loved that flag, Virginia. You love it still. I say in all sincerity, may you always love it. May the day come when this Nation, North and South, may look back upon it with reverence. Thousands upon thousands of brave Americans have died under it for what they believed was right. But may the day come again when you will love that flag you see there now—Washington's flag—better still."

He stopped, and the tears were wet upon Virginia's lashes. She could not have spoken then.

Mr. Lincoln went over to his desk and sat down before it. Then he began to write, slouched forward, one knee resting on the floor, his lips moving at the same time. When he got up again he seemed taller than ever.

"There!" he said, "I guess that will fix it. I'll have that sent to Sherman. I have already spoken to him about the matter."

They did not thank him. It was beyond them both. He turned to Stephen with that quizzical look on his face he had so often seen him wear.

"Steve," he said, "I'll tell you a story. The other night Harlan was here making a speech to a crowd out of the window, and my boy Tad was sitting behind him.

"'What shall we do with the Rebels?' said Harlan to the crowd.

"'Hang 'em!' cried the people.

"'No,' says Tad, 'hang on to 'em.'

"And the boy was right. That is what we intend to do,—hang on to 'em. And, Steve," said Mr. Lincoln, putting his hand again on Virginia's shoulder, "if you have the sense I think you have, you'll hang on, too."

For an instant he stood smiling at their blushes,—he to whom the power was given to set apart his cares and his troubles and partake of the happiness of others. For of such was his happiness.

Then the President drew out his watch. "Bless me!" he said, "I am ten minutes behind my appointment at the Department. Miss Virginia, you may care to thank the Major for the little service he has done you. You can do so undisturbed here. Make yourselves at home."

As he opened the door he paused and looked back at them. The smile passed from his face, and an ineffable expression of longing—longing and tenderness—came upon it.

Then he was gone.

For a space, while his spell was upon them, they did not stir. Then Stephen sought her eyes that had been so long denied him. They were not denied him now. It was Virginia who first found her voice, and she called him by his name.

"Oh, Stephen," she said, "how sad he looked!"

He was close to her, at her side. And he answered her in the earnest tone which she knew so well.

"Virginia, if I could have had what I most wished for in the world, I should have asked that you should know Abraham Lincoln."

Then she dropped her eyes, and her breath came quickly.

"I—I might have known," she answered, "I might have known what he was. I had heard you talk of him. I had seen him in you, and I did not know. Do you remember that day when we were in the summer-house together at Glencoe, long ago? When you had come back from seeing him?"

"As yesterday," he said.

"You were changed then," she said bravely. "I saw it. Now I understand. It was because you had seen Mr. Lincoln."

"When I saw him," said Stephen, reverently, "I knew how little and narrow I was."

Then, overcome by the incense of her presence, he drew her to him until her heart beat against his own. She did not resist, but lifted her face to him, and he kissed her.

"You love me, Virginia!" he cried.

"Yes, Stephen," she answered, low, more wonderful in her surrender than ever before. "Yes—dear." Then she hid her face against his blue coat. "I—I cannot help it. Oh, Stephen, how I have struggled against it! How I have tried to hate you, and couldn't. No, I couldn't. I tried to insult you, I did insult you. And when I saw how splendidly you bore it, I used to cry."

He kissed her brown hair.

"I loved you through it all," he said. " Virginia!"

"Yes, dearest."

"Virginia, did you dream of me?"

She raised her head quickly, and awe was in her eyes.

"How did you know?"

"Because I dreamed of you," he answered. "And those dreams used to linger with me half the day as I went about my work. I used to think of them as I sat in the saddle on the march."

"I too treasured them," she said. "And I hated myself for doing it."

"Virginia, will you marry me?"

"Yes."

"To-morrow?"

"Yes, dear, to-morrow." Faintly, "I—I have no one but you—now."

Once more he drew her to him, and she gloried in his strength.

"God help me to cherish you, dear," he said, "and guard you well."

She drew away from him, gently, and turned toward the window.

"See, Stephen," she cried, "the sun has come out at last."

For a while they were silent, looking out; the drops glistened on blade and leaf, and the joyous new green of the earth entered into their hearts.

1901

Edwin Markham

A schoolteacher from northern California, Markham (1852–1940) created a literary sensation in 1899 with the publication of his first collection of poetry, *The Man with a Hoe*. He was then asked by the Republican Club of New York to compose a poem for recitation at their Lincoln birthday dinner in 1900. The resulting verse, which became the highlight of his 1901 collection *Lincoln and Other Poems*, celebrates "The Man of the People" as an exemplary frontier hero while stressing his empathy for the common man and his oneness with the very earth he had once tilled (though, in truth, Lincoln hated farm work). Markham presents Lincoln as "an abstract embodiment of the ancient and cosmic forces of genius and wisdom," as Lincoln scholar Roy Basler perceptively observed, with "no flaw in the cast of the heroic figure."

Lincoln, the Man of the People

When the Norn-Mother saw the Whirlwind Hour,
Greatening and darkening as it hurried on,
She bent the strenuous Heavens and came down
To make a man to meet the mortal need.
She took the tried clay of the common road—
Clay warm yet with the genial heat of Earth,
Dashed through it all a strain of prophecy;
Then mixed a laughter with the serious stuff.
It was a stuff to wear for centuries,
A man that matched the mountains, and compelled
The stars to look our way and honor us.

The color of the ground was in him, the red earth;
The tang and odor of the primal things—
The rectitude and patience of the rocks;
The gladness of the wind that shakes the corn;
The courage of the bird that dares the sea;
The justice of the rain that loves all leaves;

The pity of the snow that hides all scars;
The loving-kindness of the wayside well;
The tolerance and equity of light
That gives as freely to the shrinking weed
As to the great oak flaring to the wind—
To the grave's low hill as to the Matterhorn
That shoulders out the sky.

                         And so he came.
From prairie cabin up to Capitol,
One fair Ideal led our chieftain on.
Forevermore he burned to do his deed
With the fine stroke and gesture of a king.
He built the rail-pile as he built the State,
Pouring his splendid strength through every blow,
The conscience of him testing every stroke,
To make his deed the measure of a man.

So came the Captain with the mighty heart:
And when the step of Earthquake shook the house,
Wrenching the rafters from their ancient hold,
He held the ridgepole up, and spiked again
The rafters of the Home. He held his place—
Held the long purpose like a growing tree—
Held on through blame and faltered not at praise.
And when he fell in whirlwind, he went down
As when a kingly cedar green with boughs
Goes down with a great shout upon the hills,
And leaves a lonesome place against the sky.

                                           1901

Mark Twain

In the summer of 1861 Samuel Clemens (1835–1910) served for two weeks with a Confederate militia in his native Missouri, then escaped from the Civil War by traveling west with his brother Orion, the recently appointed secretary of Nevada Territory—a position Orion had obtained through the influence of Missouri's Edward Bates, attorney general in the new Lincoln administration. More than four decades later, Mark Twain would lend his support to a successful campaign to preserve Lincoln's birthplace near Hodgenville, Kentucky, as a national monument. (The late President's own descendants showed no enthusiasm for the project.) In the remarks printed here, Twain argues that it was "no accident" that the future President was "a man of the border," someone "who knew slavery not from books only, but as a living thing," and who "understood the evil not merely as it affected the negroes, but in its hardly less baneful influence on the poor whites"—a description that fit not only Lincoln, but the author of *Adventures of Huckleberry Finn* as well.

A Lincoln Memorial

There is a natural human instinct that is gratified by the sight of anything hallowed by association with a great man or with great deeds. So people make pilgrimages to the town whose streets were once trodden by Shakespeare, and Hartford guarded her Charter Oak for centuries because it had once had a hole in it that helped to save the liberties of a Colony. But in most cases the connection between the great man or the great event and the relic we revere is accidental. Shakspeare might have lived in any other town as well as in Stratford, and Connecticut's charter might have been hidden in a woodchuck hole as well as in the Charter Oak. But it was no accident that planted Lincoln on a Kentucky farm, half way between the Lakes and the Gulf. The association there had substance in it. Lincoln belonged just where he was put. If the Union was to be saved, it had to be a man of such an origin that should save it. No wintry New England Brahmin could have done it, or any torrid cotton planter, regarding the distant Yankee as a species of obnoxious foreigner. It needed a man of the border, where civil war meant the grapple of brother and brother and disunion a raw and gaping wound. It needed one who knew slavery not from books only, but as a living thing, knew the good that was mixed with its evil, and knew the evil not merely as it affected the negroes, but in its hardly less baneful influence upon the poor whites. It needed one who knew how human all the parties to the quarrel were, how much alike they were at bottom, who saw them all reflected in himself, and felt their dissensions like the tearing apart of his own soul. When the war came Georgia sent an army in gray and Massachusetts an army in blue, but Kentucky raised armies for both sides. And this man, sprung from Southern poor whites, born on a Kentucky farm and transplanted to an Illinois village, this man, in whose heart knowledge and charity had left no room for malice, was marked by Providence as the one to "bind up the Nation's wounds." His birthplace is worth saving.

January 13, 1907

James Whitcomb Riley

In this verse Riley (1849–1916), the prolific and highly popular author of "Little Orphant Annie" and "When the Frost Is on the Punkin," crystallized the new sentimental and inspirational focus of 20th-century Lincoln poetry. His linking of the "boy he must have been" with the "loving man he was" offered readers a reassuring illustration of the maxim "the child is father of the man," while his invocation of childhood simplicity and innocence evaded the question of how many Americans of the period truly believed that all men were "kith and kin."

Lincoln—the Boy

O simple as the rhymes that tell
   The simplest tales of youth,
Or simple as a miracle
   Beside the simplest truth—
So simple seems the view we share
   With our Immortals, sheer
From Glory looking down to where
   They were as children here.

Or thus we know, nor doubt it not,
   The boy he must have been
Whose budding heart bloomed with the thought
   All men are kith and kin—
With love-light in his eyes and shade
   Of prescient tears:—Because
Only of such a boy were made
   The loving man he was.

1907

Leo Tolstoy

There may be no stronger evidence that Lincoln's fame had spread worldwide than the interview with the great Russian novelist Leo Tolstoy (1828–1910) that appeared in the *New York World* shortly before the Lincoln centennial. The headline introducing the piece declared "Great Russian Tells of Reverence for Lincoln Even Among Barbarians," and the story that followed offered an irresistible tribute, recounting how a tribal chief in the Caucasus had offered Tolstoy a prize horse if only he would relate the inspirational tale of the "greatest ruler of the world." A similar claim for Lincoln's universality was made in Edward William Thomson's poem "We Talked of Lincoln," published that same year: "We talked of Abraham Lincoln in the night, / Ten fur-coat men on North Saskatchewan's plain— / Pure zero cold and all the prairie white— / Englishman, Scotchman, Scandinavian, Dane, / Two Irish, four Canadians . . ."

Tolstoi Holds Lincoln World's Geatest Hero
by Count S. Stakelberg
(Written Especially for The World.)

Visiting Leo Tolstoi in Yasnaya with the intention of getting him to write an article on Lincoln, I unfortunately found him not well enough to yield to my request. However, he was willing to give me his opinion of the great American statesman, and this is what he told me:

"Of all the great national heroes and statesmen of history Lincoln is the only real giant. Alexander, Frederick the Great, Caesar, Napoleon, Gladstone and even Washington stand in greatness of character, in depth of feeling and in a certain moral power far behind Lincoln. Lincoln was a man of whom a nation has a right to be proud; he was a Christ in miniature, a saint of humanity, whose name will live thousands of years in the legends of future generations. We are still too near to his greatness, and so can hardly appreciate his divine power; but after a few centuries more our posterity will find him considerably bigger than we do. His genius is still too strong and too powerful for the common understanding, just as the sun is too hot when its light beams directly on us.

"If one would know the greatness of Lincoln one should listen to the stories which are told about him in other parts of the world. I have been in wild places, where one hears the name of America uttered with such mystery as if it were some heaven or hell. I have heard various tribes of barbarians discussing the New World, but I heard this only in connection with the name of Lincoln. Lincoln as the wonderful hero of America is known by the most primitive nations of Asia. This may be illustrated through the following incident:

"Once while travelling in the Caucasus I happened to be the guest of a Caucasian chief of the Circassians, who, living far away from civilized life in the mountains, had but a fragmentary and childish comprehension of the world and its history. The fingers of civilization had never reached him nor his tribe, and all life beyond his native valleys was a dark mystery. Being a Mussulman he was naturally opposed to all ideas of progress and education.

"I was received with the usual Oriental hospitality and after our meal was asked by my host to tell him something of my life. Yielding to his request I began to tell him of my profession, of the development of our industries and inventions and of the schools. He listened to everything with indifference, but when I began to tell about the great statesmen and the great generals of the world he seemed at once to become very much interested.

"'Wait a moment,' he interrupted, after I had talked a few minutes. 'I want all my neighbors and my sons to listen to you. I will call them immediately.'

"He soon returned with a score of wild looking riders and asked me politely to continue. It was indeed a solemn moment when those sons of the wilderness sat around me on the floor and gazed at me as if hungering for knowledge. I spoke at first of our Czars and of their victories; then I spoke of the foreign rulers and of some of the greatest military leaders. My talk seemed to impress them deeply. The story of Napoleon was so interesting to them that I had to tell them every detail, as, for instance, how his hands looked, how tall he was, who made his guns and pistols and the color of his horse. It was very difficult to satisfy them and to meet their point of view, but I did my best. When I declared that I had finished my talk, my host, a gray-bearded, tall rider, rose, lifted his hand and said very gravely:

"'But you have not told us a syllable about the greatest general and greatest ruler of the world. We want to know something about him. He was a hero. He spoke with a voice of thunder; he laughed like the sunrise and his deeds were strong as the rock and as sweet as the fragrance of roses. The angels appeared to his mother and predicted that the son whom she would conceive would become the greatest the stars had ever seen. He was so great that he even forgave the crimes of his greatest enemies and shook brotherly hands with those who had plotted against his life. His name was Lincoln and the country in which he lived is called America, which is so far away that if a youth should journey to reach it he would be an old man when he arrived. Tell us of that man.'

"'Tell us, please, and we will present you with the best horse of our stock,' shouted the others.

"I looked at them and saw their faces all aglow, while their eyes were burning. I saw that those rude barbarians were really interested in a man whose name and deeds had already become a legend. I told them of Lincoln and his wisdom, of his home life and youth. They asked me ten questions to one which I was able to answer. They wanted to know all about his habits, his influence upon the people and his physical strength. But they were very astonished to hear that Lincoln made a sorry figure on a horse and that he lived such a simple life.

"'Tell us why he was killed,' one of them said.

"I had to tell everything. After all my knowledge of Lincoln was exhausted they seemed to be satisfied. I can hardly forget the great enthusiasm which they expressed in their wild thanks and desire to get a picture of the great American hero. I said that I probably could secure one from my friend in the nearest town, and this seemed to give them great pleasure.

"The next morning when I left the chief a wonderful Arabian horse was brought me as a present for my marvellous story, and our farewell was very impressive.

"One of the riders agreed to accompany me to the town and get the promised picture, which I was now bound to secure at any price. I was successful in getting a large photograph from my friend, and I handed it to the man with my greetings to his associates. It was interesting to witness the gravity of his face and the trembling of his hands when he received my present. He gazed for several minutes silently, like one in a reverent prayer; his eyes filled with tears. He was deeply touched and I asked him why he became so sad. After pondering my question for a few moments he replied:

"'I am sad because I feel sorry that he had to die by the hand of a villain. Don't you find, judging from his picture, that his eyes are full of tears and that his lips are sad with a secret sorrow?'

"Like all Orientals, he spoke in a poetical way and left me with many deep bows.

"This little incident proves how largely the name of Lincoln is worshipped throughout the world and how legendary his personality has become.

"Now, why was Lincoln so great that he overshadows all other national heroes? He really was not a great general like Napoleon or Washington; he was not such a skilful statesman as Gladstone or Frederick the Great; but his supremacy expresses itself altogether in his peculiar moral power and in the greatness of his character. He had come through many hardships and much experience to the realization that the greatest human achievement is love. He was what Beethoven was in music, Dante in poetry, Raphael in painting, and Christ in the philosophy of life. He aspired to be divine—and he was.

"It is natural that before he reached his goal he had to walk the highway of mistakes. But we find him, nevertheless, in every tendency true to one main motive, and that was to benefit mankind. He was one who wanted to be great through his smallness. If he had failed to become President he would be, no doubt, just as great as he is now, but only God could appreciate it. The judgment of the world is usually wrong in the beginning, and it takes centuries to correct it. But in the case of Lincoln the world was right from the start. Sooner or later Lincoln would have been seen to be a great man, even though he had never been an American President. But it would have taken a great generation to place him where he belongs.

"Lincoln died prematurely by the hand of the assassin, and naturally we condemn the criminal from our viewpoint of justice. But the question is, was his death not predestined by a divine wisdom, and was it not better for the nation and for his greatness that he died just in that way and at that particular moment? We know so little about that divine law which we call fate that no one can answer. Christ had a presentiment of His death, and there are indications that also Lincoln had strange dreams and presentiments of something tragic. If that was really the fact, can we conceive that human will could have prevented the outcome of the universal or divine will? I doubt it. I doubt also that Lincoln could have done more to prove his greatness than he did. I am convinced we are but instruments in the hands of an unknown power and that we have to follow its bidding to the end. We have a certain apparent independence, according to our moral character, wherein we may benefit our fellows, but in all eternal and universal questions we follow blindly a divine predestination. According to that eternal law the greatest of national heroes had to die, but an immortal glory still shines on his deeds.

"However, the highest heroism is that which is based on humanity, truth, justice and pity; all other forms are doomed to forgetfulness. The greatness of Aristotle or Kant is insignificant compared with the greatness of Buddha, Moses and Christ. The greatness of Napoleon, Caesar or Washington is only moonlight by the sun of Lincoln. His example is universal and will last thousands of years. Washington was a typical American, Napoleon was a typical Frenchman, but Lincoln was a humanitarian as broad as the world. He was bigger than his country—bigger than all the Presidents together. Why? Because he loved his enemies as himself and because he was a universal individualist who wanted to see himself in the world—not the world in himself. He was great through his simplicity and was noble through his charity.

"Lincoln is a strong type of those who make for truth and justice, for brotherhood and freedom. Love is the foundation of his life. That is what makes him immortal and that is the quality of a giant. I hope that his centenary birth day will create an impulse toward righteousness among the nations. Lincoln lived and died a hero, and as a great character he will live as long as the world lives. May his life long bless humanity!"

February 7, 1909

Theodore Roosevelt

No American president ever revered Lincoln more than Theodore Roosevelt (1858–1919), who as a six-year-old boy in Manhattan watched the martyred leader's New York funeral proceed along Broadway. In 1905 he wore a ring bearing a few strands of Lincoln's hair— a gift from John Hay—to his own inauguration, and thereafter kept Lincoln's photograph displayed behind his desk. "When I am confronted with a great problem," he told a reporter, "I look up to that picture, and I do as I believe Lincoln would have done." In the waning days of his own presidency, Roosevelt delivered the centennial address at Lincoln's Kentucky birthplace; the ceremony included the cornerstone laying for a memorial hall enclosing the so-called "traditional" log cabin, now widely believed to be a replica. In his address Roosevelt stressed his predecessor's combination of high ideals and common sense, tenderness and vitality, and determination in the face of harsh criticism. Not surprisingly, the portrait sounded as much like Theodore Roosevelt as Abraham Lincoln, and marked yet another occasion in which Roosevelt enlisted Lincoln's memory in the cause of pragmatic progressivism and a reinvigorated and dynamic presidency. When Roosevelt sought a third term in 1912, Lincoln's then-elderly son Robert bitterly opposed him.

Centenary Address at Hodgenville, Kentucky

We have met here to celebrate the hundredth anniversary of the birth of one of the two greatest Americans; of one of the two or three greatest men of the nineteenth century; of one of the greatest men in the world's history. This rail-splitter, this boy who passed his ungainly youth in the dire poverty of the poorest of the frontier folk, whose rise was by weary and painful labor, lived to lead his people through the burning flames of a struggle from which the nation emerged, purified as by fire, born anew to a loftier life. After long years of iron effort, and of failure that came more often than victory, he at last rose to the leadership of the Republic, at the moment when that leadership had become the stupendous world-task of the time. He grew to know greatness, but never ease. Success came to him, but never happiness, save that which springs from doing well a painful and a vital task. Power was his, but not pleasure. The furrows deepened on his brow, but his eyes were undimmed by either hate or fear. His gaunt shoulders were bowed, but his steel thews never faltered as he bore for a burden the destinies of his people. His great and tender heart shrank from giving pain; and the task allotted him was to pour out like water the life-blood of the young men, and to feel in his every fibre the sorrow of the women. Disaster saddened but never dismayed him. As the red years of war went by they found him ever doing his duty in the present, ever facing the future with fearless front, high of heart, and dauntless of soul. Unbroken by hatred, unshaken by scorn, he worked and suffered for the people. Triumph was his at the last; and barely had he tasted it before murder found him, and the kindly, patient, fearless eyes were closed forever.

As a people we are indeed beyond measure fortunate in the characters of the two greatest of our public men, Washington and Lincoln. Widely though they differed in externals, the Virginia landed gentleman and the Kentucky backwoodsman, they were alike in essentials, they were alike in the great qualities which made each able to render service to his nation and to all mankind such as no other man of his generation could or did render. Each had lofty ideals, but each in striving to attain these lofty ideals was guided by the soundest common sense. Each possessed inflexible courage in adversity, and a soul wholly unspoiled by prosperity. Each possessed all the gentler virtues commonly exhibited by good men who lack rugged strength of character. Each possessed also all the strong qualities commonly exhibited by those towering masters of mankind who have too often shown themselves devoid of so much as the understanding of the words by which we signify the qualities of duty, of mercy, of devotion to the right, of lofty disinterestedness in battling for the good of others. There have been other men as great and other men as good; but in all the history of mankind there are no other two great men as good as these, no other two good men as great. Widely though the problems of to-day differ from the problems set for solution to Washington when he founded this nation, to Lincoln when he saved it and freed the slaves, yet the qualities they showed in meeting these problems are exactly the same as those we should show in doing our work to-day.

Lincoln saw into the future with the prophetic imagination usually vouchsafed only to the poet and the seer. He had in him all the lift toward greatness of the visionary, without any of the visionary's fanaticism or egotism, without any of the visionary's narrow jealousy of the practical man and inability to strive in practical fashion for the realization of an ideal. He had the practical man's hard common sense and willingness to adapt means to ends; but there was in him none of that morbid growth of mind and soul which blinds so many practical men to the higher things of life. No more practical man ever lived than this homely backwoods idealist; but he had nothing in common with those practical men whose consciences are warped until they fail to distinguish between good and evil, fail to understand that strength, ability, shrewdness, whether in the world of business or of politics, only serve to make their possessor a more noxious, a more evil member of the community, if they are not guided and controlled by a fine and high moral sense.

We of this day must try to solve many social and industrial problems, requiring to an especial degree the combination of indomitable resolution with cool-headed sanity. We can profit by the way in which Lincoln used both these traits as he strove for reform. We can learn much of value from the very attacks which following that course brought upon his head, attacks alike by the extremists of revolution and by the extremists of reaction. He never wavered in devotion to his principles, in his love for the Union, and in his abhorrence of slavery. Timid and lukewarm people were always denouncing him because he was too extreme; but as a matter of fact he never went to extremes, he worked step by step; and because of this the extremists hated and denounced him with a fervor which now seems to us fantastic in its deification of the unreal and the impossible. At the very time when one side was holding him up as the apostle of social revolution because he was against slavery, the leading abolitionist denounced him as the "slave hound of Illinois." When he was the second time candidate for President, the majority of his opponents attacked him because of what they termed his extreme radicalism, while a minority threatened to bolt his nomination because he was not radical enough. He had continually to check those who wished to go forward too fast, at the very time that he overrode the opposition of those who wished not to go forward at all. The goal was never dim before his vision; but he picked his way cautiously, without either halt or hurry, as he strode toward it, through such a morass of difficulty that no man of less courage would have attempted it, while it would surely have overwhelmed any man of judgment less serene.

Yet perhaps the most wonderful thing of all, and, from the standpoint of the America of to-day and of the future, the most vitally important, was the extraordinary way in which Lincoln could fight valiantly against what he deemed wrong and yet preserve undiminished his love and respect for the brother from whom he differed. In the hour of a triumph that would have turned any weaker man's head, in the heat of a struggle which spurred many a good man to dreadful vindictiveness, he said truthfully that so long as he had been in his office he had never willingly planted a thorn in any man's bosom, and besought his supporters to study the incidents of the trial through which they were passing as philosophy from which to learn wisdom and not as wrongs to be avenged; ending with the solemn exhortation that, as the strife was over, all should reunite in a common effort to save their common country.

He lived in days that were great and terrible, when brother fought against brother for what each sincerely deemed to be the right. In a contest so grim the strong men who alone can carry it through are rarely able to do justice to the deep convictions of those with whom they grapple in moral strife. At such times men see through a glass darkly; to only the rarest and loftiest spirits is vouchsafed that clear vision which gradually comes to all, even to the lesser, as the struggle fades into distance, and wounds are forgotten, and peace creeps back to the hearts that were hurt. But to Lincoln was given this supreme vision. He did not hate the man from whom he differed. Weakness was as foreign as wickedness to his strong, gentle nature; but his courage was of a quality so high that it needed no bolstering of dark passion. He saw clearly that the same high qualities, the same courage, and willingness for self-sacrifice, and devotion to the right as it was given them to see the right, belonged both to the men of the North and to the men of the South. As the years roll by, and as all of us, wherever we dwell, grow to feel an equal pride in the valor and self-devotion, alike of the men who wore the blue and the men who wore the gray, so this whole nation will grow to feel a peculiar sense of pride in the man whose blood was shed for the union of his people and for the freedom of a race; the lover of his country and of all mankind; the mightiest of the mighty men who mastered the mighty days: Abraham Lincoln.

Februray 12, 1909

Booker T. Washington

Born into slavery in Virginia, Washington (1856?–1915) founded the Tuskegee Institute in 1881 and rose to national prominence with his conciliatory speech on race relations at the Atlanta Exposition in 1895. Delivered seven months after the death of Frederick Douglass, it made Washington the country's leading new African-American public figure, equally famous but less confrontational, a model citizen as much as an advocate. Washington once wrote that Lincoln's was "almost the first name I learned . . . I confess that the more I learn of Lincoln's life the more I am disposed to look at him much as my mother and those early freedmen did." On Lincoln's 100th birthday the author of *Up from Slavery* delivered this address in New York City. Emphasizing Lincoln's twin virtues of "patience" and "courage," Washington introduced a new element to Lincoln's image in African-American memory, that of the self-made man worthy not only of "thanksgiving" but also of imitation. Urging white America to shun racial prejudice while encouraging black Americans to strive for equality through self-improvement, the eminent educator redeclared Lincoln a "Great Emancipator" and praised his lack of hatred, even in the face of rancorous criticism. (The "Armstrong" mentioned in the speech is Samuel Chapman Armstrong, the Union officer and Freedmen's Bureau agent who founded the Hampton Institute, where Washington was educated.)

Address on Abraham Lincoln
Before the Republican Club of New York City

Mr. Chairman, Ladies and Gentlemen: You ask that which he found a piece of property and turned into a free American citizen to speak to you tonight on Abraham Lincoln. I am not fitted by ancestry or training to be your teacher tonight for, as I have stated, I was born a slave.

My first knowledge of Abraham Lincoln came in this way: I was awakened early one morning before the dawn of day, as I lay wrapped in a bundle of rags on the dirt floor of our slave cabin, by the prayers of my mother, just before leaving for her day's work, as she was kneeling over my body earnestly praying that Abraham Lincoln might succeed, and that one day she and her boy might be free. You give me the opportunity here this evening to celebrate with you and the nation the answer to that prayer.

Says the Great Book somewhere, "Though a man die, yet shall he live." If this is true of the ordinary man, how much more true is it of the hero of the hour and the hero of the century—Abraham Lincoln! One hundred years of the life and influence of Lincoln is the story of the struggles, the trials, ambitions, and triumphs of the people of our complex American civilization. Interwoven into the warp and woof of this human complexity is the moving story of men and women of nearly every race and color in their progress from slavery to freedom, from poverty to wealth, from weakness to power, from ignorance to intelligence. Knit into the life of Abraham Lincoln is the story and success of the nation in the blending of all tongues, religions, colors, races into one composite nation, leaving each group and race free to live its own separate social life, and yet all a part of the great whole.

If a man die, shall he live? Answering this question as applied to our martyred President, perhaps you expect me to confine my words of appreciation to the great boon which, through him, was conferred upon my race. My undying gratitude and that of ten millions of my race for this and yet more! To have been the instrument used by Providence through which four millions of slaves, now grown into ten millions of free citizens, were made free would bring eternal fame within itself, but this is not the only claim that Lincoln has upon our sense of gratitude and appreciation.

By the side of Armstrong and Garrison, Lincoln lives today. In the very highest sense he lives in the present more potently than fifty years ago; for that which is seen is temporal, that which is unseen is eternal. He lives in the 32,000 young men and women of the Negro race learning trades and useful occupations; in the 200,000 farms acquired by those he freed; in the more than 400,000 homes built; in the forty-six banks established and 10,000 stores owned; in the $550,000,000 worth of taxable property in hand; in the 28,000 public schools existing, with 30,000 teachers; in the 170 industrial schools and colleges; in the 23,000 ministers and 26,000 churches.

But, above all this, he lives in the steady and unalterable determination of ten millions of black citizens to continue to climb year by year the ladder of the highest usefulness and to perfect themselves in strong, robust character. For making all this possible, Lincoln lives.

But, again, for a higher reason he lives tonight in every corner of the republic. To set the physical man free is much. To set the spiritual man free is more. So often the keeper is on the inside of the prison bars and the prisoner on the outside.

As an individual, grateful as I am to Lincoln for freedom of body, my gratitude is still greater for freedom of soul—the liberty which permits one to live up in that atmosphere where he refuses to permit sectional or racial hatred to drag down, to warp and narrow his soul.

The signing of the Emancipation Proclamation was a great event, and yet it was but the symbol of another, still greater and more momentous. We who celebrate this anniversary should not forget that the same pen that gave freedom to four millions of African slaves at the same time struck the shackles from the souls of twenty-seven millions of Americans of another color.

In any country, regardless of what its laws say, wherever people act upon the idea that the disadvantage of one man is the good of another, there slavery exists. Wherever in any country the whole people feel that the happiness of all is dependent upon the happiness of the weakest, there freedom exists.

In abolishing slavery, Lincoln proclaimed the principle that, even in the case of the humblest and weakest of mankind, the welfare of each is still the good of all. In reestablishing in this country the principle that, at bottom, the interests of humanity and of the individual are one, he freed men's souls from spiritual bondage; he freed them to mutual helpfulness. Henceforth no man of any race, either in the North or in the South, need feel constrained to fear or hate his brother.

By the same token that Lincoln made America free, he pushed

back the boundaries of freedom everywhere, gave the spirit of liberty a wider influence throughout the world, and reestablished the dignity of man as man.

By the same act that freed my race, he said to the civilized and uncivilized world that man everywhere must be free, and that man everywhere must be enlightened, and the Lincoln spirit of freedom and fair play will never cease to spread and grow in power till throughout the world all men shall know the truth, and the truth shall make them free.

Lincoln in his day was wise enough to recognize that which is true in the present and for all time: that in a state of slavery and ignorance man renders the lowest and most costly form of service to his fellows. In a state of freedom and enlightenment he renders the highest and most helpful form of service.

The world is fast learning that of all forms of slavery there is none that is so harmful and degrading as that form of slavery which tempts one human being to hate another by reason of his race or color. One man cannot hold another man down in the ditch without remaining down in the ditch with him. One who goes through life with his eyes closed against all that is good in another race is weakened and circumscribed, as one who fights in a battle with one hand tied behind him. Lincoln was in the truest sense great because he unfettered himself. He climbed up out of the valley, where his vision was narrowed and weakened by the fog and miasma, onto the mountain top, where in a pure and unclouded atmosphere he could see the truth which enabled him to rate all men at their true worth. Growing out of this anniversary season and atmosphere, may there crystallize a resolve throughout the nation that on such a mountain the American people will strive to live.

We owe, then, to Lincoln physical freedom, moral freedom, and yet this is not all. There is a debt of gratitude which we as individuals, no matter of what race or nation, must recognize as due Abraham Lincoln—not for what he did as chief executive of the nation, but for what he did as a man. In his rise from the most abject poverty and ignorance to a position of high usefulness and power, he taught the world one of the greatest of all lessons. In fighting his own battle up from obscurity and squalor, he fought the battle of every other individual and race that is down, and so helped to pull up every other human who was down. People so often forget that by every inch that the lowest man crawls up he makes it easier for every other man to get up. Today, throughout the world, because Lincoln lived, struggled, and triumphed, every boy who is ignorant, is in poverty, is despised or discouraged, holds his head a little higher. His heart beats a little faster, his ambition to do something and be something is a little stronger, because Lincoln blazed the way.

To my race, the life of Abraham Lincoln has its special lesson at this point in our career. In so far as his life emphasizes patience, long suffering, sincerity, naturalness, dogged determination, and courage—courage to avoid the superficial, courage to persistently seek the substance instead of the shadow—it points the road for my people to travel.

As a race we are learning, I believe, in an increasing degree that the best way for us to honor the memory of our Emancipator is by seeking to imitate him. Like Lincoln, the Negro race should seek to be simple, without bigotry and without ostentation. There is great power in simplicity. We as a race should, like Lincoln, have moral courage to be what we are, and not pretend to be what we are not. We should keep in mind that no one can degrade us except ourselves; that if we are worthy, no influence can defeat us. Like other races, the Negro will often meet obstacles, often be sorely tried and tempted; but we must keep in mind that freedom, in the broadest and highest sense, has never been a bequest; it has been a conquest.

In the final test, the success of our race will be in proportion to the service that it renders to the world. In the long run, the badge of service is the badge of sovereignty.

With all his other elements of strength, Abraham Lincoln possessed in the highest degree patience and, as I have said, courage. The highest form of courage is not always that exhibited on the battlefield in the midst of the blare of trumpets and the waving of banners. The highest courage is of the Lincoln kind. It is the same kind of courage, made possible by the new life and the new possibilities furnished by Lincoln's Proclamation, displayed by thousands of men and women of my race every year who are going out from Tuskegee and other Negro institutions in the South to lift up their fellows. When they go, often into lonely and secluded districts, with little thought of salary, with little thought of personal welfare, no drums beat, no banners fly, no friends stand by to cheer them on; but these brave young souls who are erecting schoolhouses, creating school systems, prolonging school terms, teaching the people to buy homes, build houses, and live decent lives are fighting the battles of this country just as truly and bravely as any persons who go forth to fight battles against a foreign foe.

In paying my tribute of respect to the Great Emancipator of my race, I desire to say a word here and now in behalf of an element of brave and true white men of the South who, though they saw in Lincoln's policy the ruin of all they believed in and hoped for, have loyally accepted the results of the Civil War, and are today working with a courage few people in the North can understand to uplift the Negro in the South and complete the emancipation that Lincoln began. I am tempted to say that it certainly required as high a degree of courage for men of the type of Robert E. Lee and John B. Gordon to accept the results of the war in the manner and spirit in which they did, as that which Grant and Sherman displayed in fighting the physical battles that saved the Union.

Lincoln also was a Southern man by birth, but he was one of those white men, of whom there is a large and growing class, who resented the idea that in order to assert and maintain the superiority of the Anglo-Saxon race it was necessary that another group of humanity should be kept in ignorance.

Lincoln was not afraid or ashamed to come into contact with the lowly of all races. His reputation and social position were not of such a transitory and transparent kind that he was afraid that he would lose them by being just and kind, even to a man of dark skin. I always pity from the bottom of my heart any man who feels that somebody else must be kept down or in ignorance in order that he may appear great by comparison. It requires no courage for a strong man to kick a weak one down.

Lincoln lives today because he had the courage which made him refuse to hate the man at the South or the man at the North when they did not agree with him. He had the courage as well as the patience and foresight to suffer in silence, to be misunderstood, to be abused, to refuse to revile when reviled. For he knew that, if he was right, the ridicule of today would be the applause of tomorrow. He knew, too, that at some time in the distant future our nation would repent of the folly of cursing our public servants while they live and blessing them only when they die. In this connection I cannot refrain from suggesting the question to the millions of voices raised today in his praise: "Why did you not say it yesterday?" Yesterday, when one word of approval and gratitude would have meant so much to him in strengthening his hand and heart.

As we recall tonight his deeds and words, we can do so with grateful hearts and strong faith in the future for the spread of righteousness. The civilization of the world is going forward, not backward. Here and there for a little season the progress of mankind may seem to halt or tarry by the wayside, or even appear to slide backward, but the trend is ever onward and upward, and will be until someone can invent and enforce a law to stop the progress of civilization. In goodness and liberality the world moves forward. It goes forward beneficently, but it moves forward relentlessly. In the last analysis the forces of nature are behind the moral progress of the world, and these forces will crush into powder any group of humanity that resists this progress.

As we gather here, brothers all, in common joy and thanksgiving for the life of Lincoln, may I not ask that you, the worthy representatives of seventy millions of white Americans, join heart and hand with the ten millions of black Americans—these ten millions who speak your tongue, profess your religion—who have never lifted their voices or hands except in defense of their country's honor and their country's flag—and swear eternal fealty to the memory and the traditions of the sainted Lincoln? I repeat, may we not join with your race, and let all of us here highly resolve that justice, good will, and peace shall be the motto of our lives? If this be true, in the highest sense Lincoln shall not have lived and died in vain.

And, finally, gathering inspiration and encouragement from

this hour and Lincoln's life, I pledge to you and to the nation that my race, in so far as I can speak for it, which in the past, whether in ignorance or intelligence, whether in slavery or in freedom, has always been true to the Stars and Stripes and to the highest and best interests of this country, will strive to so deport itself that it shall reflect nothing but the highest credit upon the whole people in the North and in the South.

February 12, 1909

Julia Ward Howe

Nearly half a century after meeting Lincoln, Howe, then in her 90th year, turned her thoughts back to the Civil War president with this simple poem likening the "man of homely, rustic ways" to George Washington. The effort reiterated her unchanging view—shared by most of the rapidly disappearing survivors of those times—that the founder and the preserver of the Union had achieved unmatched places of honor in the American pantheon.

Abraham Lincoln

*Read by Mrs. Howe at the Lincoln centenary meeting in
Symphony Hall, Boston, February 12, 1909*

Through the dim pageant of the years
A wondrous tracery appears:
A cabin of the western wild
Shelters in sleep a new-born child.

Nor nurse, nor parent dear can know
The way those infant feet must go;
And yet a nation's help and hope
Are sealed within that horoscope.

Beyond is toil for daily bread,
And thought, to noble issues led,
And courage, arming for the morn
For whose behest this man was born.

A man of homely, rustic ways,
Yet he achieves the forum's praise,
And soon earth's highest meed has won,
The seat and sway of Washington.

No throne of honors and delights;
Distrustful days and sleepless nights,
To struggle, suffer, and aspire,
Like Israel, led by cloud and fire.

A treacherous shot, a sob of rest,
A martyr's palm upon his breast,
A welcome from the glorious seat
Where blameless souls of heroes meet;

And, thrilling through unmeasured days,
A song of gratitude and praise;
A cry that all the earth shall heed,
To God, who gave him for our need.

1909

Edwin Arlington Robinson

Easily overlooked as a contributor to the tradition of Lincoln poetry, Robinson (1869–1935) helped define a new Lincoln for a new era: not so much a child of the earth who stumbled toward fame guided by fate, but an all-seeing "Titan" who clearly saw himself a savior of his own generation and a teacher for future ones—not to mention a humorist who could laugh in the face of venom. Louis Untermeyer believed Robinson came "nearer Lincoln than any of his compatriots," calling this poem "one of the few that maintains a genuine nobility and practically the only one that does not try to show the man's intimate humanity by some reference to rail-splitting and the use of 'Honest Abe.'"

The Master*

(*LINCOLN*)

A flying word from here and there
Had sown the name at which we sneered,
But soon the name was everywhere,
To be reviled and then revered:
A presence to be loved and feared,
We cannot hide it, or deny
That we, the gentlemen who jeered,
May be forgotten by and by.

He came when days were perilous
And hearts of men were sore beguiled;
And having made his note of us,
He pondered and was reconciled.
Was ever master yet so mild
As he, and so untamable?
We doubted, even when he smiled,
Not knowing what he knew so well.

*Supposed to have been written not long after the Civil War.

407

He knew that undeceiving fate
Would shame us whom he served unsought;
He knew that he must wince and wait—
The jest of those for whom he fought;
He knew devoutly what he thought
Of us and of our ridicule;
He knew that we must all be taught
Like little children in a school.

We gave a glamour to the task
That he encountered and saw through,
But little of us did he ask,
And little did we ever do.
And what appears if we review
The season when we railed and chaffed?
It is the face of one who knew
That we were learning while we laughed.

The face that in our vision feels
Again the venom that we flung,
Transfigured to the world reveals
The vigilance to which we clung.
Shrewd, hallowed, harassed, and among
The mysteries that are untold,
The face we see was never young
Nor could it ever have been old.

For he, to whom we had applied
Our shopman's test of age and worth,
Was elemental when he died,
As he was ancient at his birth:
The saddest among kings of earth,
Bowed with a galling crown, this man
Met rancor with a cryptic mirth,
Laconic—and Olympian.

The love, the grandeur, and the fame
Are bounded by the world alone;
The calm, the smouldering, and the flame
Of awful patience were his own:
With him they are forever flown
Past all our fond self-shadowings,
Wherewith we cumber the Unknown
As with inept, Icarian wings.

For we were not as other men:
'Twas ours to soar and his to see
But we are coming down again,
And we shall come down pleasantly;
Nor shall we longer disagree
On what it is to be sublime,
But flourish in our perigee
And have one Titan at a time.

1910

Vachel Lindsay

A longtime resident of Springfield whose Kentucky-born father had opposed Lincoln in politics, Lindsay (1879–1931) came to see the town's most famous citizen as a touchstone for his own utopian vision of America, and for a world that needed liberation from tyranny. Inspired by the outbreak of World War I, his poem is at one level a rumination on Lincoln's vivid presence in his imperfect hometown, and on another a quaint suggestion that his disturbed ghost wandered restlessly not merely to haunt residents and enchant tourists, but because it was angry that despots continued to tyrannize mankind. In many ways, Lindsay hated Springfield—he called it the "City of my Discontent"—especially after two black men were lynched there during a race riot that inspired the founding of the NAACP. Afterward Lindsay wrote: "We must have many Lincoln-hearted men. / A city is not builded in a day. / And they must do their work, and come and go, / While countless generations pass away."

Abraham Lincoln Walks at Midnight
(*In Springfield, Illinois*)

It is portentous, and a thing of state
That here at midnight, in our little town
A mourning figure walks, and will not rest,
Near the old court-house pacing up and down,

Or by his homestead, or in shadowed yards
He lingers where his children used to play,
Or through the market, on the well-worn stones
He stalks until the dawn-stars burn away.

A bronzed, lank man! His suit of ancient black,
A famous high top-hat and plain worn shawl
Make him the quaint great figure that men love,
The prairie-lawyer, master of us all.

He cannot sleep upon his hillside now.
He is among us:—as in times before!
And we who toss and lie awake for long
Breathe deep, and start, to see him pass the door.

His head is bowed. He thinks on men and kings.
Yea, when the sick world cries, how can he sleep?
Too many peasants fight, they know not why,
Too many homesteads in black terror weep.

The sins of all the war-lords burn his heart.
He sees the dreadnaughts scouring every main.
He carries on his shawl-wrapped shoulders now
The bitterness, the folly and the pain.

He cannot rest until a spirit-dawn
Shall come;—the shining hope of Europe free:
The league of sober folk, the Workers' Earth,
Bringing long peace to Cornland, Alp and Sea.

It breaks his heart that kings must murder still,
That all his hours of travail here for men
Seem yet in vain. And who will bring white peace
That he may sleep upon his hill again?

1914

Edgar Lee Masters

While practicing law in Chicago, Masters (1868–1950) was inspired by his reading of ancient Greek epigrammatic verse to write a series of poems about the inhabitants of the small Illinois towns he had grown up in. *Spoon River Anthology* appeared in the magazine *Reedy's Mirror* in 1914–15 and then appeared in book form to great success. In the sections channeling Lincoln's long-deceased prairie intimates, witnesses rise to speak hauntingly of his unbreakable connection with his hardscrabble past: Anne Rutledge, resurrected here as Lincoln's true love and eternal consort and comfort, and Hannah Armstrong, the earth mother who testifies to the President's merciful release of her sick son from the army. Unmentioned in the poem was that her son was the "Duff" Armstrong Lincoln had successfully defended against a murder charge in the famous "almanac trial" of 1858.

FROM
Spoon River Anthology

Anne Rutledge

Out of me unworthy and unknown
The vibrations of deathless music;
"With malice toward none, with charity for all."
Out of me the forgiveness of millions toward millions,
And the beneficent face of a nation
Shining with justice and truth.
I am Anne Rutledge who sleep beneath these weeds,
Beloved in life of Abraham Lincoln,
Wedded to him, not through union,
But through separation.
Bloom forever, O Republic,
From the dust of my bosom!

Hannah Armstrong

I wrote him a letter asking him for old times' sake
To discharge my sick boy from the army;
But maybe he couldn't read it.
Then I went to town and had James Garber,
Who wrote beautifully, write him a letter;
But maybe that was lost in the mails.
So I traveled all the way to Washington.
I was more than an hour finding the White House.
And when I found it they turned me away,
Hiding their smiles. Then I thought:
"Oh, well, he ain't the same as when I boarded him
And he and my husband worked together
And all of us called him Abe, there in Menard."
As a last attempt I turned to a guard and said:
"Please say it's old Aunt Hannah Armstrong
From Illinois, come to see him about her sick boy
In the army."
Well, just in a moment they let me in!
And when he saw me he broke in a laugh,
And dropped his business as president,
And wrote in his own hand Doug's discharge,
Talking the while of the early days,
And telling stories.

1915

Carl Sandburg

Among all the 20th-century interpreters of Lincoln and his memory, Sandburg (1878–1967) did the most to define him in both prose and poetry, as influential as a biographer as he was as a balladeer, easily the most dominant popular force in the field for more than 50 years. Neither of the two poems printed here were published in Sandburg's lifetime. In the first, the Illinois-born writer—who grew up in the thrall of elderly Civil War veterans with vivid Lincoln stories of their own to tell—imagines Lincoln's corpse as an "inextinguishable symbol of toil, thought, sacrifice," inspiring onlookers to fight against "the exploitation of man by man." Then, in a brilliantly conceived reversal of perspective, Sandburg takes Lincoln's admirers back in time from beatification to birth—and beyond, to the evolutionary origins of man and the inexplicable mystery that is somehow responsible for the existence of Lincoln.

Journey and Oath

When Abraham Lincoln received a bullet in the head and was
    taken to the Peterson house across the street,
He passed on and was swathed in emulsions and prepared for
    a journey to New York, Niagara, across Ohio, Indiana,
    back to Illinois—

As he lay looking life-like yet not saying a word,
Lay portentous and silent under a glass cover,
Lay with oracular lips still as a winter leaf,
Lay deaf to the drums of regiments coming and going,
Lay blind to the weaving causes of work or war or peace,
Lay as an inextinguishable symbol of toil, thought, sacrifice—

There was an oath in the heart of this man and that:
> By God, I'll go as a Man;
> When my time comes I'll be ready.
> I shall keep the faith that nothing
>   is impossible with man, that one
>   or two illusions are good as money.

> By God, I'll be true to Man
> As against hog, louse, fox, snake, wolf,
> As against these and their counterparts
>   in the breast of Man.
> By God, I'll fight for Man
> As against famine, flood, storm,
> As against crop gambling, job gambling,
> As against bootlickers on the left hand,
> As against bloodsuckers on the right hand,
> As against the cannibalism of the exploitation
>   of man by man,
> As against insecurity of the sanctities of human life.

1915

———

> Paint his head against lavender shadows.
> Fling stars around howsoever you choose.
> The wing tips of birds circling sunset
> Arches of measureless fading gates.
> Put in mystery without end.
> This man was mystery.
> And yet at the end of your hands technique
> Of fixing mystery around a head,
> Let up on the mystery. Mix in among the
> Lavender shadows the gorilla far back
> And the jungle cry of readiness for death
> Or struggle—and the clean breeds who live on
> In the underbrush. Mix in farther back yet
> Breeds out of the slime of the sea.

Put in a high green of a restless sea.
Insinuate chlorine and mystic salts,
The make-up of vertebrates,
The long highway of mammals who chew
Their victims and feed their children
From milk at a breast. Let him cry from silence
How the fathers and the women went hungry
And battled hunger and tore each other's jugulars
Over land and women, laughter and language.
Put in mystery without end. Then add mystery.

1915

Woodrow Wilson

The struggle between Republicans and Democrats for the mantle of Lincoln was well underway when Wilson (1856–1924) made his own presidential pilgrimage to Hodgenville. The occasion was the official presentation of the birthplace memorial to the federal government, but it was lost on few observers that the President would be speaking in the midst of his close re-election campaign. As a historian, Wilson had seen Lincoln as an exception, not a model, observing that he "made the presidency the government." But once he assumed the office himself, Wilson had confessed he felt "the closest kinship" to Lincoln "in principle and in political lineament." In his Hodgenville speech he went even further in his praise, describing Lincoln's unexpected rise to greatness as "the sacred mystery of democracy." Left entirely unmentioned in Wilson's eloquent address were slavery and emancipation—omissions that were not surprising in light of Wilson's segregation of black government employees and his effusive praise for D. W. Griffith's racist screen epic *The Birth of a Nation*.

Address at Hodgenville, Kentucky

No more significant memorial could have been presented to the nation than this. It expresses so much of what is singular and noteworthy in the history of the country; it suggests so many of the things that we prize most highly in our life and in our system of government. How eloquent this little house within this shrine is of the vigor of democracy! There is nowhere in the land any home so remote, so humble, that it may not contain the power of mind and heart and conscience to which nations yield and history submits its processes. Nature pays no tribute to aristocracy, subscribes to no creed of caste, renders fealty to no monarch or master of any name or kind. Genius is no snob. It does not run after titles or seek by preference the high circles of society. It affects humble company as well as great. It pays no special tribute to universities or learned societies or conventional standards of greatness, but serenely chooses its own comrades, its own haunts, its own cradle even, and its own life of adventure and of training. Here is proof of it. This little hut was the cradle of one of the great sons of men, a man of singular, delightful, vital genius who presently emerged upon the great stage of the nation's history, gaunt, shy, ungainly, but dominant and majestic, a natural ruler of men, himself inevitably the central figure of the great plot. No man can explain this, but every man can see how it demonstrates the vigor of democracy, where every door is open, in every hamlet and countryside, in city and wilderness alike, for the ruler to emerge when he will and claim his leadership in the free life. Such are the authentic proofs of the validity and vitality of democracy.

Here, no less, hides the mystery of democracy. Who shall guess this secret of nature and providence and a free polity? Whatever the vigor and vitality of the stock from which he sprang, its mere vigor and soundness do not explain where this man got his great heart that seemed to comprehend all mankind in its catholic and benignant sympathy, the mind that sat enthroned behind those brooding, melancholy eyes, whose vision swept many an horizon which those about him dreamed not of,—that mind that comprehended what it had never seen, and understood the language of affairs with the ready ease of one to the manner born,—or that nature which seemed in its varied richness to be the familiar of men of every way of life. This is the sacred mystery of democracy, that its richest fruits spring up out of soils which no man has prepared and in circumstances amidst which they are the least expected. This is a place alike of mystery and of reassurance.

It is likely that in a society ordered otherwise than our own Lincoln could not have found himself or the path of fame and power upon which he walked serenely to his death. In this place it is right that we should remind ourselves of the solid and striking facts upon which our faith in democracy is founded. Many another man besides Lincoln has served the nation in its highest places of counsel and of action whose origins were as humble as his. Though the greatest example of the universal energy, richness, stimulation, and force of democracy, he is only one example among many. The permeating and all-pervasive virtue of the freedom which challenges us in America to make the most of every gift and power we possess every page of our history serves to emphasize and illustrate. Standing here in this place, it seems almost the whole of the stirring story.

Here Lincoln had his beginnings. Here the end and consummation of that great life seem remote and a bit incredible. And yet there was no break anywhere between beginning and end, no lack of natural sequence anywhere. Nothing really incredible happened. Lincoln was unaffectedly as much at home in the White House as he was here. Do you share with me the feeling, I wonder, that he was permanently at home nowhere? It seems to me that in the case of a man,—I would rather say of a spirit,—like Lincoln the question *where* he was is of little significance, that it is always *what* he was that really arrests our thought and takes hold of our imagination. It is the spirit always that is sovereign. Lincoln, like the rest of us, was put through the discipline of the world,—a very rough and exacting discipline for him, an indispensable discipline for every man who would know what he is about in the midst of the world's affairs; but his spirit got only its schooling there. It did not derive its character or its vision from the experiences which brought it to its full revelation. The test of every American must always be, not where he is, but what he is. That, also, is of the essence of democracy, and is the moral of which this place is most gravely expressive.

We would like to think of men like Lincoln and Washington as typical Americans, but no man can be typical who is so unusual as these great men were. It was typical of American life that it should produce such men with supreme indifference as to the manner in which it produced them, and as readily here in this hut as amidst the little circle of cultivated gentlemen to whom Virginia owed so much in leadership and example. And Lincoln and Washington were typical Americans in the use they made of their genius. But there will be few such men at best, and we will not look into the mystery of how and why they come. We will only keep the door open for them always, and a hearty welcome,—after we have recognized them.

I have read many biographies of Lincoln; I have sought out

with the greatest interest the many intimate stories that are told
of him, the narratives of nearby friends, the sketches at close
quarters, in which those who had the privilege of being associated with him have tried to depict for us the very man himself
"in his habit as he lived"; but I have nowhere found a real intimate of Lincoln's. I nowhere get the impression in any narrative
or reminiscence that the writer had in fact penetrated to the
heart of his mystery, or that any man could penetrate to the heart
of it. That brooding spirit had no real familiars. I get the impression that it never spoke out in complete self-revelation, and
that it could not reveal itself completely to anyone. It was a very
lonely spirit that looked out from underneath those shaggy
brows and comprehended men without fully communing with
them, as if, in spite of all its genial efforts at comradeship, it
dwelt apart, saw its visions of duty where no man looked on.
There is a very holy and very terrible isolation for the conscience of every man who seeks to read the destiny in affairs for
others as well as for himself, for a nation as well as for individuals. That privacy no man can intrude upon. That lonely search
of the spirit for the right perhaps no man can assist. This strange
child of the cabin kept company with invisible things, was born
into no intimacy but that of its own silently assembling and de-
ploying thoughts.

I have come here today, not to utter a eulogy on Lincoln; he
stands in need of none, but to endeavor to interpret the meaning
of this gift to the nation of the place of his birth and origin. Is
not this an altar upon which we may forever keep alive the vestal
fire of democracy as upon a shrine at which some of the deepest
and most sacred hopes of mankind may from age to age be rekindled? For these hopes must constantly be rekindled, and
only those who live can rekindle them. The only stuff that can
retain the life-giving heat is the stuff of living hearts. And the
hopes of mankind cannot be kept alive by words merely, by constitutions and doctrines of right and codes of liberty. The object
of democracy is to transmute these into the life and action of
society, the self-denial and self-sacrifice of heroic men and
women willing to make their lives an embodiment of right and
service and enlightened purpose. The commands of democracy

are as imperative as its privileges and opportunities are wide and generous. Its compulsion is upon us. It will be great and lift a great light for the guidance of the nations only if we are great and carry that light high for the guidance of our own feet. We are not worthy to stand here unless we ourselves be in deed and in truth real democrats and servants of mankind, ready to give our very lives for the freedom and justice and spiritual exaltation of the great nation which shelters and nurtures us.

September 4, 1916

Witter Bynner

Offering yet another tribute to the folkloric Lincoln, Bynner (1881–1968) recalled Lincoln through the rheumy eyes of the aging generation who could still claim to have met and talked to him. A parallel tradition abounded in the oral histories of former slaves recorded in the 1920s and 1930s—the earnest testimony of African Americans who insisted they had seen Lincoln wandering unnoticed through the South before and during the Civil War. The notion of Lincoln as spectral totem was both intimate and mythical.

A Farmer Remembers Lincoln

"Lincoln?—
Well, I was in the old Second Maine,
The first regiment in Washington from the Pine Tree State.
Of course I didn't get the butt of the clip;
We was there for guardin' Washington—
We was all green.

"I ain't never ben to but one theater in my life—
I didn't know how to behave.
I ain't never ben since.
I can see as plain as my hat the box where he sat in
When he was shot.
I can tell you, sir, there was a panic
When we found our President was in the shape he was in!
Never saw a soldier in the world but what liked him.

"Yes, sir. His looks was kind o' hard to forget.
He was a spare man,
An old farmer.
Everything was all right, you know,
But he wan't a smooth-appearin' man at all—
Not in no ways;

Thin-faced, long-necked,
And a swellin' kind of a thick lip like.

"And he was a jolly old fellow—always cheerful;
He wan't so high but the boys could talk to him their
    own ways.
While I was servin' at the Hospital
He'd come in and say, 'You look nice in here,'
Praise us up, you know.
And he'd bend over and talk to the boys—
And he'd talk so good to 'em—so close—
That's why I call him a farmer.
I don't mean that everything about him wan't all right,
    you understand,
It's just—well, I was a farmer—
And he was my neighbor, anybody's neighbor.

"I guess even you young folks would 'a' liked him."

1917

John Gould Fletcher

The Arkansas-born Fletcher (1886–1950) wrote this poem in 1916 and published it five years later in his collection *Breakers and Granite*. Amy Lowell thought it "the finest poem on Lincoln which has been written" because it identified him as "a man and an aspiration, a recollection and a goal," while Roy Basler wrote that it could "only be assessed as a mystical yearning after something abstract and ultimate in this strange, heroic god."

Lincoln

I

Like a gaunt, scraggly pine
Which lifts its head above the mournful sandhills;
And patiently, through dull years of bitter silence,
Untended and uncared for, starts to grow.

Ungainly, labouring, huge,
The wind of the north has twisted and gnarled its branches;
Yet in the heat of mid-summer days, when thunder clouds
    ring the horizon,
A nation of men shall rest beneath its shade.

And it shall protect them all,
Hold everyone safe there, watching aloof in silence;
Until at last, one mad stray bolt from the zenith
Shall strike it in an instant down to earth.

II

There was a darkness in this man; an immense and hollow
    darkness,
Of which we may not speak, nor share with him nor enter;
A darkness through which strong roots stretched downwards
    into the earth,
Towards old things;

Towards the herdman-kings who walked the earth and spoke
    with God,
Towards the wanderers who sought for they knew not what,
    and found their goal at last;
Towards the men who waited, only waited patiently when all
    seemed lost,
Many bitter winters of defeat;

Down to the granite of patience,
These roots swept, knotted fibrous roots, prying, piercing,
    seeking,
And drew from the living rock and the living waters about it,
The red sap to carry upwards to the sun.

Not proud, but humble,
Only to serve and pass on, to endure to the end through
    service,
For the axe is laid at the roots of the trees, and all that bring
    not forth good fruit
Shall be cut down on the day to come and cast into the fire.

III

There is a silence abroad in the land to-day,
And in the hearts of men, a deep and anxious silence;
And, because we are still at last, those bronze lips slowly
    open,
Those hollow and weary eyes take on a gleam of light.

Slowly a patient, firm-syllabled voice cuts through the
    endless silence,
Like labouring oxen that drag a plough through the chaos of
    rude clay-fields;
"I went forward as the light goes forward in early Spring,
But there were also many things which I left behind.

"Tombs that were quiet;
One, of a mother, whose brief light went out in the darkness,
One of a loved one, the snow on whose grave is long falling,
One only of a child, but it was mine.

"Have you forgotten your graves? Go, question them in
     anguish,
Listen long to their unstirred lips. From your hostages to
     silence
Learn there is no life without death, no dawn without sun-
     setting,
No victory but to him who has given all."

The clamour of cannon dies down, the furnace-mouth of the
     battle is silent,
The midwinter sun dips and descends, the earth takes on
     afresh its bright colours.
But he whom we mocked and obeyed not, he whom we
     scorned and mistrusted,
He has descended, like a god, to his rest.

Over the uproar of cities,
Over the million intricate threads of life weaving and
     crossing,
In the midst of problems we know not, tangling, perplexing,
     ensnaring,
Rises one white tomb alone.

Beam over it, stars,
Wrap it 'round, stripes—stripes red for the pain that he bore
     for you—
Enfold it forever, O, flag, rent, soiled, but repaired through
     your anguish;
Long as you keep him there safe, the nations shall bow to
     your law.

Strew over him flowers:
Blue forget-me-nots from the north and the bright pink
        arbutus
From the east, and from the west rich orange blossom,
But from the heart of the land take the passion-flower;

Rayed, violet, dim,
With the nails that pierced, the cross that he bore and the
        circlet,
And beside it there lay also one lonely snow-white magnolia,
Bitter for remembrance of the healing which has passed.

April 19th, 1916.

1921

Robert Russa Moton

Born in Virginia and educated at Hampton Institute, Moton (1867–1940) succeeded Booker T. Washington as principal of Tuskegee Institute in 1915. A leading "accommodationist" who had advised the Wilson and Harding administrations on racial issues, Moton was predictably chosen to speak on behalf of his race at the dedication of the Lincoln Memorial in Washington, D.C., on May 30, 1922. Yet the draft address he submitted two weeks before the ceremony to Chief Justice William Howard Taft, the chairman of the Memorial Commission, proved too outspoken for the event's organizers, and Moton was advised to mute his criticism of the racial status quo. In the address he eventually gave, Moton replaced the concluding section of his draft (pages 432.31–434.23 in this volume) with more anodyne passages praising Lincoln and America's progress in achieving better race relations, although he did end his oration with a plea for "equal justice and equal opportunity for all." A further irony marked the ceremony: while the organizers treated Moton with respect, granting him his rightful place on the speakers' platform not far from Robert Lincoln, military ushers, many of them Southern-born, rudely herded all of the black spectators into a roped-off "colored section" to the rear of the vast crowd. In his speech Chief Justice Taft never mentioned slavery, while President Warren Harding assured the audience that Lincoln had seen emancipation only as a means to "the great end—maintained union and nationality." The text of Moton's address printed here is taken from the original typescript draft in the Library of Congress; it was never delivered and has remained unpublished until now.

Draft of Speech at the Lincoln Memorial

When the Pilgrim Fathers set foot upon the shores of America in 1620, they laid the foundations of our national existence upon the bed-rock of liberty. From that day to this, liberty has been the watchword, liberty has been the rallying call, liberty has been the battle-cry of our united people. In 1776, the altars of a new nation were set up in the name of liberty and the flag of freedom unfurled before the nations of the earth. In 1812, in the name of liberty, we bared our youthful might, and struck for the freedom of the seas. Again, in '61, when the charter of the nation's birth was assailed, the sons of liberty declared anew the principles of their fathers and liberty became co-extensive with the union. In '98, the call once more was heard and freedom became co-extensive with the hemisphere. And as we stand in solemn silence here today before this newly consecrated shrine of liberty, there still come rumbling out of the East the slowly dying echoes of the last great struggle to make freedom co-extensive with the seven seas. Freedom is the life-blood of the nation. Freedom is the heritage bequeathed to all her sons. For sage and scholar, for poet and prophet, for soldier and statesman, freedom is the underlying philosophy of our national existence.

But at the same time, another influence was working within the nation. While the Mayflower was riding at anchor preparing for her epoch-making voyage, another ship had already arrived at Jamestown, Virginia. The first was to bear the pioneers of freedom, freedom of thought and freedom of conscience; the latter had already borne the pioneers of bondage, a bondage degrading alike to body, mind and spirit. Here then, upon American soil, within a year, met the two great forces that were to shape the destiny of the nation. They developed side by side. Freedom was the great compelling force that dominated all and, like a great and shining light, beckoned the oppressed of every nation to the hospitality of these shores. But slavery like a brittle thread in a beautiful garment was woven year by year into the fabric of the nation's life. They who for themselves sought liberty and paid the price thereof in precious blood and priceless treasure, somehow still found it possible while defending its eternal principles for themselves, to deny that same precious boon to others.

And how shall we account for it, except it be that in the Providence of God the black race in America was thrust across the path of the onward-marching white race to demonstrate not only for America, but for the world whether the principles of freedom were of universal application. From the ends of the earth were brought together the extremes of humanity to prove whether the right to life, liberty and the pursuit or happiness should apply with equal force to all mankind.

In the process of time, these two great forces met, as was inevitable, in open conflict upon the field of battle. And how strange it is that by the same over-ruling Providence, the children of those who bought and sold their fellows into bondage should be the very ones to cast aside ties of language, of race, of religion and even of kinship, in order that a people not of their own race, nor primarily of their own creed or color, but brethren withal, should have the same measure of liberty and freedom which they enjoyed.

What a costly sacrifice upon the altar of freedom! How costly the world can never know nor estimate. The flower of the nation's manhood and the accumulated treasure of two hundred and fifty years of unremitting toil: and at length, when the bitter strife was over, when the marshalled hosts had turned again to broken, desolated firesides, a cruel fate, unsatisfied with the awful toll of four long years of carnage, struck at the nation's head and brought to the dust the already wearied frame of him, whose patient fortitude, whose unembittered charity, whose never failing trust in the guiding hand of God had brought the nation, weltering through a sea of blood, yet one and indivisible, to the placid plains of peace. On that day, Abraham Lincoln laid down his life for America, the last and costliest sacrifice upon the altar of freedom.

We do well to raise here this symbol of our gratitude. Here today assemble all those who are blessed by that sacrifice. The united nation stands about this memorial mingling its reverent praise with tokens of eternal gratitude: and not America only, but every nation where liberty is loved and freedom flourishes, joins the chorus of universal praise for him, who with his death, sealed forever the pledge of liberty for all mankind.

But in all this vast assemblage, there are none more grateful, none more reverent, than those who, representing twelve millions of black Americans, gather with their fellow-citizens of every race and creed to pay devout homage to him who was for them, more truly than for any other group, the author of their freedom. There is no question that this man died to save the union. It is equally true that to the last extremity he defended the rights of states. But, when the last veteran has stacked his arms on fame's eternal camping ground; when only the memory of high courage and deep devotion remains to inspire the noble sons of valiant fathers; at such a time, the united voice of grateful posterity will say: the claim of greatness for Abraham Lincoln lies in this, that amid doubt and distrust, against the counsel of his chosen advisors, in the hour of the nation's utter peril, he put his trust in God and spoke the word that gave freedom to a race, and vindicated the honor of a nation conceived in liberty and dedicated to the proposition that all men are created equal.

But someone will ask: Has such a sacrifice been justified? Has such a martyrdom produced its worthy fruits? I speak for the Negro race. Upon us, more perhaps than upon any other group of the nation, rests the immediate obligation to justify so dear a price for our emancipation. In answer let me review the Negro's past upon American soil. No group has been more loyal. Whether bond or free, he has served alike his country's need. Let it never be omitted from the nation's annals that the blood of a black man—Crispus Attucks—was the first to be shed for the nation's freedom; and first his name appears in the long list of the nation's martyred dead. So again, when a world was threatened with disaster and the deciding hand of America was lifted to stay the peril, her black soldiers were among the first to cross the treacherous sea; and when the cause was won, and the record made of those who shared the cruel hardship, these same black soldiers had been longest in the trenches, nearest to the enemy and first to cross their border. All too well does the black man know his wrongs. No one is more sensible than he of his incongruous position in the great American republic. But be it recorded to his everlasting credit, that no failure on the part of the nation to deal fairly with him as a citizen has, in the least degree, every qualified his loyalty.

In like manner has he served his country in the pursuits of peace. From the first blows that won the virgin soil from the woods and wilderness to the sudden, marvelous expansion of our industry that went so far to win the war, the Negro has been the nation's greatest single asset in the development of its vast resources. Especially is this true in the South where his unrequited toil sustained the splendors of that life which gave to the nation a Washington and a Jefferson, a Jackson and a Lee. And afterwards, when devastating war had levelled this fair structure with the ground, the labor of the freedman restored it to its present proportions more substantial than before.

While all this was going on, in spite of limitations within and restrictions without, he still found the way to buy land, to build homes, to erect churches, to establish schools and to lay the foundations of future development in industry, integrity and thrift. It is no mere accident that Negroes in America after less than sixty years of freedom own 22,000,000 acres of land, 600,000 homes and 45,000 churches. It is no mere accident that after so short a time Negroes should operate 78 banks, 100 insurance companies, and 50,000 business enterprises representing a combined capital value of more than $150,000,000. Neither is it an accident that there are within the race 60,000 professional men, 44,000 school teachers and 400 newspapers and magazines; that general illiteracy has been reduced to twenty per cent. Still the Negro race is only in the infancy of its development, so that, if anything in its history could justify the sacrifice that has been made, it is this: that a race that has exhibited such wonderful capacities for advancement should have the restrictions of bondage removed and be given the opportunity in freedom to develop its powers to the utmost, not only for itself, but for the nation and for humanity. Any race that could produce a Frederick Douglass in the midst of slavery, and a Booker Washington in the aftermath of reconstruction has a just claim to the fullest opportunity for developments.

But Lincoln died, not for the Negro alone, but to vindicate the honor of a nation pledged to the sacred cause of human freedom. Upon the field of Gettysburg he dedicated the nation to the great unfinished work of making sure that "government of the people, for the people and by the people should not perish from the earth". And this means ALL the people. So long as any group within our nation is denied the full protection of the law; that task is still unfinished. So long as any group within the nation is denied an equal opportunity for life, liberty and the pursuit of happiness, that task is still unfinished. So long as any group is denied the fullest privilege of a citizen to share both the making and the execution of the law which shapes its destiny— so long as any group does not enjoy every right and every privilege that belongs to every American citizen without regard to race, creed or color, that task for which the immortal Lincoln gave the last full measure of devotion—that task is still unfinished. What nobler thing can the nation do as it dedicates this shrine for him whose deed has made his name immortal—what nobler thing can the nation do than here about this shrine to dedicate itself by its own determined will to fulfill to the last letter the lofty task imposed upon it by the sacred dead?

More than sixty years ago he said in prophetic warning: "This nation cannot endure half slave and half free: it will become all one thing or all the other." With equal truth, it can be said today: no more can the nation endure half privileged and half repressed; half educated and half uneducated; half protected and half unprotected; half prosperous and half in poverty; half in health and half in sickness; half content and half in discontent; yes, half free and half yet in bondage.

My fellow citizens, in the great name which we honor here today, I say unto you that this memorial which we erect in token of our veneration is but a hollow mockery, a symbol of hypocrisy, unless we together can make real in our national life, in every state and in every section, the things for which he died. This is a fair and goodly land. Much right have we, both black and white, to be proud of our achievements at home and our increasing service in all the world. In like manner, there is abundant cause for rejoicing that sectional rancours and racial antagonisms are softening more and more into mutual understanding and increasing sectional and inter-racial cooperation. But unless here at home we are willing to grant to the least and humblest citizen the full enjoyment of every constitutional privilege, our boast is but a mockery and our professions as sounding brass and a tinkling cymbal before the nations of the earth. This is the only way to peace and security at home, to honor and respect abroad.

Sometimes I think the national government itself has not

always set the best example for the states in this regard. A government which can venture abroad to put an end to injustice and mob-violence in another country can surely find a way to put an end to these same evils within our own borders. The Negro race is not insensible of the difficulties that such a task presents; but unless we can together, North and South, East and West, black and white, find the way out of these difficulties and square ourselves with the enlightened conscience and public opinion of all mankind, we must stand convicted not only of inconsistency and hypocrisy, but of the deepest ingratitude that could stain the nation's honor. Twelve million black men and women in this country are proud of their American citizenship, but they are determined that it shall mean for them no less than for any other group, the largest enjoyment of opportunity and the fullest blessings of freedom. We ask no special privileges; we claim no superior title; but we do expect in loyal cooperation with all true lovers of our common country to do our full share in lifting our country above reproach and saving her flag from stain or humiliation. Let us, therefore, with malice toward none, with charity for all, with firmness in the right as God gives us to see the right—let us strive on to finish the work which he so nobly began, to make America the symbol for equal justice and equal opportunity for all.

May 1922

W.E.B. Du Bois

A Harvard-educated scholar, writer, and social activist, Du Bois (1868–1963) helped found the NAACP in 1910 and edited its magazine *The Crisis* for nearly a quarter century. A leading critic of Booker T. Washington, Du Bois also expressed skepticism about African-American loyalty to the Republican party and had endorsed Wilson for the presidency in 1912. His irreverent remarks about Lincoln, published in *The Crisis* in May 1922—the month in which the Memorial was dedicated—predictably stirred up controversy. In a subsequent article, Du Bois made a spirited defense of his position and offered a more detailed historical review of Lincoln's changing racial views. His realistic analysis and willingness to embrace Lincoln in all of his contradictions and inconsistencies proved enormously influential to future historians and commentators, both black and white.

FROM

The Crisis

Abraham Lincoln

May 1922

Abraham Lincoln was a Southern poor white, of illegitimate birth, poorly educated and unusually ugly, awkward, ill-dressed. He liked smutty stories and was a politician down to his toes. Aristocrats—Jeff Davis, Seward and their ilk—despised him, and indeed he had little outwardly that compelled respect. But in that curious human way he was big inside. He had reserves and depths and when habit and convention were torn away there was something left to Lincoln—nothing to most of his contemners. There was something left, so that at the crisis he was big enough to be inconsistent—cruel, merciful; peace-loving, a fighter; despising Negroes and letting them fight and vote; protecting slavery and freeing slaves. He was a man—a big, inconsistent, brave man.

Again, Lincoln

September 1922

We love to think of the Great as flawless. We yearn in our imperfection toward Perfection—sinful, we envisage Righteousness.

As a result of this, no sooner does a great man die than we begin to whitewash him. We seek to forget all that was small and mean and unpleasant and remember the fine and brave and good. We slur over and explain away his inconsistencies and at last there begins to appear, not the real man, but the tradition of the man—remote, immense, perfect, cold and dead!

This sort of falsehood appeals to some folk. They want to dream their heroes true; they want their heroes all heroic with no feet of clay; and they are astonished, angered, hurt if some one speaks the grim, forgotten truth. They can see but one motive for such digging up of filth, for such evil speaking of the dead—and that is prurient love of evil.

Thus many of my readers were hurt by what I said of Lincoln in the July CRISIS.

I am sorry to hurt them, for some of them were tried friends of me and my cause—particularly one like the veteran, wounded at Chickamauga and a staunch defender of our rights, who thinks my words "unkind and uncalled for."

First and foremost, there comes a question of fact. Was what I said true or false? This I shall not argue. Any good library will supply the books, and let each interested reader judge. Only they should remember that, as one of my naive critics writes, "I know that there are among his early biographers those who say something to the same effect"; but against these he marshalls the later words of those who want to forget. I leave the matter there. If my facts were false, my words were wrong—but were my facts false?

Beyond this, there is another and deeper question on which most of my critics dwell. They say, What is the use of recalling evil? What good will it do? or as one phrases, "Is this proper food for your people"? I think it is.

Abraham Lincoln was perhaps the greatest figure of the nineteenth century. Certainly of the five masters,—Napoleon,

Bismarck, Victoria, Browning and Lincoln, Lincoln is to me the most human and lovable. And I love him not because he was perfect but because he was not and yet triumphed. The world is full of illegitimate children. The world is full of folk whose taste was educated in the gutter. The world is full of people born hating and despising their fellows. To these I love to say: See this man. He was one of you and yet he became Abraham Lincoln.

Some may prefer to believe (as one correspondent intimates) that he was of Mayflower ancestry through the "Lincolns of Hingham!" Others may refuse to believe his taste in jokes and political maneuvers and list him as an original abolitionist and defender of Negroes. But personally I revere him the more because up out of his contradictions and inconsistencies he fought his way to the pinnacles of earth and his fight was within as well as without. I care more for Lincoln's great toe than for the whole body of the perfect George Washington, of spotless ancestry, who "never told a lie" and never did anything else interesting.

No! I do not love evil as evil; I do not retail foul gossip about either the living or the dead; but I glory in that crucified humanity that can push itself up out of the mud of a miserable, dirty ancestry; who despite the clinging smirch of low tastes and shifty political methods, rose to be a great and good man and the noblest friend of the slave.

Do my colored friends really believe the picture would be fairer and finer if we forgot Lincoln's unfortunate speech at Charleston, Illinois, in 1858? I commend that speech to the editors who have been having hysterics. Abraham Lincoln said:

> I will say, then, that I am not, nor ever have been, in favor of bringing about in any way the social and political equality of the white and black races—that I am not, nor ever have been, in favor of making voters or jurors of Negroes, nor of qualifying them to hold office, nor to intermarry with white people; and I will say in addition to this, that there is a physical difference between the white and black races which I believe will forever forbid the two races living together on terms of social and political equality. And

inasmuch as they cannot so live, while they do remain together there must be the position of superior and inferior,
and I, as much as any other man, am in favor of having the
superior position assigned to the white race.

This was Lincoln's word in 1858. Five years later he declared
that black slaves "are and henceforward shall be free." And in
1864 he was writing to Hahn of Louisiana in favor of Negro
suffrage.

The difficulty is that ignorant folk and inexperienced try continually to paint humanity as all good or all evil. Was Lincoln
great and good? He was! Well, then, all evil alleged against him
are malicious lies, even if they are true.

"Why should you wish to hold up to public gaze those defects
of character you claim he possessed, knowing that he wrought
so well?"

That is the very reason for telling the Truth. That is the reason for painting Cromwell's mole as it was and not as some artists conceive it ought to have been.

The scars and foibles and contradictions of the Great do not
diminish but enhance the worth and meaning of their upward
struggle: it was the bloody sweat that proved the human Christ
divine; it was his true history and antecedents that proved Abraham Lincoln a Prince of Men.

May–September 1922

H. G. Wells

Now remembered primarily for his classic science-fiction novels, Wells (1866–1946) also achieved great success as the author of *The Outline of History* (1920) and *A Short History of the World* (1922). It was as a popular historian that Wells gave the 1922 magazine interview excerpted here, in which he was asked to name the six greatest men in history. After choosing Jesus, Buddha, Aristotle, Asoka, and Roger Bacon, Wells addressed the perennial American question: who was greater, Washington or Lincoln? His choice of Lincoln was no small judgment from a writer who saw himself as something of a prophet.

FROM
The Six Greatest Men in History

"Now, when you come down nearer to our own times and ask for a sixth name to complete the list, the problem is difficult. There is one striking phenomenon in modern history, however. That phenomenon is America. It represents something so new, so tremendous, so full of promise for the future of the world, that it seems as if America ought surely to have the right to nominate at least one member to our list. Shall it be Washington or Lincoln? Without Washington, there would hardly have been a United States; and yet Washington is not the typical American. He was essentially an English gentleman. All his tastes, all his traditions and many of his associations and friendships ran back to the mother country.

"America might have imported her Washington, full grown, from the old world. She had to grow her own Lincoln.

"He, better than any other, seems to me to embody the essential characteristics of America. He stands for your equality of opportunity, for the right and the chance of the child of the humblest home to reach the highest place. His simplicity, his humor, his patience, his deep abiding optimism, based on the conviction that right will prevail and that things *must* work themselves out—all these seem to typify the best that you have to give. And they are very rich gifts indeed.

"It is interesting and significant to the historian that the Lincoln legend has already grown to such proportions. He has been dead only half a century, yet already he has a secure and permanent place in the affections of men, not only over here, but everywhere. I think we are safe in including Abraham Lincoln in our list of permanently great figures: not merely because of his own greatness, but because of the greatness of the spirit of America, which he, better than any other American, embodies and exemplifies."

July 1922

H. L. Mencken

Just as Lincoln had once proposed that "cold calculating reason" replace dangerous passion in political rhetoric, Mencken (1880–1956)
decried the mythologizing of Lincoln in this brief but powerful essay,
assailing biographers and portraitists alike for robbing him of his
"human weaknesses" and converting a complex man into a "plaster
saint." One can imagine how this prototypical effort at debunking
outraged Mencken's enemies—the conventional thinkers he labeled
the "booboisie"—as well as those who did not share Mencken's views
regarding self-determination and secession. But lurking behind the
author's signature dyspepsia was an important and incontrovertible
point: that where Lincoln was concerned, the myth had all but swallowed the man.

FROM
Prejudices: Third Series

The backwardness of the art of biography in These States is
made shiningly visible by the fact that we have yet to see a
first-rate life of either Lincoln or Whitman. Of Lincolniana, of
course, there is no end, nor is there any end to the hospitality of
those who collect it. Some time ago a publisher told me that
there are four kinds of books that never, under any circumstances,
lose money in the United States—first, detective stories; secondly, novels in which the heroine is forcibly debauched by the
hero; thirdly, volumes on spiritualism, occultism and other such
claptrap, and fourthly, books on Lincoln. But despite all the vast
mass of Lincolniana and the constant discussion of old Abe in
other ways, even so elemental a problem as that of his religious
faith—surely an important matter in any competent biography
—is yet but half solved. Here, for example, is the Rev. William
E. Barton, grappling with it for more than four hundred large
pages in "The Soul of Abraham Lincoln." It is a lengthy inquiry
—the rev. pastor, in truth, shows a good deal of the habitual gar-
rulity of his order—but it is never tedious. On the contrary, it is

curious and amusing, and I have read it with steady interest, including even the appendices. Unluckily, the author, like his predecessors, fails to finish the business before him. Was Lincoln a Christian? Did he believe in the Divinity of Christ? I am left in doubt. He was very polite about it, and very cautious, as befitted a politician in need of Christian votes, but how much genuine conviction was in that politeness? And if his occasional references to Christ were thus open to question, what of his rather vague avowals of belief in a personal God and in the immortality of the soul? Herndon and some of his other close friends always maintained that he was an atheist, but Dr. Barton argues that this atheism was simply disbelief in the idiotic Methodist and Baptist dogmas of his time—that nine Christian churches out of ten, if he were alive to-day, would admit him to their high privileges and prerogatives without anything worse than a few warning coughs. As for me, I still wonder.

The growth of the Lincoln legend is truly amazing. He becomes the American solar myth, the chief butt of American credulity and sentimentality. Washington, of late years, has been perceptibly humanized; every schoolboy now knows that he used to swear a good deal, and was a sharp trader, and had a quick eye for a pretty ankle. But meanwhile the varnishers and veneerers have been busily converting Abe into a plaster saint, thus making him fit for adoration in the chautauquas and Y.M.C.A.'s. All the popular pictures of him show him in his robes of state, and wearing an expression fit for a man about to be hanged. There is, so far as I know, not a single portrait of him showing him smiling—and yet he must have cackled a good deal, first and last: who ever heard of a storyteller who didn't? Worse, there is an obvious effort to pump all his human weaknesses out of him, and so leave him a mere moral apparition, a sort of amalgam of John Wesley and the Holy Ghost. What could be more absurd? Lincoln, in point of fact, was a practical politician of long experience and high talents, and by no means cursed with inconvenient ideals. On the contrary, his career in the Illinois Legislature was that of a good organization man, and he was more than once denounced by reformers. Even his handling of the slavery question was that of a politician, not that of a fanatic. Nothing alarmed him more than the suspicion that he was an Abolitionist. Barton tells of an occasion when he actually fled town to avoid meeting the issue squarely. A genuine Abolitionist would have published the Emancipation Proclamation the day after the first battle of Bull Run. But Lincoln waited until the time was more favorable—until Lee had been hurled out of Pennsylvania, and, more important still, until the political currents were safely running his way. Always he was a wary fellow, both in his dealings with measures and in his dealings with men. He knew how to keep his mouth shut.

Nevertheless, it was his eloquence that probably brought him to his great estate. Like William Jennings Bryan, he was a dark horse made suddenly formidable by fortunate rhetoric. The Douglas debate launched him, and the Cooper Union speech got him the presidency. This talent for emotional utterance, this gift for making phrases that enchanted the plain people, was an accomplishment of late growth. His early speeches were mere empty fireworks—the childish rhodomontades of the era. But in middle life he purged his style of ornament and it became almost baldly simple—and it is for that simplicity that he is remembered to-day. The Gettysburg speech is at once the shortest and the most famous oration in American history. Put beside it, all the whoopings of the Websters, Sumners and Everetts seem gaudy and silly. It is eloquence brought to a pellucid and almost child-like perfection—the highest emotion reduced to one graceful and irresistible gesture. Nothing else precisely like it is to be found in the whole range of oratory. Lincoln himself never even remotely approached it. It is genuinely stupendous.

But let us not forget that it is oratory, not logic; beauty, not sense. Think of the argument in it! Put it into the cold words of everyday! The doctrine is simply this: that the Union soldiers who died at Gettysburg sacrificed their lives to the cause of self-determination—"that government of the people, by the people, for the people," should not perish from the earth. It is difficult to imagine anything more untrue. The Union soldiers in that battle actually fought against self-determination; it was the Confederates who fought for the right of their people to govern themselves. What was the practical effect of the battle of Gettysburg?

What else than the destruction of the old sovereignty of the States, *i.e.*, of the people of the States? The Confederates went into battle an absolutely free people; they came out with their freedom subject to the supervision and vote of the rest of the country—and for nearly twenty years that vote was so effective that they enjoyed scarcely any freedom at all. Am I the first American to note the fundamental nonsensicality of the Gettysburg address? If so, I plead my æsthetic joy in it in amelioration of the sacrilege.

1922

William Carlos Williams

In another sardonic rumination on the excesses of Lincoln legend-making, Williams (1883–1963) concluded his iconoclastic book of essays *In the American Grain* with this stream-of-consciousness rant pondering the feminization of Lincoln and its impact on the collapsing American masculine ideal. (The "great broad hipped" Mengelberg is a reference to Willem Mengelberg, the Dutch conductor who was music director of the New York Philharmonic at the time.)

FROM
In the American Grain

The Great Railsplitter's, "All I am or ever hope to be I owe to my angel mother"; the walking up and down in Springfield on the narrow walk between the two houses, day after day, with a neighbor's baby, borrowed for the occasion, sleeping inside his cape upon his shoulder to give him stability while thinking and composing his coming speeches; and apart from its cowardice, the blinding stupidity of his murderer's *sic semper tyrannis*, after he had shot him in the back—in this trinity is reflected the brutalizing desolation of life in America up to that time; yet perversely flowering.

Mengelberg, a great broad hipped one, conducts an orchestra in the same vein. It is a woman. He babies them. He leans over and floods them with his insistences. It is a woman drawing to herself with insatiable passion the myriad points of sound, conferring upon each the dignity of a successful approach, relieving each of his swelling burden (but particularly, by himself), in the overtowering symphony— It is the balm of command. The violins, surrounded, yet feel that they have come alone, in silence and in secret, singly to be heard.

It is Lincoln pardoning the fellow who slept on sentry duty. It is the grace of the Bixby letter. The least private would find a woman to caress him, a woman in an old shawl—with a great bearded face and a towering black hat above it, to give unearthly reality.

Brancusi should make his statue—of wood—after the manner of his Socrates, with the big hole in the enormous mass of the head, save that this would be a woman—

The age-old torture reached a disastrous climax in Lincoln. Failing of relief or expression, the place tormented itself into a convulsion of bewilderment and pain—with a woman, born somehow, aching over it, holding all fearfully together. It was the end of THAT period.

1925

Carl Sandburg

The poet began conducting serious Lincoln research as early as 1914, determined to obtain "a better understanding of this man who the Republican party and the G.A.R. and the preachers magnified until he was too big to see." Originally planning a children's book, Sandburg realized he was onto something potentially more influential, and in 1926 he published the two-volume biography from which these six brief chapters are excerpted. The work proved enormously popular; a sequel, *The War Years*, appeared in four volumes in 1939 and won the Pulitzer Prize. Sandburg became America's leading apostle for what he claimed to be Lincoln's greatest virtues: humility, tolerance, and the ability to grow to meet changing needs and times. Many scholars who rued Sandburg's refusal to employ a systematic system of bibliography and footnoting still conceded that his prose elevated his books above their own. Edmund Wilson disagreed— characterizing *The Prairie Years* as "corn," he memorably cracked that "the cruellest thing that has happened to Lincoln since he was shot by Booth has been to fall into the hands of Carl Sandburg."

FROM
Abraham Lincoln: The Prairie Years

Chapter 6

Seven-year-old Abe walked four miles a day going to the Knob Creek school to learn to read and write. Zachariah Riney and Caleb Hazel were the teachers who brought him along from A B C to where he could write the name "A-b-r-a-h-a-m L-i-n-c-o-l-n" and count numbers beginning with one, two, three, and so on. He heard twice two is four.

The schoolhouse was built of logs, with a dirt floor, no window, one door. The scholars learned their lessons by saying them to themselves out loud till it was time to recite; alphabets, multiplication tables, and the letters of spelled words were all in the air at once. It was a "blab school"; so they called it.

The Louisville and Nashville pike running past the Lincoln

cabin had many different travelers. Covered wagons came with settlers moving south and west, or north to Ohio and Indiana; there were peddlers with knickknacks to spread out and tell the prices of; congressmen, members of the legislature meeting at Lexington, men who had visited Henry Clay at Ashland.

Coming back from a fishing trip, with one fish, Abe met a soldier who came from fighting in the Battle of New Orleans with General Jackson, and Abe, remembering his father and mother had told him to be good to soldiers, handed the soldier the one fish.

The Lincolns got well acquainted with Christopher Columbus Graham, a doctor, a scientist, who was beginning to study and write books about the rocks, flowers, plants, trees, and wild animals of Kentucky; Graham slept in the bed while the Lincolns slept on the floor of the cabin, more than once; he told in the evening talk about days camping with Daniel Boone, and running backward with Boone so as to make foot-tracks pointing forward to mislead the Indians; he talked about stones, leaves, bones, snake-skins he was carrying in a sack back to Louisville; he mentioned a young storekeeper at Elizabethtown, named John James Audubon, who had marvelous ways with birds and might some day write a great book about birds. The boy Abe heard traveling preachers and his father talk about the times when they held church meetings in cabins, and every man had his rifle by his side, and there were other men with rifles outside the cabin door, ready for Indians who might try to interrupt their Sabbath worship. And the boy never liked it when the talkers slung around words like "independent" and "predestination," because he lay awake thinking about those long words.

Abe was the chore-boy of the Knob Creek farm as soon as he grew big enough to run errands, to hold a pine-knot at night lighting his father at a job, or to carry water, fill the woodbox, clean ashes from the fireplace, hoe weeds, pick berries, grapes, persimmons for beer-making. He hunted the timbers and came back with walnuts, hickory and hazel nuts. His hands knew the stinging blisters from using a hoe-handle back and forth a summer afternoon, and in autumn the mash of walnut-stain that wouldn't wash off, with all the rinsing and scrubbing of Nancy

Hanks's homemade soap. He went swimming with Austin Gollaher; they got their backs sunburnt so the skin peeled off.

Wearing only a shirt—no hat nor pants—Abe rode a horse hitched to a "bull-tongue" plow of wood shod with iron. He helped his father with seed corn, beans, onions, potatoes. He ducked out of the way of the heels of the stallion and brood mares his father kept and paid taxes on.

The father would ride away to auctions, once coming home with dishes, plates, spoons, and a wash basin, another time with a heifer, and again with a wagon that had been knocked down to the highest bidder for $8\frac{1}{2}$ cents.

Abe and his sister picked pails of currants and blueberries for mother Nancy to spread in the sun to dry and put away for winter eating. There were wild grapes and pawpaws; there were bee trees with wild honey; there were wild crabapples and red haws. If it was a good corn year, the children helped shell the corn by hand and put it between two big flat stones, grinding it into cornmeal. The creeks gave them fish to fry. Tom Lincoln took his gun and brought back prairie turkey, partridge, rabbit, sometimes a coon, a bear, or a deer; and the skins of these big animals were tanned, cut and sewed into shirts, trousers, moccasins; the coonskins made caps.

There were lean times and fat, all depending on the weather, the rains or floods, how Tom Lincoln worked and what luck he had fishing and hunting. There were times when they lived on the fat of the land and said God was good; other times when they just scraped along and said they hoped the next world would be better than this one.

It was wilderness. Life dripped with fat and ease. Or it took hold with hunger and cold. All the older settlers remembered winter in the year 1795, when "cold Friday" came; Kentucky was "cold as Canada," and cows froze to death in the open fields. The wilderness is careless.

Between the roadway over the top of Muldraugh's Hill and the swimming-hole where Abe Lincoln and Austin Gollaher ducked each other, there are tall hills more correctly called limestone bluffs. They crowd around Knob Creek and shape the valley's form. Their foundations are rocks, their measurements seem to be those of low mountains rather than hills. They seem to be aware of proportions and to suggest a quiet importance and secrets of fire, erosion, water, time, and many repeated processes that have stood them against the sky so that human settlers in the valley feel that around them are speakers of reserves and immensities.

The valley through which Knob Creek wanders there near Muldraugh's Hill, shooting its deep rushes of water when the hill rains flush the bottoms, has many keepers of the darker reticences of the crust of the earth and the changers that hold on to their lives there. That basic stream has a journal of its movement among pools inconceivably quiet in their mirrorings during days when the weather is fair and the elements of the sky at ease, and again of movement among those same pools when the rampages between the limestone banks send the water boiling and swirling. The naming of Muldraugh's Hill was a rich act in connotation, for it has whisperings of namelessly shrewd and beautiful wishes that the older and darker landscapes of Ireland breathe.

Trees crowd up its slopes with passionate footholds as though called by homes in the rocky soil; their climbings have covered sides and crests till they murmur, "You shall see no tall hills here unless you look at us." Caverns and ledges thrust their surprises of witchery and wizardry, of gnomes and passwords, or again of old-time intimations and analogues, memories of reckless rains leaving wave-prints to hint or say Muldraugh's Hill and the Knob Creek valley are old-timers in the making of the world, old-timers alongside of the two-footed little mover known as man. In the bottom lands the honeysuckle ranges with a strength nothing less than fierce; so deep are its roots that, unless torn away by the machines of man, the bees count on every year a boomer harvest of its honey-stuff; black and brown butterflies, spotted and streaked with scrolls and alphabets of unknown tongues from the world of wings—these come back every year to the honeysuckle.

Redbud, wild rose, and white daisies that look like scatterings of snow on green levels rise up with their faces yearly. Birds have made the valley a home; oncoming civilization has not shut off their hopes; homes for all are here; the martins learned a thousand years before the white man came that ten martins that fight with despair can kill and pick the eyes out of the head of a hawk that comes to slaughter and eat martins. And horses have so loved the valley, and it has so loved them in return, that some of the fastest saddle and riding nags remembered of men got their flying starts here.

Such was the exterior of the place and neighborhood where Abe Lincoln grew up from three to seven years of age, where he heard travelers talk, where he learned to write and sign his name, where, in fact, he first learned the meanings of names and how to answer, "Yes, it's me," if his mother called in the dark, "Is that you, Abe?"

Chapter 7

In the year 1816 Tom Lincoln was appointed road surveyor. The paper naming him for that office said he was named in place of George Redman to repair the road "leading from Nolen to Pendleton, which lies between the Bigg Hill and the Rolling Fork." It further commanded "that all hands that assisted said Redman do assist Lincoln in keeping said road in repair." It was a pasty red clay road. That the county was beginning to think about good roads showed that civilization was breaking through on the wilderness. And that Tom Lincoln was named as road surveyor showed they were holding some respect for him as a citizen and taxpayer of that community. At the county courthouse the recorder of deeds noticed that Thomas Lincoln signed his name, while his wife, Nancy, made her mark.

Knob Creek settlers taking their corn to Hodgens Mill or riding to Elizabethtown to pay their taxes at the court or collect bounties on wolfskins at the county courthouse, talked a good deal about land-titles, landowners, landlords, land-laws, land-lawyers, land-sharks. Tom Lincoln about that time was chopping down trees and cutting brush on the Knob Creek land so as to clear more ground, raise corn on it and make a farm out of it. And he wasn't satisfied; he was suspicious that even if he did get his thirty acres cleared and paid for, the land might be taken away from him. This was happening to other settlers; they had the wrong kind of papers. Pioneers and settlers who for years had been fighting Indians, wolves, foxes, mosquitoes, and malaria had seen their land taken away; they had the wrong kind of papers. Daniel Boone, the first man to break a path from civilization through and into the Kentucky wilderness, found himself one day with all his rich, bluegrass Kentucky lands gone, not an acre of his big farms left; he had the wrong kind of papers; that was why he moved from Kentucky to Missouri.

Though Tom Lincoln was paying taxes on his thirty-acre farm, he was sued as a "tresspasser." He had to prove he wasn't a squatter—which he did. He went to court and won his suit. His little thirty-acre piece was only one of many pieces of a 10,000-acre tract surveyed in 1784 and patented to one man, Thomas Middleton, in 1786.

Poor white men were having a harder time to get along. Hardin County had been filling up with negroes, slave black men, bought and sold among the rich and well-to-do. The Hodgens, La Rues, and other first families usually had one or two, or six or a dozen, negroes. More than half the population of Hardin County were colored. And it seemed that as more slave black men were brought in, a poor white man didn't count for so much; he had a harder time to get along; he was free with the freedom of him who cannot be sold nor bought, while the black slave was free with the security of the useful horse, mule, cow, goat, or dog whose life and health is worth money to the owner.

Already, in parts of Kentucky and farther south, the poor white men, their women and children, were using the name of "nigger" for the slaves, while there were black slaves in families of quality who used the name of "po' w'ite" for the white people who owned only their clothes, furniture, a rifle, an ax, perhaps a horse and plow, and no land, no slaves, no stables, and no property to speak of.

While these changes were coming in Kentucky, the territory of Indiana came into the Union as a state whose law declared "all men are born equally free and independent" and "the holding any part of the human creation in slavery, or involuntary servitude, can only originate in usurpation and tyranny." In crossing the Ohio River's two shores, a traveler touched two soils, one where the buying and selling of black slaves went on, the other where the negro was held to be "part of human creation" and was not property for buying and selling. But both soils were part of the Union of states.

Letters and reports reaching Hardin County about this time told of rich, black lands in Indiana, with more bushels of corn to the acre than down in Kentucky, Government land with clear title, the right kind of papers, for two dollars an acre. This helped Tom Lincoln to decide in the year 1816 to move to Indiana. He told the family he would build a flatboat, load the household goods on it, float by creeks to the Ohio River, leave the household goods somewhere along the river while he went afoot up into Indiana, located his land, and registered it. Then he would come back, and the family, afoot and on horseback, would move to the new farm and home.

Chapter 8

The boy, Abe, had his thoughts, some running ahead wondering how Indiana would look, some going back to his seven little years in Kentucky. Here he had curled around his mother's apron, watched her face and listened to her reading the Bible at the cabin log-fire, her fingers rambling through his hair, the hands patting him on the cheek and under the chin. God was real to his mother; he tried to make pictures in his head of the face of God far off and away in the sky, watching Kentucky, Hodgenville, Knob Creek, and all the rest of the world He had made. His thoughts could go back to the first time on a winter night around the fire when he lay flat on his stomach listening to his father as he told about his brothers, Mordecai and Josiah, and their father, Abraham Lincoln, who had staked out claims for more than 2,000 acres of land on the Green River. One day Abraham Lincoln and his three boys were working in a field; all of a sudden the father doubled up with a groan of pain and crumpled to the ground, just after the boys had heard a rifle-shot and the whining of a bullet. "Indians," the boys yelled to each other.

And Mordecai ran to a cabin, Josiah started across the fields and woods to a fort to bring help, while Tom Lincoln—little knee-high Tom—stooped over his father's bleeding body and wondered what he could do. He looked up to see an Indian standing over him, and a shining bangle hanging down over the Indian's shoulder close to the heart.

The Indian clutched upward with his hands, doubled with a groan and crumpled to the ground; Mordecai with a rifle at a peephole in the cabin had aimed his rifle at the shining bangle hanging down close to the Indian's heart, and Tom was so near he heard the bullet plug its hole into the red man.

And for years after that Mordecai Lincoln hated Indians with a deadly hate; if he heard that Indians were loose anywhere in a half-day's riding, he took his best rifles, pistols, and knives, and went Indian-killing.

There was Dr. Christopher Columbus Graham from Louis-ville, telling how the Indians were chasing Daniel Boone, and Boone saw a grapevine climbing high up a big oak; and he cut the grapevine near the root, took a run and a swing and made a jump of forty feet, so the Indians had to lose time finding sight and smell of his foot-tracks again.

And there were caves, worth remembering about in that part of Kentucky, and especially the biggest one of all, Mammoth Cave, fifty miles south; they said a thousand wagons could drive in and there would be room for another thousand.

And there was the foxy Austin Gollaher, his playmate. Up a tree he climbed one time, Abe dropped a pawpaw down into a coonskin cap; he guessed it was Austin's cap he was putting a smear of pawpaw mash in, but Austin had seen the trick coming and changed caps. So he had to wipe the smear out of his own cap.

Once he was walking on a log across Knob Creek when the

rains had raised the creek. Just under the log, and under his feet, was the rush of the yellow muddy water. The log was slippery, his feet slippery. His feet went up in the air, he tumbled to the bottom of the creek; he came up, slipped again, came up with his nose and eyes full of water, and then saw Austin Gollaher on the bank holding out a long pole. He took hold of the pole and Austin pulled him to the bank.

Maybe he would grow up; his feet would be farther away from his head and his chin if he grew up; he could pick apples without climbing a tree or throwing clubs—if he grew up. Maybe then, after growing up, he would know more about those words he heard men saying, "in-de-pend-ent," "pre-des-ti-na-tion." Daniel Boone—yes, he could understand about Daniel Boone—wearing moccasins and a buckskin shirt. But George Washington and Thomas Jefferson, and the President in Washington, James Madison—they were far off; they were sort of like God; it was hard to make pictures of their faces.

How many times he had gone to the family Bible, opened the big front cover, and peeped in at the page which tells what the book is! There were the words: "The Holy Bible, containing the Old and New Testaments, with Arguments prefixed to the Different Books and Moral and Theological Observations illustrating each Chapter, composed by the Reverend Mr. Osterwald, Professor of Divinity." And then pages and pages filled with words spelled out like the words in the spelling-book he had in school. So many words: heavy words—mysterious words!

About wolf heads, he could understand. He saw a man in Elizabethtown one time carrying two big wolf heads. The man had shot the wolves and was going to the courthouse, where they paid money for wolf heads. Yes, this he could understand. Wolves kill sheep and cattle in the fields; they come to the barns for pigs and chickens; he had heard them howling and sniffing on winter nights around the Knob Creek cabin and up the hills and gorges.

And there was his mother, his "mammy," the woman other people called Nancy or Nancy Hanks. . . . It was so dark and strange about her. There was such sweetness. Yet there used to be more sweetness and a fresher sweetness. There had been one baby they buried. Then there was Sally—and him, little Abe. Did the children cost her something? Did they pull her down? . . . The baby that came and was laid away so soon, only three days after it came, in so little a grave: that hurt his mother; she was sick and tired more often after that. . . . There were such lights and shadows back in her eyes. She wanted—what did she want? There were more and more days he had to take care of her, when he loved to bring cool drinking water to her—or anything she asked for.

Well—a boy seven years old isn't supposed to know much; he goes along and tries to do what the big people tell him to do. . . . They have been young and seen trouble: maybe they know. . . . He would get up in the morning when they called him; he would run to the spring for water. . . . He was only seven years old—and there were lots of frisky tricks he wanted to know more about.

He was a "shirt-tail boy." . . . Three boys teased him one day when he took corn to Hodgen's Mill; they wouldn't be satisfied till he had punched their noses. . . . A clerk in the store at Elizabethtown gave him maple sugar to sit on a syrup keg and suck while his mother bought salt and flour. And the clerk was the only man he knew who was wearing store clothes, Sunday clothes, every day in the week. . . . The two pear trees his father planted on the Rock Spring farm . . . the faces of two goats a man kept down in Hodgenville . . . Dennis Hanks saying, "Abe, your face is solemn as a papoose."

It wouldn't be easy to forget that Saturday afternoon in corn-planting time when other boys dropped the seed-corn into all the rows in the big seven-acre field—and Abe dropped the pumpkin seed. He dropped two seeds at every other hill and every other row. The next Sunday morning there came a big rain in the hills; it didn't rain a drop in the valley, but the water came down the gorges and slides, and washed ground, corn, pumpkin seeds, and all clear off the field.

A dark blur of thoughts, pictures, memories and hopes moved through the head of little seven-year-old Abe. The family was going to move again. There was hope of better luck up north in Indiana. Tom's older brother, Josiah, was farming along the Big

Blue River. Rich black corn-land was over there in "Indianny," more bushels to the acre than anywhere in Kentucky.

Chapter 9

In the fall of the year 1816, Abe watched his father cut down trees, cut out logs, and fasten those logs into a flatboat on Knob Creek. Abe ran after tools his father called for, sometimes held a hammer, a saw and a knife in his hands ready to give his father the next one called for. If his father said, "Fetch me a drink of water," the boy fetched; his legs belonged to his father. He helped carry chairs, tables, household goods, and carpenter's tools, loading them onto the flatboat. These, with four hundred gallons of whisky, "ten bar'ls," Tom had loaded onto the boat, made quite a cargo. Tom Lincoln, who was not much of a drinking man, had traded his farm for whisky, which was a kind of money in that day, and $20.00 cash.

Nancy Hanks and Sarah and Abe stayed on the farm while the husband and father floated down Knob Creek to Salt River and into the Ohio River. Tom was out of luck when the flatboat turned over so that the tool chest, household goods and four barrels of whisky slid out of the boat. Most of the whisky and some of the other goods he managed to fish up from the river bottom. Then he crossed the Ohio River, landed on the Indiana side at Thompson's Ferry and left his whisky and household goods at the house of a man called Posey.

He started off on foot into the big timbers of what was then Perry County, later divided into Spencer County. He decided to live and to farm on a quarter-section of land on Little Pigeon Creek; he notched the trees with his ax, cleared away brush and piled it, as the Government land-laws required. This was his "claim," later filed at the Land Office in Vincennes, Indiana, as the Southwest Quarter of Section Thirty-two, Town Four South, Range Five West, to be paid for at $2.00 an acre. His Indiana homestead was now ready for a cabin and a family; he walked back to the Knob Creek home in Kentucky and told the family he reckoned they'd all put in the winter up in "Indianny."

They had fifty miles to go, in a straight line "as the crow flies," but about one hundred miles with all the zigzags and curves around hills, timbers, creeks, and rivers.

Pots, pans, kettles, blankets, the family Bible, and other things were put into bags and loaded on two horses. Nancy and Sarah climbed on one horse, Tom and Abe on the other. When it was hard going for the horses, the father and mother walked. Part of the way on that hundred-mile ride made little Abe's eyes open. They were going deeper into the wilderness. In Kentucky there were ten people to the square mile and in Indiana only three. As Abe sat on the horse plodding along, he saw miles and miles of beeches, oaks, elms, hard and soft maples, hung and run over with the scarlet streamers and the shifting gray hazes of autumn.

Then they came to the Ohio River. The Frenchmen years before named it "La Belle Rivière," meaning it was a sheen of water as good to look at as a beautiful woman. There she lay— the biggest stretch of shining water his eyes had ever seen. And Abe thought how different it was from Knob Creek, which he could walk across on a log—if he didn't let his feet slip from under. They crossed the river, and at the house of the man called Posey they got a wagon, loaded the barrels of whisky and the household goods, and drove sixteen miles to their "claim." The trail was so narrow that a few times Tom Lincoln got off the wagon with an ax and cut brush and trees so the wagon could pass through. It was a hired wagon and horses they came with, and the wagon and horse-team were taken back to Posey.

Tom Lincoln, his wife, boy, and girl, had arrived on a claim at Little Pigeon Creek, without a horse or a cow, without a house, with a little piece of land under their feet and the wintry sky high over. Naked they had come into the world; almost naked they came to Little Pigeon Creek, Indiana.

The whole family pitched in and built a pole-shed or "half-faced camp." On a slope of ground stood two trees about fourteen feet apart, east and west. These formed the two strong corner-posts of a sort of cabin with three sides, the fourth side open, facing south. The sides and the roof were covered with poles, branches, brush, dried grass, mud; chinks were stuffed where the wind or the rain was trying to come through. At the open side a log-fire was kept burning night and day. In the two far corners inside the camp were beds of dry leaves on the ground. To these beds the sleepers brought their blankets and bearskins.

Here they lived a year. In the summer time and fair weather, the pole-shed was snug enough. When the rain storms or wind and snow broke through and drenched the place, or when the south or southwest wind blew the fire-smoke into the camp so those inside had to clear out, it was a rough life.

The mother sang. Nancy Hanks knew songs her mother, Lucy, had heard in Virginia. The ballad of Fair Ellender told of the hero coming home with the Brown Girl who had lands and gold. Fair Ellender taunted: "Is this your bride? She seemeth me plagued brown." And for that, the Brown Girl leaped over a table corner and put a slim little knife through Fair Ellender's heart. Then out came the hero's sword and he cut off the Brown Girl's head and "slung it agin the wall." Then he put the sword through his own heart.

And there was the ballad of Wicked Polly, who danced and ran wild and told the old folks, "I'll turn to God when I get old, and He will then receive my soul." But when death struck her down while she was young and running wild, she called for her mother, and with rolling eyeballs, cried, "When I am dead, re-member well, your wicked Polly screams in hell."

Tom chopped logs for a cabin forty yards away while Abe did the best he could helping Nancy and Sarah trim the branches off the logs, cut brush, clear ground for planting, hoe weeds, tend the log-fire. The heaviest regular chore of the children was walking a mile away to a spring and carrying a bucket of water back home. Their food was mostly game shot in the woods near by; they went barefoot most of the year; in the winter their shoes were homemade moccasins; they were up with the sun and the early birds in the morning; their lighting at night was fire-logs and pine-knots. In summer and early fall the flies and mosquitoes swarmed.

In the new cabin Tom Lincoln was building, and on this little Pigeon Creek farm, the Lincoln family was going to live four-teen years.

Chapter 10

As Abe Lincoln, seven years old, going on eight, went to sleep on his bed of dry leaves in a corner of the pole-shed there on Little Pigeon Creek, in Indiana, in the winter of 1816, he had his thoughts, his feelings, his impressions. He shut his eyes, and looking-glasses began to work inside his head; he could see Kentucky and the Knob Creek farm again; he could see the Ohio River shining so far across that he couldn't begin to throw a stone from one side to the other.

And while his eyes were shut he could see the inside of the pole-shed, the floor of earth and grass, the frying-pan, the cooking-pot, the water-pail he and his sister carried full of water from the spring a mile away, and the log-fire always kept burning. And sometimes his imagination, his shut eyes and their quick-changing looking-glasses would bring the whole outdoor sky and land indoors, into the pole-shed, into the big shifting looking-glasses inside of his head. The mystery of imagination, of the faculty of reconstruction and piecing together today the things his eyes had seen yesterday, this took hold of him and he brooded over it.

One night he tried to sleep while his head was working on the meaning of the heavy and mysterious words standing dark on the pages of the family Bible; the stories his mother told him from those pages; all the people in the world drowned, the world covered with water, even Indiana and Kentucky, all people drowned except Noah and his family; the man Jonah swallowed by a whale and after days coming out of the belly of the whale; the Last Day to come, the stars dropping out of the sky, the world swallowed up in fire.

And one night this boy felt the southwest wind blowing the log-fire smoke into his nostrils. And there was a hoot-owl crying, and a shaking of branches in the beeches and walnuts outside, so that he went to the south opening of the shed and looked out on a winter sky with a high quarter-moon and a white shine of thin frost on the long open spaces of the sky.

And an old wonder took a deeper hold on him, a wonder

about the loneliness of life down there in the Indiana wilderness, and a wonder about what was happening in other places over the world, places he had heard people mention, cities, rivers, flags, wars, Jerusalem, Washington, Baltimore.

He might have asked the moon, "What do you see?" And the moon might have told him many things.

That year of 1816 the moon had seen sixteen thousand wagons come along one turnpike in Pennsylvania, heading west, with people hungry for new land, a new home, just like Tom Lincoln. Up the Mississippi River that year had come the first steamboat to curve into the Ohio River and land passengers at Louisville. The moon had seen the first steamboat leave Pittsburgh and tie up at New Orleans. New wheels, wagons, were coming, an iron horse snorting fire and smoke. Rolling-mills, ingots, iron, steel, were the talk of Pennsylvania; a sheet copper mill was starting in Massachusetts.

The moon could see eight million people in the United States, white men who had pushed the Indians over the eastern mountains, fighting to clear the Great Plains and the southern valleys of the red men. At Fallen Timbers and at Tippecanoe in Indiana, and down at the Great Bend of the Tallapoosa, the pale faces and copper faces had yelled and grappled and Weatherford had said, "I have done the white people all the harm I could; if I had an army I would fight to the last; my warriors can no longer hear my voice; their bones are at Talladega, Tallushatches, Emuckfaw, and Tohopeka; I can do no more than weep." The red men had been warned by Jefferson to settle down and be farmers, to double their numbers every twenty years as the white people did, the whites in "new swarms continually advancing upon the country like flocks of pigeons."

The moon had seen two men, sunburned, wind-bitten and scarred, arrive at the White House just four years before Abe Lincoln was born. The two men had been on a three-year trip, leaving Washington in 1802, riding and walking across the Great Plains, the Rockies and Sierras, to the Pacific Coast country, and then back to Washington. What those two, Lewis and

Clark, had to tell, opened the eyes of white people to what a rich, big country they lived in. Out along that trail Jefferson could see "new swarms advancing like flocks of pigeons."

And how had these eight million people come to America, for the moon to look down on and watch their westward swarming? Many were children of men who had quarreled in the old countries of Europe, and fought wars about the words and ways of worshiping God and obeying His commandments. They were Puritans from England, French Huguenots, German Pietists, Hanoverians, Moravians, Saxons, Austrians, Swiss, Quakers, all carrying their Bibles. Also there were Ulster Presbyterians from North Ireland, and Scotch Presbyterians. They came by their own wish. Others who came not by their own wish were fifty thousand thieves and murderers sent from British prisons and courts. Dr. Samuel Johnson, the same man who said, "Patriotism is the last refuge of a scoundrel," had called Americans "a race of convicts." Convicted men in England, offered the choice of hanging or being shipped to America, had given the answer, "Hang me."

The moon had seen boys and girls by thousands kidnaped off the streets of English cities and smuggled across to America. And each year for fifty years there had come a thousand to fifteen hundred "indentured servants," men and women who had signed papers to work for a certain master, the law holding them to work till their time was up.

The moon had seen sailing-ships start from ports in Europe and take from six weeks to six months crossing the Atlantic. Aboard, those ships often were "stench, fumes, vomiting, many kinds of sicknesses, fever, dysentery, scurvey, the mouth-rot, and the like, all of which come from old and sharply salted food and meat, also from bad and foul water."

Such were a few of the things known to the fathers and grandfathers of part of the eight million people in America that the moon was looking down on in the winter nights of 1816. And in the years to come the moon would see more and more people coming from Europe.

Seldom had the moon in its thousands of years of looking down on the earth and the human family seen such a man as the

Napoleon Bonaparte whose bayonets had been going in Europe for fifteen years, shoving kings off thrones, changing laws, maps, books, raising armies, using them up, and raising new armies, until people in some regions were saying, "The red roses of this year grow from the blood-wet ground of the wars we fought last year." And at last the terrible Napoleon was caged, jailed, on the lonely island of St. Helena. Crying for the "liberty and equality" of France to be spread over the world, he had led armies to believe and dream of beating down all other armies in Europe that tried to stand against him. Then he was a lean shadow; he had become fat; the paunch stuck out farther than is allowed to conquerors. He had hugged armfuls of battle-flags to his breast while telling an army of soldiers, "I cannot embrace you all, but I do so in the person of your general." It hurt his ears when, captured and being driven in an open carriage, he heard sarcastic people along the streets mock at him with the call, "Long live the Emperor!" He would die far from home, with regrets, the first man to be Napoleonic.

When Napoleon sold to Jefferson the Great Plains between the Mississippi River and the Rocky Mountains, the moon saw only a few Indians, buffalo hunters and drifters, living there. The price for the land was fifteen million dollars; Jefferson had to argue with people who said the price was too high. Such things the moon had seen. Also, out of war-taxed and war-crippled Europe the moon could see steady lines of ships taking people from that part of the Round World across the water to America. Also, lines of ships sailing to Africa with whisky, calico, and silk, and coming back loaded with negroes.

And as the wagons, by thousands a year, were slipping through the passes of the Allegheny Mountains, heading west for the two-dollar-an-acre Government land, many steered clear of the South; they couldn't buy slaves; and they were suspicious of slavery; it was safer to go farming where white men did all the work. At first the stream of wagons and settlers moving west had kept close to the Ohio River. Then it began spreading in a fan-shape up north and west.

The moon could see along the pikes, roads, and trails heading west, broken wagon-wheels with prairie grass growing up over the spokes and hubs. And near by, sometimes, a rusty skillet, empty moccasins, and the bones of horses and men.

In the hot dog-days, in the long rains, in the casual blizzards, they had stuck it out—and lost. There came a saying, a pithy, perhaps brutal folk proverb, "The cowards never started and the weak ones died by the way."

Such were a few of the many, many things the moon might have told little Abe Lincoln, nearly eight years old, on a winter night in 1816 on Little Pigeon Creek, in the Buckhorn Valley, in southern Indiana—a high quarter-moon with a white shine of thin frost on the long open spaces of the sky.

He was of the blood and breath of many of these things, and would know them better in the years to come.

Chapter 11

During the year 1817, little Abe Lincoln, eight years old, going on nine, had an ax put in his hands and helped his father cut down trees and notch logs for the corners of their new cabin, forty yards from the pole-shed where the family was cooking, eating, and sleeping.

Wild turkey, ruffed grouse, partridge, coon, rabbit, were to be had for the shooting of them. Before each shot Tom Lincoln took a rifle-ball out of a bag and held the ball in his left hand; then with his right hand holding the gunpowder horn he pulled the stopper with his teeth, slipped the powder into the barrel, followed with the ball; then he rammed the charge down the barrel with a hickory ramrod held in both hands, looked to his trigger, flint, and feather in the touch-hole—and he was ready to shoot—to kill for the home skillet.

Having loaded his rifle just that way several thousand times in his life, he could do it in the dark or with his eyes shut. Once Abe took the gun as a flock of wild turkeys came toward the new log cabin, and, standing inside, shot through a crack and killed one of the big birds; and after that, somehow, he never felt like pulling the trigger on game-birds. A mile from the cabin was a salt lick, where deer came; there the boy could have easily shot the animals, as they stood rubbing their tongues along the salty slabs or tasting of a saltish ooze. His father did the shooting; the deer killed gave them meat for Nancy's skillet; and the skins were tanned, cut, and stitched into shirts, trousers, mitts, moccasins. They wore buckskin; their valley was called the Buckhorn Valley.

After months the cabin stood up, four walls fitted together with a roof, a one-room house eighteen feet square, for a family to live in. A stick chimney plastered with clay ran up outside. The floor was packed and smoothed dirt. A log-fire lighted the inside; no windows were cut in the walls. For a door there was a hole cut to stoop through. Bedsteads were cleated to the corners of the cabin; pegs stuck in the side of a wall made a ladder for young Abe to climb up in a loft to sleep on a hump of dry leaves; rain and snow came through chinks of the roof onto his bearskin cover. A table and three-legged stools had the top sides smoothed with an ax, and the bark-side under, in the style called "puncheon."

A few days of this year in which the cabin was building, Nancy told Abe to wash his face and hands extra clean; she combed his hair, held his face between her two hands, smacked him a kiss on the mouth, and sent him to school—nine miles and back—Abe and Sally hand in hand hiking eighteen miles a day. Tom Lincoln used to say Abe was going to have "a real eddication," explaining, "You air a-goin' to larn readin', writin', and cipherin'."

He learned to spell words he didn't know the meaning of, spelling the words before he used them in sentences. In a list of "words of eight syllables accented upon the sixth," was the word "incomprehensibility." He learned that first, and then such sentences as "Is he to go in?" and "Ann can spin flax."

Some neighbors said, "It's a pore make-out of a school," and Tom complained it was a waste of time to send the children nine miles just to sit with a lot of other children and read out loud all day in a "blab" school. But Nancy, as she cleaned Abe's ears in corners where he forgot to clean them, and as she combed out the tangles in his coarse, sandy black hair, used to say, "Abe, you go to school now, and larn all you kin." And he kissed her and said, "Yes, Mammy," and started with his sister on the nine-mile walk through timberland where bear, deer, coon, and wildcats ran wild.

Fall time came with its early frost and they were moved into the new cabin, when horses and a wagon came breaking into the clearing one day. It was Tom and Betsy Sparrow and their seventeen-year-old boy, Dennis Hanks, who had come from Hodgenville, Kentucky, to cook and sleep in the pole-shed of the Lincoln family till they could locate land and settle. Hardly a year had passed, however, when both Tom and Betsy Sparrow were taken down with the "milk sick," beginning with a whitish coat on the tongue. Both died and were buried in October on a little hill in a clearing in the timbers near by.

Soon after, there came to Nancy Hanks Lincoln that white coating of the tongue; her vitals burned; the tongue turned brownish; her feet and hands grew cold and colder, her pulse slow and slower. She knew she was dying, called for her children, and spoke to them her last choking words. Sarah and Abe leaned over the bed. A bony hand of the struggling mother went out, putting its fingers into the boy's sandy black hair; her fluttering guttural words seemed to say he must grow up and be good to his sister and father.

So, on a bed of poles cleated to the corner of the cabin, the body of Nancy Hanks Lincoln lay, looking tired . . . tired . . . with a peace settling in the pinched corners of the sweet, weary mouth, silence slowly etching away the lines of pain and hunger drawn around the gray eyes where now the eyelids closed down in the fine pathos of unbroken rest, a sleep without interruption settling about the form of the stooped and wasted shoulder-bones, looking to the children who tiptoed in, stood still, cried their tears of want and longing, whispered "Mammy, Mammy," and heard only their own whispers answering, looking to these little ones of her brood as though new secrets had come to her in place of the old secrets given up with the breath of life.

And Tom Lincoln took a log left over from the building of the cabin, and he and Dennis Hanks whipsawed the log into planks, planed the planks smooth, and made them of a measure for a box to bury the dead wife and mother in. Little Abe, with a jackknife, whittled pine-wood pegs. And then, while Dennis and Abe held the planks, Tom bored holes and stuck the whittled pegs through the bored holes. This was the coffin, and they carried it the next day to the same little timber clearing near by, where a few weeks before they had buried Tom and Betsy Sparrow. It was in the way of the deer-run leading to the saltish water; light feet and shy hoofs ran over those early winter graves.

So the woman, Nancy Hanks, died, thirty-six years old, a pioneer sacrifice, with memories of monotonous, endless everyday chores, of mystic Bible verses read over and over for their promises, and with memories of blue wistful hills and a summer when the crab-apple blossoms flamed white and she carried a boy-child into the world.

She had looked out on fields of blue-blossoming flax and hummed "Hey, Betty Martin, tiptoe, tiptoe"; she had sung of bright kingdoms by and by and seen the early frost leaf its crystals on the stalks of buttonweed and redbud; she had sung:

> You may bury me in the east,
> You may bury me in the west,
> And we'll all rise together in that morning.

Chapter 12

Some weeks later, when David Elkin, elder of the Methodist church, was in that neighborhood, he was called on to speak over the grave of Nancy Hanks. He had been acquainted with her in Kentucky, and to the Lincoln family and a few neighbors he spoke of good things she had done, sweet ways she had of living her life in this Vale of Tears, and her faith in another life yonder past the River Jordan.

The "milk sick" took more people in that neighborhood the same year, and Tom Lincoln whipsawed planks for more coffins. One settler lost four milch cows and eleven calves. The nearest doctor for people or cattle was thirty-five miles away. The wilderness is careless.

Lonesome and dark months came for Abe and Sarah. Worst of all were the weeks after their father went away, promising to come back.

Elizabethtown, Kentucky, was the place Tom Lincoln headed for. As he footed it through the woods and across the Ohio River, he was saying over to himself a speech—the words he would say to Sarah Bush Johnston, down in Elizabethtown. Her husband had died a few years before, and she was now in Tom's thoughts.

He went straight to the house where she was living in Elizabethtown, and, speaking to her as "Miss Johnston," he argued: "I have no wife and you no husband. I came a-purpose to marry you. I knowed you from a gal and you knowed me from a boy. I've no time to lose; and if you're willin' let it be done straight off."

Her answer was, "I got debts." She gave him a list of the debts; he paid them; a license was issued; and they were married on December 2, 1819.

He could write his name; she couldn't write hers. Trying to explain why the two of them took up with each other so quickly, Dennis Hanks at a later time said, "Tom had a kind o' way with women, an' maybe it was somethin' she took comfort in to have a man that didn't drink an' cuss none."

Little Abe and Sarah, living in the lonesome cabin on Little Pigeon Creek, Indiana, got a nice surprise one morning when four horses and a wagon came into their clearing, and their father jumped off, then Sarah Bush Lincoln, the new wife and mother, then John, Sarah, and Matilda Johnston, Sarah Bush's three children by her first husband. Next off the wagon came a feather mattress, feather pillows, a black walnut bureau, a large clothes-chest, a table, chairs, pots and skillets, knives, forks, spoons.

Abe ran his fingers over the slick wood of the bureau, pushed his fist into the feather pillows, sat in the new chairs, and wondered to himself, because this was the first time he had touched such fine things, such soft slick things.

"Here's your new mammy," his father told Abe as the boy looked up at a strong, large-boned, rosy woman, with a kindly face and eyes, with a steady voice, steady ways. The cheek-bones of her face stood out and she had a strong jaw-bone; she was warm and friendly for Abe's little hands to touch, right from the beginning. As one of her big hands held his head against her skirt he felt like a cold chick warming under the soft feathers of a big wing. She took the corn-husks Abe had been sleeping on, piled them in the yard and said they would be good for a pig-pen later on; and Abe sunk his head and bones that night in a feather pillow and a feather mattress.

Ten years pass with that cabin on Little Pigeon Creek for a home, and that farm and neighborhood the soil for growth. There the boy Abe grows to be the young man, Abraham Lincoln.

Ten years pass and the roots of a tree spread out finding water to carry up to branches and leaves that are in the sun; the trunk thickens, the forked limbs shine wider in the sun, they pray with their leaves in the rain and the whining wind; the tree arrives, the mystery of its coming, spreading, growing, a secret not even known to the tree itself; it stands with its arms stretched to the corners the four winds come from, with its murmured testimony, "We are here, we arrived, our roots are in the earth of these years," and beyond that short declaration, it speaks nothing of the decrees, fates, accidents, destinies, that made it an apparition of its particular moment.

Abe Lincoln grows up. His father talks about the waste of time in "eddication"; it is enough "to larn readin', writin', cipherin'"; but the stanch, yearning stepmother, Sarah Bush Lincoln, comes between the boy and the father. And the father listens to the stepmother and lets her have her way.

1926

Stephen Vincent Benét

Benét (1898–1943) wrote his epic *John Brown's Body* while living in France, a country Lincoln himself never visited, but where his reputation remained high. While there, Benét assiduously conducted library research on slavery, John Brown, and the rebellion, but also relied heavily on personal childhood memories of his father's extensive Civil War bookshelf, which included the invaluable multivolume collection *Battles and Leaders of the Civil War*. Benét's book-length poem won the 1929 Pulitzer Prize, though Harriet Monroe, the editor of the influential *Poetry*, dismissed it as "cinematic." While never filmed, the work was staged by Charles Laughton in 1953 as a dramatic reading featuring Tyrone Power, Judith Anderson, and Raymond Massey. (Benét did, however, work on the screenplay for the 1930 D. W. Griffith film *Abraham Lincoln*.) The excerpts on Lincoln printed here—which open and close with depictions of the President as a "gaunt" and haunted man—celebrate his enduring patience, which Benét describes as his greatest virtue.

FROM
John Brown's Body

Lincoln, six feet one in his stocking feet,
The lank man, knotty and tough as a hickory rail,
Whose hands were always too big for white-kid gloves,
Whose wit was a coonskin sack of dry, tall tales,
Whose weathered face was homely as a plowed field—
Abraham Lincoln, who padded up and down
The sacred White House in nightshirt and carpet-slippers,
And yet could strike young hero-worshipping Hay
As dignified past any neat, balanced, fine
Plutarchan sentences carved in a Latin bronze;
The low clown out of the prairies, the ape-buffoon,
The small-town lawyer, the crude small-time politician,
State-character but comparative failure at forty
In spite of ambition enough for twenty Caesars,

Honesty rare as a man without self-pity,
Kindness as large and plain as a prairie wind,
And a self-confidence like an iron bar:
This Lincoln, President now by the grace of luck,
Disunion, politics, Douglas and a few speeches
Which make the monumental booming of Webster
Sound empty as the belly of a burst drum,
Lincoln shambled in to the Cabinet meeting
And sat, ungainly and awkward. Seated so
He did not seem so tall nor quite so strange
Though he was strange enough. His new broadcloth suit
Felt tight and formal across his big shoulders still
And his new shiny top-hat was not yet battered
To the bulging shape of the old familiar hat
He'd worn at Springfield, stuffed with its hoard of papers.
He was pretty tired. All week the office-seekers
Had plagued him as the flies in fly-time plague
A gaunt-headed, patient horse. The children weren't well
And Mollie was worried about them so sharp with her
        tongue.
But he knew Mollie and tried to let it go by.
Men tracked dirt in the house and women liked carpets.
Each had a piece of the right, that was all most people could
        stand.

Look at his Cabinet here. There were Seward and Chase,
Both of them good men, couldn't afford to lose them,
But Chase hates Seward like poison and Seward hates Chase
And both of 'em think they ought to be President
Instead of me. When Seward wrote me that letter
The other day, he practically told me so.
I suppose a man who was touchy about his pride
Would send them both to the dickens when he found out,
But I can't do that as long as they do their work.
The Union's too big a horse to keep changing the saddle
Each time it pinches you. As long as you're sure
The saddle fits, you're bound to put up with the pinches

And not keep fussing the horse.
                                    When I was a boy
I remember figuring out when I went to town
That if I had just one pumpkin to bump in a sack
It was hard to carry, but once you could get two pumpkins,
One in each end of the sack, it balanced things up.
Seward and Chase'll do for my pair of pumpkins.
And as for me—if anyone else comes by
Who show me that he can manage this job of mine
Better than I can—well, he can have the job.
It's harder sweating than driving six cross mules,
But I haven't run into that other fellow yet
And till or supposing I meet him, the job's my job
And nobody else's.
                        Seward and Chase don't know that.
They'll learn it, in time.
                            Wonder how Jefferson Davis
Feels, down there in Montgomery, about Sumter.
He must be thinking pretty hard and fast,
For he's an able man, no doubt of that.
We were born less than forty miles apart,
Less than a year apart—he got the start
Of me in age, and raising too, I guess,
In fact, from all you hear about the man,
If you set out to pick one of us two
For President, by birth and folks and schooling,
General raising, training up in office,
I guess you'd pick him, nine times out of ten
And yet, somehow, I've got to last him out.

These thoughts passed through the mind in a moment's flash,
Then that mind turned to business.
                                    It was the calling
Of seventy-five thousand volunteers.

————

Horace Greeley has written Lincoln an hysterical letter—he has not slept for seven nights—in New York, "on every brow sits sullen, scorching, black despair."

He was trumpeting "On to Richmond!" two weeks ago. But then the war was a thing for an editorial—a, triumphal parade of Unionists over rebels. Now there has been a battle and a defeat. He pleads for an armistice—a national convention—anything on almost any terms to end this war.

Many think as he does; many fine words ring hollow as the skull of an orator, the skull of a maker of war. They have raised the Devil with slogans and editorials, but where is the charm that will lay him? Who will bind the Devil aroused?

Only Lincoln, awkwardly enduring, confused by a thousand counsels, is neither overwhelmed nor touched to folly by the madness that runs along the streets like a dog in August scared of itself, scaring everyone who crosses its path.

Defeat is a fact and victory can be a fact. If the idea is good, it will survive defeat, it may even survive the victory.

His huge, patient, laborious hands start kneading the stuff of the Union together again; he gathers up the scraps and puts them together; he sweeps the corners and the cracks and patches together the lost courage and the rags of belief.

The dough didn't rise that time—maybe it will next time. God must have tried and discarded a lot of experiment-worlds before he got one even good enough to whirl for a minute—it is the same with a belief, with a cause.

It is wrong to talk of Lincoln and a star together—that old rubbed image is a scrap of tinsel, a scrap of dead poetry—it dries up and blows away when it touches a man. And yet Lincoln had a star, if you will have it so—and was haunted by a prairie-star.

Down in the South another man, most unlike him but as steadfast, is haunted by another star that has little to do with tinsel, and the man they call "Evacuation" Lee begins to grow taller and to cast a longer shadow.

———

The head of the snake is captured—the tail gripped fast—
But the body in between still writhes and resists,
Vicksburg is still unfallen—Grant not yet master—
Sheridan, Sherman, Thomas still in the shadow.
The eyes of the captains are fixed on the Eastern game,
The presidents—and the watchers oversea—
For there are the two defended kings of the board,
Muddy Washington, with its still-unfinished Capitol,
Sprawling, badly-paved, beset with sharp hogs
That come to the very doorsteps and grunt for crumbs,
Full of soldiers and clerks, full of all the baggage of war,
"Bombproof" officers, veterans back on leave,
Recruits, spies, spies on the spies, politicians, contractors,
Reporters, slackers, ambassadors, bands and harlots,
Negro-boys who organize butting-matches
To please the recruits, tattooers and fortune-tellers,
Rich man, poor man, soldier, beggarman, thief,
And one most lonely man in a drafty White House
Whose everlasting melancholy runs
Like a deep stream under the funny stories,
The parable-maker, humble in many things
But seldom humble with his fortitude,
The sorrowful man who cracked the sure-fire jokes,
Roared over Artemus Ward and Orpheus C. Kerr
And drove his six cross mules with a stubborn hand.
He has lost a son, but he has no time to grieve for him.
He studies tactics now till late in the night
With the same painful, hewing industry
He put on studying law.
               McClellan comes,
McClellan goes, McClellan bustles and argues,
McClellan is too busy to see the President,
McClellan complains of this, complains of that,
The Government is not supporting him,
The Government cannot understand grand strategy,
The Government—
               McClellan feels abused.
McClellan is quite sincere and sometimes right.

They come to the lonely man about McClellan
With various tales.
                McClellan lacks respect,
McClellan dreams about a dictatorship,
McClellan does that and this.
                     The lonely man
Listens to all the stories and remarks,
"If McClellan wins, I will gladly hold his horse."

———

It was still hot in Washington, that September,
Hot in the city, hot in the White House rooms,
Desiccate heat, dry as a palm-leaf fan,
That makes hot men tuck cotton handkerchiefs
Between their collars and their sweaty necks,
And Northern girls look limp at half-past-four,
Waiting the first cool breath that will not come
For hours yet.
            The sentinel on post
Clicks back and forth, stuffed in his sweltering coat,
And dreams about brown bottles of cold beer
Deep in a cellar.
             In the crowded Bureaus
The pens move slow, the damp clerks watch the clock.
Women in houses take their corsets off
And stifle in loose gowns.
                They could lie down
But when they touch the bed, the bed feels hot,
And there are things to do.
                The men will want
Hot food when they come back from work.
                     They sigh
And turn, with dragging feet, to the hot kitchens.

Sometimes they pause, and push a window up
To feel the blunt, dry buffet of the heat
Strike in the face and hear the locust-cry
Of shrilling newsboy-voices down the street,

"News from the army—extra—ter-ble battle—
Terr-r-ble vic'try—ter-r-ble defeat—
Lee's army trapped invading Maryland—
McClellan—Sharpsburg—fightin'—news from the front—"
The women at the windows sigh and wonder
"I ought to buy a paper—No, I'll wait
Till Tom gets home—I wonder if it's true—
Terrible victory—terrible defeat—
They're always saying that—when Tom gets home
He'll have some news—I wonder if the army—
No, it's too hot to buy a paper now—"

A hot, spare day of waiting languidly
For contradictory bits of dubious news.

It was a little cooler, three miles out,
Where the tall trees shaded the Soldiers' Home.
The lank man, Abraham Lincoln, found it so,
Glad for it, doubtless, though his cavernous eyes
Had stared all day into a distant fog
Trying to pierce it.
                    "General McClellan
Is now in touch with Lee in front of Sharpsburg
And will attack as soon as the fog clears."

It's cleared by now. They must be fighting now.

We can't expect much from the first reports.
Stanton and Halleck think they're pretty good
But you can't tell. Nobody here can tell.
We're all too far away.
                        You get sometimes
Feeling as if you heard the guns yourself
Here in the room and felt them shake the house
When you keep waiting for the news all day.
I wish we'd get some news.
                            Bull Run was first.
We got the news of Bull Run soon enough.

First that we'd won, hands down, which was a lie,
And then the truth.
                    It may be that to-day.
I told McClellan not to let them go,
Destroy them if he could—but you can't tell.
He's a good man in lots of different ways,
But he can't seem to finish what he starts
And then, he's jealous, like the rest of them,
Lets Pope get beaten, wanted him to fail,
Because he don't like Pope.
                         I put him back
Into command. What else was there to do?
Nobody else could lick those troops in shape.
But, if he wins, and lets Lee get away,
I'm done with him.
                    Bull Run—the Seven Days—
Bull Run again—and eighteen months of war—
And still no end to it.
                    What is God's will?

They come to me and talk about God's will
In righteous deputations and platoons,
Day after day, laymen and ministers.
They write me Prayers From Twenty Million Souls
Defining me God's will and Horace Greeley's.
God's will is General This and Senator That,
God's will is those poor colored fellows' will,
It is the will of the Chicago churches,
It is this man's and his worst enemy's.
But all of them are sure they know God's will.
I am the only man who does not know it.

And, yet, if it is probable that God
Should, and so very clearly, state His will
To others, on a point of my own duty,
It might be thought He would reveal it me
Directly, more especially as I
So earnestly desire to know His will.

The will of God prevails. No doubt, no doubt—
Yet, in great contests, each side claims to act
In strict accordance with the will of God.
Both may, one must be wrong.

       God could have saved
This Union or destroyed it without war
If He so wished. And yet this war began,
And, once begun, goes on, though He could give
Victory, at any time, to either side.
It is unfathomable. Yet I know
This, and this only. While I live and breathe,
I mean to save the Union if I can,
And by whatever means my hands can find
Under the Constitution.

       If God reads
The hearts of men as clearly as He must
To be Himself, then He can read in mine
And has, for twenty years, the old, scarred wish
That the last slave should be forever free
Here, in this country.

       I do not go back
From that scarred wish and have not.

         But I put
The Union, first and last, before the slave.
If freeing slaves will bring the Union back
Then I will free them; if by freeing some
And leaving some enslaved I help my cause,
I will do that—but should such freedom mean
The wreckage of the Union that I serve
I would not free a slave.

       O Will of God,
I am a patient man, and I can wait
Like an old gunflint buried in the ground
While the slow years pile up like moldering leaves
Above me, underneath the rake of Time,
And turn, in time, to the dark, fruitful mold
That smells of Sangamon apples, till at last

There's no sleep left there, and the steel event
Descends to strike the live coal out of me
And light the powder that was always there.

That is my only virtue as I see it,
Ability to wait and hold my own
And keep my own resolves once they are made
In spite of what the smarter people say.
I can't be smart the way that they are smart.
I've known that since I was an ugly child.
It teaches you—to be an ugly child.
It teaches you—to lose a thing you love.
It sticks your roots down into Sangamon ground
And makes you grow when you don't want to grow
And makes you tough enough to wait life out,
Wait like the fields, under the rain and snow.

I have not thought for years of that lost grave
That was my first hard lesson in the queer
Thing between men and women we call love.
But when I think of it, and when I hear
The rain and snow fall on it, as they must,
It fills me with unutterable grief.

We've come a good long way, my hat and I,
Since then, a pretty lengthy piece of road,
Uphill and down but mostly with a pack.
Years of law-business, years of cracking jokes,
And watching Billy Herndon do his best
To make me out, which seemed to be a job;
Years trying how to learn to handle men,
Which can be done, if you've got heart enough,
And how to deal with women or a woman
And that's about the hardest task I know.
For, when you get a man, you've got the man
Like a good big axehandle in your fist,
But you can't catch a woman like an axe.

She'll run like mercury between your hands
And leave you wondering which road she went,
The minute when you thought you knew her ways.

I understand the uses of the earth,
And I have burned my hands at certain fires
Often enough to know a use for fire,
But when the genius of the water moves,
And that's the woman's genius, I'm at sea
In every sense and meaning of the word,
With nothing but old patience for my chart,
And patience doesn't always please a woman.

Bright streams of water, watering the world,
Deep seas of water that all men must sail
Or rest half-men and fill the narrow graves,
When will I understand or comprehend
Your salt, sweet taste, so different from the taste
Of Sangamon russets, weighing down the bough?
You can live with the water twenty years
And never understand it like the earth
But that's the lesson I can't seem to learn.

"Abraham Lincoln, his hand and pen,
He will be good, but God knows when."
He will be wise, but God knows when.

It doesn't matter. If I had some news—
News from that fog—
                              I'll get the hypo, sure,
Unless I watch myself, waiting for news.
I can't afford to get the hypo now,
I've got too much to do.
                              Political years,
Housekeeping years of marrying and begetting
And losing, too, the children and the town,
The wife, the house, the life, the joy and grief,
The profound wonder still behind it all.

I had a friend who married and was happy.
But something haunted him that haunted me
Before he did, till he could hardly tell
What his own mind was, for the brooding veil
And immaterial horror of the soul
Which colors the whole world for men like that.

I do not know from whence that horror comes
Or why it hangs between us and the sun
For some few men, at certain times and days,
But I have known it closer than my flesh,
Got up with it, lain down and walked with it,
Scotched it awhile, but never killed it quite,
And yet lived on.
                    I wrote him good advice,
The way you do, and told him this, for part,
"Again you fear that that Elysium
Of which you've dreamed so much is not to be.
Well, I dare swear it will not be the fault
Of that same black-eyed Fanny, now your wife.
And I have now no doubt that you and I,
To our particular misfortune, dream
Dreams of Elysium far exceeding all
That any earthly thing can realize."

I wrote that more than twenty years ago,
At thirty-three, and now I'm fifty-three,
And the slow days have brought me up at last
Through water, earth and fire, to where I stand,
To where I stand—and no Elysiums still.

No, no Elysiums—for that personal dream
I dreamt of for myself and in my youth
Has been abolished by the falling sledge
Of chance and an ambition so fulfilled
That the fulfillment killed its personal part.

My old ambition was an iron ring
Loose-hooped around the live trunk of a tree.
If the tree grows till bark and iron touch
And then stops growing, ring and tree are matched
And the fulfillment fits.
                          But, if by some
Unlikely chance, the growing still keeps on,
The tree must burst the binding-ring or die.

I have not once controlled the circumstances.
They have controlled me. But with that control
They made me grow or die. And I have grown.
The iron ring is burst.
                          Three elements,
Earth, water and fire. I have passed through them all,
Still to find no Elysium for my hands,
Still to find no Elysium but growth,
And the slow will to grow to match my task.

Three elements. I have not sought the fourth
Deeply, till now—the element of air,
The everlasting element of God,
Who must be there in spite of all we see,
Who must be there in spite of all we bear,
Who must exist where all Elysiums
Are less than shadows of a hunter's fire
Lighted at night to scare a wolf away.

I know that wolf—his scars are in my hide
And no Elysiums can rub them out.
Therefore at last, I lift my hands to You
Who Were and Are and Must Be, if our world
Is anything but a lost ironclad
Shipped with a crew of fools and mutineers
To drift between the cold forts of the stars.

I've never found a church that I could join
Although I've prayed in churches in my time

And listened to all sorts of ministers.
Well, they were good men, most of them, and yet—
The thing behind the words—it's hard to find.
I used to think it wasn't there at all
Couldn't be there. I cannot say that, now.
And now I pray to You and You alone.
Teach me to know Your will. Teach me to read
Your difficult purpose here, which must be plain
If I had eyes to see it. Make me just.

There was a man I knew near Pigeon Creek
Who kept a kennel full of hunting dogs,
Young dogs and old, smart hounds and silly hounds.
He'd sell the young ones every now and then,
Smart as they were and slick as they could run.
But the one dog he'd never sell or lend
Was an old half-deaf foolish-looking hound
You wouldn't think had sense to scratch a flea
Unless the flea were old and sickly too.
Most days he used to lie beside the stove
Or sleeping in a piece of sun outside.
Folks used to plague the man about that dog
And he'd agree to everything they said,
"No—he ain't much on looks—or much on speed—
A young dog can outrun him any time,
Outlook him and outeat him and outleap him,
But, Mister, that dog's hell on a cold scent
And, once he gets his teeth in what he's after,
He don't let go until he knows he's dead."

I am that old, deaf hunting-dog, O Lord,
And the world's kennel holds ten thousand hounds
Smarter and faster and with finer coats
To hunt your hidden purpose up the wind
And bell upon the trace you leave behind.
But, when even they fail and lose the scent,
I will keep on because I must keep on
Until You utterly reveal Yourself

And sink my teeth in justice soon or late.
There is no more to ask of earth or fire
And water only runs between my hands,
But in the air, I'll look, in the blue air,
The old dog, muzzle down to the cold scent,
Day after day, until the tired years
Crackle beneath his feet like broken sticks
And the last barren bush consumes with peace.

I should have tried the course with younger legs,
This hunting-ground is stiff enough to pull
The metal heart out of a dog of steel;
I should have started back at Pigeon Creek
From scratch, not forty years behind the mark.
But you can't change yourself, and, if you could,
You might fetch the wrong jack-knife in the swap.
It's up to you to whittle what you can
With what you've got—and what I am, I am
For what it's worth, hypo and legs and all.
I can't complain. I'm ready to admit
You could have made a better-looking dog
From the same raw material, no doubt,
But, since You didn't, this'll have to do.

Therefore I utterly lift up my hands
To You, and here and now beseech Your aid.
I have held back when others tugged me on,
I have gone on when others pulled me back
Striving to read Your will, striving to find
The justice and expedience of this case,
Hunting an arrow down the chilly airs
Until my eyes are blind with the great wind
And my heart sick with running after peace.
And now, I stand and tremble on the last
Edge of the last blue cliff, a hound beat out,
Tail down and belly flattened to the ground,
My lungs are breathless and my legs are whipped,

Everything in me's whipped except my will.
I can't go on. And yet, I must go on.

I will say this. Two months ago I read
My proclamation setting these men free
To Seward and the rest. I told them then
I was not calling on them for advice
But to hear something that I meant to do.
We talked about it. Most of them approved
The thing, if not the time. Then Seward said
Something I hadn't thought of, "I approve
The proclamation—but, if issued now
With our defeats in everybody's mouth
It may be viewed as a last shriek for help
From an exhausted, beaten government.
Put it aside until a victory comes,
Then issue it with victory."
                                    He was right.
I put the thing aside—and ever since
There has been nothing for us but defeat,
Up to this battle now—still no news.

If I had eyes to look to Maryland!
If I could move that battle with my hands!
No, it don't work. I'm not a general.
All I can do is trust the men who are.

I'm not a general, but I promise this,
Here at the end of every ounce of strength
That I can muster, here in the dark pit
Of ignorance that is not quite despair
And doubt that does but must not break the mind!
The pit I have inhabited so long
At various times and seasons, that my soul
Has taken color in its very grains
From the blind darkness, from the lonely cave
That never hears a footstep but my own

Nor ever will, while I'm a man alive
To keep my prison locked from visitors.

What if I heard another footstep there,
What if, some day—there is no one but God,
No one but God who could descend that stair
And ring his heavy footfalls on the stone.
And if He came, what would we say to Him?

That prison is ourselves that we have built,
And, being so, its loneliness is just,
And, being so, its loneliness endures.
But, if another came,
                  What would we say?
What can the blind say, given back their eyes?

No, it must be as it has always been.
We are all prisoners in that degree
And will remain so, but I think I know
This—God is not a jailor. . . .
                      And I make
A promise now to You and to myself.
If this last battle is a victory
And they can drive the Rebel army back
From Maryland, back over the Potomac,
My proclamation shall go out at last
To set those other prisoners and slaves
From this next year, then and forever free.

So much for my will. Show me what is Yours!

That must be news, those footsteps in the hall,
Good news, or else they wouldn't come so fast.

What is it, now? Yes, yes, I'm glad of that.
I'm very glad. There's no mistake this time?
We have the best of them? They're in retreat?

This is a great day, Stanton. . . . .
. . . . If McClellan
Can only follow up the victory now!

Lord, I will keep my promise and go on,
Your will, in much, still being dark to me,
But, in this one thing, as I see it, plain.

And yet—if Lee slips from our hands again
As he well may from all those last reports
And the war still goes on—and still no end—
Even after this Antietam—not for years—

I cannot read it but I will go on,
Old dog, old dog, but settled to the scent
And with fresh breath now from this breathing space,
Almighty God.
                    At best we never seem
To know You wholly, but there's something left,
A strange, last courage.
                    We can fail and fail,
But, deep against the failure, something wars,
Something goes forward, something lights a match,
Something gets up from Sangamon County ground
Armed with a bitten and a blunted axe
And after twenty thousand wasted strokes
Brings the tall hemlock crashing to the ground.

———

The gaunt man, Abraham Lincoln, lives his days.
For a while the sky above him is very dark.
There are fifty thousand dead in these last, bleak months
And Richmond is still untaken.
                    The papers rail,
Grant is a butcher, the war will never be done.
The gaunt man's term of office draws to an end,
His best friends muse and are doubtful. He thinks himself
For a while that when the time of election comes

He will not be re-elected. He does not flinch.
He draws up a paper and seals it with his own hand.
His cabinet signs it, unread.

                       Such writing might be
A long historic excuse for defeated strength.
This is very short and strict with its commonsense.
"It seems we may not rule this nation again.
If so, we must do our best, while we still have time,
To plan with the new rulers who are to come
How best to save the Union before they come,
For they will have been elected upon such grounds
That they cannot possibly save it, once in our place."

The cloud lifts, after all. They bring him the news.
He is sure of being President four years more.
He thinks about it. He says, "Well, I guess they thought
They'd better not swap horses, crossing a stream."
The deserters begin to leave the Confederate armies. . . .

————

Richmond is fallen—Lincoln walks in its streets,
Alone, unguarded, stops at George Pickett's house,
Knocks at George Pickett's door. George Pickett has gone
But the strange, gaunt figure talks to George Pickett's wife
A moment—she thinks she is dreaming, seeing him there—
"Just one of George Pickett's old friends, m'am."

                            He turns away.
She watches him down the street with wondering eyes.
The red light falls upon him from the red sky.
Houses are burning, strange shadows flee through the streets.
A gang of loafers is broaching a liquor-barrel
In a red-lit square. The liquor spills on the cobbles.
They try to scoop it up in their dirty hands.

A long, blue column tramps by, shouting "John Brown's Body."
The loafers scatter like wasps from a half-sucked pear,
Come back when the column is gone.

                       A half-crazy slave

Mounts on a stoop and starts to preach to the sky.
A white-haired woman shoos him away with a broom.
He mumbles and reels to the shadows.
                                        A general passes,
His escort armed with drawn sabres. The sabres shine
In the red, low light.
                        Two doors away, down the street,
A woman is sobbing the same long sob all night
Beside a corpse with crossed hands.
                                        Lincoln passes on.

———

The gaunt man, Abraham Lincoln, woke one morning
From a new dream that yet was an old dream
For he had known it many times before
And, usually, its coming prophesied
Important news of some sort, good or bad,
Though mostly good as he remembered it.

He had been standing on the shadowy deck
Of a black formless boat that moved away
From a dim bank, into wide, gushing waters—
River or sea, but huge—and as he stood,
The boat rushed into darkness like an arrow,
Gathering speed—and as it rushed, he woke.

He found it odd enough to tell about
That day to various people, half in jest
And half in earnest—well, it passed the time
And nearly everyone had some pet quirk,
Knocking on wood or never spilling salt,
Ladders or broken mirrors or a Friday,
And so he thought he might be left his boat,
Especially now, when he could breathe awhile
With Lee surrendered and the war stamped out
And the long work of binding up the wounds
Not yet begun—although he had his plans
For that long healing, and would work them out

In spite of all the bitter-hearted fools
Who only thought of punishing the South
Now she was beaten.
                    But this boat of his.
He thought he had it.
                    "Johnston has surrendered.
It must be that, I guess—for that's about
The only news we're waiting still to hear."
He smiled a little, spoke of other things.

That afternoon he drove beside his wife
And talked with her about the days to come
With curious simplicity and peace.
Well, they were getting on, and when the end
Came to his term, he would not be distressed.
They would go back to Springfield, find a house,
Live peaceably and simply, see old friends,
Take a few cases every now and then.
Old Billy Herndon's kept the practice up,
I guess he'll sort of like to have me back.
We won't be skimped, we'll have enough to spend,
Enough to do—we'll have a quiet time,
A sort of Indian summer of our age.

He looked beyond the carriage, seeing it so,
Peace at the last, and rest.

They drove back to the White House, dressed and ate,
Went to the theatre in their flag-draped box.
The play was a good play, he liked the play,
Laughed at the jokes, laughed at the funny man
With the long, weeping whiskers.
                        The time passed.
The shot rang out. The crazy murderer
Leaped from the box, mouthed out his Latin phrase,
Brandished his foolish pistol and was gone.

Lincoln lay stricken in the flag-draped box.
Living but speechless. Now they lifted him
And bore him off. He lay some hours so.
Then the heart failed. The breath beat in the throat.
The black, formless vessel carried him away.

1928

Honoré Willsie Morrow

Born Honoré McCue in Ottumwa, Iowa, Morrow (1880–1940) graduated from the University of Wisconsin, edited the women's magazine *The Delineator*, and published several novels set in the Southwest before turning her attention to Lincoln in her "Great Captain" trilogy of novels, *Forever Free* (1927), *With Malice Toward None* (1928), and *The Last Full Measure* (1930). Morrow created a new and unprecedented romantic image of Lincoln in *Forever Free* by having her fictitious Confederate spy "Miss Ford" fall in love with the President while serving as Mary Lincoln's social secretary. In the chapter printed here from *With Malice Toward None*, Morrow paints a sympathetic picture of a politician transforming himself almost re-luctantly into a nation-preserving liberator. Her portrait vivified Lincoln's own claim in 1864 that "events have controlled me," an assertion that made his more controversial decisions seem either in-evitable or compelled by public opinion, and not the result of his own keen political acumen.

FROM

With Malice Toward None

CHAPTER IV

Created Equal

S hortly after supper that evening, Billy Stoddard came into the office and closed the reception room door behind him to say in a low voice:

"Mr. Hamlin has just come in with Fred Douglass, sir, and the other visitors are making it uncomfortable for Douglass. How about taking him into the secretaries' office?"

"Bring him in here," returned Lincoln.

With a little smile, Stoddard went out. A moment later Ham-lin entered, followed by a tall, well-built colored man in the con-ventional black broadcloth frock suit. Douglass was handsome

in a brooding and tragic way. The story of his heroic struggle
was written in the distrustful curve of his thin, well-cut mouth
and in the unbelief of his dark eyes: eyes set far apart under
quizzical brows and a broad forehead. His nose was the Indian's
rather than the negro's, well arched, with close nostrils. His high
cheek bones and hollow cheeks gave his whole face the look of
austerity that marks the thinker rather than the fighter. His chin
was concealed by a short black beard and his whole aspect was
rendered doubly striking by the mass of black hair that stood up
like a great halo round his head.

Lincoln shook hands with him. "I reckon we need no introduction, Mr. Douglass. You were a long time getting here."

"I've been up in Canada, Your Excellency. I was in hopes that
some of the fugitive slaves up there would come back and help
me preach the gospel of freedom. I was much troubled when I
learned I'd been keeping Your Excellency waiting."

"I'd rather be called plain Mr. Lincoln, if you please, Mr.
Douglass. Sit down and let's talk. How about the draft bill,
Hamlin? Will it go through before the session ends?"

"It'll go through to-morrow," answered the Vice President,
sinking into the Cabinet chair next to the one Douglass had
taken, while Lincoln took the rocker and slowly elevated his feet
to the mantel.

"I sweat when I think what enforcing that measure'll mean,"
he mused.

"Papa day," called Tad, curled up on a sofa with his kitten,
"you wememba what motha said about you' feet?"

"Jings, yes!" exclaimed the President, dropping the offending
members. "Will the bill go through as I last saw it, Hamlin?"

"Yes, Mr. Lincoln," replied Hamlin who had twisted about to
glare at Tad.

"I've been out of touch with the papers," said Douglass.
"Will you tell me if you draw the color line in the bill, Mr. Vice
President?"

Hamlin turned back to the fire. "All able-bodied male citizens between eighteen and forty-five are made subject to call
after July 1, 1863. Drafted persons can furnish a substitute or
pay $300 bounty for exemption!"

"I don't like the bounty idea," commented Lincoln, "but Chase is jubilant over it. Says it will be a full meat course to the Treasury." He turned abruptly to Douglass. "Mr. Douglass, how do you and your colored friends feel about the Emancipation Proclamation?"

"That it's thoughtful, cautious and well guarded," answered Douglass.

"Come now, that's no answer!" cried Lincoln. "The average run of colored man thinks nothing of the kind."

Douglass smiled. "You asked me what I and my friends thought, sir! Most of my people are enthusiastic, if they are anything. I was in Boston on January first with that great mass of people of every color waiting in Tremont Temple to hear by telegraph whether or not you'd signed the Proclamation. It was midnight before word came over the wire, 'It's signed!' People all over the hall began to sob for joy. It looked for a little while as if we could find no other way to express our feelings until a colored preacher with a glorious voice jumped up and began to sing 'Sound the loud timbrel o'er Egypt's dark sea, Jehovah hath triumphed, His people are free—' Everybody joined him. It was superb—this report pleases you more, doesn't it, Mr. Lincoln?"

Lincoln stared at Douglass. This was like no negro he'd ever known. There was no least trace of servility here. Come to think of it, this was the first time he'd ever observed the man beneath the mask of bondage, the first time he'd seen the negro as he showed himself to his own race, never to the white. Douglass actually was sneering at him!

Lincoln found it more stimulating than irritating. He glanced at Hamlin's anxious face and thought with amusement that the Vice President would like to give Douglass an admonitory nudge.

"I'm going to the wrong barrel for soft soap, eh, Mr. Douglass?" he said. "You're not grateful to us for the Proclamation?"

Douglass' tragic face softened. "There's not a colored man who knows of you who wouldn't die for you, Mr. Lincoln, but we wish you weren't so timid. We don't believe you'll really finally end slavery when it comes to reconstructing the Union."

"Et tu, Brute!" grunted Lincoln. "What would you have me do?"

"Organize colored regiments at once on an exactly equal status with white regiments. Let us fight for our freedom ourselves," replied Douglass quickly.

"Colored men have larger motives for being soldiers than white men," declared Lincoln grimly, "and should be grateful for a chance to enlist on any terms."

Douglass leaned forward, his hands on his knees and spoke across Hamlin as though he and the President were alone. "Mr. Lincoln, this war is something the white race has brought on itself by its own hoggishness. So the negro feels. And unless you understand clearly how we feel you will never be able to enforce emancipation or handle reconstruction. It's very hard for us negroes to feel gratitude toward any but God. As a race we have no more inherent loyalty to the whites than they have to us. But we're not fools. We see in this war an opportunity to break our chains and you can't offer us a task too hard for us to tackle. But for God's sake, offer us tasks as you'd give them to men and not to beasts of burden."

James came in to renew the fire just as Douglass finished his plea. His black eyes widened as he saw Douglass, and as he heard his words he dropped the tongs with a clatter that caused the kitten to spit and Tad to giggle.

"Tad," said Lincoln, "you go ask your mother for a plate of those Vermont greenings."

"I'll fetch 'em, Massa Lincum, sah," proffered James with alacrity.

The President nodded and looked broodingly into the flames for a moment before he said, "I've never tried to fool myself about this war, Mr. Douglass. I know we're working out in bitter humiliation the sins of two hundred years. We're drinking the dreadful cup to the dregs. But all this being acknowledged, I still in my humility must face facts as facts. And one fact is that white folks up to now have had an insuperable prejudice against using negroes in the army for anything but servants. I've no such prejudice myself but I've felt I must wait until our need for men was so great that colored soldiers would be welcomed before forming negro regiments."

"Surely that time has come now, Mr. Lincoln!" ejaculated Hamlin. "Our regiments hardly average more than four hundred men. The country's in despair over its losses."

"I can't see why you're so sure colored men would enlist," said Lincoln, looking not at Hamlin but closely at Douglass. "All efforts to organize black troops last year proved, if not actually abortive, at least ineffectual. I'd hoped after the Edict of Freedom was signed that Fortress Monroe and Yorktown might be garrisoned by colored troops to free the whites for weak spots where they're badly needed. But out of all the colored population down there, General Dix found only four or five willing to take up arms. They said they'd work but not fight."

"They're too close to their old masters down there!" exclaimed Douglass. "They fear reprisals. Try Massachusetts negroes."

"Why don't they come North?" insisted Lincoln. "Why has the Proclamation failed to bring them over the line?"

"Most of them have never heard of the Proclamation," answered Douglass. "The South would see to that."

"Ah! now we're getting down to the marrow!" exclaimed the President. "Douglass, how shall we get word to those people that it's time to come over into Canaan?"

"More than a word's needed, sir! There must be a promise that they shall not only be free but shall have equality. If you'll assure me of that, I'll go down into the Richmond country myself, even though I'm liable to be taken as a slave, and spread the tidings. You'll see them swarm across the Red Sea then."

"How can I promise any such thing!" ejaculated Lincoln, his heart sinking at this reiterated shortsightedness with all its implications. "Who can know the Southern attitude on that matter better than you? We can free the slaves by winning this war. We could give them the vote. But you know and I know that we'd have to exterminate the whites in the South before we could give the slave the kind of equality you want. I can't give them that equality. If they are given freedom, and when they've had education, the right to vote, the rest they'll have to earn through the generations to come—and that you and I or our children won't see, Douglass."

The colored man twisted his work-scarred hands together in a gesture of despair. "Oh, that Sumner or Chase were here in your place, sir!"

Lincoln shook his head impatiently. "And you actually believe that a scratch of my pen, or Sumner's or Chase's at my desk there, would change your color to the only shade the white has ever been willing to acknowledge covers his social equal? God knows, I want to see the negro eventually enjoy every civic right and privilege, Douglass, but—"

"'Scuse me, Massa Lincum!" James, almost as black as his clothes, his round face twitching with excitement, appeared before Lincoln with a huge plate of apples which turned to green bronze in the firelight. "'Scuse me but I got to have my say, sah! An' I'm going to say I ain't one of those niggers that's always wanting to set at the white man's table. I got my freedom and Massa Sumner's fixed it so's my chilluns and all colored chilluns is getting a white schooling right hea' in Washington. If you'll fix it so's my chilluns when they's grown kin hev the vote so's to help make the laws they live under, that's all I want. And what's more, Fred Douglass, his own self, knows if he went down below the line and gathered together all the niggers for a thousand miles and tried to lead 'em North, he couldn't lead 'em. Niggers is so jealous among theyselves they don't want to trust or help out a nigger that's gone ahead like Fred Douglass. There's Massa Sumner! What does he know about colored folks? He's too good to 'em. You're the one that knows 'em, Massa Lincum. Not Massa Sumner, or Massa Chase, or, 'scuse me, Massa Hamlin!"

He paused and banged the apples down on the scarred oak Cabinet table, then waved his arm toward the sofa. "You might better give little mischievous Massa Tad over there the vote than the niggers the way they are to-day. Those Southern Massas would make the niggers vote theyselves back into slavery again! I'm telling you truth. Yassa!"

He crossed to the sofa, lifted the sleeping Tad and the purring kitten into his arms and disappeared into the private passage into the living room. No one spoke until Lincoln broke the silence.

"What I wanted to propose to you, Mr. Douglass, is this. Are you willing to organize a group of intelligent colored men into a company of scouts who will scatter themselves through the South and tell the slaves what we're trying to do up here and ask them to come up and help us fight? I'll guarantee to make them into soldiers, eventually, if I can just get the right men to officer them."

"I'll supply you with one white officer now!" exclaimed Hamlin.

"Who's that, Hamlin?"

"My son, Captain Cyrus Hamlin. He and a group of his friends, such as the sons of James Russell Lowell and Thomas W. Higginson, are tormenting the life out of me to get you to let them raise colored regiments and go under fire."

In Hamlin's face was a touching mixture of pride and sadness.

Lincoln felt quick tears flush his eyes. These New England Abolitionists! Of such stuff were martyrs immemorially made. All his caution was not proof against this.

"I'll give you a letter to Stanton to-night to let Cyrus go ahead. The passing of the draft bill to-morrow is going to put a different face on the negro soldier question, anyhow." He took a huge bite out of an apple.

"Do you mean it?" shouted Hamlin, jumping to his feet. As Lincoln nodded, Hamlin placed pen and paper before the President with one sweep of the hand. "Write that order now, sir, and I'll take it to my boy this minute! How about your boys, Mr. Douglass?"

"My three sons enlisted last year, Mr. Hamlin," replied Douglass.

Lincoln wrote the order and signed his name and smiled up at Hamlin who seized the paper and departed almost at a run.

"You haven't answered my question, Mr. Douglass," Lincoln said, when they were alone.

"I'm afraid our friend James answered for me, sir," replied Douglass. "I would need a white man identified in their minds with you to accompany me South, else the slaves wouldn't believe me."

Lincoln finished his apple and threw the core into the fire. "I think I can help you out there," he said finally. "My oldest son Bob is a levelheaded fellow, almost through his law course at Harvard. How would it do for him to go along with you?"

Douglass stared as though he couldn't believe his ears. "Will your son agree to that, Mr. Lincoln?"

"If Cyrus Hamlin can do his job, I reckon my son can do his," answered the President.

"Then, Mr. Lincoln," exclaimed Douglass, "all I can say is that all that I have is at your service." He rose as the President rose and after a moment in which he fought to control his quivering lips he added, "Sir, Mr. Secretary Chase has had me eat at his own table. Senator Sumner, John Brown, Wendell Phillips, have fraternized with me. And yet, in spite of our topic of conversation to-day, you're the only man who's ever made me for a moment forget the curse of my color."

"The thing I don't like to remember is that it's we white men who've made a curse of that color," said Lincoln. "But be patient with us, Mr. Douglass. We're trying to make it right—with our heart's blood." He shook hands and added, "You work out a scheme and come to me when it's finished." He walked with Douglass to the door, came back and looked at his watch. He must see the waiting folk in the reception room before reading the dispatches on his desk and it was now nine o'clock. He rang the bell for Stoddard.

Although the break with Sumner was now the most consuming of Lincoln's anxieties, it was impossible for him to give to it the best of his thought. The public dissatisfaction with himself and with his generals, particularly with Grant, pressed upon him with ever-increasing violence and would not be ignored for a moment, day or night.

A few days after his momentous five-o'clock tea party, he asked Nicolay to bring him the week's vintage of aspersions on Grant's character and ability. Nicolay's solemn face did not change as he with James' help brought in two great baskets heaped with telegrams and letters.

"Here's a part of 'em, sir," he said as they emptied the baskets on the Cabinet table. "I'll bring more when you're finished. We've divided them into States. These are all from Wisconsin, Iowa and Illinois. The newspaper comments aren't filed as yet."

Lincoln grunted, took a turn or two around the table with his hands clasped behind his back, looked out the window, blurred by rain, and shook his head. "Lord, how I dread to wade in! I don't want to see the newspapers, George. These are closer to the people." He seized a handful of letters and began running rapidly through them. "Looks as if Grant were about as popular as I am! 'Can't hope to keep confidence of nation if you permit General Grant to continue his futile butchery before Vicksburg. —Grant, a drunken bum—a common roysterer . . . lazy . . . Rosecrans the real general—'" He dropped the letters. "Oh, take them away again, George! They give me the hiccoughs."

Nicolay carefully began to re-stack the letters. Lincoln watched him, talking half to himself, half to his secretary as had become his custom under the influence of Nicolay's understanding and sympathy. "What's the truth about Grant?—I'm not going to get myself into another blind road like I did with McClellan—I never even saw Grant.—He has no personal hold on me.—But he *fights*, though he mostly loses.—Most of 'em don't fight. They argue. I wish I *knew* about Grant. I have a feeling that he's the general I almost think is a fabled giant. George, I'd like to send you out there to look him over. No, I can't spare you. I'll send Charles Dana. You know, that old newspaper man who did such a fine job investigating cotton speculations in the army last year for Stanton?—I'll make my decision as to Grant on Dana's report on him, plus anything Grant may do in the meantime, plus my own feelings about him—"

He fell into silence, watching Nicolay pile the letters with a growing unease. After all, he ought not to put these messages by with nothing but a grunt.

"The thing I get most strongly from those messages, Nicolay, is that the people are in a dangerous state of gloom. They feel ugly because they feel helpless. They've found their military leaders and they've found me continually failing them. Confidence in man is dead and suspicion reigns. It's a time when every foul bird comes abroad and every dirty reptile rises up. The people need a new sign-post. The only one I can refer them to is the One above—and that's a preacher's job. I'm no preacher, God knows, but perhaps if I tell them how my own mind runs just now it would help. I can put it into the proclamation of the national fast day the Senate has asked for."

He had forgotten Nicolay. He walked to the windows and stood staring out blindly at the dim top of the half-finished Washington monument. Nicolay dropped the packets of letters and listened eagerly to the muttered fragments that reached him. After a moment, he took out his pencil and began to jot them down in his notebook.

"—And insomuch as we know that by his divine law, nations, like individuals, are subjected to punishments and chastisements in this world, may we not justly fear that the awful calamity of civil war which now desolates the land may be but a punishment inflicted on us for our presumptuous sins to the needful end of our national reformation as a whole people? We have been the recipients of the choicest bounties of Heaven. We have been preserved these many years in peace and prosperity. We have grown in numbers, wealth and power as no other nation ever has grown, but we have forgotten God. We have forgotten the gracious hand which preserved us in peace and multiplied and enriched and strengthened us; and we have vainly imagined, in the deceitfulness of our hearts, that all these blessings were produced by some superior wisdom and virtue of our own. Intoxicated with unbroken success, we have become too self-sufficient to feel the necessity of redeeming and preserving grace, too proud to pray to the God that made us:

"It behooves us then to humble ourselves before the offended Power, to confess our national sins and pray for clemency and forgiveness:

"Now, therefore . . . I do by this my proclamation designate and set apart Thursday, the 30th day of April, 1863, as a day of national humiliation, fasting and prayer. And I do hereby request all the people to abstain on that day from all their secular pursuits and to unite at their several places of public worship, and their respective homes to keep the day holy to the Lord and devoted to the humble discharge of the religious duties proper to that solemn occasion.—All this being done in sincerity and truth, let us then rest humbly in the hope authorized by divine teaching that the united cry of the nation will be heard on high and answered with blessings no less than the pardon of our national sins, and the restoration of our now divided and suffering country to its former happy condition of unity and peace—"

He experienced a peculiar relaxation of the nerves as he turned from the window to his desk. In uncovering the signpost for the people he had once more given to himself the final justification of the dreadful responsibility he had assumed.

1928

Dale Carnegie

A former salesman, Chautauqua lecturer, and failed actor, Carnegie (1888–1955) began teaching public speaking techniques in 1912 and went on to almost single-handedly invent the modern American self-improvement genre. His most famous book, *How to Win Friends and Influence People*, became an enormous bestseller following its publication in 1936. Four years earlier Carnegie had published *Lincoln the Unknown*, his inevitable biography of the ultimate American success story. Carnegie adhered to the tried-and-true log cabin to the White House school of Lincoln memory in an undisguised attempt to inspire his own generation of self-help followers. The two chapters printed here offer a harsh depiction of Lincoln's early years, perhaps echoing Carnegie's own childhood recollections of growing up poor on a Missouri farm.

FROM
Lincoln the Unknown

2

Lincoln's mother, Nancy Hanks, was brought up by her aunt and uncle, and probably had no schooling at all. We know she could not write, for she made her mark when signing a deed.

She lived deep in the somber woods and made few friends; and, when she was twenty-two, she married one of the most illiterate and lowly men in all Kentucky—a dull, ignorant day-laborer and deer-hunter. His name was Thomas Lincoln, but the people in the backwoods and canebrake settlements where he lived called him "Linkhorn."

Thomas Lincoln was a rover, a drifter, a ne'er-do-well, floating about from one place to another, taking any kind of job he could get when hunger drove him to it. He worked on roads, cut brush, trapped bear, cleared land, plowed corn, built log cabins; and the old records show that on three different occasions he was employed to guard prisoners, with a shot-gun. In 1805 Hardin

County, Kentucky, paid him six cents an hour for catching and whipping recalcitrant slaves.

He had no money sense whatever: he lived for fourteen years on one farm in Indiana, and during that period he was unable to save and pay as much as ten dollars a year on his land. At a time when he was so poor that his wife had to pin her dresses together with wild thorns, he went to a store in Elizabethtown, Kentucky, and bought a pair of silk suspenders for himself—and bought them on credit. Shortly after that, at an auction sale, he paid three dollars for a sword. Probably he wore his silk suspenders and carried his sword even when going barefoot.

Shortly after his marriage he moved to town and tried to make a living as a carpenter. He got a job building a mill, but he did not square his timbers or cut them the right length. So his employer sharply refused to pay him for his bungling efforts, and three lawsuits followed.

Tom Lincoln had come from the woods, and, dull as he was, he soon realized now that he belonged to the woods. He took his wife back to a poor, stony farm on the edge of the forest, and never again did he have the temerity to forsake the soil for the village.

Not far from Elizabethtown there was a vast stretch of treeless land known as "the barrens." For generations the Indians had started fires there and burned away the forests and brush and undergrowth, so that the coarse prairie-grass could grow in the sun, and the buffaloes would come there to wallow and graze.

In December, 1808, Tom Lincoln purchased a farm on "the barrens" for sixty-six and two thirds cents per acre. There was a hunter's hut on it, a crude sort of cabin surrounded with wild crab-apple trees; and half a mile away flowed the South Fork of Nolin Creek, where the dogwood blossomed in the spring. In the summertime, hawks circled lazily in the blue overhead, and the tall grasses surged in the wind like an illimitable sea of green. Few people had had the poor judgment to settle there. So in the wintertime it was one of the most lonely and desolate regions in all Kentucky.

And it was in a hunter's hut on the edge of these lonely barrens, deep in the winter of 1809, that Abraham Lincoln came into the world. He was born on a Sunday morning—born on a bed of poles covered with corn husks. It was storming outside, and the February wind blew the snow through the cracks between the logs and drifted it across the bearskin that covered Nancy Hanks and her baby. She was destined to die nine years later, at the age of thirty-five, worn out by the strain and hardships of pioneer life. She never knew much of happiness. Wherever she lived, she was hounded by gossip about her illegitimate birth. What a pity she could not have looked into the future that morning, and seen the marble temple that a grateful people have now erected on the spot which she then consecrated with her suffering!

The paper money in circulation at that time, in the wilderness, was often of very doubtful value. Much of it was worthless. So hogs, venison hams, whisky, coon-skins, bear-hides, and farm produce were much used as mediums of exchange. Even preachers sometimes took whisky as part pay for their services. In the autumn of 1816, when Abraham was seven years old, old Tom Lincoln bartered his Kentucky farm for about four hundred gallons of corn whisky, and moved his family into the gloom and solitude of the wild and desolate forests of Indiana. Their nearest neighbor was a bear-hunter; and all about them the trees and brush and grape-vines and undergrowth were so thick that a man had to cut and hack his way through it. This was the spot, "Rite in the Brush," as Dennis Hanks described it, where Abraham Lincoln was to spend the next fourteen years of his life.

The first snow of winter was already falling when the family arrived; and Tom Lincoln hastily built what was then known as "a three-faced camp." To-day it would be called a shed. It had no floor, no door, no windows—nothing but three sides and a roof of poles and brush. The fourth side was entirely open to wind and snow and sleet and cold. Nowadays an up-to-date farmer in Indiana wouldn't winter his cattle or hogs in such a crude shelter, but Tom Lincoln felt it was good enough for himself and his family all during the long winter of 1816–17, one of the severest and most violent winters in our history.

Nancy Hanks and her children slept there that winter like

dogs, curled up on a heap of leaves and bearskins dumped on the dirt floor in a corner of the shed.

As for food, they had no butter, no milk, no eggs, no fruit, no vegetables, not even potatoes. They lived chiefly on wild game and nuts.

Tom Lincoln tried to raise hogs, but the bears were so hungry that they seized the hogs and ate them alive.

For years, there in Indiana, Abraham Lincoln endured more terrible poverty than did thousands of the slaves whom he would one day liberate.

Dentists were almost unknown in that region, and the nearest doctor was thirty-five miles away; so when Nancy Lincoln had a toothache, probably old Tom Lincoln did what the other pioneers did; he whittled out a hickory peg, set the end of it against the complaining molar, and hit the peg a hard blow with a rock.

From the earliest times in the Middle West the pioneers suffered from a mysterious malady known as the "milk sick." It was fatal to cattle, sheep, and horses, and sometimes carried off entire communities of people. No one knew what caused it, and for a hundred years it baffled the medical profession. It was not until the beginning of the present century that science showed that the poisoning was due to animals eating a plant known as white snakeroot. The poison was transmitted to humans through the milk of cows. White snakeroot thrives in wooded pastures and deeply shaded ravines, and to this day it continues to take its toll of human life. Every year the Department of Agriculture of the State of Illinois posts placards in the county court-houses, warning farmers that if they do not eradicate this plant, they may die.

In the autumn of 1818 this dreadful scourge came to the Buckhorn Valley of Indiana, wiping out many families. Nancy Lincoln helped nurse the wife of Peter Brooner, the bear-hunter, whose cabin was only half a mile away. Mrs. Brooner died, and Nancy herself suddenly felt ill. Her head swam, and sharp pains shot through her abdomen. Vomiting severely, she was carried home to her wretched pallet of leaves and skins. Her hands and feet were cold, but her vitals seemed to be on fire. She kept calling for water. Water. Water. More water.

Tom Lincoln had a profound faith in signs and omens; so, on the second night of her illness, when a dog howled long and piteously outside the cabin, he abandoned all hope and said she was going to die.

Finally Nancy was unable even to raise her head from the pillow, and she could not talk above a whisper. Beckoning Abraham and his sister to her, she tried to speak. They bent over to catch her words: she pleaded with them to be good to each other, to live as she had taught them, and to worship God.

These were her last words, for her throat and entire intestinal tract were already in the first stages of paralysis. She sank into a prolonged coma, and finally died on the seventh day of her illness, October 5, 1818.

Tom Lincoln put two copper pennies on her eyelids, to hold them shut; and then went out into the forest and felled a tree and cut it into rough, uneven boards and fastened these together with wooden pegs; and in this crude coffin he placed the tired, worn body of the sad-faced daughter of Lucy Hanks.

Two years before, he had brought her into this settlement on a sled; and now, again on a sled, he hauled her body to the summit of a thickly wooded hill, a quarter of a mile away, and buried her without service or ceremony.

So perished the mother of Abraham Lincoln. We shall probably never know what she looked like or what manner of woman she was, for she spent most of her short life in the gloomy forests, and made only a faint impression upon the few people who crossed her path.

Shortly after Lincoln's death one of his biographers set out to get some information about the President's mother. She had been dead then for half a century. He interviewed the few people living who had ever seen her, but their memories were as vague as a faded dream. They were unable to agree even as to her physical appearance. One described her as a "heavy built, squatty woman," but another said she had a "spare, delicate form." One man thought she had black eyes, another described them as hazel, another was sure they were bluish green. Dennis Hanks, her cousin, who had lived under the same roof with her for fifteen years, wrote that she had "lite hair." After further reflection, he reversed himself and said her hair was black.

For sixty years after her death there was not so much as a stone to mark her resting-place, so that to-day only the approximate position of her grave is known. She is buried beside her aunt and uncle, who reared her; but it is impossible to say which of the three graves is hers.

A short time before Nancy's death Tom Lincoln had built a new cabin. It had four sides, but no floor, no windows, no door. A dirty bearskin hung over the entrance, and the interior was dark and foul. Tom Lincoln spent most of his time hunting in the woods, leaving his two motherless children to run the place. Sarah did the cooking, while Abraham kept the fire going and carried water from the spring a mile away. Having no knives and forks, they ate with their fingers, and with fingers that were seldom clean, for water was hard to get and they had no soap. Nancy had probably made her own soft lye soap, but the small supply that she left at her death had long since vanished, and the children didn't know how to make more; and Tom Lincoln wouldn't make it. So they lived on in their poverty and dirt.

During the long, cold winter months they made no attempt to wash their bodies; and few, if any, attempts to wash their soiled and ragged garments. Their beds of leaves and skins grew filthy. No sunlight warmed and purified the cabin. The only light they had was from the fireplace or from hog fat. We know from accurate descriptions of other cabins on the frontier what the womanless Lincoln cabin must have been like. It smelled. It was infested with fleas, crawling with vermin.

After a year of this squalor even old Tom Lincoln could stand it no longer; he decided to get a new wife who would clean up.

Thirteen years before he had proposed to a woman in Kentucky named Sarah Bush. She had refused him then and married the jailer of Hardin County, but the jailer had since died and left her with three children and some debts. Tom Lincoln felt that the time was auspicious now for renewing his proposal; so he went to the creek, washed up, scrubbed his grimy hands and face with sand, strapped on his sword, and started back through the deep, dark woods to Kentucky.

When he reached Elizabethtown he bought another pair of silk suspenders, and marched whistling down the street.

That was in 1819. Things were happening, and people were talking of progress. A steamship had crossed the Atlantic Ocean!

3

When Lincoln was fifteen he knew his alphabet and could read a little but with difficulty. He could not write at all. That autumn—1824—a wandering backwoods pedagogue drifted into the settlement along Pigeon Creek and started a school. Lincoln and his sister walked four miles through the forests, night and morning, to study under the new teacher, Azel Dorsey. Dorsey kept what was known as a "blab" school; the children studied aloud. In that way the teacher believed he could tell whether or not they were applying themselves. He marched about the room, switch in hand, giving a cut to those who were silent. With such a premium on vociferousness, each pupil strove to out-blab the others. The uproar could often be heard a quarter of a mile away.

While attending this school Lincoln wore a cap of squirrel-skin, and breeches made from the hide of a deer. The breeches failed by a considerable stretch to meet the top of his shoes, leaving several inches of sharp, blue shinbone exposed to the wind and snow.

The school was held in a crude cabin barely high enough for the teacher to stand up in. There were no windows; a log had been left out at each side, and the opening covered with greased paper to let in the light. The floor and seats were made of split logs.

Lincoln's reading lessons were chapters from the Bible; and in his writing exercises he took the chirography of Washington and Jefferson as his models. His handwriting resembled theirs. It was unusually clear and distinct. People commented on it, and the illiterate neighbors walked for miles to have Abraham write their letters.

He was finding a real tang and zest, now, in learning. The

hours at school were all too short, he carried his studies home. Paper was scarce and high, so he wrote on a board with a charcoal stick. Sometimes he ciphered on the flat sides of the hewn logs that formed the cabin walls. Whenever a bare surface became covered with figures and writing he shaved them off with a drawing-knife and began anew.

Too poor to buy an arithmetic, he borrowed one and copied it on sheets of paper about the size of an ordinary letter-head. Then he sewed them together with twine, and so had a home-made arithmetic of his own. At the time of his death his stepmother still had portions of this book.

Now he began to exhibit a trait which sharply distinguished him from the rest of the backwoods scholars. He wanted to write out his opinions on various topics; at times he even broke into verse. And he took his verse and prose composition to William Wood, a neighbor, for criticism. He memorized and recited his rhymes, and his essays attracted attention. A lawyer was so impressed with his article on national politics that he sent it away and had it published. A newspaper in Ohio featured an article he wrote on temperance.

But this was later. His first composition here in school was inspired by the cruel sports of his playmates. They used to catch terrapins and put burning coals on their backs. Lincoln pleaded with them to stop it, and ran and kicked off the coals with his bare feet. His first essay was a plea for mercy to animals. Already the boy was showing that deep sympathy for the suffering which was to be so characteristic of the man.

Five years later he attended another school irregularly—"by littles," as he phrased it.

Thus ended all his formal attempts at education, with a total of not more than twelve months of schooling.

When he went to Congress in 1847 and filled out a biographical blank, he came to the question, "What has been your education?" He answered it with one word: "Defective."

After he was nominated for the Presidency he said: "When I came of age, I did not know much. Still, somehow, I could read, write, and cipher to the rule of three; but that was all. I have not been to school since. The little advance I now have upon this store of education, I have picked up from time to time under the pressure of necessity."

And who had been his teachers? Wandering, benighted pedagogues who had faith in witches and believed that the world was flat. Yet, during these broken and irregular periods, he had developed one of the most valuable assets any man can have, even from a university education: a love of knowledge and a thirst for learning.

The ability to read opened up a new and magic world for him, a world he had never dreamed of before. It changed him. It broadened his horizon and gave him vision; and, for a quarter of a century, reading remained the dominant passion of his life. His stepmother had brought a little library of five volumes with her: the Bible, Æsop's Fables, "Robinson Crusoe," "The Pilgrim's Progress," and "Sinbad the Sailor." The boy pored over these priceless treasures. He kept the Bible and Æsop's Fables within easy reach and read them so often that they profoundly affected his style, his manner of talking, his method of presenting arguments.

But these books weren't enough. He longed for more things to read, but he had no money. So he began to borrow books, newspapers, anything in print. Walking down to the Ohio River, he borrowed a copy of the Revised Laws of Indiana from a lawyer. Then, for the first time, he read the Declaration of Independence and the Constitution of the United States.

He borrowed two or three biographies from a neighboring farmer for whom he had often grubbed stumps and hoed corn. One was the Life of Washington by Parson Weems. It fascinated Lincoln, and he read it at night as long as he could see; and, when he went to sleep, he stuck it in a crack between the logs so that he could begin it again as soon as daylight filtered into the hut. One night a storm blew up, and the book was soaked. The owner refused to take it back, so Lincoln had to cut and shock fodder for three days to pay for it.

But in all his book-borrowing expeditions, he never made a richer find than "Scott's Lessons." This book gave him instruction in public speaking, and introduced him to the renowned speeches of Cicero and Demosthenes and those of Shakespeare's characters.

With "Scott's Lessons" open in his hand, he would walk back and forth under the trees, declaiming Hamlet's instructions to the players, and repeating Antony's oration over the dead body of Cæsar: "Friends, Romans, countrymen, lend me your ears; I come to bury Cæsar, not to praise him."

When he came across a passage that appealed especially to him, he would chalk it down on a board if he had no paper. Finally he made a crude scrap-book. In this he wrote all his favorites, using a buzzard's quill for a pen and pokeberry juice for ink. He carried the scrap-book with him and studied it until he could repeat many long poems and speeches by heart.

When he went out in the field to work his book went with him. While the horses rested at the end of the corn row he sat on the top rail of a fence and studied. At noontime, instead of sitting down and eating with the rest of the family, he took a corn-dodger in one hand and a book in the other and, hoisting his feet higher than his head, lost himself in the lines of print.

When court was in session Lincoln would often walk fifteen miles to the river towns to hear the lawyers argue. Later, when he was out working in the fields with other men, he would now and then drop the grub-hoe or hay-fork, mount a fence, and repeat the speeches he had heard the lawyers make down at Rockport or Boonville. At other times he mimicked the shouting hard-shell Baptist preachers who held forth in the Little Pigeon Creek church on Sundays.

Abe often carried "Quinn's Jests," a joke-book, to the fields; and when he sat astride a log and read parts of it aloud, the woods resounded with the loud guffaws of his audience; but the weeds throve in the corn rows and the wheat yellowed in the fields.

The farmers who were hiring Lincoln complained that he was lazy, "awful lazy." He admitted it. "My father taught me to work," he said, "but he never taught me to love it."

Old Tom Lincoln issued peremptory orders: all this foolishness had to stop. But it didn't stop; Abe kept on telling his jokes and making his speeches. One day—in the presence of others—

the old man struck him a blow in the face and knocked him down. The boy wept, but he said nothing. There was already growing up between father and son an estrangement that would last for the rest of their lives. Although Lincoln looked after his father financially in his old age, yet when the old man lay on his death-bed, in 1851, the son did not go to see him. "If we met now," he said, "it is doubtful whether it would not be more painful than pleasant."

In the winter of 1830 the "milk sick" came again, spreading death once more through the Buckhorn Valley of Indiana.

Filled with fear and discouragement, the roving and migratory Tom Lincoln disposed of his hogs and corn, sold his stump-infested farm for eighty dollars, made a cumbersome wagon—the first he had ever owned—loaded his family and furniture into it, gave Abe the whip, yelled at the oxen, and started out for a valley in Illinois which the Indians called the Sangamon, "the land of plenty to eat."

For two weeks the oxen crept slowly forward as the heavy wagon creaked and groaned over the hills and through the deep forests of Indiana and out across the bleak, desolate, uninhabited prairies of Illinois, carpeted then with withered yellow grass that grew six feet tall under the summer sun.

At Vincennes Lincoln saw a printing-press for the first time; he was then twenty-one.

At Decatur the emigrants camped in the court-house square; and, twenty-six years later, Lincoln pointed out the exact spot where the wagon had stood.

"I didn't know then that I had sense enough to be a lawyer," he said.

Herndon tells us:

> Mr. Lincoln once described this journey to me. He said the ground had not yet yielded up the frosts of winter; that during the day the roads would thaw out on the surface and at night freeze over again, thus making travelling, especially with oxen, painfully slow and tiresome. There were, of course, no bridges, and the party were consequently driven to ford the streams, unless by a circuitous route they could

avoid them. In the early part of the day the latter were also frozen slightly, and the oxen would break through a square yard of thin ice at every step. Among other things which the party brought with them was a pet dog, which trotted along after the wagon. One day the little fellow fell behind and failed to catch up till after they had crossed the stream. Missing him they looked back, and there, on the opposite bank, he stood, whining and jumping about in great distress. The water was running over the broken edges of the ice, and the poor animal was afraid to cross. It would not pay to turn the oxen and wagon back and ford the stream again in order to recover a dog, and so the majority, in their anxiety to move forward, decided to go on without him. "But I could not endure the idea of abandoning even a dog," related Lincoln. "Pulling off shoes and socks I waded across the stream and triumphantly returned with the shivering animal under my arm. His frantic leaps of joy and other evidences of a dog's gratitude amply repaid me for all the exposure I had undergone."

While the oxen were pulling the Lincolns across the prairies Congress was debating with deep and ominous emotion the question of whether or not a State had a right to withdraw from the Union; and during that debate Daniel Webster arose in the United States Senate and, in his deep, golden, bell-like voice, delivered a speech which Lincoln afterward regarded "as the grandest specimen of American oratory." It is known as "Webster's Reply to Hayne" and ends with the memorable words which Lincoln later adopted as his own political religion: "Liberty and Union, now and forever, one and inseparable!"

This cyclonic issue of secession was to be settled a third of a century later, not by the mighty Webster, the gifted Clay, or the famous Calhoun, but by an awkward, penniless, obscure driver of oxen who was now heading for Illinois, wearing a coonskin cap and buckskin trousers, and singing with ribald gusto:

> "Hail Columbia, happy land,
>   If you ain't drunk, then I'll be damned."

Langston Hughes

Born in Missouri, Hughes (1902–1967) spent part of his childhood in Lincoln, Illinois, which in 1853 had become the first American town named for the future President—probably in gratitude for his role in developing the area, both as a state legislator and as a lawyer for the Chicago & Mississippi Railroad. (According to tradition, Lincoln personally christened the town with a pair of watermelons.) Hughes published an early version of this poem while a student at Lincoln University in Pennsylvania in 1926; the final version appeared in 1932 in his book *The Dream Keeper*. His use of Lincoln to measure the passage of time and unfulfilled promises anticipates his famous lines from decades later about "a dream deferred."

Lincoln Monument: Washington

Let's go see old Abe
Sitting in the marble and the moonlight,
Sitting lonely in the marble and the moonlight,
Quiet for ten thousand centuries, old Abe.
Quiet for a million, million years.

Quiet—

And yet a voice forever
Against the
Timeless walls
Of time—
Old Abe.

1932

Rosemary Benét

Rosemary Carr Benét (1898–1962), a graduate of the University of Chicago, married Stephen Vincent Benét in France in 1921. They collaborated on *A Book of Americans*, a collection of poems for children published in 1933. "Nancy Hanks," one of her contributions to the volume, was later used in the opening titles of the 1939 John Ford film *Young Mr. Lincoln*.

Nancy Hanks

1784–1818

If Nancy Hanks
Came back as a ghost,
Seeking news
Of what she loved most,
She'd ask first
"Where's my son?
What's happened to Abe?
What's he done?

"Poor little Abe,
Left all alone
Except for Tom,
Who's a rolling stone;
He was only nine
The year I died.
I remember still
How hard he cried.

"Scraping along
In a little shack,
With hardly a shirt
To cover his back,
And a prairie wind
To blow him down,

Or pinching times
If he went to town.

"You wouldn't know
About my son?
Did he grow tall?
Did he have fun?
Did he learn to read?
Did he get to town?
Do you know his name?
Did he get on?"

1933

Carl Sandburg

As diligently as he worked to analyze and portray Lincoln in prose, Sandburg customarily emphasized his subject's innate mystery in his poetry. In this section from *The People, Yes*—the longest of his Lincoln works in verse—Sandburg deftly interweaves speculation and Lincoln's own words to craft the image of the inexplicable populist of destiny. He ended by transposing the opening lines of Lincoln's 1858 "House Divided" address into free verse—demonstrating what many writers had long observed: that Lincoln had been himself a poet, even in his political speeches.

FROM
The People, Yes

57

Lincoln?
He was a mystery in smoke and flags
saying yes to the smoke, yes to the flags,
yes to the paradoxes of democracy,
yes to the hopes of government
of the people by the people for the people,
no to debauchery of the public mind,
no to personal malice nursed and fed,
yes to the Constitution when a help,
no to the Constitution when a hindrance,
yes to man as a struggler amid illusions,
each man fated to answer for himself:
Which of the faiths and illusions of mankind
must I choose for my own sustaining light
to bring me beyond the present wilderness?

Lincoln? was he a poet?
and did he write verses?
"I have not willingly planted a thorn
in any man's bosom."

"I shall do nothing through malice; what
        I deal with is too vast for malice."

Death was in the air.
So was birth.
What was dying few could say.
What was being born none could know.

He took the wheel in a lashing roaring
        hurricane.
And by what compass did he steer the course
        of the ship?
"My policy is to have no policy," he said in
        the early months,
And three years later, "I have been controlled
        by events."

He could play with the wayward human mind, saying at Charles-
        ton, Illinois, September 18, 1858, it was no answer to an
        argument to call a man a liar.
"I assert that you [pointing a finger in the face of a man in the
        crowd] are here today, and you undertake to prove me a liar
        by showing that you were in Mattoon yesterday.
"I say that you took your hat off your head and you prove me a
        liar by putting it on your head."

He saw personal liberty across wide horizons.
"Our progress in degeneracy appears to me to be pretty rapid,"
        he wrote Joshua F. Speed, August 24, 1855. "As a nation we
        began by declaring that 'all men are created equal, except
        negroes.' When the Know-Nothings get control, it will
        read 'all men are created equal except negroes and foreign-
        ers and Catholics.' When it comes to this, I shall prefer
        emigrating to some country where they make no pretense
        of loving liberty."

Did he look deep into a crazy pool
and see the strife and wrangling

with a clear eye, writing the military
head of a stormswept area:
"If both factions, or neither, shall abuse
you, you will probably be about right. Beware of being assailed by one and praised
by the other"?

Lincoln? was he a historian?
did he know mass chaos?
did he have an answer for those
who asked him to organize chaos?
"Actual war coming, blood grows hot, and blood is spilled.
   Thought is forced from old channels into confusion. Deception breeds and thrives. Confidence dies and universal
   suspicion reigns.
"Each man feels an impulse to kill his neighbor, lest he be first
   killed by him. Revenge and retaliation follow. And all this,
   as before said, may be among honest men only; but this is
   not all.
"Every foul bird comes abroad and every dirty reptile rises up.
   These add crime to confusion.
"Strong measures, deemed indispensable, but harsh at best,
   such men make worse by maladministration. Murders for
   old grudges, and murders for pelf, proceed under any cloak
   that will best cover for the occasion. These causes amply
   account for what has happened in Missouri."

Early in '64 the Committee of the New York Workingman's
   Democratic Republican Association called on him with assurances and he meditated aloud for them, recalling race
   and draft riots:
"The most notable feature of a disturbance in your city last
   summer was the hanging of some working people by other
   working people. It should never be so.
"The strongest bond of human sympathy, outside of the family
   relation, should be one uniting all working people, of all
   nations and tongues and kindreds.
"Let not him who is houseless pull down the house of another,

but let him labor diligently and build one for himself, thus
by example assuring that his own shall be safe from violence when built."

Lincoln? did he gather
the feel of the American dream
and see its kindred over the earth?

"As labor is the common burden of our race,
so the effort of some to shift
their share of the burden
onto the shoulders of others
is the great durable curse of the race."

"I hold,
if the Almighty had ever made a set of men
that should do all of the eating
and none of the work,
he would have made them
with mouths only, and no hands;
and if he had ever made another class,
that he had intended should do all the work
and none of the eating,
he would have made them
without mouths and all hands."

"—the same spirit that says, 'You toil and work and earn
bread, and I'll eat it.' No matter in what shape it
comes, whether from the mouth of a king who seeks
to bestride the people of his own nation and live by
the fruit of their labor, or from one race of men as
an apology for enslaving another race, it is the same
tyrannical principle."

"As I would not be a *slave*, so I would not be a *master*.
This expresses my idea of democracy. Whatever
differs from this, to the extent of the difference, is
no democracy."

"I never knew a man who wished to be himself a slave.
      Consider if you know any *good* thing that no man
      desires for himself."

"The sheep and the wolf
      are not agreed upon a definition
      of the word liberty."

"The whole people of this nation
      will ever do well
      if well done by."

"The plainest print cannot be read
      through a gold eagle."

"How does it feel to be President?" an Illinois friend
      asked.

"Well, I'm like the man they rode out of town on a rail.
      He said if it wasn't for the honor of it he would just
      as soon walk."

            Lincoln? he was a dreamer.
            He saw ships at sea,
            he saw himself living and dead
            in dreams that came.

Into a secretary's diary December 23, 1863 went an entry:
      "The President tonight had a dream. He was in a
      party of plain people, and, as it became known who
      he was, they began to comment on his appearance.
      One of them said: 'He is a very common-looking
      man.' The President replied: 'The Lord prefers
      common-looking people. That is the reason he
      makes so many of them.'"

He spoke one verse for then and now:
    "If we could first know where we are,
    and whither we are tending,
    we could better judge
    what to do, and how to do it."

                                    1936

Marsden Hartley

Unique among those who have interpreted Lincoln memory, Hartley (1877–1943) was an artist as well as a poet. He produced three widely praised Lincoln canvases, *Young Worshipper of the Truth* (1939), *Weary of the Truth* (1940), and *Great Good Man* (1942), all modeled after familiar photographs, but all imaginatively deconstructing Lincoln's features and paraphrasing them as monumental icons clearly influenced by Gutzon Borglum's Mount Rushmore memorial. In the words of his biographer Townsend Ludington, Hartley saw Lincoln with "geographical grandeur," a characterization reinforced by his trinity of paintings. In fact, in the second of these admiring portraits, Lincoln is made to loom so large that his signature top hat competes with the Capitol dome and the Washington Monument (the former under construction during much of Lincoln's term, the latter actually left unfinished until years later) to dominate the Washington skyline. Hartley's poetic tribute to Lincoln was no less obsessed with his subject's physical grandeur, but offered a fascinating glimpse into his own creative impulse and the challenges facing artists who dared to tamper with the Lincoln image, even with admiring intentions.

American Ikon—Lincoln

I have walked up and down the
valleys
of his astounding face
I have witnessed all the golgothas
I have climbed the steep declivities
of all his dreams
listened to the whickering of the
wind
around them
like a lilliput I have sat, quietly
upon his haggard chin
looked up at the breaking rain
falling from his furrowed lids.

I have for once heard God calling
all things to order here.
I have seen infinite mercies
on his woman's lower lip
in the same way I have seen
determination
upon his man's upper.
Pity has poured out from between
these massive portals
majesty of love has walked out
of them
clothed in amazingly decent garments
the only voice worth hearing has sounded
great beauty in my ear
because I have walked where I have
walked
I have scaled the sheer surface of his
dignities
watching the flaming horizon
with calm.

c. 1939

Weary of the Truth, oil painting by Marsden Hartley (1940). *Yale University Art Gallery; gift of Donald Gallup.*

Robert E. Sherwood

A successful playwright turned presidential speechwriter, Sherwood (1896–1955) did more perhaps than any writer of his day to take ownership of Lincoln memory away from the Republicans and give it to the Democrats. A wounded World War I veteran, Sherwood won a Pulitzer Prize for his anti-war play *Idiot's Delight* (1936), but then became increasingly alarmed by the dangers of foreign totalitarianism. Inspired by Sandburg's *The Prairie Years*, he wrote *Abe Lincoln in Illinois*, which traced the future President's life from 1831 to 1861 in 12 scenes. The play opened on Broadway in October 1938, just two weeks after the signing of the Munich agreement. "If you substitute the word dictatorship for the word slavery throughout Sherwood's script," said Raymond Massey, its star, "it becomes electric for our time." Sherwood purposely de-emphasized Lincoln's ambition, portraying him as a reluctant leader who must be convinced to commit himself to the struggle for freedom. After the release early in 1940 of the screen version—also starring Massey—Sherwood became a White House speechwriter and helped Franklin D. Roosevelt prepare the nation for war. Under the playwright's tutelage, Roosevelt began referring to Lincoln with increasing frequency at press conferences and in speeches, eventually likening the challenges America faced from foreign enemies to those Lincoln had faced—and overcome—from domestic foes the century before. The three scenes from *Abe Lincoln in Illinois* printed here take the hero from reluctant candidate to president-elect, and end with a farewell speech to Springfield that expands on—but reduces the impact of—Lincoln's magnificent original. They are accompanied by the fascinating notes Sherwood wrote for the published version of the play to illuminate his transformation of history into drama.

Abe Lincoln in Illinois

ACT THREE

SCENE X

Parlor of the Edwards home, now being used by the Lincolns. After-noon of a day in the early Spring of 1860.

    ABE *is sitting on the couch at the right, with his seven-year-old son,* TAD, *on his lap. Sitting beside them is another son,* WILLIE, *aged nine. The eldest son,* ROBERT, *a young Harvard student of seventeen, is sitting by the window, importantly smoking a pipe and listening to the story* ABE *has been telling the children.* JOSHUA SPEED *is sitting at the left.*

ABE

You must remember, Tad, the roads weren't much good then—mostly nothing more than trails—and it was hard to find my way in the darkness. . . .

WILLIE

Were you scared?

ABE

Yes—I was scared.

WILLIE

Of Indians?

ABE

No—there weren't any of them left around here. I was afraid I'd get lost, and the boy would die, and it would be all my fault. But, finally, I found the doctor. He was very tired, and wanted to go to bed, and he grumbled a lot, but I made him come along with me then and there.

WILLIE

Was the boy dead?

ABE

No, Willie. He wasn't dead. But he was pretty sick. The doctor gave him a lot of medicine.

TAD

Did it taste bad, Pa?

ABE

I presume it did. But it worked. I never saw those nice people again, but I've heard from them every so often. That little boy was your age, Tad, but now he's a grown man with a son almost as big as you are. He lives on a great big farm, in a valley with a river that runs right down from the tops of the snow mountains. . . .

(MARY *comes in.*)

MARY

Robert! You are smoking in my parlor!

ROBERT (*wearily*)

Yes, Mother. (*He rises.*)

MARY

I have told you that I shall not tolerate tobacco smoke in my parlor or, indeed, in any part of my house, and I mean to . . .

ABE

Come, come, Mary—you must be respectful to a Harvard man. Take it out to the woodshed, Bob.

ROBERT

Yes, Father.

MARY

And this will not happen again!

ROBERT

No, Mother. (*He goes out.*)

ABE

I was telling the boys a story about some pioneers I knew once.

MARY

It's time for you children to make ready for your supper.

(*The* CHILDREN *promptly get up to go.*)

WILLIE

But what happened after that, Pa?

ABE

Nothing. Everybody lived happily ever after. Now run along.

(WILLIE *and* TAD *run out.*)

JOSH

What time *is* it, Mary?

MARY

It's nearly half past four. (*She is shaking the smoke out of the curtains.*)

JOSH

Half past four, Abe. Those men will be here any minute.

ABE (*rising*)

Good Lord!

MARY (*turning sharply to* ABE)

What men?

ABE

Some men from the East. One of them's a political leader named Crimmin—and there's a Mr. Sturveson—he's a manufacturer—and . . .

MARY (*impressed*)

Henry D. Sturveson?

ABE

That's the one—and also the Reverend Dr. Barrick from Boston.

MARY (*sharply*)

What are they coming here for?

ABE

I don't precisely know—but I suspect that it's to see if I'm fit to be a candidate for President of the United States.

(MARY *is, for the moment, speechless.*)

I suppose they want to find out if we still live in a log cabin and keep pigs under the bed. . . .

MARY (*in a fury*)

And you didn't *tell* me!

ABE

I'm sorry, Mary—the matter just slipped my . . .

MARY

You forgot to tell me that we're having the most important guests who ever crossed the threshold of my house!

ABE

They're not guests. They're only here on business.

MARY (*bitterly*)

Yes! Rather important business, it seems to me. They want to see us as we *are*—crude, sloppy, vulgar Western barbarians, living in a house that reeks of foul tobacco smoke.

ABE

We can explain about having a son at Harvard.

MARY

If I'd only *known*! If you had only given me a little time to prepare for them. Why didn't you put on your best suit? And those filthy old boots!

ABE

Well, Mary, I clean forgot. . . .

MARY

I declare, Abraham Lincoln, I believe you would have treated me with much more consideration if I had been your slave, instead of your wife! You have never, for one moment, stopped to think that perhaps I have some interests, some concerns, in the life we lead together. . . .

ABE

I'll try to clean up my boots a little, Mary.

(*He goes out, glad to escape from this painful scene.* MARY *looks after him. Her lip is quivering. She wants to avoid tears.*)

MARY (*seating herself; bitterly*)

You've seen it all, Joshua Speed. Every bit of it-—courtship, if you could call it that, change of heart, change back again, and marriage, eighteen years of it. And you probably think just as all the others do—that I'm a bitter, nagging woman, and I've tried to kill his spirit, and drag him down to my level. . . .

(JOSH *rises and goes over to her.*)

JOSH (*quietly*)

No, Mary. I think no such thing. Remember, I know Abe, too.

MARY

There never could have been another man such as he is! I've read about many that have gone up in the world, and all of them seemed to have to fight to assert themselves every inch of the way, against the opposition of their enemies and the lack of understanding in their own friends. But he's never had any of that. He's never had an enemy, and every one of his friends has always been completely confident in him. Even before I met him, I was told that he had a glorious future, and after I'd known him a day, I was sure of it myself. But he didn't believe it—or, if he did, secretly, he was so afraid of the prospect that he did all in his power to avoid it. He had some poem in his mind, about a life of woe, along a rugged path, that leads to some future doom, and it has been an obsession with him. All these years, I've tried and tried to stir him out of it, but all my efforts have been like so many puny waves, dashing against the Rock of Ages. And now, opportunity, the greatest opportunity, is coming here, to him, right into his own house. And what can I do about it? He *must* take it! He *must* see that this is what he was meant for! But I can't persuade him of it! I'm tired—I'm tired to death! (*The tears now come.*) I thought I could help to shape him, as I knew he should be, and I've succeeded in nothing—but in breaking myself. . . . (*She sobs bitterly.*)

(JOSH *sits down beside her and pats her hand.*)

JOSH (*tenderly*)

I know, Mary. But—there's no reason in heaven and earth for you to reproach yourself. Whatever becomes of Abe Lincoln is in the hands of a God who controls the destinies of all of us, including lunatics, and saints.

(ABE *comes back.*)

ABE (*looking down at his boots*)

I think they look all right now, Mary. (*He looks at* MARY, *who is now trying hard to control her emotion.*)

MARY

You can receive the gentlemen in here. I'll try to prepare some refreshment for them in the dining-room.

(*She goes out.* ABE *looks after her, miserably. There are a few moments of silence. At length,* ABE *speaks, in an off-hand manner.*)

ABE

I presume these men *are* pretty influential.

JOSH

They'll have quite a say in the delegations of three states that may swing the nomination away from Seward.

ABE

Suppose, by some miracle, or fluke, they did nominate me; do you think I'd stand a chance of winning the election?

JOSH

An excellent chance, in my opinion. There'll be four candidates in the field, bumping each other, and opening up the track for a dark horse.

ABE

But the dark horse might run in the wrong direction.

JOSH

Yes—you can always do that, Abe. I know *I* wouldn't care to bet two cents on you.

ABE (*grinning*)

It seems funny to be comparing it to a horse-race, with an old, spavined hack like me. But I've had some mighty energetic jockeys—Mentor Graham, Bowling Green, Bill Herndon, you, and Mary—most of all, Mary.

JOSH (*looking at* ABE)

They don't count now, Abe. You threw 'em all, long ago. When you finally found yourself running against poor little Douglas, you got the bit between your teeth and went like greased lightning. You'd do the same thing to him again, if you could only decide to get started, which you probably won't . . . (*The door-bell jangles.* JOSH *gets up.*)

ABE

I expect that's them now.

JOSH

I'll go see if I can help Mary. (*He starts for the door but turns and looks at* ABE, *and speaks quietly.*) I'd just like to remind you, Abe— there are pretty nearly thirty million people in this country; most of 'em are common people, like you. They're in serious trouble, and they need somebody who understands 'em, as you do. So—when these gentlemen come in—try to be a *little* bit polite to them. (ABE *grins.* JOSH *looks off.*) However—you won't listen to any advice from me.

(JOSH *goes. The door is opened by a* MAID *and* STURVESON, BARRICK, *and* CRIMMIN *come in.* STURVESON *is elderly, wealthy and bland.* BARRICK *is a soft Episcopalian dignitary.* CRIMMIN *is a shrewd, humorous fixer.*)

ABE

Come right in, gentlemen. Glad to see you again, Mr. Crim-min.

(*They shake hands.*)

CRIMMIN

How de do, Mr. Lincoln. This is Dr. Barrick of Boston, and Mr. Sturveson, of Philadelphia.

DR. BARRICK

Mr. Lincoln.

STURVESON

I'm honored, Mr. Lincoln.

LINCOLN

Thank you, sir. Pray sit down, gentlemen.

STURVESON

Thank you.

(*They sit.*)

CRIMMIN

Will Mrs. Lincoln seriously object if I light a seegar?

LINCOLN

Go right ahead! I regret that Mrs. Lincoln is not here to receive you, but she will join us presently. (*He sits down.*)

BARRICK (*with great benignity*)

I am particularly anxious to meet Mrs. Lincoln, for I believe, with Mr. Longfellow, that 'as unto the bow the cord is, so unto the man is woman.'

STURVESON (*very graciously*)

And we are here dealing with a bow that is stout indeed.

(ABE *bows slightly in acknowledgment of the compliment.*)

And one with a reputation for shooting straight. So you'll forgive us, Mr. Lincoln, for coming directly to the point.

ABE

Yes, sir. I understand that you wish to inspect the prairie politician in his native lair, and here I am.

STURVESON

It is no secret that we are desperately in need of a candidate—one who is sound, conservative, safe—and clever enough to skate over the thin ice of the forthcoming campaign. Your friends—

and there's an increasingly large number of them throughout the country—believe that you are the man.

ABE

Well, Mr. Sturveson, I can tell you that when first I was considered for political office—that was in New Salem, twenty-five years ago—I assured my sponsors of my conservatism. I have subsequently proved it, by never progressing anywhere.

BARRICK (*smiling*)

Then you agree that you are the man we want?

ABE

I'm afraid I can't go quite that far in self-esteem, Dr. Barrick, especially when you have available a statesman and gentleman as eminent as Mr. Seward who, I believe, is both ready and willing.

STURVESON

That's as may be. But please understand that this is not an inquisition. We merely wish to know you better, to gain a clearer idea of your theories on economics, religion and national affairs, in general. To begin with—in one of your memorable debates with Senator Douglas, your opponent indulged in some of his usual demagoguery about industrial conditions in the North, and you replied shrewdly that whereas the slaves in the South . . .

ABE

Yes, I remember the occasion. I replied that I was thankful that laborers in free states have the right to strike. But that wasn't shrewdness, Mr. Sturveson. It was just the truth.

STURVESON

It has gained for you substantial support from the laboring classes, which is all to the good. But it has also caused a certain amount of alarm among business men, like myself.

ABE

I cannot enlarge on the subject. It seems obvious to me that this nation was founded on the supposition that men have the right to protest, violently if need be, against authority that is unjust or oppressive. (*He turns to* BARRICK.) The Boston Tea Party was a kind of strike. So was the Revolution itself. (*Again to* STURVESON.) So was Nicholas Biddle's attempt to organize the banks against the Jackson administration.

STURVESON

Which is all perfectly true—but—the days of anarchy are over. We face an unprecedented era of industrial expansion—mass production of every conceivable kind of goods—railroads and telegraph lines across the continent—all promoted and developed by private enterprise. In this great work, we must have a free hand, and a firm one, Mr. Lincoln. To put it bluntly, would you, if elected, place the interests of labor above those of capital?

ABE

I cannot answer that, bluntly, or any other way; because I cannot tell what I should do, if elected.

STURVESON

But you must have inclinations toward one side or the other. . . .

ABE

I think you know, Mr. Sturveson, that I am opposed to slavery.

BARRICK

And we of New England applaud your sentiments! We deplore the inhumanity of our Southern friends in . . .

ABE (*to* BARRICK)

There are more forms of slavery than that which is inflicted upon the Negroes in the South. I am opposed to all of them. (*He turns again to* STURVESON.) I believe in our democratic system— the just and generous system which opens the way to all—gives hope to all, and consequent energy and progress and improvement of condition to all, including employer and employee alike.

BARRICK

We support your purpose, Mr. Lincoln, in steadfastly proclaiming the rights of men to resist unjust authority. But I am most anxious to know whether you admit One Authority to whom devotion is unquestioned?

ABE

I presume you refer to the Almighty?

BARRICK

I do.

ABE

I think there has never been any doubt of my submission to His will.

BARRICK

I'm afraid there is a great deal of doubt as to your devotion to His church.

ABE

I realize that, Doctor. They say I'm an atheist, because I've always refused to become a church member.

BARRICK

What have been the grounds of your refusal?

ABE

I have found no churches suitable for my own form of worship. I could not give assent without mental reservations to the long, complicated statements of Christian doctrine which characterize their Articles of Belief and Confessions of Faith. But I can promise you, Dr. Barrick—I shall gladly join any church at any time if its sole qualification for membership is obedience to the Saviour's statement of Law and Gospel: 'Thou shalt love the Lord thy God with all thy heart and with all thy soul and with all thy mind, and thou shalt love thy neighbor as thyself.' . . . But—I beg you gentlemen to excuse me for a moment. I believe Mrs. Lincoln is preparing a slight collation, and I must see if I can help with it. . . .

CRIMMIN

Certainly, Mr. Lincoln.

(ABE *goes, closing the door behind him.* CRIMMIN *looks at the door, then turns to the others.*) Well?

BARRICK

The man is unquestionably an infidel. An idealist—in his curious, primitive way—but an infidel!

STURVESON

And a radical!

CRIMMIN

A radical? Forgive me, gentlemen, if I enjoy a quiet laugh at that.

STURVESON

Go ahead and enjoy yourself, Crimmin—but I did not like the way he evaded my direct question. I tell you, he's as unscrupulous a demagogue as Douglas. He's a rabble rouser!

CRIMMIN

Of course he is! As a dealer in humbug, he puts Barnum himself to shame.

STURVESON

Quite possibly—but he is not *safe*!

CRIMMIN

Not safe, eh? And what do you mean by that?

STURVESON

Just what I say. A man who devotes himself so whole-heartedly to currying favor with the mob develops the mob mentality. He becomes a preacher of discontent, of mass unrest. . . .

CRIMMIN

And what about Seward? If we put him up, he'll start right in demanding liberation of the slaves—and then there *will* be discontent and unrest! I ask you to believe me when I tell you that this Lincoln *is* safe—in economics and theology and everything else. After all—what is the essential qualification that we demand of the candidate of our party? It is simply this: that he be able to get himself elected! And there is the man who can do that. (*He points off-stage.*)

STURVESON (*smiling*)

I should like to believe you!

BARRICK

So say we all of us!

CRIMMIN

Then just keep faith in the eternal stupidity of the voters, which is what *he* will appeal to. In that uncouth rail splitter you may observe one of the smoothest, slickest politicians that ever hoodwinked a yokel mob! You complain that he evaded your questions. Of course he did, and did it perfectly! Ask him about the labor problem, and he replies, "I believe in democracy." Ask his views on religion, and he says, "Love thy neighbor as thyself." Now—you know you couldn't argue with that, either of you. I tell you, gentlemen, he's a vote-getter if I ever saw one. His very name is right—Abraham Lincoln! Honest Old Abe! He'll play the game with us now, and he'll go right on playing it when we get him into the White House. He'll do just what we tell him. . . .

DR. BARRICK (*cautioning him*)

Careful, Mr. Crimmin. . . .

(ABE *returns*.)

ABE

If you gentlemen will step into the dining-room, Mrs. Lincoln would be pleased to serve you with a cup of tea.

BARRICK

Thank you.

STURVESON

This is most gracious.

(*He and* BARRICK *move off toward the door*.)

ABE

Or perhaps something stronger for those who prefer it.

(STURVESON *and* BARRICK *go*. CRIMMIN *is looking for a place to throw his cigar*.)

ABE (*heartily*)

Bring your seegar with you, Mr. Crimmin!

CRIMMIN

Thank you—thank you!

(*He smiles at* ABE, *gives him a slap on the arm, and goes out,* ABE *following. The lights fade.*)

END OF SCENE X

SCENE XI

Lincoln campaign headquarters in the Illinois State House. The evening of Election Day, November 6th, 1860.

It is a large room with a tall window opening out on to a wide balcony. There are doors upper right and upper left. At the left is a table littered with newspapers and clippings. There are many chairs about, and a liberal supply of spittoons.

At the back is a huge chart of the thirty-three states, with their electoral votes, and a space opposite each side for the posting of bulletins. A short ladder gives access to Alabama and Arkansas at the top of the list.

On the wall at the left is an American flag. At the right is a map of the United States, on which each state is marked with a red, white or blue flag.

ABE *is sitting at the table, with his back to the audience, reading newspaper clippings. He wears his hat and has spectacles on.* MRS. LINCOLN *is sitting at the right of the table, her eyes darting nervously from* ABE, *to the chart, to the map. She wears her bonnet, tippet and muff.*

ROBERT LINCOLN *is standing near her, studying the map.* NINIAN EDWARDS *is sitting at the left of the table and* JOSH SPEED *is standing near the chart. They are both smoking cigars and watching the chart.*

The door at the left is open, and through it the clatter of telegraph instruments can be heard. The window is partly open, and we can hear band music from the square below, and frequent cheers from the assembled mob, who are watching the election returns flashed from a magic lantern on the State House balcony.

Every now and then, a telegraph operator named JED *comes in from the left and tacks a new bulletin up on the chart. Another man named* PHIL *is out on the balcony taking bulletins from* JED.

ROBERT

What do those little flags mean, stuck into the map?

JOSH

Red means the state is sure for us. White means doubtful. Blue means hopeless.

(ABE *tosses the clipping he has been reading on the table and picks up another.*)

(JED *comes in and goes up to pin bulletins opposite Illinois, Maryland and New York.*)

NINIAN (*rising to look*)

Lincoln and Douglas neck and neck in Illinois.

(JOSH *and* ROBERT *crowd around the chart.*)

JOSH

Maryland is going all for Breckenridge and Bell. Abe—you're nowhere in Maryland.

MARY (*with intense anxiety*)

What of New York?

JED (*crossing to the window*)

Say, Phil—when you're not getting bulletins, keep that window closed. We can't hear ourselves think.

PHIL

All right. Only have to open 'er up again. (*He closes the window.*)

MARY

What does it say about New York?

   (JED *goes.*)

NINIAN

Douglas a hundred and seventeen thousand—Lincoln a hundred and six thousand.

MARY (*desperately, to* ABE)

He's winning from you in New York, Abe!

JOSH

Not yet, Mary. These returns so far are mostly from the city where Douglas is bound to run the strongest.

ABE (*interested in a clipping*)

I see the New York *Herald* says I've got the soul of a Uriah Heep encased in the body of a baboon. (*He puts the clipping aside and starts to read another.*)

NINIAN (*who has resumed his seat*)

You'd better change that flag on Rhode Island from red to white, Bob. It looks doubtful to me.

   (ROBERT, *glad of something to do, changes the flag as directed.*)

MARY

What does it look like in Pennsylvania, Ninian?

NINIAN

There's nothing to worry about there, Mary. It's safe for Abe. In fact, you needn't worry at all.

MARY (*very tense*)

Yes. You've been saying that over and over again all evening. There's no need to worry. But how can we help worrying when every new bulletin shows Douglas ahead.

JOSH

But every one of them shows Abe gaining.

NINIAN (*mollifying*)

Just give them time to count all the votes in New York and then you'll be on your way to the White House.

MARY

Oh, why don't they hurry with it? Why don't those returns come in?

ABE (*preoccupied*)

They'll come in—soon enough.

(BILLY HERNDON *comes in from the right. He has been doing a lot of drinking but has hold of himself.*)

BILLY

That mob down there is sickening! They cheer every bulletin that's flashed on the wall, whether the news is good or bad. And they cheer every picture of every candidate, including George Washington, with the same, fine, ignorant enthusiasm.

JOSH

That's logical. They can't tell 'em apart.

BILLY (*to* ABE)

There are a whole lot of reporters down there. They want to know what will be your first official action after you're elected.

NINIAN

What do you want us to tell 'em, Abe?

ABE (*still reading*)

Tell 'em I'm thinking of growing a beard.

JOSH

A beard?

NINIAN (*amused*)

Whatever put that idea into your mind?

ABE (*picking up another clipping*)

I had a letter the other day from some little girl. She said I ought to have whiskers, to give me more dignity. And I'll need it—if elected.

(JED *arrives with new bulletins.* BILLY, NINIAN, JOSH *and* ROBERT *huddle around* JED, *watching him post the bulletins.*)

MARY

What do they say now?

(JED *goes to the window and gives some bulletins to* PHIL.)

MARY

Is there anything new from New York?

NINIAN

Connecticut—Abe far in the lead. That's eleven safe electoral votes anyway. Missouri—Douglas thirty-five thousand—Bell thirty-three—Breckenridge sixteen—Lincoln, eight. . . .

(*Cheers from the crowd outside until* PHIL *closes the window.* JED *returns to the office at the left.*)

MARY

What are they cheering for?

BILLY

They don't know!

ABE (*with another clipping*)

The Chicago *Times* says, "Lincoln breaks down! Lincoln's heart fails him! His tongue fails him! His legs fail him! He fails all over! The people refuse to support him! They laugh at him! Douglas is champion of the people! Douglas skins the living dog!"

(*He tosses the clipping aside.* MARY *stands up.*)

MARY (*her voice is trembling*)

I can't stand it any longer!

ABE

Yes, my dear—I think you'd better go home. I'll be back before long.

MARY (*hysterical*)

I won't go home! You only want to be rid of me. That's what you've wanted ever since the day we were married—and before that. Anything to get me out of your sight, because you hate me! (*Turning to* JOSH, NINIAN *and* BILLY.) And it's the same with all of you—all of his friends—you hate me—you wish I'd never come into his life.

JOSH

No, Mary.

(ABE *has stood up, quickly, at the first storm signal. He himself is in a fearful state of nervous tension—in no mood to treat* MARY *with patient indulgence. He looks sharply at* NINIAN *and at the others.*)

ABE

Will you please step out for a moment?

NINIAN

Certainly, Abe.

(*He and the others go into the telegraph office.* JOSH *gestures to* ROBERT *to go with them.* ROBERT *casts a black look at his mother and goes. . . .* ABE *turns on* MARY *with strange savagery.*)

ABE

Damn you! Damn you for taking every opportunity you can to

make a public fool of me—and yourself! It's bad enough, God knows, when you act like that in the privacy of our own home. But here—in front of people! You're not to do that again. Do you hear me? You're never to do that again!

(MARY *is so aghast at this outburst that her hysterical temper vanishes, giving way to blank terror.*)

MARY (*in a faint, strained voice*)

Abe! You cursed at me. Do you realize what you did? You cursed at me.

(ABE *has the impulse to curse at her again, but with considerable effort, he controls it.*)

ABE (*in a strained voice*)

I lost my temper, Mary. And I'm sorry for it. But I still think you should go home rather than endure the strain of this—this Death Watch.

(*She stares at him, uncomprehendingly, then turns and goes to the door.*)

MARY (*at the door*)

This is the night I dreamed about, when I was a child, when I was an excited young girl, and all the gay young gentlemen of Springfield were courting me, and I fell in love with the least likely of them. This is the night when I'm waiting to hear that my husband has become President of the United States. And even if he does—it's ruined, for me. It's too late. . . .

(*She opens the door and goes out. ABE looks after her, anguished, then turns quickly, crosses to the door at the left and opens it.*)

ABE (*calling off*)

Bob!

(ROBERT *comes in.*)

Go with your Mother.

ROBERT

Do I have to?

ABE

Yes! Hurry! Keep right with her till I get home.

(ROBERT *has gone. ABE turns to the window. PHIL opens it.*)

PHIL

Do you think you're going to make it, Mr. Lincoln?

ABE

Oh—there's nothing to worry about.

CROWD OUTSIDE (*singing*)

Old Abe Lincoln came out of the wilderness
Out of the wilderness
Out of the wilderness
Old Abe Lincoln came out of the wilderness
Down in Illinois!

(NINIAN, JOSH, BILLY, *and* JED *come in, the latter to post new bulletins. After* JED *has communicated these,* PHIL *again closes the window.* JED *goes.*)

NINIAN

It looks like seventy-four electoral votes sure for you. Twenty-seven more probable. New York's will give you the election.

(ABE *walks around the room.* JOSH *has been looking at* ABE.)

JOSH

Abe, could I get you a cup of coffee?

ABE

No, thanks, Josh.

NINIAN

Getting nervous, Abe?

ABE

No. I'm just thinking what a blow it would be to Mrs. Lincoln if I should lose.

NINIAN

And what about me? I have ten thousand dollars bet on you.

BILLY (*scornfully*)

I'm afraid that the loss to the nation would be somewhat more serious than that.

JOSH

How would you feel, Abe?

ABE (*sitting on the chair near the window*)

I guess I'd feel the greatest sense of relief of my life.

(JED *comes in with a news despatch.*)

JED

Here's a news despatch. (*He hands it over and goes.*)

NINIAN (*reads*)

"Shortly after nine o'clock this evening, Mr. August Belmont stated that Stephen A. Douglas has piled up a majority of fifty thousand votes in New York City and carried the state."

BILLY

Mr. Belmont be damned!

(CRIMMIN *comes in, smoking a cigar, looking contented.*)

CRIMMIN

Good evening, Mr. Lincoln. Good evening, gentlemen—and how are you all feeling *now*?

(*They all greet him.*)

NINIAN

Look at this, Crimmin. (*He hands the despatch to* CRIMMIN.)

CRIMMIN (*smiles*)

Well—Belmont is going to fight to the last ditch, which is just what he's lying in now. I've been in Chicago and the outlook there is cloudless. In fact, Mr. Lincoln, I came down tonight to protect you from the office-seekers. They're lining up downstairs already. On the way in I counted four Ministers to Great Britain and eleven Secretaries of State.

(JED *has come in with more bulletins to put on the chart and then goes to the window to give* PHIL *the bulletins.*)

BILLY (*at the chart*)

There's a bulletin from New York! Douglas a hundred and eighty-three thousand—Lincoln a hundred and eighty-*one* thousand!

(JED *goes.*)

JOSH

Look out, Abe. You're catching up!

CRIMMIN

The next bulletin from New York will show you winning. Mark my words, Mr. Lincoln, this election is all wrapped up tightly in a neat bundle, ready for delivery on your doorstep tonight. We've fought the good fight, and we've won!

ABE (*pacing up and down the room*)

Yes—we've fought the good fight—in the dirtiest campaign in the history of corrupt politics. And if I have won, then I must cheerfully pay my political debts. All those who helped to nominate and elect me must be paid off. I have been gambled all around, bought and sold a hundred times. And now I must fill all the dishonest pledges made in my name.

NINIAN

We realize all that, Abe—but the fact remains that you're winning. Why, you're even beating the coalition in Rhode Island!

ABE

I've got to step out for a moment. (*He goes out at the right*.)

NINIAN (*cheerfully*)

Poor Abe.

CRIMMIN

You gentlemen have all been close friends of our Candidate for a long time so perhaps you could answer a question that's been puzzling me considerably. Can I possibly be correct in supposing that he doesn't want to win?

JOSH

The answer is—yes.

CRIMMIN (*looking toward the right*)

Well—I can only say that, for me, this is all a refreshingly new experience.

BILLY (*belligerently*)

Would *you* want to become President of the United States at this time? Haven't you been reading the newspapers lately?

CRIMMIN

Why, yes—I try to follow the events of the day.

BILLY (*in a rage*)

Don't you realize that they've raised ten thousand volunteers in South Carolina? They're arming them! The Governor has issued a proclamation saying that if Mr. Lincoln is elected, the State will secede tomorrow, and every other state south of the Dixon line will go with it. Can you see what that means? War! Civil War! And *he'll* have the whole terrible responsibility for it—a man who has never wanted anything in his life but to be let alone, in peace!

NINIAN

Calm down, Billy. Go get yourself another drink.

  (JED *rushes in*.)

JED

Mr. Edwards, here it is! (*He hands a news despatch to* NINIAN, *then rushes to the window to attract* PHIL'S *attention and communicate the big news.*)

NINIAN (*reads*)

"At 10:30 tonight the New York *Herald* conceded that Mr. Lincoln has carried the state by a majority of at least twenty-five thousand and has won the election!" (*He tosses the despatch in the air.*) He's won! He's won! Hurrah!

(*All on the stage shout, cheer, embrace and slap each other.*)

BILLY

God be praised! God be praised!

CRIMMIN

I knew it! I never had a doubt of it!

(JED *is on the balcony, shouting through a megaphone.*)

JED

Lincoln is elected! Honest Old Abe is our next President!

(*A terrific cheer ascends from the crowd below.* ABE *returns. They rush at him.* BILLY *shakes hands with him, too deeply moved to speak.*)

NINIAN

You've carried New York, Abe! You've won! Congratulations!

CRIMMIN

My congratulations, Mr. President. This is a mighty achievement for all of us!

(JED *comes in and goes to* ABE.)

JED

My very best, Mr. Lincoln!

ABE (*solemnly*)

Thank you—thank you all very much.

(*He comes to the left.* JOSH *is the last to shake his hand.*)

JOSH

I congratulate you, Abe.

ABE

Thanks, Josh.

NINIAN

Listen to them, Abe. Listen to that crazy, howling mob down there.

CRIMMIN

It's all for you, Mr. Lincoln.

NINIAN

Abe, get out there and let 'em see you!

ABE

No. I don't want to go out there. I—I guess I'll be going on home, to tell Mary. (*He starts toward the door.*)

(*A short, stocky officer named* KAVANAGH *comes in from the right. He is followed by two soldiers.*)

CRIMMIN

This is Captain Kavanagh, Mr. *President.*

KAVANAGH (*salutes*)

I've been detailed to accompany you, Mr. Lincoln, in the event of your election.

ABE

I'm grateful, Captain. But I don't need you.

KAVANAGH

I'm afraid you've got to have us, Mr. Lincoln. I don't like to be alarming, but I guess you know as well as I do what threats have been made.

ABE (*wearily*)

I see . . . Well—Good night, Josh—Ninian—Mr. Crimmin—Billy. Thank you for your good wishes.

(*He starts for the door. The others bid him good night, quietly.*)

KAVANAGH

One moment, Sir. With your permission, I'll go first.

(*He goes out,* ABE *after him, the two other soldiers follow. The light fades.*)

END OF SCENE XI

SCENE XII

The yards of the railroad station at Springfield. The date is February 11, 1861.

At the right, at an angle toward the audience, is the back of a railroad car. From behind this, off to the upper left, runs a ramp. Flags and bunting are draped above.

In a row downstage are soldiers, with rifles and bayonets fixed, and packs on their backs, standing at ease. Off to the left is a large crowd, whose excited murmuring can be heard.

KAVANAGH *is in the foreground. A* BRAKEMAN *with a lantern is inspecting the wheels of the car, at the left. A* WORKMAN *is at the right, polishing the rails of the car.* KAVANAGH *is pacing up and down, chewing a dead cigar. He looks at his watch. A swaggering* MAJOR *of militia comes down the ramp from the left.*

MAJOR

I want you men to form up against this ramp. (*To* KAVANAGH; *with a trace of scorn.*) You seem nervous, Mr. Kavanagh.

KAVANAGH

Well—I am nervous. For three months I've been guarding the life of a man who doesn't give a damn what happens to him. I heard today that they're betting two to one in Richmond that he won't be alive to take the oath of office on March the 4th.

MAJOR

I'd like to take some of that money. The State Militia is competent to protect the person of our Commander-in-Chief.

KAVANAGH

I hope the United States Army is competent to help. But those Southerners are mighty good shots. And I strongly suggest that your men be commanded to keep watch through every window of every car, especially whenever the train stops—at a town, or a tank, or anywhere. And if any alarm is sounded, at any point along the line . . .

MAJOR (*a trifle haughty*)

There's no need to command my men to show courage in an emergency.

KAVANAGH

No slur was intended, Major—but we must be prepared in advance for everything.

(*A brass band off to the left strikes up the campaign song, "Old Abe Lincoln came out of the wilderness." The crowd starts to sing it, more and more voices taking it up. A* CONDUCTOR *comes out of the car and looks at his watch. There is a commotion at the left as* NINIAN *and* ELIZABETH EDWARDS, *and* JOSH, BILLY *and* CRIMMIN *come in and are stopped by the soldiers. The* MAJOR *goes forward, bristling with importance.*)

MAJOR

Stand back, there! Keep the crowd back there, you men!

NINIAN

I'm Mr. Lincoln's brother-in-law.

MAJOR

What's your name?

KAVANAGH

I know him, Major. That's Mr. and Mrs. Edwards, and Mr. Speed and Mr. Herndon with them. I know them all. You can let them through.

MAJOR

Very well. You can pass.

(*They come down to the right. The* MAJOR *goes off at the left.*)

CRIMMIN

How is the President feeling today? Happy?

NINIAN

Just as gloomy as ever.

BILLY (*emotionally*)

He came down to the office, and when I asked him what I should do about the sign, "Lincoln and Herndon," he said, "Let it hang there. Let our clients understand that this election makes no difference to the firm. If I live, I'll be back some time, and then we'll go right on practising just as if nothing had happened."

ELIZABETH

He's always saying that—"If I live" . . .

(*A tremendous cheer starts and swells offstage at the left. The* MAYOR *comes on, briskly.*)

MAJOR (*to* KAVANAGH)

The President has arrived! (*To his men*) Attention! (*The* MAJOR *strides down the platform and takes his position by the car, looking off to the left.*)

KAVANAGH (*to* NINIAN *and the others*)

Would you mind stepping back there? We want to keep this space clear for the President's party.

(*They move upstage, at the right. The cheering is now very loud.*)

MAJOR

Present—Arms!

(*The soldiers come to the Present. The* MAJOR *salutes. Preceded by soldiers who are looking sharply to the right and left, ABE comes in from the left, along the platform. He will be fifty-two years old tomorrow. He wears a beard. Over his shoulders is his plaid shawl. In his right hand, he carries his carpet-bag; his left hand is leading TAD. Behind him are MARY, ROBERT and WILLIE, and the MAID. All, except MARY, are also carrying bags. She carries a bunch of flowers. When they come to the car, ABE hands his bag up to the CONDUCTOR, then lifts TAD up. MARY, ROBERT, WILLIE and the MAID get on board, while ABE steps over to talk to NINIAN and the others. During this, there is considerable commotion at the left, as the crowd tries to surge forward.)*

MAJOR *(rushing forward)*

Keep 'em back! Keep 'em back, men!

(The SOLDIERS have broken their file on the platform and are in line, facing the crowd. KAVANAGH and his men are close to ABE. Each of them has his hand on his revolver, and is keeping a sharp lookout.)

KAVANAGH

Better get on board, Mr. President.

(ABE climbs up on to the car's back platform. There is a great increase in the cheering when the crowd sees him. They shout: "Speech! Speech! Give us a speech, Abe! Speech, Mr. President! Hurray for Old Abe!" Etc. . . . ABE turns to the crowd, takes his hat off and waves it with a half-hearted gesture. The cheering dies down.)

NINIAN

They want you to say something, Abe.

(For a moment, ABE stands still, looking off to the left.)

ABE

My dear friends—I have to say good-bye to you. I am going now to Washington, with my new whiskers—of which I hope you approve.

(The crowd roars with laughter at that. More shouts of "Good Old Abe!" In its exuberant enthusiasm, the crowd again surges forward, at and around the SOLDIERS, who shout, "Get back, there! Stand back, you!")

ABE *(to the MAJOR)*

It's all right—let them come on. They're all old friends of mine.

(The MAJOR allows his men to retreat so that they form a ring about the back of the car. KAVANAGH and his men are on the car's

steps, watching. The crowd—an assortment of townspeople, including some Negroes—fills the stage.)

ABE

No one, not in my situation, can appreciate my feelings of sadness at this parting. To this place, and the kindness of you people, I owe everything. I have lived here a quarter of a century, and passed from a young to an old man. Here my children have been born and one is buried. I now leave, not knowing when or whether ever I may return. I am called upon to assume the Presidency at a time when eleven of our sovereign states have announced their intention to secede from the Union, when threats of war increase in fierceness from day to day. It is a grave duty which I now face. In preparing for it, I have tried to enquire: what great principle or ideal is it that has kept this Union so long together? And I believe that it was not the mere matter of separation of the colonies from the motherland, but that sentiment in the Declaration of Independence which gave liberty to the people of this country and hope to all the world. This sentiment was the fulfillment of an ancient dream, which men have held through all time, that they might one day shake off their chains and find freedom in the brotherhood of life. We gained democracy, and now there is the question whether it is fit to survive. Perhaps we have come to the dreadful day of awakening, and the dream is ended. If so, I am afraid it must be ended forever. I cannot believe that ever again will men have the opportunity we have had. Perhaps we should admit that, and concede that our ideals of liberty and equality are decadent and doomed. I have heard of an eastern monarch who once charged his wise men to invent him a sentence which would be true and appropriate in all times and situations. They presented him the words, "And this too shall pass away." That is a comforting thought in time of affliction—"And this too shall pass away." And yet— (*Suddenly he speaks with quiet but urgent authority.*) —let us believe that it is not true! Let us live to prove that we can cultivate the natural world that is about us, and the intellectual and moral world that is within us, so that we may secure an individual, social and political prosperity, whose course shall be forward, and which, while the earth endures, shall not pass away. . . . I commend you to the care of the Almighty, as I hope that in your prayers you will remember me. . . . Goodbye, my friends and neighbors.

(*He leans over the railing of the car platform to say good-bye to* NINIAN, ELIZABETH, JOSH, BILLY *and* CRIMMIN, *shaking each by the hand. The band off-stage strikes up "John Brown's Body." The cheering swells. The* CONDUCTOR *looks at his watch and speaks to the* MAJOR, *who gets on board the train. The crowd on stage is shouting "Good-bye, Abe," "Good-bye, Mr. Lincoln," "Good luck, Abe," "We trust you, Mr. Lincoln.")*

(*As the band swings into the refrain, "Glory, Glory Hallelujah," the crowd starts to sing, the number of voices increasing with each word.*)

(KAVANAGH *tries to speak to* ABE *but can't be heard. He touches* ABE'S *arm, and* ABE *turns on him, quickly.*)

KAVANAGH

Time to pull out, Mr. President. Better get inside the car.

(*These words cannot be heard by the audience in the general uproar of singing.* NINIAN, ELIZABETH, JOSH *and* BILLY *are up on the station platform. The* SOLDIERS *are starting to climb up on to the trains.* ABE *gives one last wistful wave of his hat to the crowd, then turns and goes into the car, followed by* KAVANAGH, *the* MAJOR *and the* SOLDIERS. *The band reaches the last line of the song.*)

ALL (*singing*)

His soul goes marching on.

(*The* BRAKEMAN, *downstage, is waving his lantern. The* CONDUCTOR *swings aboard. The crowd is cheering, waving hats and handkerchiefs. The shrill screech of the engine whistle sounds from the right.*)

CURTAIN

————

SCENE 10 (1860)

The three characters who enter this scene—Sturveson, Barrick and Crimmin—are of course apocryphal and not based on any of Lincoln's contemporaries. Their purpose in the play, obviously, is to represent the world into which the crossroads politician was being drawn.

Lincoln's views on religion, as expressed in his reply to Doctor Barrick, are taken from F. B. Carpenter's *Six Months at the White House with Abraham Lincoln*. Mrs. Lincoln once said of her husband, "He never joined a church, but he was still a religious man. But it was a kind of poetry in his nature, and he never was a technical Christian." That was as good a way as any of accounting for the manifold, unfathomable mysteries in Abraham Lincoln: "It was a kind of poetry in his nature." That is why Sandburg is the perfect biographer.

Later on, in Washington, Lincoln attended regularly the Presbyterian Church, but never joined it. Stephenson has written, "His religion flowered in his later temper. It did not, to be sure, overcome his melancholy. That was too deeply laid. Furthermore, we fail to discover in the surviving evidences any certainty that it was a glad phase of religion. Neither the ecstatic joy of the wild women, which his mother had, nor the placid joy of the ritualist, which he did not understand, nor those other variants of the joy of faith, were included in his portion. It was a lofty but grave religion. . . ." In fact, a form of religion inherited from his forebears of Puritan New England but qualified by his own eternal doubts and broadened by his own essential liberalism. If he knew any form of spiritual gladness, it was what has been called by another descendant of the Puritans, Mr. Justice Oliver Wendell Holmes, "the secret isolated joy of the thinker."

Lincoln's most vigorous statements on the relationship of capital and labor were made in an address delivered to a gathering of Wisconsin farmers at the State Fair in Milwaukee on September 30th, 1859, and he repeated these statements and enlarged upon them in his Message to Congress in December, 1861. Near the beginning of the Milwaukee speech you may find a paragraph which is a superb example of his humor and his artful method of winning the attention and affection of a crowd of strangers. He said, "I presume I am not expected to employ the time assigned me in the mere flattery of the farmers as a class. My opinion of them is that, in proportion to numbers, they are neither better nor worse than other people. In the nature of things they are more numerous than any other class; and I believe there really are more attempts at flattering them than any other, the reason of which I can not perceive, unless it be that they can cast more votes than any other. On reflection, I am not quite sure that there is not cause of suspicion against you in selecting me, in some sort a politician and in no sort a farmer, to address you." (A year later, in the Presidential election, he carried Wisconsin by a handsome majority.)

This tenth scene (and I have mentioned this point before in these notes) may seem to over-emphasize Lincoln's shrinking from great responsibility, suggesting again that he never sought public office for himself, but was always being thrust into it by others. Such was not my intention in writing the play, but it is evidently the impression that has been conveyed to many.

It is true that Lincoln's friends always displayed more confidence in him than he did in himself, and that his *persona* (to employ just one word out of psychoanalysis) was that of a man who is reluctant to advance, indifferent to fame and fortune. Nevertheless, it is a mistake to assume that he never pulled any strings on his own behalf. He pulled many, and he did it with consummate skill. He was, in fact, one of the most artful campaigners that ever lived. When he could finally make up his mind that he wanted office and that he was fitted for it he went about the getting of it in a manner that was infinitely crafty. I don't know just when the Presidential bee entered his bonnet, but it was probably a lot earlier than any one knew at the time. He wrote a great number of letters to influential men, choosing his words carefully so as not to commit himself but still managing to suggest that he might be available. All of these letters ended with strict injunctions to secrecy—"burn this," etc.—but fortunately his orders were not always obeyed. In politics, as in everything else (except perhaps his humor) he was a profoundly subtle man. But—in politics, as in everything else, he was a bewilderingly contradictory one.

He worked hard, if silently, to win the Republican nomination. He sent $100 to a Kansas friend to help him get to the Chicago Convention, and he enclosed many instructions with the money. Others of his friends, such as Judge David Davis, Orville H. Browning, Judge Stephen T. Logan, Norman B. Judd and Leonard Swett, many of whom had known him since the New Salem days, were in Chicago working furiously, bargaining, trading, playing off such masters of the craft as Thurlow Weed and Horace Greeley against one another, preparing one of the most astounding coups in the history of political chicanery. While the Convention was in session, Lincoln was in Springfield, playing handball and (according to Herndon) steadying his nerves with an occasional glass of beer. But he was in close touch with his own shock troops at the front.

Nobody of any prominence in the highest councils of the party thought that Lincoln had the remotest chance of winning the nomination. Seward was far in the lead, and certainly deserved to win. But Lincoln's strategy had been brilliantly prepared, and his lieutenants were not too heavily burdened with the scruples that have wrecked many a political boom. The crisis came during the night before the first ballot was taken. Judge Davis and the others were sweating and struggling to win various delegations, notably Pennsylvania's, by munificent offers of jobs. It was at that crucial moment that Lincoln let them down.

Whether his conscience triumphed over his political ambition, or his nerve failed him, he suddenly shrank back and refused to go through with the disreputable business. Davis telegraphed him that they could make a deal to capture the Pennsylvania delegates if Lincoln would promise the office of Secretary of the Treasury to that dubious politician, Governor Simon Cameron. Lincoln replied, "I authorize no bargains and will be bound by none." Later, at literally the eleventh hour, he sent a messenger to Chicago with a heavily underlined message, "Make no contracts that will bind me."

This strange reneging by their candidate caused consternation among the frantic men in Lincoln headquarters. Jesse K. Dubois said, "Damn Lincoln!" Judge Davis, more practically, said, "Lincoln ain't here, and don't know what we have to meet, so we will go ahead, as if we hadn't heard from him, and he must ratify it!"

So the corrupt bargains were made, and Lincoln gained the nomination, and he did ratify it—although with a bitterness that found expression in these words (which are quoted in the next scene): "They have gambled me all around, bought and sold me a hundred times. I can not begin to fill the pledges made in my name."

Cameron became Secretary of War in a cabinet which ranks amongst the worst that have ever sat about a White House table.

Nevertheless, if Lincoln played ball with the boys before he became President, he stopped it afterward. He provided many stunning surprises for those (including the estimable Seward) who thought he would be malleable, tractable, and take orders. There is probably no other Chief Executive in our history who so thoroughly deserved the term Chief. Lincoln came to rule with an iron hand, taking but little advice and no orders from any one. In this way he gained the hatred and the attempted insubordination of those who had thought he would be easily bossed, but he gained the admiration and the invaluable friendship of Seward.

A memorandum which Lincoln read to his Cabinet in the last year of the Civil War is eloquent: "I must myself be the judge how long to retain in and when to remove any of you from his position. It would greatly pain me to discover any of you endeavoring to procure another's removal, or in any way to prejudice him before the public . . . My wish is that on this subject no remark be made nor question asked by any of you, here or elsewhere, now or hereafter."

Thus the humble Illinois sucker. Eight hours after his death, leaders of the Republican Party gathered and discussed plans "to get rid of the last vestige of Lincolnism." (You will find a fine description of this in Claude G. Bowers' powerful, shocking book, *The Tragic Era*.) At that meeting of political gangsters the horrors of the Reconstruction Period were gleefully plotted. One of those present was George Washington Julian, chairman of the Committee of Public Lands in the House of Representatives, and it is to his long unpublished diary that we are indebted for the knowledge that among his associates "The hostility for Lincoln's policy of conciliation and contempt for his weakness" were "undisguised" and that "his death is a Godsend to our cause."

The boys in the back room were grateful to John Wilkes Booth for killing that one, solitary, strong man whose policy was based on the belief that "a just and lasting peace" might be achieved "with malice toward none; with charity for all."

Any one who doubts that Lincoln was absolute ruler of the United States of America during four years of emergency has only to contemplate the chaotic orgy of corruption which followed his death. Andrew Johnson turned out to be an honorable man, but neither he nor Seward nor any one else in the administration had the personal power of control which went to the grave with Lincoln.

However—I'm straying far from this play.

SCENE 11 (1860)

The Presidential election which was held on November 6, 1860, was the most terrific in its excitement in our history. Not that there was any particular uncertainty as to the count of the votes, for Lincoln's election was virtually assured; but the country knew that these ballots could start fires of hatred which might never be put out. As was said at the time, Southern patriots were working to gain victory in this election, but they would not accept defeat!

As the nation went to the polls that day, Lincoln could read in the newspapers that Governor Gist of South Carolina had recommended the use of all available means for arming every man in the State between the ages of eighteen and forty-five, urging the need for such drastic action because, as he told the Legislature, "of the probability of the election to the Presidency of a sectional candidate by a party committed to the support of measures which if carried out will inevitably destroy our equality in the Union, and ultimately reduce the Southern States to mere provinces of a consolidated despotism."

These sentiments were wildly cheered throughout the South and other States were preparing to take similar measures. Small wonder that Lincoln was moved to say that "the task before me is greater than that which rested on Washington."

It is worth remembering that no man ever assumed the Presidency with so little of experience in public life to guide him. All other Presidents down to the present day had gained some substantial prominence as statesmen, soldiers, or, at least, as vote-getters, before receiving nomination to the highest office. Even those Vice-Presidents who acceded through death—Tyler, Johnson, Arthur, Theodore Roosevelt and Coolidge—had far more in their records to recommend them than did Lincoln, who had served only in the State Assembly when he was in his twenties and one inconspicuous term in Congress when he was in his thirties, and had never done anything to reveal any degree of executive ability. But he faced the greatest task of them all. He had reason for nervousness on November 6, 1860.

In this eleventh scene is one speech that has been much criticized and deplored by good people who revere Lincoln's memory and who cannot believe that he ever cursed at his wife. There is certainly overwhelming evidence of the fact that, in the years in the White House, he treated the obstreperous Mrs. Lincoln with unfailing courtesy and tender considerateness. This was his public behavior and, so far as any one can know, his private behavior, as well.

Nevertheless, I did not feel that this play concerning a part of the tragedy of Lincoln's life would be complete in its attempted honesty if I did not include the admission that, on occasion, his monumental patience snapped. That it did, before the move from Springfield, there can be no doubt. Usually he met her tirades with stony silence, or abrupt departure, or with laughter (the most infuriating response of all). But Herndon records that at least once, when she had run him out of the house and was chasing him down Eighth Street, and they approached some church-goers, he turned on her, picked her up, spanked her, and thrust her back into the house, saying, "There, now, stay in the house and don't be a damned fool before the people."

Feeling that one such outburst from Lincoln to his wife was necessary, I placed it in this scene on Election Night, considering that this was the most appropriate moment, with the nerves of both so severely strained.

In this eleventh scene is reference to the letter from a little girl suggesting that Lincoln should grow a beard. Her name was Grace Bedell, of New York, and Lincoln's reply to her, written two weeks before the election, was as follows:

"My dear little Miss: Your very agreeable letter of the 15th is received. I regret the necessity of saying I have no daughter. I have three sons—one seventeen, one nine, and one seven years of age. They, with their mother, constitute my whole family. As to the whiskers, having never worn any, do you not think people would call it a piece of silly affectation if I were to begin it now? Your very sincere well-wisher, A. Lincoln."

In the election, Lincoln received about 40 per cent of the popular vote, Douglas about 30 per cent, with the rest divided between Breckenridge and Bell. In the Electoral College, Lincoln had 180 votes to 123 for the other three.

SCENE 12 (1861)

There is no exaggeration in the suggestion that Lincoln's life was constantly threatened after his election, or that he himself was unresponsive to the attempts to guard him from assassination. He knew that there were many brave, desperate men determined to prevent him from taking the oath of office on March 4th, but he protested against bodyguards by saying, "What's the use of putting up a gap when the fence is down all around?" He did send Thomas S. Mather, Adjutant-General of Illinois, to Washington to sound out General Winfield Scott, a Virginian, on his loyalty to the new administration. Scott, who was known as "Old Fuss and Feathers," sent back these words: "Say to him that, when once here, I shall consider myself responsible for his safety. If necessary I'll plant cannon at both ends of Pennsylvania Avenue, and if any show their hands or even venture to raise a finger, I'll blow them to hell." On his journey East Lincoln was warned to keep out of the free city of Baltimore, and a plot was discovered to blow up his train. He was compelled to travel from Harrisburg to Washington in strictest secrecy, so that he literally slunk into the capital.

The farewell speech from the train platform in this final scene, like the Douglas debate speech, is a blend of several of Lincoln's utterances, starting with the moving words he actually delivered to his neighbors on this occasion. The lines about the "sentiment in the Declaration of Independence," were from his speech in Independence Hall, in Philadelphia, on Washington's

Birthday, eleven days later. The mystic lines about the Eastern monarch and his wise men were from the address given to farmers in Milwaukee a year and a half previously.

There is, in this farewell speech, one group of words which seems to me a particularly fine example of Lincoln's poetry: "not knowing when or whether ever I may return." That strange and beautiful construction is comparable to "The world will little note nor long remember . . ." in the Gettysburg address.

The play ends with words written by Thomas Brigham Bishop (not, as many people suppose, by Julia Ward Howe): "His soul goes marching on." They referred originally to John Brown, whose body lay a-mouldering in the grave when the first regiments marched off to war in 1861; but they express now the most important of all facts about Abraham Lincoln—the fact that, by the eternal nature of the truths that he uttered, he can never die.

In these notes I have quoted many authorities on his life, and I shall now quote from an article, published in the *Locomotive Engineers Journal*, which provides stirring testimony to the extent of his influence upon men of good will the world over. It was written by the late B. Charney Vladeck shortly after he first came to this country, a Jewish refugee from oppression in Tsarist Russia. Vladeck had been a member of the Bolshevist Party, had voted at the meeting which had elected Lenin their leader, and had served in prison for his revolutionary activities. He then emigrated to America, a man whose heart was filled with bitterness—and he learned here that those illusive words, liberty and equality, may have profound meaning. He became a good and useful American citizen, and in the last year of his life was chosen leader of the coalition of liberal Republicans, Democrats and Labor Party members of the Council of the City of New York.

"One of my first and most memorable lessons in Americanization," he wrote, "was Lincoln's Gettysburg address. When I read it and reread it and learned it by heart, struck by its noble clearness and sweeping faith in America, I felt as if the whole past of this country had been lit up by a row of warm and beautiful lights; as if some unknown friend had taken me by the hand on a dark and uncertain road, saying gently: 'Don't doubt and don't despair. This country has a soul and a purpose and, if you so wish, you may love it without regrets' . . .

"On the winding highway of American history I picture Lincoln as a sad but gentle landscape, permeated with the beauty of eternity. I ennobled myself by trying to understand him, and I am grateful to America for making him possible."

Here, in these glowing words from one who had been a deeply skeptical alien, is the essence of what we like to call "Americanization," but which is actually just what Lincoln meant it to be: liberation. Those who study Lincoln most closely know that he was no chauvinistic flag-waver—and may God forgive the loud-mouthed Fourth of July orators who wave the American flag boastfully in his name. The reason that he lives today, and still inspires so many men everywhere with the will to shake off their chains and find freedom and opportunity in the brotherhood of life, is that he was essentially a citizen of the world. In a letter from the White House, he wrote: "The strongest bond of human sympathy, outside of the family relation, should be one uniting all working people, of all nations, and tongues, and kindreds." He was never parochial, never nationalistic; he was never heard to utter thanks for that providential accident of geography which gave us the protection of the Atlantic Ocean. In his recorded speeches and letters, from his earliest frontier days, he spoke not as a representative of any one community, any one faith or class, but as a member of the whole human race. He was forever conscious of the obligation of all Americans to their brethren in all other lands—to "the Liberal party throughout the world"— to make the democratic spirit live and grow.

In the speech that he gave in Independence Hall, ten days before his first Inaugural, he said: "I have often enquired of myself what great principle or idea it was that kept this Confederacy so long together. It was not the mere matter of separation of the colonies from the motherland, but that sentiment in the Declaration of Independence which gave liberty not alone to the people of this country, but hope to all the world, for all future time." And he added: "If this country can not be saved without giving up that principle, I would rather be assassinated on this spot than surrender it."

In his first Message to Congress, when he was discussing most soberly the results of the firing on Fort Sumter, he said: "This issue embraces more than the fate of these United States. It presents to the whole family of man the question whether a constitutional republic or democracy—a government of the people by the same people—can or cannot maintain its territorial integrity against its own domestic foes."

Four years later, at his second Inaugural, in the last weeks of his life, he repeated Christ's words, "Woe unto the world because of offenses! for it must needs be that offenses come; but woe to that man by whom the offense cometh!"

1939

Raymond Massey in the Broadway production of *Abe Lincoln in Illinois*, drawn for the theater playbill by Norman Rockwell (1938). *Reproduced by permission of the Norman Rockwell Family Agency, Inc.*

Carl Sandburg

Central to the durable legend of Lincoln as Everyman is the image of
the rugged frontiersman forced to awkwardly squeeze his long, lanky
frame into constricting formal clothing, compelled by Washington
society to learn social graces that he wisely saw as superficial. In truth,
Lincoln willingly purchased lavish, expensive ensembles for each of
his inaugurals and was delighted with receiving frequent gifts of hats,
canes, and other fancy accessories. If he experienced constant difficulty with gloves, it was only because his enormous hands did not
easily fit into those of commercial manufacture, not, as the poet suggests here, because he was otherwise engaged in more important
tasks, such as preserving free government.

Mr. Lincoln and His Gloves

Mr. Lincoln on his way to Washington
to be the President of the United States
stays in New York City two days
and one night goes to the Opera.
Sits in a box, his lean speaking hands
    on a red velvet railing.
And the audience notices something.
Yes, notices.
Mr. Lincoln is wearing gloves
                kid gloves
                black kid gloves.

The style
the vogue
the fashion is white kid gloves.
On the main floor
in the balcony
in the boxes
the gloves are correct and white.

A gentleman in another box tells his ladies:
"I think we ought to send some flowers over the way
to the Undertaker of the Union."

Soon we see Mr. Lincoln in Washington kissing the Bible
swearing to be true to the Constitution.

Lincoln holding in his heart these words:
"I have not willingly planted a thorn in any man's bosom.
I shall do nothing through malice.
What I deal with is too vast for malice."

Now we see Mr. Lincoln at a White House reception
His fingers swollen, his white gloves
    twisted by a mob of handshakes.
His right hand at last giving an extra strong handshake
to an Illinois man, an Illinois man he knew long ago.
Then it happens!
His right glove cracks and goes to pieces.
He holds his hand up, looks at the dangling glove.
"Well, my old friend, this is a general bustification,
you and I were never meant to wear these things."

Another time, Mr. Lincoln rides away in a White House
    carriage.
Next to him an old western friend, wearing brand new
        white kid gloves.
Mr. Lincoln notices, can't help noticing those brand
    new white tight gloves.
Mr. Lincoln digs down into his pocket.
Feels around and brings out his own brand new white
    kid gloves,
begins squeezing his fingers and thumbs in
when the old friend cries:
"No, no, Mr. Lincoln,
put up your gloves, Mr. Lincoln."

And they ride along, talk and joke, no more bother,
                   sitting pretty
                   sitting easy
                   as two old worn gloves.

Often Mr. Lincoln cannot find his gloves.
Sometimes Mr. Lincoln forgets his gloves.
Often Mrs. Lincoln gives him a new pair, a nice, correct
fashionable pair of gloves.

And one day a California newspaper man
sees him hunting in his overcoat pocket
for a pair of gloves.
Bringing out one pair
he digs deeper
and brings out another pair.
Then into another pocket.
Out comes
               three
               four
               five
               six
               seven
               more pairs of gloves.

That was one time
if Mr. Lincoln had anything plenty of
it was gloves.

You and I may be sure Mr. Lincoln never in his life
felt sorry for himself about his gloves.

When he forgot his gloves
maybe he was too deep with remembering
men fighting, men dying, on consecrated ground.
Too deep with remembering
his hope
"Government of the people

by the people
for the people
shall not perish from the earth."

And there is no good reason why you,
                        why I,
                        why we
                        should ever worry
about Mr. Lincoln and his gloves.

c. 1942

Melvin B. Tolson

Born in Moberly, Missouri, Tolson (1898–1966) graduated from Lincoln University in Pennsylvania and taught at Wiley College in Marshall, Texas, from 1923 to 1947. (His achievements as the college debate coach inspired the 2007 film *The Great Debaters*, directed by, and starring, Denzel Washington.) Tolson's first published collection of poetry, *Rendezvous with America* (1944)—from which "The Dictionary of the Wolf" is taken—demonstrated his interest in the forgotten and overlooked characters of history. The title of the poem alludes to the "the wolf's dictionary," a term Lincoln used in his 1864 address at the Baltimore Sanitary Fair to describe the rationale for slavery, and lines 1–2 and 9–12 are quotes or paraphrases from the President's speech; the last two lines, and the mysterious prediction they convey, are entirely Tolson's own.

The Dictionary of the Wolf

"We all declare for liberty," Lincoln said.
"We use the word and mean all sorts of things:
In the sweat of thy face shalt thou eat bread.
Rifle the basket that thy neighbor brings."

The grizzled axman squinted at Honest Abe,
The six feet four of him, gaunt, sad of face,
The hands to split a log or cradle a babe,
The cracked palm hat, the homespun of his race.

"The wolf tears at the sheep's throat: and the sheep
Extols the shepherd for cudgeling tyranny;
The wolf, convulsed with indignation deep,
Accuses the shepherd of murdering liberty.

"But the dictionary of the wolf is writ
In words the rats of time chew bit by bit."

1944

Carl Sandburg

A wartime ode to Lincoln's magisterial 1862 annual message to Congress—itself a haunting rumination on the past and the future—this aptly titled "litany" offers a numbing accounting of sacrifice, including the ultimate offering made by the "sad . . . cool . . . kind" leader whose wit was but a "guard and cover" for a melancholy recognition of challenges yet to come. By the time he published this poem in early 1945, Sandburg was almost universally acknowledged as the nation's premier spokesman on Lincoln. In the postwar era he would become an on-screen commentator discussing Lincoln in television documentaries, a celebrity who read the Gettysburg Address on the Ed Sullivan show, and the orator who addressed a joint session of Congress held on February 12, 1959, to mark Lincoln's 150th birthday. The "most enduring memorial to Lincoln," he suggested that day in an otherwise surprisingly prosaic speech, could be found "in the hearts of lovers of liberty . . . who understand that wherever there is freedom there have been those who fought, toiled, and sacrificed for it."

The Long Shadow of Lincoln: A Litany

(We can succeed only by concert. . . . The dogmas of the quiet past are inadequate to the stormy present. The occasion is piled high with difficulty, and we must rise with the occasion. As our case is new so we must think anew and act anew. We must disenthrall ourselves. . . . DECEMBER 1, 1862. *The President's Message to Congress*.)

> Be sad, be cool, be kind,
> remembering those now dreamdust
> hallowed in the ruts and gullies,
> solemn bones under the smooth blue sea,
> faces warblown in a falling rain.
>
> Be a brother, if so can be,
> to those beyond battle fatigue
> each in his own corner of earth

or forty fathoms undersea
beyond all boom of guns,
beyond any bong of a great bell,
each with a bosom and number,
each with a pack of secrets,
each with a personal dream and doorway
and over them now the long endless winds
      with the low healing song of time,
      the hush and sleep murmur of time.

Make your wit a guard and cover.
Sing low, sing high, sing wide.
Let your laughter come free
remembering looking toward peace:
"We must disenthrall ourselves."

Be a brother, if so can be,
to those thrown forward
for taking hardwon lines,
for holding hardwon points
      and their reward so-so,
little they care to talk about,
their pay held in a mute calm,
highspot memories going unspoken,
what they did being past words,
what they took being hardwon.
      Be sad, be kind, be cool.
            Weep if you must
      And weep open and shameless
            before these altars.

There are wounds past words.
There are cripples less broken
than many who walk whole.
      There are dead youths
      with wrists of silence
      who keep a vast music

under their shut lips,
what they did being past words,
their dreams like their deaths
beyond any smooth and easy telling,
having given till no more to give.

There is dust alive
with dreams of The Republic,
with dreams of the Family of Man
flung wide on a shrinking globe
with old timetables,
old maps, old guide-posts
torn into shreds,
shot into tatters,
burnt in a firewind,
lost in the shambles,
faded in rubble and ashes.

There is dust alive.
Out of a granite tomb,
Out of a bronze sarcophagus,
Loose from the stone and copper
Steps a whitesmoke ghost
Lifting an authoritative hand
In the name of dreams worth dying for,
In the name of men whose dust breathes
of those dreams so worth dying for,
what they did being past words,
beyond all smooth and easy telling.

Be sad, be kind, be cool,
remembering, under God, a dreamdust
hallowed in the ruts and gullies,
solemn bones under the smooth blue sea,
faces warblown in a falling rain.

Sing low, sing high, sing wide.
Make your wit a guard and cover.
Let your laughter come free
like a help and a brace of comfort.

The earth laughs, the sun laughs
over every wise harvest of man,
over man looking toward peace
by the light of the hard old teaching:
    "We must disenthrall ourselves."

1945

Adlai E. Stevenson

The national standard bearer for American liberalism in the 1950s, Stevenson (1900–1965) had family roots in both parties: his grandfather served as vice-president in Grover Cleveland's second term, while his great-grandfather Jesse W. Fell was an Illinois Republican who helped promote Lincoln's candidacy in 1860. Elected governor of Illinois by a landslide in 1948, Stevenson made these remarks at a Gettysburg ceremony commemorating the 88th anniversary of Lincoln's address. He used the occasion to enlist the 16th President in the cause of liberal internationalism, casting him as an opponent of isolationism and McCarthyism, and as a supporter of collective security—and, by implication, the ongoing war in Korea. Stevenson's eloquence won him the Democratic nomination in 1952, but proved incapable of defeating Dwight Eisenhower in the fall. On election night Stevenson ended his concession speech by quoting remarks traditionally attributed to Lincoln after an unsuccessful campaign: "He said he felt like a little boy who had stubbed his toe in the dark. He said that he was too old to cry but it hurt too much to laugh."

Remarks at Gettysburg

We are met here today on the field of a bloody, shattering battle. And we meet in reverence for the tall, gaunt man who, standing here 88 years ago, mindful of the dead and the cause for which they here died, phrased in words, clean of all ornament, the duty of the living to continue the struggle. The struggle did continue, the high fever that was Gettysburg passed, and the democratic experiment survived its mortal crisis.

More than the survival of the American Union was at issue here at Gettysburg. Upon the fate of the Union hung the fate of the new dream of democracy throughout the world. For in Lincoln's time the United States was the only major country of the world that enjoyed the democratic form of government, the only land where government was of, by, and for the people. America was democracy's proving ground. The masses of other lands looked to us with hope. If our experiment proved successful, they too might win self-government. But the cynics and the privileged, regarding our experiment with foreboding, identified it with mob rule and lawlessness, sneered and prophesied its doom. When civil war broke out they said: "We told you so."

But Lincoln saw the war in its global dimensions. He was a man of peace, yet even the horror of a brothers' war was not too great a price to save the Union and to demonstrate the viability and the superiority of government by the people.

As Lincoln saw it, the Confederate States had rejected two fundamental precepts of democracy. First, in refusing to accept him as their President and making his election their justification for withdrawing from the Union, they had violated the first rule of democratic government, the obligation of a minority to abide by the result of an election. Without such acquiescence democracy would not work. The Union must never be dissevered for any such reason as this.

Second, in making slavery the foundation stone of their new government, the Confederacy was renouncing the doctrine of the equal rights of man in favor of the creed of the master race, an idea that Lincoln abhorred. "The last, best hope of earth," in his view, was to be found in our Declaration of Independence which affirmed that all men are created equal, that they are endowed by their Creator with certain inalienable rights, among which are life, liberty, and the pursuit of happiness.

Here, in fact, was the whole pith and substance of Lincoln's political philosophy. Here, in his deep reverence for the rights of man as proclaimed in our American charter of freedom, is to be found the explanation of most of his political actions. "I have never had a feeling politically," he said, "which did not spring from the sentiments embodied in the Declaration of Independence." It was these principles, Lincoln believed, that would lift artificial weights from men's shoulders, clear the paths of laudable pursuit for all, and afford everyone an unfettered start and a fair chance in the race of life.

When we realize that Lincoln saw the dissolution of the Union as a threat to democratic aspirations throughout the world, his words at Gettysburg become more meaningful. Chancellorsville, Antietam, Chickamauga and Gettysburg were deciding more than the fate of these United States. Americans were dying for the new, revolutionary idea of the free man, even as they had died at Bunker Hill and Yorktown. They were dying to save the hope of all people everywhere.

So when Lincoln was asked to speak at the dedication of this cemetery, he welcomed the chance to tell the people what those three days of bloody battle meant and to explain what those men died for, as he saw it.

His thoughts went back four score and seven years to the revolutionary founding of this nation, conceived in liberty and dedicated to the proposition that all men are created equal. Then his mind came back to the war being fought to determine whether that nation, or any nation conceived in revolution and dedicated to such radical principles, could long endure—whether the people were capable of shaping their own destiny. He thought of the heroic dead, and of what the living owed them for their sacrifice. Mere words could not express it. The world, he thought, would little note nor long remember what was said that day. Then he looked ahead—not merely to the tomorrow, but into the far distant future, as he said: "It is for us, the living, rather to be here dedicated to the great task remaining before us . . . that these dead shall not have died in vain."

The war ended. The nation, reunited, once again offered hope for liberal yearnings everywhere. Inspired by the example of America, democracy made striking headway throughout the world, even among the so-called backward peoples of the earth. It seemed that the principles for which Lincoln fought and died would win world-wide acceptance. America took it for granted. To us it became merely a question of when and how. Busy building up a rich continent, America lost sight of its mission.

Then came the shock of World War I. But with victory, democracy took up its march again. Russia, most reactionary of all European countries, was in revolt against autocracy. Germany, Austria, Czechoslovakia, became republics. Woodrow Wilson, who, even as Lincoln, saw the fate of democracy as the prime issue of the war, went to Europe with a purpose to mark out new boundaries which would express, as nearly as possible, the people's will. Democracy was again in the ascendant. But America, mindless of her mission, following the soft voices of men of little vision, shrouded herself in isolation.

The rest is within the recollection of us all. Adolph Hitler resurrected the malevolent doctrine of the master race, and poised its ghastly death's head over Europe. And now comes imperial Communism, stalking freedom throughout the world.

The struggle for human liberty goes on. The great bearers of our tradition have believed in it not because they were born in it, but because they saw despotism as we have seen it and turned from it to rediscover the American faith in the free man.

The struggle must be re-fought by every generation and democracy is threatened not alone by hostile ideologies abroad, but by fear, greed, indifference, intolerance, demagoguery and dishonor here at home. Little men spread mistrust, confusion, fear. Careless inquisition and irresponsible accusation increase tensions, and tensions, repressions. The tyranny of organized opinion lifts its ugly head to mock the faith of the American Revolution.

No, Lincoln's fight is not finished. The far future into which he looked is here, and we are now the living. Eight and eighty years after he uttered here those immortal words, it is for us, the living, to be re-dedicated to our democratic faith; to be here dedicated to the great task, the same task, remaining before us. The fight goes on. Cemetery Ridge is shrouded in the mist of history. But American boys are dying today on Heartbreak Ridge far away for the last, best hope of collective security, of peace and of freedom for all, to choose their way of life.

Proud of the past, impatient with what Washington called "the impostures of pretended patriotism," it is for us, the living, to rekindle the hot, indignant fires of faith in the free man, free in body, free in mind, free in spirit, free to hold any opinion, free to search and find the truth for himself; the old faith that is ever new—that burned so brightly here at Gettysburg long ago.

November 19, 1951

James Agee

A novelist, essayist, screenwriter, and influential film critic, Agee (1909–1955) was commissioned in 1952 to write a program about Lincoln for the new CBS television series *Omnibus*. Broadcast in five parts between November 1952 and February 1953, *Mr. Lincoln* proved so popular that it was re-edited into a single 90-minute version, *Abraham Lincoln—The Early Years*. The series was directed by the veteran character actor Norman Lloyd, who—now in his 90s—recently described to the editor of this volume his efforts to make the production as realistic as possible, despite an often constrained budget. In an era when almost all television was studio-bound, much of *Mr. Lincoln* was shot on location in Illinois, Kentucky, Maryland, and New Jersey. (The second unit in Kentucky was directed by the 24-year-old Stanley Kubrick.) Although *Variety* hailed the production as "a superb vidpic" and film historian Mark S. Reinhart has called it "one of the finest Lincoln-related screen works ever produced," the series was criticized by the historian Allan Nevins as overly romantic, especially in its treatment of the Ann Rutledge story. The scene presented here is taken from *Abraham Lincoln—The Early Years*, the re-edited version of the series. Ann Rutledge was played by Joanne Woodward and Lincoln by Royal Dano, who later supplied the voice for the animatronic Lincoln displayed by Walt Disney at the 1964 World's Fair.

FROM

Abraham Lincoln—The Early Years

. . . ACT THREE

FADE IN:

> (*Beside the mill dam—late afternoon. The soft roar of water over the dam, o.s.* ABE *and* ANN *walk toward dam.*)
>
> (CLOSE TWO-SHOT: ABE AND ANN. *They sit by the water, mainly not looking at each other.*)

ANN.   I like your plans, Abe; they've got a lot of common sense in them.

579

ABE.   You don't think I'm a fool, not to care about money?

ANN.   (*After pause.*)   Papa thinks that if—if you only—get some *polish*—some culture—you may go a long way.

    (*A silence.*)

ABE.   (*With difficulty.*)   What became of John McNeil?

ANN.   He went back East, to see about his people.

ABE.   That's what I hear. I mean, is he—comin' back?

ANN.   He plans to.

ABE.   Do you hear from him?

ANN.   No. (*Pause.*) Not yet.

    (*Another silence.* ABE's *face shows the approach of an intensely critical moment in his life.*)

ABE.   (*At last.*)   There's a question I want you to answer me, Miss Ann.

ANN.   (*Corrects him.*)   Ann.

ABE   (*Sacredly.*)   Ann.

    (*Pause.*)

ANN.   What is it you want me to answer?

ABE.   When I first walked into town that mornin', an' met you in the street, did you—did you remember ever seein' me before? (*Pause, trying to coach her.*) I mean, the year before? When my boat went aground, right here?

    (*He indicates the dam.*)

ANN.   (*Ater pause.*) I remembered. Did you remember me?

    (*A pause; unable to speak, he nods.*)

ABE.   There's something I want to tell you.

    (*Speechless again.*)

ANN.   Well, what is it you want to tell me?

ABE.   You know why I come—came back to New Salem?

ANN.   'Cause Offut saw how you handled the boat, and gave you a job.

ABE.   No: that was just my excuse. I—it—I came back because of you.

    (*He looks at her, and quickly away; she looks at him, fondly. She starts to obey an impulse to put her hand on his, but—considering what she is about to say—resists it.*)

ANN.   (*Quietly.*)   Abe.

ABE.   (*Unable to look at her.*)   Yes'm?

ANN.   There's something I got to tell *you*.

ABE.   (*Doomed.*) Yes'm?

ANN.   Before John McNeil went back East, I promised that when he came back I'd marry him.

(*A silence.*)

ABE.   (*Almost inaudibly.*) Yes'm.

(*A silence.*)

ANN.   But I want you for a friend, Abe. I mean, if you're willing. I like you. I like talking with you. (*Pause.*) I don't ever want to lose your friendship:—if you're willing.

(*A long pause; then he brings himself to meet her eyes. The bad news has just about wrecked him. A pause.*)

ABE.   Willin'? (*Pause.*) Sure I am.

(*Their eyes hold; a long pause; both are deeply moved. In distance, we hear a* LIGHT CHURCH BELL; *a watery sound. They clasp hands, as friends, and continue looking at each other. After clasping hands, and looking at each other, and holding this* CLOSE UP *a sufficient time, they get up at leisure, turn from us, and start walking away—close, but not holding hands. Over this getting up and walking away, with* BELL *sound continuing, the* NARRATOR *speaks.*)

NARRATOR.   We have seen how a very young man, Abraham Lincoln, found his place in New Salem, and in a new world. Next we shall see how he fared in his love for Ann Rutledge; and what became of their love; and what effect this had on this young man.

FADE OUT.

FADE UP.

(THE FRONT DOOR — RUTLEDGE HOME. *Over* KNOCKING *o.s.,* ANN RUTLEDGE *hurries to open the door, disclosing a full-length portrait of a new* ABE LINCOLN, *touchingly shy and grotesque in a funereal new suit and ruffled shirt, carrying a new black hat,* NOT A STOVE PIPE.* *He looks to* ANN *sheepishly.*)

(CLOSE SHOT — REVERSE ANGLE — ANN, LOOKING UP AT HIM. *For*

---

*Stove-pipe: high hat. When Lincoln is portrayed with a hat, it is inevitably of this type.

*a moment she tries to control her affectionate laughter; then
she can't.* CLOSE SHOT—ABE, AS BEFORE. ABE *is taken aback;
then a sheepish grin.*)

ABE.   (*Lamely joking.*)   Well, a member of the State Legislature's got to dress up to his job.

ANN.   (*Mischievously.*) . . . Put it on.

ABE.   Put *what* on? Oh.
      (*He puts on the hat.*)

ANN.   Now turn around. (*A hang-dog glance; he does so.*) Now
come on in.

ABE.   I can only stay a minute. I'm already late on my way. To
Vandalia.

ANN.   (*Rather hard hit.*)   Oh.
      (CLOSE TWO-SHOT.)

ABE.   I just wanted to tell you good-by, first.

ANN.   Well, I should *hope* so.

ABE.   I'm goin' to miss you. (*She all but laughs at the inadequacy
of the words, and keeps looking at him hard. A pause. He approaches
a precipice, braces himself, and goes over.*) There's somethin' I
want to say to you. (*Seated.*) It's just this. If I was a man that
was engaged to a girl like you, and I had to go away a while—
if I was that John McNeil, I'd have wrote you. Written you.
That's what!
      (ANN *says nothing; he supposes he has offended her.*)

ABE.   (*Miserable but intense.*)   I just had to speak my mind.
      (*Pause. Now* ANN *makes her big turn in the relationship. She
      does it quietly, with a touch of mischief; confident of the result.*)

ANN.   I'm glad you did because it helps me make up *my* mind.
A woman *needs* a man's help in that, you know. I'm going to
write John tonight, and break off the engagement.
      (*She clearly expects the wow reactions of the suddenly accepted
      suitor; so do we, for he is clearly very much in love. Instead:*)

ABE.   Oh. (*Pause.*) Oh!
      (*He is clearly flabbergasted; so is she, by him:*)

ANN.   I should have thought that was *good* news.

ABE.   *Oh. Yeah. Sure*, Ann. It just sorta knocks the wind outa
me.
      (*Pause.*)

ANN.   Well?

ABE.   Well! *Well!*

(*He is so helpless that tenderness enters her look and voice.*)

ANN.   What troubles you, Abe? (*He looks at her like a doomed calf.*) Can't you tell me—even as a friend?

(*He looks at her in helpless woe. Pause. He shakes his head.*)

ABE.   I'm sorry. *Awful* sorry.

(*Silence.* ANN *rises.*)

ANN.   (*Very quiet.*)   Good-by, Abe. (*This all but ruins him.*) For now. (*He is greatly relieved.*) Try to settle your mind. When you can. *If* you can.

ABE.   Good-by.

ANN.   (*Thinking of* MCCNEIL.)   *You* write me.

ABE.   *Oh! . . . Yeah!*

(*Pause. In painful conflict between his love and his fear,* ABE *seems on the verge of coming through.*)

ABE.   (*Desperate and momentous.*)   Ann!

(*Words fail him.*)

ANN.   (*Ready again.*)   Yes, Abe?

(*They're on the brink of embracing; he can't make it. He shoves out a hand, which she takes.*)

ABE.   (*Just audibly.*)   Good-by.

(*He turns and walks quickly out of the shot. We hold on* ANN, *watching after him, as we hear him ride away. Her eyes dampen with tenderness, frustration, and fury.*)

ANN.   (*Softly.*)   Oh, you fool! (*New thought. She calls out.*) Good-by, Abe! Good luck!

DISSOLVE TO

INTERIOR — VANDALIA — LOBBY

MCCLASON.   (*O.s.*)   Mr. Lincoln!

(WE PULL OR PAN MCCLASON INTO AN ABRUPT TWO-SHOT AND STOP AS ABE STOPS. *They shake hands.* MCCLASON *is a political big shot; prosperous, citified, middle-aged—far above the ward-heeler type.*)

ABE.   Why, howdy Senator McClason!

MCCLASON.   I want a word with you.

ABE.   Glad ye caught me. I was headin' fer home.

MCCLASON.   So am I.

BEEKMAN.   Say, Abe, I'd like to have a word with you before you go.

ABE.   Sure. I'll see you before I go.
   (*They go aside.*)

MCCLASON.   Young man, I've been keeping an eye on you.

ABE.   Afraid I haven't given you much to look at, Senator.

MCCLASON.   Oh, I know your kind: quiet—and smart as a whip. The fact is, I think you're a comer, and so do quite a little group of us, from around Springfield.

BEEKMAN.   Don't forget I want to speak with you, Abe.

ABE.   Oh, I won't forget, Jonathan. (*Very quiet.*) What's your proposition, Senator?

MCCLASON.   (*Taken a little aback.*)   You probably know, there's been talk of moving the capital out of this mud hole. (ABE *nods.*) Well: *we* intend to make *Springfield* the capital.

ABE.   That ought to suit *my* constituents.

MCCLASON.   Well there's a lot of people it doesn't suit, and that's where *you* come in. (ABE *is silent.*) You've got a way with people, young man—'specially, with the country folks. Swing 'em our way. You have my word you won't regret it.
   (ABE *reflects; then, in a curiously cold yet friendly drawl, his eyes hardening:*)

ABE.   Well: I reckon I can swing a thing or two: but there'll be some considerations. (MCCLASON *is taken slightly aback.*) I don't mean money, Senator.
   (MCCLASON *bursts out laughing.*)

MCCLASON.   Don't you worry about "considerations," my boy. We'll settle all that next fall. (*He shakes* ABE's *hand warmly.*) In the meantime, have a good summer.

DISSOLVE TO: EXT.—THE RUTLEDGE DOOR—DAY.

(CLOSE DOWN-SHOT . . . OVER ABE, KNOCKING; ANN *opens the door and looks up at him, serious, speechless, waiting, proud. For her, it is clearly the showdown.*)

(CLOSE UP-SHOT—HER VIEWPOINT. *It's the showdown for him, too. He is in intense conflict and we can expect him to dodge out again; but after a moment, in a sudden reflex of love, he stoops, almost in tears, hands forward, saying:)*

ABE.   I missed you so bad!

CUT TO:

(CLOSE TWO-SHOT: *At first favoring* ANN, *as he takes her by the shoulders and they turn into a* BALANCED TWO-SHOT, *gazing at each other, almost incredulous. Pause. They both feel shaky, smile acknowledgment.)*

(Hands linked, they lead each other to two chairs or a bench on porch or beside door, and sit. They continue to gaze. Silence.)

(More gazing; then they kiss. Parting from it, each, over-whelmed, withdraws for a moment into his private fog of wonder and joy. When their eyes meet again he is a gone goose and she regards herself, almost, as an achieved and happily mar-ried woman. She begins to laugh softly. He looks inquiry; she explains, through her soft laughter.)

ANN.   Those awful *letters* of yours! "Friend Ann." "Affection-ately, your friend, A. Lincoln." Oh, you *jackass!* Do you have any idea how close I was to parting company with you forever?

(This nearly kills him, even now; her tenderness overwhelms him.)

ANN.   *(Tender and luminous.)*   Well, my dear one: thank Heaven it's all over—but the shouting.

(She means, of course, "Marry me now," and awaits that re-sponse confidently. He is terribly drawn by that realization and his own desire but, after silent struggle:)

ABE.   Ann, my dearest: we *can't* marry yet a while.

ANN.   And why not, if you please?

ABE.   I'm a poor man. *Very* poor. And I've got debts. *Bad.* And the only knack I've got with money is to get worse in debt.

(She nods, with loving humor, after each of these statements.)

ANN.   *(Gently.)*   Abe: what sort of woman do you take me for! You think *I* care how poor we are?

ABE.   You're gonna hate the sight of me. But it's the least I owe you, to try. *(Pause.)* All right: *(In quiet despair.)* I don't even want to *waste time*, makin' a livin'. Ann, if we marry now it'll be the finish of me, before I even get started.

ANN.   Appears to me you've made a *pretty good* start.

ABE.   Oh, if *politickin'* was all!

CUT TO:

(CLOSE SHOT—ABE. ANN IN CLOSE SHOT, *listening and watching as well as speaking; her reactions very deeply restrained.*)

ABE.   No, it's a kind of *feeling*, Ann. That there's something *in* me, that I've got to live up to, and take care of, no matter what, or it'd be better if I'd never been born.

ANN.   Can't you tell me what the feeling is?

ABE.   All I know now is, it's something to do with people. Just—how I look up to 'em, Ann. Their sadness. The hard work it is, just being alive. And how *brave* they are about it mostly; and so cheerful. Oh there's times I could just about die, there's so much I wish I could *do* for 'em.

ANN.   You couldn't start by doing for a wife and children?

(*A soft, agonized laugh breaks from* ABE.)

ABE.   I sure can't see why not, most of the time. Other times I know it's like a gun at my head: there isn't time or room to do right by both; not in a lifetime. (*A silence. He's sure he is lost, now; but has a tremendous compulsion at least to be honest with her.*) So I guess I'm just a man who's got to travel light.

CUT TO:

(CLOSE TWO-SHOT.)

ANN.   (*Very quiet.*)   Well. You're even worse off than I guessed. (*Silence; they keep looking at each other; he can't stand it any longer.*)

ABE.   (*Wildly.*)   Oh, what do *I* care! I'll quit *everything*, to do right for you, Ann! I mean it, I want to!

(*He smiles at her desperately; really does mean it; and in a way is happy.*)

ANN.   You do, and I'll never speak to you again. (*He is utterly bewildered.*) Why do you suppose I love you so much!

ABE.   (*Incredulous.*)   You'd still have me?

ANN.   If I can get you.

ABE.   (*Barely daring it.*)   You'll wait?

ANN.   If that's what you think you need.

ABE.   Ann—this'll all clear up—quicker than we can imagine. I'll get those debts paid off. It won't be so long to wait. And meantime we'll be seein' each other. Every bit we can. Why, we're *young*, Ann! We've got a *world* o' time ahead of us! *All our lives*, sweetheart.

(*On this closing phrase we abruptly* PAN TO LOSE ABE *and bring* ANN, *quietly, into a sudden* HEAD CLOSE UP.)

ANN.   All our lives.

DISSOLVE TO: INTERIOR — A SMALL COUNTRY COURT.

(*Held at the house of the local justice, in this case* BOWLING GREEN. CLOSE SHOT: A RURAL SHYSTER *is summing up before the jury of six—i.e., the camera. While he talks we* INTERCUT THE FOLLOWING GROUP AND CLOSE SHOTS WITH HIS OWN SHOT. THE DEFENDANTS, *two very young men, looking sly and smug.* ABE, *nodding calm agreement with his opponent's points.* ABE'S CLIENT, *a pathetic, destitute old guy, terribly dismayed as he watches* ABE. BOWLING GREEN, *on the bench, likewise puzzled by* ABE. MCCLASON *watchful, curious and surprised about* ABE.)

THE SHYSTER.   Gentlemen of the Jury, this old man claims that my clients swindled him out of two heifers. And my clients freely admit to that. But gentlemen, permit me to remind you: at that time, these young men were both under the legal age of twenty-one, therefore, *infants* at that time; and *not morally responsible for their actions*: and therefore they do not come under the jurisdiction of this court, or of any court in the land. You cannot therefore find them guilty, gentlemen.

(*He bows, with a triumphant smirk.* ABE'S *concern for the boys is completely genuine, yet in his speaking manner and his eye, there are shadings of a weird and mischievous gaiety.* ABE *rises.*)

ABE.   Gentlemen of the Jury, as you can see the plaintiff is not an infant. He is of age, and morally responsible, and destitute. You can't hurt him, any more than the years already have; nor can you do much to help him. So let's quit bothering about him. Gentlemen, I stand here on behalf of these two young men. They are *indeed* infants; and mighty smart infants. I think they'll go far. But it's your responsibility, gentlemen, *which way* they'll go far. I am very sorry for these two young men, for at this moment they are in a grievous danger. They stand at a fork in the road. If they leave this courtroom free of guilt, this will be only the beginning of a lifetime wasted, in getting away with wrongdoing. But gentlemen, you can give them a chance to become morally responsible—I mean, to become *men*, rather than older and older *infants*—then I am confident that I can read in their young faces that they will welcome that new chance, and make the best of it. I beseech you: give them their chance. I ask that you return a verdict of guilty against them; that the heifers be restored to their rightful owner, and that the penalty be light.

(*Loud* MURMURS *o.s.*, *of many more people than we at any time see.* CLOSE SHOT—GREEN— *stifling his hilarity and pleasure*)

GREEN.   (*To jury.*)   Gentlemen, you will now retire, deliberate, and reach a verdict.

FOREMAN.   If it please the Court, this jury don't want to retire *or* deliberate, for we have already reached a verdict. We find the defendants guilty as charged, and we ask clemency.

GREEN.   The jury is discharged.

(*A roar of pleasure and applause o.s.* GREEN, *laughing his head off, bangs with his gavel and then gives up.*)

(CLOSE GROUP SHOT—ABE: PEOPLE *crowd in around him, shaking his hand. A solid din of ad lib talk; the old man, grinning with joy and gratitude; a couple of extras we've not seen before;* MCCLASON, *practically ready to knight* ABE; GREEN, *laughing; the two defendants, one of them teary; they fervently pump his hand, thanking him.* CUT IN A COUPLE OF NEW ANGLES *if need be, to point expressions. Through this crush,* JACK *struggles forward, grave and urgent.* ABE *sees him.*)

ABE.   (*Calling over din.*)   You want to see me, Jack? (JACK *nods.* ABE *struggling toward him, continues:*) Thank ye, I'm obliged to ye. 'Scuse me. 'Scuse me.

(NEW ANGLE— *as he reaches* JACK. PAN *as he takes* JACK'S *elbow and they walk aside. Din continues o.s.*)

ABE.   What's the trouble?

JACK.   It's Ann, Abe. She sent me for you.

ABE.   (*He grabs* JACK *by both shoulders.*)   She's . . .

(*The realized possibility deprives him of words.*)

JACK.   It don't look good.

(ABE *gasps and jacknifes over, hands to his caved-in belly.* JACK *puts a hand on his shoulder and, as he speaks, pats the shoulder harder than he knows.*)

JACK.   Come on, boy. Come on, boy.

(ABE *straightens up,* JACK *takes his arm and, as we* PAN, *they walk shakily away from us toward the open door.*)

DISSOLVE TO:

(FULL SHOT — EXT. THE RUTLEDGE HOME — DAY.)

(. . . JAMES RUTLEDGE *sits outside the door.* ALLEN'S *horse is hitched in f.g. Fast hoofbeats o.s.;* JACK *and* ABE *ride into shot, dismount, hitch their horses, and walk fast toward the house.* RUTLEDGE *stands up. He and* ABE *solemnly shake hands.* RUTLEDGE *gestures toward inner house;* ABE *starts for door—which opens as he is about to enter;* DR. ALLEN *comes out.*)

CUT TO: INT. RUTLEDGE HOME.

(CLOSE UP-SHOT — ANN'S DOOR, FROM OUTSIDE, *as it is opened.*)

(CLOSE DOWN-SHOT — ANN, *in her bed, looking up as* ABE *enters o.s. She is as wasted away as make-up can manage, yet has a fierce, unearthly beauty—above all, in the eyes. They epitomize everything she will say and feel in their two hours together. After a moment she lifts her arms forward as if for an embrace.* CLOSE UP-SHOT — ABE, *struck to a standstill at the door. His face is still young in tragedy; he must save a lot for later shots. A moment; then he shuts the door softly behind him and advances into* EXTREME CLOSE SHOT, *his eyes wet.*)

(HEAD-ON, MEDIUM CLOSE SHOT — THE RUTLEDGE DOOR — EXT.)

(WE PAN TO BRING IN RUTLEDGE AND JACK *where they sit, motionless, staring at nothing; and on past them to the corner of the house and the shadow it makes on the ground.* JACK *with horses.*)

LAP DISSOLVE TO: SAME ANGLE AS ABOVE SHOT.

(*Now the shadow has shifted to later in the day. We* REVERSE THE PAN, BRINGING IN JACK AND RUTLEDGE *as before; over them we hear footsteps and they react heavy-heartedly; we* WHIP-SHOT THE PAN TO CATCH ABE, *close as he comes out. His face is terribly altered. Looking at nobody and saying nothing, he walks as close as possible past* CAMERA *and we . . .*)

CUT TO:

(REVERSE ANGLE—FROM WITHIN THE FRAMING, OPEN DOOR *as he walks straight ahead, away from us.*)

(DOWN SHOT—DAY—ANN'S GRAVE—*flowers disintegrating on it.* ABE *lies beside it, face down.* LITERALLY *face down; the face flattened into the ground. His left arm is flung across the grave and nearby there is a large butcher knife.*)

UP-SHOT—JACK.

(*He is exhausted, and half sick with shock, compassion and help-lessness: breathing hard still, as if he had just arrived.*)

CUT OVER THIS TO: CLOSE TWO-SHOT:

(*As* JACK *squats beside* ABE, *gently picks up and conceals the knife, and turns him over and sits him up.* ABE'S *head hangs low so that for a while we hardly see his face. He neither resists* JACK *nor helps him.* JACK *half carries him away from grave.*)

OPEN COUNTRY— MID-MORNING.

(MEDIUM LONG SHOT, PANNING—ABE— *unless his success in not doing so will be misunderstood—never turns his head to look at the grave. But early in the shot, he removes his hat; and at the very last of the shot, if it can be held long enough, he slowly puts it on again.*)

(WE SHOOT FROM A LOW HILLSIDE, DOWN TOWARD A COUNTRY ROAD. *After a couple of seconds,* ABE *enters the shot, riding, at a walk. We* PASS WITH HIM. *Very likely it is clear from the start that we are in a graveyard; in any case, with* MID-PAN, *we* PAN IN ON ANN'S GRAVE, QUITE CLOSE— *if feasible, the* HEADSTONE, *which for a few moments blocks* ABE *from sight. As we* CENTER THE GRAVE OR STONE, WE STOP PANNING, NOT MORE THAN TWO SECONDS; THEN RESUME PANNING, CENTERING ABE, AND PASS HIM OUT OF SIGHT ON INTO DIS-TANCE, AS WE . . . FADE OUT.)

1953

Irving Stone

By the time he turned his attention to the Lincoln marriage, Stone (1903–1989) had already written popular fictionalized biographies of Vincent van Gogh, Jack London, Jessie Benton Frémont, Eugene Debs, and Andrew Jackson's wife, Rachel. Building on the sympathetic assessment presented by Ruth Painter Randall in *Mary Lincoln: Biography of a Marriage* (1953), Stone sought to persuade readers that Abraham and Mary had shared a love deep and genuine enough to withstand the death of two children, the pressures of fratricidal war, and the jealous invective of a legion of misguided critics. Though the positive Randall-Stone interpretation has been tempered by the work of scholars such as Jean H. Baker, Catherine Clinton, and Jason Emerson, it did provide a counterview to the myth of unrelenting Lincoln marital misery advanced in the 19th century by William H. Herndon. As the following excerpt shows, Stone added a sexual element missing from all previous (and most future) accounts. His Mary rises naked from a bath, Abraham makes his entrance wearing a revealing robe, and the new Mrs. Lincoln all but purrs as she gratefully acknowledges that love is not only "eternal" (the words her husband had inscribed on her wedding band), but also "corporeal."

Love Is Eternal

It Is Abraham's Turn Now

I

She sat soaking in the hot water of the round tin tub; out the north window snow hung like a sheet on a clothesline, but the room was bright with the fire on the hearth and redolent of lavender water. Abraham had gone down to the men's bathing room just off the kitchen of the hotel, carrying his soap, towel, razor and comb.

She rubbed the Windsor soap on her slender hips and stomach, then leaned back against the circular rim, her eyes roaming the room which she had converted from a conventional hotel chamber into something peculiarly their own: the shelves of

books against the south wall with a vase of evergreen branches
flanked on either side by an ivory figurine; the crimson calico
curtains she had sewn and hung in place of the mustard velvets;
the round table she had bought to put in front of the fire, covered by bowls of oranges and walnuts, stacks of the Lexington
Observer, the Baltimore *Niles' Register*, the New York *Tribune*
and a volume of Bancroft's *History of the United States*. On the
bureau next to their four-poster were her silver combs, brushes
and scent jars. She had not been able to avoid the Globe Tavern;
she would be here a full year, perhaps two, and so she had used
one of her cash wedding gifts to buy an oil painting and prints
for the walls, a fluffy white yarn hearth carpet on which Abraham liked to stretch out at night and read poetry to her, and a tiny
French escritoire which she placed in front of the bookshelves
for her papers and correspondence with the family in Lexington.

She stepped out of the tub and onto the warm rug, dried herself with a big towel, slipped into her underthings, stockings,
petticoats and low leather slippers, then a swiss muslin lace-
trimmed dressing robe. She pulled the bell cord for the servants
to come and carry out the tub of water. In a few moments she
heard Abraham coming down the hall; he appeared in the doorway dressed in the blue wool robe and buckskin slippers she had
given him for Christmas. He was wearing his side hair considerably longer now; it came down his cheeks to a point level with
the bottom of his ears. On top, his hair was cut shorter, falling
in a wide part on the right side, the main lock covering the
rounded forehead.

Marriage becomes him, she thought; he's looking better than
I've ever seen him. He has good color, the web of anxiety lines
is gone from under his eyes. Love might be eternal, but how
nice that it could also be corporeal!

He put the comb and razor on his worktable under the
window, then turned and opened his arms to her. She nestled
against his bosom while he kissed her shoulder, murmuring,
"Ummm, you smell good."

"So do you. It's that castile soap, isn't it? I must get you
more." She leaned back a little, studying his face. "Though I
says it as shouldn't, I'm good for you." Imitating his high nasal

tone, she mimicked, "In this matter of looking at one another, I'm soon going to have the advantage."

He threw his head back and laughed.

"Now that we're both so scrubbed and beautiful, I wish I had thought to have my good suit pressed for Breese's levee."

"You did."

"Did we also remember to have a clean white shirt and collar?"

"Bottom drawer of the bureau. We can't have you getting nostalgic about the good old days above Josh Speed's store."

He stood still for a moment, his head turned to one side, his eyes puzzled.

"Molly, why were Speed and I so mortally frightened of marriage? For a year and a half we exchanged letters, trying to answer each other's anxieties and misgivings."

"And now?"

The seriousness of his mood passed.

"Anything I might tell you in the privacy of our boudoir would not be admissible as legal evidence in court. But I did write a letter to a lawyer, Sam Marshall, and in it I said, 'Nothing new here, except my marrying, which to me is a matter of profound wonder.' It wasn't until I'd mailed that old letter that I realized how fast and irrevocably I had committed myself."

She took his hand, led him to the comfortable rocker before the fire, then dropped on her knees before him.

"You committed yourself even faster and more irrevocably than you know."

"How do you mean, Molly?"

"My dear . . . I'm with child."

His gray eyes were round in astonishment.

"Are you sure? My, that was fast, wasn't it?"

"Instantaneous would be the better word. But then, what should I have expected from a man who can raise two ax heads off the ground?"

A flush spread over his neck and face.

"Why, Abraham," she exclaimed, "you're blushing. I didn't know you could."

He raised her from her knees, cradled her in his arms. She

saw that his face did not know what expression his mind was wearing.

"And after I promised you a carefree year . . ."

"Oh, I couldn't be more free from care. Married less than two months and already with tangible proof that my husband loves me . . . written in his own handwriting to a client, admissible as legal evidence in any court of law!"

It was only two blocks east on Adams from the Globe to the American House, but fresh snow lay heavy on the walks and so they shared a carriage with their next-door neighbors, Albert T. Bledsoe, a West Point graduate who was practicing law on the Eighth Circuit, and his wife Harriet from New Jersey.

When they entered the candlelit ballroom of the American House Mary was puzzled to see but a scattering of ladies among the three hundred men present. The only folk who had come to Sidney Breese's levee to celebrate his election to the United States Senate were his fellow legislators.

The orchestra began a waltz. Abraham held out his arms. Mary danced away with him, her full lemon-yellow silk skirts swirling against his polished boots. Stephen Douglas claimed her for the next dance. His dark blue eyes were big and burning, the wavy hair combed back pompadour style over the splendid head.

"Steve, I expected to find you glum, since you were expecting to give this celebration party yourself. Yet here you are, bright-eyed and confident."

Douglas's laugh was a deep baritone. "Breese never could have been elected if I hadn't released my people. I made a deal with him: after he serves one term he must support me. When I get into the United States Senate I'll stay there forever because I won't have anybody back here plotting for their turn. Clever, Mary?"

A sudden stir went through the hall; all eyes turned to the entrance foyer. Standing against a background of twelve disciples in white military uniform, she saw a man in a blue dress coat with a black velvet vest and white cravat. She recognized him as the Prophet, Joseph Smith, leader of the Mormons who had built a prosperous community at Nauvoo.

Joseph Smith was mixed into the memories of her secret meetings with Abraham at the Simeon Francis house, for this was the time Simeon had been publishing the letters of John C. Bennett, who not only accused Joseph Smith of having ordered the shooting of former Governor Boggs of Missouri but of setting up a system of prostitution for the benefit of the church officials, of maintaining a band of Destroying Angels to assassinate the Prophet's enemies, and the creation of a western dynasty which he would rule as emperor. Abraham had done his best to persuade Simeon not to publish the attacks, but Simeon had persisted; Governor Ford then issued a belated warrant for Smith's arrest on the grounds of instigating the attempted assassination of Governor Boggs.

Mary left Douglas's side and went to her husband. "Could I meet him, Abraham?"

"Now, Molly, Mr. Smith is alleged to have seven wives, and I have one little one. Surely you wouldn't send me back to the Butlers after only two months?"

"It's a *soupçon* too late for me to send you anywhere. But I'll confess I'm fascinated. Please do introduce me."

Joseph Smith accepted the introduction with dignity. Abraham moved away to join Benjamin Edwards. Mary found herself gazing into a pair of the most magnetic blue eyes she had ever encountered. Was this man truly chosen of God? Had the Lord led him to the hiding place of the golden plates of the Angel Moroni, and then given Joseph the power to decipher them? Could the Book of Mormon be an authentic new Bible? Certainly thousands of good and honest people believed so, and more were being converted every day.

"May I bid you welcome to Springfield, Mr. Smith?" she said. "Most of us feel you are being persecuted."

"Thank you, Mrs. Lincoln." His voice was a powerful throbbing organ. "The Lord has given us friends in Springfield."

"More important, if I may say so, the Lord has kept you on the side of the law. Mr. Lincoln believes there are no legal grounds for Illinois to send you back to Missouri."

Smith flashed her a taunting smile.

"Mrs. Lincoln, if ever you become disillusioned with your

chosen church—Episcopal?—Presbyterian?—come to Nauvoo and let me reveal the true religion to you."

"Thank you," she replied with a full curtsy, "it's always gratifying to be wanted."

When he had moved on she joined Abraham where he was standing with Benjamin Edwards and his wife Helen. Helen greeted her excitedly.

"Mary, Ben and I have bought the Houghan house."

Mary forced back the hot stinging tears which came instantly to her eyes.

"I have news too," Benjamin cried. "Your cousin Stuart asks if I'd like to form a partnership with him when he returns from Washington."

"Does that mean Cousin Stuart is not running for Congress again?" she asked after a barely perceptible pause.

"Yes, he said two terms were quite enough." Edwards turned to Abraham. "Is it your turn next, Lincoln?"

"I certainly hope so. If you hear of anyone saying Lincoln doesn't want to go to Congress, you tell him you know it isn't so."

When the orchestra struck up and Ben and Helen had glided away Mary looked at Abraham with high color in her cheeks.

"For your Victory Ball we're going to have a party like this, only all of Springfield society will be here to help you celebrate."

"Yes, indeed, Mrs. Lincoln, I have to look sharply to the future. Election to the Congress takes place next August . . . and my child will be born . . . let me see . . . in August too? Ain't that a caution? He shall be the first to call me the Honorable Mr. Lincoln."

2

It was pleasant to do one's New Year's calling with one's husband, to leave cards reading *Mr. and Mrs. A. Lincoln* in the baskets hung on front doorknobs.

They returned to the Globe at nine in the evening, walking arm in arm through the cold night air. The Globe was on Adams, next to a blacksmith shop, a two-story building fronted by elms and maples; the tavern had changed hands every two or three years, each new owner adding rooms so that it now looked like an oversized barn. The inside was comfortable; the women's parlor to the left as they entered the vestibule, the big dining room beyond that facing on Adams. A staircase led upstairs to the ell with its six rooms on either side of a narrow hallway for the permanent guests such as themselves, the Bledsoe family, Mrs. Bournedot, a widow and brilliant pianist, such attorneys as Justin Butterfield and Judge Nathaniel Pope. Occupying this upper floor, they were able to avoid the day-by-day confusion of arriving and departing guests. It was needed, Mary thought, to compensate for the clanging locomotive bell placed on top of the main building, which was rung by a pull rope at the desk every time a stage drew up or a traveler arrived on horseback.

She carried easily, as Elizabeth and Frances had. They went out a good deal, to the marriage of Ann Rodney, to Ninian's party for the baptism of his new daughter, Elizabeth, to the band concert at the Hall of Representatives, the fair at Watson's given by the First Presbyterian Church, to dinner parties and cotillions. But she enjoyed equally the quiet evenings in their room with Abraham at his worktable drawn up before the fire, writing with a steel pen and blue ink on long sheets of foolscap an appeal to the Whigs of Sangamon County.

His joy in the written word and the hours he spent at his desk led her to believe that he was basically a literary man.

"From childhood I've had an ambition to master a style," he told her; "that's why I write verses sometimes, to see if I can make words rhyme. But it's discouraging: I still write by ear."

"Yet it's lucible. You state the essence of a matter with the least possible verbiage."

He flashed her a look of gratitude, then began striding the narrow paths between the four-poster, French wardrobe, small sofa and escritoire.

"If only I can convince the Whigs to adopt the convention system for all nominations. What does it matter that the plan was originated by Stephen Douglas; it's been responsible for the overwhelming Democratic victories in Illinois. I've got to convince them that union is strength, and that 'a house divided against itself cannot stand.'"

She wished she could hear him make his speech, but no ladies were admitted to the meeting. For the next three weeks he campaigned through Sangamon County. The Whigs accepted his platform almost exactly as he had written it. Yet he returned from the convention with a glum look. To her repeated questions of what had happened he replied bleakly:

"The people of Sangamon have cast me off . . . our delegation is instructed to go for Edward Baker." He brought his left hand upward and outward, dismissingly. "Things didn't go well for me on the early ballots, my strength was getting weaker, so I dropped out before I lost all my support."

"You didn't!" she cried. "You should never withdraw, never."

He turned away from her, stood gazing out the east window toward the cupola of the state house. She placed her hand on his shoulder:

"Forgive me, Abraham, you did what you thought right. It just wasn't fair of them to reject you altogether . . ."

"Oh, not altogether," he interrupted with a wry smile. "They appointed me one of the delegates to the Pekin convention; so that in trying to get Baker the nomination there I shall be fixed a good deal like the fellow who is made groomsman to the man what has cut him out, and is marrying his own dear gal."

She smiled, relieved to see that he could laugh at his disappointment.

The following day she learned that she had contributed to his rejection: some of Baker's supporters had claimed that since Abraham's marriage he had become "the candidate of wealth, pride and aristocratic family distinction."

"They yanked up your vest, and there was I!" she said to Abraham *sotto voce* that night at supper. "It was our first flight after marriage and I was so sure it would succeed."

She was grateful that the Sangamon Circuit Court opened the next morning, for Logan and Lincoln had a number of cases on the docket, and Abraham would have no time to brood about his defeat. A number of the cases involved fair sums of money so that it should be a remunerative session for them.

She had seen steady growth in her husband as a lawyer since he had become Logan's partner, particularly in the abstract principles of the law in which Logan had been a student all his life. She knew that her cousin was a severe taskmaster, obliging Abraham to write out their long and intricately reasoned briefs; there were times, too, when she sensed that he was smarting at being treated as a perennial junior law student.

"Cousin Logan loves the law as a science," he complained one evening, "but that's all he does read, the law. When he sees me reading history or poetry or politics he thinks I'm wasting my time."

She had expected that Abraham would bring home his important legal associates, state officers, businessmen, as her father had, but with the exception of the Simeon Francises he never appeared with a guest. Her husband apparently preferred to keep his friendships out of his marriage, meeting these men in the lobby of the state house, the *Journal* office, the post office, the drugstores, the street corners where they congregated to talk. He was still, as Edwin Webb had said, a man's man.

Nor did he consider it necessary to reciprocate for the many fine dinners and dances to which they were invited. Aside from the one dinner she had given here at the Globe for her family, he did not want to entertain. Already in the last couple of weeks Mr. and Mrs. Abraham Lincoln had not been included in two or three *distingué* affairs.

She had put off explaining to him about this; he did not like big parties anyway. He would say that one of the main reasons they had come to the Globe, which cost them only four dollars a week, was that they could save their money, pay off his debts, and put away some capital. However when they were quite pointedly not included in William Thornton's party here at the Globe to which Thornton had invited all the doctors, lawyers and honorables of the capital, and rightly so, thought Mary, since Thornton had already entertained the Lincolns at two dinner parties at the American House without being invited back, she decided to broach the subject.

She chose a night when a white hailstorm bombarded their north window, making the night impenetrable and their bright fire the cozier.

"Abraham, since you intend to pay off every dollar of those New Salem debts, and so much of our lives seems to be circumscribed by them, why not let me sell my Indiana farm land? Then we could start out fresh and free."

He looked up from his book, the puzzled expression on his face asking, Now what brought up this subject?

"No, Mary, I can't let you sell your land and use the money to pay off debts that are mine and mine alone."

"I don't follow your reasoning," she retorted, her expression serious. "If you use current income to pay past debts, doesn't that make them equally mine? I understand your need to repay what you owe, but there is an obligation which I have been brought up to consider equally binding: my social debts."

She saw a frown cross his face; he went back to his reading.

In the middle of March her sister Ann arrived to fill the vacancy in the Edwards house. She had changed little in the three and a half years since Mary had seen her; she was still thin of face, sharp-featured and flat-chested. Mary invited her to the Globe for dinner to meet Abraham. After a few minutes he came in with a group of men, stood in the doorway talking. Ann asked:

"Which one is Mr. Lincoln?"

"The one towering over the rest . . . with the mop of black hair."

Ann studied her new brother-in-law, making no attempt to conceal her disappointment. "Not the one with the dark, lined face . . . ? Well, you certainly didn't help my chances in the Springfield matrimonial mart by that unlikely choice!"

Mary gazed pointedly at her sister's bosom and said with kitchen-knife sharpness:

"If you had more of the *milk* of human kindness in you, Ann, you would not think, let alone say, cruel things like that."

Ann's manner was so unresponsive that Abraham soon caught on.

"I'm afraid I've been a disappointment to your little sister,

Mary. Guess I'll have to tell her what the state's prosecuting attorney said the other day: An ugly man stands upon his own merits; nature has done nothing for him, and he feels he must labor to supply the deficit by amiability and good conduct. A pretty man, on the contrary, trusts his face to supply head, heart and everything."

Ann chewed on this for a moment, her eyes cast down, then she looked up, saw the grin on Abraham's face, answered his smile. Mary thought, I fight fire with fire; he extinguishes fire with laughter.

At the beginning of April, Abraham and most of the town's lawyers went out on circuit. Mary persuaded him to rent a buggy from the Globe stables rather than make the journey on horseback. His first note told of miserable roads, deep sloughs, execrable bridges, swollen streams; a mile or two beyond the Sangamon River he had plunged into a bad mudhole when the horse fell and the buggy broke a shaft; the next day while rolling rapidly down a hill his wheel had come off. Next time could he please ride a horse, since a horse rarely slipped a linchpin and lost a wheel?

Mary missed him, but she was never lonely. She spent her afternoons at Elizabeth's or Frances's home sewing for the coming baby. On the rare occasions when she felt ill, her neighbor Harriet Bledsoe took care of her. Once or twice a week she invited friends in for midday dinner, Mercy Conkling or Helen Edwards. She paid for these guests with her own money rather than have the meals go on the bill.

One noon Mercy arrived waving a letter triumphantly in the air. Both of their husbands were in Bloomington, about sixty miles north, attending a full week's court session.

"Mary, you certainly have your husband eating out of your hand: look at this letter I just received from James."

Mary took the sheet of paper, read the line that Mercy was indicating:

> I reached Bloomington Monday afternoon, and found Lincoln desperately homesick, turning his head frequently towards the south.

Her eyes misted.

Abraham was due to arrive in Pekin early in May for the Whig state convention. She was completely astonished when, dressing to go to Elizabeth's for Sunday dinner, she heard familiar footsteps coming down the hallway. She threw open the door, and there stood Abraham, tired, dusty and disheveled. He picked her up with a tremendous swoop, carried her to the rocker in front of the fire and sat down with her in his lap, burning the tender skin of her face with his rough beard stubble. When she got her breath back she exclaimed:

"How did you manage it? Aren't you due in Livingston?"

"I just couldn't stand being away from you any longer. When court closed Friday I rented a horse . . . thought I never would cover those sixty miles. We have today and tomorrow together before I start out again."

While he was down in the bathing room, and she laid out his fresh linen on the sofa she thought, He's the only lawyer who came home for the week end to be with his wife. May the Lord forgive me my vanity, but I'm going to show him off all over town!

3

With the coming of spring she developed a series of headaches, brought on in part by the clanging locomotive bell on top of the Globe. When it awakened her from sleep she sat up in bed trembling. Her hands and feet were cold, she shivered under the blankets at night, holding herself close to her husband to garner warmth. She tried to conceal as much of this as she could from Abraham, but when he came home at midday and found her with the blinds drawn and the covers over her head, she had to explain that it was necessary for her to shun both light and noise because of the intensity of the pain.

When the Globe's chef quit a new cook was installed. Mary did not know whether it was her condition or his cooking but she found the food inedible; he used too much saleratus, making the buckwheat cakes yellow and the corncakes and short biscuits sour.

"It's a good thing our bodies are not glass bottles and tightly corked," she commented grimly, "or we'd be blown to pieces in excessive fermentation."

"Why, Mary Todd of the Bluegrass Todds: that's the first time I've heard you make a barnyard joke!"

She found it increasingly distasteful now that she was big with child to cross the lobby and go through the dining room three times a day under the gaze of changing male eyes. Once when she was passing the men's parlor she overheard a whispered comment:

"Mrs. Lincoln sure must have become pregnant the first time Lincoln dropped his pants across the foot of the bed."

She burned with indignation at the raucous laughter and could swallow no bite of her dinner. She felt worse when she sensed that they were beginning to count on their fingers; the suddenness of their marriage was known, and she imagined these men checking back in terms of time to see if her child were legitimate. The thought of their prying pierced her composure, yet she could utter no word of protest, neither to her family nor to her husband, for her cousin Stuart's wife had conceived and given birth in this very bed, and so had her sister Frances.

She went to see Dr. Wallace and told her brother-in-law her troubles, not omitting the fact that she was upset by conditions which had not disturbed his wife.

"William, please talk to me as a doctor. Tell me what is wrong."

Dr. Wallace had noncombative eyes, a right eyebrow that went upward and a left eyebrow that turned down, giving his face a quizzical look. Unable to achieve robust health for himself, he managed to cure most people of their illnesses; owner of a drugstore out of which he operated as a physician, he urged his patients to stay away from all medication.

"If you're worrying about your physical health, Mary, or about the child, forget it. But let's assume that a man had a leg as badly broken as your nerves were damaged during your separation from Abraham. It would take a long time to get that leg back to its full strength, and if the break were bad enough, there might always be a little limp. Isn't that so?"

"Go on, William."

"What I am trying to say, Mary, is that during that twenty months of extreme tension you suffered an illness, as surely as though you had been stricken by diphtheria. Your reunion with Abraham, and your marriage, put an end to the illness; but that did not mean that your nerves had recovered."

"William, how long will it take before I am completely well . . . as though that separation never happened?"

Dr. Wallace filled a pipe from the bowl on his desk, then put it down without lighting it.

"That's difficult to say, Mary. You must have a long tranquil period."

She walked back to the Globe slowly, letting the bright spring sun warm her face and bathe her tired eyes. She stopped at the desk to ask the attendant to please send Sarah Beck to her. Mrs. Beck was a strapping rawboned woman with iron-gray hair and severe facial lines; her husband, long dead, had trained her in tavern keeping on the National Road in Pennsylvania and West Virginia.

Mary had no sooner settled in the comfortable rocker than Mrs. Beck knocked and stood in the doorway. Mary explained that she desired certain services which she knew were not customary, but which her health demanded, and for which she was willing to pay.

"A carryin' woman is entitled," replied Mrs. Beck in a deep voice.

Mary then asked that all her meals be served in her room; that she be permitted to use her own linens, and to bring in her cleaning materials and keep her own chamber.

She went through the lobby only once a day now, at a quiet hour when she was on her way to the Edwardses' or to visit with Mercy or Julia. At first she asked Abraham to have his dinner and supper with her, but she soon saw that this was a deprivation to him: he missed the camaraderie of the laughing, arguing, yarn-spinning men; he liked to meet his friends from over the state who brought news of political strengths and developments, of business and of possible cases. She released him to his cronies around the big bachelor table in the dining room.

Nor were they being invited out any more; six months of no

reciprocation had cut their social life down to visits with her sisters and cousins and the Simeon Francises, where they were expected every Friday night for supper.

She settled back to await her day, confident that once her child was born their "carefree year" would be over and she would be able to persuade Abraham to go to housekeeping. Then she would establish their rightful place.

Abraham returned from the Pekin convention with a small-boy expression: her cousin John J. Hardin had turned up with more support than Edward Baker, so Abraham had persuaded Baker to nominate Hardin, then had introduced a resolution that the convention recommend Baker as a suitable person to be voted for by the Whigs for Representative to Congress in the election of 1844.

"I understand: the rotation system," she commented, nodding her head up and down vigorously; "Cousin Hardin and Baker will then support you in 1846?"

"If I support them both with all my strength, in all likelihood they will support me the same way."

She remembered that this was the plan Stephen Douglas had worked out for himself.

"Then we must wait four years for our turn?"

He spread out his long-fingered hands before her in a gesture of resignation.

"What else could I do, Molly? I was running a poor third. This way we have an objective to work toward."

"But you end the arrangement, the same as Stephen Douglas does with the Democrats? You won't be obliged to announce for only one term?"

He gulped. "I had to take the same stand as the others. Cousin Logan also wants to go to Congress. . . ."

"Well, I do declare," she said, lapsing into her early southern drawl. "I thought mothers had to be patient, carrying for nine long months, but I'm the merest tyro compared to you. You're going to wait for four years to get one session as a congressman. And after your term is over where do we go from there?"

His eyes were twinkling now.

"I'll throw the question right back to you, Mary: after your baby is born, where do we go from there? Why, we have more babies, of course. And we'll have more offices, too, if we plan ahead. . . ."

"I guess you're right, Abraham, but I'm certainly glad it's not as difficult to become a mother as it is to become a congressman."

1954

Sir Winston Churchill

Churchill (1874–1965), the most famous Englishman of the 20th century, was half-American by birth and enjoyed a lifelong fascination with the United States and its history that sometimes took unexpected form. In December 1930 he published an early exercise in counterfactual history, "If Lee Had Not Won the Battle of Gettysburg," in *Scribner's Magazine*. The article recounted how a Confederate victory in Pennsylvania led to the Southern capture of Washington, a declaration of emancipation by Lee, a peace treaty between North and South, an Anglo-Confederate alliance, and the creation in 1905 by Theodore Roosevelt, Arthur Balfour, and Confederate President Woodrow Wilson of the English-Speaking Association, which in turn prevented the outbreak of a catastrophic European war in 1914, and opened the way for the possible creation of a "United States of Europe." Abraham Lincoln's assigned role in these events was to lose gracefully: "Never did his rugged yet sublime common sense render a finer service to his countrymen. He was never greater than in the hour of fatal retreat." Churchill would return to the events of the Civil War more realistically nearly three decades later in *The Great Democracies*, the fourth and final volume of *A History of the English-Speaking Peoples* (1956–58). The first excerpt printed here describes events in the fall of 1862 and in particular Lincoln's difficulties with General George B. McClellan—a situation Churchill, who appointed and then dismissed several wartime commanders in North Africa, could readily identify with. In the second excerpt, Churchill pays heartfelt tribute to Lincoln in terms reminiscent of "The Moral of the Work" he used to preface each volume of his magisterial history of World War II: "In War: Resolution, In Defeat: Defiance, In Victory: Magnanimity, In Peace: Good Will."

FROM

A History of the English-Speaking Peoples

Lincoln had hoped for a signal victory. McClellan at the Antietam presented him with a partial though important success. But the President's faith in the Union cause was never dimmed by disappointments. He was much beset by anxieties, which led him to cross-examine his commanders as if he were still a prosecuting attorney. The Generals did not relish it. But Lincoln's popularity with the troops stood high. They put their trust in him. They could have no knowledge of the relentless political pressures in Washington to which he was subjected. They had a sense however of his natural resolution and generosity of character. He had to draw deeply on these qualities in his work at the White House. Through his office flowed a stream of politicians, newspaper editors, and other men of influence. Most of them clamoured for quick victory, with no conception of the hazards of war. Many of them cherished their own amateur plans of operation which they confidently urged upon their leader. Many of them too had favourite Generals for whom they canvassed. Lincoln treated all his visitors with patience and firmness. His homely humour stood him in good stead. A sense of irony helped to lighten his burdens. In tense moments a dry joke relieved his feeling. At the same time his spirit was sustained by a deepening belief in Providence. When the toll of war rose steeply and plans went wrong he appealed for strength in his inmost thoughts to a power higher than man's. Strength was certainly given him. It is sometimes necessary at the summit of authority to bear with the intrigues of disloyal colleagues, to remain calm when others panic, and to withstand misguided popular outcries. All this Lincoln did. Personal troubles also befell him. One of his beloved sons died in the White House. Mrs Lincoln, though devoted to her husband, had a taste for extravagance and for politics which sometimes gave rise to wounding comment. As the war drew on Lincoln became more and more gaunt and the furrows on his cheeks and brow bit deep. Fortitude was written on his countenance.

The Antietam and the withdrawal of Lee into Virginia gave the President an opportunity to take a momentous step. He proclaimed the emancipation of all the slaves in the insurgent states. The impression produced in France and Britain by Lee's spirited and resolute operations, with their successive great battles, either victorious or drawn, made the Washington Cabinet fearful of mediation, to be followed, if rejected, by recognition of the Confederacy. The North was discouraged by disastrous and futile losses and by the sense of being out-generalled. Recruitment fell off and desertion was rife. Many urged peace, and others asked whether the Union was worthy of this slaughter, if slavery was to be maintained. By casting down this final challenge and raising the war to the level of a moral crusade Lincoln hoped to rally British public opinion to the Union cause and raise a new enthusiasm among his own fellow-countrymen.

It was a move he had long considered. Ever since the beginning of the war the Radicals had been pressing for the total abolition of slavery. Lincoln had misgivings about the effects on the slave-owning states of the border which had remained loyal. He insisted that the sole object of the war was to preserve the Union. As he wrote to the New York publisher, Horace Greeley, "My paramount object is to save the Union, and is not either to save or to destroy slavery. . . . What I do about slavery and the coloured race, I do because it helps to save the Union; and what I forbear, I forbear because I do not believe it would help to save the Union." Meanwhile he was meditating on the timing of his Proclamation and on the constitutional difficulties that stood in the way. He believed he had no power to interfere with slavery in the border states. He felt his Proclamation could be legally justified only as a military measure, issued in virtue of his office as Commander-in-Chief of the Army and Navy. Its intention was to deprive the Confederacy of a source of its strength. When the Proclamation was published, with effect from January, 1st, 1863, it therefore applied only to the rebel states. Slavery in the rest of the Union was not finally abolished until the passing of the Thirteenth Amendment in December 1865. In the South the Proclamation only came into force as the Federal armies advanced. Nor were the broader results all that Lincoln had hoped. In Britain it was not understood why he had not declared Abolition outright. A political manœuvre on his part was suspected. In America itself the war assumed an implacable character, offering to the South no alternative but subjugation. The Democratic Party in the North was wholly opposed to the Emancipation Edict. In the Federal armies it was unpopular, and General McClellan, who might be expected to become the

Democratic candidate for the Presidency, had two months earlier sent Lincoln a solemn warning against such an action. At the Congressional elections in the autumn of 1862 the Republicans lost ground. Many Northerners thought that the President had gone too far, others that he had not gone far enough. Great, judicious, and well-considered steps are thus sometimes at first received with public incomprehension.

The relations between the Washington Government and its General remained deplorable. McClellan might fairly claim to have rendered them an immense service after the panic at Manassas. He had revived the Army, led it to the field, and cleared Maryland. For all the Government knew, he had saved the capital. In fact he had done more. Lord Palmerston in England had decided that summer on mediation. News of the Antietam made him hesitate. This averted the danger to the North that the Confederacy would be recognised by the Powers of Europe. But it was not immediately apparent in the Union. Gladstone, Chancellor of the Exchequer in Palmerston's Government, delivered a speech at Newcastle in the autumn which enraged Northern opinion. He said: "We know quite well that the people of the Northern states have not yet drunk of the cup—they are still trying to hold it from their lips—which all the world sees they nevertheless must drink of. We may have our own opinions about slavery, we may be for or against the South, but there is no doubt that Jefferson Davis and other leaders of the South have made an Army; they are making, it appears, a Navy; and they have made what is more than either, they have made a Nation." Gladstone had not been informed that Palmerston had changed his mind.

Meanwhile between the politicians and the Commander-in-Chief upon the Potomac there was hatred and scorn on both sides. Bitter party politics aggravated military divergence. The President desired a prompt and vigorous advance. McClellan, as usual, magnified Confederate numbers and underrated their grievous losses. He was determined to run no unmilitary risks for a Government which he knew was eager to stab him in the back. Five weeks passed after the battle before he began to cross the Potomac in leisurely fashion and move forward from Harpers Ferry to Warrenton.

Lee withdrew by easy marches up the Shenandoah valley. He had sent "Jeb" Stuart on his second romantic ride round McClellan in mid-October, had harried the Federal communications and acquired much valuable information. He now did not hesitate to divide his army in the face of McClellan's great hosts. He left Jackson in the valley to keep Washington on tenterhooks, and rested himself with Longstreet, near Culpeper Court House. If pressed he could fall back to Gordonsville, where he judged Jackson could join him in time. McClellan however had now at length prepared his blow. He planned to strike Lee with overwhelming strength before Jackson could return. At this moment he was himself taken in rear by President Lincoln. On the night of November 7, 1862, he was ordered to hand over his command to General Burnside, and at the same time Porter, his most competent subordinate, was placed under arrest. The Government had used these men in their desperation. They now felt strong enough to strike them down. McClellan was against the abolition of slavery, and he never changed his view. The dominant Radical wing of the Republican Party was out for his blood. They were convinced that McClellan would never set himself to gain a crushing victory. They suspected him of tender feelings for the South and a desire for a negotiated peace. They also feared that the General would prove to be a potent Democratic candidate for the Presidency. Lincoln allowed himself to be persuaded by the Radical Republicans that McClellan had become a liability to his Government. He had long stood up for his commander against the attacks and whisperings of the politicians. Now he felt he must give way. But it was without animosity, for that viper was never harboured in Lincoln's breast.

———

Lincoln had entered Richmond with Grant, and on his return to Washington learned of Lee's surrender. Conqueror and master, he towered above all others, and four years of assured power seemed to lie before him. By his constancy under many varied strains and amid problems to which his training gave him no key he had saved the Union with steel and flame. His thoughts were bent upon healing his country's wounds. For this he possessed all the qualities of spirit and wisdom, and wielded besides incomparable authority. To those who spoke of hanging Jefferson Davis he replied, "Judge not that ye be not judged." On April 11 he proclaimed the need of a broad and generous temper and urged the conciliation of the vanquished. At Cabinet on the 14th he spoke of Lee and other Confederate leaders with kindness, and pointed to the paths of forgiveness and goodwill. But that very night as he sat in his box at Ford's Theatre a fanatical actor, one of a murder gang, stole in from behind and shot him through the head. The miscreant leapt on the stage, exclaiming, "*Sic semper tyrannis,*" and although his ankle was broken through his spur catching in an American flag he managed to escape to Virginia, where he was hunted down and shot to death in a barn. Seward, Secretary of State, was also stabbed at his home, though not fatally, as part of the same plot.

Lincoln died next day, without regaining consciousness, and with him vanished the only protector of the prostrate South. Others might try to emulate his magnanimity; none but he could control the bitter political hatreds which were rife. The assassin's bullet had wrought more evil to the United States than all the Confederate cannonade. Even in their fury the Northerners made no reprisals upon the Southern chiefs. Jefferson Davis and a few others were, indeed, confined in fortresses for some time, but afterwards all were suffered to dwell in peace. But the death of Lincoln deprived the Union of the guiding hand which alone could have solved the problems of reconstruction and added to the triumph of armies those lasting victories which are gained over the hearts of men.

Who overcomes
By force hath overcome but half his foe.

1958

Mark Van Doren

A professor of English at Columbia University for nearly four decades, Van Doren (1894–1972) was also a novelist and a Pulitzer Prize–winning poet. Written for the 1959 sesquicentennial, *The Last Days of Lincoln* examines the final weeks of the President's life in six scenes, with Lincoln speaking in prose while the characters around him declaim in blank verse. Van Doren's depiction of the tension between Lincoln and the Republican senators who visit him reflects much of the mainstream historical thinking of the period, which viewed Radical Reconstruction with disfavor. Although Van Doren's play has rarely been staged, it was praised by Roy Basler and other Lincoln scholars, and it offers a convincing portrait of Lincoln's personal and political acuteness in his dealing with such powerful personalities as Edwin M. Stanton.

FROM

The Last Days of Lincoln

SCENE FIVE

The same as Scene Two. Morning, April 10th.

JOSHUA SPEED *is waiting in the office; he is looking out of a window through which sounds of cheering, singing, and fired salutes pour in.*

Enter STANTON, *without being seen at first by* SPEED, *who when he hears* STANTON *speak turns and answers without enthusiasm.*

STANTON:
Hello, Speed. What have you done with the President?
    SPEED:
Mr. Stanton, now you flatter me.
I can do nothing with a man so torn
Between his joy that General Lee has quit
And his own doubts of what may happen next.
    STANTON:
He's right for once. But where in God's name is he?

SPEED:

I think he went for news of Mr. Seward.
He called on him last night, you know, the first thing
After his boat had docked. He came because
Of that. He found the Secretary better—
And better still because the war was ending.
He told him so, and Mr. Seward smiled—
Though it hurt to do it, with those injuries.

STANTON:

A pretty time for an important man
To let himself be thrown out of his carriage!
What if we all did that—what if *I* did!

SPEED:

You never would, we know. But here he is.

> LINCOLN *enters, evidently expecting to see only* SPEED, *but gives*
> STANTON *his attention*

LINCOLN:

Well, Mars, good morning—for the second time today. You will
be glad to learn that Seward continues to mend. Our Secretary
of State thrives on good news. Even last night, when I told him
how things looked in Virginia, he brightened up like an old dollar. But that was before word came of the surrender. I can imagine him then, in that horse collar of his the doctors put on to
keep him from nodding his head and breaking his neck—he
must have flickered like a lantern at the bottom of a well. It was
all I could do this morning to restrain myself from going over
there; he must have heard the guns and the yelling, just as we did,
and I'd have liked to hear him on the subject. I miss Seward.

STANTON:

We all do. But I came in here to tell you——

LINCOLN:

I miss the way he says things. He is a wicked, unbelieving man—
people say so, and I have no direct evidence to the contrary—
but he has been almost my best company these four years. I
remember him on New Year's Day in Sixty-Three. Orville
Browning, whom no one has ever found too witty, called to say
he thought the Emancipation Proclamation was a mistake
because unnecessary. Well, Seward took care of my old friend by

telling him of a New Englander who kicked because a Liberty Pole was being erected at some expense to his village, and therefore to him. We have the liberty, he said, so why the pole? And someone answered: What is liberty without a pole? So Seward answered Browning: What is War without a Proclamation?

STANTON:

I heard him. Mr. Lincoln, I came to tell you——

LINCOLN:

He might have said, of course, What is Emancipation without a Proclamation? But that would have been rubbing it into Congress that I had freed the slaves before it did—or *told* them they were free; they weren't yet; there was only a Proclamation, and this was Seward's point—that I had done whatever I did for my own reasons; which were, as I confessed then, more military than moral. The Senate, my dear Stanton, is dreadfully moral. Or it says it is. But you came here to tell me what?

STANTON:

Two things, Mr. Lincoln; and some Senators
Agree with what I'll say.

LINCOLN:

As to both things?

STANTON:

Certainly. And we are but a few
Of those who will be wondering tomorrow,
When everything is public, who surrendered
To who at Appomattox.

LINCOLN:

Don't you know? I saw you reading the telegrams. And I'm sure your windows rattled when the cannon boomed. What do you suppose all this singing in the streets could be about? Are we in Richmond?

STANTON:

You know, I think, precisely what I mean.

LINCOLN:

You and some Senators. Let's see. Could Sumner be among them? Wade, and Chandler? Julian? Not my old friend Trumbull, I think. A wonder they didn't burst in here. They still may. I'll try not to be engaged.

STANTON:

I am not one of them, though on these points——

LINCOLN:

Why, Stanton, you're not a Senator at all.

STANTON:

I stand on no ground that is not my ground.

LINCOLN:

Of course, of course.

Abandons his sarcasm

That is how you came to win the war when nobody else could. I know this, Mr. Secretary; nor do I lump you with those others. You can't be lumped. Now this may seem a strange time to tell you how often I have thought you right. You told somebody once I was a damned fool, and he repeated the opinion to me, expecting fireworks. But there were no fireworks; I said you knew what you were talking about if any man did.

STANTON:

Softening

I was harassed that day. I apologize.

LINCOLN:

No, don't. I would rather have you as you are than have any other man on my own terms. I may not always appear to believe this; but the fact is, I do.

STANTON:

Thank you.

His voice steadily rises to its original pitch

       Nevertheless I find them furious,

And can't, with a good conscience, reassure them.

They say that Grant fell over his own feet

To be magnanimous at Appomattox;

That Lee will move in on our sentiments now

Till he has reached the center; and that Richmond,

For all our victory, will govern Washington.

They say that——

LINCOLN:

His sarcasm returning

What? Do they say more? They must have talked since sunrise

—one spelling the other, as we used to ride and tie on the roads

in Illinois: one man would ride the horse a mile ahead, tie him
to a tree, and walk on until the second man——

STANTON:
Yes, they say more. They say that Justice Campbell
Is to yourself as Lee is to the man
Who whipped him. They are swearing that Virginia
Must never be permitted such a meeting
As you consented to six days ago.
They think there is a strange resemblance suddenly
Between you and the General—as if
At City Point, perhaps, you became partners—
And Sherman, crazy Sherman, for a third.
God knows, if this is so, what he and Johnston
Will sign and seal down there in Carolina—
After, of course, kissing each other's hands.

LINCOLN:
   Gentler again
Now as to Justice Campbell—plain Judge is what I called him,
and I hope I offended no propriety. Lee's surrender yesterday puts
quite a new complexion on the meeting he proposed and I—
provisionally, mind you—accepted. The purpose of the meeting
was surrender. Well, it has happened; and so we shall have to
think about the meeting. I see little reason for it now.

STANTON:
He probably has reasons by the dozen.

LINCOLN:
Who, Campbell? Let us not speculate about somebody's reasons
for wanting something there is no reason to think he will get.
Now as to Grant and Lee. I did talk to Grant, and Grant talked
to me; and there was no difficulty in our understanding each
other. Sherman was there, too, and Admiral Porter. Sherman,
somewhat to my surprise, thought what I thought and Grant
thought. In short, the Commander in Chief and his two best
generals discussed the terms upon which they would accept surrender. These were the terms—in Grant's case—that came to you
by telegram this morning. They are the terms everyone will
know tomorrow, as you say. They are the terms the Secretary of
War is bound to honor.

STANTON *looks at him sharply.* LINCOLN *appears not to notice*
The substance of them is that Lee's army will cease to be an army
and go home; and further, as long as its members, both officers
and men, abide by their paroles, they will not be molested by
you, by me, by anybody. Is this your understanding of them?

STANTON:

You say I am bound to honor them—like that.

> *Snaps his fingers*

LINCOLN:

> *After a second's hesitation*

I say the Secretary of War is.

STANTON:

Is this a threat? You ask me to resign?

LINCOLN:

Nothing would be more painful to me, Stanton. Is *that* a
threat?

STANTON:

Then you are not consulting me as Secretary.

LINCOLN:

> *Hesitates again*

No, I am not.

STANTON:

You are ordering me to honor what four Senators,
An hour ago, denounced as rank dishonor.
You force me to suppress my right desire,
My natural desire, that those who hurt us—
Well, so *much*—shall themselves be hurt
That much and more. And *now*. Now is the time
To break them into bits. You leave them whole.

LINCOLN:

I have seen them, Stanton, since you did. They were badly broken,
let me tell you. As for the bits, would you obliterate all of those, or
simply some? The brightest, say? The wisest? Is that your natural
desire? I think it isn't, quite. As for the Senators——

STANTON:

Nevertheless you are ordering me and them——

LINCOLN:

No, I am ordering *you*. Four Senators or forty—I cannot order

them. And neither must the Secretary of War. You *are* that man?
I'm not mistaken?

> STANTON *stamps up and down before the desk, then turns*

STANTON:

No, Mr. President, you are not mistaken.

LINCOLN:

Good!

> *Breathes deeply and straightens up*

Good!

STANTON:

Not as to me, I mean. But as to Lee——

LINCOLN:

> *Wearily*

Lee and the country, Mr. Stanton. Think of it that way. The war
must really end. It has been destroying us all, and it must really
end—must be, in so far as such a thing is possible, as if it never
were.

STANTON:

Sumner thinks that is the way to lose it.

LINCOLN:

But we have won it, Stanton. And now I want it to stay won in
such a way that it can be forgotten. This is how we do that.
Sumner is wrong.

STANTON:

And if the entire Cabinet should say *you* were——

LINCOLN:

Why, I should overrule them.

STANTON:

I remember how you told us, when you read
The Proclamation to us, that your mind
Was perfectly made up. You only wanted
Suggestions as to the text; the idea—no.

LINCOLN:

But it was *your* idea. So you didn't mind.

STANTON:

True, I didn't. But responsibility——

LINCOLN:

I take it all.

To SPEED

Joshua, hello. You haven't heard any of this, have you? Mr. Stanton wouldn't like to think you had.

STANTON *waves a hand brusquely and starts pacing the floor again*

I have been meaning to tell you, Joshua, about a picture of Lee my boy Robert showed me at City Point. He brought it in at breakfast, one morning on the *Malvern*. I told him it was the face of a good man. One of our best men—I have always thought so, and I think so now. Terribly mistaken, but a good man. A pity when a good man is mistaken. Of course I have never doubted that he was mistaken; and neither has he, perhaps, though he would have had his own way of realizing this, just as he would have had his own way of realizing that I could think I was mistaken too. I could, you know. I have.

SPEED:

You have indeed—too many times, of course,

For your own happiness. A deep disease.

MARY LINCOLN *comes in, unnoticed except by* STANTON, *who continues to pace the stage*

LINCOLN:

Like SPEED, *unaware of* MARY LINCOLN's *presence near the door*

You know it best, and once you were afflicted with it too. Otherwise, I suppose, we should never have got on so comfortably together, like a pair of old shoes both of which pinched in the same place. But I haven't told you the most interesting fact about Lee's face. His doubts have never made him ugly. Mine—well, they haven't made me beautiful. Only once have I been called beautiful.

Dips his head, makes a face, and smiles

That was last year, when Mrs. Harvey, widow of the Governor of Wisconsin, came to see me about certain hospitals she wanted built. Her husband had gone down after the battle of Shiloh to move supplies for his wounded troops, and the poor man was drowned. She went South herself, and became convinced that more men in the hospitals there were dying of the heat than of their wounds. So she asked for hospitals in the Northwest, and particularly of course in Wisconsin. I told her No, but she came the next day—came every day until she broke me down. She was a fine woman. I liked to have her here.

Swings his arm to indicate the room

She was handsome; I admired her will. I confess I deceived her toward the end. I kept on saying No when the truth was that I had got an order written—remember, Stanton?—I had to convince you after she convinced me—

Stanton *pays no attention to this*

an order for at least three hospitals to be built. Then on the last day I had to say Yes. I showed her the order—one of the hospitals was to be named for her husband—and for the first time she was speechless. I almost was myself, though I didn't cry as she did. Then something possessed me—I can't imagine what—to say to her: "You almost think I am good-looking, don't you?" And she exclaimed: "Why, Mr. President, I think you are beautiful!" Of course she was in no state then to judge such things.

Speed *laughs—then breaks off as* Mary Lincoln *comes forward, raging*

Mary Lincoln:

What woman was that! Tell me, who was that!

Lincoln, *turning and seeing her, crosses over to where she stands. He shows great distress, and holds out both hands as if to help her. But* She *steps back, away from him*

Handsome! And you admired her! And she called you
Beautiful! No dead or living woman
Must speak of you that way. At City Point
I had enough of Mrs. General Ord,
And for that matter Mrs. General Grant—
Who wants, I still think, to be mistress here!

Lincoln, *appalled, looks back in turn at* Speed *and* Stanton, *his shoulders sagging, but with no shame in his voice when he begins to speak*

Lincoln:

Now, Mother, remember I said at breakfast that this was bound to be one of my busiest days.

Mary Lincoln:

Don't think I care if Joshua is listening,

Or that man Stanton. *He* should *fire* a general
Whose wife can play the wanton as she did—
That woman Ord, whose mouth, when she came over,
Wouldn't have melted butter. There she had been
Closer to you than I was—riding, oh,
So cleverly on that ridiculous horse,
Right by the President, and she no more
Than a poor general's wife. Oh, she came over,
Once the review was done, and made such scrapes,
Such curtseys! She was so *entranced* to see me.
And all the time her eyes were rolling, rolling,
At no one else but you—and Mrs. Grant,
Who seemed to be in on the secret also.
I know *she* wants to be here where *I* am.
I told her so, and she denied it—oh,
So sweetly. It was *very nice*, I said,
To be here where *I* am. But anyhow,
I had enough of *her*. And now I hear
Of Mrs. Harvey! *Who* is Mrs. *Harvey*?
How dared she say such things to you—how *dared* she!

> LINCOLN *waits until he is sure she has finished, then turns again
> to* SPEED *and* STANTON

LINCOLN:

Gentlemen, you will excuse me I know for a few minutes.

> *He goes past her to the door, which he holds open until, suddenly,*
> SHE *starts weeping*

MARY LINCOLN:

Oh, my dear, I'm sorry. What I said
I never meant to say. And now it's more,
I know, than you can bear—or I can live with.
What's to become of me? I'm *so* afraid.

> *He pats her shoulder, then lets her go out under his arm.* HE
> *follows, closing the door behind him*

SPEED:

> *After a silence*

A terrible change in her. This is the worst,
However, I have seen.

Stanton:
                    And so with me.
A pity, certainly. I feel for him.
She is a whole day's work for any man;
And every day for *him*, as if no other
Trouble ever was. I feel for him.
    Speed:
        Looks carefully at Stanton
Thank you for that. I was afraid you wouldn't——
    Stanton:
Wouldn't! Wouldn't! Well, you know it now.
All sorts of people have all sorts of notions
Of what I can or cannot feel—*cannot*
Is usually their guess, and usually
They're right; though *will* not would come closer home.
No time for such indulgences, I say;
And mean it. Yet his case is extraordinary,
Because *he* is. You may not know it, Speed—
Few do—but I have more love for that man,
In spite of his misjudgments, than I have
For any other living; and I include
Myself.
    Does not smile
            Now this reminds me—why do you think
She said "no living or dead woman"? Dead!
Living, of course; you should have heard the tales
Of how she cut and slashed poor Mrs. Ord
At City Point—for the offense of cantering
Abreast of him while he reviewed the troops;
And then poor Mrs. Grant for trying to soothe her
By explaining that the lady had been asked:
That Mrs. Lincoln was late to the review,
And someone had to ride. His gentleness
With her that day was unbelievable,
They tell me, unless witnessed. But why no dead one?
Dead—what could she mean? Or is she mad?
    Speed:
I don't know, Mr. Stanton. All these years

She probably has doubted that he loved her—
Completely, anyway. She must remember—
Of course she does—how hard it was to make him
Come to the mark and marry her. He suffered
Equally with her because of that;
I knew him well, and thought *he* would go mad,
So shamed he was by his irresolution:
A quality in himself he rather enjoyed
Till it afflicted others; till it—you know—
Humiliated her. I have supposed
That she imagines women before and after—
Long ago and now—whom he could love
Without such hesitation: all the way
And simply, as his genius would direct him;
And that among them there might be some girl
Who died; and so his only love sleeps there.
I say I have supposed this. I don't know.
He never told me anything of the kind.
So it would have to be, as I have said,
Imagined. She is capable of that.
    STANTON:
I see. Well, it's absurd. He is immune
To females. They are nothing to him, nothing.
    SPEED:
Oh, but you're wrong.
    STANTON:
                            You think so?
    SPEED:
                                    He is powerful
That way too; he sees and feels immensely—
And it ends there. She has as little cause
For jealousy as certain Senators
Have to be doubtful of his loyalty—
Not to them merely, I mean, but to us all.
    STANTON:
    Snapping out of his mood
All us Kentuckians?

SPEED:

You can't be serious.
You know I mean to all of us there are,
Past, coming, and to come. He keeps no less
Than that in steady view. It is remarkable
How easily he does it.

STANTON:

Or how stubbornly
He tells us that he does it. Not that I doubt
His honesty.

SPEED:

Who does?

STANTON:

Why, every rebel.
To them he is compounded of low cunning
And highfalutin phrases. But they plan
To profit by the phrases.

Turns

I must go.

SPEED:

Don't leave, or he will think you censure *her*.

STANTON:

A luxury I simply can't afford,
To stay and reassure him.

The door opens, admitting LINCOLN *and* JUDGE DAVID DAVIS,
who is very fat. LINCOLN *does a fair job of looking as if nothing
has happened*

Mr. President,

I was about to go. If I see Sumner,
I think I know your views—if he should ask.

LINCOLN:

Here is Judge Davis.

Then, as if only now hearing STANTON

Oh, he will ask. But it won't be a bona fide question. When
Sumner asks you what *you* think his only purpose is to tell you
what *he* thinks. I know what that is, on every point. And he
knows my opinions; or if he doesn't he is entitled to guess. I

think I'll let him do some guessing. Mind you, I regard Sumner as my friend. He is the sincerest of his faction. Some of the others I can suspect, as our Northern Democrats do, of a desire to ruin the South so that the North—particularly the North*east*—will grow richer than it already is. It was rich to begin with, or the war might never have been won. But the war has made it *very* wealthy, and it wants to keep that wealth: even at the cost of a continuing blight where slavery used to be. They will blame the blight on slavery, and call it a punishment even unto the third generation. But greed will be the mainspring of their action—so the Democrats say, and I pay more attention to them than they give me credit for.

STANTON:
Shall I inform them?
Sarcastically

It would make them happy.

LINCOLN:
Ignoring this
But they are wrong if they find this true of Sumner. His sincerity is that of a fanatic—terrible too, yet it is pure and simple. One thing that keeps me awake at night, gentlemen,
He includes them all
is the fear that the violence of this war has created a violent nation—*one* nation, in a sense that it never was before, and wild at heart. The future of it is beyond our present imagination; and the power of it is a serious matter to contemplate. My hope is that it will recover its reason. My fear is that this may prove so difficult that most men will give it up as impossible and let the worst do what they will.
Comes to as from a trance
Now here is Judge Davis—I should call him Justice Davis now that he is a member of the Supreme Court, but I can't forget our days together on the circuit in Illinois—the Eighth Judicial District.

DAVIS:
Or, Mr. President, the nights.
To the others

We held
An Orgmathorial Court, before the fire
In some cold county seat—Urbana, Danville,
Charleston, or Decatur—and this lawyer
Often was fined because of his exorbitant
Fees—exorbitantly small. They threatened,
Some of us thought, the life of our profession.
    Chuckles, unaware that STANTON *is not amused*
  STANTON:
I have a thousand things to do this morning.
    Starts to go
  DAVIS:
But Mr. Secretary, I find it fortunate
That you are here. I came to ask,
And might as well ask you—not as a Justice,
    Smiles at LINCOLN
But merely as one member of a violent
Nation,
    Ceases to smile
        whether martial law continues
Long with us or short. It may be soon
To ask it, but I wonder.
  STANTON:
    Snapping the words
                That is a matter
For my decision, under the President.
As long, certainly, as it is needed.
  DAVIS:
Of course, of course. Only, was it ever
Needed where no armies were in danger?
  STANTON:
You mean in Indiana and Ohio.
    LINCOLN *listens carefully*
  DAVIS:
I merely ask you, as a million might,
Whether the end is visible of law
By generals, not judges.

STANTON:

　　　　　　And I say,

That is a matter for decision *here*.

> *Stamps on the floor. Both* MEN *look at* LINCOLN, *who has started walking back and forth by the window*

LINCOLN:

> *As if to himself*

We may look black in history for filling Federal prisons with thousands of men who shouldn't have been there, since their worst crime was to tell us of our faults. I could have done more than I did to temper this procedure. It pains me when I hear it said that I gave new rights to one race and robbed another of its old ones. The question is, of course, whether I would have looked blacker had I been too weak and lost the government—as the old farmer said of his wife who wasn't in the wagon when he got home—"somewhere between here and hell." It is a difficult question, and good men disagree.

STANTON:

The second error would have been the worse.

LINCOLN:

Yes, yes, I really think that. Yet the names some Northern Democrats call me have a certain sound, Mr. Secretary, to which I am more sensitive than you are.

> HE *has stopped walking, and is looking down through the window*

Now here comes a new test of how thick my skin is. Gentlemen, I must ask you to leave me alone with Shadrach, Meshach, and Abednego. They will be here in less than a minute.

> *Goes to the door and calls through*

John, send the Senators right in. But Joshua, you come back. Mr. Secretary, I know you are busy. Judge, did you have something special on your mind? That is, besides——

> SPEED *nods and leaves, following* STANTON

DAVIS:

No, Mr. President. It was broad and general.

> LINCOLN *smiles and holds his hands as far apart as* DAVIS' *girth is, measuring.* DAVIS *smiles too*

I came, if you must know, chiefly to see
With my own eyes how tired you have become,
And how much older one more year has made you.
They told me stories, and I wanted facts.

Lincoln:

Well?

Davis:

My diagnosis: you will thrive again.

Lincoln:

My excellent old friend!

Shakes Davis' *hand vigorously as he goes out—passing* Wade,
Chandler, *and* Sumner *as they enter;* Wade, *however, looks
back at* Davis *curiously*

Well, gentlemen, I expected you. In fact, I saw you crossing the
avenue, arm in arm.

Sumner:

*He wears a brown cape under which can be seen a maroon vest
and lavender pantaloons. He flourishes a gold-headed cane*

But Mr. President, that wasn't so.

Lincoln:

Then, Mr. Sumner, mind in mind. You came as one man anyhow. Which of you will speak for all? Mr. Wade? Mr. Chandler?
Did you meet Mr. Stanton, by the way?

All:

Stanton?

Lincoln:

He stayed longer than he intended, so that if you sent him——

Sumner:

But Mr. President, we sent nobody.
We come as one man—it is true—to ask
What you intend to say tomorrow night.

Lincoln:

Tomorrow night! Isn't that a long way off? But even so, I don't
quite understand why you think you can ask me.

Wade *snorts as if he could make it clear, but* Chandler *re-
strains him, indicating that* Sumner *is the spokesman, as he
proves to be—pompously*

SUMNER:

The times are perilous, as of course you know,
With much in them that no event resolves
Unless it be the work of many minds.

LINCOLN:

Mine too?

SUMNER:

Certainly, Mr. President. None more.

LINCOLN:

Thank you, Senator. Otherwise I have been wasting my time in
the composition of a speech to be delivered from the balcony of
this house tomorrow night. You seem to have heard that I promised something less impromptu than serenades require. You must
agree that I should study what I say.

SUMNER:

We do. And that is why we three are here.

LINCOLN:

You will be impatient with me, though, when I tell you I haven't
fully decided. The speech is not finished.

SUMNER:

So much the better, Mr. President.
There is so much now that is unresolved.
Victory, yes. And happily, a surrender——

WADE:

Who surrendered?

SUMNER:

                That is not our question.

WADE:

It's *my* question.

SUMNER:

                No. We must accept
The fact of a surrender; then go on
To counsel with you as to what should follow:
The Negroes, first of all, and then the States.

LINCOLN:

Why not the States and then the Negroes? The Negroes, bless
them, will have to live in States—or are there to *be* States, gen-

tlemen? I am assuming so in my address; I am even assuming
that a few exist already—barely exist, to be sure, but——
    CHANDLER:
Barely is just the word. You mean those little
Governments it pleased you so to make
When no one else was watching.
    WADE:
                    Zach, be still.
    LINCOLN:
        To WADE:
That's all right, Senator. He means Louisiana, for instance. I'm
glad he recognizes Louisiana.
    CHANDLER:
Recognizes!
        The SENATORS *look at one another, embarrassed into silence for*
        a moment
    SUMNER:
            Well! But there are others.
    LINCOLN:
        As if unaware that a sensitive issue has been exposed
Now I have been putting down some thoughts about Louisiana,
and I am delighted that you all agree it should be mentioned.
    WADE:
Mentioned! That's sarcasm. Well, it goes
With something else I've noticed. Mr. President,
I know the world's regard for you, and share it.
        LINCOLN *looks at him doubtfully*
But the world is not informed, as after years
I am, of your unconquerable pride.
        LINCOLN *stiffens a little*
They call me blunt, they say I am a bull,
A very mule for stubbornness; and so
You say, out loud; I've heard you. And they call
You humble.
        LINCOLN *listens intently*
            They don't see you as I do:
A difficult, deep man whose one assumption,
If I may say so, is superiority.

Glances at Sumner *for confirmation, but* Sumner *is looking uncomfortably at* Lincoln, *who is looking at the floor*

You may not like the word, yet it explains
The hard time we have here.

Chandler:

Frowning

Ben, be quiet.

Lincoln:

After a silence which he breaks by throwing his head back and raising his voice to indicate that he has made one decision out of many that were possible

Let him talk. But it won't be to me, however much he sounds like someone I saw recently in Richmond. I've had enough of that, true or untrue. Gentlemen, I leave you here

Starts toward the door

to tell one another anything you please. The walls do not have ears. Meanwhile, I have much to do—a speech to write, some unimportant people to see, and about sixty documents to endorse. You must excuse me now.

Shows each a chair and resumes his way to the door, pretending not to know that they are on his heels

Sumner:

But, Mr. President, we have advice!

Lincoln:

Good! Give it to yourselves. Pass it back and forth and polish it up. It may be a little rough in its present state.

Chandler:

It's rough enough, and ought to be, considering——

Lincoln:

Gentlemen, good morning! Day after tomorrow, possibly, we can talk to better purpose. For we must keep on talking. You are not my enemies, I know. This is not good-by.

Sumner:

With him at the door, Wade *and* Chandler *behind*

I am your one devoted friend among us;
And so I say, in true and tried affection:
Mr. President, you may regret this.

LINCOLN:

So I may. But I'd be sorrier, Senator, if I said all I am tempted to say.

Suddenly relaxes

We might never again go to the theater together. That would be terrible, for I enjoy seeing a good play with you. Or even a bad one.

SUMNER:

And I with you.

Arranges the folds of his cape with great care, then takes a step toward LINCOLN, *smiling and lowering his voice a little*

Next week, I understand,

There is one to which we both can feel *superior.*

CHANDLER *nudges* WADE

LINCOLN:

Excellent!

Smiles briefly, then addresses all three as before

But of course I can't plan any playgoing now. This other matter presses me too hard. Tomorrow night, that is, or if not then, soon after, I have some things to say—quite simply and directly— to the South if it will listen. I am studying now, or should be, how to catch their ears. Your only thought is about how they must learn to live again with us. You don't appear to consider that we must live with them, and that this will take some learning too. I'm doing my best to remember both parties to the divorce —a miserable divorce, if any at all, for neither party could move away. Meanwhile, gentlemen, let us all study to avoid a certain dictatorial tone—it may be mine, it may be yours—that is not to be tolerated in such perilous times. It is what makes the times perilous. Such is my conclusion, gentlemen, as of this painful moment.

He appears to suspect for the first time that they intend to leave him. THEY *are close together at the door;* CHANDLER *has his hand on the knob*

But aren't you staying? You are very welcome.

THEY *look at one another; hesitate; but none of them speaks*

Good day, then, gentlemen.

HE *holds the door wide open for them, and* THEY *go out—*
SUMNER *last, puzzled.* LINCOLN *does not follow, for* SPEED
enters

SPEED:

You told me to come back. I wasn't far.

LINCOLN:

Why, Joshua, you must have been in the keyhole.

    Sits down, exhausted

Did you hear anything?

SPEED:

Of course not. But they must have made you madder,
Lincoln, than you ever like to be.

LINCOLN:

Oh, I don't know. A little anger may be good for the soul—if
there is a soul, and I'm more inclined to think so than I used to
be when I was a young philosopher in New Salem. In those days
I could be sarcastic because I felt superior. Now I feel merely
equal, and sarcasm doesn't go with that. But Joshua, I wonder if
I'm too tired to make my speech tomorrow night as short as it
should be. It threatens to be long. And legal. Yet why not legal?
If law is coming home again, it had better be made welcome in
its native language. Nevertheless, nobody may listen.

SPEED:

The best of them will listen best, as always.

LINCOLN:

But it could be that I have too much to say; though some will
think I have too little. I must make it clear—this is confidential,
understand—

    SPEED *nods*

how unimportant it is to decide whether the seceded States have
ever properly been out of the Union; that is, whether they anything more than *said* they seceded. For four years they have disliked my doubts upon this point; now they may like them better.
Anyhow, here the States are where they always were; and the
only question that seems real to me concerns the practical relation they shall have henceforth with the rest of us. The relation
must be practical. What I am most tired of, Joshua, is righteousness
and rant. I want to sit down quietly and work things out. Also, I

must try to save the Negroes from Sumner and his friends. That sounds funny, but he wants them all to vote tomorrow; whereas I want to see them educated first, however long that takes. Of course a few now are; well, let them vote, and send the others off to school. But there's my speech, and it threatens to be windy. Pray, Joshua, that it be short and good, and that they listen.

SPEED:

You never used to ask that favor—prayer.

LINCOLN:

No, but I didn't dream then. I don't sleep, and yet I dream. Did you know that could be? It can. I dream of ships and moving shores; of rich men looking at themselves in mirrors, and seeing poor men there; of poor men looking, and laughing at what they see. I dream, Joshua, of being dead.

SPEED:

You *are* tired. Nobody knows how tired.

LINCOLN:

Nobody needs to know. It isn't important, considering all those who are truly dead. *They* don't dream any more. I understand, Joshua, that there are half a million of them.

SPEED:

More, Stanton says. But not a million.
He says it will be far short of a million.

LINCOLN:

A comfort, I suppose.

Smiles wryly

Joshua, I do hope you understand that I don't feel superior any more.

SPEED:

I never thought you did, even in *those* days.

LINCOLN:

Well, then, I fooled you; for that was how I felt—and have, actually, in days more recent than you would guess. Wade thinks I still do.

SPEED:

Wade? But the pot thinks every kettle black.

LINCOLN:

Looking out of the window

I wish Judge Douglas were alive.

SPEED:

Douglas?

LINCOLN:

Why not?

Musing

The Little Giant. He was ambitious, but so was I—only Mary knows how much.

He waits to see if SPEED *will discuss* MARY LINCOLN, *and when he does not, continues*

We were rivals for everything; last of all, for this place here. They say I rose on his shoulders, and I guess I did. They were strong shoulders—honorable shoulders—and it would do me good to tell him so as I never did while he still lived; even, Joshua, when the war had just begun and he went West to tell the Democrats they must support me. That effort, and the cold spring weather, killed him. And now I dream I am dead beside him.

SPEED:

Abe! Don't say that word again. Now don't.

LINCOLN:

"Dream"?

SPEED:

"Dead."

LINCOLN:

All right, Joshua, I never will,

Gets up

at least in your hearing.

Shouts outside

There is a new party on the lawn, expecting some remarks. I must go out and ask them to wait until tomorrow night. What then, Joshua? What then? Pray for my speech, that it may say the one right thing. What *is* the right thing, Joshua?

SPEED:

The thing that you will say. I have no doubts.

LINCOLN:

Good, Joshua. You never did. I had them for us both.

SPEED:

Have them for neither of us, Mr. President.

LINCOLN:

All right, if you say so.

Starts out, then pauses

My job, you know, is beginning only now.

Straightens up suddenly and smiles

SPEED:

You mean out there? You mean tomorrow night?

LINCOLN:

Oh, no. I mean, I am free at last to be President of the United States. This has been everything but that, Joshua; and a long time to wait. Think of it, Joshua! The United States!

As he goes out, the shouting increases and there is the noise of a brass band, and firecrackers

Curtain

1959

Jacques Barzun

Barzun (b. 1907) immigrated to the United States from his native France in 1920. A professor of history at Columbia University from 1929 to 1967, he has written on a wide range of subjects in European and American cultural and intellectual history. First published during the sesquicentennial in *The Saturday Evening Post*, "Lincoln the Writer" reads very much like a classroom lesson by a master teacher, as Barzun challenges his audience to rethink the familiar—the question of Lincoln's literary style and its relation to his subject matter—and then leads them through a careful explication of the "four main qualities of Lincoln's literary art." But his essay is more than an inquiry into style; it is also an argument about personality. Determined to free "Lincoln the artist" from the confines of sentimental convention, Barzun recasts him as a Romantic type he calls "the dark outcast" and speculates that Lincoln "hugged a secret wound" that ultimately made him "an artist-saint." Not surprisingly, Barzun is an admiring reader of William H. Herndon, who is again shown to have created as much in the way of Lincoln mythology as he ever succeeded in dispelling.

Lincoln the Writer

A great man of the past is hard to know, because his legend, which is a sort of friendly caricature, hides him like a disguise. He is one thing to the man in the street and another to those who study him closely—and who seldom agree. And when a man is so great that not one but half a dozen legends are familiar to all who recognize his name, he becomes once more a mystery, almost as if he were an unknown.

This is the situation that Lincoln occupies in the United States on the 150th anniversary of his birth. Everybody knows who he was and what he did. But what was he like? For most people, Lincoln remains the rail splitter, the shrewd country lawyer, the cracker-barrel philosopher and humorist, the statesman who saved the Union, and the compassionate leader who saved many a soldier from death by court-martial, only to meet his own end as a martyr.

Not being a Lincoln scholar, I have no wish to deal with any of these images of Lincoln. I want only to help celebrate his sesquicentennial year by bringing out a Lincoln who I am sure is real though unseen. The Lincoln I know and revere is a historical figure who should stand—I will not say, instead of, but by the side of all the others. No one need forget the golden legends, yet anyone may find it rewarding to move them aside a little so as to get a glimpse of the unsuspected Lincoln I have so vividly in mind.

I refer to Lincoln the artist, the maker of a style that is unique in English prose and doubly astonishing in the history of American literature, for nothing led up to it. The Lincoln who speaks to me through the written word is a figure no longer to be described wholly or mainly by the old adjectives, shrewd, humorous, or saintly, but rather as one combining the traits that biography reports in certain artists among the greatest—passionate, gloomy, seeming-cold, and conscious of superiority.

These elements in Lincoln's makeup have been noticed before, but they take on a new meaning in the light of the new motive I detect in his prose. For his style, the plain, undecorated language in which he addresses posterity, is no mere knack with words. It is the manifestation of a mode of thought, of an outlook which colors every act of the writer's and tells us how he rated life. Only let his choice of words, the rhythm and shape of his utterances, linger in the ear, and you begin to feel as he did—hence to discern unplumbed depths in the quiet intent of a conscious artist.

But before taking this path of discovery, it is necessary to dispose of a few too familiar ideas. The first is that we already know all there is to know about Lincoln's prose. Does not every schoolchild learn that the Gettysburg Address is beautiful, hearing this said so often that he ends by believing it? The belief is general, of course, but come by in this way, it is not worth much. One proof of its little meaning is that most Americans also believe that for fifty years Lincoln's connection with the literary art was to tell racy stories. Then, suddenly, on a train journey to

Gettysburg he wrote a masterpiece. This is not the way great artists go to work—so obviously not, that to speak of Lincoln as an *artist* will probably strike some readers as a paradox or a joke. Even so, the puzzle remains: How did this strange man from Illinois produce, not a few happy phrases, but an unmistakable style?

On this point the books by experts do no better than the public. The latest collective attempt to write a literary history of the United States does indeed speak of Lincoln's styles, in the plural: but this reference is really to Lincoln's various tones, ranging from the familiar to the elevated. Like all other books that I have searched through, this authoritative work always talks of the subject or the occasion of Lincoln's words when attempting to explain the power of his best-known pieces. It is as if a painter's genius were explained by the landscapes he depicted.

Lincoln has indeed had praise as a writer, but nearly all of it has been conventional and absentminded. The few authors of serious studies have fallen into sentimentality and incoherence. Thus, in the Hay and Nicolay edition of Lincoln's works, a famous editor of the nineties writes: "Of style, in the ordinary use of the word, Lincoln may be said to have had little. There was nothing ambitiously elaborate or self-consciously simple in Lincoln's way of writing. He had not the scholar's range of words. He was not always grammatically accurate. He would doubtless have been very much surprised if anyone had told him that he 'had' a style at all."

Here one feels like asking: Then why discuss "Lincoln as a writer"? The answer is unconvincing: "And yet, because he was determined to be understood, because he was honest, because he had a warm and true heart, because he had read good books eagerly and not coldly, and because there was in him a native good taste, as well as a strain of imagination, he achieved a singularly clear and forcible style, which took color from his own noble character and became a thing individual and distinguished. . . ."

*

So the man who had no style had a style—clear, forcible, individual and distinguished. This is as odd a piece of reasoning as that offered by the late Senator Beveridge: "The cold fact is that not one faint glimmer appears in his whole life, at least before his Cooper Union speech, which so much as suggests the radiance of the last two years." Perhaps a senator is never a good judge of what a president writes: this one asks us to believe in a miracle. One would think the "serious" critics had simply failed to read their author.

Yet they must have read him, to be so obviously bothered. "How did he do it?" they wonder. They think of the momentous issues of the Civil War, of the grueling four years in Washington, of the man beset by politicians who were too aggressive and by generals who were not enough so, and the solution flashes upon them: "It was the strain that turned homespun into great literature." This is again to confuse a literary occasion with the literary power which rises to it. The famous documents —the two inaugurals, the Gettysburg Address, the letter to Mrs. Bixby—marvelous as they are, do not solve the riddle. On the contrary, the subjects have such a grip on our emotions that we begin to think almost anybody could have moved us. For all these reasons—inadequate criticism, overfamiliarity with a few masterpieces, ignorance of Lincoln's early work and the consequent suppression of one whole side of his character—we must go back to the source and begin at the beginning.

Pick up any early volume of Lincoln's works and start reading as if you were approaching a new author. Pretend you know none of the anecdotes, nothing of the way the story embedded in these pages comes out. Your aim is to see a life unfold and to descry the character of the man from his own words, written, most of them, not to be published, but to be felt.

Here is Lincoln at twenty-three telling the people of his district by means of a handbill that they should send him to the state legislature: "Upon the subjects of which I have treated, I have spoken as I thought. I may be wrong in regard to any or all of them; but holding it a sound maxim that it is better to be only sometimes right than at all times wrong, so soon as I discover

my opinions to be erroneous, I shall be ready to renounce them."
And he closes his appeal for votes on an unpolitical note suggestive of melancholy thoughts: "But if the good people in their
wisdom shall see fit to keep me in the background, I have been
too familiar with disappointments to be very much chagrined."

One does not need to be a literary man to see that Lincoln
was a born writer, nor a psychologist to guess that here is a youth
of uncommon mold—strangely self-assertive, yet detached, and
also laboring under a sense of misfortune.

For his handbill Lincoln may have had to seek help with his
spelling, which was always uncertain, but the rhythm of those
sentences was never taught by a grammar book. Lincoln, as he
himself said, went to school "by littles," which did not in the
aggregate amount to a year. Everybody remembers the story of
his reading the Bible in the light of the fire and scribbling with
charcoal on the back of the shovel. But millions have read the
Bible and not become even passable writers. The neglected
truth is that not one but several persons who remembered his
childhood remarked on the boy's singular determination to express his thoughts in the best way.

His stepmother gave an account of the boy which prefigures
the literary artist much more than the rail splitter: "He didn't
like physical labor. He read all the books he could lay his hands
on. . . . When he came across a passage that struck him, he
would write it down on boards if he had no paper and keep it
there till he did get paper, then he would rewrite it, look at it,
repeat it." Later, Lincoln's law partner, William H. Herndon,
recorded the persistence of this obsessive habit with words: "He
used to bore me terribly by his methods. . . . Mr. Lincoln
would doubly explain things to me that needed no explanation. . . . Mr. Lincoln was a very patient man generally,
but . . . just go at Lincoln with abstractions, glittering generalities, indefiniteness, mistiness of idea or expression. Here he
flew up and became vexed, and sometimes foolishly so."

In youth, Lincoln had tried to be a poet, but found he lacked
the gift. What he could do was think with complete clarity in
words and imagine the workings of others' minds at the same

time. One does not read far in his works before discovering that as a writer he toiled above all to find the true order for his thoughts—order first, and then a lightninglike brevity. Here is how he writes in 1846, a young politician far from the limelight, and of whom no one expected a lapidary style: "If I falsify in this you can convict me. The witnesses live, and can tell." There is a fire in this, and a control of it, which shows the master.

That control of words implied a corresponding control of the emotions. Herndon described several times in his lectures and papers the eccentric temperament of his lifelong partner. This portrait the kindly sentimental people have not been willing to accept. But Herndon's sense of greatness was finer than that of the admirers from afar, who worship rather storybook heroes than the mysterious, difficult, unsatisfactory sort of great man— the only sort that history provides.

What did Herndon say? He said that Lincoln was a man of sudden and violent moods, often plunged in deathly melancholy for hours, then suddenly lively and ready to joke; that Lincoln was self-centered and cold, not given to revealing his plans or opinions, and ruthless in using others' help and influence; that Lincoln was idle for long stretches of time, during which he read newspapers or simply brooded; that Lincoln had a disconcerting power to see into questions, events, and persons, never deceived by their incidental features or conventional garb, but extracting the central matter as one cores an apple; that Lincoln was a man of strong passions and mystical longings, which he repressed because his mind showed him their futility, and that this made him cold-blooded and a fatalist.

In addition, as we know from other sources, Lincoln was subject to vague fears and dark superstitions. Strange episodes, though few, marked his relations with women, including his wife-to-be, Mary Todd. He was subject, as some of his verses show, to obsessional gloom about separation, insanity, and death. We should bear in mind that Lincoln was orphaned, reared by a step-mother, and early cast adrift to make his own way. His strangely detached attitude toward himself, his premonitions and depressions, his morbid regard for truth and abnormal suppression of aggressive impulses, suggest that he hugged a secret wound which ultimately made out of an apparent common man the unique figure of an artist-saint.

Lincoln moreover believed that his mother was the illegitimate daughter of a Virginia planter, and like others who have known or fancied themselves of irregular descent, he had a powerful, unreasoned faith in his own destiny—a destiny he felt would combine greatness and disaster.

Whatever psychiatry might say to this, criticism recognizes the traits of a type of artist one might call "the dark outcast." Michelangelo and Byron come to mind as examples. In such men the sense of isolation from others is in the emotions alone. The mind remains a clear and fine instrument of common sense— Michelangelo built buildings, and Byron brilliantly organized the Greeks in their revolt against Turkey. In Lincoln there is no incompatibility between the lawyer-statesman, whom we all know, and the artist, whose physiognomy I have been trying to sketch.

Lincoln's detachment was what produced his mastery over men. Had he not, as president, towered in mind and will over his cabinet, they would have crushed or used him without remorse. Chase, Seward, Stanton, the Blairs, McClellan had among them enough egotism and ability to wreck several administrations. Each thought Lincoln would be an easy victim. It was not until he was removed from their midst that any of them conceived of him as an apparition greater than themselves. During his life their dominant feeling was exasperation with him for making them feel baffled. They could not bring him down to their reach. John Hay, who saw the long struggle, confirms Herndon's judgments: "It is absurd to call him a modest man. No great man was ever modest. It was his intellectual arrogance and unconscious assumption of superiority that men like Chase and Sumner could never forgive."

This is a different Lincoln from the clumsy country lawyer who makes no great pretensions, but has a trick or two up his sleeve and wins the day for righteousness because his heart is pure. Lincoln's purity was that of a supremely conscious genius, not of an innocent. And if we ask what kind of genius enables a man to master a new and sophisticated scene as Lincoln did, without the aid of what are called personal advantages, with little experience in affairs of state and no established following, the answer is: military genius or its close kin, artistic genius.

The artist contrives means and marshals forces that the beholder takes for granted and that the bungler never discovers for himself. The artist is always scheming to conquer his material and his audience. When we speak of his craft, we mean quite literally that he is crafty.

Lincoln acquired his power over words in the only two ways known to man—by reading and by writing. His reading was small in range and much of a kind: the Bible, Bunyan, Byron, Burns, Defoe, Shakespeare, and a then-current edition of Aesop's Fables. These are books from which a genius would extract the lesson of terseness and strength. The Bible and Shakespeare's poetry would be less influential than Shakespeare's prose, whose rapid twists and turns Lincoln often rivals, though without imagery. The four other British writers are all devotees of the telling phrase, rather than the suggestive. As for Aesop, the similarity of his stories with the anecdotes Lincoln liked to tell —always in the same words—is obvious. But another parallel occurs, that between the shortness of a fable and the mania Lincoln had for condensing any matter into the fewest words:

"John Fitzgerald, eighteen years of age, able-bodied, but without pecuniary means, came directly from Ireland to Springfield, Illinois, and there stopped, and sought employment, with no present intention of returning to Ireland or going elsewhere. After remaining in the city some three weeks, part of the time employed, and part not, he fell sick, and became a public charge. It has been submitted to me, whether the City of Springfield, or the County of Sangamon is, by law, to bear the charge."

As Lincoln himself wrote on another occasion, "This is not a long letter, but it contains the whole story." And the paragraph would prove, if it were necessary, that style is independent of attractive subject matter. The pleasure it gives is that of lucidity and motion, the motion of Lincoln's mind.

In his own day, Lincoln's prose was found flat, dull, lacking in taste. It differed radically in form and tone from the accepted models—Webster's or Channing's for speeches, Bryant's or Greeley's for journalism. Once or twice, Lincoln did imitate their genteel circumlocutions or resonant abstractions. But these were exercises he never repeated. His style, well in hand by his thirtieth year and richly developed by his fiftieth, has the eloquence which comes of the contrast between transparency of medium and density of thought. Consider this episode from a lyceum lecture written when Lincoln was twenty-nine:

"Turn, then, to that horror-striking scene at St. Louis. A single victim was only sacrificed there. His story is very short; and is, perhaps, the most highly tragic of anything of its length that has ever been witnessed in real life. A mulatto man by the name of McIntosh was seized in the street, dragged to the suburbs of the city, chained to a tree, and actually burned to death; and all within a single hour from the time he had been a freeman, attending to his own business, and at peace with the world."

Notice the contrasting rhythm of the two sentences: "A single victim was only sacrificed there. His story is very short." The sentences are very short, too, but let anyone try imitating their continuous flow or subdued emotion on the characteristic Lincolnian theme of the swift passage from the business of life to death.

Lincoln's prose works fall into three categories: speeches, letters, and proclamations. The speeches range from legal briefs and arguments to political debates. The proclamations begin with his first offer of his services as a public servant and end with his presidential statements of policy or calls to Thanksgiving between 1861 and 1865. The letters naturally cover his life span and a great diversity of subjects. They are, I surmise, the crucible in which Lincoln cast his style. By the time he was in the White House, he could frame, impromptu, hundreds of messages such as this telegram to General McClellan: "I have just read your despatch about sore-tongued and fatigued horses. Will you pardon me for asking what the horses of your army have done since the battle of Antietam that fatigues anything?"

Something of Lincoln's tone obviously comes from the practice of legal thought. It would be surprising if the effort of mind that Lincoln put into his profession had not come out again in his prose. After all, he made his name and rose to the presidency over a question of constitutional law. Legal thought encourages precision through the imagining and the denial of alternatives. The language of the law foresees doubt, ambiguity, confusion, stupid or fraudulent error, and one by one it excludes them. Most lawyers succeed at least in avoiding misunderstanding, and this obviously is the foundation of any prose that aims at clear expression.

As a lawyer Lincoln knew that the courtroom vocabulary would achieve this purpose if handled with a little care. But it would remain jargon, obscure to the common understanding. As an artist, therefore, he undertook to frame his ideas invariably in one idiom, that of daily life. He had to use, of course, the technical names of the actions and documents he dealt with. But all the rest was in the vernacular. His first achievement, then, was to translate the minute accuracy of the advocate and the judge into the words of common men.

To say this is to suggest a measure of Lincoln's struggle as an artist. He started with very little confidence in his stock of knowledge, and having to face audiences far more demanding than ours, he toiled to improve his vocabulary, grammar, and logic. In the first year of his term in Congress he labored through six books of Euclid in hopes of developing the coherence of thought he felt he needed in order to demonstrate his views. Demonstration was to him the one proper goal of argument; he never seems to have considered it within his power to convince by disturbing the judgment through the emotions. In the few passages where he resorts to platform tricks, he uses only irony or satire, never the rain-barrel booming of the Fourth-of-July orator.

One superior gift he possessed from the start and developed to a supreme degree, the gift of rhythm. Take this fragment, not from a finished speech, but from a jotting for a lecture on the law:

"There is a vague popular belief that lawyers are necessarily dishonest. I say vague, because when we consider to what extent confidence and honors are reposed in and conferred upon lawyers by the people, it appears improbable that their impression of dishonesty is very distinct and vivid. Yet the impression is common, almost universal. Let no young man choosing the law for a calling for a moment yield to the popular belief—resolve to be honest at all events; and if in your own judgment you cannot be an honest lawyer, resolve to be honest without being a lawyer."

Observe the ease with which the theme is announced: "There is a vague popular belief that lawyers are necessarily dishonest." It is short without crackling like an epigram, the word "necessarily" retarding the rhythm just enough. The thought is picked up with hardly a pause: "I say vague, because, when we consider . . ." and so on through the unfolding of reasons, which winds up in a kind of calm: "it appears improbable that their impression of dishonesty is very distinct and vivid." Now a change of pace to refresh interest: "Yet the impression is common, almost universal." And a second change, almost immediately, to usher in the second long sentence, which carries the conclusion: "Let no young man choosing the law . . ."

The paragraph moves without a false step, neither hurried nor drowsy; and by its movement, like one who leads another in the dance, it catches up our thought and swings it into willing compliance. The ear notes at the same time that none of the sounds grate or clash: the piece is sayable like a speech in a great play; the music is manly, the alliterations are few and natural. Indeed, the paragraph seems to have come into being spontaneously as the readiest incarnation of Lincoln's thoughts.

From hints here and there, one gathers that Lincoln wrote slowly—meaning, by writing, the physical act of forming letters on paper. This would augment the desirability of being brief. Lincoln wrote before the typewriter and the dictating machine, and wanting to put all his meaning into one or two lucid sentences, he thought before he wrote. The great compression came after he had, lawyerlike, excluded alternatives and hit upon right order and emphasis.

Obviously this style would make use of skips and connections unsuited to speechmaking. The member of the cabinet who received a terse memorandum had it before him to make out at leisure. But an audience requires a looser texture, just as it requires a more measured delivery. This difference between the written and the spoken word lends color to the cliché that if Lincoln had a style, he developed it in his presidential years. Actually, Lincoln, like an artist, adapted his means to the occasion. There was no pathos in him before pathos was due. When he supposed his audience intellectually alert—as was the famous gathering at Cooper Union in 1860—he gave them his concentrated prose. We may take as a sample a part of the passage where he addresses the South:

"Again, you say we have made the slavery question more prominent than it formerly was. We deny it. We admit that it is more prominent, but we deny that we made it so. It was not we, but you, who discarded the old policy of the fathers. We resisted, and still resist, your innovation; and thence comes the greater prominence of the question. Would you have that question reduced to its former proportions? Go back to that old policy. What has been, will be again, under the same conditions. If you would have the peace of the old times, readopt the precepts and policy of the old times."

This is wonderfully clear and precise and demonstrative, but two hours of equally succinct argument would tax any but the most athletic audience. Lincoln gambled on the New Yorkers' agility of mind, and won. But we should not be surprised that in the debates with Stephen A. Douglas, a year and a half before, we find the manner different. Those wrangles lasted three hours, and the necessity for each speaker to interweave prepared statements of policy with improvised rebuttals of charges and "points" gives these productions a coarser grain. Yet on Lincoln's side, the same artist mind is plainly at work:

"Senator Douglas is of world-wide renown. All the anxious politicians of his party, or who have been of his party for years past, have been looking upon him as certainly, at no distant day, to be the President of the United States. They have seen in his round, jolly, fruitful face, post offices, land offices, marshalships, and cabinet appointments, chargéships and foreign missions, bursting and sprouting out in wonderful exuberance ready to be laid hold of by their greedy hands."

The man who could lay the ground for a splendid yet catchy metaphor about political plums by describing Douglas's face as round, jolly and *fruitful* is not a man to be thought merely lucky in the handling of words. The debates abound in happy turns, but read less well than Lincoln's more compact productions. Often, Douglas's words are more polished:

"We have existed and prospered from that day to this thus divided and have increased with a rapidity never before equaled in wealth, the extension of territory, and all the elements of power and greatness, until we have become the first nation on the face of the globe. Why can we not thus continue to prosper?"

It is a mistake to underrate Douglas's skill, which was that of a professional. Lincoln's genius needs no heightening through lowering others. Douglas was smooth and adroit, and his arguments were effective, since Lincoln was defeated. But Douglas —not so Lincoln—sounds like anybody else.

Lincoln's extraordinary power was to make his spirit felt, a power I attribute to his peculiar relation to himself. He regarded his face and physique with amusement and dismay, his mind and destiny with wonder. Seeming clumsy and diffident, he also showed a calm superiority which he expressed as if one half of a double man were talking about the other.

In conduct, this detachment was the source of his saintlike forebearance; in his art, it yielded the rare quality of elegance. Nowhere is this link between style and emotional distance clearer than in the farewell Lincoln spoke to his friends in Springfield before leaving for Washington. A single magical word, easy to pass over carelessly, holds the clue:

"My friends: No one, not in my situation, can appreciate my feeling of sadness at this parting. To this place, and the kindness of these people, I owe everything. . . ." If we stop to think, we ask: "This place"?—yes. But why "*these* people"? Why not "you people," whom he was addressing from the train platform, or "this place and the kindness of *its* people"? It is not, certainly, the mere parallel of *this* and *these* that commanded the choice. "These" is a stroke of genius, which betrays Lincoln's isolation from the action itself—Lincoln talking to himself about the place and the people whom he was leaving, foreboding the possibility of his never returning, and closing the fifteen lines with one of the greatest cadences in English speech: "To His care commending you, as I hope in your prayers you will commend me, I bid you an affectionate farewell."

The four main qualities of Lincoln's literary art—precision, vernacular ease, rhythmical virtuosity, and elegance—may at a century's remove seem alien to our tastes. Yet it seems no less odd to question their use and interest to the present when one considers one continuing strain in our literature. Lincoln's example, plainly, helped to break the monopoly of the dealers in literary plush. After Lincoln comes Mark Twain, and out of Mark Twain come contemporaries of ours as diverse as Sherwood Anderson, H. L. Mencken, and Ernest Hemingway. Lincoln's use of his style for the intimate genre and for the sublime was his alone; but his workaday style is the American style par excellence.

1959

Delmore Schwartz

Schwartz (1913–1966), the Brooklyn-born poet whose self-destructive genius inspired Saul Bellow's novel *Humboldt's Gift*, published an early version of this poem in *Genesis* (1943), an autobiographical work in prose and verse, and then revised it for inclusion in *Summer Knowledge*, a selection of his poems published in 1959—the year of the Lincoln sesquicentennial. Harsh, provocative, and full of rage, Schwartz positions himself as the anti-Sandburg, eager to tell his countrymen that the "prairie Christ" they have made to "sate the need coarse in the national heart" was no more than "a tricky lawyer," an indecisive, opportunistic, suicidal figure mostly worthy of their pity and scorn. Equally derided by Schwartz is the possibility that the Civil War had any victor besides the "stupid deity" of capitalism. With its furious evocation of futility and insanity, Schwartz's poem serves as a prescient overture to the iconoclastic 1960s.

Lincoln

Manic-depressive Lincoln, national hero!
How just and true that this great nation, being conceived
In liberty by fugitives should find
—Strange ways and plays of monstrous History—
This Hamlet-type to be the President—

This failure, this unwilling bridegroom,
This tricky lawyer full of black despair—

He grew a beard, becoming President,
And took a shawl as if he guessed his role,
Though with the beard he fled cartoonists' blacks,
And many laughed and were contemptuous,
And some for four years spoke of killing him—

He was a politician—of the heart!—
He lived from hand to mouth in moral things!
He understood quite well Grant's drunkenness!
It was for him, before Election Day,
That at Cold Harbor Grant threw lives away
In hopeless frontal attack against Lee's breastworks!

O how he was the Hamlet-man, and this,
After a life of failure made him right,
After he ran away on his wedding day,
Writing a coward's letter to his bride—
How with his very failure, he out-tricked
The florid Douglas and the abstract Davis,
And all the vain men who, surrounding him,
Smiled in their vanity and sought his place—

Later, they made him out a prairie Christ
To sate the need coarse in the national heart—

His wife went insane, Mary Todd too often
Bought herself dresses. And his child died.
And he would not condemn young men to death
For having slept, in weakness. And he spoke
More than he knew and all that he had felt
Between outrageous joy and black despair
Before and after Gettysburg's pure peak—

He studied law, but knew in his own soul
Despair's anarchy, terror and error,
—Instruments had to be taken from his office
And from his bedroom in such days of horror,
Because some saw that he might kill himself:
When he was young, when he was middle-aged,
How just and true was he, our national hero!

Sometimes he could not go home to face his wife,
Sometimes he wished to hurry or end his life!
But do not be deceived. He did not win,

And, it is plain, the South could never win
(Despite the gifted Northern generals!)
—Capitalismus is not mocked, O no!
This stupid deity decided the War—

In fact, the North and South were losers both:
—Capitalismus won the Civil War—

—Capitalismus won the Civil War,
Yet, in the War's cruel Colosseum,
Some characters fulfilled their natures' surds,
Grant the drunkard, Lee the noble soldier,
John Brown in whom the Bible soared and cried,
Booth the unsuccessful Shakespearean,
—Each in some freedom walked and knew himself,
Then most of all when all the deities
Mixed with their barbarous stupidity
To make the rock, root, and rot of the war—

"This is the way each only life becomes,
Tossed on History's ceaseless insane sums!"

1959

Norman Corwin

A onetime journalist and film publicist, Corwin (b. 1910) began writing and producing radio broadcasts for CBS in 1938. Over the next decade he created original programs on the Bill of Rights, wartime England, and the Allied victory in Europe, as well as adaptations of literary works such as *Spoon River Anthology*, *The Red Badge of Courage*, and Carl Sandburg's *The People, Yes*. Corwin made his last program for CBS in 1949; the following year he was one of 151 persons named in the booklet *Red Channels*, which became the basis for the blacklist in broadcasting—though he was still able to write the screenplays for several Hollywood films under his own name during the 1950s. *The Rivalry*, his stage play about the 1858 Lincoln-Douglas Senate race, toured the United States in 1957–58 in a production starring Raymond Massey as Lincoln, Martin Gabel as Douglas, and Agnes Moorehead as Adele Douglas, and a Broadway production with Richard Boone, Gabel, and Nancy Kelly ran for 81 performances in 1959. Although much of the dialogue in the play was drawn from the 1858 debate transcripts, the dramatically compressed stage version ended up much closer in format to the Kennedy-Nixon debates of 1960 than the actual Lincoln-Douglas encounters, each of which opened with a 60-minute speech, followed by a 90-minute reply, and then concluded with a 30-minute rejoinder. The first excerpt printed below takes place during the 1858 campaign, while the second recounts Douglas's response to the threat of secessionism in 1860–61.

FROM

The Rivalry

ADELE

(*To audience*) There was only one other time during the debates when I exchanged a few words with Mr. Lincoln. Stephen and I were staying at the Tremont House in Chicago and so was Mr. Lincoln. I met him in the lobby. Stephen had forgotten something, and had gone up to get it; Mr. Lincoln was sitting alone, in a big leather chair. (*Turns toward him*) He looked tired.

I never saw a more thoughtful or dignified face. I never saw so sad a face.

LINCOLN

Good evening, Mrs. Douglas.

ADELE

Good evening, Mr. Lincoln. You look weary. Are you well?

LINCOLN

Oh, yes, thank you . . . but I *am* a little used up.

ADELE

So is the Senator. You certainly have had *at* each other.

LINCOLN

I'm afraid campaigning is not one of the gentler arts.

ADELE

I had no illusions that you would be *tender* with each other, but the *brickbats*—

LINCOLN

Kind words about a man are usually saved up until after he's dead . . . on the theory, I suppose, that they won't go to his head then.

ADELE

That *is* a little late for vanity.

LINCOLN

Even post-mortem, of course, there's some question as to how one will be treated when he gets where he's going. In the cemetery up in New Salem, there's an epitaph on the grave of an old Indian chief named Johnny Kangapod:

> "Here lies Johnny Kangapod—
> Be gentle to him, gracious God,
> As he would be if he were God,
> And You were Johnny Kangapod."

ADELE

Now why can't you tell stories like that in the debates? I mean when you both run out of arguments?

LINCOLN

Do you think the Judge will ever let that happen?

ADELE

Frankly, no.

LINCOLN

Do you know the story of the backwoods housewife, who lived in a messed-up log cabin? —One day a wandering preacher came along and wanted to sell her a Bible. She answered sharply that she already *owned* a Bible. "Let's see it," said the preacher. So she started to look for it, but couldn't find it. She called in her children, and they joined in the hunt. At last, after turning the place upside down, one of the children held up in triumph a few torn and ragged pages of Holy Writ. The preacher tried to argue that this was no Bible and how could she pretend it was? But the lady stuck to her claims. "Of *course* it's a Bible," she said—"But I had no idea we were so nearly *out*."

ADELE

(*Laughs*) Where *do* you get your stories, Mr. Lincoln? They are always so *apt*. It's uncanny!

LINCOLN

Maybe my ideas move in pairs, Mrs. Douglas, like the beasts entering Noah's Ark.

ADELE

I've heard it said that story-telling is characteristic of the country you were raised in.

LINCOLN

It's good enough country without stories, ma'am.

ADELE

I have no doubt. —Where Stephen was brought up, in Vermont, they're unusually tight-lipped.

LINCOLN

I believe that's one tradition he left behind him in New England. I say that very respectfully.

ADELE

I know you do. —The last time we met, Mr. Lincoln, you mentioned your indifference to innuendo and insinuation. Since then I've read an attack on you that even I, in the camp of the enemy, know to be full of errors, if not outright lies. Do you mean to say you don't intend to write a letter setting the facts straight?

LINCOLN

I guess I'm not really mad enough. —Mrs. Douglas, I do the

very best I know how. I mean to keep doing so. If the end brings me out all right, what's said against me won't amount to anything. If the end brings me out wrong, ten thousand angels swearing I was right would make no difference.

ADELE

But you seem to be a man of high principle. Is there no principle involved in this?

LINCOLN

Yes, but one picks carefully the principles he wants to stand up to defend. For example, a rich client came to my law office in Springfield one day, determined to sue a poor attorney for $2.50. I urged him to let the matter drop. I said, "You can make nothing out of him, and it will cost you a good deal more than the amount of the debt, for you to bring suit." But my client was determined to have his way. "Principle!" he said. "It's the *principle* of the thing!" So I finally took the case, and said my fee would be $10, which he paid me on the spot. As soon as he left the office, I hunted up the poor lawyer, told him about the suit, and handed him half of the $10. Together we went over to the squire's office, where he confessed judgment, and paid the $2.50 that he owed. That was the only way I could see to make things satisfactory—in principle—for my rich client as well as the poor debtor.

ADELE

(*Laughing*) A profitable deal all the way around.

LINCOLN

How are you bearing up under the debates, Mrs. Douglas?

ADELE

I'm not really. I find them frightening at times. I don't at all like the way it's assumed in some quarters that the issue of war and peace depends on you and my husband, as though you had personally invented abolitionism, and he slavery. I have no humor whatever when it comes to the subject of war. I think it's the foulest abomination of mankind.

LINCOLN

I'm sure I feel just as you do about it.

ADELE

(*Sees* DOUGLAS *entering at R*) Well . . . the Judge will be looking for me. One last question before I go, if I may: Was the town of Lincoln in this state named after you?

LINCOLN

Well—all I can tell you is that *it* was named after *I* was.

ADELE

(*Smiling; as she starts off*) Good evening, Mr. Lincoln.

———

ADELE

He went South. He spoke in a dozen cities. The Slave States didn't like his arguments against secession; he was threatened with physical violence all the time we traveled down there. In some places eggs were thrown at him . . . but he was not deterred for a moment. —And then came the election. Well, Stephen was the model of a good loser. I think I can say that with modesty and pride. On the very evening the Lincolns arrived in Washington an ailing Stephen called on the President at Willard's Hotel. . . . (DOUGLAS *enters from R,* LINCOLN *a moment later, from L. He greets* DOUGLAS *warmly, and offers him a chair*)

LINCOLN

Judge . . .

DOUGLAS

It's good to see you, Mr. President. (DOUGLAS *starts to sit, but holds up until* LINCOLN *precedes him.* LINCOLN *notices this, and motions for him to sit . . . a friendly waiving of formalities between them . . .*)

LINCOLN

No, no, sit down, sit down. . . . (*Concerned*) I've heard you're not well.

DOUGLAS

(*Dismissing it*) Oh, it's nothing. —Mr. President, we have said many harsh things to each other within the hearing of the whole country. But we have never, for a moment, disagreed in the conviction that the Union must not and shall not be destroyed. —I have come here tonight to assure you that I and my friends pledge ourselves with all our strength and energy to aid you. I am with you, Mr. President . . . and God bless you. (LINCOLN, *moved, looks at him silently.* HE *makes a move, a subtle indication that*

HE *wants to reply . . . but perhaps an excess of emotion chokes him.* DOUGLAS *goes on*) I'm also concerned about the threats to do violence to you at the inauguration. Have the proper precautions been taken?

LINCOLN

If I were to worry about threats like that, I could never get on with this job.

DOUGLAS

Well, I want you to know that if any man attacks you, he attacks me too! I shall be there when you take the oath!

LINCOLN

(*After a moment*) Judge, when I first heard you called The Little Giant, I was satisfied that the name fitted—but you've never lived up to it more than you have just now. . . .

DOUGLAS

(*Moved*) Thank you.

LINCOLN

No, no—with all my heart I thank *you*. The people with us, and God helping us, all will yet be well.

DOUGLAS

I earnestly hope so. (*Rising*) Don't hesitate to call upon me if there's anything I can do.

LINCOLN

(*Slowly rising*) Well now, there may be. —As you know, there's trouble in our own state. The secessionists are busy again.

DOUGLAS

(*Shaking his head*) They never sleep, do they?

LINCOLN

We can take no chances of losing Illinois. As I remember now, you seem to have some influence back home. —Would you help me out by going there?

DOUGLAS

Of course I'd go. Whenever you say. I'd be honored to go.

LINCOLN

(*After a pause in which* HE *studies* DOUGLAS' *face*) Thank you Stephen. Thank you. I'll never forget this.

DOUGLAS

Mr. President . . . (DOUGLAS *exits at stage R.* LINCOLN, *after a moment, slowly exits at L.* ADELE *enters from L and resumes narration*)

ADELE

On the day of the inaugural, on the platform itself, my husband stood just a little behind Mr. Lincoln, holding his hat. And at the Inaugural Ball that night, the President led the grand march, followed by Mrs. Lincoln hand-in-hand with Stephen. My husband and the first lady were partners in the quadrille. (*A little wistfully—this might have been herself*) To all of us it seemed that it must be the happiest night in her life. —Then, in spite of everything, or perhaps because of everything war came! The President did ask Stephen to go to Illinois, where there was growing anxiety. Tired and sick as he was, Stephen went . . . and I went with him. (ADELE *retires to the back of the platform, where* SHE *remains standing.* DOUGLAS *enters from L.* HE *looks worn, haggard.* HE *is sick.* HE *has trouble beginning his speech*)

DOUGLAS

(*Brokenly*) It is with a grief that I have never before experienced . . . that I contemplate this fearful struggle. —Bloody, calamitous it will be. —But I believe in my conscience that it is a duty we owe ourselves . . . and our children . . . and our God . . . to protect this government, and our flag, from every assailant . . . *BE HE WHO HE MAY!* (*Moves forward, as though to be closer to his audience, as though to plead with every last man*) Unite . . . unite as a band of brothers . . . and rescue your Government . . . and its capital . . . and your country . . . from the enemies who have been the author of our calamity! (HE *finishes.* HE *is cold, clammy; sweat is on his brow.* HE *is silent and still for a moment; then* HE *turns and looks long, looks lovingly, silently at* ADELE. *With that,* HE *turns and very slowly walks off . . . a sick man, a dying man*) (ADELE *comes forward again, after which her husband leaves . . . for what is the last time*)

ADELE

He saved Illinois for the Union. (SHE *pauses as though affected emotionally, before* SHE *goes on*) Shortly after, Stephen became very ill. It was in Chicago. He was worn out, exhausted. And he had a strange fever. He became delirious . . . and yet in his delirium his mind was taken with the nation's sickness rather than his own. Once he cried out in his sleep: "Telegraph to the President, and let the column move on!" At about 5 o'clock on the morning of June third, in his 48th year, he asked that the blinds be thrown back and the window opened. He seemed to revive for a moment, but then sank back on the pillow and uttered the word "Death" three times. That was the end. (*The lights dim.* LINCOLN *enters from the wing in a deep shadow, and speaks into the darkness:*)

LINCOLN

Drape the public buildings of the city in mourning, and the White House in deep black. Let all regimental colors be draped and in mourning also, in honor of this man who nobly discarded party for his country.

ADELE

Well . . . the war ground on. The blood of young Americans soaked into earth that should never have been contested. And it was not many seasons before the Capital was draped in black for the Commander-in-Chief himself. God knows that all of us who lived through those days, saw enough of struggle and anguish. At times the hatred and malice was thick about us, like a dense smoke. But when I was most discouraged, I remembered the principles that Stephen had stood for at the end; how he had worked for Union and for peace . . . and I remember also the words of his lifelong friend and opponent, back in the very year of the Debates, at a time when I gave them little heed . . . when it seemed to me that denying one man's rights couldn't possibly lead to trouble, so long as that man was inferior to others. . . . (LINCOLN *appears now in a dim, ghostly light, which has faded up unobtrusively during the fade down on* ADELE)

LINCOLN

What constitutes the bulwark of our liberty and independence? Not our frowning battlements, our army and navy . . . our defence is in the spirit which prizes liberty as the heritage of all men, in all lands everywhere. Destroy this spirit and you have planted the seeds of despotism at your doors. Familiarize yourself with the chains of bondage and you prepare your own limbs to wear them. Accustomed to trample on the rights of others, you have lost the genius of your own independence and become fit subjects for the first cunning tyrant who rises among you. Whether it is right or wrong to trample on the rights of others— that is the real issue . . . the issue that will continue in this country long after the poor tongues of Judge Douglas and myself shall be silent. (*The light fades, and the stage is in darkness*)

THE END

1960

MacKinlay Kantor

The genre of counterfactual history—especially counterfactual historical fiction—has boasted few persuasive practitioners in the Lincoln field. Kantor (1904–1977) was a rare exception. A graduate of one of the nation's innumerable high schools named for Lincoln, he grew up in Webster City, Iowa, listening to grizzled Civil War veterans spinning battle stories. Their tales helped inspire two of his early novels, *Long Remember* (1934) and *Arouse and Beware* (1936), as well as his masterpiece of historical fiction, *Andersonville* (1955), which won the Pulitzer Prize for its depiction of the suffering of Union soldiers held in the infamous Confederate prison camp. In his subsequent book of speculative fiction from which the following excerpts are taken, Kantor imagined Lincoln himself as a humbled prisoner of war following an imagined Confederate victory. The fictionalized emasculation was designed to evoke horror in readers accustomed to the treasured myth of a Lincoln endowed with reassuring powers of tenacity and resistance.

FROM
If the South Had Won the Civil War

July turned unseasonably chilly following torrential rains in the Washington, D.C. region on the 3rd and 4th.

By Monday evening, Ward Hill Lamon, the President's close personal friend, and Marshal of the District of Columbia, was obsessed by fears for Mr. Lincoln's safety. Twice during the day lawless crowds had endeavored to storm into the White House, and were driven back by bayonets of the infantry on guard.

Lamon himself disappeared from the scene before sunset, and did not return for nearly three hours. A rumor had reached him and he wanted to explore it.

When Lamon returned to the White House, where he had been in residence since the first news of military calamities arrived (each night he had slept with loaded pistols beside him, on a rug outside the President's door), he was accompanied by half a dozen horsemen who wore mackintosh capes over their other clothing. The little cavalcade was followed closely by a large van used for delivery of ice during the summer months; but two New York cavalrymen occupied the driver's seat.

Marshal Lamon entered the White House, while his unidentified companions waited in shadows outside the west door. According to a later statement made by the marshal, he found President Lincoln lying on a sofa, alone, in the darkened East Room. The President had a severe headache, and a damp handkerchief was folded across his eyes.

Lamon's first words brought Abraham Lincoln to his feet. "You shan't stay here an hour longer! I can't be responsible for your safety if you remain—no one could."

The President smiled bleakly. "Just where might we go? The railroads to the North are cut, and you tell me that all of Maryland is in revolt."

"True, true," cried Lamon impatiently, "but I have other plans for you."

"Well, Hill, I have news for you as well: I am going no place."

The mighty Lamon took a deep breath. "You will go if I have to pick you up in my arms and carry you. Go—if I have to clout you over the head and render you unconscious! I have already informed Mrs. Lincoln and Bob, and they're preparing for a journey. If you persist in being stubborn," Lamon finally exploded, "you'll have to answer to her, as well as to me!"

Lamon said later that the President made his way upstairs without another word. Lamon watched him go, then hastened outside to make arrangements.

Raggle-taggle throngs were still clustered beyond the fence north of the White House, facing Lafayette Park. From the park itself rose the scream and mumble of crowds surrounding a couple of speakers who ranted on barrelheads in the glow of torchlight.

Lamon personally superintended the removal of some settees and hassocks, which were placed in the back of the ice-van. Then he reached the stairway in time to meet Mrs. Lincoln, who came down, sobbing wildly, with ten-year-old Tad clinging to her. Several servants carried a mass of luggage. Lamon knew well enough that there would be no room for such weighty impedimenta; but, in the wisdom of long experience, he said nothing to the President's wife. He drew her maid aside and ordered that only the most necessary bags be carried out. Robert Lincoln came from his room a moment later and escorted his weeping mother and little brother to the west door.

Lamon stood waiting for the President. When Mr. Lincoln appeared he was wearing a shabby old overcoat and toying with a crushed felt hat which he held in his hands.

"Hill," he said to Lamon, "remember how I wore these duds when I came into Washington, before the Inauguration?"

"I do indeed, sir. And I'm glad to see that you're no longer resisting my efforts for your safety and the safety of your family."

Lincoln walked slowly toward the west door. He repeated, as it were a litany: "I wore these duds when I came to Washington, and I might as well wear them going out."

Mrs. Lincoln and the boys were already in the van. The President halted a moment on the step and gazed sadly about, taking in the big wagon with its closed body, and the strange figures of mackintosh-draped horsemen alongside.

"Mr. President," said Lamon, joining him on the steps, "I have an introduction to perform." At his words one of the strangers stepped forward.

"Permit me, Mr. President, to introduce Major John Singleton Mosby of the Confederate States Army. He has very kindly expressed his willingness to accompany us, and I feel that we are in good custody."

The President shook hands with the young guerrilla leader. "Oh, yes," he said, but still speaking as if in a dream. "Mosby. Indeed I have heard of you."

Only after he was in the van and established on a settee opposite his wife, did he inquire of Lamon: "Just where are we bound?"

"To Richmond, Mr. President. I think 'twill be the safest place for you and the folks."

Lincoln made no reply, but reached across and stroked the

head of the frightened Tad. Then he quoted in a dry whisper: "It is finished."

Major Mosby came to the rear of the van to assure the Lincolns that the furniture had been lashed firmly into place, and they need have no fear of an upset. The van began to move. It went rumbling out into 17th Street, with Lamon and Mosby and five of Mosby's men riding in escort.

There were catcalls, then a faint cheer from some of the disorderly rovers in the street, then sounds of a fist fight breaking out. Several young men started at a dogtrot, following the van; but they fell back when two of the Confederate troopers halted and swung their mounts about to face them.

The fleeing party turned, moved east through the President's Park, crossed 15th Street, and turned south to reach the Long Bridge by a devious route. When they were a few blocks away from the White House, they met only with casually curious stares from people encountered.

Lamon had planned this flight adroitly and under pressure. He had learned that Stuart's cavalry were closing in north of the city, eager to be the first Confederate troops to enter the Nation's capital. But the slightly built Partisan Ranger had come on into town in advance, with a few of his men: a characteristic act in one who had explored the route for Stuart's famous Ride-around-McClellan the year before.

On reaching the Virginia side of the Potomac, the two Federal troopers got down from the wagon (they had no wish to go to Richmond!) and their places were taken by two of Mosby's men. Mosby led the party on south, bent on avoiding Alexandria by traveling on back roads which he knew so well.

————

However much Lee and others—North and South—might have desired those "regularly constituted authorities" to sit as a peace commission, and immediately, it was the middle of September before representatives of the two governments met in their historic conclave.

Meanwhile Federal troops finally brought order to the cities, expediting the martial law which prevailed almost throughout the Union. At first the status of the Presidency itself was in grave doubt. Who indeed *was* President of the United States? Was it Lincoln, who had fled to Richmond (or *deserted* to the Confederate cause, as his enemies proclaimed)? Or was it Hannibal Hamlin, formerly Vice-President, now automatically in succession? Even members of the Supreme Court were divided in their opinions. Indeed there were almost as many opinions as there were editors (once the process of the press was restored) or orators eager to prate from rostrum or wagon-tail.

The most puzzling aspects of the situation were dispelled on the receipt of a letter of resignation, unquestionably valid, from Mr. Lincoln himself. He addressed the Congress and the people of the United States at large.

"In the hallowed year of Seventeen-seventy-six," he wrote, "our fathers established, before the eyes of the world, a new Nation. But it now appears that Divine wisdom has dictated that that Nation shall henceforth be in twain."

Abraham Lincoln went on to acknowledge that the military events of recent date had demonstrated that the United States of America could no longer be held together by force of arms. He tendered his formal resignation from the Presidency.

"Let Americans all," he said, "North and South, blue and gray, now affirm that our respective dead shall not have perished without purpose. Let us pray that our two governments shall have a new birth in freedom."

Mr. Lincoln's last word was interpreted variously by newspapers and statesmen alike. On the whole the public reaction was anything but complimentary, except in the case of the few fanatical devotees who never believed that Lincoln could commit an error. As for the ex-President himself, he had been invited to take up quarters in President Davis's mansion, once he was escorted to Richmond by Mosby. To be a guest in the home of the Secessionist President was not, however, to Mr. Lincoln's liking, although he was willing that his family should be cared for, politely if austerely, by their late enemies.

"No, Mr. Davis," Lamon recalls Lincoln's saying flatly to the Confederate dignitary, "it's just a case of which pen you happen to drive the calf into. Now, if you'd come our way, I suppose the public would have demanded that I put you in the Old Capitol prison. So pray to make whatever substitution for that famous edifice you can manage! Hill, please affirm to Mr. Jefferson Davis the fact that you would have clapped him in irons, had he ventured into your bailiwick."

"Not irons, sir," Lamon remonstrated, turning to Davis, "but I would have been compelled to incarcerate you."

Davis shrugged. "Let it be as you say."

Thereupon a section of Castle Thunder was vacated and scrubbed, and Abraham Lincoln was established there. Lamon wished to share his imprisonment.

"I am a Virginian by birth," he declared, "and, as such, I demand the right to accompany the President of the United States into exile, into a dungeon, or to the scaffold itself!"

It was decided that Lamon's status as Marshal of the District of Columbia was sufficient to allow him to become a prisoner of State. He was ensconced in a cell adjacent to that of Mr. Lincoln. Lamon's role became that of a glorified secretary who spent most of his time acting as a bulwark between Abraham Lincoln and those who desired to see him, either to revile or—in some rare cases—to commiserate.

While Lincoln lived behind bars, the scissors of History and of Fate slashed at the map of the United States.

There sounded still the chatter of musketry, the pounding of cannon. A simultaneous collapse and defeat of the two stoutest armies which the North had put into the field was not accepted as *prima facie* evidence of a National surrender by certain doughty commanders whose far-flung forces still resisted. Men died during July, hopelessly or with supreme dedication, at lonely places in Arkansas and West Virginia, and in the South Central States. But the scale of the Confederacy had hurled itself aloft, the pan of the Union struck the ground with a disheartening thud.

In the general disorganization of government and of the military establishment, there could be no efficient supply or reinforcement of those units not directly affected by the obliteration of armies at Vicksburg and in the East. No one could count or name the last shot fired in a pitched battle, but certainly it spoke its echo into the hot air before the end of July. And, long since, the State of Maryland (following the brutal assassination of pro-Union Governor Augustus W. Bradford) had elected to join the Southern Confederacy—to be followed, in opinion and action, by Kentucky only five days later.

The loss of these two States did not come as a surprise to most of the North. It was recognized that Maryland and Kentucky had sent huge bodies of troops to support the Confederate arms. The delighted Secessionists contended spiritedly that neither State truly desired to remain as part of the Yankee structure, but had been held there either by trickery or by force.

Missouri, however, was quite another matter. Here there extended no Mason and Dixon line, nor was the Ohio River flowing within Missouri's boundaries. True, the Missouri River did flow there, but its demarcation was neither geographical nor soundly political. A preponderance of Confederate sentiment bulked heavily in the northern counties: Sterling Price, the Marmadukes, Claiborne Fox Jackson and their adherents all came from that region. The mass of pro-Yankee sentiment was in the southern portion of the state—in the highlands, with the highlanders' traditional adherence to the *status quo* and their disinclination to change. Also there existed a solid core of pro-Nationalist sympathy among the Germans in St. Louis (a sturdy factor in the original decision that Missouri should remain with the North).

Kansas was no problem: a blanket of National troops had taken care of that: the Kansas question was *per se* long since solved. But the "bleeding Kansas" of yore found a counterpart in the "murderous Missouri" of the several months following July. From the leaders of both Confederate and United States governments issued appeals for tolerance, human sympathy, human decency. It was no more feasible for Federal troops to attempt upholding a northern Missouri regime by the strength of bayonets than it was for the Confederate States' Government to send a punitive expedition through the Ozarks, though both courses were advocated by firebrands of either camp. Vicious

raids by irresponsible freebooters did nothing to help the situation, no more than did the duels (these were a momentary disgrace): duels fought, many of them, by men prominent in the
life of the State.

In the autumn, however, the State legislature, which could by
no stretch of imagination be called a rump, established Missouri's
adherence to the North beyond any shadow of a doubt. Then,
as in 1861, an official appeal was made for Federal troops. These
were forthcoming, and remained on guard until 1866.

The Confederacy had little desire to expend blood in order
to add doubtful territory to its possessions, when such rich and
populous commonwealths as Kentucky and Maryland had swept
into the Southern ranks without coercion. The pro-slavery and
pro-Secessionist groups and families of the northern Missouri
counties promptly washed their hands of the whole situation,
and the most ardent of these chose to take up residence within
the Confederacy. Many pathetic or humorous accounts of the
hegira which ensued have since become a portion of Americana.
The "Sixty-three-ers" and "Sixty-four-ers" of Missouri legendry
have almost as firm a hold on our traditional affection as the
Forty-niners. Rich slave-holding families sold out—in most
cases, to remarkable advantage, since there were many bidders
for every inch of property. They moved to Kentucky, Tennessee
and Arkansas, to be received with open arms by their late comrades. A former Confederate general, Sterling Price, eventually
became a Confederate senator from Tennessee.

The retention of Missouri in the Union was regarded as an
event of signal importance in the West, and as a matter especially vital to her closest neighbors—Kansas, Nebraska, Iowa and
Illinois. Attention in the East, however, was focused upon the
future status of West Virginia, the struggle for the eastern shore
of Maryland, and the problem of Washington, D.C.

In Richmond, Virginia's more vociferous patriots demanded
immediate reacquisition of those counties of northwestern Virginia which had formed a new State and so recently attached
themselves to the United States (formal admission: June 19th,
1863). Following the piecemeal destruction of the Army of the
Potomac, Confederate commanders of troops in the Harper's

Ferry region and further up the Valley of Virginia had, on their own responsibility, thrown out columns through mountains to the west. (In one case at least there was out-and-out expression of intent to seize and subjugate the city of Charleston.) The advancing Secessionists were halted with heavy losses, inflicted by Federal troops still holding the region, together with West Virginia militia and hastily armed parties of enraged citizens. Governor Arthur I. Boreman issued a manifesto in which he declared that the mother state, Virginia, stood guilty of abrogating morally the doctrine of Secession which had now achieved a dignity of historical stature. Quoting the *lives, fortunes and sacred honor* phrase of the original Declaration of Independence, Governor Boreman flung back in the teeth of the Secessionists their own statements, uttered devoutly in earlier years.

"We West Virginians stand as intentioned spiritually as we do physically," he declared, "to uphold the doctrine of self-determination as staunchly as any Virginian, living or dead, ever upheld it against the fancied domination of the North." *Save West Virginia!* became a rallying cry throughout southeastern Ohio and southwestern Pennsylvania. Within three days after the publication of this firm stand, Federal artillery brigades were wheeling into position in the mountains.

In Richmond ex-President Lincoln was reputed to have pleaded personally with Jefferson Davis to avoid further bloodshed. Lamon, in his memoirs,* hints that a meeting came about, but gives few details. Whether he was impressed by Boreman's plea or not, or whether he was considerate merely of the practical military problems involved (obviously these were tremendous, because of the nature of the terrain), Davis soon persuaded his impetuous commanders not to proceed further on what might have turned out to be an exceedingly ill-starred campaign. The admission of West Virginia to the Union was acknowledged by the Southern Confederacy, and was included as an integral part of the Washington Treaty, signed on December 16th, 1863.

No longer was there an auburn-haired Kate Chase wielding

Recollections of a Cavalier. Ward Hill Lamon. Philadelphia: J. B. Lippincott Company, 1887.

the imperious wand of her beauty, no longer was there a Mary Todd Lincoln to set tongues gossiping by the extravagance of her gowns. Mrs. Kate Chase Sprague was now circulating a little less imperiously in dull, crowded Philadelphia. And Mary Todd Lincoln was in Illinois.

So was her husband, the only President of the United States to resign his office. Released from detention in Richmond a month before (as a pronounced gesture of international amity), he had withdrawn quietly to his former home at Springfield.

There patiently he endured the flood of calumny, vituperation and mere criticism which rushed around him; there he received the rare affirmation of personal loyalty and affection from friends who still clung; and from there he went, a few months afterward, to practice law in Chicago, along with the stout Lamon.

More profitable legal business than he might have believed possible came Mr. Lincoln's way. "Hill," he said to his worshiping partner in March, "I thought to be turned out to grass, and winter-killed grass at that. Never did I expect to discover a downright clover patch!"

On the evening of April 14th, 1865, he went to McVickers Theatre in the Chicago Loop, where Taylor's trivial play, *Our American Cousin*, was being presented. There, while seated with friends in a box, he was shot to death by an actor whose hatred for Abraham Lincoln had survived all changes of status and of capitals, all affirmations of Peace.

1961

Marianne Moore

After publishing poetry for more than 35 years, Moore (1887–1972) achieved wide acclaim with her *Collected Poems* (1951), which won the Pulitzer Prize, the National Book Award, and the Bollingen Prize, and a degree of celebrity for her fondness for three-cornered hats and black capes and passion for New York baseball. "Abraham Lincoln and the Art of the Word" first appeared in *Lincoln for the Ages* (1960), an anthology of Lincoln tributes assembled by the Chicago bibliophile Ralph G. Newman; a revised and expanded version was included in *A Marianne Moore Reader* the following year. Weaving her way with economy and precision through a carefully assembled array of quotations from his works, Moore identifies the "persuasive expedients" Lincoln used to convey "*the meaning*, clear and unadorned." For Moore, his writing reveals an art she memorably calls "a 'grasp of eternal grace.'"

Abraham Lincoln and
the Art of the Word

"I dislike an oath which requires a man to swear he *has* not done wrong. It rejects the Christian principle of forgiveness on terms of repentance. I think it is enough if the man does no wrong hereafter."* It was Abraham Lincoln who said this—his controlled impetuosity exemplifying excellences both of the technician and of the poet.

The malcontent attacks greatness by disparaging it—by libels on efficiency, interpreting needful silence as lack of initiative, by distortion, by ridicule. "As a general rule," Lincoln said, "I abstain from reading attacks upon myself, wishing not to be provoked by that to which I cannot promptly offer an answer." Expert in rebuttal, however, as in strategy, he often won juries

---

*Quotations from Lincoln are taken from Earl S. Miers and Paul M. Angle, editors, *The Living Lincoln* (New Brunswick, N.J.: Rutgers University Press, 1955); and from Roy P. Basler, editor, *Abraham Lincoln: His Speeches and Writings* (New York: World, 1946).

and disinterested observers alike, by anecdote or humorous implication that made argument unnecessary. His use of words became a perfected instrument, acquired by an education largely self-attained—"'picked up,'" he said, "under pressure of necessity." That the books read became part of him is apparent in phrases influenced by the Bible, Shakespeare, *The Pilgrim's Progress*, *Robinson Crusoe*, Burns, Blackstone's *Commentaries*; and not least, by some books of Euclid—read and "nearly mastered," as he says, after he had become a member of Congress. The largeness of the life entered into the writing, as with a passion he strove to persuade his hearers of what he believed, his adroit, ingenious mentality framing an art which, if it is not to be designated poetry, we may call a "grasp of eternal grace"—in both senses, figurative and literal. Nor was he unaware of having effected what mattered, as we realize by his determined effort, when a first attempt failed, to obtain from the *Chicago Press and Tribune* "a set of the late debates (if they may be so called)" he wrote, "between Douglas and myself . . . two copies of each number . . . in order to lay one away in the raw and to put the other in a scrapbook." One notes that he did not neglect to say, "if any debate is on *both* sides of one sheet, it will take two sets to make one scrapbook."

Of persuasive expedients, those most constant with Lincoln are antithesis, reiteration, satire, metaphor; above all *the meaning*, clear and unadorned. A determination "to express his ideas in simple terms became his ruling passion," his every word natural, impelled by ardor. In his address at the Wisconsin Agricultural Fair, he said—regarding competitive awards about to be made— "exultations and mortifications . . . are but temporary; the victor shall soon be vanquished, if he relax in his exertion; and . . . the vanquished this year may be the victor next, in spite of all competition." At the Baltimore Sanitary Fair of 1864, in an address conspicuously combining antithesis with reiteration, he said, "The world has never had a good definition of liberty. . . . We all declare for liberty; but in using the same *word* we do not all mean the same *thing*. With some the word may mean for each man to do as he pleases with himself, and the product of his labor; while with others the same word may mean for some men to do as they please with other men, and the product of other men's labor. Here are two, not only different, but incompatible things, called by the same name—liberty. . . . The shepherd drives the wolf from the sheep's throat, for which the sheep thanks the shepherd as a *liberator*, while the wolf denounces him for the same act as the destroyer of liberty, especially as the sheep was a black one." In Lincoln's use of italics, one perceives that he is not substituting emphasis for precision but is impersonating speech. In declining an invitation to the Jefferson birthday dinner of 1859, he wrote, "The principles of Jefferson are the axioms of a free society. One dashingly calls them 'glittering generalities'; another bluntly calls them 'self-evident lies.'" And in combating repeal of the Missouri Compromise (which would have ended slavery), he said, "Repeal the Missouri Compromise—repeal all compromises—repeal the Declaration of Independence—repeal all history—you cannot repeal human nature."

Crystalline logic indeed was to be his passion. He wrote to James Conkling, "You desire peace; and you blame me that we do not have it. But how can we attain it? There are but three conceivable ways. First, force of arms. . . . Are you for it? . . . A second way is to give up the Union. Are you for it? If you are, you should say so plainly. If not for force, nor yet for dissolution, Compromise. I am against that. I do not believe any compromise is now possible." And to General Schurz he said, "You think I could do better; therefore you blame me. I think I could not do better, therefore I blame you for blaming me."

Unsurpassed in satire, Lincoln said that Judge Douglas, in his interpretation of the Declaration of Independence, offered "the arguments that kings have made for enslaving the people in all ages of the world. They always bestrode the necks of the people, not that they wanted to do it, but that the people were better off for being ridden." Of slavery as an institution he said, "Slavery is strikingly peculiar in this, that it is the only good thing which no man seeks the good of for *himself*."

Metaphor is a force, indeed magnet, among Lincoln's arts of the word. Urgent that the new government of Louisiana be affirmed, he said, "If we reject it, we in effect say, 'You are worthless. We will neither help nor be helped by you.' To the blacks we say, 'This cup of liberty which these, your old masters, hold to your lips, we will dash from you, . . . discouraging and paralyzing both white and black. . . . If on the contrary, we recognize and sustain the new government, we are supporting its efforts to this end, to make it, to us, in your language, a Union of hearts and hands as well as of states.'" Passionate that the Union be saved, he uses a metaphor yet stronger than the cup of liberty. He says, "By general law, life, *and* limb must be protected; yet often a limb must be amputated to save a life; but a life is never wisely given to save a limb. . . . I could not feel that, . . . to save slavery, . . . I should permit the wreck of government, country, and constitution altogether."

Diligence underlay these verbal expedients—one can scarcely call them devices—so rapt Lincoln was in what he cared about. He had a genius for words but it was through diligence that he became a master of them—affording hope to the most awkward of us. To Isham Reavis he wrote, "If you are resolutely determined to make a lawyer of yourself, the thing is half done already. It is a small matter whether you read *with* anybody or not. . . . It is of no consequence to be in a large town. . . . I read at New Salem, which never had three hundred people living in it. The *books* and your *capacity* for understanding them, are just the same in all places."

Diligence was basic. Upon hearing that George Latham, his son Robert's classmate at the Phillips Exeter Academy, had failed entrance examinations to Harvard, Lincoln wrote, "having made the attempt you *must* succeed in it. '*Must*' is the word . . . you *can* not fail if you resolutely determine that you *will* not." This intensity we see heightened in Lincoln's torment of anxiety, during the war, that the struggle be ended. "The subject is on my mind day and night," he said. During August, 1862, in a letter to Colonel Haupt on the 29th, he begged, "What news from the direction of Manassas?" On that same day to General McClellan he wrote, "What news from the direction of Manassas Junction?" On August 30th, to General Banks, "Please tell me what news?" and again "What news?" on August 30th to Colonel Haupt. The result was a man wearing down under

continuous desperation when General Meade, unable to conclude the war at Gettysburg, allowed the Confederate forces to
retreat south.

In speeches and in letters, Lincoln made articulate an indomitable ideal—that what the framers of the Constitution embodied in it be preserved—"and that something is the principle of
'Liberty for all,' that clears the *path* for all—gives *hope* to all—
and by consequence *enterprise* and *industry* to all." Inflexible
when sure he was right—as in his reply to Isaac Schermerhorn,
who was dissatisfied with the management of the war, he said,
"This is not a question of sentiment or taste but one of physical
force which may be measured and estimated as horse-power and
Steam-power are measured and estimated. . . . Throw it away
and the Union goes with it."

There is much to learn from Lincoln's respect for words
taken separately, as when he said, "It seems to me very important that the statute laws should be made as plain and intelligible
as possible, and be reduced to as small compass as may consist
with the fullness and precision of the will of the legislature and
the perspicuity of its language." He was "determined to be so
clear," he said, "that no honest man can misunderstand me, and
no dishonest one can successfully misrepresent me." Exasperated to have been misquoted, he deplored "a specious and fantastic arrangement of words, by which a man can prove a horse-
chestnut to be a chestnut horse." Consulted regarding a more
perfect edition of his Cooper Institute speech, he said, "Of course
I would not object, but would be pleased rather . . . but I do
not wish the sense changed or modified, to a hair's breadth.
Striking out 'upon' leaves the sense too general and incomplete. . . . The words 'quite,' 'as,' and 'or,' on the same page, I
wish retained." Of Stephen Douglas he said, "Cannot the Judge
perceive the difference between a purpose and an expectation? I
have often expressed an expectation to die but I have never expressed a *wish* to die." The Declaration of Independence he
made stronger by saying, "I think the authors of that notable
instrument intended to include *all* men but they did not intend
to declare all men were equal *in all respects*." And to quibblers,
after the surrender of the South, he replied "whether the se-

ceded states, so-called, are in the Union or out of it, the question is bad . . . a pernicious abstraction!" Indelible even upon a feeble memory—we recall the phrase, "With malice toward none and charity for all," and in the second inaugural address, "Let us strive on to finish the work we are in." We are *in*. Lincoln understood in the use of emphasis that one must be *natural*. Instead of using the word "confidential" in a letter to A. H. Stephens, he wrote in italics at the head of the page, "*For your eye only.*" The result of this intensified particularity was such that in his so-called Lost Speech of 1856, which unified the Republican party, "newspapermen forgot paper and pad . . . to sit enraptured," and instead of taking down his eulogy of Henry Clay, "dropped their pens and sat as under enchantment from near the beginning, to quite the end."

Lincoln attained not force only, but cadence, the melodic propriety of poetry in fact, as in the Farewell Address from Springfield he refers to "the weight of responsibility on George Washington"; then says of "that Divine being without which I cannot succeed, with that assistance, I cannot fail." Consider also the stateliness of the three cannots in the Gettysburg Address: "We cannot dedicate—we cannot consecrate—we cannot hallow—this ground. The brave men, living and dead, who struggled here, have consecrated it far above our poor power to add or detract. The world will little note nor long remember what we may say here, but it can never forget what they did here." Editors attempting to improve Lincoln's punctuation by replacing dashes with commas, should refrain—the dash, as well known, signifying prudence.

With consummate reverence for God, with insight that illumined his every procedure as a lawyer, that was alive in his every decision as a President with civilian command of an army at bay, Lincoln was notable in his manner of proffering consolation; studiously avoiding insult when relieving an officer of his command; instantaneous with praise. To General Grant—made commander of the Union army after his brilliant flanking maneuver at Vicksburg—he said, "As the country trusts you, so, under God, it will sustain you." To Grant "alone" he ascribed credit for terminating the war. Constrained almost to ferocity by the sense of fairness, he begs recognition for "black men who can remember that with silent tongues, and clenched teeth, and steady eye and well-poised bayonet, they have helped mankind to this consummation" (preserving the Union). He managed to take time to retrieve the property of a barber, a Negro, who had not recorded the deed to land he owned. Emphasizing by vivid addendum his request for promotion of a "brave drummer-boy" who "had accompanied his division under heavy fire," Lincoln said, "he should have his chance." For a poor widow whose son was serving a long sentence without pay—recommending the son for reenlistment with pay—he wrote, "she says she cannot get it acted on. Please do it." In constant disfavor with officers in charge of penalties, he said, "Must I shoot a simple soldier boy who deserts while I must not touch a hair of the wily agitator who induces him to desert? To silence the agitator and save the boy is not only constitutional but withal a great mercy." Of Captain McKnabb, dismissed on the charge of being a disunionist, Lincoln wrote, "He wishes to show that the charge is false. Fair play is a jewel. Give him a chance if you can." Afflicted by self-obsessed factions in Missouri, where private grievances should have been settled locally, he summarized the matter: "I have exhausted my wits and nearly my patience in efforts to convince both [sides] that the evils they charged on the others are inherent. I am well satisfied that the preventing of the remedial raid into Missouri was the only safe way to avoid an indiscriminate massacre, including probably more innocent than guilty. Instead of condemning, I therefore approve what I understand General Schofield did in that respect. . . . Few things have been so grateful to my anxious feeling as when . . . the local force in Missouri aided General Schofield to so promptly send a large force to the relief of General Grant then investing Vicksburg and menaced by General Johnston. . . . My feeling obliges nobody to follow me and I trust obliges me to follow nobody."

With regard to presidential appointments, it was in 1849, during Zachary Taylor's administration, that Lincoln said, "I take the responsibility. In that phrase were the 'Samson's locks' of General Jackson, and we dare not disregard the lessons of experience"—lessons underlying the principle which he put into practice when appointing Governor Chase Secretary of the Treasury. Pressed, in fact persecuted, to appoint General Cameron, he said, "It seems to me not only highly proper but a *necessity* that Governor Chase shall take that place. His ability, firmness, and purity of character produce the propriety." Purity of character—the phrase is an epitome of Lincoln. To a young man considering law as a career, he said, "There is a vague popular belief that lawyers are necessarily dishonest. If you cannot be an honest lawyer, resolve to be honest without being a lawyer." Deploring bombast, yet tactful, he opposed investigating the Bank of Illinois: "No, Sir, it is the *politician* who is first to sound the alarm (which, by the way, is a false one). It is he, who, by these unholy means, is endeavoring to blow up a storm that he may ride upon and direct it. . . . I say this with the greater freedom, because, being a politician, none can regard it as personal." Firm in resisting pressure, he was equally strong in exerting it, as when he wrote to "Secretary Seward & Secretary Chase" jointly, "You have respectively tendered me your resignations . . . but, after most anxious consideration, my deliberate judgment is, that the public interest does not admit of it. I therefore have to request that you will resume the duties of your departments respectively. Your Obt. Servt."

In faithfulness to a trust, in saving our constitutional freedom and opportunity for all, declaring that "no grievance is a fit object of redress by mob violence," made disconsolate by what he termed "a conspiracy" to "nationalize slavery," Lincoln—dogged by chronic fatigue—was a monumental contradiction of that conspiracy. An architect of justice, determined and destined to win his "case," he did not cease until he had demonstrated the mightiness of his "proposition." It is a Euclid of the heart.

1961

Edmund Wilson

Like countless authors from previous generations, the literary critic
Edmund Wilson (1895–1972) admired Lincoln as a writer. But in the
startling, and still much-debated, assessment of Lincoln's motives and
politics included in *Patriotic Gore: Studies in the Literature of the American Civil War* (1962), Wilson emboldened a generation of psychobiographers to portray the 16th President as a fatherless boy who
imagined America's founding fathers as his true ancestors, and longed
to make history, however bloody, in order to join them in the national pantheon. Although he acknowledged Lincoln's personal suffering and exonerated him from blame for the "exaggeration" with
which other writers had celebrated him, Wilson focused on what he
claimed the "epic" story had misleadingly omitted: that Lincoln was
more a tyrant than an American saint. Brilliantly written, particularly
in its breathtakingly original interpretation of Lincoln's first major
speech, the 1838 Springfield Lyceum Address, Wilson's observations
in the Lincoln chapter of *Patriotic Gore* have fueled the so-called anti-
Lincoln tradition for more than 40 years. In his highly polemical
introduction to the volume, Wilson went even further in his iconoclasm, comparing Lincoln to Bismarck and Lenin. All three men, he
argued, had presided over the unification of a great new modern
power, they were "all men of unusual intellect and formidable tenacity of character, of historical imagination combined with powerful
will," and each of them "became an uncompromising dictator."

FROM
Patriotic Gore

What precisely did Alexander Stephens mean when he said
that for Lincoln the Union had risen to the sublimity of
religious mysticism?

Whether or not it is true that Lincoln was troubled by the
eloquence of the Methodist preacher mentioned by Francis
Grierson, there is no evidence that, in early maturity, he ever saw
the approaching crisis as an apocalyptic judgment or the possible
war as a holy crusade. He was not a member of any church, and

it is plain that in his earlier days, before he had become a great public figure, he was what was called a free-thinker. William Herndon, his law partner in Springfield, tells us that the young Lincoln had been associated, during his years at New Salem, with persons who had been strongly influenced by the skepticism of the eighteenth century, and that he had read Voltaire, Volney and Tom Paine. Later, in Springfield, when Herndon had brought to the office the books of Darwin, Spencer and Feuerbach, Lincoln had dipped into these. "He soon grew into the belief," says Herndon, "of a universal law, evolution, and from this he never deviated. Mr. Lincoln became a firm believer in evolution and [in] law. Of the truth of this there is no doubt and can be none. Mr. Lincoln believed in laws that imperiously ruled both matter and mind. With him there could be no miracles outside of law; he held that the universe was a grand mystery and a miracle. Nothing to him was lawless, everything being governed by law. There were no accidents in his philosophy. Every event had its cause. The past to him was the cause of the present and the present including the past will be the cause of the grand future and all are one, links in the endless chain, stretching from the infinite to the finite. Everything to him was the result of the forces of Nature, playing on matter and mind from the beginning of time," which would continue to do so "and will to the end of it . . . giving the world other, further, and grander results." Herndon says that Lincoln did not believe "that Jesus was . . . the son of God any more than any man," or "that the Bible was the special divine revelation of God as the Christian world contends," and he goes on to tell us that Lincoln, at some point in his middle twenties, before he had left New Salem, had even composed a long essay setting forth his views on religion, which he wanted to bring out as a pamphlet. But when he read it to the proprietor of the general store in which he was then working, his scandalized employer asked to look at it, then quickly thrust it into the stove. In 1842, when the thirty-three-year-old Lincoln delivers a remarkable address before the Springfield Temperance Society, it is quite evident that his hopes for the world are still confined to a human utopianism which does not yet embody the will of God. "Of our political revolution of '76 we are all justly proud," he says. "It has given us a degree of political freedom, far exceeding that of any other of the nations on the earth. In it the world has found a solution of the long mooted problem, as to the capability of man to govern himself. In it was the germ which has vegetated, and still is to grow and expand into the universal liberty of mankind." The march of this cause of political freedom, "cannot fail," he continues, "to be on and on, till every son of earth shall drink in rich fruition, the sorrow quenching draughts of perfect liberty. Happy day, when, all appetites controlled, all passions subdued, all matters subjected, *mind*, conquering *mind*, shall live and move the monarch of the world. Glorious consummation! Hail fall of Fury! Reign of Reason, all hail!"

But when Lincoln was running for Congress in 1846, his Democratic opponent, a Methodist preacher, denounced him for infidelity. The candidate then made a point of writing and publishing in a local paper a statement of his religious views, the only one he ever made, which seems to have satisfied his public. When, however, we examine this closely, we discover that the supposed clarification is not really a confession of faith: it does not commit Lincoln to anything. Lincoln says that he has "never denied the truth of the Scriptures," but he does not say that he affirms this truth. "I have never spoken with intentional disrespect of religion in general, or of any denomination of Christians in particular"—which, of course, does not imply agreement. "It is true that in early life I was inclined to believe in what I understand is called the 'Doctrine of Necessity'—that is, that the human mind is impelled to action, or held in rest, by some power over which the mind itself has no control"; but he adds that he has only discussed this "with one, two or three, but never publicly," and has "entirely left off for more than five years." "I have always understood this same opinion to be held by several of the Christian denominations"—with which denominations, however, it is plain that he does not associate himself. He ends by remarking that he would not care to support any man for office "whom I know to be an open enemy of, and scoffer at, religion"—on the ground that no man "has the right to insult the feelings, and injure the morals, of the community in which he may live." There is nothing, so far, to conflict with Herndon's version of Lincoln's views Herndon admits that Lincoln's "Doctrine of Necessity" had a conception of divinity behind it. "He firmly believed in an overruling Providence, Maker, God, and the great moral of Him written in the human soul. His—late in life—conventional use of the word God must not by any means be interpreted that he believed in a personal God. I know that it is said Mr. Lincoln changed his views. There is no evidence of this." This overruling Providence, this Deity, which we find, in the degree to which Lincoln advances to political prominence, taking the place of such words as *Reason* and *mind* in such an utterance as the Temperance Society speech, wears sometimes the more secular aspect of the creative or the fatal operation of "history."

This conception of history as a power which somehow takes possession of men and works out its intentions through them is most familiar today as one of the characteristic features of Marxism, in which "history" has become the object of a semi-religious cult and has ended by supplying the stimulus for a fanaticism almost Mohammedan. But it was very widespread in the nineteenth century, and appeared in other contexts, at the time when the scientific study of the past had not yet disentangled itself from the doctrine of divine Providence. When we find Lincoln speaking as follows, in 1858, in the course of his debates with Stephen A. Douglas, we are made to feel the menace of "history" as a kind of superhuman force that vindicates and overrides and that manipulates mankind as its instruments: "Accustomed to trample on the rights of others, you have lost the genius of your own independence and become the fit subjects of the first cunning tyrant who rises among you. And let me tell you that all these things are prepared for you with the logic of history, if the elections shall promise that the next Dred Scott decision and all future decisions will be quietly acquiesced in by the people." And again, in his message to Congress of December 1, 1862: "Fellow-citizens, we cannot escape history. We of this Congress and this administration, will be remembered in spite of ourselves. No personal significance, or insignificance, can spare one or another of us. The fiery trial through which we pass, will light us down, in honor or dishonor, to the latest generation." But he needed something more in keeping than this doctrine of historical necessity with the Scriptural religious conceptions of most of his fellow Americans. His Methodist competitor for Congress had come close to injuring his reputation (just as Herndon's account in his *Life* of Lincoln's early skepticism was to give rise to such an outcry on the part of the clergy that the book on its first appearance, as a result of their influence, was virtually banned; though several times reprinted, it has never been popular). But it was not really easy for Lincoln's public to suspect him of a critical attitude toward the Scriptures, for the Bible was the book he knew best; he had it at his fingertips and quoted it more often than anything else. And he must now have deliberately adopted the practice of stating his faith in the Union and his conviction of his own mission in terms that would not be repugnant to the descendants of the New England Puritans and to the evangelism characteristic of his time. In this he went much further than Herndon, with his confidence in Spencer and Darwin, was willing to recognize. Lincoln's speeches, on the eve of his inauguration, are full of appeals to the Deity. "A duty devolves upon me," he says in his farewell address at Springfield, "which is, perhaps, greater than that which has devolved upon any other man since the days of Washington. He never would have succeeded except for the aid of Divine Providence upon which he at all times relied. I feel that I cannot succeed without the same Divine aid which sustained him, and on the same Almighty Being I place my reliance for support, and I hope you, my friends, will all pray that I may receive that Divine assistance without which I cannot succeed, but with which success is certain." He continues in this vein in his subsequent speeches; and we find him at last in his inaugural address describing the situation in the following terms: "If the Almighty Ruler of nations, with his eternal truth and justice, be on your side of the North or on yours of the South, that truth, and that justice, will surely prevail, by the judgment of this great tribunal, the American people"; and, "Intelligence, patriotism, Christianity, and a firm reliance on Him who has never yet forsaken this favored land, are still competent to adjust, in the best way, all our present difficulty."

He is to revert several times in the years that follow to the attitude of God toward the war; and as the struggle continues undecided, he becomes a good deal less sure that the moral issue is perfectly clear, that the Almighty Ruler of nations is committed to the side of the North. "The will of God prevails," we find him writing in a document to which Nicolay and Hay gave the title *Meditation on the Divine Will*, a note found after his death, which dates from the autumn of 1862, at a time when he was much discouraged by the failures of George McClellan, his General-in-chief. "In great contests each party claims to act in accordance with the will of God. Both may be, and one must be, wrong. God cannot be for and against the same thing at the same time. In the present civil war it is quite possible that God's purpose is something different from the purpose of either party; and yet the human instrumentalities, working just as they do, are of the best adaption to effect his purpose. I am almost ready to say that this is probably true; that God wills this contest, and wills that it shall not end yet. By his mere great power on the minds of the now contestants, he could have either saved or destroyed the Union without a human contest. Yet the contest began. And, having begun, he could give the final victory to either side any day. Yet the contest proceeds." Two years later, in a letter to a Quaker lady, "we hoped," he writes, "for a happy termination of this terrible war long before this; but God knows best, and has ruled otherwise. . . . Surely he intends some great good to follow this mighty convulsion, which no mortal could make, and no mortal could stay." This line of anxious speculation is to culminate in the Second Inaugural Address. "Both," he writes there of the North and the South, "read the same Bible, and pray to the same God; and each invokes His aid against the other. It may seem strange that any men should dare to ask a just God's assistance in wringing their bread from the sweat of other men's faces; but let us judge not that we be not judged. The prayers of both could not be answered; that of neither has been answered fully. The Almighty has his own purposes.

'Woe unto the world because of offences! for it must needs be that offences come; but woe to that man by whom the offence cometh!' If we shall suppose that American Slavery is one of those offences which, in the providence of God, must needs come, but which, having continued through His appointed time, He now wills to remove, and He gives to both North and South this terrible war, as the woe due to those by whom the offence came, shall we discern therein any departure from those divine attributes which the believers in a Living God always ascribe to Him? Fondly do we hope—fervently do we pray—that this mighty scourge of war may speedily pass away. Yet, if God wills that it continue, until all the wealth piled by the bond-man's two hundred and fifty years of unrequited toil shall be sunk, and until every drop of blood drawn with the lash, shall be paid by another drawn with the sword, as was said three thousand years ago, so still it must be said 'the judgments of the Lord are true and righteous altogether!' "

We are far here from Herndon's office, closer to Harriet Beecher Stowe. If the need on Lincoln's part, as a public man, to express himself in phrases congenial to his public may have had some part in inducing him to heighten and personify the formulas of his eighteenth-century deism, if it is true that as the war went on and gave rise to more and more disaffection, it became more and more to his interest to invoke the traditional Lord of Hosts, it is nevertheless quite clear that he himself came to see the conflict in a light more and more religious, in more and more Scriptural terms, under a more and more apocalyptic aspect. The vision had imposed itself.

And now let us put aside this Scriptural phraseology and examine Lincoln's view of the war as a crisis in American history and his conception of himself as an American leader. Both of these emerge very early. Lincoln had always felt himself very close to the American Revolution. He had been seventeen when Jefferson died; his great hero was Henry Clay, who, in putting through the Missouri Compromise, had averted a break with the slave interests. He has from youth been acutely aware that the survival of the Union may still be threatened, and he has already had dreams of defending it. In a speech on *The Perpetuation of Our Political Institutions*, made before the Young Men's Lyceum of Springfield in 1838, when Lincoln was twenty-nine, he mounts up to the following impassioned climax. At the time of the American Revolution, he says of its heroes and leaders, "all that sought celebrity and fame, and distinction, expected to find them in the success of that experiment. . . . They succeeded. The experiment is successful, and thousands have won their deathless names in making it so. . . . This field of glory is harvested, and the crop is already appropriated. But new reapers will arise, and *they*, too, will seek a field. It is to deny what the history of the world tells us is true to suppose that men of ambition and talents will not continue to spring up amongst us. And when they do, they will as naturally seek the gratification of their ruling passion as others have so done before them." You may assume that the young Lincoln is about to exhort his auditors to follow the example of their fathers, not to rest on the performance of the past but to go on to new labors of patriotism; but the speech takes an unexpected turn. "The question, then, is, can that gratification be found in supporting and maintaining an edifice that has been erected by others? Most certainly it cannot." He has been, it seems, preparing to deliver a warning: "Towering genius," he tells them, "disdains a beaten path. It seeks regions unexplored. . . . It *denies* that it is glory enough to serve under any chief. It scorns to tread in the footsteps of *any* predecessor, however illustrious. It thirsts and burns for distinction; and, if possible, it will have it, whether at the expense of emancipating slaves or enslaving freemen. Is it unreasonable then to expect that some man possessed of the loftiest genius, coupled with ambition sufficient to push it to its utmost stretch, will, at some time, spring up among us? And when such a one does, it will require the people to be united with each other, attached to the government and laws, and generally intelligent, to successfully frustrate his designs." Now, the effect of this is somewhat ambiguous: it is evident that Lincoln has projected himself into the role against which he is warning them. And a little less than two years later we find one of his political speeches winding up with the following peroration: "The *probability* that we may fall in the struggle *ought not* to deter us from the support of a cause we believe to be just: it *shall not* deter me. If ever I feel the soul within me elevate and expand to those dimensions not entirely unworthy of its Almighty Architect, it is when I contemplate the cause of my country, deserted by all the world beside, and I standing up boldly alone and hurling defiance at her victorious oppressors."

The young Lincoln, then, was extremely ambitious; he saw himself in an heroic role. He is aware in the earlier of these two speeches that the political tug-of-war going on between the two sections of the country gives a chance for "some man possessed of the loftiest genius" to perform a spectacular feat. Such a man would "thirst and burn for distinction . . . whether at the expense of emancipating slaves or enslaving freemen." And which was Lincoln to choose? He was not unsympathetic with the South. His father had come from Kentucky, and he told Herndon that his mother's father had been "a well-bred Virginia planter." He has started his political career with the party of the propertied interests, the Whigs, and he never shows anything of the animus of the leader who has come up from poverty. He did not approve of slavery, but he did not much resent the slaves' masters, and he was accustomed to say that if they of the North had found themselves in their opponents' situation they would undoubtedly have behaved like the planters. He is at first philosophic about slavery. Lincoln was once taken by a Springfield friend, Joshua F. Speed, for a visit to the latter's family on their plantation near Louisville, Kentucky, and on his return he wrote to Speed's half-sister (letter to Mary Speed, September 27, 1841) telling of their journey back: "By the way, a fine example was presented on board the boat for contemplating the effect of *condition* upon human happiness. A gentleman had purchased twelve negroes in different parts of Kentucky and was taking them to a farm in the South. They were chained six and six together. A small iron clevis was around the left wrist of each, and this fastened to the main chain by a shorter one at a convenient distance from, the others; so that the negroes were strung together precisely like so many fish upon a trot-line. In this condition they were being separated forever from the scenes of their childhood, their friends, their fathers and mothers, and brothers and sisters, and many of them, from their wives and children, and going into perpetual slavery where the lash of the master is proverbially more ruthless and unrelenting than any other where; and yet amid all these distressing circumstances, as we would think them, they were the most cheerful and apparantly happy creatures on board. One, whose offence for which he had been sold was an over-fondness for his wife, played the fiddle almost continually; and the others danced, sung, cracked jokes, and played various games with cards from day to day. How true it is that 'God tempers the wind to the shorn lamb,' or in other words, that He renders the worst of human conditions tolerable, while He permits the best, to be nothing better than tolerable." Years later, in a letter to the same friend (August 24, 1855), in which he discusses their political disagreements, he gives this incident a somewhat different emphasis: "You suggest that in political action now, you and I would differ. I suppose we would; not quite as much, however, as you may think. You know I dislike slavery; and you fully admit the abstract wrong of it. So far there is no cause of difference. But you say that sooner than yield your legal right to the slave—especially at the bidding of those who are not themselves interested, you would see the Union dissolved. I am not aware that *any one* is bidding you to yield that right; very certainly *I* am not. I leave that matter entirely to yourself. I also acknowledge *your* rights and *my* obligations, under the constitution, in regard to your slaves. I confess I hate to see the poor creatures hunted down, and caught, and carried back to their stripes, and unrewarded toils; but I bite my lip and keep quiet. In 1841 you and I had together a tedious low-water trip, on a Steam Boat from Louisville to St. Louis. You may remember, as I well do, that from Louisville to the mouth of the Ohio there were, on board, ten or a dozen slaves, shackled together with irons. That sight was a continual torment to me; and I see something like it every time I touch the Ohio, or any other slave-border. It is hardly fair for you to assume, that I have no interest in a thing which has, and continually exercises, the power of making me miserable. You ought rather to appreciate how much the great body of the Northern people do crucify their feelings, in order to maintain their loyalty to the constitution and the Union."

But in the critical year of 1858, the forty-nine-year-old Lincoln, now a public figure, who has served in Congress and is running against Stephen A. Douglas for the Senate, takes definitely a new stand. The struggle over slavery in Kansas and Nebraska was intensifying political antagonisms. The new Republican party had already been organized—in 1854—by Democratic and Whig opponents of the Kansas-Nebraska Act, and northern Democrats who had not become Republicans were now being alienated by the efforts of the Democratic President, James Buchanan, to forestall secession by appeasing the South. The debates, in their campaign for the Senate, between the Republican Lincoln and one of these anti-Buchanan Democrats drove Lincoln to make bold statements and to formulate a point of view which still exerts a very strong authority over the Northerner's conception of the Civil War. He had already in Springfield, on June 16, made his "House Divided" speech which reverberated all through the political world and which is echoing still in our minds: "'A house divided against itself cannot stand.' I believe this government cannot endure, permanently half *slave* and half *free*. I do not expect the Union to be *dissolved*—I do not expect the house to *fall*—but I *do* expect it will cease to be divided. It will become *all* one thing, or *all* the other." How much Lincoln had staked on this speech is attested by W. H. Herndon, who tells Weik, in one of his letters, that Lincoln "was a good while preparing it . . . he was at it off and on about one month." When he read it to Herndon, "I emphatically said to him: 'Lincoln, deliver and publish your speech just as you have written it.'" This speech figured constantly in the debates with Douglas, and after Lincoln was defeated by him, "hundreds of friends," says Herndon, "flocked into the office and said to Lincoln, 'I told you that speech would kill you.'"

While the Lincoln-Douglas debates were going on, Senator W. H. Seward of New York State, taking his cue from Lincoln, delivered in Rochester, on October 25, another anti-slavery speech, which was also to have long reverberations:

"Russia yet maintains slavery, and is a despotism. Most of the other European states have abolished slavery and adopted the system of free labor. It was the antagonistic political tendencies of the two systems which the first Napoleon was contemplating when he predicted that Europe would ultimately be either all Cossack or all republican. Never did human sagacity utter a more pregnant truth. The two systems are at once perceived to be incongruous. But they are more than incongruous—they are incompatible. They never have permanently existed together in one country, and they never can. It would be easy to demonstrate this impossibility, from the irreconcilable contrast between their great principles and characteristics. . . .

"Hitherto, the two systems have existed in different states, but side by side within the American Union. This has happened because the Union is a confederation of states. But in another aspect the United States constitute only one nation. Increase of population, which is filling the states out to their very borders, together with a new and extended net-work of railroads and other avenues, and an internal commerce which daily becomes more intimate, is rapidly bringing the states into a higher and more perfect social unity or consolidation. Thus, these antagonistic systems are continually coming into closer contact, and collision results.

"Shall I tell you what this collision means? They who think that it is accidental, unnecessary, the work of interested or fanatical agitators, and therefore ephemeral, mistake the case altogether. It is an irrepressible conflict between opposing and enduring forces, and it means that the United States must and will, sooner or later, become either entirely a slaveholding nation, or entirely a free-labor nation. Either the cotton and rice-fields of South Carolina and the sugar plantations of Louisiana will ultimately be tilled by free labor, and Charleston and New Orleans become marts for legitimate merchandise alone, or else the rye-fields and wheat-fields of Massachusetts and New York must again be surrendered by their farmers to slave culture and to the production of slaves, and Boston and New York become once more markets for trade in the bodies and souls of men."

This social-political issue was thus dramatized by the rising and militant Republicans as presenting sensational alternatives, a choice which would affect all history; but the issue had also to be shown as fundamentally a moral one. In the last of his debates with Douglas (October 15), Lincoln speaks with a frankness and a vehemence which, in the previous ones, he has hardly released: his answer to his opponent becomes a sermon. Slavery is a *wrong* and not merely "social and political" but "moral." "That is the real issue. That is the issue that will continue in this country when these poor tongues of Judge Douglas and myself shall be silent. It is the eternal struggle between these two principles—right and wrong—throughout the world. They are the two principles that have stood face to face from the beginning of time; and will ever continue to struggle. The one is the common right of humanity and the other the divine right of kings. It is the same principle in whatever shape it develops itself. It is the same spirit that says, 'You work and toil and earn bread, and I'll eat it.' [Loud applause.] No matter in what shape it comes, whether from the mouth of a king who seeks to bestride the people of his own nation and live by the fruit of their labor, or from one race of men as an apology for enslaving another race, it is the same tyrannical principle."

In his more famous Cooper Institute speech of February 27, 1860, on the eve of his campaign for the presidency, he reiterates this with even more eloquence: "If slavery is right, all words, acts, laws, and constitutions against it, are themselves wrong, and should be silenced, and swept away. If it is right, we cannot justly object to its nationality—its universality; if it is wrong, they cannot justly insist upon its extension—its enlargement. All they ask, we could readily grant, if we thought slavery right; all we ask, they could as readily grant, if they thought it wrong. Their thinking it right, and our thinking it wrong, is the precise fact upon which depends the whole controversy. Thinking it right, as they do, they are not to blame for desiring its full recognition, as being right; but, thinking it wrong, as we do, can we yield to them? Can we cast our votes with their view, and against our own? . . . Neither let us be slandered from our duty by false accusations against us, nor frightened from it by menaces of destruction to the Government nor of dungeons to ourselves.

LET US HAVE FAITH THAT RIGHT MAKES MIGHT, AND IN THAT FAITH, LET US, TO THE END, DARE TO DO OUR DUTY AS WE UNDERSTAND IT."

Now, Lincoln—as he explains in his debates with Douglas—did not think that, aside from his right to be free, the Negro deserved to be set on a basis of equality with the white man. "I have no purpose," he says, "to introduce political and social equality between the white and black races. There is a physical difference between the two, which, in my judgment, will probably forever forbid their living together on the footing of perfect equality, and inasmuch as it becomes a necessity that there must be a difference, I as well as Judge Douglas am in favor of the race to which I belong having the superior position. [Cheers, 'That's the doctrine.']" Nor had he approved of the Abolitionists. He believed that their furious agitation only made the situation worse; and even later, when the Republican party included a strong Abolitionist element, he took pains to dissociate himself from it. Yet his declarations that slavery was a *moral* issue, his talk about "right" and "wrong," made a connection between his policies and the spirit of the New England crusaders who were to turn the conflict of interests between the Northern and Southern states into a Holy War led by God. Though Lincoln was defeated in his contest with Douglas, his rivalry had prodded the latter into giving full expression to views sufficiently unfavorable to slavery to be quite inacceptable to the slave-owners and had thus deepened the split in the Democratic party which was to give the Republicans their chance; and Lincoln himself now stood out as a formidable public figure. He had indeed his heroic role, in which he was eventually to seem to tower—a role that was political through his leadership of his party; soldierly through his rank of commander-in-chief of the armies of the United States; spiritual—for persons like Grierson—as the prophet of the cause of righteousness. And he seems to have known that he was born for this.

Now, aside from this self-confident ambition, what kind of man was Lincoln? There has undoubtedly been written about him more romantic and sentimental rubbish than about any other American figure, with the possible exception of Edgar Allan Poe; and there are moments when one is tempted to feel that the cruellest thing that has happened to Lincoln since he was shot by Booth has been to fall into the hands of Carl Sandburg. Yet Carl Sandburg's biography of Lincoln, insufferable though it sometimes is, is by no means the worst of these tributes. It is useless if one tries to consult it for the source of some reported incident, but it does have its unselective value as an album of Lincoln clippings. It would, however, be more easily acceptable as a repository of Lincoln folk-lore if the compiler had not gone so far in contributing to this folk-lore himself. Here is Sandburg's intimate account of the behavior of Lincoln's mother, about whom almost nothing is known: "She could croon in the moist evening twilight to the shining face in the sweet bundle, 'Hush thee, hush thee, thy father's a gentleman!' She could toss the bundle into the air against a far, hazy line of blue mountains, catch it in her two hands as it came down, let it snuggle to her breast and feed, while she asked, 'Here we come—where from?' And after they had both sunken in the depths of forgetful sleep, in the early dark and past midnight, the tug of a mouth at her nipples in the grey dawn matched in its freshness the first warblings of birds and the morning stars leaving the earth to the sun and dew." And here is his description of Lincoln in the days when, according to Herndon, he was in love with Ann Rutledge, about whom we know hardly more than we do about Lincoln's mother: "After the first evening in which Lincoln had sat next to her and found that bashful words tumbling from his tongue's end really spelled themselves out into sensible talk, her face, as he went away, kept coming back. So often all else would fade out of his mind and there would be only this riddle of a pink-fair face, a mouth and eyes in a frame of light corn-silk hair. He could ask himself what it meant and search his heart for an answer and no answer would come. A trembling took his body and dark waves ran through him sometimes when she spoke so simple a thing as, 'The corn is getting high, isn't it?'" The corn is getting high, indeed! To one of the most vigorous passages in Lincoln's debates with Douglas, his biographer has added the following comment: "He [Lincoln] was a sad lost man chanting a rhythm of the sad and lost."*

Carl Sandburg is not obnoxious when he is strumming his homely guitar and singing American ballads or in his chunks of Middle Western rhapsody that combine the density of a Chicago block with the dryness of a Kansas drought; but Lincoln took him out of his depth, and the result was a long sprawling book that eventually had Lincoln sprawling. The amorphous and coarse-meshed Sandburg is incapable of doing justice to the tautness and the hard distinction that we find when, disregarding legends, we attack Lincoln's writings in bulk. These writings do not give the impression of a folksy and jocular countryman swapping yarns at the village store or making his way to the White House by uncertain and awkward steps or presiding like a father, with a tear in his eye, over the tragedy of the Civil War. Except in the debates with Douglas and some of his early productions, there is very little humor in these writings, and only the gravest sentiment. The dignity of the public utterances and the official correspondence of the Presidency is only infrequently varied by some curtly sarcastic note to a persistently complaining general or an importunate office-seeker. This is a Lincoln intent, self-controlled, strong in intellect, tenacious of purpose.

The raw realities of Lincoln's origins—the sordidness of his childhood environment, the boorishness of his first beginnings—are unflinchingly presented by Herndon, and the public has always found them repellent; but Herndon brings into the foreground Lincoln's genius and his will to succeed as the more romantic writers do not. From those who knew Lincoln best, we learn that he was naturally considerate, but essentially cold and aloof, not really caring much, Herndon tells us, about anyone but his wife and children. He seems always to have had the conviction of his own superiority. The legend of the log-cabin, the illiterate father, the rail-splitting, the flat-boat and all the rest has vulgarized Lincoln for the vulgar even in making him a backwoods saint. Aside from the possibility of his finding himself

---

*It should be noted that in a new edition of Sandburg's *Lincoln* a good deal of this matter has been removed.

sustained by his belief that he came from good stock, he was able to derive self-confidence from knowing that, through physical strength, through sound character, through active brains and through personal charm, he had been able, with no other advantages, to establish himself as a person of importance in rude pioneer Illinois, where most people started from scratch and where one had to have sound qualifications in order to command respect. Though Henry Adams makes a point of telling us that Lincoln, at his Inaugural Ball, had difficulty in managing his gloves, we never feel that he is seriously ill at ease or that he finds himself with others at any sort of disadvantage. "Mr. Lincoln was a curious being," says Herndon in a letter to Weik. "He had an idea that he was equal to, if not superior to, all things; thought he was fit and skilled in all things, master of all things, and graceful in all things,"—adding, however, that he "had not good judgments; he had no sense of the fitness, appropriateness, harmony of things." "With all [Lincoln's] awkwardness of manner," wrote Don Piatt, a journalist who had seen a good deal of him, "and utter disregard of social conventionalities that seemed to invite familiarity, there was something about Abraham Lincoln that enforced respect. No man presumed on the apparent invitation to be other than respectful. I was told at Springfield that this accompanied him through life. Among his rough associates, when young, he was a leader, looked up to and obeyed, because they felt of his muscle and its readiness in use. Among his associates at the bar it was attributed to his wit, which kept his duller associates at a distance. But the fact was that this power came from a sense of reserve force of intellectual ability that no one took account of save in its results." John Hay, who was Lincoln's secretary and observed him at close range all the time he was the White House, insisted that it was "absurd to call him a modest man. No great man is ever modest. It was his intellectual arrogance and unconscious assumption of superiority that men like Chase and Sumner could never forgive." It was this, too, that made it possible, even in suppressing opponents, for him to exercise a magnanimity unusual for a politician, especially in a period of crisis—as when he continued to keep Salmon P. Chase in his cabinet at the time when the latter was working against him and allowing Chase's followers to attack him in leaflets which he refused to read.

Two other descriptions of Lincoln by persons who had closely observed him insist upon his intellectual qualities. "Mr. Lincoln's perceptions," said Herndon, in a speech after Lincoln's death, "were slow, cold, clear and exact. Everything came to him in its precise shape and colour. To some men the world of matter and of man comes ornamented with beauty, life and action, and hence more or less false and inexact. No lurking illusion or other error, false in itself, and clad for the moment in robes of splendour, ever passed undetected or unchallenged over the threshold of his mind—that point that divides vision from the realm and home of thought. Names to him were nothing, and titles naught—assumption always standing back abashed at his cold, intellectual glare. Neither his perceptions nor intellectual visions were perverted, distorted or diseased. He saw all things through a perfect mental lens. There was no diffraction or refraction there. He was not impulsive, fanciful, or imaginative, but calm and precise." Add to this the following passages from the letters of the Marquis de Chambrun, writing to his mother from America. "Mr. Lincoln," he says, "stopped to admire an exceptionally tall and beautiful tree growing by the roadside and applied himself to defining its particular beauties: powerful trunk, vigorous and harmoniously proportioned branches, which reminded him of the great oaks and beeches under whose shade his youth had been passed. Each different type he compared, in technical detail, to the one before us. His dissertation certainly showed no poetic desire to idealize nature; but if not that of an artist, it denoted extraordinary observation, mastery of descriptive language and absolute precision of mind. . . . No one who heard him express personal ideas, as though thinking aloud, upon some great topic or incidental question, could fail to admire his accuracy of judgment and rectitude of mind. I have heard him give opinions on statesmen and argue political problems with astounding precision. I have heard him describe a beautiful woman and discuss the particular aspects of her appearance, differentiating what is lovely from what might be open to criticism, with the sagacity of an artist. In discussing literature, his judgment showed a delicacy and sureness of taste which would do credit to a celebrated critic."

It must have been the Frenchman who turned Lincoln's attention to literature and beautiful women. But it is true that his sense of style was developed to a high degree. His own style was cunning in its cadences, exact in its choice of words, and yet also instinctive and natural; and it was inseparable from his personality in all of its manifestations. This style pervades Lincoln's speeches, his messages to Congress, his correspondence with his generals in the field as well as with his friend and family, his interviews with visitors to the White House and his casual conversation. Lincoln's editor, Mr. Roy P. Basler, in a study of Lincoln's style prefixed to a volume of selections from his writings, explains that the literary education of Lincoln was a good deal more thorough than used to be thought. "A careful examination," he says, of the books on elocution and grammar "which Lincoln studied both in and out of school will not impress anyone with Lincoln's poverty of opportunity for the study of grammar and rhetoric. It is safe to say that few children today learn as much through twelve years of formal schooling in these two subjects as one finds in the several textbooks which Lincoln is supposed to have studied." For it is true that the schoolbooks of the early nineteenth century taught not only the mechanics of writing—that is, of grammar and syntax—but also the art of rhetoric—that is, of what used to be called "harmonious numbers" and of dramatic and oratorical effectiveness. Here is a passage from a private letter dealing with personal matters which was written by Lincoln in his thirty-third year: "The second [cause of his correspondent's melancholy] is, the *absence* of *all business* and *conversation of friends*, which might divert your mind, and give it occasional rest from that *intensity* of thought, which will sometimes wear the sweetest idea threadbare and turn it to the bitterness of death." Here, in the final phrases, the balance of vowels and consonants, the assonance and alliteration, the progression from the long "e"s of "sweetest idea," over which one would want to linger, to the short and closed vowels of "bitterness of death," which chill the lyrical rhythm and bite it off at the end—all this shows a training of the literary ear that is not often taught in modern schools. The satirical *Letter from the Lost Townships*, written in 1842, which nearly cost Lincoln a duel, handles colloquial language with a similar sense of style: it is quite a successful experiment in the vein of homely frontier humor that Mark Twain was to bring to perfection; and the poems that Lincoln wrote four years later, when he revisited his old home in Indiana, show even a certain skill in a medium in which he was less at home. He is describing a neighbor who had gone insane and whose daft doleful singing he now remembers:

> I've heard it oft, as if I dreamed,
>   Far-distant, sweet, and lone;
> The funeral dirge it ever seemed
>   Of reason dead and gone.
>
> To drink its strains, I've stole away,
>   All silently and still,
> Ere yet the rising god of day
>   Had streaked the Eastern hill.
>
> Air held his breath; the trees all still
>   Seemed sorr'wing angels round.
> Their swelling tears in dew-drops fell
>   Upon the list'ning ground.

In his *Eulogy on Zachary Taylor*, delivered in 1850, in striving for a loftier eloquence, he resorts, with less successful results, to a kind of constricted blank verse. Yet in prose, as in verse, he is working for the balance of eighteenth-century rhythms, and he learns to disembarrass these of eighteenth-century pomposity. He will discard the old-fashioned ornaments of forensic and congressional oratory, but he will always be able to summon an art of incantation with words, and he will know how to practice it magnificently—as in the farewell to Springfield, the Gettysburg speech and the Second Inaugural Address—when a special occasion demands it. Alone among American Presidents, it is possible to imagine Lincoln, grown up in a different milieu, becoming a distinguished writer of a not merely political kind. But actually the poetry of Lincoln has not all been put into his

writings. It was acted out in his life. With nothing of the deliberate histrionics of the Roosevelts or of the evangelical mask of
Wilson, he created himself as a poetic figure, and he thus imposed himself on the nation.

For the molding by Lincoln of American opinion was a
matter of style and imagination as well as of moral authority, of
cogent argument and obstinate will. When we put ourselves
back into the period, we realize that it was not at all inevitable
to think of it as Lincoln thought, and we come to see that Lincoln's conception of the course and the meaning of the Civil
War was indeed an interpretation that he partly took over from
others but that he partly made others accept, and in the teeth of
a good deal of resistance on the part of the North itself. If you
are tempted to suspect that the Lincoln myth is a backward-
reading invention of others, a closer acquaintance with the subject will convince you that something like the reverse is true.
Though Lincoln is not responsible for the element of exaggeration, humorous or sentimental, with which he himself has been
treated, we come to feel that the mysticism of a Grierson in his
Lincoln and *The Valley of Shadows*, as well as the surprising nobility, at once classical and peculiarly American, of the Grant of the
Personal Memoirs, are in some sense the creations of Lincoln,
and that Lincoln has conveyed his own legend to posterity in an
even more effective way than he did to the America of the sixties.

Should we, too, have accepted this vision if we had lived at
the time of the Civil War? Can an American be sure he would
have voted for Lincoln, that he would even have wanted him as
a candidate, in the election of 1864? The war was then in its
fourth year, and hundreds of thousands of men had been killed
without, as it seemed to many, having brought a decision nearer.
Lincoln had just called for a draft of half a million more, though
the draft of the summer before had set off in New York City a
series of riots in which a thousand people had been killed or
injured: Negroes had been shot and lynched, and Unionists'
houses had been burned to the ground. The writ of habeas corpus had been suspended by Lincoln in spite of much public dis-
approval and an obstinate filibuster in Congress, and one of

Lincoln's bitterest critics, the Democratic Congressman Clement L. Vallandigham, who had demanded that the fighting be stopped and the quarrel submitted to foreign arbitration, had been sent to jail for the duration of the war (though his sentence was later commuted to banishment behind the Confederate lines). To the Albany Democratic Convention, which had passed a set of resolutions condemning the suppression of civil liberties, the President had addressed a retort which asserted his uncompromising policy and showed his argumentative style at its most compelling: "The man who stands by and says nothing when the peril of his government is discussed, cannot be misunderstood. If not hindered, he is sure to help the enemy; much more if he talks ambiguously—talks for his country with *buts* and *ifs* and *ands*" (he should have said *ans*). Could this nasty situation have been averted? Should the war not have earlier been brought to an end? Could it not, in fact, have been prevented? Should Fort Sumter have been relieved? Would it not have been a good deal less disastrous if the South had been allowed to secede? All these questions have been debated; and yet—except, of course, in the South—the ordinary American does not often ask them. He does not doubt now that Lincoln was right. Did he not, by reducing the Confederacy to an unconditional surrender, save the Union and liberate the slaves? Lincoln's conduct of the Civil War is usually now accepted as one of the most conclusive and most creditable exploits of our history. If the war left a lasting trauma, and resulted in, not an apocalypse, but, on the one hand, a rather gross period of industrial and commercial development and, on the other, a severe disillusionment for the idealists who had been hoping for something better, these are matters about which we in the North have rarely thought and even less often spoken. We have, in general, accepted the epic that Lincoln directed and lived and wrote. Since it was brought to an end by his death the moment after the war was won, we are able to dissociate him entirely from the ignominies and errors of the Reconstruction and to believe he would have handled its problems better.

But let us see what Lincoln's epic leaves out. Of the strategy of the economic interests at work in the Civil War, which has been analyzed by Charles A. Beard in *The Rise of American Civilization*—a highly unconventional book when it was published in 1927—you will get no inkling from Lincoln, for the reason that he had none himself. The tariff for the benefit of the Northern manufacturers—which prevented the South from buying goods from England more cheaply than they could from the North and had constituted one of their grievances—was raised higher during the years of the war than it ever had been before; the government presented enormous grants to the various railroad companies; and a prospect of high wages for labor encouraged by the absence of men in the army was averted, on behalf of the employers, by the Immigration Act of 1864, which authorized the importing of labor under terms that could compel the immigrant to pay for the cost of his journey by pledging his wages for as long as twelve months. At the end of the Civil War, the industrialists were firmly in the saddle, but of what this implied for the future Lincoln had had no idea.

He refers on several occasions to the relations of capital and labor, and does not seem to be aware how completely the Republican party is already the champion of the former, for he always arrives at the conclusion that capital overrates its importance, since labor can get along without capital whereas capital cannot get along without labor, and is, in fact, as he says, "the fruit of labor, and could never have existed if labor had not first existed." Though he examined the mechanical devices that were brought to him in the years of his Presidency and is reported to have understood them, he does not seem to have been much impressed by the development of machinery in America or even much interested in it. In a speech before the Wisconsin State Agricultural Society, in 1859, he takes rather a dubious view of the prospects of the steam plow, and a lecture delivered in the same year on the subject of "Discoveries, Inventions, and Improvements" is a curious production for its period and was quite comprehensibly not a success, since most of the speech was devoted to extolling the value to humanity of language and the art of writing, the only discovery, invention or improvement that appears to have excited his enthusiasm. This was perfectly natural for Lincoln, since he evidently felt that the use of the Word

was the only technique he needed; and for him, in his impoverished youth, it had been also a discovery and an improvement.
Nor did he compensate for his indifference to industry by a sympathetic solicitude for agriculture. He does not seem to have
looked back with pleasure on his labors in his boyhood on his
father's farm, much publicized though these were, and when he
writes to a friend who is working the land, it is usually in the
vein of "I am so glad it is you and not I who are trying to run
that farm." Though he tells his Wisconsin audience that, since
the farmers in the United States constitute the largest occupa-
tional group, they are "most worthy of all to be cherished and
cultivated," he hopes that he will not be expected to flatter them
"as a class" or "to impart to you much specific information on
agriculture," because, as he says, "you have no reason to believe,
and do not believe, that I possess it."

Lincoln begins as a provincial lawyer and soon becomes a
politician of more than provincial importance. His real vocation
was for what we call statesmanship, and, as a statesman, he was
entirely absorbed by the problems created by secession—though,
under pressure of the necessity of winning the war, he was
forced to become something of a military strategist. From the
moment of his advent to the Presidency just after the withdrawal
of seven states, he had of course little opportunity to occupy
himself with anything else.

It is partly these limitations that give Lincoln's career its unity,
its consistency, its self-contained character. He is not tempted to
dissipate his energies; he has no serious conflicts of interest.
Everything hangs together. He is conscious from the first of his
public role, not only in relation to the history of his country but
also in relation to the larger world, for which all the old values
will be modified, the social relations altered, if it is possible to
prove to it the practicability of the principles of our revolutionary documents. With conviction and persistence he performs
this role, and he is always articulate in it. He has always had a
sense of drama, as appears in the debates with Douglas, which
seem actually to have proved effective when they were recently
put on the stage, and now every word that he utters belongs to

his part as President. In order to appreciate Lincoln's lines, you have, of course, to know the whole drama. A foreigner who did not know our history might be able to hear the music of the Second Inaugural and the Gettysburg Addresses yet at the same time not fully grasp the reasons for the powerful emotional effect that they have on Lincoln's fellow-Americans; and as for the letter to Mrs. Bixby, such a visitor might be quite at a loss to account for the elaborate trouble that has been taken to track Mrs. Bixby down and to authenticate that the letter is really by Lincoln and not by his secretary John Hay. These things must be felt in their contexts, where they speak to us with all the power of Lincoln's inspired conception of his role in the Civil War.

The dreams and premonitions of Lincoln are also a part of this drama, to which they contribute an element of imagery and tragic foreshadowing that one finds sometimes in the lives of poets—Dante's visions or Byron's last poem—but that one does not expect to encounter in the career of a political figure: Lincoln's recurrent dream of a ship on its steady way to some dark and indefinite shore, which seemed to prophesy that the war would be going well, since it had always been followed by a victory; his ominous hallucination, after the election of 1860, when, lying exhausted on a sofa, he saw in a mirror on the wall a double reflection of his face, with one image paler than the other, which his wife had taken as a sign that he would be elected to a second term but that he would not live to complete it. He repeated this story to John Hay and others the night of his second election, and a few days before his death he had spoken of a more recent dream, in which he had seen a crowd of people hurrying to the East Room of the White House and, when he followed them, found his own body laid out and heard voices saying, "Lincoln is dead." Herndon tells us that in the early days in Springfield, Lincoln would say to him, "Billy, I fear that I shall meet with some terrible end." But although he had been shot at in '62 when he was riding in the streets of Washington, he would not have a bodyguard; he explained that he wanted the people to know that "I come among them without fear." He would take walks in the middle of the night alone. It was only in the November of 1864 that four plain-clothesmen were posted at the White House. On his way back to Washington from his visit to Richmond just after the city's surrender, he read to his companions on the boat the scene from *Macbeth* that contains the lines:

> Duncan is in his grave;
> After life's fitful fever he sleeps well;
> Treason has done his worst: nor steel, nor poison,
> Malice domestic, foreign levy, nothing,
> Can touch him further.

The night before Lincoln was murdered, he dreamed again of the ship approaching its dark destination. He had foreseen and accepted his doom; he knew it was part of the drama. He had in some sense imagined this drama himself—had even prefigured Booth and the aspect he would wear for Booth when the latter would leap down from the Presidential box crying, "*Sic semper tyrannis!*" Had he not once told Herndon that Brutus was created to murder Cæsar and Cæsar to be murdered by Brutus? And in that speech made so long before to the Young Men's Lyceum in Springfield, he had issued his equivocal warning against the ambitious leader, describing this figure with a fire that seemed to derive as much from admiration as from apprehension—that leader who would certainly arise among them and "seek the gratification of [his] ruling passion," that "towering genius" who would "burn for distinction, and, if possible . . . have it, whether at the expense of emancipating slaves or enslaving freemen." It was as if he had not only foreseen the drama but had even seen all around it with a kind of poetic objectivity, aware of the various points of view that the world must take toward its protagonist. In the poem that Lincoln lived, Booth had been prepared for, too, and the tragic conclusion was necessary to justify all the rest.

It is not to be doubted that Lincoln, in spite of his firm hand on policy, had found his leadership a harrowing experience. He had himself, one supposes, grown up in pain. The handicaps imposed by his origins on his character and aspirations must have constrained him from his earliest years, and his unhappy relations with women, the tantrums and pretensions of his rather vulgar wife, and the death of two of his sons must have saddened and worried and humiliated him all through his personal life. The humorous stories and readings that his cabinet sometimes found so incongruous only served, as he once explained, as a relief from his fits of despondency, his constant anxiety about the war. Though not warm in his personal relationships, he was sensitive to the pain of others. He had remembered from fourteen years before that the sight of the slaves on the steamboat had been "a continual torment," and though he had pardoned, whenever it was possible, the soldiers who had been sentenced to death, he had been compelled by his office to authorize the executions of two hundred and sixty-seven men. He must have suffered far more than he ever expressed from the agonies and griefs of the war, and it was morally and dramatically inevitable that this prophet who had crushed opposition and sent thousands of men to their deaths should finally attest his good faith by laying down his own life with theirs.

1962

Cartoon by Bill Mauldin, *Chicago Sun-Times*, November 23, 1963. *Copyright ©
1963 by Bill Mauldin. Courtesy of the Bill Mauldin Estate, LLC.*

John Dos Passos

A highly innovative novelist whose politics moved over time from radical socialism to Goldwaterite conservatism, Dos Passos (1896–1970) brought the documentary sensibility that had informed much of his epic *U.S.A.* trilogy to this rumination on Lincoln's historic trip to Gettysburg in November 1863. Contemplating Lincoln's early life and education, Dos Passos memorably asserts that merely by exemplifying America's westward migration and forming his intellect in the mold of the Bible, the unschooled Lincoln could claim to be "the best educated man in the United States," and a pioneer in a new American cultural tradition that included Mark Twain and Walt Whitman.

Lincoln and His Almost Chosen People

The story of that day has been so often repeated that it is as if you had been there yourself. It is as if we personally remembered the neat streets of Gettysburg jingling with horsemen and carriages that Indian summer morning, the ladies in hoopskirts and shawls, the bearded Amish in their flat black hats, the hobbling convalescents in weatherstained blue from the military hospitals, and the gleam of the Marine Band that led the cavalcade of blackcoated dignitaries out the Taneytown road to Cemetery Ridge. Right behind the band President Lincoln's dark gangling frame, topped by a tall silk hat, towers above the dumpy figures of cabinet members and secretaries. For once he rides a horse that suits him, a fine big chestnut. Even his most querulous critics admit that he sits his horse well.

A square wooden platform had been erected at the cemetery. It bustled with governors and congressmen and diplomats, interlarded here and there with a general in uniform. The speakers faced the multitude of raw graves and the shallow valley and the ridges where nearly forty-five thousand men fell dead or wounded in the three-day battle which ended Lee's invasion of the North.

Beyond the ridges and the russet woods of late fall smooth blue hills shimmered in the smoky distance.

The opening prayer, which was described as touching and beautiful, was also remembered for its extreme length. Then the band played "Old Hundred," and the stately figure of Edward Everett, ex-Senator, former Secretary of State, four-term governor of Massachusetts, the first American to win a doctorate in a German university, apostle of Hellenic studies, ex-president of Harvard College, Brahmin of the Brahmins, and the fashionable orator of the day, advanced to the podium with a sheaf of papers in his hand.

"Standing beneath this serene sky," he began, in the voice which had been described as equal in melody to that of the prodigious Webster, "overlooking these broad fields now reposing from the labors of the waning year, the mighty Alleghenies towering before us, the graves of our brethren beneath our feet, it is with hesitation that I raise my poor voice to break the eloquent silence of God and Nature."

Mr. Everett's voice broke the silence for something like two hours, according to the reporter from the *New York Times*, who went on to describe the sightseers wandering over the slopes in search of souvenirs, and the great number of carcasses of dead horses which had been left to rot in the fields.

Listeners on the edge of the crowd, too far away to follow the learned Bostonian as he led them, in measured periods, through human history from Pericles' funeral oration to the Union successes of the past summer, may well have been regaling each other with fresh tales of the President's oddities. When he had been called to speak to one throng waiting at a train stop the day before, he had smiled at them wryly from the back platform. "Well, you've seen me," he said, "and according to general experience you have seen less than you expected to see." When a military band came out in the moonlight to serenade him at Judge Wills's house in Gettysburg, he appeared tall and grim at a second story balcony, and told the people thronging the street below he was sure that they would listen to him if he did make a speech but that tonight he had no speech to make. He added that in his position it was important for him not to say foolish things. "Not if you can help it," came a voice from the crowd. "It often happens that the only way to help it is to say nothing at all." The President made his bow and retired. Some people appreciated this kind of humor, but a great many didn't.

It was hard for people to understand that Abraham Lincoln was not an off-the-cuff speaker. Every sentence he uttered had to be phrased and rephrased, and written out in his careful hand. He had worked long and hard over the scant two pages he was planning to read as his share of the dedicatory remarks.

We were most of us brought up on the story of the notes scribbled on the back of an envelope, but the record seems to show that Lincoln started drafting the Gettysburg Address back in Washington at the Executive Mansion, and finished it at Judge Wills' house before going to bed the night he arrived in Gettysburg.

He was never quite satisfied with it. His invitation to speak was an afterthought on the part of the Cemetery Commission. The press of executive business left him little time to arrange his thoughts for the address. He was preoccupied with the message to Congress he was preparing for early December. In spite of two great victories for the Union cause that had ushered in the summer's campaign, Gettysburg and Vicksburg, it had been a heavy year. Draft riots in New York. Copperhead agitation in the Middle West. At that very moment Bragg's Confederates seemed to have a federal army bottled up in Chattanooga. Grant was on his way to the rescue. After having allowed Lee to make good his retreat across the Potomac, Meade was facing him along the Rapidan. Again Meade had let the wily strategist choose his own ground: Lincoln trembled for the result. As if he hadn't enough public worries, his dearest little Tad had taken sick. He had left Mrs. Lincoln, who had never recovered from their son Willie's death the year before, in a state near hysterics.

Just before starting for the cemetery the President was handed a cheering telegram from Secretary of War Stanton. Grant had things in hand at Chattanooga. Mrs. Lincoln reported the boy was better.

Even so late in his career Lincoln was a nervous speaker. His voice was shrill and his delivery mechanical at the start. Sitting with an air of respectful attention through Edward Everett's oratorical set piece, which a Philadelphia reporter described as like Greek sculpture, "beautiful but cold as ice," Lincoln had time to collect his thoughts. He even made a couple of last-minute changes in the order of words. A hymn, specially composed for the occasion and sung by the Baltimore Glee Club, rose out of the "thundering applause" that greeted Edward Everett's patriotic peroration. During the singing Mr. Lincoln was seen to put on his eyeglasses. He ran his eyes hastily down the two sheets he had brought out of his pocket. His strapping young friend and junior partner Ward Hill Lamon, whom he had appointed a United States marshal and who acted as a private bodyguard, rose to his feet and introduced "The President of the United States."

Accounts differ as to the immediate effect on the audience of the Gettysburg Address. Young John Hay, then one of Lincoln's secretaries, thought the Ancient, as he called him, acquitted himself well. Others found his delivery high pitched and tremulous with taut nerves. A reporter wrote of his "sharp unmusical treble voice." The speech was over so soon that a photographer who had meant to photograph the President delivering it didn't have time to focus his lens. There was applause, but Lincoln felt it perfunctory. "Lamon," he is reported to have whispered to his friend as he stepped back from the edge of the platform, "that speech went sour. It is a flat failure and the people are disappointed."

But the address stuck in people's minds. The more they remembered it, the more they were impressed. Edward Everett wrote Lincoln handsomely next day: "I should be glad, if I could flatter myself that I came as near to the central idea of the occasion in two hours, as you did in two minutes." *Harper's Weekly* in New York found the speech "simple," "felicitous," "earnest." Even among New Englanders who had been so scornful of the rail-splitting attorney from backwoods Illinois the address was spoken of as "one of the wonders of the day."

As the years went by, memorized by every schoolchild, the Gettysburg Address became, along with the Declaration of

Independence, one of the grand showpieces of the American heritage.

Why should these few words have rung so true? Why should they have evoked such response from so many different kinds of people? Wasn't it perhaps that Lincoln, by birth and education, was the man of his time best fitted to speak from the main stream of national culture? The great underlying fact which motivated the history of the United States throughout the mid-nineteenth century was the migration westward. As a boy and youth, Lincoln had lived that migration. The inner spirit and the external ethics of the nation were based on the Protestant Bible. The Bible was the mold of Lincoln's intellectual formation.

In that sense Lincoln was the best educated man in the United States. The college-trained gentry along the Eastern seaboard were thrown off by his canny use of the ignorant country-boy pose which he found such an asset politically. They couldn't see that education was a profounder matter than college courses. Literate Americans were still shut up too tight in their provincial backwater of the English literary tradition to appreciate the energy or the depth of the national culture then forming. Based on the Bible and on the traditions of the Scotch-Irish borderers it was part of the main stream of the culture of the English-speaking peoples. As a wielder of words Lincoln was among the forerunners of the new tradition: Lincoln, Walt Whitman, Mark Twain.

Born in Kentucky, where his father and grandfather had moved from Rockingham County, Virginia, as part of the first wave of settlers across the Appalachians, his earliest memory was being told how his grandfather Abraham was killed by an Indian while clearing the forest behind his cabin. Lincoln described his father Thomas as "a wandering labor boy . . . who never did more in the way of writing than bunglingly write his own name." The family legend had it that it was Abraham Lincoln's mother who taught his father that much; certainly she seems to have started young Abraham reading the Bible at an early age.

Thomas Lincoln worked as a carpenter and odd job man. He drifted westward with the tide. Having trouble getting title to the land he had cleared in Kentucky, he moved the family to Indiana where the homesteader had a better chance. Lincoln wrote of himself as a boy as large for his age . . . "and had an axe put in his hands at once; and from that till within his twenty-third year he was almost constantly handling that most useful instrument."

When he was nine his mother died of an epidemic known as "the milk-sick." Thomas Lincoln, who seems to have been luckier with the ladies than with crops or land titles, went back home to Kentucky and picked himself a new wife. Abraham and his sister needed a woman's care.

This was a competent widow with three children, said to have been a childhood sweetheart. Children were an asset to a pioneer family. Many hands made light work. She was tolerably well furnished with this world's goods in the shape of house furnishings and farming equipment, and Abraham Lincoln affectionately remembered her care and kindness. Perhaps she encouraged him to pay attention to his schooling when he could get it, "by littles," he described it.

Abe grew up with a reputation for great strength. The neighbors thought he was lazy. Most of them agreed with his father that reading a book never cleared an acre of land. A cousin, John Hanks, told Herndon, reminiscing about the days when he and Abe worked together in the field as shambling teenagers: "When Abe and I returned to the house from work he would go to the cupboard, snatch a piece of corn bread, sit down, take a book, cock his legs up as high as his head and read. We grubbed, plowed, mowed and worked together barefooted in the field. Whenever Abe had a chance in the field while at work, or at the house, he would stop and read."

Outside of the famous "school of hard knocks" Lincoln got his early education almost exclusively from the Bible, *Pilgrim's Progress*, and *Aesop's Fables*. The shrewd and salty comments of the Hebrew chroniclers made more of an impression on him than the miracles. He instinctively recognized that the Old Testament encompassed an entire literature; the mythology, the poetry, as well as the traditional history and the religion of the tribes of Israel. Lincoln once remarked that, compared with other books that came into his hand, it was the truthfulness of the characterizations that impressed him. Saul and David were real men. The chronicler did not gloss over their sins and weaknesses. The boy could compare them with men he knew.

The border life of the Lincoln and Hanks families wasn't too different from the life of the Israelites. Though there had been some improvement in tools, their technology had not advanced too far from the technology of the days of Abraham the patriarch. Though the machine age was imminent, the first twenty years of Lincoln's life were spent in the age of handicraft.

Pilgrim's Progress and *Aesop's Fables* fitted in with pioneer culture where storytelling was an art. When he came to *Robinson Crusoe*, it fitted in perfectly: that was how young Abe lived most of the time. Added to that were scraps of oratory and quotations from the classics he found in his school readers. From these quotations and from the Biblical teachings, he could assemble a body of standards to judge the world by. Then when he read Parson Weems' *George Washington*, his whole soul kindled with the thought that there were nobler things to do in the world than hoe corn. Ambition started to stir in him to do something grander than splitting rails.

Of course his reading broadened when he moved to New Salem and then later to Springfield. Gibbon gave him a touch of the ironic and Augustan view of history. Volney and Tom Paine disparaged the Biblical miracles that the revivalist sects he was brought up with based their faith on. For a while he fancied himself a freethinker. Eventually the inconsistencies of the freethinkers struck him as forcibly as the inconsistencies of the Biblical mythmakers. He was never a church member and had no interest at all in sectarian dogmas, but in the last analysis he was as profoundly imbued with the religion of the Bible as any man who ever lived.

Lincoln was bound he would push out into the world for himself the day he turned twenty-one. Before he could leave home he had to help his father's family in one more migration, this time into the black loam country of Illinois. He helped his father build wagons and load them with the plows and the hoes and the bedding brought from Kentucky, and they set off for a new location.

When he described the journey for John L. Scripps, who was getting up a campaign biography in 1860, his words naturally fell into the Old Testament cadences: "March 1, 1830, Abraham having just completed his twenty-first year, his father and family, with the families of the two daughters and sons-in-law of his stepmother, left the old homestead in Indiana and came to Illinois. Their mode of conveyance was wagons drawn by oxteams, and Abraham drove one of the teams. They reached the county of Macon, and stopped there some time within the same month of March. . . . His father and family settled a new place at the junction of the timberland and the prairie," Lincoln's narrative continued. "Here they built a log cabin, into which they removed, and made sufficient of rails to fence ten acres of ground, fenced and broke the ground, and raised a crop of sown corn upon it the same year."

Compare the cadence with this passage from Chronicles: "And they went to the entrance of Gedor, even unto the east side of the valley to seek pasture for their flocks.

"And they found fat pasture and good, and the land was wide and quiet and peaceable; for they of Ham had dwelt there of old."

These were probably the last rails Abraham Lincoln ever split in his life. He was on the lookout for better ways of making a living. He once told a friend that his father had "learned him to work but had never taught him to like it." While he still lived at Pigeon Creek, he worked as helper with the ferryman and occasionally brought passengers ashore from the Ohio River steamboats in his own skiff. At nineteen he made his first trip down river to New Orleans as a hired hand on a flatboat.

The family had hardly settled near Decatur before Lincoln began to show interest in public affairs. His signature appeared on a petition to the county commissioners to change the location of the polling place. It was during the political campaign that same fall that he made his maiden speech when the candidates for the legislature came to Decatur. "Pictured out the future of Illinois," noted a listener. He added that one of the candidates said "he was a bright one."

Young Lincoln was an enthusiast for "internal improvements." Steamboats were taking the place of flats and bateaux. The difficulties of a second trip poling a flatboat down the Sangamon and then drifting down the Illinois and the Mississippi to New Orleans brought home the need for quick and cheap transportation to open up the Western country. When he was the Civil War President years later, no one had to explain to Abraham Lincoln the importance of the Mississippi. The knowledge had come with the calluses on his hands as he tugged at the steering oar past the settlement at Walnut Hills that was to become Vicksburg.

This trip was in the interest of a storekeeper named Offutt. On his return Lincoln clerked in Offutt's store and helped him run his mill at New Salem. Clerking in a store gave him leisure to read and to exchange droll tales with the customers. Already he had a local reputation as a storyteller. Lincoln used to figure that his whole schooling barely covered a year, but he could write, read, and spell a great deal better than most of his neighbors. He was in demand to draft public documents. For a while he couldn't decide whether to study law or blacksmithing. The law won out. Old-timers told Herndon that Lincoln was hardly ever seen in those days without a book under his arm. He devoured the newspapers.

When Offutt's business showed signs of going on the rocks, Lincoln decided he had made enough friends around New Salem to take a fling at running for office. The lineups were forming for the presidential contest between Andrew Jackson and Henry Clay. Though Lincoln's family and friends were all Jacksonian Democrats, reading Henry Clay's speeches convinced Lincoln he ought to be a Whig. It was as a Whig he decided to run for the legislature. We tend to forget what a conservative man Lincoln was.

His appeal to the voters was disarming. He discussed the feasibility of constructing a railroad across the state. (This was 1832. Construction was only beginning on the first line of the Baltimore and Ohio. New Salem wasn't such a backwater as people have tried to make out.) Right at the present, reflected young Lincoln, a railroad would cost too much to be financed in Sangamon County. The aspirant legislator presented a detailed scheme for canalizing the Sangamon River. He spoke up in favor of public schools. His arguments in favor of universal education was Jeffersonian: "That every man may receive at least a moderate education and thereby be enabled to read the histories of his own and other countries, by which he may duly appreciate the value of our free institutions"; and he noted furthermore "the satisfaction to be derived from all being able to read the Scriptures." He apologized for his youth and ended on a very characteristic note:

> Every man is said to have his peculiar ambition. Whether it be true or not, I can say for one that I have no other so great as that of being truly esteemed by my fellow men, by rendering myself worthy of their esteem. [The phrase still smacks of the copybook: he was just turned twenty-three. That copybook was to become the imperative of his career.] . . . I am young and unknown to many of you. I was born and have ever remained in the most humble walks of life. I have no wealthy or popular relations to recommend me. My case is thrown exclusively upon the independent voters of this county, and if elected they will have conferred a favor upon me, for which I shall be unremitting in my labors to compensate. But if the good people in their wisdom shall see fit to keep me in the background I have been too familiar with disappointments to be very much chagrined.

This was a busy summer. Besides running for the legislature Lincoln hired out to a certain Captain Bogue who was trying to establish a steamboat service from Beardstown on the Illinois to the fast-growing settlement of Springfield about twenty miles above New Salem on the Sangamon. This was internal improvements put in practice. Lincoln's job was to hew with a long-handled axe, cutting away snags and fallen trees that impeded the passage of the good ship *Talisman*. The *Talisman* never reached Springfield. She stuck on a dam when she had to turn back on account of the falling water. The enterprise was a failure.

Steamboating on the Sangamon proved unprofitable. It was probably the experience of this trip that caused Lincoln a few years later to dope out and patent a contraption for easing boats over sandbars.

Back in New Salem with forty dollars in his pocket, and at loose ends, Lincoln enlisted in the militia. The occasion was an expedition to drive Black Hawk and his Sauk warriors back across to the farther side of the Mississippi River. Lincoln was elected captain by his company. Describing his part in that campaign in a sardonic speech he made in Congress many years later, he said he hadn't seen any Indians, but he had shed some blood in his struggles with the mosquitoes. He was mustered out in time to lose his election, but he had the satisfaction of carrying New Salem by a large majority. "The only time," he stated with some solemnity in his autobiography, "that Abraham was ever beaten by a vote of the people."

Well-wishers got him appointed postmaster as a consolation. He picked up a little income as assistant to the county surveyor. Reading the surveyors' manual interested him in geometry. When he was finally elected to the legislature, he took Euclid along to study in slack moments. One of his colleagues lent him law books and eventually took him into his office, when Springfield became the state capital, as a partner. About that time he discovered Shakespeare and memorized scene after scene. Shakespeare's people, like the characters in Chronicles and Kings, were men and women like the people he knew.

According to Herndon, his partner in later years, Lincoln wasn't much of a reader while he was practicing law. Herndon thought he absorbed more information talking to people than reading books.

By the time he became a successful lawyer and married a lady of somewhat upperclass breeding, Lincoln's own education was complete. From the experience of pioneer life and canoeing on the Sangamon and flatboating on the Mississippi and drawing plats for Illinois boom towns and passing the time of day with all comers at the post office, and from absorption in the Bible and from reading Shakespeare's plays and the speeches of Henry Clay, he had already assembled the moral and intellectual tools with which he was going to cope with events and problems for the rest of his life. His outlook was tinged by the crackerbarrel humor of the country store and by a peculiar note of melancholy best expressed by a stanza of his favorite poem, which he found in a newspaper and quoted again and again in all sorts of contexts:

> T'is the wink of an eye, t'is the draught of a breath
> From the blossoms of health to the paleness of death,
> From the gilded saloon to the bier and the shroud.
> Oh, why should the spirit of mortal be proud?

The classics of this particular mid-American mid-nineteenth-century culture formed the mental bank which Lincoln could draw upon whenever political life demanded that he put his notions into words. They had to be words people would understand. They had to be words people would feel. His phrases sank into the minds of his hearers because their education, too, was based on the King James Bible. When Lincoln, in the Gettysburg Address, describes self-government as "government of the people, by the people, for the people" he touched his audience to the quick. The words aroused something more personal than the rubber-stamp response to a political slogan. They aroused unspoken memories of marking the ballots at the polling place, serving on jury duty, petitions to the legislature, political debates in the grand manner, such as the still freshly remembered oratorical contest between Lincoln himself and Stephen A. Douglas which had done so much to polarize Republican opinion during Lincoln's losing campaign for the Senate. Behind the first meanings of the words he used were resonances that struck deep chords of feeling among stored recollections out of Bible reading and hymn-singing in church. To many he seemed a minor prophet come back to life out of the Old Testament.

Lincoln never denied that he was a professional politician. He was a professional of self-government. Implicit in many of his speeches was the effort to explain the paradoxical relationship between the leader and the led which was buried deep in the phrase, "government of the people, by the people, for the people." He felt that this balanced interplay was something the people of the United States had that nobody else in the world had. It was easy to feel but hard to pin down in a precise statement.

He had come very close to saying what he meant in an address he delivered before the New Jersey senate in the course of his extended speaking tour on his way to Washington for his first inauguration in the winter of 1861. He had been ingratiating himself with the assembled legislators with reminiscences of what the name Trenton had meant to him:

> May I be pardoned if upon this occasion I mention that a way back in my childhood, the earliest days of my being able to read, I got hold of a small book, such a one as few of the younger members have ever seen, Weems's *Life of Washington*. I remember all the accounts there given of the battlefields and struggles for the liberties of the country, and none fixed themselves upon my imagination so deeply as the struggles here at Trenton, New-Jersey. The crossing of the river; the contest with the Hessians; the great hardships endured at that time, all fixed themselves on my memory more than any single revolutionary event; and you all know, for you have all been boys, how these early impressions last longer than any others. I recollect thinking then, boy even though I was, that there must have been something more than common that those men struggled for. I am exceedingly anxious that that thing which they struggled for; that something even more than National Independence; that something that held out a great promise to all the people of the world to all time to come; I am exceedingly anxious that this Union, the Constitution, and the liberties of the people shall be perpetuated in accordance with the original idea for which that struggle was made, and I shall be most happy indeed if I shall be an humble instrument in the bands of the Almighty, and of this, his almost chosen people, for perpetuating the object of that great struggle.

In using the phrase "his almost chosen people" Lincoln was picking his words with care. He was saying that the application of the principles laid down in the Constitution and the Declaration of Independence was a continuing process, not yet completed. This was the theme he resumed in those great phrases in the Gettysburg Address that toll like a bell: "It is for us, the living, rather, to be dedicated here to the unfinished work . . . that these dead shall not have died in vain—that this nation, under God, shall have a new birth. . . ."

A hundred years later what do the words of the care-worn national prophet who spoke at Gettysburg mean to us? Have our basic preconceptions changed so completely that we have lost the frame of reference that gave them meaning?

There are two ways of answering this question.

An uncommitted observer from an alien culture (say an Arab journalist) might well search in vain, under the opulence, the crime, the daily exploitation of everything that is shoddiest in human nature which forms so much of the surface of our national life, for any of the deep-seated responses that Lincoln relied on to give meaning to his phrases.

Lincoln was no sectarian, but his outlook was profoundly Christian. Our uncommitted observer might well discover that the bases of Christian conviction were so eroded in the United States that there was little left but the compulsive do-goodism of social service. He might find that the only people who understood what the word liberty meant were refugees from the communist countries where liberty had ceased to exist. He would find the Bible, which was the fountainhead both of individual Protestant Christianity and of the literary tradition of the English-speaking peoples, not only neglected at home, but chased out of the schools. He might suspect, that if the atheists carried their victory to its logical extreme, the Good Book might soon be removed from public libraries. He would find that many Americans had so lost faith in the concept of nationality they didn't care whether the United States was chosen or not. He might find it hard to see how Lincoln's words could meet with anything but a perfunctory or ritual response if they were spoken for the first time today.

This uncommitted observer might well discover, against the background of a type of widespread material well-being which the human race has never had to cope with in its previous history, that the concept which for Lincoln was embodied in the expression "the people," had been so disfigured by the manipulations of mass communication as to be unrecognizable. He might even suspect that the technological advances which so changed the shape of society as to raise hob with the ethical norms of the population were in danger of bogging down through a failure of the inventing and improvising imagination. Having read "Mene, Mene, Tekel, Upharsin" off the walls of the banquet hall, our uncommitted observer might well hasten to shake the dust of these states from his shoes. Babylon, too, was prosperous in its day.

But we are not uncommitted. "This nation under God" is our country. "His almost chosen people" is our people. As Americans we are irrevocably committed to that "something more than common" that Washington's Continentals fought for when they surprised the Hessians at Trenton. "That something that held out a great promise to all the people of the world to all time to come" is the cement which reunited the nation when Lincoln won his war against the Confederacy. It is that something added to the political and religious and literary traditions of the English-speaking peoples which has bound together the congeries of immigrants of various origins through the hundred years since Lincoln's short speech at Gettysburg.

It has been a hundred years of dizzy technological development. It has been a period of social change so drastic as to affect the whole gamut of human behavior.

Lincoln spoke at Trenton of his anxiety "that this Union, the Constitution, and the liberties of the people shall be perpetuated in accordance with the original idea for which that struggle was made." This idea was based on belief in individual liberty and individual responsibility. It depended upon the belief that there was a divine spirit in man which ever strove for the good. The truth of this conviction cannot be tested by logic or proved by scientific experiment, but the contrary cannot be proved either. Inevitably the moment comes when we have to take the leap of faith.

Faith is a big word. Lincoln wouldn't have needed to explain it, but today it has become one of those bugle words that leave an emotional blob in the mind instead of a sharp definition. By faith I mean whatever conviction produced a feeling of participation in a common enterprise. A civilization is a common enterprise. When faith is lost, civilizations coast along on their momentum for a while, but soon they start to rot and disintegrate. Much more than on material well-being or on technological successes their survival depends on an inner imperative which causes men to reach for what is good for them instead of what is bad for them. Self-governing institutions particularly depend on individual responsibility for the choice between what is right and what is wrong.

If Americans cease to be dedicated to "that something more than common" that Lincoln spoke of, the republic he gave his life for has no more reason for being. The continuing process that faces the generations alive today is the adjustment of the methods of self-government and of the aspirations of individual men for a full life to the changing shape of mass-production society. There is nothing easy about such an assignment. The alternative is the soggy despotism that pervades two-thirds of the globe. Even partial success will call for the rebirth of some sort of central faith as strong as Lincoln's was. Only then may we continue to entertain the hope that this "government of the people, by the people, for the people, shall not perish from the earth."

1964

Reinhold Niebuhr

A second-generation minister, Niebuhr (1892–1971) was ordained in the Evangelical Synod of North America in 1913. After serving as the pastor of a Detroit church for 13 years, he joined the faculty of the Union Theological Seminary in New York in 1928 and remained there until his retirement in 1960. Always committed to social action, Niebuhr moved away from his earlier socialism and pacifism as he developed the doctrine of Christian Realism, in which an awareness of sin and human fallibility led to a rejection of utopianism and an acceptance of the tragic necessity of confronting evil. A co-founder in 1947 of the liberal anti-Communist group Americans for Democratic Action, his writings influenced Martin Luther King Jr. as well as Alcoholics Anonymous, which adopted (and adapted) his famous "serenity prayer." In his essay on Lincoln's religion, Niebuhr bypassed earlier disputes regarding whether Lincoln was an orthodox Christian and focused instead on his sense of providence, lack of fanaticism, avoidance of self-righteousness, and willingness to share in "the moral ambiguity of the political order itself" regarding slavery. Nonetheless, Niebuhr did not question Lincoln's fundamental opposition to slavery and enlisted his memory on behalf of the ongoing civil rights struggle—an identification other commentators would soon call into question.

The Religion of Abraham Lincoln

Analysis of Abraham Lincoln's religion in the context of the prevailing religion of his time and place and in the light of the polemical use of the slavery issue, which corrupted religious life in the days before and during the Civil War, must lead to the conclusion that Lincoln's religious convictions were superior in depth and purity to those held by the religious as well as by the political leaders of his day.

This judgment may seem extravagant, and the casual reader may suspect that it has been influenced by the hagiography which envelops the heroes of a nation, substituting symbolic myths for sober reality. It is true of course that Lincoln, the savior and therefore the second father of his nation, is enveloped in historical myth. But only poetic symbol adequately describes the status of Lincoln as a more authentic embodiment of American democracy than was the 18th century aristocrat George Washington, who holds first place in the national pantheon as the "father" of his country.

It is nevertheless easy to validate the judgment as derived from sober history: Lincoln's superior religious convictions are attested to in part by the fact that, though he was of deeply religious temperament, he joined none of the religious sects of the frontier. His abstention has led some historians to number him among the religious skeptics. Lincoln was not a sophisticated modern, but he was a thoughtful and well read man; one must suppose that this was why he did not share the orthodox beliefs of the frontier or make common cause with the frontier evangelist Peter Cartwright (who, incidentally, was one of his political opponents).

Lincoln's religious faith was informed primarily by a sense of providence, as is indeed the case with most of the world's statesmen past and present. In his eloquent second inaugural address he voiced his belief thus:

> The Almighty has His own purposes. "Woe unto the world because of offenses! for it must needs be that offenses come; but woe to that man by whom the offense cometh." If we shall suppose that American slavery is one of those offenses which, in the providence of God, must needs come, but which, having continued through his appointed time, he now wills to remove, and that he gives to both North and South this terrible war as the woe due to those by whom offense came, shall we discern therein any departure from those divine attributes which the believers in a living God always ascribe to him?

It is to be noted that both the pious and the skeptical veins in Lincoln's faith are expressed in these words. When he speaks of the "divine attributes which the believers in a living God always ascribe to him," he does not explicitly number himself among

the believers. As he goes on to spell out the workings of providence one can sense why there were in him, as in all men except
the most conventional believers, both faith and skepticism concerning the concept of providence. For while the drama of history is shot through with moral meaning, the meaning is never
exact. Sin and punishment, virtue and reward are never precisely proportioned.

Lincoln spells out the dilemma of faith as he applies the idea
of providence to the issue of slavery: in the words of Scripture,
his concept involves the "sins of the fathers" being visited on the
children of another generation. The second inaugural continues:

> Fondly do we hope, fervently do we pray, that this mighty
> scourge of war may speedily pass away. Yet, if God wills that
> it continue until all the wealth piled by the bondsman's two-
> hundred and fifty years of unrequited toil shall be sunk, and
> until every drop of blood drawn with the lash shall be paid
> by another drawn with the sword, as was said three thou-
> sand years ago, so still it must be said, "The judgments of
> the Lord are true and righteous all together."

Lincoln's faith is closely akin to that of the Hebrew prophets,
who first conceived the idea of a meaningful history. If there was
an element of skepticism in his grand concept, one can only observe that Scripture itself, particularly the Book of Job, expresses
some doubts about giving the providential aspects of history
exact meanings in neat moral terms. Incidentally, this eloquent
passage surely expresses Lincoln's moral abhorrence of slavery.
The point is important because the abolitionists had expressed
some doubt on this issue.

As a responsible statesman, Lincoln was not primarily an
abolitionist; rather he confessed that his primary purpose was to
save the union. But the chief evidence of the purity and profun-
dity of Lincoln's sense of providence is the fact that he was able
to resist the natural temptation to do what all political leaders,
indeed all men, have done through the ages: identify providence
with the cause to which he was committed. Alone among statesmen of the ancient and modern periods, Lincoln had a sense of
historical meaning so high as to cast doubt on the intentions of

both sides, to put the enemy into the same category of ambiguity as the nation to which his life was committed. In his second inaugural address Lincoln put the whole tragic drama of the Civil War in a religio-dramatic setting:

> Neither party expected for the war the magnitude or the duration which it has now attained. Neither anticipated that the cause of the conflict might cease with, or even before, the conflict itself should cease. Each looked for an easier triumph, and a result less fundamental and astounding. Both read the same Bible; and pray to the same God; and each invokes His aid against the other.

There follows a thoughtful passage which shows—more precisely, I think, than has any other statesman or any theologian—the relation of our moral commitments in history to our religious reservations about the partiality of our moral judgments. First, the moral judgment: "It may seem strange that any men should dare to ask a just God's assistance in wringing their bread from the sweat of other men's faces." Then, the religious reservation: "But let us judge not, that we be not judged. The prayers of both could not be answered—that of neither have been answered fully."

Surely such a nice balance of moral commitment and religious reservation in regard to the partiality of all historic commitments of biased men is a unique achievement It is particularly remarkable for a responsible political leader; for it is the very nature of political commitments that those who make them claim more ultimate virtues for their cause than either a transcendent providence or a neutral posterity will validate. It was Lincoln's achievement to embrace a paradox which lies at the center of the spirituality of all Western culture: affirmation of a meaningful history along with religious reservation about the partiality and bias which human actors and agents betray in their definition of that meaning.

To embrace this paradox was an important achievement. For the evil by-product of the historical dynamism of Western culture was a fanaticism which confused partial meanings and contingent purposes with the ultimate meaning of life itself. Lincoln's lack of fanaticism, his spirit of magnanimity, was revealed in many of his policies but most of all in his attitude toward the defeated secessionists, a spirit beautifully expressed in his second inaugural: "With malice toward none; with charity for all; with firmness in the right, as God gives us to see the right, let us strive on to finish the work we are in. . . ." Unfortunately his untimely death at the hands of an assassin prevented him from carrying out his design of pacification and launched the nation into a terrible period characterized by vindictive crushing of a vanquished foe—a disaster from which we have not yet recovered. The stubbornness of the south's resistance to the present integration movement is part of the price we pay for the vindictiveness which Lincoln would have avoided.

But since the spirit of magnanimity grew from his apprehension of the biased character of all historic judgments and did not annul those judgments, we must turn to Lincoln's scheme of moral principles, his hierarchy of values, to ascertain the complexity of his compound of moral preferences, political and personal. His abhorrence of slavery was variously expressed but most vividly in the second inaugural. Yet Lincoln was not an abolitionist. The secessionist, he said in his first inaugural, had "no oath registered in Heaven to destroy the government," but he himself had a "most solemn one to 'defend, preserve and protect' it." One might regard this preference as that of a patriot expressing a nation's primal impulse for collective survival. But his preference represented more than mere national patriotism. He had a Jeffersonian belief in the mission of the new nation to initiate, extend and preserve democratic self-government. Thus for him not only national survival, but the survival of democracy itself was involved in the fortunes of the Civil War.

In his brief but eloquent Gettysburg address, Lincoln defined the mission of the new nation in Jeffersonian terms: ". . . our fathers brought forth on this continent a new nation conceived in liberty and dedicated to the proposition that all men are created equal. Now we are engaged in a great civil war testing whether that nation, or any nation so conceived and so dedicated, can long endure." Lincoln evidently believed that the whole democratic cause was being tested in the destiny of our own nation—a belief which was natural in the middle of the 19th century when many European critics were prophesying the failure of our system of government and when the trends of history which would make democracy a universal, pattern of government in western Europe were not yet apparent. The peroration of the Gettysburg address returned to the same theme: "that we here highly resolve that these dead shall not have died in vain, that this nation under God shall have a new birth of freedom, and that government of the people, by the people, for the people, shall not perish from the earth."

Lincoln's passion for saving the union was viewed by some critics an a personal concept of the irrevocable character of the covenant of the Constitution. A very high-minded leader of the secessionist states, Robert E. Lee, had a different conception; though he detested slavery, he felt himself bound in loyalty to his state of Virginia rather than to the nation. Since the Civil War itself, not to speak of the many unifying forces which made the nation one, subsequently altered the loyalties of our citizens, making state loyalty subordinate to national loyalty, it is safe to say that if Lincoln's conception of the irrevocable character of the national covenant was a personal conviction, it was eventually transmuted into a national one. In his first inaugural Lincoln argued in favor of the irrevocability of the covenant in words which many of his contemporaries did not accept but which we take for granted:

> I hold that, in contemplation of universal law and of the Constitution, the Union of these states is perpetual. Perpetuity is implied, if not expressed, in the fundamental law of all national governments. It is safe to assert that no government proper ever had a provision in its organic law for its own termination. To the extent of my ability I shall take care, as the Constitution expressly enjoins me, that all the laws shall be faithfully executed in all the states.

There was of course a residue of moral ambiguity in Lincoln's devotion to national union. Sometimes that devotion involved his abhorrence of slavery. Thus:

> When he [Stephen A. Douglas] invites any people, willing
> to have slavery, to establish it, he is blowing out the moral
> lights around us. When he says he "cares not whether slav-
> ery is voted down or voted up—that it is a sacred right of
> self-government"—he is, in my judgment, penetrating the
> human soul and eradicating the light of reason and the love
> of liberty in this American people.

This absolute rejection of slavery seems at variance with the
sentiment Lincoln expressed in a letter to Horace Greeley, assuring him that his "paramount object" was to save the union,
and that if he could save it half slave and half free, he would do
it. The contradiction in the two attitudes may be explained by
the fact that the point at issue in the Douglas debates was the
extension of slavery into free territories, as provided in the
Kansas-Nebraska act. Lincoln was violently opposed to this policy, the more so since he believed that if the institution could be
restricted to the original slave states, it would gradually die. In
holding to this position he felt himself in firm accord with the
founding fathers:

> The framers of the Constitution found the institution of
> slavery amongst their other institutions at the time. They
> found that by an effort to eradicate it, they might lose much
> of what they had already gained. They were obliged to bow
> to this necessity. They gave power to Congress to abolish
> the slave trade at the end of twenty years. They also prohib-
> ited slavery in the territories where it did not exist. They
> did what they could and yielded to necessity for the rest. I
> also yield to all which follows from that necessity.

Lincoln's opposition to slavery cannot be questioned. If there
is moral ambiguity in his position, it is an ambiguity which he
shared with the founding fathers, the author of the Declaration
of Independence, with all responsible statesmen who pursue
their ideals within the framework of the harmony and survival
of the community. In short, he exhibited not his own moral ambiguity but the moral ambiguity of the political order itself.
    Lincoln's attitude toward the principle of the Declaration of

Independence "that all men are created equal" was, of course, informed by the ethos of his day. It was not the same as our present ethos, when we are charged with eliminating the last vestiges of slavery from our national life. Lincoln's attitude toward racial equality exhibited that compromise between the ideal of equality and the customary inequality which the institution of slavery had introduced into the ethos of the nation, which presumably was exhibited in the attitude of Thomas Jefferson, author of the Declaration.

In one of his debates with Douglas, Lincoln said:

> I do not understand the Declaration to mean that all men are created equal in all respects. They are not our equal in color, but I suppose that it does mean to declare that all men are equal in some respects; they are equal in their right to "life, liberty, and the pursuit of happiness." Certainly, the Negro is not our equal in color—perhaps not in many other respects; still, in the right to put into his mouth the bread that his own hands have earned, he is the equal of every other man.

That affirmation of basic human equality is beyond reproach. One might argue that the assumption of a difference in color implies inequality; Lincoln either shared the color prejudices of his and our day or he was politically astute enough not to challenge popular prejudices too radically.

The chief source of tension between Lincoln and the abolitionists was his hesitancy to free the slaves. That hesitancy was not personal; it was the political calculation of a responsible statesman concerned to retain the loyalty of the border states (Lincoln reprimanded the commanders who freed the slaves in those states). And when he finally issued the Emancipation Proclamation (postponed for a year until victory would ensure that it was not regarded as a final desperate effort of a defeated nation), it was made applicable only to the Negroes in territories under Union arms. And in the words of a distinguished historian, "it had the eloquence of a bill of lading."

Not only our own abolitionists but also the critical British liberals failed to be moved by the proclamation. But both its timing and its immediate scope were the fruits of statesmanlike calculations; they revealed that Lincoln was primarily not a moral prophet but a responsible statesman. All his actions and attitudes can be explained and justified by his hierarchy of values, succinctly expressed in his statement to Greeley, "My paramount object in this struggle is to save the Union."

A conscientious politician is compelled to relate all the moral aspirations and all the moral hesitancies of the social forces of a free society to the primary goal, the survival of the community. In the political order, the value of justice takes an uneasy second place behind that of internal order. In reviewing Lincoln's catalogue of values one must come to the conclusion that his sense of justice was strong enough to give that value a position immediately beneath survival, not only of the nation's physical life but also of its system of democratic self-government, which he identified—perhaps too simply, as did all our fathers—with the survival of democracy throughout the world.

It may be significant that the moral ambiguities in the idealism of this man proved themselves religiously superior to the pure moral idealism of the abolitionists—the Horace Greeleys, the William Lloyd Garrisons, the Wendell Phillipses. This fact does not prove that responsible statesmen are morally superior to pure idealists; the idealists' opposition to slavery was an indispensable contribution to the dramatic struggle which saved the nation and purged it of the hated institution of human bondage. In his message to Congress in 1862 Lincoln, with caution prompted by diverse sentiments on the issue within the union, revealed both the moral imperatives which prompted emancipation and the political considerations which made him more cautious than the abolitionists wished:

> Among friends of the Union there is great diversity of sentiment and policy in regard to slavery and the African race amongst us. Some would perpetuate slavery; some would abolish it suddenly and without compensation; some would remove the freed people from among us—some would abolish it gradually and with compensation; and some would retain them with us; and there are yet other minor diversities.

Because of these diversities we waste much strength in struggle among ourselves. By concession we should harmonize and act together.

As President, however, Lincoln acted for the nation, and the moral imperative of the emancipation was eloquently expressed in these words from the same message:

> In giving freedom to the slave we assure freedom to the free—honorable alike in what we give and what we preserve. We shall nobly save or meanly lose the last, best hope of earth. Other means may succeed; this could not fail. The way is plain, peaceful, generous, just—a way which if followed the world will forever applaud and God must forever bless.

Lincoln's sense of the indivisibility of freedom and his conviction that emancipation of the slaves implied the opportunity to "nobly save . . . the last, best hope of earth"—the cause of democratic government—is particularly significant for a generation called upon to remove the last remnants of human bondage from our national life. It reminds us that as we give freedom we preserve our freedom and the prestige of free institutions. It is clear that Lincoln believed that in a nation "conceived in liberty and dedicated to the proposition that all men are created equal," moral ambiguity is limited to the field of tactics; in his case it was prompted by the diversity of opinion on the issue of slavery. But the ambiguity ends in the strategy. The emancipation of the slaves gave and preserved liberty, gave it to the slave and preserved it for all free men. Lincoln's 1862 message to Congress throws light not only on the moral problems of politics in general but on our current integration problems.

Lincoln's moral superiority over the idealists stemmed primarily not from his conscientiousness as a statesman but from the depth and height of his religious sense of the meaning of the drama of history; from his consequent sensitivity to the problem posed by the taint of self-interest in the definitions of meaning, by the way human agents corrupt the meaning in which they are involved; and from the magnanimity which was the natural fruit of this sensitivity.

The idealists were—as are most if not all idealists—self-righteous and consequently vindictive. Garrison may have made the southern response to the abolitionist movement the more stubborn because he interpreted social attitudes and evils as the fruits of criminal tendencies. He did not understand that good men may inherit social attitudes and become the bearers of social evil, even though their own consciences may be not perverse but merely conventional.

Failure to understand the complex causes of historical and societal evil made for the vindictiveness exhibited by the victors in the Civil War and for the consequent horrors of Reconstruction. As we try now, a century later, to eliminate the last vestiges of slavery, we frequently encounter resentments in the south which are the fruits not so much of the terrible conflict as of the vengeance displayed in Reconstruction, when the actions of men from the north revealed that without humility idealism can be easily transmuted into cruelty.

If we analyze the whole import of the relation of moral idealism to fanaticism and of religious humility and contrition to magnanimity, and if we set the tension between Lincoln and the abolitionists in the context of this problem, the conclusion is inevitable: Abraham Lincoln was not only a statesman who saved the nation in the hour of its greatest peril but also a rare and unique human being who could be responsible in the discharge of historic tasks without equating his interpretation of the task with divine wisdom.

It is not too much to claim that, more adequately than any other statesman of modern history, Lincoln demonstrated the paradox of all human spirituality, and of Western historical dynamism in particular. The measure of his spiritual achievement becomes apparent when we compare him with the religiously inspired idealists among statesmen of the modern period—from Oliver Cromwell to Woodrow Wilson.

February 1965

Lerone Bennett Jr.

After a century of intermittent criticism, the image of Lincoln as the Great Emancipator came under full-scale assault in the 1960s as a consequence of the civil rights and Black Power movements. One of the most significant revisionist appraisals of Lincoln's record on slavery and race came from Lerone Bennett Jr. (b. 1928), a senior editor at *Ebony* and the author of the highly successful *Before the Mayflower: A History of the Negro in America, 1619–1962* (1962). "Was Abe Lincoln a White Supremacist?" appeared in *Ebony* in February 1968 and quickly elicited an indignant response, "Was Lincoln Just a Honkie?," from the journalist Herbert Mitgang in *The New York Times Magazine*. Intended as a challenge to mainstream historical understanding and to Lincoln's special place in African-American memory, Bennett's article helped prompt a re-examination of Lincoln's words and deeds regarding race and emancipation by historians such as Vincent Harding, LaWanda Cox, Stephen Oates, and James McPherson. Bennett himself would later expand his article into a book, *Forced into Glory: Abraham Lincoln's White Dream*, published in 2000. As scholars debated the historical record, Lincoln's standing among the African-American public continued to fall; in a 1991 poll, only 35 percent of the black respondents named Lincoln as one of the three greatest presidents.

Was Abe Lincoln a White Supremacist?

The presidential campaign was over and the victor was stretching his legs and shaking off the cares of the world in his temporary office in the State Capitol in Springfield, Ill. Surrounded by the perquisites of power, at peace with the world, the president-elect was regaling old acquaintances with hilarious stories of his early days as a politician. One of the visitors interrupted this entertaining monologue and remarked that it was a shame that "the vexatious slavery matter" would be the first question of public policy the new President would have to deal with in Washington.

The President-elect's eyes twinkled and he said he was remined of a story. According to eyewitness Henry Villard, President-elect Abraham Lincoln "told the story of the Kentucky Justice of the Peace whose first case was a criminal prosecution for the abuse of slaves. Unable to find any precedent, he exclaimed at last angrily: 'I will be damned if I don't feel almost sorry for being elected when the niggers is the first thing I have to attend to.'"

This story, shocking as it may sound to Lincoln admirers, was in character. For the President-elect had never shown any undue interest in black people, and it was altogether natural for him to suggest that he shared the viewpoint of the reluctant and biased justice of the peace.

In one of the supreme ironies of history, the man who told this story was forced by circumstances to attend to the Negroes. And within five years he was enshrined in American mythology as "the Great Emancipator who freed the Negroes with a stroke of the pen out of the goodness and compassion of his heart."

Over the years, the Mythology of the Great Emancipator has become a part of the mental landscape of America. Generations of schoolchildren have memorized its cadences. Poets, politicians, and long-suffering blacks have wept over its imagery and drama.

No other American story is so enduring. No other American story is so comforting. No other American story is so false.

Abraham Lincoln was *not* the Great Emancipator. As we shall see, there is abundant evidence to indicate that the Emancipation Proclamation was not what people think it is and that Lincoln issued it with extreme misgivings and reservations. Even more decisive is the fact that the real Lincoln was a tragically flawed figure who shared the racial prejudices of most of his white contemporaries.

If, despite the record, Lincoln has been misunderstood and misinterpreted, it is not his fault. A conservative Illinois lawyer, cautious and conventional in social matters, Lincoln never pretended to be a racial liberal or a social innovator. He said repeatedly, in public and in private, that he was a firm believer in white supremacy. And his acts supported his assertions. Not only that: Lincoln had profound doubts about the possibility of realizing the rhetoric of the Declaration of Independence and the Gettysburg Address on this soil; and he believed until his death that black people and white people would be much better off separated—preferably with the Atlantic Ocean or some other large and deep body of water between them.

The man's character, his way with words, and his assassination, together with the psychological needs of a racist society, have obscured these contradictions under a mountain of myths which undoubtedly would have amused Lincoln, who had a wonderful sense of the ironic and ridiculous. The myth-makers have not only buried the real Lincoln; they have also managed to prove him wrong. He said once that it was impossible to fool all of the people all of the time. But his apotheosis clearly proves that it is possible to fool enough of them long enough to make a conservative white supremacist a national symbol of racial tolerance and understanding.

If the Lincoln myths were the harmless fantasies of children at play, it would be possible to ignore them. But when the myths of children become adult daydreams and when the daydreams are used to obscure deep social problems and to hide historical reality, it becomes a social duty to confront them. When, at the height of the summer rebellion season, President Lyndon B. Johnson said he intended to follow a Lincolnian course, Professor Vincent P. Harding of Spelman College rebuked him, pointing out in a letter to the New York Times that Lincoln's vacillating Civil War posture was a prescription for social disaster today.

Because, as Professor Harding suggested, we are environed by dangers and because we need all the light we can get; because Abraham Lincoln is not the light, because he is in fact standing in the light, hiding our way; because a real emancipation proclamation has become a matter of national survival and *because no one has ever issued such a document in this country*—because, finally, lies enslave and because the truth is always seemly and proper, it has become urgently necessary to reevaluate the Lincoln mythology. The need for such a reevaluation has already been recognized in some scholarly circles. Some scholars have confronted the ambiguities of the Emancipation Proclamation and have suggested that Lincoln's reputation would be more securely based if it were grounded not on that document but on his services as leader of the victorious North. Analyzing the same evidence, David Donald said in *Lincoln Reconsidered* that perhaps "the secret of Lincoln's continuing vogue is his essential ambiguity. He can be cited on all sides of all questions." Donald was not quite correct, for Lincoln cannot be cited on the side of equal rights for black people, a fact that has discomfited more than one Lincoln Day orator. Commenting on Lincoln's determined opposition to a policy of emancipation, Professor Kenneth Stampp wrote: "Indeed it may be said that if it was Lincoln's destiny to go down in history as the Great Emancipator, rarely has a man embraced his destiny with greater reluctance than he."

To understand Lincoln's reluctance and his painful ambivalence on the question of race, one must see him first in the background of his times. Born into a poor white family in the slave state of Kentucky and raised in the anti-black environments of southern Indiana and Illinois, Lincoln was exposed from the very beginning to racism.

It would have been difficult, if not impossible, for young Abraham Lincoln to emerge unscathed from this environment. By an immense effort of transcendence, worthy of admiration and long thought, Lincoln managed to free himself of most of the crudities of his early environment. But he did not—and perhaps could not—rise above the racism that was staining the tissue of the nation's soul.

It appears from the record that Lincoln readily absorbed the Negro stereotypes of his environment, for he ever afterwards remained fond of Negro dialect jokes, blackface minstrels and Negro ditties. "Like most white men," Professor Benjamin Quarles wrote, "Lincoln regarded the Negro as such as funny." More to the point, Lincoln, as Quarles also noted, regarded the Negro as inferior.

There is a pleasant story of Lincoln awakening to the realities of slavery on a visit to New Orleans in 1841. According to the traditional account, an aroused Lincoln said: "If I ever get a chance to hit that thing [slavery] I'll hit it hard." Since the man who reported this statement did not accompany Lincoln to

New Orleans, the story is of dubious value. More telling is the fact that Lincoln distinguished himself as a public official by a reluctance to hit slavery at all.

In the general literature, Lincoln is depicted as an eloquent and flaming idealist, whaling away at the demon of slavery. This view is almost totally false. In the first place, Lincoln was an opportunist, not an idealist. He was a man of the fence, a man of the middle, a man who stated the principle with great eloquence but almost always shied away from rigid commitments to practice. Contrary to reports, Lincoln was no social revolutionary. As a matter of fact, he was an archetypal example of the cautious politician who assails the extremists on both sides. It is not for nothing that cautious politicians sing his praises.

It should be noted, secondly, that Lincoln's position on slavery has been grossly misrepresented. Lincoln was not opposed to slavery; he was opposed to the *extension* of slavery. More than that: Lincoln was opposed to the extension of slavery out of devotion to the interests of white people, not out of compassion for suffering blacks. To be sure, he did say from time to time that slavery was "a monstrous injustice." But he also said, repeatedly, that he was not prepared to do anything to remove that injustice where it existed. On the contrary, he said that it was his duty to tolerate and, if necessary, to give practical support to an evil supported by the U.S. Constitution.

More damaging is the fact that Lincoln apparently believed that immediate and general emancipation would be a greater evil than slavery itself. Eulogizing Henry Clay on July 6, 1852, he associated himself with that slaveowner's colonization ideas and said that Clay "did not perceive, as I think no wise man has perceived, how it [slavery] could be at *once* eradicated, without producing a greater evil, even to the cause of human liberty itself." In other speeches of the same period, Lincoln commended travel to black people and noted with admiration that "the children of Israel . . . went out of Egyptian bondage in a body."

A third point of significance is that Lincoln's opposition to the extension of slavery was a late and anomalous growth. In the 1830s and 1840s, in the midst of one of the greatest moral crises in the history of America, Lincoln remained silent and lamentably inactive. In his few public utterances on the subject in the 30s and 40s, he very carefully denounced both slavery and the opponents of slavery.

For many white Northerners, the most agonizing moral issue of the day was the fugitive slave law, which required all Americans to assist in the capture and return of runaway slaves. Many whites, some of them quite conservative, refused to obey the law. Others, more daring, organized an open resistance movement, moving runaway slaves from station to station on the Underground Railway.

Instead of aiding this effort, Lincoln opposed it, publicly announcing his support of the fugitive slave law. In a private letter to Joshua F. Speed in 1855, he said: "I confess I hate to see the poor creatures hunted down, and caught, and carried back to their stripes, and un-rewarded toils, but I bite my lip and keep quiet."

Lincoln came down off the fence, rhetorically, in the 50s when the Kansas-Nebraska act reopened the whole question of the extension of slavery to the largely uninhabited territories of the West. This was, he said, a clear and present threat to free white men and to what he called "the white man's charter of freedom" —the Declaration of Independence. In his public speeches of this period, Lincoln was given to saying in the same speech that he believed in white supremacy as a practical matter and in the Declaration of Independence as an abstract matter of principle.

The Lincoln years in Illinois were years of oppression and reaction. Black people could not vote, testify against white people in court or attend public schools. It was a crime for free black people to settle in the state. Although Lincoln was a powerful figure in state politics for more than a quarter of a century, he made no audible protest against this state of affairs. In fact, he said he preferred it that way. When H. Ford Douglas, a militant black leader, asked Lincoln to support a movement to repeal the law banning black testimony, Lincoln refused.

In the famous series of debates with Stephen Douglas, Lincoln made his position crystal clear. He was opposed, he said, to Negro citizenship and to "the niggers and the white people marrying together." Speaking at Charleston, Illinois, on September 18, 1858, Lincoln said: "I will say, then, that I am not, nor ever have been, in favor of bringing about in any way the social and political equality of the white and black races; (applause) that I am not, nor ever have been, in favor of making voters or jurors of Negroes, nor of qualifying them to hold office, nor to intermarry with white people; and I will say, in addition, to this, that there is a physical difference between the white and black races which I believe will forever forbid the two races living together on terms of social and political equality. And inasmuch as they cannot so live, while they do remain together there must be the position of superior and inferior, and I as much as any other man am in favor of having the superior position assigned to the white race."

Lincoln grew during the war—but he didn't grow much. On every issue relating to the black man—on emancipation, confiscation of rebel land and the use of black soldiers—he was the very essence of the white supremacist with good intentions. In fact, Lincoln distinguished himself as President by sustained and consistent opposition to the fundamental principle of the Proclamation that guaranteed his immortality. Incredible as it may seem now, the man who would go down in history as the Great Emancipator spent the first 18 months of his administration in a desperate and rather pathetic attempt to save slavery where it existed. He began his Presidential career by saying that he had neither the power nor the desire to interfere with slavery in the states. And he endorsed a proposed Thirteenth Amendment which would have guaranteed that slavery would never be molested in existing states and Washington, D.C.

"My policy," Lincoln said, "is to have no policy." In this famous statement, Lincoln was something less than candid. For he did have a policy and that policy was to win the war without touching slavery. "It is the desire of the President," Secretary of War Simon Cameron wrote a general on August 8, 1861, "*that all existing rights in all states be fully respected and maintained.*" When Lincoln's policy foundered on the reef of Southern intransigence, Lincoln complained sadly to a friend: "I *struggled* nearly a year and a half to get along without touching the 'institution.' . . ."

In accordance with the real policy of the Lincoln Administration, the War Department refused to accept black troops and Union generals vied with each other in proving their fealty to slavery. Some generals returned fugitive slaves to rebel owners; others said that if black slaves staged an uprising behind enemy lines they would stop fighting the enemy and turn their fire on their black friends. Union officers who refused to go along with the "soft-on-slavery" policy were court-martialed and cashiered out of the service. When, in August, 1861, General John C. Fremont emancipated Missouri slaves, Lincoln angrily counter-manded the proclamation, telling Fremont's wife that "General Fremont should not have dragged the Negro into it . . ." A year later, when General David Hunter freed the slaves in three Southern states, Lincoln again countermanded the order, say-ing that emancipation was a Presidential function.

That this policy was changed at all was due not to Lincoln's humnanitarianism but to rebel battlefield brilliance and the compassion and perseverance of a small band of Radical Repub-licans. Foremost among these men were Charles Sumner, the U.S. senator from Massachusetts; Wendell Phillips, the brilliant agitator from Boston; Frederick Douglass, the bearded black abolitionist; and Thaddeus Stevens, the Pennsylvania congress-man who virtually supplanted Abraham Lincoln as the leader of the Republican party. As the war continued and as Northern casualties mounted, the Radical Republicans put events to use and mobilized a public pressure Lincoln could not ignore. Del-egation after delegation waited on the President and demanded that he hit the South where it would hurt most by freeing the slaves and arming them. Lincoln parried the pressure with heat and conviction, citing constitutional, political and military rea-sons to justify his anti-emancipation stand. Lincoln usually ex-pressed his opposition to emancipation in a troubled but polite tone. But he could be pushed across the border of politeness. When Edward L. Pierce urged the President to adopt a more enlightened policy, Lincoln, according to Pierce, exploded and denounced "the itching to get niggers into our lives."

The traditional image of Lincoln is of a harried and large-hearted man fending off "extremists of the left and right" only to emerge at the precise psychological moment to do what he had always wanted to do. This image clashes, unfortunately, with evidence which suggest that sudden and general emancipation was never Lincoln's policy.

Lincoln was given to saying that his constitutional duties prevented him from doing anything substantial to give point to his "oft-expressed *personal* wish that all men everywhere could be free." But it is obvious from the evidence that Lincoln's problems were deeper than that. For when his duty was clear, he refused to act. On several occasions he refused to take anti-slavery action which was mandated by Congress and he sabotaged some anti-slavery legislation by executive inaction. Somehow, duty, in Lincoln's view, almost always worked against the black man.

Lincoln defenders say that he resisted emancipation pressures because of his fear that premature action would alienate white supporters in Northern and Border States and endanger the prosecution of war. But this view does not come to grips with the fact that Lincoln was *personally* opposed to sudden and general emancipation before 1861 and the further fact that he continued to oppose sudden and general emancipation after the circulating Proclamation proved that his fears were groundless. Nor does the traditional Lincoln apologia touch the mass of evidence—in Lincoln letters as well as in private and public statements—which shows that Lincoln was personally opposed to sudden emancipation on social and racial grounds.

It was not the fear of emancipation but the fear of what would happen afterwards that palsied Lincoln's hand. He was deeply disturbed by the implications of turning loose four million black people in a land he considered the peculiar preserve of the white man. He spoke often of "the evils of sudden derangement" and warned Congress against "the vagrant destitution which must largely attend immediate emancipation in localities where their numbers are very great." He said and over again that it was his considered judgment that "gradual, and not sudden, emancipation is better for all." Count Adams Gurowski believed Lincoln was concerned about poor white fear of black competition. "Be sure," he wrote in a May 7, 1862, letter, "that Lincoln is at heart with Slavery. He considers that *emancipation is a job which will smother the free States. Such are his precise words.*"

Lincoln also feared racial conflict. Like many white liberals, he was consumed by fears of black violence. More than one visitor to the White House found him in agony over the possibility of a Nat Turner-like uprising behind the enemy's lines.

An additional factor in Lincoln's opposition to the principle of sudden emancipation was his racial bias. He considered black people unassimilable aliens. There was not, in his view, enough room in America for black and white people. He didn't believe white people would sanction equal rights for black people and he didn't ask white people to sanction equal rights for black people. Since he did not propose to confront racism, he told black people they would have to travel or accept a subordinate position in American life.

Insofar as it can be said that Lincoln had an emancipation policy, it was to rid America of slaves and Negroes. When he failed in his attempt to end the war without touching slavery, he fell back to a second plan of gradual and compensated emancipation extending over a 37-year-period. This was linked in his thinking with a companion policy of colonizing black people in South America or Africa.

As the pressure for emancipation rose, Lincoln argued passionately and eloquently for his plan of gradual emancipation and abrupt emigration. On August 14, 1862, he called a hand-picked group of black men to the White House and proposed a black exodus. In "a curious mixture of condescension and kindness," to use James M. McPherson's phrase, Lincoln told the black men that it was their duty to leave America. "You and we," he said, "are different races. We have between us a broader difference than exists between almost any other two races. Whether it is right or wrong I need not discuss, but this physical difference is a great disadvantage to us both, as I think your race suffer very greatly, many of them by living among us while ours suffer from your presence."

Lincoln did not seek the opinions of his visitors. He did not propose, he said, to discuss racism, to debate whether it was found on reality or justice. He was simply, he said, presenting a fact: white people didn't want black people in America and therefore black people would have to go. "There is," he said, "an unwillingness on the part of our people, harsh as it may be, for you free colored people to remain with us." The only solution, Lincoln said, was a black exodus. "It is better for us both," he said, ". . . to be separated." He proposed a black settlement on Central American land, "rich in coal;" and he asked his vistors to help him find black settlers "capable of thinking as white men."

Although Lincoln's plan received a generally hostile reception in the black community, he pursued it with passion and conviction. For several months after the signing of the Emancipation Proclamation, he was deeply involved in a disastrously abortive attempt to settle black people on an island off the coast of Haiti. When that venture failed, he shifted to the Southwest, conferring with contractors on the feasibility of settling black people in the state of Texas.

While Lincoln was trying to send black people away, Congress was busy emancipating. In the spring and summer of 1862, Congress forbade military officers to return fugitive slaves, authorized the President to accept black soldiers, and emancipated the slaves in Washington, D.C. Finally, on July 17, 1862, Congress passed the Second Confiscation Act, which freed the slaves of all rebels. This act, which has received insufficient attention in general media, was actually more sweeping than the preliminary Emancipation Proclamation, which came two months later.

Lincoln followed Congress' lead slowly and grudgingly, signing most of these acts with evident displeasure. But the drift of events was unmistakable, and Lincoln changed steps, saying with great honesty that he had not controlled events but had been controlled by them. Conferring with the member of a congressional committee charged with drafting a plan for buying the slaves and sending them away, Lincoln urged speed, saying: "You had better come to an agreement. Niggers will never be cheaper."

Orthography apart, Lincoln caught here the spirit of the times. At that moment, in late July of 1862, the Union war effort was bogged down in the marshes of Virginia, and England and France were on the verge of intervening on the side of the Confederacy. At home, the heat was rising fast, fueled by mounting

Northern casualties. Faced with mushrooming pressures at home and abroad, Lincoln reversed his course and "conditionally determined," to use his words, to touch the institution of slavery.

Lincoln adopted the new policy from necessity, not conviction. In public and in private, he made it clear that he was not motivated by compassion for the slaves. Taking his stand on the ground of military necessity, he said his new policy was designed to weaken Southern white men and to strengthen the hand of Northern white men. "Things," he said later, "had gone from bad to worse, till I felt we had reached the end of the rope on the plan of operation we had been pursuing, and that we had about played our last card." Lincoln said he was driven to the "alternative of either surrendering the Union, and with it, the Constitution, or of laying a strong hand upon the colored element."

There was truth in this, but it was not the whole truth. There is evidence that Lincoln was forced to adopt the new policy by political pressures. Edward Stanly, military governor of North Carolina, said Lincoln told him that "the proclamation had become a civil necessity to prevent the Radicals from openly embarrassing the government in the conduct of the war. The President expressed the belief that, without the proclamation for which they had been clamoring, the Radicals would take the extreme step in Congress of withholding supplies for carrying on the war—leaving the whole land in anarchy." Count Gurowski gave a similar version of Lincoln's metamorphosis and concluded, in a fine phrase, that Lincoln was literally "whipped" into glory.

Responding to a parallelogram of pressures, Lincoln issued a preliminary Emancipation Proclamation on September 22, 1862. In this document, he warned the South that he would issue a final Emancipation Proclamation in 100 days if the rebellion had not ended by that time. The proclamation outlined a future policy of emancipation, but Lincoln had no joy in the black harvest. To a group of serenaders who congratulated him on the new policy, Lincoln said: "I can only trust in God I have made no mistake." To his old friend, Joshua F. Speed, Lincoln expressed misgivings and said he had "been anxious to avoid it." To Congressman John Covode of Pennsylvania, Lincoln explained that he had been "*driven to it*," adding: "But although my duty is plain, it is in some respects painful. . . ." Still another visitor, Edward Stanly, received a dramatic account of Lincoln's resistance to policy of emancipation. "Mr. Lincoln said," according to Stanly, "that he had prayed to the Almighty to save him from this necessity, adopting the very language of our Saviour. 'If it be possible, let this cup pass from me,' but the prayer had not been answered."

On Thursday, January 1, 1863, Lincoln drank from the cup, and apparently he liked neither the flavor nor the color of the draught. When he started to sign the document, his arm trembled so violently, an eyewitness said, that he could not hold the pen. Lincoln, who was very superstitious, paused, startled. Then, attributing his shakes to hours of hand-shaking at a New Year's Day reception, he scrawled his name, saying he did not want the signature to be "tremulous" because people would say "he had some compunctions."

He had "compunctions."

Nothing indicates this better than the Emancipation Proclamation which is, as J. C. Randall and Richard N. Current indicated, "more often admired than read." Cold, forbidding, with all the moral grandeur of a real estate deed, the Proclamation does not enumerate a single principle hostile to slavery and it contains not one quotable sentence. As a document, it lends weight to the observation of Lincoln's law partner, William Herndon, who wrote: "When he freed the slaves, there was no heart in the act."

There wasn't much else in it, either. Rightly speaking, the Emancipation Proclamation, as Ralph Korngold wrote, was "not an Emancipation Proclamation at all." The document was drafted in such a way that it freed few, if any, slaves. It did not apply to slaves in the Border States and areas under federal control in the South. In other words, Lincoln "freed" slaves where he had no power and left them in chains where he had power. The theory behind the Proclamation, an English paper noted, "is not that a human being cannot justly own another, but that he cannot own him unless he is loyal to the United States."

The Proclamation argues so powerfully against itself that

some scholars have suggested that Lincoln was trying to do the
opposite of what he said he was doing. In other words, the suggestion is that the Emancipation Proclamation was a political
stratagem by which Lincoln hoped to outflank the Radicals, buy
time and forestall a definitive act of emancipation. This is not
the place to review the political stratagem theory in detail. Suffice it to say that on the basis of the evidence one can make a
powerful case for the view that Lincoln never intended to free
the slaves, certainly not immediately.

Lincoln's post-Proclamation behavior lends substance to this
view. For contrary to all logic, he continued to agitate against
his own policy. On the eve of the Proclamation, he again recommended to Congress his favorite plan of gradual and compensated emancipation. And he continued, according to several
witnesses, to doubt the wisdom of the Emancipation Proclamation. Three weeks after signing the document, he reportedly
told Wendell Phillips that the Proclamation was "a great mistake." Two months later, he told Congressman George W.
Julian that the Proclamation had "done about as much harm as
good." In the following months, Lincoln repeatedly said that he
still favored a gradual emancipation plan which contradicted
the spirit of his own Proclamation.

To this bleak picture one should add in all justice that Lincoln can be quoted on both sides of the issue. He reportedly said
later that the Proclamation and the arming of black soldiers
constituted the heaviest blows against the rebellion. It should
also be said that Lincoln, after a period of vacillation and doubt,
helped to win passage of the Thirteenth Amendment, which
made the paper freedom of the Proclamation real. Having said
that, it remains to be said that Lincoln never fully accepted the
fundamental principle of the Proclamation and the Thirteenth
Amendment. As late as February, 1865, he was still equivocating
on the issue of immediate emancipation. At an abortive peace
conference with Confederate leaders at Hampton Roads, Virginia, Lincoln said, according to Alexander Stephens, that he
had never been in favor of immediate emancipation, even by the
states. He spoke of the "many evils attending" immediate emancipation and suggested, as he had suggested on other occasions,

a system of apprenticeship "by which the two races could gradually live themselves out of their old relations to each other."

At Gettysburg, Lincoln shifted gears and announced a new policy of liberation and social renewal. America, he said, was engaged in a great war testing whether it or any other nation "conceived in liberty and dedicated to the proposition that all men are created equal" could long endure. The war, he said, would decide whether "government of the people, by the people, for the people" would perish from the earth. But 20 days later when he unveiled his own postwar policy, it was obvious that *all* meant the same thing to Lincoln that it had always meant: all white people. In his Proclamation of Amnesty and Reconstruction, Lincoln said he would recognize any rebel state in which one-tenth of the white voters of 1860 took an oath of allegiance to the United States and organized a government which renounced slavery. What of black people? Slavery apart, Lincoln ignored them. Incredibly, the commander-in-chief of the U.S. Army abandoned his black soldiers to the passions of Confederate veterans who feared and hated them. Lincoln barely suggested "privately" that it would be a good thing for Southern states to extend the ballot "to the very intelligent [Negroes], and especially those who have fought gallantly in our ranks." But these were private sentiments, not public acts; and they were expressed in an extremely hesitant manner at that. Lincoln didn't require fair or equal treatment for the freedmen. In fact, he didn't make any demands at all. Reconstruction, Lincoln style, was going to be a Reconstruction of the white people, by the white people and for the white people.

It seems that Lincoln never reconciled himself to the implications of emancipation. Shortly before his death, Lincoln summoned General Benjamin F. Butler to inquire about the possibilities of "sending the blacks away." According to Butler, he said, "I wish you would examine the question and give me your views upon it and go into figures as you did before in some degree as to show whether the Negroes can be exported." Butler went away and came back two days later with a sad story. "Mr. President," he said, "I have gone very carefully over my calculation as to the power of the country to export the Negroes of the South and I assure you that, using all your naval vessels and all the merchant marine fit to cross the seas with safety, it will be impossible for you to transport to the nearest place fit for them . . . half as fast as Negro children will be born here."

Lincoln's assassination and the aggressive dissemination of the "Massa Linkun myth" pushed the real Lincoln with his real limitations into the background. And black people were soon pooling their pennies to erect a monument to the mythical emancipator. When, on April 14, 1876, this monument was unveiled, with President U.S. Grant and other high officials in attendance, Frederick Douglass punctured the myths and looked frankly at the man. Douglass praised Lincoln's growth, but he also rehearsed his limitations.

Truth [Douglass said] *is proper and beautiful at all times and in all places, and it is never more proper and beautiful in any case than when speaking of a great public man whose example is likely to be commended for honor and imitation long after his departure to the solemn shades, the silent continent of eternity. It must be admitted, truth compels me to admit, even here in the presence of the monument we have erected to his memory, Abraham Lincoln was not, in the fullest sense of the word, either our man or our model. In his interests, in his associations, in his habits of thought, and in his prejudices, he was a white man. He was preeminently the white man's President, entirely devoted to the welfare of white men . . . In all his education and feeling he was an American of the Americans.*

Speaking thus of interests and passion and public acts, Frederick Douglass, who knew Lincoln well, sounded the discordant notes of a national, not a personal tragedy. For, in the final analysis, Lincoln must be seen as the embodiment, not the transcendence, of the American tradition, which is, as we all know, a racist tradition. In his inability to rise above that tradition, Lincoln, often called "the noblest of all Americans," holds up a flawed mirror to the American soul. And one honors him today, not by gazing fixedly at a flawed image, not by hiding warts and excrescences, but by seeing oneself in the reflected ambivalences of a life which calls us to transcendence, not imitation.

February 1968

Shelby Foote

Born in Greenville, Mississippi, Foote (1916–2005) published his first novel in 1949; his fourth, *Shiloh* (1952), told the story of the Civil War's first great bloodletting from the perspective of seven Union and Confederate participants. Impressed by its attention to historical detail, Bennett Cerf of Random House suggested that he write a single-volume history of the Civil War, and Foote, who was struggling to make progress on a sprawling fictional saga set in the Mississippi Delta, agreed. The result was *The Civil War: A Narrative*, published in three volumes between 1958 and 1974 and acclaimed by many of its admirers as the American *Iliad*. After its completion Foote returned to writing fiction, then became an overnight celebrity as a commentator in the 1990 Ken Burns television series *The Civil War*. The excerpt from the third volume of Foote's narrative, *Red River to Appomattox*, printed below begins with Robert Anderson, the commander of Fort Sumter in 1861, toasting the President in Charleston four years later, and then shifts to the capital to follow Lincoln through his last day and night on earth.

FROM
The Civil War: A Narrative

R obert Anderson, having performed what he called "perhaps the last act of my life, of duty to my country," had a somewhat let-down feeling as the ceremony ended and he and the rest got aboard boats to return to Charleston. At the outset he had urged Stanton to keep the program brief and quiet, but it had turned out to be neither. What was more, he faced still another speaking ordeal that night at a formal dinner Gillmore was giving for him and other guests of honor, including the old-line abolitionist Garrison, who had been hanged and burned in effigy on a nearby street corner, thirty-odd years before, in reaction to the Nat Turner uprising in Virginia. Garrison spoke, as did Beecher again—impromptu this time, and to better effect—and John Nicolay, who had been sent from Washington to

deliver the Chief Executive's regrets that he himself was unable
to attend. Others held forth at considerable length, interrupted
from time to time by the crump and crackle of a fireworks display being staged in the harbor by Dahlgren's fleet, with Battery
wharves and rooftops nearly as crowded as they had been for a
grimmer show of pyrotechnics, four years ago this week. In the
banquet hall of the Charleston Hotel the evening wore on as
speaker after speaker, not sharing Anderson's aversion to exposure, had his say. At last, the various orators having subsided, the
Kentuckian's turn came round.

He rose, glass in hand, and haltingly, with no mention of
Union victory or Confederate defeat, of which so much had
already been said by the others, proposed a toast to "the man
who, when elected President of the United States, was compelled to reach the seat of government without an escort, but a
man who now could travel all over our country with millions of
hands and hearts to sustain him. I give you the good, the great,
the honest man, Abraham Lincoln."

The man to whom the celebrants raised their glasses down in
Charleston this Good Friday evening was seated in a box at Ford's
Theater, attentive to the forced chatter of a third-rate farce which
by then was into its second act. Apparently he was enjoying himself, as he generally did at the theater, even though he had come
with some reluctance, if not distaste, and more from a sense of
obligation than by choice. "It has been advertised that we will be
there," he had said that afternoon, "and I cannot disappoint the
people. Otherwise I would not go. I do not want to go."

In part this was because of a last-minute withdrawal by Grant,
who earlier had accepted an invitation for him and his wife to
come along, and whose presence, as the hero of Appomattox,
would have lent the presidential box a glitter that outdid anything under limelight on the stage. Besides, Lincoln had looked
forward to the general's company as a diversion from the strain
of the daily grind, which the advent of peace had not made any
less daily or less grinding. Today, for example, he was in his
office by 7 o'clock as usual, attending to administrative matters
in advance of the flood of supplicants who would descend on

him later. After issuing a call for a cabinet meeting at 11, he went back upstairs for breakfast with Mrs Lincoln and their two sons. Robert, just up from Virginia, brought with him a photograph of R. E. Lee which he presented to his father at the table, apparently as a joke. Lincoln did not take it so. He polished his glasses on a napkin, studied the portrait, then said quietly: "It's a good face. I am glad the war is over."

This last was repeated in varied phrasings through the day. Returning to his office he conferred first with Speaker Colfax, who was slated for a cabinet post—probably Stanton's, who more than anything wanted a seat on the Supreme Court as soon as one became vacant—and then with Senator John Creswell, who had done much to keep Maryland in the Union during the secession furor. "Creswell, old fellow," Lincoln hailed him, "everything is bright this morning. The war is over. It has been a tough time, but we have lived it out. Or some of us have." His face darkened, then lightened again. "But it is over. We are going to have good times now, and a united country." He approved a number of appointments, granted a military discharge, sent a messenger over to Ford's on 10th Street to reserve the State Box for the evening performance—not forgetting to inform the management that Grant would be a member of his party, which would help to increase the normally scant Good Friday audience—and wrote on a card for two Virginians requesting passes south: "No pass is necessary now to authorize anyone to go and return from Petersburg and Richmond. People go and return just as they did before the war." Presently, as the hour approached for the cabinet meeting he had called, he walked over to the War Department, hoping for news from Sherman of Johnston's surrender. There was nothing, but he was not discouraged. He said later at the meeting that he was convinced some such news was on the way, and soon would be clicking off the wire, because of a dream he had had the night before.

Grant was there by special invitation, having arrived from City Point just yesterday. Welcomed and applauded as he entered the cabinet room, he told of his pursuit of Lee and the closing scene at Appomattox, but added that no word had come from Carolina, where a similar campaign was being mounted against Joe Johnston, hopefully with similar results. The President said he was sure they would hear from Sherman soon, for he had had this dream the night before. What sort of dream? Welles asked. "It relates to your element, the water," Lincoln replied, and told how he had been aboard "some singular, indescribable vessel" which seemed to be "floating, floating away on some vast and indistinct expanse, toward an unknown shore." The dream was not so strange in itself, he declared, as in the fact that it was recurrent; that "each of its previous occurrences has been followed by some important event or disaster." He had had it before Sumter and Bull Run, he said, as well as before such victories as Antietam, Stones River, Gettysburg, Vicksburg, and Wilmington. Grant—who seldom passed up a chance to take a swipe at Rosecrans—remarked that Stones River was no victory; he knew of no great results it brought. In any case, Lincoln told him, he had had this dream on the eve of that battle, and it had come to him again last night. He took it as a sign that they would "have great news very soon," and "I think it must be from Sherman. My thoughts are in that direction."

After a brief discussion of dreams and their nature, the talk returned to Appomattox. Grant's terms there had assured that no member of the surrendered army, from Lee on down, would ever be prosecuted by the government for treason or any other crime, so long as he observed the conditions of his parole and the laws in force where he resided. Lincoln's ready approval of this assurance gave Postmaster General William Dennison the impression that he would like to have it extended to the civilian leaders—a number of whom by now were fugitives, in flight for their lives amid the ruins of the rebellion—if only some way could be found to avoid having them hauled into court. "I suppose, Mr President," he half-inquired, half-suggested, "that you would not be sorry to have them escape out of the country?" Lincoln thought it over. "Well, I should not be sorry to have them out of the country," he replied, "but I should be for following them up pretty close to make sure of their going." Having said as much he said still more to others around the table. "I think it is providential that this great rebellion is crushed just as Congress has adjourned and there are none of the disturbing elements of that body to hinder and embarrass us. If we are wise and discreet we shall reanimate the states and get their governments in successful operation, with order prevailing and the Union reëstablished before Congress comes together in December." Returning to the question of what should be done with the rebel leaders, he became more animated both in speech and gesture. "I hope there will be no persecution, no bloody work after the war is over. No one need expect me to take any part in hanging or killing these men, even the worst of them. Frighten them out of the country; open the gates; let down the bars." He put both hands out, fluttering the fingers as if to frighten sheep out of a lot. "Shoo; scare them off," he said; "enough lives have been sacrificed."

It was for this, the consideration of reconstruction matters and incidentals preliminary to them, that the cabinet had been assembled in the first place, midway between its regular Tuesday gatherings. In the absence of Seward—still on his bed of pain, he was represented at the meeting by his son Frederick—Stanton had come armed with a plan, drawn up at the President's request, for bringing the states that had been "abroad" back into what Lincoln, in his speech three nights ago, had called "their proper practical relation with the Union." The War Secretary's notion was that military occupation should precede readmission, and in this connection he proposed that Virginia and North Carolina be combined in a single district to simplify the army's task. Welles took exception, on grounds that this last would destroy the individuality of both states and thus be "in conflict with the principles of self-government which I deem essential." So did Lincoln. After some earnest discussion, back and forth across the green-topped table, he suggested that Stanton revise his plan in this regard and provide copies for the other cabinet members to study between now and their next meeting, four days off. Congress would no doubt have its say when it returned in December, but as for himself he had already reached certain bedrock conclusions. "We can't undertake to run state governments in all these southern states. Their own people must do that—though I reckon that at first some of them may do it badly."

By now it was close to 2 o'clock, and the meeting, nearly
three hours long, adjourned. Grant however remained behind
to talk with Lincoln: not about army matters, it turned out, but
to beg off going to the theater that night. His wife, he said, was
anxious to catch the late-afternoon train for Philadelphia, en
route to a visit with their young sons in Burlington, New Jersey.
Lincoln started to press him, but then refrained, perhaps realizing from the general's embarrassed manner that the real reason was Julia Grant, who was determined not to expose herself
to another of Mary Lincoln's tirades, this time in full view of the
audience at Ford's. Disappointed, Lincoln accepted the excuse
—reinforced just then by a note from Mrs Grant, reminding her
husband not to be late for their 6 o'clock departure—and went
upstairs for lunch, faced with the unpleasant job of informing
his wife that the social catch of the season would not be going
with them to the theater that evening. If he also told her, as he
would tell others between now and curtain time, that he too no
longer wanted to go, it made no difference; Grant or no Grant,
she was set on attending what the papers were calling the "last
appearance of Miss Laura Keene in her celebrated comedy of
Our American Cousin."

He was back in his office by 3 o'clock, in time for an appointment with the Vice President, the first since the scandalous scene
at his swearing in. They talked for twenty minutes or so, and
though neither left any record of what was said, witnesses noted
that Lincoln called him "Andy," shaking him vigorously by the
hand, and that Johnson seemed greatly relieved to find himself
greeted cordially after nearly six weeks of pointed neglect. This
done, Lincoln attended to some paper work, including an appeal on behalf of a soldier convicted for desertion. So far in the
war he had approved 267 death sentences for military offenses,
but not this one. "Well, I think the boy can do us more good
above ground than under ground," he drawled as he fixed his
signature to a pardon. Before setting out on a 4.30 carriage ride
with his wife—"Just ourselves," he had said at lunch when she
asked if he wanted anyone else along—he walked over to the
War Department, in hope that some word had come at last from
Sherman. Again there was nothing, which served to weaken his

conviction that the news of "some important event or disaster" would shake the capital before the day was over. Time was running out, and he was disappointed. It was then, on the way back from the telegraph office, that he told his bodyguard Crook that he did not want to go to the theater that night, and would not go, except for notices in the papers that he would be there. Crook was about to go off shift, and when they reached the White House door Lincoln paused for a moment and turned to face him. He seemed gloomy, depressed. "Goodbye, Crook," he said, to the guard's surprise. Always before, it had been "Good night, Crook," when they parted. Now suddenly it was goodbye; "Goodbye, Crook."

Still, by the time the carriage rolled out of the driveway a few minutes later, on through streets that glittered with bright gold April sunshine, he had recovered his spirits to such an extent that he informed his wife: "I never felt better in my life." What was more—even though, just one month ago today, he had been confined to his bed with what his doctor described as "exhaustion, complete exhaustion"—he looked as happy as he said he felt. The recent City Point excursion, his first extended vacation of the war, had done him so much good that various cabinet members, after observing him at the midday meeting—in contrast to the one a month ago, when they gathered about his sickbed—remarked on the "expression of visible relief and content upon his face." One said that he "never appeared to better advantage," while another declared that "the weary look which his face had so long worn . . . had disappeared. It was cheerful and happy." They were glad to see him so. But Mary Lincoln, whose moods were quite as variable as his own, had a different reaction when he told her he had never felt better in his life. "Don't you remember feeling just so before our little boy died?" she asked. He patted her hand to comfort her, and spoke of a trip to Europe as soon as his term was up. After that they would return to Springfield, where he would resume the practice of law and perhaps buy a farm along the Sangamon. "We must both be more cheerful in the future," he told her. "Between the war and the loss of our darling Willie, we have both been very miserable."

The good mood held. Seeing two old friends just leaving as
the open barouche turned into the White House driveway an
hour later, he stood up and called for them to wait. They were
Richard Oglesby, the new governor of Illinois, and his adjutant
general Isham Haynie, a combat brigadier who had left the
army to work for him and Lincoln in the recent campaign. Lincoln led the way inside, where he read to them from the latest
collection of "Letters" by Petroleum V. Nasby, a humorist he
admired so much that he once said he would gladly swap his
present office for the genius to compose such things. "Linkin
rides into Richmond!" he read from the final letter. "A Illinois
rale-splitter, a buffoon, a ape, a goriller, a smutty joker, sets hisself down in President Davis's cheer and rites dispatchis! . . .
This ends the chapter. The Confederasy hez at last consentratid
its last consentrate. It's ded. It's gathered up its feet, sed its last
words, and deceest. . . . Farewell, vane world." The reading
went on so long—four letters, with time out for laughter and
thigh-slapping all around—that supper was delayed, as well as
his departure for the theater. Even so, with the carriage waiting,
he took time to see Colfax, who called again to ask if a special
session of Congress was likely to interrupt a Rocky Mountain
tour he was planning. The President said there would be no
special session, and they went on talking until Mrs Lincoln appeared in the office doorway. She wore a low-necked evening
dress and was pulling on her gloves, by way of warning her husband that 8 o'clock had struck.

He excused himself and they started out, only to be interrupted by two more men, a Massachusetts congressman and a
former congressman from Illinois, both of whom had political
favors to collect. One wanted a hearing for a client who had a
sizeable cotton claim against the government; Lincoln gave him
a card that put him first on tomorrow's list of callers. What the
other wanted no one knew, for he whispered it into the presidential ear. Lincoln had entered and then backed out of the
closed carriage, cocking his head to hear the request. "Excuse
me now," he said as he climbed in again beside his wife. "I am
going to the theater. Come and see me in the morning."

Stopping en route at the home of New York Senator Ira

Harris to pick up their substitute guests, the senator's daughter
Clara and her fiancé, Major Henry Rathbone, the carriage rolled
and clopped through intersections whose streetlamps glim-
mered dimly through the mist. It was close to 8.30, twenty minutes past curtain time, when the coachman drew rein in front of
Ford's, on 10th Street between E and F, and the two couples
alighted to enter the theater. Inside, about midway of Act I, the
performance stopped as the President and his party came down
the side aisle, and the orchestra struck up "Hail to the Chief" as
they entered the flag-draped box to the right front. A near-
capacity crowd of about 1700 applauded politely, masking its
disappointment at Grant's absence. Clara Harris and Rathbone
took seats near the railing; the First Lady sat a little behind
them, to their left, and Lincoln slumped into a roomy, uphol-
stered rocker toward the rear. This last represented concern for
his comfort and was also the management's way of expressing
thanks for his having been here at least four times before, once
to see Maggie Mitchell in *Fanchon the Cricket*, once to see John
Wilkes Booth in *The Marble Heart*—"Rather tame than otherwise," John Hay had complained—and twice to see James Hackett play Falstaff in *Henry IV* and *The Merry Wives of Windsor*.
Tonight's play resumed, and Lincoln, as was his habit, at once
grew absorbed in the action down below: though not so absorbed that he failed to notice that the major was holding his
fiancée's hand, for he reached out and took hold of his wife's.
Pleased by the attention he had shown her on their carriage ride
that afternoon, and now by this further expression of affection,
Mary Lincoln reverted to her old role of Kentucky belle. "What
will Miss Harris think of my hanging onto you so?" she whispered, leaning toward him. Lincoln's eyes, fixed on the stage,
reflected the glow of the footlights. "Why, she will think nothing
about it," he said, and he kept his grip on her hand.

Act I ended; Act II began. Down in Charleston the banquet-
ers raised their glasses in response to Anderson's toast, and here
at Ford's, in an equally festive mood, the audience enjoyed *Our
American Cousin* with only occasional sidelong glances at the
State Box to see whether Grant had arrived. He might have
done so without their knowledge, for though they could see the

young couple at the railing and Mrs Lincoln half in shadow
behind them, the President was screened from view by the box
curtains and draped flags. Act II ended; Act III began. Lincoln,
having at last released his wife's hand and settled back in the
horsehair rocker, seemed to be enjoying what was happening
down below. In the second scene, which opened shortly after
10 o'clock, a three-way running dialogue revealed to Mrs
Mountchessington that Asa Trenchard, for whom she had set
her daughter's cap, was no millionaire after all.

—No heir to the fortune, Mr Trenchard?

—Oh, no.

—What! No fortune!

—Nary a red. . . .

Consternation. Indignation.

—Augusta, to your room.

—Yes, ma. The nasty beast!

—I am aware, Mr Trenchard, that you are not used to the
manners of good society, and that alone will excuse the imperti-
nence of which you have been guilty.

Exit Mrs Mountchessington, trailing daughter. Trenchard
alone.

—Don't know the manners of good society, eh? Wal, I guess
I know enough to turn you inside out, you sockdologizing old
mantrap!

Then it came, a half-muffled explosion, somewhere between
a boom and a thump, loud but by no means so loud as it sounded
in the theater, then a boil and bulge of bluish smoke in the presidential box, an exhalation as of brimstone from the curtained
mouth, and a man coming out through the bank and swirl of it,
white-faced and dark-haired in a black sack suit and riding
boots, eyes aglitter, brandishing a knife. He mounted the ledge,
presented his back to the rows of people seated below, and let
himself down by the handrail for the ten-foot drop to the stage.
Falling he turned, and as he did so caught the spur of his right
boot in the folds of a flag draped over the lower front of the high
box. It ripped but offered enough resistance to bring all the
weight of his fall on his left leg, which buckled and pitched him
forward onto his hands. He rose, thrust the knife overhead in a

broad theatrical gesture, and addressed the outward darkness of the pit. "Sic semper tyrannis," he said in a voice so low and projected with so little clarity that few recognized the state motto of Virginia or could later agree that he had spoken in Latin. "Revenge for the South!" or "The South is avenged!" some thought they heard him cry, while others said that he simply muttered "Freedom." In any case he then turned again, hobbled left across the stage past the lone actor standing astonished in its center, and vanished into the wings.

Barely half a minute had passed since the jolt of the explosion, and now a piercing scream came through the writhing tendrils of smoke—a full-voiced wail from Mary Lincoln. "Stop that man!" Rathbone shouted, nursing an arm slashed by the intruder, and Clara Harris, wringing her hands, called down from the railing in a tone made falsely calm by shock: "Water. Water." The audience began to emerge from its trance. "What is it? What happened?" "For God's sake, what is it?" "What has happened?" The answer came in a bellow of rage from the curtained orifice above the spur-torn flag: "He has shot the President!" Below, men leaped from their seats in a first reaction of disbelief and denial, not only of this but also of what they had seen with their own eyes. "No. For God's sake, no! It can't be true." But then, by way of reinforcement for the claim, the cry went up: "Surgeon! A surgeon! Is there a surgeon in the house?"

The young doctor who came forward—and at last gained admission to the box, after Rathbone removed a wooden bar the intruder had used to keep the hallway door from being opened while he went about his work—thought at first that he had been summoned to attend a dead man. Lincoln sat sprawled in the rocker as if asleep, knees relaxed, eyes closed, head dropped forward so that his chin was on his chest. He seemed to have no vital signs until a closer examination detected a weak pulse and shallow breathing. Assuming that he had been knifed, as Rathbone had been, the doctor had him taken from the chair and laid on the floor in a search for a stab wound. However, when he put his hands behind the patient's head to lift it, he found the back hair wet with blood from a half-inch hole where a bullet had entered, three inches to the right of the left ear. "The course of the ball was obliquely forward," a subsequent report would state, "toward the right eye, crossing the brain in an oblique manner and lodging a few inches behind that eye. In the track of the wound were found fragments of bone driven forward by the ball, which was embedded in the anterior lobe of the left hemisphere of the brain." The doctor—Charles A. Leale, assistant surgeon, U.S. Volunteers, twenty-three years old and highly familiar with gunshot wounds—did not know all this; yet he knew enough from what he had seen and felt, here in the crowded box for the past five minutes, as well as in casualty wards for the past year, to arrive at a prognosis. Everything was over for Abraham Lincoln but the end. "His wound is mortal," Leale pronounced. "It is impossible for him to recover."

Two other surgeons were in the box by then, both senior to Leale in rank and years, but he remained in charge and made the decision not to risk a removal to the White House, six cobblestone blocks away. "If it is attempted the President will die before we reach there," he replied to the suggestion. Instead, with the help of four soldier volunteers, the three doctors took up their patient and carried him feet first down the stairs and aisle, out onto 10th Street—packed nearly solid with the curious and grieving, so that an infantry captain had to draw his sword to clear a path for the seven bearers and their awkward burden, bawling excitedly: "Out of the way, you sons of bitches!" —up the front steps, down a narrow hall, and into a small back ground-floor bedroom in one of a row of modest houses across the way. Let by the night by its owner, a Swedish tailor, the room was mean and dingy, barely fifteen by nine feet in length and width, with a threadbare rug, once Turkey red, and oatmeal-colored paper on the walls. The bed itself was too short for the long form placed diagonally on the cornshuck mattress; Lincoln's booted feet protruded well beyond the footboard, his head propped on extra pillows so that his bearded chin was on his chest, as it had been when Leale first saw him in the horsehair rocker, back at Ford's. By then the time was close to 11 o'clock, some forty-five minutes after the leaden ball first broke into his skull, and now began a painful, drawn-out vigil, a death watch that would continue for another eight hours and beyond.

Three more doctors soon arrived, Surgeon General Joseph Barnes, his chief assistant, and the family physician, who did what he could for Mary Lincoln in her distress. Barnes took charge, but Leale continued his ministrations, including the removal of the patient's clothing in a closer search for another wound and the application of mustard plasters in an attempt to improve his respiration and heartbeat. One did as little good as the other; for there was no additional wound and Lincoln's condition remained about the same, with stertorous breathing, pulse a feeble 44, hands and feet corpse-cold to the wrists and ankles, and both eyes insensitive to light, the left pupil much contracted, the right dilated widely. Gideon Welles came in at this point and wrote next day in his diary of "the giant sufferer" as he saw him from his post beside the bed. "He had been stripped of his clothes. His large arms, which were occasionally exposed, were of a size which one would scarce have expected from his spare appearance. His slow, full respiration lifted the bedclothes with each breath that he took. His features were calm and striking. I had never seen them appear to better advantage than for the first hour, perhaps, that I was there." Presently, though, their calm appearance changed. The left side of the face began to twitch, distorting the mouth into a jeer. When this desisted, the upper right side of the face began to darken, streaked with purple as from a blow, and the eye with the ball of lead behind it began to bulge from its socket. Mary Lincoln screamed at the sight and had to be led from the room, while a journalist noted that Charles Sumner, "seated on the right of the President's couch, near the head, holding the right hand of the President in his own," was about equally unstrung. "He was sobbing like a woman, with his head bowed down almost on the pillow of the bed on which the President was lying."

By midnight, close to fifty callers were in the house, all of sufficient prominence to gain entrance past the guards and most of them wedged shoulder to shoulder in the death chamber, at one time or another, for a look at the final agony of the man laid diagonally on the bed in one corner. Andrew Johnson was there—briefly, however, because his presence was painful to Mrs Lincoln, who whimpered at the sight of her husband's imminent successor—as were a number of Sumner's colleagues from the House and Senate, Robert Lincoln and John Hay, Oglesby and Haynie again, a pair of clergymen—one fervent, the other unctuous—and Laura Keene, who claimed a star's prerogative, first in the box at the theater, where she had held the President's bleeding head in her lap, and now in the narrow brick house across the street, where she helped Clara Harris comfort the distraught widow-to-be in the tailor's front parlor, what time she was not with her in the crowded bedroom toward the rear. All members of the cabinet were on hand but the Secretary of State, and most of the talk that was not of Lincoln was of him. He too had been attacked and grievously wounded, along with four members of his household, by a lone assassin who struck at about the same time as the one at Ford's: unless, indeed, it was the same man in rapid motion from one place to the other, less than half a mile away. Seward had been slashed about the face and throat, and he was thought to be dying, too, except that the iron frame that bound his jaw had served to protect him to some extent from the knife. "I'm mad, I'm mad," the attacker had said as he ran out into the night to vanish as cleanly as the other—or he—had done when he—or the other—leaped from the box, crossed the stage, entered the wings, and exited into the alley behind Ford's, where he—whoever, whichever he was—mounted his waiting horse and rode off in the darkness.

In this, as in other accounts concerning other rumored victims—Grant, for one, and Andrew Johnson for another, until word came that the general was safe in Philadelphia and the Vice President himself showed up unhurt—there was much confusion. Edwin Stanton undertook on his own the task of sifting and setting the contradictions straight, in effect taking over as head of the headless government. "[He] instantly assumed charge of everything near and remote, civil and military," a subordinate observed, "and began issuing orders in that autocratic manner so superbly necessary to the occasion." Among other precautions, he stopped traffic on the Potomac and the railroads, warned the Washington Fire Brigade to be ready for mass arson, summoned Grant back to take charge of the capital defenses, and alerted guards along the Canadian border, as well as in all major eastern ports, to be on the lookout for suspicious persons attempting to leave the country. In short, "he continued throughout the night acting as president, secretary of war, secretary of state, commander in chief, comforter, and dictator," all from a small sitting room adjacent to the front parlor of the tailor's house on 10th Street, which he turned into an interrogation chamber for grilling witnesses to find out just what had happened in the theater across the street.

From the outset, numbers of people who knew him well, including members of his profession, had identified John Wilkes Booth as Lincoln's attacker, and by now the twenty-six-year-old matinee idol's one-shot pocket derringer had been found on the floor of the box where he had dropped it as he leaped for the railing to escape by way of the stage and the back alley. Identification was certain. Even so, and though a War Department description eventually went out by wire across the land—"height 5 feet 8 inches, weight 160 pounds, compact build; hair jet black, inclined to curl, medium length, parted behind; eyes black, heavy dark eyebrows; wears a large seal ring on little finger; when talking inclines head forward, looks down"—Stanton was intent on larger game. Apparently convinced that the President could not have been shot by anyone so insignificant as an actor acting on his own, he was out to expose a full-scale Confederate plot, a conspiracy hatched in Richmond "and set on foot by rebels under pretense of avenging the rebel cause."

So he believed at any rate, and though he gave most of his attention to exploring this assumption—proceeding with such misdirected and disjointed vigor that he later aroused revisionist suspicions that he must have wanted the assassin to escape: as, for instance, by his neglect in closing all city bridges except the one Booth used to cross into Maryland—he still had time for periodic visits to the small back room, filled with the turmoil of Lincoln's labored breathing, and to attend to such incidental administrative matters as the preparation of a message giving Johnson formal notice that the President had died. His purpose in this, with the hour of death left blank to be filled in later, was to avoid delay when the time came, but when he read the rough draft aloud for a stenographer to take down a fair copy he produced a premature effect he had not foreseen. Hearing a strangled cry behind him, he turned and found Mary Lincoln standing in the parlor doorway, hands clasped before her in entreaty, a stricken expression on her face. "Is he dead? Oh, is he dead?" she moaned. Stanton tried to explain that what she had heard was merely in preparation for a foreseen contingency, but she could not understand him through her sobbing and her grief. So he gave it up and had her led back into the parlor, out of his way; which was just as well, an associate declared, for "he was full of business, and knew, moreover, that in a few hours at most she must be a widow."

It was by then about 1.30; Good Friday was off the calendar at last, and Mary Lincoln was into what everyone in the house, doctors and laymen alike, could see would be the first day of her widowhood. At intervals, supported on either side by Clara Harris and Laura Keene, she would return to the crowded bedroom and sit or stand looking down at her husband until grief overcame her again and the two women would half-guide half-carry her back to the front parlor, where she would remain until enough strength returned for her to repeat the process. She made these trips about once an hour, and each was more grueling than the last, not only because of her own cumulative exhaustion, but also because of the deteriorating condition of the sufferer on the bed, which came as a greater shock to her each time she saw him. Earlier, there had been a certain calm and dignity about him, as if he were in fact aboard "some singular, indescribable vessel . . . floating, floating away on some vast and indistinct expanse, toward an unknown shore." Now this was gone, replaced by the effects of agony. The dream ship had become a rack, and the stertorous uproar of his breathing, interspersed with drawn-out groans, filled the house as it might have filled a torture chamber. "Doctor, save him!" she implored first one and then another of the attending physicians, and once she said in a calmer tone: "Bring Tad. He will speak to Tad, he loves him so." But all agreed that would not do, either for the boy or for his father, who was beyond all knowledgeable contact with anything on earth, even Tad, and indeed had been so ever since

Booth's derringer crashed through the laughter in the theater at 10.15 last night. All the while, his condition worsened, especially his breathing, which not only became increasingly spasmodic, but would stop entirely from time to time, the narrow chest expanded between the big rail-splitter arms, and then resume with a sudden gusty roar through the fluttering lips. On one such occasion, with Mrs Lincoln leaning forward from a chair beside the bed, her cheek on her husband's cheek, her ear near his still, cyanotic mouth, the furious bray of his exhalation —louder than anything she had heard since the explosion in the box, five hours ago—startled and frightened her so badly that she shrieked and fell to the floor in a faint. Stanton, interrupted in his work by the piercing scream, came running down the hall from his improvised Acting President's office up front. When he saw what it was he lost patience entirely. "Take that woman out," he ordered sternly, thrusting both arms over his head in exasperation, "and do not let her in again."

He was obeyed in this as in all his other orders, and she remained in the front parlor until near the very end. Meantime dawn came through, paling the yellow flare of gas jets. A cold rain fell on the people still keeping their vigil on the street outside, while inside, in the dingy room made dingier by daylight, Lincoln entered the final stage of what one doctor called "the saddest and most pathetic deathbed scene I ever witnessed." Interruptions of his breathing were more frequent now, and longer, and whenever this happened some of the men about the bed would take out their watches to note the time of death, then return them to their pockets when the raucous sound resumed. Robert Lincoln—"only a boy for all his shoulder straps," the guard Crook had said—"bore himself well," according to one who watched him, "but on two occasions gave way to overpowering grief and sobbed aloud, turning his head and leaning on the shoulder of Senator Sumner." At 7 o'clock, with the end at hand, he went to bring his mother into the room for a last visit. She tottered in, looked at her husband in confusion, saying nothing, and was led back out again. Stanton was there full-time now, and strangely enough had brought his hat along, standing motionless with his chin on his left hand, his right hand holding the hat and supporting his left elbow, tears running down his face into his beard.

By this time Lincoln's breathing was fast and shallow, cheeks pulled inward behind the closed blue lips. His chest heaved up in a last deep breath, then subsided and did not rise again. It was 7.22; the nine-hour agony was over, and his face took on what John Hay described as "a look of unspeakable peace." Surgeon General Barnes leaned forward, listened carefully for a time to the silent chest, then straightened up, removed two silver half-dollars from his pocket, and placed them carefully on the closed eyes. Observing this ritual, Stanton then performed one of his own. He stretched his right arm out deliberately before him, clapped his hat for a long moment on his head, and then as deliberately removed it, as if in salute. "Now he belongs to the ages," he said, or anyhow later saw to it that he was quoted as having said. "Let us pray," one of the parsons intoned, and sank to his knees on the thin red carpet beside the bed.

Soon thereafter Mary Lincoln was brought back into the room. "Oh, why did you not tell me he was dying?" she exclaimed when she saw her husband lying there with coins on his eyes. Then it came home to her, and her grief was too great to be contained. "Oh my God," she wailed as she was led out, weeping bitterly, "I have given my husband to die!" Presently she was taken from the house, and the other mourner witnesses picked their way through the wet streets to their homes and hotels near and far.

Bells were tolling all over Washington by the time Lincoln's body, wrapped in a flag and placed in a closed hearse, was on its way back to the White House, escorted (as he had not been when he left, twelve hours before) by an honor guard of soldiers and preceded by a group of officers walking bareheaded in the rain. He would lie in state, first in the East Room, then afterwards in the Capitol rotunda, preparatory to the long train ride back to Springfield, where he would at last be laid to rest. "Nothing touches the tired spot," he had said often in the course of the past four years. Now Booth's derringer had reached it.

1974

Robert Lowell

A great-grandnephew of James Russell Lowell, Robert Lowell (1917–1977) found inspiration for much of his verse in history, including that of the Civil War. One of his best-known poems, "For the Union Dead," is a meditation on the Augustus Saint-Gaudens monument to Colonel Robert Gould Shaw and the 54th Massachusetts Regiment, and he would later eulogize his kinsman Colonel Charles Russell Lowell, who was killed at Cedar Creek in 1864. Lowell himself served five months in prison in 1943 after refusing to be drafted in protest against the Allied policy of unconditional surrender and the bombing of German cities, a pacifist stance reflected in the accusations he directs at Lincoln for waging a murderous war and then shooting the deserters who sought to escape it. Yet his anger is balanced by his admiration for "our one genius in politics," whom he had earlier called "the last President of the United States who could genuinely use words," lauding the Gettysburg Address as "a symbolic and sacramental act." Lowell published three versions of this poem within seven years (this volume prints the last), and much of its power comes from the sense that Lincoln may be ultimately unknowable to the poet, and perhaps to ourselves.

Abraham Lincoln

All day I bang and bang at you in thought,
as if I had the license of your wife. . . .
If War is the continuation of politics—
is politics the discontinuation of murder?
You may have loved underdogs and even mankind,
this one thing made you different from your equals . . .
you, our one genius in politics . . . who followed
the bull to the altar . . . to death in unity.
J'accuse, j'accuse, j'accuse, j'accuse, j'accuse!

Say it in American. Who shot the deserters?
Winter blows sparks in the face of the new God,
who breathes-in fire and dies with cooling faith,
as the firebrand turns black in the black hand,
and the squealing pig darts sidewise from his foot.

1976

Stanley Kunitz

In 1937 Mary Lincoln Isham, the President's granddaughter, donated a box to the Library of Congress that held the contents of Lincoln's pockets on the night he was assassinated. It remained in a vault until February 12, 1976, when it was opened by Daniel J. Boorstin, the Librarian of Congress; it contained a handkerchief, a watch fob, a sleeve button, a pocket knife, a lens polisher, two pairs of spectacles, and a brown wallet holding a Confederate $5 bill and nine newspaper clippings, including one from 1863 reporting disaffection among Confederate soldiers and another reprinting a letter from John Bright to Horace Greeley, in which the English reformer praised Lincoln for his "grand simplicity of purpose" and unfaltering patriotism. "Abraham Lincoln is mythologically engulfed," said Boorstin, adding: "We should try to humanize him." In "The Lincoln Relics," Stanley Kunitz (1905–2006), who was serving as Poetry Consultant to the Library of Congress when the box was opened, chose instead to openly address Lincoln's peculiar role as a national saint, and in doing so to express the sense of anguish and loss felt by many Americans in the aftermath of Vietnam and Watergate.

The Lincoln Relics

"A Lincoln exhibit on view in the Great Hall makes the 16th President of the United States, born 167 years ago, seem very real. Displayed are the contents of his pockets the night he was assassinated, a miniature portrait never before exhibited, and two great documents from the Library's collections, the Gettysburg Address and the Second Inaugural Address."

—Library of Congress Information Bulletin,
February 1976

I

Cold-eyed, in Naples once,
while the congregation swooned,
I watched the liquefaction
of a vial of precious blood,

773

and wondered only
how the trick was done.
Saint's bones are only bones
to me, but here,
where the stage is set
without a trace of gore,
these relics on display—
watchfob and ivory pocket knife,
a handkerchief of Irish linen,
a button severed from his sleeve—
make a noble, dissolving music
out of homely fife and drum,
and that's miraculous.

                    2

His innocence was to trust
the better angels of our nature,
even when the Union cracked
and furious blood
ran north and south
along the lines of pillage.
Secession grieved him
like the falling-out of brothers.
After Appomattox he laid
the white flower of forgiving
on Lee's crisp sword.
What was there left for him to do?
When the curtain rose
on *Our American Cousin*
he leaned forward in his chair
toward the last absurdity,
that other laughable country,
for which he was ready with his ransom—
a five-dollar Confederate note
in mint condition, and nine
newspaper accolades
neatly folded in his wallet.

It was time for him now
to try on his gold-rimmed spectacles,
the pair with the sliding temples
mended with a loop of string,
while the demon of the absolute,
who had been skulking in the wings,
leaped into focus,
waving a smoking pistol.

3

In the Great Hall of the Library,
as in a glass aquarium,
Abe Lincoln is swimming around,
dressed to the nines
in his stovepipe hat
and swallowtail coat,
effortlessly swimming,
propelled by sudden little kicks
of his gunboat shoes.
His billowing pockets hang
inside out; he is swimming
around, lighter at each turn,
giddy with loss,
while his memory sifts
to the sticky floor.
He is slipping away from us
into his legend and his fame,
having relinquished, piece by piece,
what he carried next to his skin,
what rocked to his angular stride,
partook of his man-smell,
shared the intimacy of his needs.
Mr. President,
in this Imperial City,
awash in gossip and power,
where marble eats marble
and your office has been defiled,

I saw the piranhas darting
between the rose-veined columns,
avid to strip the flesh
from the Republic's bones.
Has no one told you
how the slow blood leaks
from your secret wound?

4

To be old and to be young
again, inglorious private
in the kitchens of the war
that winter of blackout,
walking by the Potomac
in melancholy khaki,
searching for the prairie star,
westward scanning the horizon
for its eloquent and magnanimous light,
yearning to be touched by its fire:
to be touched again, with the years
swirling at my feet, faces
blowing in the wind
around me where I stand,
withered, in the Great Hall.

5

He steps out from the crowd
with his rawboned, warty look,
a gangling fellow in jeans
next to a plum-colored sari,
and just as suddenly he's gone.
But there's that other one
who's tall and lonely.

                                        1978

Allen Ginsberg

It is hardly surprising that Ginsberg (1926–1997), the foremost Beat disciple of Walt Whitman, would pay poetic tribute to Whitman's hero Lincoln, or that he would choose to do so in homage to another of his literary influences, the Chilean poet Pablo Neruda (1904–1973). Neruda originally published "Que despierte el leñador" in his epic history of the Americas, *Canto General* (1950); the first English version, translated by his friend Waldeen (born Waldeen Falkenstein; 1914–1993), appeared the same year in *Let the Railsplitter Awake and Other Poems*, a selection of Neruda's verse issued by the left-wing publisher Masses and Mainstream. Ginsberg made this adaptation from the Waldeen version in collaboration with the poet and playwright Sidney Goldfarb (b. 1942), giving the poem a renewed colloquial fluidity—and, by removing it from proximity to Neruda's effusive and repeated praise of Joseph Stalin, a more democratic context.

ADAPTED FROM
Neruda's "Que despierte el leñador"

V

Let the Railsplitter Awake!
Let Lincoln come with his axe
and with his wooden plate
to eat with the farmworkers.
May his craggy head,
his eyes we see in constellations,
in the wrinkles of the live oak,
come back to look at the world
rising up over the foliage
higher than Sequoias.
Let him go shop in pharmacies,
let him take the bus to Tampa
let him nibble a yellow apple,
let him go to the movies, and
talk to everybody there.

Let the Railsplitter awake!

Let Abraham come back, let his old yeast
rise in green and gold earth of Illinois,
and lift the axe in his city
against the new slavemakers
against their slave whips
against the venom of the print houses
against all the bloodsoaked
merchandise they want to sell.
Let the young white boy and young black
march singing and smiling
against walls of gold,
against manufacturers of hatred,
against the seller of his own blood,
singing, smiling and winning at last.

Let the Railsplitter awake!

1982

Donggill Kim

Judged solely by the number of philatelic tributes issued around the world to mark the Lincoln sesquicentennial in 1959, America's quintessential leader had fully evolved into an international hero by the middle of the 20th century. Over the next 50 years Nelson Mandela, Lech Walesa, and Mikhail Gorbachev (who cited him in his attempts to preserve the Soviet Union) would all invoke Lincoln as an ally in their own campaigns and quests. In South Korea, Kim (b. 1928) would go even further, comparing Lincoln to Confucius and concluding that the two men, though separated by 2,300 years and some 9,000 miles, had shared a common belief in man's innate goodness, a boundless patience, a love of poetry, and an innate moderation. Educated at Yonsei University in Seoul and in the United States, Kim originally wrote *Abraham Lincoln: An Oriental Interpretation* (from which the excerpt below is taken) as his doctoral dissertation at Boston University. (Kim used "Oriental" to refer to the Confucian societies of China, Korea, and Japan.) A popular professor of history at Yonsei and public lecturer throughout South Korea, Kim was imprisoned in 1974 and again in 1980 for his advocacy of democracy and human rights; he later served a term (1992–96) in the National Assembly.

Lincoln and Confucian Virtues

Some might reject as ridiculous and absurd the idea of a comparison between Confucius, the Sage, and Lincoln, the Politician. There is a vast distance of nearly nine thousand miles between Shantung Province, China, and Hodgenville, Kentucky, not to mention the enormous time differential of two thousand three hundred years between the two. To understand the "Master" is almost impossible because of the large amount of legend and tradition that has accumulated so thickly about his name over the centuries. It is thus not easy to fathom the plain truth. Compared to "the Confucian myth," the "Lincoln myth" is relatively uncomplicated. But, from sources that may be accepted as reliable, a brief account of Confucius' career in simple language can be determined, and it reveals certain similarities between the lives of the Great Teacher and the Great Emancipator that may amaze the student of Lincoln.

Confucius was born in the small state of Lu in the year 551 B.C. What his ancestry was we cannot know, but it is probable that there were aristocrats among his forebears. At any rate, as a young man he had to make his own living at tasks that were more or less menial. Once Tzu-kung, one of his disciples, said in reply to the question raised by the Grand Minister who wanted to know if the Master was a Divine Sage: "Heaven certainly intended him to become a Sage." The Grand Minister went on to ask: "If so, how comes it that he has many practical accomplishments?" Tzu-kung again replied that it was also true that he had many accomplishments. The Master heard of the conversation and said: "The Grand Minister is quite right about me. When I was young, I was in humble circumstances; that is why I have many practical accomplishments in regard to simple, everyday matters."[1] Lincoln once confessed that there was no romance nor anything heroic in his early life. He quoted from Thomas Gray's "An Elegy Written in a Country Churchyard" to describe his life: "The short and simple annals of the poor."[2] That humbleness was in both of them. Both learned to study and both were largely self-taught.

At the age of seventeen, Confucius was made an inspector of the corn-marts, and distinguished himself by his industry and energy in repressing fraud, and in introducing order and integrity into the whole business. He also had considerable difficulties with his wife.[3] The following words of his own give us some clue on this matter: "Women and people of low birth [*hsiao-jen* —small men] are very hard to deal with. If you are friendly with them, they get out of hand, and if you keep your distance, they resent it."[4]

Confucius was next appointed inspector-general of pastures and flocks, and the result of his judicious measures, we are told, was a general improvement in the cultivation of the country and the condition of the people. The death of his mother, which happened in his twenty-third year, brought him to a turning point. He shut himself up in his house to pass in solitude the three years of mourning for his mother. It was his moral expression of his love for the deceased parent. Lincoln's own mother died when he was nine. He did not mourn for three years, but all his life he cherished and adored the image of his mother. For him, she was a noble, affectionate, good, and kind mother. It is commonly assumed that it was Lincoln who said: "All that I am, or hope to be, I owe to my angel mother."[5] According to Carl Sandburg, one of the best loved American poets and Lincoln biographers, on the morning of the funeral of Willie, the third son of the President, Lincoln confided to Mrs. Rebecca Pomeroy of Chelsea, Massachusetts: "I had a good Christian mother, and her prayers have followed me thus far through life."[6]

Confucius returned to his home state, Lu. But an unworthy change of magistrates made him unhappy and restless. He then proceeded to Chen, where he was not much appreciated; and afterwards to Tze, where he became one of the King's ministers. He was dismissed after a short time through the intrigue of cunning courtiers. He began to wander again, but state after state refused his efforts at reform. He was misunderstood and in some instances persecuted. Once he was imprisoned, and nearly starved; and finally, seeing no hope of securing the favorable attention of his countrymen while alive, he returned in extreme poverty to his native state, and spent his last years in the composition of literary works, by which posterity at least might be instructed.

On the other hand, Lincoln's wanderings came to an end at relatively an early stage of his life. His life pattern in reality, however, remarkably coincides with what Confucius suggested as ideal. Evidently in his old age the Sage said:

At fifteen I set my heart upon Learning.
At thirty, I had planted my feet firm upon the ground.
At forty, I no longer suffered from perplexities.
At fifty, I knew what were the biddings of Heaven.
At sixty, I heard them with docile ear.
At seventy, I could follow the dictates of my own heart; for what I desired no longer overstepped the boundaries of right.[7]

Lincoln, of course, did not live long enough to reach sixty or seventy. He was struck down in his fifties. Therefore, Lincoln at sixty or Lincoln at seventy cannot but be a mere speculation. However, it may not be presumptuous to say that he had the potential to hear "the biddings of Heaven" "with docile ear," and to be able to "follow the dictates" of his "own heart," without transgressing the standards of right. It is true that Lincoln constantly sought the "divine will" during the difficult war days. Even earlier, when leaving Springfield, Illinois, "with a task . . . greater than that which rested upon Washington," Lincoln said: "Without the assistance of that Divine Being, Who ever attended him, I cannot succeed. With that assistance I cannot fail. Trusting in Him, who can go with me, and remain with you and be everywhere for good, let me confidently hope that all will yet be well."[8] In his "Last Public Address" on April 11, 1865, Lincoln clearly stated:

> We meet this evening, not in sorrow, but in gladness of heart. The evacuation of Petersburg and Richmond, and the surrender of the principal insurgent army, give hope of a righteous and speedy peace whose joyous expression can not be restrained. In the midst of this, however, He, from Whom all blessings flow, must not be forgotten. A call for a national thanksgiving is being prepared, and will be duly promulgated.[9]

From such utterances as these, it seems safe to assume that Lincoln, indeed, could follow the dictates of his own heart without overstepping the boundaries of right.

Furthermore, in the light of Confucian teachings, it can be reasonably asserted that Lincoln was the type of leader that Confucius was so anxious to give to the world as an ideal human being, *chün-tzu*. What is a *chün-tzu*? The word *chün-tzu* originally meant a son of a ruler. A descendant of the ruling house in any state could be called *chün-tzu*. He is a gentleman to be bound by a particular code of morals and manners. Therefore, superiority of birth alone is inadequate; *chün-tzu* must possess superiority of character and behavior. Finally the requisite of birth is discarded. The Master declared:

If the offspring of a brindled ox is ruddy-coated and has grown its horns, however most people might hesitate to use it, would the hills and streams really reject it?[10]

He who follows the Way of the *chün-tzu* is a *chün-tzu*; he who follows the Way of "small" people is common. And what is the Way of the Gentleman? "At home in his native village his manner is simple and unassuming, as though he did not trust himself to speak."[11] "At Court when conversing with the Under Ministers his attitude is friendly and affable."[12]

Robert G. Ingersoll, in reminiscing about Abraham Lincoln, called him "the gentlest memory of our world," and gave his account of Lincoln's personality in these words:

> Lincoln was an immense personality—firm but not obstinate. Obstinacy is egotism—firmness, heroism. He influenced others without effort, unconsciously; and they submitted to him as men submit to nature, unconsciously. He was severe with himself, and for that reason lenient with others. He appeared to apologize for being kinder than his fellows. He did merciful things as stealthily as others committed crimes. Almost ashamed of tenderness, he said and did the noblest words and deeds with that charming confusion—that awkwardness—that is the perfect grace of modesty. . . .
>
> A great man stooping, not wishing to make his fellows feel that they were small or mean.[13]

Moderation in conduct and opinion is a well-known hallmark of the true gentleman. The *chün-tzu* avoids the absolute, avoids the extreme.[14] Mencius tells us that Confucius was one who abstained from extremes.[15] Asked by Tzu-kung which was the better, Shih or Shang, the Master said: "Shih goes too far and Shang does not go far enough . . . To go too far is as bad as not to go far enough."[16]

When Lincoln said his policy was to have no policy, it was an expression of his determination to take a road of moderation even if it was crooked and winding. In fact, he never had a policy. He "simply tried to do what seemed best as each day came."[17]

His purpose was in avoiding extremes, knowing that to exceed was as bad as not to reach.

But the *chün-tzu*, the gentleman, should be keen and alert all the time. If he gets dull and insensitive, he is no longer a gentleman. Master K'ung said:

> The gentleman has nine cares. In seeing he is careful to see clearly, in hearing he is careful to hear distinctly, in his looks he is careful to be kindly; in his manner to be respectful, in his words to be loyal, in his work to be diligent. When in doubt he is careful to ask for information; when angry he has a care for the consequences, and when he sees a chance of gain, he thinks carefully whether the pursuit of it would be consonant with the right.[18]

Moderation cannot be achieved unless it is accompanied by the determination to be right. Both Confucius and Mencius assume that the nature of man is originally good. At the same time they admit that this wicked world is full of temptations to corrupt man's goodness. Therefore, the *chün-tzu* has to base his character on righteousness while conducting himself according to propriety, expressing himself in modesty, and becoming complete in sincerity.[19] The *chün-tzu* holds righteousness in the highest esteem.[20] But, without courage, how can one remain both moderate and right? To our comfort, "Lincoln, the Liberal Statesman" always had the courage to carry out his middle-of-the-road policy. He was not only a man of velvet but also a man of steel. J. G. Randall, in describing Lincoln's personality, seems to have summarized all the qualities of the *chün-tzu*:

> Lincoln's greatness arose from a combination of qualities in a balanced personality. One could never define his conduct as springing from mere automatic reaction. It came rather from informed study and mature reflection. Mere slogans and stereotypes did not impress him. He was a simple man—he was unpretentious in manner and straightforward in expression—but he was never extravagant. He combined humanitarianism with practical common sense. He attained a position of lofty eminence and moved among the great

without making other men feel small. . . . He could assert himself without becoming a dictator. He had ambition, but without selfishness. If a colleague, a subordinate, or a cabinet member were attacked, he would take the blame upon his own shoulders. Sometimes he would write a letter as an outlet for overwrought feeling, think it over, realize that it might wound the recipient, and then withhold it.[21]

Master K'ung would have been exceedingly happy if he had found one like Lincoln among his disciples! The gentleman cultivates himself so as to give rest to the troubled world.[22] Those who have abilities but act arrogantly are no gentlemen because they break the harmony of the world. This world can maintain its harmony through the gentlemen who cultivate themselves in order to make all people live in peace and happiness. Lincoln had this quality of the Oriental gentleman. Confucius has finally found a real *chün-tzu*!

The teachings of Confucius, as noted above, put emphasis on human relationships and teach men how to live in harmony with one another. So far as has been observed, Lincoln has admirably met the standards of a *chün-tzu* in moral conduct set forth by Master K'ung himself. But, a few more steps are needed for an individual to become a perfect gentleman. In the Confucian ethical system poetry, rites, and music are important and essential for the training of a *chün-tzu*. The Master said: "Let a man be first incited by the *Songs*, then given a firm footing by the study of ritual, and finally perfected by music."[23] In other words, personal cultivation begins with poetry, is established by rites, and is perfected by music.

Orientals seem to make a distinction between literature that instructs and literature that pleases, or literature that is the vehicle of truth and literature that is the expression of emotions. The distinction is easy to see; the former is objective and expository, while the latter is subjective and lyrical. They all pretend that the former is of greater value than the latter, because it improves the people's minds and uplifts society's morals. From this point of view, they tend to look down upon novels and dramas as minor arts, unworthy of inclusion in the Hall of Great

Literature. The only exception is poetry, which they cultivate and honor more intensively and generally than in the West. As a matter of fact, all Confucian scholars are poets, or pretend to be, and about fifty percent of the contents of a scholar's collected works usually consists of poetry. And Chinese national examinations, ever since the T'ang Period, have always included the composition of poems among the important tests of literary ability. The Master himself earnestly encouraged his pupils to study the *Odes*, the *Songs*:

> Why is it that none of you study the *Songs*? For the *Songs* will help you to incite people's emotions, to observe their feelings, to keep company, to express your grievances. They may be used at home in the service of one's father; abroad, in the service of one's prince. Moreover, they will widen your acquaintance with the names of birds, beasts, plants and trees.[24]

Confucius loved poems because they expressed joy without being licentious and grief without being injurious.[25]

It is an undeniable fact that Abraham Lincoln was fond of poetry. In fact his very first extant writing was done in the form of verse:

> Abraham Lincoln
> his hand and pen
> he will be good but
> god knows When[26]

The originality of this verse has been questioned. However, the authenticity of his own poem entitled "My Childhood-Home I See Again" composed in 1846 at the age of thirty-seven is clearly established. A man does not write poems at that age unless he has some talent or at least some propensity for verse. Jacques Barzun, acknowledging Lincoln's "literary genius" maintains that Lincoln had a literary style that was "clear, forcible, individual and distinguished." Referring to the handbill prepared by Lincoln at the age of twenty-three, Barzun says:

One does not need to be a literary man to see that Lincoln was a born writer, nor a psychologist to guess that here is a youth of uncommon mold—strangely self-assertive, yet detached, and also laboring under a sense of misfortune.[27]

Barzun challenges the validity of the assertion made by the late Senator Albert J. Beveridge concerning Lincoln's life prior to his Cooper Union speech. Beveridge said: "The cold fact is that not one faint glimmer appears in his whole life, at least before his Cooper Union speech, which so much as suggests the radiance of the last two years." But Barzun maintains that even Lincoln's early writings all indicate that he was born with genius. "Perhaps a senator is never a good judge of what a President writes."[28]

> My childhood-home I see again,
>   And gladden with the view;
> And still as mem'ries crowd my brain,
>   There's sadness in it too.
>
> O memory! thou mid-way world
>   'Twixt Earth and Paradise,
> Where things decayed, and loved ones lost
>   In dreamy shadows rise.[29]

This Lincolnian verse can be compared with Liu Yushi's poem about the decay of the Black-Gown Alley, which once was the home of the great Wang and Hsieh families. The backgrounds are different, but there is the same sentiment, the same pathos:

Now by the Redsparrow Bridge wild grasses are growing,
And on the Black-Gown Alley the ev'ning sun is glowing,
And the swallows which once graced the Wang and Hsieh halls,
Now feed in common people's homes—without their knowing.

But Lincoln stopped composing verses as his public responsibilities grew heavier. A man of his caliber left to the world fewer than five poems! The traditional Oriental mind might regard the fact as tragic and regrettable.

Personal cultivation for a *chün-tzu* is to be established by rites. Then, what are rites? *Li* is the Chinese character for rites. *Li* is to govern the moral, social and religious activities of a man. Etymologically, *li* is religious in nature, and in the course of its evolution, it came to include all forms of rituals and everything in connection with the proper conduct of the *chün-tzu*. The original meaning of *li* was to sacrifice; it still has this sense in modern Chinese. Confucius thought, if rulers were gravely serious in sacrificing to their ancestors, why should they not be equally so in attending to the government of the realm? If ministers treated one another with courtesy, in the daily intercourse of the court, why should they not be equally considerate toward the common people, who were the backbone of the state? Thus he said to one of his disciples that, wherever he went in the world, he should treat all those with whom he came in contact as if he were receiving an important guest.[30]

Even in some of the so-called Confucian classics we find the most minute directions for behavior, which tell one exactly where each finger should be placed in picking up a ritual object. But Confucius himself conceived of *li* quite differently. It was the spirit that counted, and he was contemptuous of those who believed that, by mere ostentatious show of expensive trappings they could excel in *li*. The Master was quite upset when he said: "Ritual, ritual! Does it mean no more than presents of jade and silk?"[31]

Lincoln was a completely unconventional American, it has been said. He seemed to disregard clothing, and in privacy wore as little of it as possible. But this does not mean he was rude and unmannered. He has been pictured as a hopelessly ill-clad man. However, all the pictures in Stefan Lorant's picture story of Lincoln indicate that he never failed to dress properly according to his status in life and society. When he was a prairie lawyer, he dressed like a prairie lawyer. When he became the President, he dressed like the President of the United States, to be sure.[32]

Lincoln was thoughtful and careful even in small matters. He wrote to Thurlow Weed on March 15, 1865, and said: "Everyone likes a compliment. Thank you for yours on my little inaugural address."[33] Frederick Douglass remembered Lincoln's courteous manner and friendly gesture: "I could not have been more than ten feet from him when Mr. Lincoln saw me; his countenance lighted up and he said in a voice which was heard all around, 'Here comes my friend Douglass.'" According to Douglass, the President gave him a cordial shake, and even asked for his opinion about the inaugural address.[34] In other words, the Confucian concept of *li* was not far from what Lincoln practiced all his life. He had an ambition in life, and that was, in his own words, a "peculiar one." He said in 1832: ". . . I have no other so great as that of being truly esteemed of my fellow men, by rendering myself worthy of their esteem."[35] In order to make himself worthy of his fellow men's esteem Lincoln practiced *li* all his life. Is this not the true foundation of *li*, the highly cultivated way of Oriental life?

Finally, a man ought to be perfected by music if he is to be counted as *chün-tzu*. Did Lincoln know anything about music? After an exhaustive study on Lincoln and the music of the Civil War, Kenneth A. Bernard concludes:

> Abraham Lincoln was one of our most "unmusical" Presidents. He never studied music, never had any training in it, and knew nothing of its technical aspects; he could not play any instrument (except possibly the harmonica), could not read music, nor could he really sing. Lincoln, the railsplitter, the circuit lawyer, the saver of the Union and the Emancipator, was, in short, no musician.
>
> Yet two significant facts are clearly evident when one thinks of Lincoln and music. He was extremely fond of music and, as President, he heard more music than any other occupant of the White House.[36]

It is said that when the Master was in Ch'i, he heard the *Shao* music and for three months he forgot the taste of meat, saying that he never thought music could be so beautiful.[37]

In view of all those Confucian virtues that Lincoln possessed so abundantly, it is appropriate to call him a real *chün-tzu*, a perfect gentleman in the eyes of educated Orientals.

———

[1]*Analects*, IX, 6.

[2]Thomas Gray, a noted English poet, lived from 1716 to 1771. Most famous of his works is "An Elegy" (1750).

[3]There is some evidence that Confucius married at the age of nineteen, but divorced his wife four years later. However, this point is still considered unsettled.

[4]*Analects*, XVII, 25.

[5]Isaac Newton Arnold, *The Life of Abraham Lincoln* (Chicago: Jansen, McClurg & Company, 1885), p. 20. However, the date and its source are not determined. Louis A. Warren maintains: "Lincoln's own mother was once despised and censured by most of those who wrote about her. She has now emerged from the purely traditional and misty background which made her a waif and an irresponsible wanderer to an honorable place in the family history of her noble son." *Lincoln Lore*, No. 526 (May 8, 1939).

[6]Quoted from an unidentified source by Carl Sandburg, *Abraham Lincoln: The War Years* (New York: Harcourt, Brace & Company, 1939), III, 378.

[7]*Analects*, II, 4.

[8]Farewell Address at Springfield, Illinois, February 11, 1861, Lincoln, *Works*, IV, 190.

[9]Last Public Address, April 11, 1865, Lincoln, *Works*, VIII, 399–400.

[10]*Analects*, VI, 4.

[11]*Ibid.*, X, 1.

[12]*Ibid.*, X, 2.

[13]Robert G. Ingersoll, "The Gentlest Memory of Our World," in Allen Thorndike Rice, ed., *Reminiscences of Abraham Lincoln by Distinguished Men of His Times* (New York: Harper & Brothers Publishers, 1909), p. 426.

[14]*Han Fei Tzu*, 33, (Roll XII): adapted in *Tao Te Ching*, XXIX.

[15]*Mencius*, IV, 2, X.

[16]*Analects*, XI, 14.

[17]Sandburg, *Abraham Lincoln: The War Years*, III, 663.

[18]*Analects*, XVI, 10.

[19]*Ibid.*, XV, 17.

[20]*Ibid.*, XVII, 23.

[21]J. G. Randall, *Lincoln: The Liberal Statesman* (New York: Dodd, Mead & Company, 1947), p. 205.

[22]*Analects*, XIV, 14.

[23]*Ibid.*, VIII, 8.

[24]*Ibid.*, XVII, 9.

[25]*Ibid.*, III, 20.

[26]Lincoln, *Works*, I, 1.

[27]Jacques Barzun, "Lincoln the Literary Genius," *The Saturday Evening Post*, February 14, 1959, p. 62.

[28]*Ibid.*

[29]Lincoln, "My Childhood-Home I See Again," *Works*, I, 367.

[30]*Analects*, XII, 2.

[31]*Ibid.*, XVII, 11.

[32]See Stefan Lorant, *Lincoln: A Picture Story of His Life*; Hamilton and Ostendorf, *Lincoln in Photographs*.

[33]Lincoln to Thurlow Weed, March 15, 1865, Lincoln, *Works*, VIII, 356.

[34]"Abraham Lincoln: Frederick Douglass's Reminiscence," in *New York Tribune*, July 5, 1885.

[35]Communication to the People of Sangamon County, March 9, 1832, Lincoln, *Works*, I, 8.

[36]Kenneth A. Bernard, *Lincoln and the Music of the Civil War* (Caldwell, Idaho: The Caxton Printers, 1966), xvii.

[37]*Analects*, VII, 13.

1983

William Kennedy

The bard of Albany, New York, a city that showed little support for Lincoln during his lifetime—its voters proved overwhelmingly Democratic, and its few Republicans preferred their local hero from Auburn, William H. Seward—Kennedy has yet to explore the Lincoln theme in any of his riveting novels. But in *O Albany!*, his 1983 nonfiction love letter to his hometown, he recounts in almost novelistic style the visit made by the President-elect to New York's capital city en route to his inauguration in 1861. Did John Wilkes Booth, Kennedy wondered, appearing at the time at a local theater, glimpse Lincoln during that day's subdued parade from the railroad depot? Did Lincoln, in turn, notice the well-known actor? Kennedy left these "preposterous" questions unanswered, but brought a tangible thrill to the speculation. (The tragic story of Henry Rathbone and Clara Harris, briefly told by Kennedy here, would later become the subject of *Henry and Clara*, an acclaimed historical novel published by Thomas Mallon in 1994.)

FROM

O Albany! An Urban Tapestry

The Myers' collapse was touted as Albany's worst disaster, but it hardly qualified after two and a half centuries of riverboat sinkings, plagues, fires, massacres, wars, and epidemics. Cholera, for instance, killed four hundred in 1832, another three hundred and twenty in 1849. The Great Fire of August 17, 1848, was a tragedy of a different order, not in loss of life, but of property—six hundred homes destroyed in the most densely populated part of the city. It started from a washerwoman's bonnet, says the legend, inside a shed next to the Albion Hotel at Broadway and Herkimer Street. The area, no longer inhabited, now forms part of the arterial highway network. Then it was all houses, down to the Basin and the pier. Thirty-seven acres burned—or one thirtieth of the city—and the damage on Broadway, Church, Herkimer, Dallius, and Hudson streets and the pier was estimated at $3 million. Four days later the Common Council decreed that no wooden building could thereafter be built east of Lark Street.

Edwin Booth, America's greatest tragedian, was in Albany during the fire, as was his brother, the infamous hambone John Wilkes Booth. Edwin heroically fought the fire; John was only a boy of ten at the time. Edwin played here at Tweddle Hall, doing Othello, Shylock, and Hamlet on a bare stage, with a huge American flag dropped as a curtain between acts. John, on February 18, 1861, was in town again, having a few nights earlier played Iago, and on this night taking the role of another villainous character named Pescara, in *The Apostate*, a play created for his father, Junius Brutus Booth. Wilkes Booth, as the newspapers called him, was performing at the Gayety and staying at Stanwix Hall on Broadway, three blocks down from the Delavan House, where the man he would assassinate, President-elect Abraham Lincoln, was stopping overnight en route to Washington.

Lincoln had arrived in the afternoon by train, his car pulled by a highly polished locomotive bearing the name *Erastus Corning, Jr.* (after the son of Albany's premier businessman, Erastus Corning, president of the New York Central Railroad). As the train passed the Central's West Albany shops a signal was flashed to a military unit at the Dudley Observatory on Arbor Hill, and a twenty-one-gun salute then welcomed the President to the city.

Officials met him at the Broadway rail crossing near Lumber Street (Livingston Avenue), but he did not immediately emerge, for the Twenty-fifth Regiment, the first Northern detachment to enter Virginia after the assault on Fort Sumter, was half an hour late to escort him. The crowd grew impatient: "Show us the rail-splitter . . . trot out old Abe" were the cries some remembered. Mayor George Hornell Thacher rode with the newly bearded, stovepipe-hatted President in the horse-drawn barouche, down Broadway and up State Street. WELCOME TO THE CAPITAL OF THE EMPIRE STATE—NO MORE COMPROMISE, a banner proclaimed.

"That Negro-lover will never get to the Executive Mansion," said a bystander, and Henry Burns, a Civil War veteran who heard that, said he then saw "a big burly fellow . . . one of the

Mullen boys" hit the President's critic, knock him down, and bloody his face. Lincoln doffed his hat, stood and waved to the mob. Burns said, "I thought him the tallest man I ever saw and he didn't seem homely to me." Wilkes Booth also watched Lincoln pass in front of Stanwix Hall, where he, too, had made hostile remarks about the President and been cautioned for it.

Lincoln rode to the old Capitol, addressed the legislature in a brief, undistinguished speech, dined with Governor Edwin D. Morgan, then received the Albany citizenry at the Delavan, which was, said one account, "crowded to suffocation." The *Albany Atlas and Argus*, a newspaper hostile to Lincoln, found his face "indicates more intelligence and less character" than expected, and noted that Albany's "Republican crowd" followed Lincoln around with "vulpine eagerness." Albany—city and county—was Democratic, and had voted against Lincoln, and would again in 1864. The *Albany Journal* noted his departure briefly on page two the following day. On page one it effusively noted Wilkes Booth's performance at the Gayety—"one of the finest bits of lifelike acting we ever saw . . . undoubtedly one of the finest actors this country ever produced."

Had Lincoln noticed Wilkes Booth? Had the President and his assassin-to-be made eye contact, perhaps? Albany asked itself such preposterous questions for an age to come.

Lincoln's tragic death at Wilkes Booth's hand brought on another tragedy involving an Albany couple who were present on that baleful Good Friday night, April 14, 1865, when Booth entered the presidential box at Ford's Theater in Washington. A month earlier, March 15, Booth had given his last performance there in *The Apostate*, the role that had won him a rave in Albany.

Sitting behind the President and Mrs. Lincoln at Ford's Theater were two Albanians: U.S. Army Major Henry Rathbone, twenty-eight, and his fiancée, Clara Harris, daughter of U.S. Senator and Albany attorney Ira Harris. Rathbone's father, Jared, had been mayor of Albany, and his cousin, the precocious John, would grow so wealthy from the enormous Rathbone foundry in Albany that he would retire at thirty-five.

The young Albanians were substitute guests for General

Ulysses S. Grant and his wife, Julia, who had begged off joining the Lincolns; and so it was young Major Rathbone, instead of General Grant, who grappled with the assassin after the shooting. Booth stabbed Rathbone with a dagger, inflicting a severe gash on his upper arm. And when Booth leaped from the balcony to the stage it was Rathbone who called out, "Stop that man!"— which no one did. When a young doctor came to the box and diagnosed the President's head wound as mortal, Rathbone spoke the phrase "I'm bleeding to death," but as a newsman wrote, "all medical attention was for Lincoln." Rathbone fainted from loss of blood and was two months recuperating.

He later married Clara Harris and retired from the Army. They stayed in the Senator's home on Cherry Tree Lane in Loudonville, and a legend grew that twice Clara saw Lincoln's ghost sitting in a rocking chair in her room. They lived Downtown for a time, at 28 Eagle Street, Rathbone moving inexorably into melancholia—guilty, said his friends, over not preventing Lincoln's death. His depression turned to violence, and in Germany in 1883 he shot and killed Clara and stabbed himself five times with a dagger, but didn't die. He was tried for murder, but when the German court heard of his response to Lincoln's death, the trial was curtailed; Rathbone was adjudged insane and sent to an asylum, where he died in 1911.

Lincoln came back to Albany after his death (and so did Grant, who died in 1885 at Mount McGregor, near Saratoga, after finishing his memoirs, a grueling task but a legacy to his financially bereft family, whom he knew he was soon to leave— another form of heroism in the man. Grant's bier was on display in the new Capitol for two days). Lincoln's funeral train stopped in Albany en route to his burial in Springfield, Illinois, and his body lay in state for thirteen hours at the Assembly Chamber of the old Capitol. The *Atlas and Argus* was more reverential in reporting on the President this time, noting on April 27, 1865: "Aside from the slow tread of the procession, not a sound was to be heard in the streets. . . . Never upon a sabbath morning did the city present a stillness so complete."

All businesses were closed and no vehicles ran during the procession, which took thirty minutes to pass a given point, so many groups were in line: the Twenty-fifth Regiment (on time), the German Literary Society, the Iron Moulders Union, the Fenian Brotherhood, the St. Andrew's Society, the International Order of Odd Fellows, and many more. Some eighty thousand people were in the city, all hotels full, restaurants open all night to feed the mobs, hundreds of people sleeping in the streets. "Such a mass of human beings . . . was never before seen in the streets of Albany," said the *A and A*.

While the President's open coffin was on view, some fifty thousand people filed past, the line extending from the Capitol to Broadway. When the coffin was closed—with thousands still waiting in line—the procession began anew: up State Street, over Dove Street, down Washington Avenue to State, and up Broadway to the railroad crossing. Eight white horses drew the coffin on its catafalque trimmed in white silk; four bands played "Auld Lang Syne" and "Love Not." And then Lincoln was put into the Hearse Car, which was draped with "emblems of sorrow," and he left Albany forever.

The *A and A* had said that despite the crowds "the city was never more orderly." But on subsequent days it noted that certain disorderly events had occurred during the procession. From 132 Lark Street, burglars took eleven silver spoons; from 187 Hudson, thirty silver spoons; and from 196 Hudson, twelve silver spoons, a lady's gold watch, and a pair of armlets marked FANNIE.

Furthermore, George Murray and William Kennan were arrested for stealing a Mr. Van Vechten's watch on State Street while the cortege was passing, Patrick Roddy and Thomas Brown were arrested for fighting, Betsey Farrell for spitting in the face of Catherine Gray, and Johnson Noble for seducing Ann Miller by proposing marriage.

A famous Albany clergyman, Rabbi Isaac Mayer Wise, whose story is told elsewhere in this book, spoke in Cincinnati about the President and claimed him as a Jew. "Brethren," said the rabbi, "the lamented Abraham Lincoln is believed to be bone from our bone, flesh from our flesh. He was supposed to be a descendant of Hebrew parentage. He said so in my presence.

And indeed he preserved numerous features of the Hebrew race, both in countenance and character."

The same day that the *A and A* reported this, it also noted that the *New York World* had said Wilkes Booth was of Jewish descent.

1983

Tom Wicker

A journalist who joined *The New York Times* in 1960, Wicker (b. 1926) came to national prominence three years later for his brilliant reporting on the assassination and funeral of President John F. Kennedy. During his long career with the *Times* he served as its Washington bureau chief and as an associate editor, while also writing a column that ran for 25 years. The author of numerous works of both fiction and nonfiction, Wicker depicted the Second Battle of Manassas in his Civil War novel *Unto This Hour* (1984). The first excerpt printed here portrays President Lincoln waiting for news from the front at the War Department telegraph office, while in the second he holds an off-the-record conversation with a newspaper correspondent. In his postscript, Wicker writes that while Grady, the cipher operator, and Hale, the reporter, are his imaginary creations, the telegraph office scenes in the novel were derived from *Lincoln in the Telegraph Office* (1907), a memoir by a former wartime telegraph operator, David Homer Bates, and that Lincoln's remark to the fictitious Hale about General George B. McClellan wanting General John Pope, the Union commander at Second Manassas, to fail was actually recorded by John Hay in his diary on September 5, 1862. Although the claim, first made by Bates and accepted by Wicker, that Lincoln painstakingly drafted the preliminary Emancipation Proclamation during his visits to the telegraph office has been disputed by some historians, there is no question that in August 1862 the President was anxiously awaiting a military success that would allow him to issue the proclamation.

FROM

Unto This Hour

August 29—
Midnight to Dawn

Night had brought no relief from the heat; in Washington in August, it seldom did. Even the five broad windows that looked out over Pennsylvania Avenue from the War Department

798

Telegraph Office could catch no hint of a breeze. Insects, drawn by the yellow glow within, fluttered and whirred around the lamps. Cipher Operator James F. Grady, sweating at his desk, wished devoutly to take off his coat and roll up his sleeves, as he often could do on night duty.

He stole a quick look over his shoulder at the gaunt, quiet man who sat with his feet on a desk by the middle window, a long black coat drawn about his lank frame as if it were already fall, rather than the shank of a fetid Washington summer. If he'd only take off that coat, Grady thought, the Telegraph Office clerks could get comfortable, too. But that wasn't likely to happen —not in the brooding mood he appeared to be in.

Grady had seldom seen him sit so quietly; usually he was restless, crossing one leg over the other, or sprawling a leg over the arm of his chair, then maybe getting up, sitting down again and turning sideways to put both legs over the chair arm. Or he'd pace the office, arms behind his back, looking down at his large feet moving solidly over the floor.

But that night, since he'd put his feet up on the desk an hour earlier and settled down to read over the day's file of military telegrams, he'd scarcely moved and had said nothing at all. Of course there'd been plenty to brood about in the file—particularly the midafternoon telegram from Colonel Haupt in Alexandria. An escaped prisoner gave eyewitness testimony that Rebs had fired and destroyed the rail bridge over Bull Run, Haupt reported.

> It is clear, therefore, that the Army of Virginia can receive no more supplies by rail at present, and must flank the enemy by a movement to the east, cut its way through, or be lost.

The only fresh news anybody in Washington had of Pope's Army of Virginia was coming in such telegrams from Haupt; some other messages were being relayed a day or more late via the roundabout route through General Burnside's headquarters far to the south at Falmouth.

Just an hour earlier, a message from Burnside had come through for Generals Halleck and McClellan; this one passed

on the word-of-mouth information of a courier dispatched to
Falmouth from Bristoe Station by General Fitz-John Porter.
The news was twenty-four hours old and no doubt superceded
by events, but nevertheless seemed important to Grady. Burnside quoted the courier from Bristoe:

> An engagement took place near there yesterday between
> Hooker and a portion of Jackson's force, which resulted in
> the withdrawal of the enemy, leaving their killed and wounded
> on the field. Our loss reported from 300 to 500; enemy's
> about the same. Warrenton Junction and Bealeton were
> being evacuated by our troops, who are moving toward
> Gainesville and Manassas Junction.

Of course, Falmouth was as far from the action as the President or Halleck in Washington were, so Burnside had cautiously
declined to vouch for this information.

Neither he nor Haupt had been able to furnish much solid
information about Pope's situation—even his whereabouts. Since
early on the evening of the 26th, when the Rebs had cut the wires
and the railroad at Bristoe and Manassas, there had been no
word directly from Pope himself. It was almost as if more than
50,000 men, with their horses and equipment, had disappeared.

But out there in the darkness beyond the Potomac, not more
than maybe a day's hard march from the Long Bridge, Grady
knew that armies were moving again on the blood-soaked plains
of Manassas, men were dying, history was being shaped. (Grady
was a romantic who cherished his own small part in the shaping.)

Yet silence hung as ominously as a thundercloud over the
vast scene (clearly imagined by Grady in the manner of the battle lithographs in *Harper's Weekly*). He thought that silence must
be maddening to the brooding man in the black coat, for no one
ever was hungrier than he for news—even bad news.

Shortly past noon—Grady had noted in the file of carbon
copies—Haupt had sent word that the Rebel forces suddenly
operating around Manassas "were large and several of their best
generals were in command." Scarcely had that message been
deciphered than another had gone back headed "War Department, August 28, 1862, 2:40 p.m." on the standard yellow tissue

paper, in the neat, tight handwriting with which all the operators had become familiar:

Colonel Haupt:
    Yours received. How do you learn that the rebel forces at
Manassas are large, and commanded by several of their best
generals?

A. Lincoln

Right to the point. No fuss and no pretense, like the man
himself. And typical of his gluttonous appetite for fact and detail. Grady was an unreserved admirer; even now, sweating like
a mule as he labored over the difficult "Blonde" cipher, meticu-
lously breaking out the gibberish of Haupt's latest telegram into
eleven lines and seven columns that would enable the message
to be read, he did not resent the deference that caused him in
the sweltering night to keep on his heavy coat as long as the
President remained wrapped in his.

Grady was used to this imposing presence at Superintendent
Eckert's desk, or wandering around the office. Frequently that
summer, Mr. Lincoln had worked for hours on the papers Eckert
would later lock up for him in a drawer of the desk; and always
when the keys were clicking and message traffic was flowing
rapidly into and out of the big room overlooking Pennsylvania
Avenue, he'd be up and about, reading the telegrams, chatting
with the operators, his height and his reedy, ready laugh domi-
nating the scene.

Grady had heard him say that the Telegraph Office was as
much a refuge for him as a source of information. He could get
a little peace and quiet there, even when it was jumping like a
hen on a hot stove; but in his office a constant stream of visitors
would be sending in their cards to distract him. In the Telegraph
Office, with the latest news at hand, Secretary of War Stanton
right next door, his own secretaries only minutes away, he could
be in charge of things and yet not be swamped by the lesser duties
of his office.

That summer, as the war had grown into a consuming monster, Superintendent Eckert had practically given up his desk to
him, and Grady had become curious about the document on

which the President had lavished so much effort and thought. It was in the drawer now, just under the crossed ankles and the big feet in their heavy boots; and Grady wished he had the nerve to ask straight out what it was that Mr. Lincoln had worked on so long and so hard.

But he didn't, although not because he feared rebuff. As far as Grady could see, very little ruffled the President's temper or disturbed his self-possession. Most of the time, he was downright genial, even garrulous. But other times—like now, as he waited for news—he would withdraw deep within his own concerns, of such gravity as Grady could hardly imagine. At such moments, Grady would not have dreamed of intruding mere curiosity on the brooding presence that permeated the Telegraph Office like the heat of the night.

Grady only wished he could decipher more positive news. He actually resented the silence from Virginia, regarding it as a sort of insult not just to the man waiting by the window but to the clattering instruments and the wires strung like nerves across the countryside. The telegraph seemed to Grady so marvelous, so precisely suited to the needs of the war, that he took Pope's silence as a kind of rejection, a rebuff to beneficial science (although he knew well enough that, in fact, the Rebs had cut the wires beyond Bull Run).

Haupt's latest message, as Grady continued to decipher it, was more of the same conjecture and fragments he had been sending, valuable but not *solid*. Except that he could definitely confirm, from the observations of one of his own men, the destruction of the bridge over Bull Run. And a wounded soldier reported Hooker and Sigel in occupation of Manassas and the Rebs gone from that place.

Grady finished breaking the cipher into the required lines and columns. In "Blonde," the first word of the actual message was on the bottom line of column six; then the message moved up that column one word to a line, then down column three, up column five and so on. At the end of each column he had to throw out a "blind" word that had no purpose but to confuse an interceptor.

The completed message contained a startling report from a captured Reb chaplain:

He saw General Lee today at Fairfax about 11 o'clock, who took the road toward Vienna with a large force, accompanied by artillery.

In more than a year of immersion in military telegrams, Grady had learned that information from the front—any front, any information—varied from the impressive (rare) to the misleading (commonplace) and not infrequently to the downright false. He took the report about General Lee being that close to Washington with a large grain of salt, as it seemed to him the cautious Haupt probably intended. The colonel's closing lines even raised doubts about the reported reoccupation:

If our forces occupy Manassas, I will endeavor to pour in supplies without delay, and reconstruct Bull Run Bridge in the shortest time possible.

H. Haupt

Grady made a straight copy and the required carbons in his angular, practiced hand, and took the message across the room. The other two clerks, Tinker and Bates, worked quietly at their desks. There was no sound but the whir of insects and the big clock ticking on the wall with a regularity that mocked the fallibility of men (although the cipher operator was too young and too optimistic to realize that).

Mr. Lincoln took his feet from the desk as Grady approached. His long legs swung awkwardly to the floor, rather like those of the wooden dolls Grady had seen in puppet shows. The black coat fell open and he sat up straight, his deep-set, dark gray eyes blinking in his long, thin face. His head was large, with a forehead so broad that Grady was certain the intellect it sheltered was of remarkable power. Under coarse dark hair, rather carelessly combed back, the President's other features were almost as prominent, particularly the heavy nose and full lips, the furrowed cheeks, and the wide mouth that could easily break into a smile.

Clearly, he had been napping; that surprised Grady, who had supposed that profound contemplation of great events occupied the still figure at Eckert's desk.

"From Colonel Haupt, Mister President."

He held out the telegram. Mr. Lincoln sighed and took it in his thick-fingered hand. He looked more tired than usual, Grady thought, and a bit disconsolate.

"Thank you, Mister Grady." The President put the telegram on the desk and leaned on one arm, reading it.

Over his bent shoulder, beyond the dark expanse of lawn in front of the War Department, Grady saw through the window a group of men on horseback trooping along Pennsylvania Avenue. They were only indistinct shapes under a dim street lamp, but the clink of metal, a barked military command, gave the moving forms identity. No doubt a military police unit or stray cavalry from the Washington defense forces. Grady had suddenly a sense of the sleeping city, unaware of its danger; he was only twenty-three years old, so it was perhaps understandable that he felt himself informed, an insider, and gloried in the feel of it.

A tiny breeze fluttered at the window and brought him a dank sniff of the sewage canal that oozed foul and viscous between the White House and the Potomac. He went back to his own desk. His post did give him unusual opportunities to know what was going on. So he was in no doubt that the present hour was desperate—even if that hadn't been signaled by the President's midnight vigil in the Telegraph Office. Whenever he stayed so late, something was bound to be up somewhere.

Barely two months before, Mr. Lincoln had been all but constantly on hand as a steady flow of news came in from General McClellan on the Peninsula. Coming each day across the wooded lawn from the White House next door, his tall hat adding almost comical height to his six feet four inches, he would stay for hours, sometimes all night, reading the dispatches as they were deciphered, sending back his persistent inquiries, chatting with the clerks and the operators and Eckert as if they might have been Cabinet members, telling his bantering stories, sometimes rapt in his deep silences.

Sometimes, usually in good humor, he would chide the press, whose reports all too often bordered on fantasy and which Mr. Stanton clearly considered a nest of traitors. Grady was inclined to agree. By the time the papers got through exaggerating some minor skirmish, he had heard the President complain to Eckert, "Revolvers have grown into horse pistols."

Back then, there had been reason enough for good humor. McClellan had been kicking at the doors of Richmond, and it was possible to hope that the war might soon be over, the Rebs gutted and crushed (as, in Grady's opinion, they deserved to be), the old Union restored to its former might.

But Grady could hardly believe all that had gone wrong in so short a time. In his youth and inexperience, he had not yet admitted to himself the truth implicit in the reams of misinformation he had deciphered in the past year. He still thought Presidents and generals made decisions and carried them out as they might order breakfast from the extensive menu at Willard's, and that the results ought to arrive as surely as the morning coffee.

But the hard facts could not be blinked—McClellan's great Peninsula offensive shattered, his army strewn in dribs and drabs from Alexandria to Aquia to Falmouth—disjointed, disheartened, lacking even a leader, with McClellan himself secluded on his steamer in a "fit of the sulks" (so Grady had heard the general's mood irately described by Secretary Stanton).

And over there somewhere in the menacing silence of northern Virginia, almost within spitting distance of the Capitol dome, Stonewall Jackson was on the loose, with Lee's whole army somewhere behind him. Before the June battles that had halted the Peninsula offensive, Grady had never heard of Lee, who in a summer's brief passing had assumed near-heroic stature. As for Jackson, everybody had known his nickname since the first battle at Bull Run; and since the Valley fighting in the spring he had seemed to be a shadow moving swiftly to cast unexpected, deadly shades.

Now the elusive Stonewall had emerged from the darkness to strike again; and nothing stood between Washington and the Rebel captain but the unknown westerner, John Pope, and his makeshift Army of Virginia—some troops whipped once by Jackson in the Valley, plus McDowell's largely untested corps, together with such units of McClellan's beaten army as might have moved out to Pope's support. Telegraph lines down, bridges burned, the railroad lifeline broken at Bull Run, supplies bound to be short, Washington at risk—Grady was too young and too optimistic and too ignorant of war to feel himself personally in danger; but he was glad he didn't have to carry the burdens of the man in the long black coat.

A hand touched his shoulder. Grady looked up, saw the dark, shadowed eyes peering down, and started to rise to his feet. But a big hand gently pressed him back into his chair. The President put a yellow sheet in front of the cipher clerk, gave his shoulder what Grady was sure was a commendatory squeeze, and turned away. In his long, deliberate stride, the long coat flapping like the rags of a scarecrow, he went back across the office to Eckert's desk, folded himself into the superintendent's squeaking swivel chair, and put his legs up again.

Turning to his work, young James Grady was as conscious of that powerful presence behind him as of his own sweating body. He ran his eye over the closely written script and saw that it did not need encipherment. From the steadily ticking clock, he noted that the time was just past midnight. He dated the telegram with the hour and the new day—August 29, 1862—and reached for his key.

Colonel Haupt:
    What news from direction of Manassas Junction? What news generally?

                                  A. Lincoln

August 29—Evening

Albert Stevens Hale came out of the White House, and stood for a moment under the north portico wondering whether to cross the lawn to the War Department to call on Assistant Secretary Watson. Then he decided that first he had to think through the startling information President Lincoln himself had just confided.

Hale set off quickly for his office on Twelfth Street. Even in the tropical heat of a Washington afternoon, his step was brisk and he was dressed in a heavy, rather formal suit. His tall black hat could not counter the fact that he was a small man. The President, escorting him to the door of his office, could almost have held an arm straight out over Hale's thinning hair.

Lucky thing he had sent in his card at just the right moment, Hale thought. He hadn't expected to see Lincoln, had merely scribbled on the card: "News from Pope?"

Most times the President replied to journalists who presented him such questions by jotting what he chose to answer on the back of the card; occasionally, however, he called the questioner in for a chat.

"You newspapermen are so often behind the scenes at the front," he'd told Williams of *The Times*, "I frequently get ideas from you that no one else can give."

Hearing that, Forney of the *Washington Chronicle* had complained, "When *I* go to see him, he asks me what's the last good joke I heard."

Hale's own experience suggested that the President's favorite question was, "What news have you?" He often felt more interviewed than informed after a talk with the genial, humorous man who bore the weight of the war on his bony shoulders. Hale was a Republican and an abolitionist who had slowly come to respect the President; but he was Washington bureau chief for a New York newspaper that was making no bones about its impatience at the slow progress of the war. And Hale shared his employer's view that Lincoln was remiss in not proclaiming freedom for southern slaves.

Wasn't that really what the struggle was about? Saying so plainly would transform a civil war into what was needed—a moral crusade. But Lincoln appeared not to grasp the overwhelming sentiment of the country for emancipation. Everybody knew that he'd told Senator Charles Sumner that a decree freeing the slaves would be "too big a lick."

To which the caustic Secretary Stanton was known to have replied—though not to the President's face—that the country "wanted big licks now."

As Hale hurried through the midafternoon heat and the stench of the sewage canal that ran below the White House and near the stump of the unfinished monument to Washington, he was more than usually anxious to get at his daily confidential report to New York. A nervous, bespectacled man, nearsighted and constantly worrying about his health, Hale was, for all that, an incessant worker. He organized and coordinated, as well as anyone could, the work of his paper's correspondents in the field; and one of his worries at the moment was that young Charlie Keach had disappeared. When the other correspondents had been forced by Halleck's order to separate themselves from Pope's Army of Virginia, Keach simply had not returned with them, nor had he been heard from since.

The bureau chief also cultivated some of the most important news sources in Washington—Secretary of State Seward, Secretary of the Treasury Chase, Assistant War Secretary Watson (Hale detested Stanton and sought out his deputy instead), Speaker Colfax, Representatives Covode and Washburne, Senator Sumner, General Wadsworth, and not infrequently the President himself. All contributed, more than they knew, not only to Hale's long and informed dispatches about the government and the conduct of the war, but also to his nightly private report to his editor, Stanley Glenn, in New York.

Just a few nights before, Hale had been able to write Glenn privately—though carefully masking his source, Secretary of the Navy Welles—that Lincoln had completed the draft of an Emancipation Proclamation three weeks before. He could not tell Glenn why its issuance had been delayed, and he had been considerably embarrassed the next day, when Lincoln's reply to Greeley's "Prayer of Twenty Million" had been printed in the *New York Tribune*:

> I would save the Union. If there be those who would not save the Union, unless they could at the same time save slavery, I do not agree with them. If there be those who would not save the Union, unless they could at the same time destroy slavery, I do not agree with them. My paramount object in this struggle is to save the Union and is not either to save or destroy slavery. If I could save the Union without freeing any slave, I would do it, and if I could save

the Union by freeing some and leaving others alone, I
would also do that . . .

Hale had perfect confidence in his impressive source, who
assured him the Proclamation was indeed down on paper in
Lincoln's own hand—the product of a summer's secret work in
the Telegraph Office. But that was not the same as having emancipation proclaimed to the world, and Hale feared Lincoln's
letter to Greeley had damaged his—Hale's—standing with Stanley Glenn.

So when the President, instead of sending back Hale's card
with a line or two in response, had invited him in for a talk, Hale
had quickly decided to press the emancipation question. But he
never got the chance; for the first time in Hale's experience,
Lincoln was in a wrathful mood. Hardly offering civil welcome,
he held up a telegram from General McClellan and began to
excoriate the general for dragging his feet in sending reinforce-
ments out to Pope.

"He's acted badly toward Pope." Lincoln draped one of his
long legs over the arm of his chair. "He really *wanted* him to
fail."

Lincoln had stopped short of showing McClellan's telegram
to Hale; apparently just received, it seemed to have set off the
President's tirade. But he did read aloud the operative sentence,
inflecting his high-pitched voice sarcastically:

"I am clear that one of two courses should be adopted: first,
to concentrate all our available forces to open communications
with Pope; second, to leave Pope to get out of his scrape, and at
once to use all our means to make the capital perfectly safe."

Leave Pope to get out of his scrape! Hale would have found
the phrase shocking even had he not already come to regard
George B. McClellan as a general moved more by personal ambition than by patriotism. His telegram amounted to a proposal
to leave a Federal army to fend for itself against forces of unknown size and disposition.

Even without these indiscretions, the telegram—as Hale
pieced together the story from Lincoln's remarks—was an act of

insubordination. In it McClellan appeared to have gone over Halleck's head to Lincoln in an effort to hold back some troops the general in chief had ordered out to Pope.

"I tell you, Hale, there's been a design, a *purpose*, in breaking down Pope without regard to the consequences to the country." Lincoln smacked his open palm on his desk. "That's atrocious. It's shocking—but there's no remedy at present. McClellan has the army with him."

Hale had never had such a story; but all correspondents understood that private conversations with Lincoln were never to be attributed to him. And he certainly couldn't publish without documentation what the President had seemed plainly to be suggesting—that Major General George B. McClellan and his toady generals had acted to cause Major General John Pope to be defeated by the Rebels—at the least had declined to assist him.

As Hale crossed Fourteenth Street, he was calculating how best to use this startling information. In the nightly letter to Glenn, of course—though he'd have to ponder whether or not to disclose even confidentially that the news was directly from Lincoln himself. Then, tomorrow, he'd get busy with War Department officials to see if he could use his information to drag the story out of them in publishable form. Maybe Watson would open up.

Of course, he had to allow for the fact that Lincoln was being driven to distraction by the lack of news from Pope. There had been no word for four days. The President could be seizing on McClellan as a scapegoat—which put Hale in mind of his own frustration.

"Where the devil's that Keach?" he muttered, causing an old gentleman passing by to stare at him suspiciously.

But Hale was too single-minded to notice or to give further thought to Keach; he hurried on, anxious to put everything down in his nightly letter.

1984

Gore Vidal

Vidal (b. 1925) had already established himself as a prolific novelist, essayist, playwright, and screenwriter when he began writing a series of novels exploring the history of the United States and recording what he saw as its transformation from a republic into an empire. *Washington, D.C.* appeared in 1967 and was followed by *Burr* (1973), *1876* (1976), and, in 1984, by *Lincoln*, which became a runaway best-seller while igniting a protracted dispute regarding its historical accuracy. An enthusiastic and experienced controversialist, Vidal mocked his academic critics as "scholar-squirrels," then gave as proof of his bona fides the pre-publication vetting of his manuscript by the eminent Harvard historian, and leading Lincoln expert, David Herbert Donald. Heavily influenced by Edmund Wilson, Vidal took enormous interpretative liberties in presenting his version of the "real" Lincoln who, constipated and perennially weary, is driven by his ambition to embrace despotism in order to heroically save the Union. Vidal was at his best in re-creating, and embellishing, scenes described only fleetingly in historical sources—usually for lack of further evidence. The chapter printed here, for example, makes Lincoln's unannounced courtesy call to the White House on his arrival in Washington in 1861 into an occasion full of challenge and portent. Nonetheless, Vidal manages in a few pages to convey his characters' various moods as they prepare themselves for an uncertain future in a suddenly divided country.

FROM
Lincoln

At eleven o'clock in the morning, Seward and Lincoln—the latter still unrecognized—crossed from Willard's to the Executive Mansion, known to those few Americans who were not addicted to the prevailing Latinate English of the nation's orators as the President's House or just plain White House. The single guard at the gate did not even look at the two soberly dressed statesmen, who proceeded up the iced-over, deep-rutted driveway to the main portico, from whose columns the

811

paint was peeling; the glass of the front windows was streaked with dust.

"Last time I was here it was 1848." Lincoln looked about with some curiosity.

"Your friend Mr. Polk was in residence then."

Lincoln nodded. "But never friendly to me, particularly after I attacked his Mexican War."

"Ah, the irrepressible speeches of one's youth!" Seward made a comical face. "You'll be hearing a lot about that speech of yours before you're done."

Lincoln grimaced. "I know. I know. Words are hostages to fortune, they say. The only problem is we never know in advance just what the fortune is."

At the front door, a short elderly Irish usher stopped them. "State your business, gentlemen. The President is *not* available. He's in Cabinet."

"Tell the President," said Seward, "that Mr. Abraham Lincoln has come to pay a call."

The usher turned very red in the face. "By heaven, if it isn't old Abe himself! Oh, forgive me, Your Excellency . . ."

"It's heaven *I* can't forgive, for making me old."

"Well, sir, they call *me* old Edward, sir. Edward McManus. I've been doorkeeper since President Taylor."

"Then I shall leave the door just as it is, in your good hands."

Old Edward smiled, revealing few teeth, dark gums. He led them across the musty entrance hall and into the Red Room, just off the foot of the great staircase. "If you'll wait here, sir, I'll go fetch the President."

As the usher hurried upstairs, Lincoln and Seward looked about the Red Room, which was true to its name but shabby withal. Lincoln touched a red damask curtain from which pieces had been hacked.

"Visitors like their souvenirs," said Seward. "When I was governor of New York, at every reception, I'd have a guard with a gun next to every curtain."

"Did you get reelected?"

Seward laughed. "I did. In fact—"

But at that moment, President James Buchanan hurried—or flurried, thought Seward—into the room. He was a tall man, with white hair and a twisted neck, which meant that his left cheek seemed always about to rest on his left shoulder. One eye had a squint, which made the old man look as if he were winking slyly at you, as if his words were not to be taken seriously.

"Mr. Lincoln! I didn't expect you until tomorrow! Mr. Seward, too. What an honor for us. Where is my niece?" This was addressed directly to Lincoln, who said, very gravely, "On my honor, I have not misplaced your niece, Mr. President."

"Of course not. You've never met her. Nor have I. That is, nor do I *know* where she is at the moment. She is looking forward so much to showing Mrs. Lincoln around the Mansion." A lifelong bachelor, Buchanan was sustained by his niece Harriet Lane, of whom a Washington wit had been heard to say, "There is no power *behind* the throne, either."

"We just wanted to pay our respects, sir . . ." Lincoln began to move toward the door. But Buchanan took his arm, firmly.

"You must meet the Cabinet. We're having a special meeting. Texas left the Union this morning. We just got the official word . . ."

They were now in the main hall. Servants—black and white —had begun to appear, to get a glimpse of the new President.

"What answer do you make to the . . . seceders?" Although Lincoln's usual word was "rebels," he used the softer word, because the Democrat Buchanan was close to the Southern wing of his party, as represented by his own Vice-President, John C. Breckinridge.

"*You* will give us inspiration, let's hope." Buchanan bowed to Seward, who could not help but think that this run-of-the-mill Pennsylvanian politician had found his true niche not as President but during the time that he was America's minister to England.

As the three men moved up the main staircase, Buchanan said, "The house is a good deal smaller than it looks. Actually, we're quite crowded up here. Our private rooms are at this end while the offices are at the other end and this corridor that connects the two is for me like the river Styx. Each day I pass like a doomed soul through crowds of people, all waiting to be given something for nothing."

They were now at the top of the stairs, the ominous dark corridor before them. "I was never up here before," said Lincoln.

"You had no private business with Mr. Polk?" Seward lit a cigar; then, to the President, "Have I your leave?"

"By all means, sir." Buchanan indicated four large doors to the left and two doors to the right. "Those are the bedrooms. And there is the bathroom. The taps do not work, of course. Nothing really does here." Buchanan led them down the dusty hall, whose only illumination came from a single large window at the living-quarters end. Midway to the offices, the President showed them a sitting room, which followed the shape of the oval Blue Room below. The room was bleakly furnished, with horsehair sofas and empty bookcases. A number of paintings hung on the walls; but they were so darkened by time and dirt that it was hard to tell who or what they were of. "This is our only *private* parlor. Even so, the people barge in on you."

The President then led them down the corridor to a wooden railing with a gate. "This is where Hades begins," he said, unlatching the gate. Back of the railing was an empty desk and behind the desk, there was a waiting room lined with benches that always put Seward in mind of a small-town railway depot. "This is where the other Edward sits, only he's not here. I can't think why. He's a colored man; and most respectable. He decides who goes into the waiting room. Then here on the left is the secretary's office, which is quite as large as mine, with a small room just off it, which is where Harriet, my niece, keeps the linen. Would you like to see these offices?"

"No, sir." Seward could tell that Lincoln was prepared for flight. But Old Buck, as the President was popularly and unpopularly known, was inexorable. "Then the Cabinet meets right here, just off the clerk's office, as you can see, and inside it connects with the President's office, which is in the corner there, and slightly larger, thank Heaven."

Buchanan had now thrown open the door to the Cabinet Room. The half-dozen men who were seated at the green-baize–

covered table got to their feet as the President ushered Lincoln and Seward into the room. "Gentlemen, the President-elect."

Briskly, Lincoln shook hands with each man. Seward noticed that he paused for a moment as he shook the hand of the Attorney-General, Edwin M. Stanton, a large, bald-headed asthmatic man with steel-rimmed spectacles and an unpleasant sneer, aimed now at Lincoln, who said, somewhat quizzically, "Well, Mr. Stanton, we meet again."

"Yes, we do . . . *sir*."

Lincoln turned to the others. "Five years ago we were a pair of lawyers trying to determine whether Mr. McCormick's reaper was his reaper or someone else's."

"I remember . . . *sir*." Stanton stood very straight, his large paunch quivering slightly.

"Yes, Mr. Stanton. So do I."

Buchanan had now drawn Lincoln over to the window with its view of the southern part of the President's estate, bounded at the far end by the old canal, now an open sewer, and the Potomac River beyond. "In the summer, sir, the smell from that canal is absolutely unbearable," said Buchanan. "Drain the canal, I tell them. Or fill it in. Naturally, Congress does nothing. But they do let me use a little stone cottage out at the Soldiers' Home. I spend the summers there and I suggest that you use it, too, if you don't want the fever."

Lincoln was staring at a pile of white marble blocks, at whose center the base of an obelisk rose. "They've still not finished that monument to Washington?"

"No, sir. In fact, nothing is ever finished here! No dome on the Capitol. No street pavings. No street lamps. Nothing's ever done to completion here except, sir, one thing." The old man's head now rested on his shoulder and the bad eye was entirely shut as, with a quiet joy, he pointed out the window. "There," he said. "Look!"

Lincoln stared at a huge red-brick wall. "The one thing that the Executive Mansion has dearly needed since Mr. Jefferson's time was a proper barn. But not a *wooden* barn, sir. No, sir. Not a barn that will catch fire or get the rot. No, sir. But a *brick* barn, sir. A barn built to outlast time itself. You don't know the pleasure it has given me these last four years to see this beautiful barn slowly rise from that swamp they call the President's Park."

"And watch the Union fall apart," said Lincoln to Seward as the two men crossed the President's Park on the way to the War Department.

"He's well-meaning, Old Buck," said Seward, pronouncing the ultimate political epitaph. "What was that between you and Stanton?"

Lincoln chuckled. "Well, Mr. Stanton was this big important lawyer on a patent case . . . sort of *your* territory, come to think of it. And I was the backwoods lawyer that was called in to help him out because I had political connections in Chicago, where the trial was supposed to be. Anyway, when the trial got moved to Cincinnati, I wasn't really needed, as he made absolutely clear. Fact, he cut me dead."

"He's a disagreeable man," said Seward. "But he's the best lawyer in the country. And he's one of us."

Lincoln gave Seward a sidelong glance. "In what sense? He's a Democrat. He was for Douglas, or so people say. He never says, I'm told."

"Last week he told the President that if he lets Fort Sumter go without a fight, he would deserve impeachment."

"Well, well," said Lincoln; and no more. The small brick War Department was surrounded by thirty loud geese which a farmer was doing his best to make move on, to the delight of the two soldiers more or less on guard.

"I shall make no references to Rome and the Capitoline geese." Seward was fond of classical allusions. He knew his Tacitus; loved his Cicero.

"Please don't." Lincoln stared with some distaste at the unexpectedly rustic scene.

"Actually, General Scott has got himself a brand-new War Department across the way there, on Seventeenth Street. This building will only be for the army, just as that one over there"— Seward pointed to a second small brick building—"is for the navy. But the whole thing will be run from Seventeenth Street." Together the two men crossed the frozen mud field that was Seventeenth Street, where stood a large building with no guards at all, not even geese. This was the War Department. As they approached the main door, Seward asked Lincoln who ought to be Secretary of War.

Lincoln's response was sharp. "Certainly, *not* the man best qualified. I think that is already understood, isn't it?" For all Lincoln's serene amiability, Seward detected a sudden edge of true bitterness. As a minority president, Lincoln could only reign by placating certain great powers and dominations. As for ruling . . . It was Seward's view, on the morning of Saturday, February 23, 1861, that Lincoln would be fortunate if he could last out his term as the figurehead president of a mere rump of the dis-United States. Since the wealth and talent of this remaining fragment of the original Union was almost entirely in the north—specifically, in New York and New England—the inexperienced outlander from the west would need a knowledgeable prime minister, a man from the wealthy part—himself, the party's leader. But Seward was in no hurry to impose himself and the so-called Albany Plan upon Lincoln. He was convinced that in the next nine days tumultuous events would make him so necessary to the new president that he would then be able to assert his dominance in order to avoid the war with the South that Lincoln might blunder into, exclude Chase and the Democrats from the Cabinet, and begin the creation of the new North American—South American and West Indian, too; why not?—empire that Seward felt would more than compensate them for the loss of the slave states.

Seward was no longer the abolitionist he had once been. He was now both more and less ambitious than when, in the very year that Lincoln was attacking Polk for making war on Mexico, he was telling an audience in Cleveland that, "slavery must be abolished and you and I must do it." Now Seward was conciliatory on the matter in general; and beautifully vague in particular. On the other hand, Lincoln was still struggling with the words that he had so proudly hurled in the face of President Polk: "Any people anywhere," Representative Lincoln had proclaimed to the Congress, "being inclined and having the power, have the right to rise up and shake off the existing government . . ." Seward knew this so-called right of revolution speech by heart, as did every Southerner; and not a day passed that these words were not used to taunt the tall, awkward-moving man who was entering the War Department for the first time.

At seventy-four, Winfield Scott was general-in-chief of the Union armies and at six feet four and a quarter inches, he was a quarter-inch taller than the new president. Estimates of his legendary weight seldom dropped below the three-hundred-pound mark.

General Scott received the Commander-in-Chief-elect in his ground-floor office—he was too large and too old to climb stairs with any ease. Although he suffered from gout, he still loved food and wine; loved glory and himself. The bejowled, red face was huge and mottled; a spider's web of tiny purple lines had netted the nose. Scott wore an elaborate uniform of his own design, gleaming with gold braid and massive epaulets. Like a glittering mountain he stood now before a painting of himself as the hero of the War of 1812. As Lincoln entered the room, the general waddled forward; they shook hands beneath a painting of Scott conquering Mexico in 1847.

"You have come, sir, when, as a nation, we are at the razor's edge." The old man's voice was still deep; but there was a tendency to quaver whenever he summoned up emotion, either real or simulated.

"It's a great privilege to meet you, General." Lincoln glanced at the painting of Scott storming Chapultepec—and looked away. Not an auspicious beginning, thought Seward. Lincoln had detested the Mexican War.

"Sit down, sir." Scott eased himself into a throne that had been designed for a very fat man to get in and out of with relative ease. "I must confess, sir, I did not vote for you—"

"Because you are a Virginian?"

"No, sir. I am a loyal Union man, which is why I am so relieved that you are here to prevent more dis-Union. I did not vote for you because I never vote."

"Well, General, *I* voted for you in 1852, when you were the last Whig candidate for president, and I was just about the last good Whig in Springfield." Seward wondered whether or not this was true. In the course of the morning, he had duly noted that Lincoln had the gift of flattery, a form of insincerity that Seward tended to think of as being peculiarly his own most delicate art. In any case, Seward regarded Scott as his own handiwork. After all, it had been Seward's idea to run the man for President; and Seward had written every single speech that Scott had delivered in the course of a disastrous campaign.

"I received," said the general, the voice of military command taking on a politician's tone, "one million three hundred eighty-six thousand five hundred and seventy-eight votes. Franklin Pierce"—as the old man said the name, the red face darkened—"got two hundred twenty thousand more votes than I. And now we are faced with a civil war. Because, sir, had I been elected, I would have strengthened the Federal forts in the south. There would have been no trouble at Fort Sumter because I would have made nearby Fort Moultrie impregnable, and Charleston would still be what it is meant to be—a harbor of the United States."

"What is to be done?" Lincoln's voice was soft.

Scott motioned to an aide, who set up a map of the Union on an easel. Scott then picked up a ferule that lay beside his throne and pointed to the various military establishments throughout the South. He presented the bad news directly. With the exception of Forts Sumter and Pickens, the rest of the Federal forts either were in rebel hands—or would soon be. Seward then expected Scott to follow their agreed-upon line: Lincoln should say to the South, "Wayward sisters, go in peace." Although Scott said no such thing, he was hardly sanguine. "We have no fleet to speak of. This Administration has deliberately weakened our military forces. But then Mr. Floyd, the late Secretary of War, is a secessionist and a traitor. You do not object to my candor, sir?"

"No, General. I had come to the same conclusion myself. Now if war *were* to come . . ." Lincoln paused. Seward sat on the edge of his chair. It had never occurred to him that Lincoln might actually have a plan and that that plan might involve a military action against the rebel states. Like most intelligent men, Seward thought that all intelligent men, given the same set of facts, would react as he did. During the last few hours, he had come to appreciate Lincoln's intelligence if not the rustic western style; now this sallow-faced man, sprawled in an arm-chair, knees working their way to his chin, was saying, "If war were to come, how long would it take us to raise an army, build a fleet, make all necessary preparations?"

"Six months, sir. What we lack now are good officers. The best of our West Pointers are Southerners. From Jefferson Davis himself, the President of the Confederacy, to—"

Lincoln cut the old man short. "General, that is a title that I do not use nor acknowledge, while the Confederacy is a place that does not exist. Is that clear?"

Seward sat bolt upright. This man Lincoln was hard, all right; or so he sounded. Intelligent men were pliant; or so Seward chose to believe.

"Yes, sir. You are right, sir. Anyway, from Mr. Davis to Colonel Lee, all our best officers are Southern."

"Maybe you should've promoted a few more Northerners—and Westerners."

"Well, sir . . ." Vaguely, Scott gestured with his ferule, which in turn reminded him of the map. "Sir, I have already devised a plan, should it be necessary to restore the Union by force." Scott paused for some response from Lincoln but there was none beyond attentiveness.

Scott continued without, as it were, the looked-for sign. "If Virginia and Maryland go out of the Union, we shall then be obliged to move the capital to Harrisburg or to Philadelphia . . ." Scott paused. Lincoln made no response; the face was impassive. Seward was growing definitely uneasy. What was this man's game? Seward, who enjoyed poker, rather thought that Lincoln was simply indulging himself in the card-player's bluff. Certainly, he hoped that that was what it was.

Scott, signless again, proceeded to divide the South with his stick. "I do not think that a straight assault on Maryland and Virginia will succeed. Virginia is the most populous of the Southern states, the wealthiest, the most ready for war. We should inflict what damage we can upon Virginia but I would say, sir, that our hope is in the west. The Mississippi River is the key. Seize the river. Knock Mississippi out of the war and whatever sections of Tennessee and Kentucky may stand against us. Split the South into two parts, and each part will die for lack of the other."

Scott paused. Lincoln slowly straightened up. "Well, I guess we'd better persuade Virginia and Maryland to stay in the Union a while longer." Seward gave an audible sigh of relief. This was the Lincoln that he had been inventing for himself ever since the election: the cautious vacillator—a Western Jesuit, in fact.

As Lincoln rose, an aide pulled Scott to his feet. "By the way, General, what would you do about Fort Sumter?"

"I would hold out as long as possible."

"And then?"

"I would evacuate the fort. Otherwise, Major Anderson and all his men will be killed or seized. We have not the sea power to dominate Charleston harbor."

"An honor to meet you, General." Lincoln turned to Seward, "My wife and family should be arriving any minute now."

"Well, the mayor will be at the depot, even if you won't be."

Lincoln frowned. "I should have stayed with the rest of the party."

"It was at my advice, sir," said Scott, "that you took the nightcars. I trust our people in Baltimore. They swore to me that you would never have got through alive."

"Well, even if you were right, General, I'm still not sure that you've done me a good turn."

"We could take no chances," said Seward.

General Scott nodded. "That's why I agreed with Mr. Seward when he said you would be safer at Willard's Hotel than in a private house."

"Was that *your* idea?" Lincoln looked at Seward, with some amusement. "I thought it was General Scott's."

Seward was amazed to find himself blushing, as he stammered about safety. Actually, the Albany Plan had dictated Lincoln's removal from a private house to a hotel where Seward and the others would have access to him and his party. The general saluted as they departed.

The weak sun had now vanished behind what looked to be

snow clouds. Lincoln and Seward walked in silence down Seventeenth Street to the corner of Pennsylvania Avenue, as usual crowded at this time of day. Carriages and cabs clattered by while the horse carriages rattled on their tracks, bells sounding.

"No soldiers," said Lincoln, watching the traffic.

"No war—so far."

"What a fix we're in," said the President-elect, stepping up on the brick sidewalk that led past the iron fence of the White House, where he would soon be quartered—caged, was more like it, thought Seward. For a brief moment—very brief, actually—he was glad that Lincoln and not he had been elected sixteenth president of what was left of the United States of America.

1984

Mario M. Cuomo

An eloquent orator who served three terms as governor of New York, Cuomo (b. 1932) was introduced to Lincoln when his sister gave him the eight-volume *Collected Works* as a gift. "I am always taken by the humor, the pathos, the determination, the compassion that resonate in those words," he wrote more than 30 years later. "And by the great ideas." Following his mesmerizing keynote address to the 1984 Democratic National Convention, which invigorated speculation that he would seek the presidency, Cuomo made several signature speeches on Lincoln, including major addresses at Gettysburg and Springfield, in which he claimed Lincoln for his own political party in the strongest terms heard since the era of Franklin D. Roosevelt. Even James Thompson, the Republican governor of Illinois, praised the Springfield oration, delivered before the Abraham Lincoln Association and printed below, as "a great work—very eloquent." Cuomo has continued the quest to complete Lincoln's "unfinished work"—and to keep Lincoln a prominent part of the national conversation—through countless speeches, television appearances, newspaper articles, a series of forums held at Cooper Union, and two books, *Lincoln on Democracy* (1990) and *Why Lincoln Matters* (2004)—both projects, it must be disclosed, in which the editor of this volume proudly played a supporting role.

Abraham Lincoln and Our "Unfinished Work"

It is an intimidating thing to stand here tonight to talk about the greatest intellect, the greatest leader, perhaps the greatest soul, America has ever produced.

To follow such legendary orators as William Jennings Bryan and Adlai Stevenson.

Only a struggling student myself, to face as imposing an audience as the Lincoln scholars: Tough-minded. Demanding. Harsh critics. Highly intelligent.

And to face so many Republicans: Tough-minded. Demanding, harsh critics.

And I certainly wasn't encouraged after I learned that when another New York governor, Franklin D. Roosevelt, announced his intention to come here to speak on Lincoln, a local political stalwart threatened him with an injunction.

To be honest with you, I feel a little like the Illinois man from one Lincoln story. When he was confronted by a local citizens' committee with the prospect of being tarred and feathered and run out of town on a rail, he announced, "If it weren't for the honor of the thing, I'd just as soon it happened to someone else."

I should tell you one more thing before I go on with my remarks. It would be foolish to deny that there has been some speculation surrounding this event about ambitions for the presidency. Let me be candid. I don't know anyone who wouldn't regard it as the highest possible political privilege to be president. And governors are, perhaps, better prepared than most to be president.

Governors like Teddy Roosevelt and FDR and even governors from places like Georgia and California. Particularly governors of great industrial states with good records. That's because governors do more than make speeches. They have to make budgets and run things—and that's what presidents do.

So, the truth is, despite what might be said about planning to run again for governor, the speculation about the presidency is plausible.

I wouldn't be a bit surprised—if the election goes well this year for him—if early next year you heard a declaration of interest from a reelected governor of a large state—Jim Thompson of Illinois.

Good Luck, Jim!

But seriously, this is an event beyond the scope of partisan politics.

When Lincoln gave his one and only speech in my capital, Albany, New York, he told the Democratic governor, "You have invited and received me without distinction of party."

Let me second that sentiment, and thank you for inviting and receiving me in the same spirit.

To be here in Springfield, instead of at the memorial in

Washington, to celebrate this "high holy day" of Lincoln remembrance gives us a special advantage.

In Washington, Lincoln towers far above us, presiding magisterially, in a marble temple.

His stony composure, the hugeness of him there, gives him and his whole life a grandeur that places him so far above and beyond us that it's difficult to remember the reality of him.

We have lifted Lincoln to the very pinnacle of our national memory. Enlarged him to gargantuan proportions in white stone recreations.

We have chiseled his face on the side of a mountain, making him appear as a voice in the heavens.

There is a danger when we enshrine our heroes, when we lift them onto pedestals and lay wreaths at their feet. We can, by the very process of elevating them, strain the sense of connection between them and the palpable, fleshy, sometimes mean concerns of our own lives.

I have come to remember Lincoln as he was. The flesh-and-blood man. Haunted by mortality in his waking and his dreaming life. The boy who had been uprooted from one frontier to another, across Kentucky and Indiana and Illinois, by a father restless with his own dreams.

To remember some of Lincoln's own words—which, taken altogether, are the best words America has ever produced.

To remember the words that he spoke ten days after his lyrical, wrenching farewell to Springfield on his way to his inauguration as our sixteenth president.

"Back in my childhood," he said then, "the earliest days of my being able to read, I got hold of a small book . . . Weems's *Life of Washington*.

"I remember all the accounts there given of the battlefields and struggles for the liberties of the country and the great hardships of that time fixed themselves on . . . my memory.

"I recollect thinking then, boy even though I was, that there must have been something *more* than *common* that those men struggled for.

"I am exceedingly anxious that the thing which they struggled for; that something even more than national independence;

that something that held out a promise to all the people of the world for all time to come; . . . shall be perpetuated in accordance with the original idea for which the struggle was made . . ."

Here was Lincoln, just before his inauguration, reminding us of the source of his strength and eventual greatness. His compelling need to understand the meaning of things and to commit to a course that was directed by reason, supported by principle, designed to achieve the greatest good. He was a man of ideas, grand and soaring ones. And he was cursed by the realization that they were achievable ideas as well, so that he could not escape the obligation of pursuing them, despite the peril and the pain that pursuit would inevitably bring.

Even as a boy he grasped the great idea that would sustain him—and provoke him—for the rest of his days. The idea that took hold of his heart and his mind. The idea that he tells us about again and again throughout his life. It became the thread of purpose that tied the boy to the man to the legend—the great idea, the dream, the achievable dream, of equality, of opportunity . . . for all.

"The original idea for which the struggle was made . . ." The proposition that all men are created equal. That they are endowed by their Creator with certain unalienable rights. That among these are life, liberty, and the pursuit of happiness.

Even by Lincoln's time, for many the words had been heard often enough so that they became commonplace, part of the intellectual and historical landscape, losing their dimension, their significance, their profoundness.

But not for Lincoln.

He pondered them. Troubled over their significance. Wrestled with their possibilities.

"We did not learn quickly or easily that all men are created equal," one Lincoln scholar has observed.

No. We did not learn those words quickly or easily. We are still struggling with them in fact.

As Lincoln did. For a whole lifetime. From the time he read

Weems's little book, until the day he was martyred, he thought and planned and prayed to make the words of the Declaration a way of life.

Equality and opportunity, for *all*. But truly, for *all*.

Lincoln came to believe that the great promise of the founding fathers was one that had only begun to be realized with the founding fathers themselves. He understood that from the beginning it was a promise that would have to be fulfilled in degrees. Its embrace would have to be widened over the years, step by step, sometimes painfully, until finally it included everyone.

That was his dream. That was his vision. That was his mission.

With it, he defined, for himself and for us, the soul of our unique experiment in government: the belief that the promise of the Declaration of Independence—the promise of equality and opportunity—cannot be considered kept until it includes everyone.

For him, that was the unifying principle of our democracy. Without it, we had no nation worth fighting for. With it, we had no limit to the good we might achieve.

He spent the rest of his life trying to give the principle meaning. He consumed himself doing it.

He reaffirmed Jefferson's preference for the human interest and the human right. "The principles of Jefferson," he said, "are the definitions and axioms of free society."

But Lincoln extended those instincts to new expressions of equality.

Always, he searched for ways to bring within the embrace of the new freedom, the new opportunity, *all* who had become Americans.

Deeply, reverently, grateful for the opportunity afforded *him*, he was pained by the idea that it should be denied others. Or limited.

He believed that the human right was more than the right to exist, to live free from oppression.

He believed it included the right to achieve, to thrive. So he reached out for the "penniless beginner."

He thought it the American promise that every "poor man" should be given his chance.

He saw what others would or could not see: the immensity of the fundamental ideas of freedom and self-determination that made his young nation such a radically new adventure in government.

But he was not intimidated by that immensity. He was willing to *use* the ideas as well as to admire them. To mold them so as to apply them to new circumstances. To wield them as instruments of justice and not just echoes of it.

Some said government should do no more than protect its people from insurrection and foreign invasion and spend the rest of its time dispassionately observing the way its people played out the cards that fate had dealt them.

He scorned that view. He called it a "do nothing" abdication of responsibility.

"The legitimate object of government," he said, "is to do for the people what needs to be done, but which they cannot, by individual effort, do at all, or do so well, for themselves. There are many such things . . ." he said.

So he offered the "poor" *more* than freedom and the encouragement of his own good example: He offered them government. Government that would work aggressively to help them find the chance they might not have found alone. He did it by fighting for bridges, railroad construction, and other such projects that others decried as excessive government.

He gave help for education, help for agriculture, land for the rural family struggling for a start.

And always at the heart of his struggle and his yearning was the passion to make room for the outsider, the insistence upon a commitment to respect the idea of equality by fighting for inclusion.

Early in his career, he spoke out for women's suffrage.

His contempt for the "do-nothings" was equaled by his disdain for the "Know-Nothings."

America beckoned foreigners, but many Americans—organized around the crude selfishness of the nativist movement—rejected them. The nativists sought to create two classes of people, the old-stock Americans and the intruders from other places, keeping the intruders forever strangers in a strange land.

Lincoln shamed them with his understanding and his strength. "I am not a Know-Nothing," he said. "How could I be? How can anyone who abhors the oppression of Negroes be in favor of degrading classes of white people? . . . As a nation we began by declaring 'all men are created equal.'

"We now practically read it: 'All men are created equal except Negroes,' When the Know-Nothings get control, it will read 'All men are created equal except Negroes, and Catholics and Foreigners.'"

Then he added: "When it comes to this I shall prefer emigrating to some country where they make no pretense of loving liberty—to Russia for instance, where despotism can be taken pure, and without the base alloy of hypocrisy."

Had Lincoln not existed, or had he been less than he was and the battle to keep the nation together had been lost, it would have meant the end of the American experiment. Secession would have bred secession, reducing us into smaller and smaller fragments until finally we were just the broken pieces of the dream.

Lincoln saved us from that.

But winning the great war for unity did not preserve us from the need to fight further battles in the struggle to balance our diversity with our harmony, to keep the pieces of the mosaic intact, even while making room for new pieces.

That work is today, as it was in 1863, still an unfinished work . . . still a cause that requires "a full measure of devotion."

For more than 100 years, the fight to include has continued:
  • In the struggle to free working people from the oppression of a ruthless economic system that saw women and children worked to death and men born to poverty and die in poverty, in spite of working all the time.
  • In the continuing fight for civil rights, making Lincoln's promise real.

- In the effort to keep the farmer alive.
- In the ongoing resistance to preserve religious freedom from the arrogance of the Know-Nothing and zealotry of those who would make their religion the state's religion.
- In the crusade to make women equal, legally and practically.

Many battles have been won. The embrace of our unity has been gradually but inexorably expanded.

But Lincoln's work is not yet done.

A century after Lincoln preached his answer to equality and mutual respect, some discrimination—of class or race or sex or ethnicity—as a bar to full participation in America still remains.

Unpleasant reminders of less enlightened times linger. Sometimes they are heard in whispers. At other times they are loud enough to capture the attention of the American people.

I have had my own encounter with this question, and I have spoken of it.

Like millions of others, I am privileged to be a first-generation American. My mother and father came to this country more than sixty years ago with nothing but their hopes. Without education, skills, or wealth.

Through the opportunity given them here to life themselves through hard work, they were able to raise a family. My mother has lived to see her youngest child become chief executive of one of the greatest states in the greatest nation in the only world we know.

Like millions of other children of immigrants, I know the strength that immigrants can bring. I know the richness of a society that allows us a whole new culture without requiring us to surrender the one our patents were born to. I know the miraculous power of this place that helps people rise up from poverty to security, and even affluence, in the course of a single lifetime. With generations of other children of the immigrants, I know about equality and opportunity and unity in a special way.

And I know how, from time to time, all this beauty can be challenged by the misguided children of the Know-Nothings, by the shortsighted and the unkind, by contempt that masks itself as humor, by all the casual or conscious bigotry that must keep the American people vigilant.

We heard such voices again recently saying things like: "Italians are not politically popular."

"Catholics will have a problem."

"He has an *ethnic* problem."

An ethnic problem.

We hear the word again. "Wop."

"We oftentimes refer to people of Italian descent as 'Wops,'" said one public figure, unabashedly.

Now, given the unbroken string of opportunity and good fortune provided me by this great country, I might simply have ignored these references. I could easily have let the words pass as inconsequential, especially remembering Lincoln, himself the object of scorn and ridicule. But the words took on significance because they were heard far beyond my home or my block or even my state. Because they were heard by others who remembered times of their own when words stung and menaced *them* and *their* people.

And because they raised a question about our system of fundamental American values that Lincoln helped construct and died for. Is it true? Are there really so many who have never heard Lincoln's voice, or the sweet sound of reason and fairness? So many who do not understand the beauty and power of this place, that they could make of the tint of your skin or the sex you were born to or the vowels of your name an impediment to progress in this, the land of opportunity?

I believed the answer would be clear. So I asked for it by disputing the voices of division. By saying, "It is not so. It is the voice of ignorance, and I challenge you to show me otherwise."

In no time at all the answer has come back from the American people. Everyone saying the same things:

"Of course it's wrong to judge a person by the place where his forebears came from. Of course that would violate all that we stand for, fairness and common sense. It shouldn't *even* have been brought up. It shouldn't *even* have been a cause for discussion."

I agree. It should not have been. But it was. And the discussion is now concluded, with the answer I was sure of and the answer I am proud of as an American. The answer Lincoln would have given: "You will rise or fall on your merits as a person and the quality of your work. All else is distraction."

Lincoln believed, with every fiber of his being, that this place, America, could offer a dream to all mankind, different than any other in the annals of history.

More generous, more compassionate, more inclusive.

No one knew better than Lincoln our sturdiness, the ability of most of us to make it on our own given the chance. But at the same time, no one knew better the idea of family, the idea that unless we helped one another, there were some who would never make it.

One person climbs the ladder of personal ambition, reaches his dream, and then turns . . . and pulls the ladder up.

Another reaches the place he has sought, turns, and reaches down for the person behind him.

With Lincoln, it was that process of turning and reaching down, that commitment to keep lifting people up the ladder, which defined the American character, stamping us forever with a mission that reached even beyond our borders to embrace the world.

Lincoln's belief in America, in the American people, was broader, deeper, more daring than any other person's of his age—and, perhaps, ours, too.

And *this* is the near-unbelievable greatness of the man—that with that belief, he not only led us; he *created* us.

His personal mythology became our national mythology.

It is as if Homer not only chronicled the siege of Troy, but conducted the siege as well.

As if Shakespeare set his play writing aside to lead the English against the Armada.

Because Lincoln embodied his age in his actions and in his words.

Words, even and measured, hurrying across three decades, calling us to our destiny.

Words he prayed, and troubled over—more than a million words in his speeches and writings.

Words that chronicled the search for his own identity as he searched for a nation's identity.

Words that were, by turns, as chilling as the night sky and as assuring as home.

Words his reason sharpened into steel, and his heart softened into an embrace.

Words filled with all the longings of his soul and of his century.

Words wrung from his private struggle, spun to capture the struggle of a nation.

Words out of his own pain to heal that struggle.

Words of retribution, but never of revenge.

Words that judged, but never condemned.

Words that pleaded, cajoled for the one belief—that the promise *must* be kept, that the dream *must* endure and grow, until it embraces everyone.

Words ringing down into the present.

All the hope and the pain of that epic caught, somehow, by his cadences: The tearing away, the binding together, the leaving behind, the reaching beyond.

As individuals, as a people, we are still reaching up, for a better job, a better education, a better society, even for the stars, just as Lincoln did.

But because of Lincoln, we do it in a way that is unique to this world.

What other people on earth have ever claimed a quality of character that resided not in a way of speaking, dressing, dancing, praying, but in an idea?

What other people on earth have ever refused to set the definitions of their identity by anything other than that idea?

No, we have not learned quickly or easily that the dream of America endures only so long as we keep faith with the struggle to include. But Lincoln, through his words and his works, has etched that message forever into our consciousness.

Lincoln showed us, for all time, what unites us.

He taught us that we cannot rest until the promise of equality and opportunity embraces every region, every race, every religion, every nationality . . . and every class. Until it includes "the penniless beginner" and the "poor man seeking his chance."

In his time, Lincoln saw that as long as one in every seven Americans was enslaved, our identity as a people was hostage to that enslavement.

He faced that injustice. He fought it. He gave his life to see it righted.

Time and again since then, we have had to face challenges that threatened to divide us.

And time and again, we have conquered them.

We reached out—hesitantly at times, sometimes only after great struggle—but always we reached out, to include impoverished immigrants, the farmer and the factory worker, women, the disabled.

To all those whose only assets were their great expectations, America found ways to meet those expectations, and to create new ones.

Generations of hardworking people moved into the middle class and beyond.

We created a society as open and free as any on earth. And we did it Lincoln's way—by founding that society on a belief in the boundless enterprise of the American people.

Always, we have extended the promise. Moving toward the light, toward our declared purpose as a people: "to form a more perfect Union," to overcome all that divides us, because we believe the ancient wisdom that Lincoln believed—"a house divided against itself cannot stand."

Step by step, our embrace grows wider.

The old bigotries seem to be dying. The old stereotypes and hatreds that denied so many their full share of an America they helped build have gradually given way to acceptance, fairness, and civility.

But still, great challenges remain.

Suddenly, ominously, a new one has emerged.

In Lincoln's time, one of every seven Americans was a slave.

Today, for all our affluence and might, despite what every day is described as our continuing economic recovery, nearly one in every seven Americans lives in poverty, not in chains—because Lincoln saved us from that—but trapped in a cycle of despair that is its own enslavement.

Today, while so many of us do so well, one of every two minority children is born poor, many of them to be oppressed for a lifetime by inadequate education and the suffocating influence of broken families and social disorientation.

Our identity as a people is hostage to the grim facts of more than 33 million Americans for whom equality and opportunity is not yet an attainable reality, but only an illusion.

Some people look at these statistics and the suffering people behind them, and deny them, pretending instead we are all one great "shining city on a hill."

Lincoln told us for a lifetime—and for all time to come—that there can be no shining city when one in seven of us is denied the promise of the Declaration.

He tells us today that we are justly proud of all that we have accomplished, but that for all our progress, for all our achievement, for all that so properly makes us proud, we have no right to rest, content.

Nor justification for turning from the effort, out of fear or lack of confidence.

We have met greater challenges with fewer resources. We have faced greater perils with fewer friends. It would be a desecration of our belief and an act of ingratitude for the good fortune we have had to end the struggle for inclusion because it is over for some of us.

So, this evening, we come to pay you our respects, Mr. Lincoln. Not just by recalling your words and revering your memory, which we do humbly and with great pleasure.

This evening, we offer you more, Mr. President. We offer you what you have asked for, a continuing commitment to live your truth, to go forward painful step by painful step, enlarging the greatness of this nation with patient confidence in the ultimate justice of the people.

Because—as you have told us, Mr. President—there is no better or equal hope in the world.

Thank you.

February 12, 1986

William Safire

Best known for his popular books on language and for his long-running column in *The New York Times*, Safire (b. 1929) was a presidential speechwriter during Richard Nixon's first term. Not long after leaving the White House in 1973, he was enraged to learn that his home phone had been wiretapped, on Nixon's orders and without court authorization, for several weeks in 1969 on the unfounded suspicion that he was giving classified information to the press. In his novel *Freedom* (1987), which follows the Lincoln administration from the first inauguration through the signing of the Emancipation Proclamation, Safire displays both his fascination, and familiarity, with the inner workings of presidential power and his concerns regarding the abuse of presidential authority and the curtailment of civil liberties. The chapter below imagines a confrontation in the fall of 1862 between Lincoln and Horatio Seymour, the Democratic candidate for governor of New York. In the note from the lengthy "Sources and Commentary" section of his book, printed at the end of the excerpt below, Safire explains how he used actual speeches and letters to artfully construct a conversation that never took place. Seymour went on to win the 1862 gubernatorial election, but lost his reelection bid two years later; in 1868 he won the Democratic presidential nomination, but was defeated by Ulysses S. Grant.

FROM
Freedom

Debate

"You and I are substantially strangers," the President began, addressing Horatio Seymour, candidate for Governor of New York, in what he intended to be a mood of friendly formality, "and I have asked you here chiefly that we may become better acquainted. I, for the time being, am at the head of a nation which is in great peril, and you are a candidate to become head of the greatest state in that nation."

"I don't claim any superior wisdom," Seymour replied, "but I am confident the opinions I hold are entertained by one half of the population of the Northern states."

Lincoln cocked an eyebrow at that sally; the urbane New Yorker, carrying the demeanor of man of wealth and executive experience, was apparently unawed by his presence in the White House and was ready for a rhetorical scrap. Might be interesting; Lincoln's purpose was to take the measure of the leader of the political opposition as the election campaign heated up, and he was secretly pleased that Seymour obviously overestimated Democratic strength. The President shrugged and allowed as how the election in four weeks would provide the answer to the candidate's contention.

Seymour nodded with civility. "I intend to show those charged with the administration of public affairs a due deference and respect," he promised. "After I am elected governor, Mr. President, I will give you just and generous support in all measures you may adopt within the scope of your constitutional powers."

His careful qualification did not escape the President. "You have been asserting that certain military arrests," Lincoln said to draw the man out, "for which I am ultimately responsible, are unconstitutional."

"I say that your suspension of habeas corpus will not only lead to military despotism," Seymour replied coolly, "it establishes military despotism. This action of your administration will determine, in the minds of more than one half of the people in the loyal states, whether this war is waged to put down rebellion in the South, or to destroy free institutions in the North."

Lincoln was not going to let him get away with that. "May I be indulged," he returned mildly, "to submit a few general remarks on the subject of arrests?"

"You have shown that you think the Constitution is somehow different in time of insurrection and invasion," Seymour continued, not indulging the President at all. "I disagree. The safeguards of the rights of the citizen against the pretensions of arbitrary power were intended especially for his protection in times of civil commotion." As Lincoln shook his head, Seymour added: "You forget, sir, that these civil rights were secured to the English people after years of protracted civil war, and were adopted into our American Constitution at the close of the Revolution."

"Wouldn't your argument be better," Lincoln asked, "if those safeguards had been adopted and applied *during* the civil wars and *during* our Revolution, instead of *after* the one and *at the close* of the other? I, too, am devotedly for them *after* civil war, and before civil war, and at all times except—and here I quote the Constitution—'except when, in cases of rebellion or invasion, the public safety may require' their suspension."

Lincoln thought he had the better of that exchange, but Seymour conceded nothing. "You are quoting the portion of the Constitution dealing with the powers of the Congress, not the President. You tried to justify your usurpation of this power in the Merryman case last year by claiming the Congress was not in session. Well, Congress is in session right now. If it is so urgent that those who disagree with you be clapped into jail without a trial, why not call on Congress to pass martial law? Who are you to override the most sacred rights of free men—solely when you choose to say the public safety requires it? You were not elected dictator."

Lincoln recognized the debating tactic: goad your opponent to anger with a personal dig. "Divested of your phraseology calculated to represent me as struggling for an arbitrary personal prerogative," Lincoln said slowly, containing his temper, "your question is simply a question of *who* shall decide, or an affirmation that *nobody* shall decide, what the public safety does require, in cases of rebellion or invasion."

"Not so. The Congress can decide."

"The Constitution contemplates the question as likely to occur for decision, but it does not expressly declare who is to decide it," Lincoln corrected him. "By necessary implication, when rebellion or invasion comes, the decision is to be made from time to time; and I think the man who, for the time the people have, under the Constitution, made commander in chief of their army and navy, is the man who holds the power and bears the responsibility of making it."

"With no restraints? No checks and balances, no appeals? That, sir, is dictatorial power."

"If he uses the power justly," Lincoln said matter-of-factly, "the same people will probably justify him; if he abuses it, he is in their hands to be dealt with by all the modes they have reserved to themselves in the Constitution."

"Do you realize what you are saying?" Seymour uncrossed his legs and leaned forward. "You are saying, 'If you don't like my arbitrary arrests, impeach me—but I can arrest you for speaking out to demand my impeachment.' No despot ever seized more power to mete out punishment."

"The purpose of these arrests is not punishment," the President said patiently. He realized he was in a dispute with a lawyer who knew his case, but Lincoln had been writing thoughts for this session on little scraps of paper for days, putting each arguing point in a drawer to be assembled for his presentation. "You claim that men may, if they choose, embarrass those whose duty it is to combat a giant rebellion, and then be dealt with only in turn as if there were no rebellion. The Constitution itself rejects this view. The military arrests and detentions which are being made are for prevention and not punishment—as injunctions to stay injury, as proceedings to keep the peace. Hence, like proceedings in such injunction cases, they are not accompanied by indictments, or trial by juries, nor in a single case by any punishment whatever beyond what is purely incidental to the prevention."

"Not punishment? To be arrested for one knows not what; to be confined, no one entitled to ask where; to be tried, no one can say when, by a law nowhere known or established, or to linger out life in a cell without trial—you call that no punishment? That is a body of tyranny which cannot be enlarged."

Lincoln could just hear those words being used effectively in a political stump speech. It was demagoguery, he knew, but, like all effective demagoguery, contained a germ of truth: Stanton had already appointed a special provost marshal in Washington to carry out the arrests, with provost marshals in every loyal state with power to ignore local court rulings. That would strike fear in traitorous hearts, as Lincoln intended, but would also send a chill into the hearts of the loyal voter.

"Habeas corpus does not discharge men who are proved to be guilty of defined crime," Lincoln instructed Seymour in the law, "and its suspension is allowed by the Constitution on purpose that men may be arrested and held who cannot be proved to be guilty of defined crime. Arrests are made, not so much for what *has* been done as for what probably *would* be done—preventive, not vindictive. In crimes against the state, the purposes of men are much more easily understood than in cases of ordinary crime."

"Oh?"

"The man who stands by and says nothing," Lincoln said, "when the peril of his government is discussed, cannot be misunderstood. If not hindered, he is sure to help the enemy—much more, if he talks ambiguously: talks for his country with 'buts' and 'ifs' and 'ands.'"

Lincoln watched Seymour burn at that imputation of disloyalty, and as Seymour said nothing, awaited the question the candidate would have to ask. Sure enough, Seymour rose to the bait: "Can you not bear to wait until a crime has been committed before meting out punishment?"

He had him. "Wait until a crime has been committed? Let me give you an example. General John Breckinridge, as well as others occupying the very highest places in the rebel war service, were all within the power of the government once the rebellion began, and were nearly as well known to be traitors then as now. Unquestionably, if we had seized and held them, the insurgent cause would be much weaker. But no one of them had then committed any crime defined in the law. If arrested, they would have been discharged on habeas corpus, were the writ allowed to operate." The President made his point triumphantly: "I think the time not unlikely to come when I shall be blamed for having made too few arrests rather than too many."

The candidate for chief executive of the state Lincoln counted on most for men and money shook his head as if in disbelief. "The Constitution provides for no limitations on the guarantees of personal liberty, except as to habeas corpus. Even granting you the usurpation of that power from Congress, do you hold that all the other rights of every man throughout the country can be annulled whenever you say the public safety requires it? Freedom of speech, of the press—"

"The benefit of the writ of habeas corpus is the great means through which the guarantees of personal liberty are conserved and made available in the last resort," Lincoln conceded. "But by the Constitution, even habeas corpus may be suspended when, in case of rebellion or invasion, the public safety may require it." Through his power to suspend that essential right, the President held the key to all the other rights.

"Can you be unaware, Mr. President, that the suppression of journals and the imprisonment of persons has been glaringly partisan? Republicans have been allowed the utmost licentiousness of criticism, while Democrats have been punished for a fair exercise of the right of discussion. For supporters of mine, even to ask the aid of counsel has been held to be an offense."

Lincoln started to interrupt, but the New York candidate pressed on: "An attempt is being made to shield the violators of law and to suppress inquiry into their motives and conduct. I warn you, sir, this attempt to conceal the abuses of power will fail. Unconstitutional acts cannot be shielded by unconstitutional laws."

"Now hold on." He did not appreciate being warned. "In this time of national peril, I would have preferred to meet you on a level one step higher than any party platform. But not all Democrats have denied me this. The Secretary of War, on whose discretionary judgment the arrests are being made, is a Democrat, having no old party affinity with me. And from all those Democrats who are nobly exposing their lives on the battlefield, I have heard from many who approve my course, and not from a single one condemning it."

If Seymour caught the subtle import of his point—that those Democrats doing the complaining were not the patriots doing the fighting—he ignored it airily. "I shall not inquire what rights states in rebellion have forfeited, but I deny that this rebellion can suspend a single right of the citizens of loyal states. I denounce your doctrine that civil war in the South takes away from the loyal North the benefits of one principle of civil liberty."

Lincoln wondered if the man would go as far as to threaten the national authority, and was astounded when Seymour did: "In the event that I am elected governor next month, I will make it plain that it is a high crime to abduct a citizen of the state of New York. I will admonish my sheriffs and district attorneys to take care that no New Yorker is imprisoned or carried by force outside the state without due process of legal authority."

The man was a danger to the Union. Seymour was, in effect, promising insurrection of another sort: a "high crime" was an offense of state, and could lead to the arrest, impeachment, and imprisonment of the arresting federal officer. And New York's police forces, added to local militia, would be more than a match for the thin federal forces in that state. If elected governor, Seymour would have the military power on the scene to back up his threat to federal authority.

"I can no more be persuaded," Lincoln told him, hoping a practical argument would take hold, "that the government can constitutionally take no strong measures in time of rebellion— because it can be shown that the same could not be lawfully taken in time of peace—than I can be persuaded that a particular drug is not good medicine for a sick man because it can be shown not to be good for a well one. Nor am I able to appreciate the danger that the American people will, by means of military arrests during the rebellion, lose the right of public discussion, the liberty of speech and the press, the law of evidence, trial by jury and habeas corpus any more than I am able to believe that a man could contract so strong an appetite for emetics during temporary illness as to persist in feeding upon them during the remainder of his healthful life."

"I suppose those homespun metaphors go over well with juries, Mr. Lincoln, but ask yourself this: did you approve of President Polk's war with Mexico?"

Lincoln frowned, not getting his opponent's sudden shift of argument. He reluctantly shook his head. Like many good Whigs in the 1840s, he had faulted Polk for provoking the war at the behest of the Texans.

"During the war with Mexico," Seymour recounted, "many of the political opponents of the Administration thought it their duty to denounce and oppose the war. With equal reason as you give now, it might have been said of them that their discussions before the people were calculated to discourage enlistments and to induce desertions. Were these people, yourself included, 'warring on the military,' to use your own phrase, and did this give the military constitutional jurisdiction to lay hands upon them?"

"I dislike to waste words on a purely personal point," answered Lincoln, "but you will find yourself at fault should you ever seek for evidence to prove your assumption that I opposed, *in discussions before the people*, the policy of the Mexican War." Lincoln had privately spoken forcefully against the start of Polk's war, but had refrained from speaking out publicly for fear of jeopardizing his political career in those early days. He realized now that as a young congressman, he had been wise to stay silent; anti-war oratory would have come home to haunt him now. Nobody could make him feel guilty now about not speaking out then. Time for an anecdote.

"Seward says that one fundamental principle of politics is to be always on the side of your country in a war," Lincoln drawled. "I remember Butterfield of Illinois was asked, at the beginning of the Mexican War, if he was not opposed to it. He said, 'No. I opposed one war and it ruined me. I am now perpetually in favor of war, pestilence, and famine.'"

Unfortunately, Seymour was too worked up for Lincoln's attempt to reduce the animosity to have the desired effect. "Do you seriously think that arresting the outspoken opposition," asked the New York candidate, "is going to preserve the public safety? I think the opposite. I think all authority is going to be weakened by your repression. Government is never strengthened by the exercise of doubtful powers: it always produces discord, suspicion, and distrust. If that is what you feel you must do, Lincoln, that is what I must run against."

Lincoln fingered the mole on his cheek; although he had flushed Seymour out and learned the campaign strategy, he was unhappy with what he had learned. He rose from his couch and walked to the desk, half sitting there. "This civil war began on very unequal terms between the parties. The insurgents had been preparing for it more than thirty years." Anna Carroll had documented the activities of the Knights of the Golden Circle in her pamphlet exposing Breckinridge. "Their sympathizers pervaded all departments of the Government, and nearly all communities of the people. Under cover of 'liberty of speech,' 'liberty of the press,' and 'habeas corpus,' they hoped to keep on foot among us a most efficient corps of spies, informers, suppliers, and aiders and abettors of their cause in a thousand ways."

"I find it hard to believe that a President of the United States swallows such a—"

"Hear me out, Seymour. They knew that in times such as they were inaugurating, by the Constitution itself the habeas corpus might be suspended; but they also knew they had friends who make a question as to *who* was to suspend it; meanwhile, their spies and others might remain at large to help on their cause."

"The person who first raised that question was the Chief Justice of the United States," Seymour said hotly. "Are you accusing him of being a part of a conspiracy to—"

Lincoln kept on going. "Or if, as has happened, the Executive should suspend the writ, without ruinous waste of time, instances of arresting innocent persons might occur—as are always likely to occur in such cases—and then a clamor could be raised in regard to this, of service to the insurgent cause."

"For God's sake, Lincoln, what about the courts? I'm not talking about arrests of bushwhackers and guerrillas in a war zone, I mean arrests of dissenters in those areas where judges now sit, empowered to hear cases."

"Nothing is better known to history than that courts of justice are utterly incompetent to such cases," Lincoln held. "Civil courts are organized chiefly for trials of individuals, or at most a few individuals acting in concert, and this in quiet times. Even in times of peace, bands of horse thieves and robbers frequently grow too numerous and powerful for the ordinary courts of justice. But what comparison, in numbers, have such bands ever borne to the insurgent sympathizers even in many of the loyal states?"

"Why are you, a lawyer, afraid of judges and juries?"

"A jury frequently has at least one member more ready to hang the panel than to hang the traitor," the President shot back. "Thoroughly imbued with a reverence for the guaranteed rights of individuals," he went on, "I was slow to adopt the strong measures indispensable to the public safety. Remember, Seymour: he who dissuades one man from volunteering, or induces one soldier to desert, weakens the Union cause as much as he who kills a Union soldier in battle. Yet this dissuasion or inducement may be so conducted as to be defined as no crime in civil court."

"Your reverence for the rule of law is overwhelming, Mr. Lincoln. I take it that you believe all of us who strive to protect the right of dissent are weakening the cause of the Union. You have become so obsessed with holding the Union together that you have forgotten that the purpose of the Union is to preserve individual freedom."

"Your own attitude, therefore," said the President, unrelenting, eager to make clear the political danger in the line Seymour had been taking, "encourages desertion, resistance to the draft, and the like, because it teaches those who incline to desert and to escape the draft to believe it is your purpose to protect them, and to hope that you will become strong enough to do so."

"We have nothing further to discuss," said Seymour, rising. "Your pretensions to more than regal authority are contemptible. You claim to have found within the Constitution a germ of arbitrary power, which in time of war expands at once into an absolute sovereignty wielded by one man, so that liberty perishes at his discretion or caprice. I will stand for election in New York, sir, and refute you. The American people will never acquiesce in your extraordinary doctrine."

"We shall see." Lincoln judged this fellow to be stronger than he had thought, and no demagogue, but felt confident he could take him in debate in '64 if it came to that, just as he had taken Stephen Douglas in '58. If he felt like debating, that was a President's prerogative. Greeley was certain that Seymour had no chance of winning the governorship next month, but Weed was worried about the undignified and unprecedented way he was traveling all over the state of New York, running instead of standing for election in the traditional way. "We shall see. I'll just have to keep pegging away."

1987

———

This scene never took place, but the quotations are genuine.

I have interspersed portions of Horatio Seymour's speeches in the campaign of 1862, taken from David G. Croly's 1868 campaign biography, *Seymour and Blair*, pp. 75–95, with Lincoln's later reply to the same and similar charges, notably in his letter to Erastus Corning and others, *CW* for June 12, 1863, and his follow-up letter to Matthew Birchard and others, *CW* for June 29, 1863.

Another source is a more direct interchange: Lincoln's letter to Seymour of March 23, 1863, and Seymour's response in *CW* for that date. Although Lincoln came to see Governor Seymour as most important to the war, as we shall see later, the two never met face to face. The anecdote about being for war, pestilence and famine, which Lincoln told in relation to Seymour, is found in Hay's real diary for August 13, 1863.

Lincoln was pleased with his long letter justifying harsh measures against dissidents to Corning and other New York Democrats, which followed the arrest of Clement Vallandigham. Congressman James Wilson of Ohio reported (Sandburg, II, p. 308) that Lincoln said: "When it became necessary for me to write that letter, I had it nearly all in there [Pointing to the drawer] . . . Often an idea about it would occur to me which seemed to have force and make perfect answer to some of the things that were said and written about my actions. I never let one of those ideas escape me, but wrote it on a scrap of paper and put it in that drawer . . . I am pleased to know that the present judgment of thoughtful men about it is so generally in accord with what I believe the future will, without serious division, pronounce concerning it." He was wrong about that; division still exists about the necessity or wisdom of his arbitrary arrests.

Garry Wills

An extraordinarily prolific writer on history, politics, religion, literature, and popular culture, Wills (b. 1934) won the Pulitzer Prize for his eloquent and insightful study *Lincoln at Gettysburg: The Words That Remade America* (1992). Arguing that Lincoln revolutionized both American political thought and American oratory on November 19, 1863, Wills demonstrates that what was radically innovative about the Gettysburg Address was not merely Lincoln's novel use of shorter words and simpler sentences—the conventional explanation for its success—but also his brilliant use of repetition to link the separate phrases and sentences together into an unforgettable whole. ("SW" is a citation for the two-volume Library of America edition *Speeches and Writings 1832–1865*.)

FROM

Lincoln at Gettysburg:
The Words That Remade America

Revolution in Style

Lincoln's speech at Gettysburg worked several revolutions, beginning with one in literary style. Everett's talk was given at the last point in history when such a performance could be appreciated without reservation. It was made obsolete within a half-hour of the time when it was spoken. Lincoln's remarks anticipated the shift to vernacular rhythms that Mark Twain would complete twenty years later. Hemingway claimed that all modern American novels are the offspring of *Huckleberry Finn*.[1] It is no greater exaggeration to say that all modern political prose descends from the Gettysburg Address.

The Address looks less mysterious than it should to those who believe there is such a thing as "natural speech." All speech is unnatural. It is artificial. Believers in "artless" or "plain" speech think that rhetoric is added to some prior natural thing, like cosmetics added to the unadorned face. But human faces are *born*, like kitten faces. Words are not born in that way. Human babies, unlike kittens, produce a later artifact called language, and they largely speak in jingles, symbols, tales, and myths during the early stages of their talk. Plain speech is a later development, in whole cultures as in individuals. Simple prose depends on a complex epistemology—it depends on concepts like "objective fact."[2] Language reverses the logic of horticulture: here the blossoms come first, and *they* produce the branches.

Lincoln, like most writers of great prose, began by writing bad poetry. Early experiments with words are almost always stilted, formal, tentative. Economy of words, grip, precision come later (if at all). A Gettysburg Address does not precede rhetoric, but burns its way through the lesser toward the higher eloquence, by a long discipline. Lincoln not only exemplifies this process, but studied it, in himself and others. He was a student of the word.

One of the more teasing entries in John Hay's diary of his service with Lincoln was made on July 25, 1863. Hay had ridden out with the Tycoon (as he called the President in the privacy of his journal) to the Retired Soldiers Home—a federal property on a wooded height outside Washington, which Lincoln used as an early version of Camp David, a retreat from Washington's swamp-fever summers. The twenty-five-year-old secretary who lived in the Executive Mansion was often favored by the President with late-night visits and long talks. These talks could become more relaxed and discursive when the two were away from their respective offices. On this night, three weeks after the disappointment of Meade's actions after Gettysburg, the subject was a recurring one: "I rode out to Soldier's Home with the Tycoon tonight. . . . Had a talk on philology for which the T. has a little-indulged inclination" (p. 72).

Philology, the study of words, was a bond between the President and this man half his age. Hay would later tell Mark Twain, after they had become friends, that he was born like Twain on the Mississippi (at Spunky Point, Illinois), and Hay would help along the vernacular revolution when, in the early 1870s, he published dialect poems of the Bret Harte sort.[3] But Hay had also gone to Brown University (where he was Class Poet), and he would become a newspaper editor, a member of Henry

Adams's exclusive circle (The Five of Hearts), and Secretary of State to Presidents William McKinley and Theodore Roosevelt. He was sure enough of his own taste to argue with "the Tycoon," and even to catch Lincoln out when the President reverted to earlier bad habits.

Hay, who admired Lincoln without succumbing to a debilitating awe, wrote about one of his boss's famous effusions:

> His last letter is a great thing. Some hideously bad rhetoric —some indecorums that are infamous—yet the whole letter takes its solid place in history, as a great utterance of a great man. [P. 91.]

Hay is just in his praise and just in his reproach. Lincoln's letter to James C. Conkling has shrewd criticisms of Conkling's desire to hasten emancipation, but its description of military successes goes from grandiosity to mushy cuteness:

> The Father of Waters again goes unvexed to the sea. Thanks to the great North-West for it. Nor yet wholly to them. Three hundred miles up, they meet New-England, Empire, Key-Stone, and Jersey, hewing their way right and left. The Sunny South too, in more colors than one, lent a hand. On the spot, their part of the history was jotted down in black and white. The job was a great national one; and let none be banned who bore an honorable part in it. And while those who have cleared the great river may well be proud, even that is not all. It is hard to say that anything has been more bravely and well done than at Antietam, Murfreesboro, Gettysburg, and on many fields of lesser note. Nor must Uncle Sam's Web-feet [marines] be forgotten. At all the watery margins they have been present. Not only on the deep sea, the broad bay, and the rapid river, but also up the narrow muddy bayou, and wherever the ground was a little damp, they have been, and made their tracks. Thanks to all. For this great republic—for the principle it lives by, and keeps alive—for man's vast future,—thanks to all. [SW 2.498]

Though this was written only three months before the Gettysburg Address, it has the poeticisms of Everett ("watery margins"), the nature lore of Waugh's John Boot in *Scoop* ("feather-footed through the plashy fen"), and the comic formality of Claudius and Gertrude:

—Thanks, Rosencrantz and gentle Guildenstern.
—Thanks, Guildenstern and gentle Rosencrantz.

Hay, whose narrow-set eyes gave him a perpetual air of intense scrutiny, was merciless in spotting such weaknesses. It is a measure of Lincoln's desire for honest literary discussion that he became ever more intimate with Hay.

Hay appreciated the ironies in this arrangement. Despite his own frontier birth, the small, trim Hay was a bit of a dandy. In the photograph of Lincoln with Hay and his young friend John Nicolay, the two presidential secretaries look like oversized (and overdressed) Lilliputians guarding a morose Gulliver. In Hay's and Nicolay's corner room on the second floor of what we now call the White House, the contrast was even more striking: Lincoln would wander in late at night to read something he had just come across. Hay records one scene, after midnight, as he was writing that day's entry in his diary: Lincoln was

utterly unconscious that he with his short shirt hanging above his long legs and setting out behind like the tail feathers of an ostrich was infinitely funnier than anything in the book he was laughing at [p. 179].

Of another such bare-legged apparition, Hay wrote that he

complimented him [Lincoln] on the amount of underpinning he still has [fifty-five looks old to one still in his twenties] & he said he weighed 180 pds. Important if true [p. 181].

The critic is apparent in those two last words.

Lincoln liked to attend the theater with the foppish Hay—opera (*Martha*), plays (several with John Wilkes Booth), and, especially, Shakespeare. Hay, like Lincoln, admired the Shakespearean actor James Hackett, who was invited to the White House and favored with a presidential correspondence.[4] Hay defended the way Hackett emphasized a word while playing Falstaff:

The President criticized H.'s reading of a passage where Hackett said "Mainly *thrust* at me," the President thinking it should read "Mainly thrust at *me*," I told the Pres^t I tho't he was wrong: that "mainly" merely meant "strongly," "fiercely." [P. 139.]

Hay is right on the narrower matter—"mainly" here is "with might and main." But Falstaff's account of his imaginary fight at Gad's Hill is funnier if he gives a plaintive emphasis to "[poor] *me*"—as in his earlier line from the same scene: "two or three and fifty upon poor old Jack" (*1 Henry IV*, 2.4.184). Orson Welles, playing Falstaff in *Chimes at Midnight*, reads the disputed line Lincoln's way, not Hay's. There was very little Hay, or any other man, could teach Lincoln about how to milk a comic remark for maximum effect.

Arguments like this, over the exact meaning of (and stress on) a single word, make us wish that Hay had described the discussions on philology held with Lincoln at the Soldiers Home. The closest we can come to that is a lecture on the subject that Lincoln wrote, and delivered several times, and wished to see in print. This began as a speech in the 1850s praising modern inventions. It was patterned after a similar performance by the historian George Bancroft.[5] The effort shows that Lincoln, like Mark Twain, like many aspiring authors of the mid-century, hoped to become a paid lecturer. But the changes he made in the text show, even more clearly, what Lincoln considered the supreme inventions of mankind—language and its modes of dissemination (writing and printing). In that age of a dawning technology, he thought the principal mark of human ingenuity was still the ancient "trick" of verbal communication. No wonder his *words* made sense of the merely destructive work of advanced weaponry in the Civil War. It is impossible, reading this early lecture, to doubt that Lincoln knew language is a human glory *because* it is "artificial," an invention:

When we remember that words are *sounds* merely, we shall conclude that the idea of representing those sounds by marks, so that whoever should, at any time after, see the marks would understand what sounds they meant, was a bold and ingenious conception, not likely to occur to one man of a million in the run of a thousand years. And, when it did occur, a distinct mark for each word, giving twenty thousand different marks first to be learned and afterwards remembered, would follow as the second thought, and would present such a difficulty as would lead to the conclusion that the whole thing was impracticable. But the *necessity* still would exist; and we may readily suppose that the idea was conceived, and lost, and reproduced, and dropped, and taken up, again and again, until at last the thought of dividing sounds into parts, and making a mark not to represent a whole sound but only a part of one, and then of combining these marks, not very many in number, upon the principles of permutation, so as to represent any and all of the whole twenty thousand words, and even any additional number, was somehow conceived and pushed into practice. This was the invention of phonetic writing, as distinguished from the clumsy picture writing of some of the nations. That it was difficult of conception and execution is apparent, as well by the foregoing reflections as by the fact that so many tribes of men have come down from Adam's time to ours without ever having possessed it. Its utility may be conceived by the reflection that to *it* we owe everything which distinguishes us from savages. Take it from us, and the Bible, all history, all science, all government, all commerce, and nearly all social intercourse, go with it. [SW 2.7–8]

Lincoln's early experiments with language have an exuberance that is almost comic in its playing with contrivances. His showy 1838 speech to the Young Men's Lyceum is now usually studied to support or refute Edmund Wilson's claim that it contains "oedipal" feelings. But its most obvious feature is the desire to express a complex situation in neatly balanced structures.

> Theirs was the task
> (and nobly they performed it)
>   to possess themselves,

and through themselves, us,
 of this goodly land;
 and to uprear upon its hills
  and its valleys
   a political edifice of liberty
   and of equal rights;
'tis ours only
to transmit these,
 the former, unprofaned by the foot of an
  invader,
 the latter, undecayed by the lapse of time,
  untorn by usurpation—
   to the latest generation that fate shall permit
   the world to know. [SW 1.28]

This is too labored to be clear. One has to look a second time to be sure that "the former" refers to "this goodly land" and "the latter" to "a political edifice." But the exercise is limbering Lincoln up for subtler uses of such balance and antithesis. The parenthetic enriching of a first phrase is something he would use to give depth to his later prose:

Theirs was the task
 (and nobly they performed it)
to possess themselves
 (and through themselves us)
  of this goodly land.

It is the pattern of

The world will little note
 (nor long remember)
  what we do here. [SW 2.536]

Or of:

Fondly do we hope
 (fervently do we pray)
  that this mighty scourge of war
  may speedily pass away. [SW 2.687]

Or:

> with firmness in the right
> (as God gives us to see the right)
> let us strive on to finish
> the work we are in. [SW 2.687]

To end, after complex melodic pairings, with a strong row of monosyllables, was an effect he especially liked. Not only "what we do here" and "the work we are in" and "the world to know" of the above examples, but:

> Trusting in Him,
> who can go with me,
> and remain with you
> and be everywhere for good,
> let us confidently hope
> that all will yet be well. [SW 2.199]

Or this, from the Second Inaugural:

> Both parties deprecated war;
> but one of them would *make* war
> rather than let the nation survive;
> and the other would *accept* war
> rather than let it perish.
> And the war came. [SW 2.686]

Or, from the 1862 message to Congress:

> In *giving* freedom to the *slave*,
> we *assure* freedom to the *free*—
> honorable alike in what we give,
> and what we preserve.
> We shall nobly save,
> or meanly lose
> the last best hope of earth. [SW 2.415]

The closing of Lincoln's early Lyceum sentence ("to the latest generation") also gives a premonition of famous statements to come.

> The fiery trial through which we pass
> will light us down
> > (in honor or dishonor)
> > to the latest generation. [SW 2.415]

Those words to Congress in 1862 were themselves forecast in Lincoln's Peoria address of 1854:

> If we do this,
> > we shall not only have saved the Union,
> > but we shall have so saved it
> > > as to make and to keep it
> > > forever worthy of the saving.
> > We shall have so saved it
> > > that the succeeding millions
> > > of free happy people
> > > > (the world over)
> > > shall rise up
> > > and call us blessed to the latest generations. [SW 1.340]

It would be wrong to think that Lincoln moved toward the plain style of the Gettysburg just by writing shorter, simpler sentences. Actually, that Address ends with a very long sentence —eighty-two words, almost a third of the whole talk's length. So does the Second Inaugural Address, Lincoln's other most famous piece of eloquence: its final sentence runs to seventy-five words. Because of his early experiments, Lincoln's words acquired a flexibility of structure, a rhythmic pacing, a variation in length of words and phrases and clauses and sentences, that make his sentences move "naturally," for all their density and scope.[6] We get inside his verbal workshop when we see how he recast the suggested conclusion to his First Inaugural given him by William Seward.[7] Every sentence is improved, in rhythm, emphasis, or clarity:

Seward	**Lincoln**
I close.	I am loth to close.
We are not, we must not be, aliens or enemies, but fellow-countrymen and brethren.	We are not enemies, but friends. We must not be enemies.
Although passion has strained our bonds of affection too hardly, they must not, I am sure they will not, be broken.	Though passion may have strained, it must not break our bonds of affection.
The mystic chords which, proceeding from so many battle-fields and so many patriot graves, pass through all the hearts and all the hearths in this broad continent of ours, will yet harmonize in their ancient music when breathed upon by the guardian angels of the nation.	The mystic chords of memory, stretching from every battlefield and patriot grave, to every living heart and hearthstone, all over this broad land, will yet swell the chorus of the Union, when again touched, as surely they will be, by the better angels of our nature. [SW 2.224]

Lincoln's lingering monosyllables in the first sentence seem to cling to the occasion, not wanting to break off the communication on which the last hopes of union depend. He simplifies the next sentence using two terms (enemies/friends) where Seward had used two *pairs* (aliens - enemies/fellow countrymen - brethren), but Lincoln repeats "enemies" in the urgent words "We *must* not be enemies." The next sentence is also simplified, to play off against the long, complex image of the concluding sentence, and to repeat the urgent "must." The *bonds* of affection become the *cords* of memory in Lincoln. The bonds and the strings are equally *physical* images. The "chords" are not musical *sounds*. Lincoln spelled "chord" and "cord" indiscriminately—they are the same etymologically. He uses the geometric term "chord" for the line across a circle's arc—as the cord on a tortoise shell gave Apollo his lute.[8] On the other hand, he spelled the word "cord" when calling the Declaration of Independence an electrical *wire* sending messages to American hearts: "the electric cord in that Declaration that links the hearts of patriotic and liberty-loving men together" (SW 1.456).

Seward knew the cord to be breathed on was a *string* (of harp or lute), though his "chords *proceeding from* graves" is grotesque. Lincoln stretches the cords *between* graves and living hearts, as in his image of the Declaration. Seward also gets ethereal when he talks of harmonies that come from breathing on the cords. Lincoln is more believable (and understandable) when he has the better angels of our nature *touch* the cords to swell the chorus of union. Finally, Seward made an odd picture to get his jingle of chords passing *through* "hearts and hearths." Lincoln stretches the lines from graves *to* hearts *and* hearthstones. He gets rid of the crude rhyme by making a chiastic (a-b-b-a) cluster of "*living*-hearts, hearth-*stone*"; the vital heart is contrasted with the inert hearth-stuff. Seward's clumsy image of stringing these two different items on a single cord has disappeared. Lincoln gives to Seward's fustian a pointedness of imagery, a euphony and interplay of short and long sentences and phrases, that lift the conclusion almost to the level of his own best prose.

Lincoln was not abandoning rhetoric in a passage like that, but taking the formal ideals of the past into the modern era, where the pace of life does not allow for the leisurely style of Lincoln's rhetorical forebears. He perfected a new classicism in this effort, since economy had always been the ancient ideal. Hugh Blair, who was still the respected expositor of ancient rhetoric in Lincoln's time, had written:

> The first rule which I shall give for promoting the strength of a sentence is to prune it of all redundant words. . . . The exact import of precision may be drawn from the etymology of the word. It comes from *precidere*, to cut off. It imports retrenching all superfluities and turning the expression so as to exhibit neither more nor less than an exact copy of his ideas who uses it.[9]

Lincoln may have known Blair directly; he certainly knew his principles from derivative texts when he undertook what Joshua Speed called "his study for composition . . . to make short sentences and a compact style."[10] His work seems the very embodiment of Blair's ideal. Take, for instance, the opening to the House Divided Speech of 1858. Don Fehrenbacher has identified the debt this speech owes to Daniel Webster's Reply to Hayne.[11] This makes the contrast in their opening paragraphs more startling. Webster began this way:

> When the mariner has been tossed for many days in thick weather and on an unknown sea, he naturally avails himself of the first pause in the storm, the earliest glance of the sun, to take his latitude, and ascertain how far the elements have driven him from his true course. Let us imitate this prudence, and, before we float farther on the waves of this debate, refer to the point from which we departed, that we may at least be able to conjecture where we now are.[12]

Here is Lincoln's simple exordium:

> If we could first know *where* we are, and *whither* we are tending, we could then better judge *what* to do, and *how* to do it. [SW 1.426]

One might read this as an implicit criticism of Webster, though Lincoln had praised Webster as one who "talked excellent sense and used good language," and he quarried thoughts as well as phrases for several of his own speeches out of the Reply to Hayne.[13] In fact, Lincoln admired all three of the giants in his own "golden age of oratory"—Clay and Calhoun as well as Webster.

The spare quality of Lincoln's prose did not come naturally but was worked at. Blair taught that it was not enough to be plain. The proper words must be thrown into prominence, even if that meant inverting the normal order of a sentence.[14] Twain said that even in swearing you must study to put the "crash-words" in emphatic places.[15] The young Lincoln attacked this problem with a kind of verbal athleticism: "Broken by it, I, too, may be; bow to it I never will" (SW 1.64). He remained fond of grammatical inversion throughout his life, but learned to make it look less studied. In the Second Inaugural, he does not say "We fondly hope and fervently pray," but "Fondly do we hope, fervently do we pray."

Blair recommended defining by balanced antitheses. He gave Pope's famous example:

> Homer was the greatest genius; Virgil the better artist: in the one, we most admire the man; in the other, the work. Homer hurries us with a commanding impetuosity; Virgil leads us with an attractive majesty. . . .[16]

Lincoln describes the hostile sections the nation had fallen into by 1854:

> The South, flushed with triumph and tempted to excesses; the North, betrayed, as they believe, brooding on wrong and burning for revenge. One side will provoke; the other resent. The one will taunt, the other defy; one aggresses, the other retaliates. [SW 1.335]

Lincoln even "shortens his members," as the rhetoricians put it, to suggest the quickening pace toward disaster.

But Blair taught that all such devices will be self-defeating if not used with honest intent to make meaning clearer and truth more compelling:

> For we may rest assured that, whenever we express ourselves ill, there is, besides the mismanagement of language, for the most part some mistake in our manner of conceiving the subject. Embarrassed, obscure and feeble sentences are generally, if not always, the result of embarrassed, obscure and feeble thought. Thought and language act and react upon each other mutually. Logic and rhetoric have here, as in many other cases, a strict connection; and he that is learning to arrange his sentences with accuracy and order is learning, at the same time, to think with accuracy and order. . . .[17]

This, surely, is the secret of Lincoln's eloquence. He not only read aloud, to think his way into sounds, but wrote as a way of ordering his thought. He had a keenness for analytical exercises. He was proud of the mastery he achieved over Euclid's Elements, which awed Herndon and others.[18] He loved the study of grammar, which some think the most arid of subjects.[19] Some claimed to remember his gift for spelling, a view that our manuscripts disprove.[20] Spelling as he had to learn it (apart from etymology) is more arbitrary than logical. It was the logical side of language—the principles of order as these reflect patterns of thought or the external world—that appealed to him.

He was also, Herndon tells us, laboriously precise in his choice of words. He would have agreed with Mark Twain that the difference between the right word and the nearly right one is that between the lightning and a lightning bug.[21] He said, debating Douglas, that his foe confused a similarity of words with a similarity of things—as one might equate a horse chestnut with a chestnut horse (SW 1.511).

Herndon's description of Lincoln's attitude toward words suggests Hugh Blair's standards. Here is Blair:

> The words which a man uses to express his ideas may be faulty in three respects. They may either not express that idea which the author intends, but some other which only resembles it or is akin to it; or they may express that idea, but not quite fully or completely; or they may express it together with something more than he intends . . . . Hardly in any language are there two words that convey precisely the same idea; a person thoroughly conversant in the propriety of the language will always be able to observe something that distinguishes them. . . . The bulk of writers are very apt to confuse them with each other, and to employ them carelessly, merely for the sake of filling up a period or of rounding and diversifying the language, as if their signification were exactly the same, while in truth it is not. Hence a certain mist, and indistinctness, is unwarily thrown over style.[22]

Twain and Herndon both used the same image, of a mist over the sentence, to suggest what the "right word" dispels. Here is Twain:

A powerful agent is the right word: it lights the reader's way and makes it plain; a close approximation to it will answer, and much traveling is done in a well-enough fashion by its help, but we do not welcome it and applaud it and rejoice in it as we do when *the* right one blazes out on us. . . . One has no time to examine the [right] word and vote upon its rank and standing, the automatic recognition of its supremacy is so immediate. There is a plenty of acceptable literature which deals largely in approximations, but it may be likened to a fine landscape seen through the rain; the right word would dismiss the rain, then you would see it better. It doesn't rain when Howells is at work.[23]

Neither, Herndon says, did it rain when Lincoln was at work:

He saw all things through a perfect mental lens. There was no diffraction or refraction there. He was not impulsive, fanciful, or imaginative; but cold, calm, and precise. He threw his whole mental light around the object, and, after a time, substance and quality stood apart, form and color took their appropriate place, and all was clear and exact in his mind. . . . In the search for words Mr. Lincoln was often at a loss . . . because there were, in the vast store of words, so few that contained the exact coloring, power, and shape of his ideas.[24]

Lincoln was merciless in pointing out his opponents' loose use of words. When Stephen Douglas said that Winfield Scott's nomination posed a peril to the Union, Lincoln replied:

Well, we ought all to be startled at the view of "peril to the Union," but it may be a little difficult for some shortsighted mortals to perceive such peril in the *nomination* of Scott. Mark you, it is the *nomination* and not the *election* which produces the peril. The Judge does not say the election, and he cannot mean the election, because he constantly assures us there is no prospect of Scott's election. He could not be so alarmed at what he is so sure will never happen. In plain truth I suppose he did mean the election, so far as he meant anything; but, feeling that his whole proposition was mere nonsense, he did not think of it distinctly enough to enable him to speak with any precision. [SW 1.277]

Like other logicians, like Lewis Carroll and Edgar Poe, Lincoln saw fantasy in the illogical use of words. Douglas accused Winfield Scott of entertaining reservations about the Whigs' platform because he had said, "I accept the nomination, with the resolution annexed."

> In the North it will be said he accepts the nomination notwithstanding the platform; that he accepts it although he defies the platform; that he accepts it although he spits upon the platform.

"Verily," Lincoln rejoined, "these are wonderful substitutes for the word 'with'"—and he suggested they be substituted for "with" in a Bible verse like "Enoch walked with [although he spat upon?] God." In a dizzy exercise, he turns Douglas's exegetical tool on his own words.

> As another example, take from Judge Douglas's ratification speech a sentence in relation to the democratic platform and the democratic ticket, Pierce and King, which is as follows:
> "With such a platform, and with such a ticket, a glorious victory awaits us."
> Now, according to the Judge's rule of criticizing General Scott's language, the above sentence of his will, without perversion of meaning, admit of being read in each of the following ways:
> "*Notwithstanding* such a platform, and notwithstanding such a ticket, a glorious victory awaits us."
> "*Although we defy* such a platform, and although we defy such a ticket, a glorious victory awaits us."
> "*Although we spit upon* such a platform and although we spit upon such a ticket, a glorious victory awaits us." [SW 1.279–80][25]

Lincoln's responsive Whig audience could anticipate where he was going, yet there was a natural climax in the way he ordered

Douglas's "synonyms," giving this passage an inexorable air of letting nonsense work itself out to its own demise.

When the Dred Scott decision said that the Constitution applied only to free subjects in the eighteenth century, Lincoln took Douglas's defense of that position and did another of his word substitutions, to reduce his opponent to absurdity:

> Suppose after you read it [the Declaration of Independence] in the old-fashioned way, you read it once more with Judge Douglas' version. It will run thus: "We hold these truths to be self-evident, that all British subjects who were on this continent eighty-one years ago, were created equal to all British subjects born and *then* residing in Great Britain." [SW 1.400]

Parker had made a similar substitution in 1848: "To make our theory accord with our practice, we ought to recommit the Declaration to the hands which drafted that great state paper and declare that 'All men are created equal, and endowed by their Creator with certain unalienable rights if born of white mothers; but if not, not.' "[26]

In his quest to use the right words himself, Lincoln often achieved a clarity that is its own source of aesthetic satisfaction. There is no better description of this effect than Blair's:

> Perspicuity in writing is not to be considered as only a sort of negative virtue, a freedom from defect. It has a higher merit. It is a degree of positive beauty. We are pleased with an author, we consider him as deserving praise, who frees us from all fatigue of searching for his meaning, who carries us through his subject without any embarrassment or confusion, whose style flows always like a limpid stream where we see to the very bottom.[27]

In a text like Lincoln's famous letter to Horace Greeley, even the sentence structure seems to present its own case. The grammar argues. By ordering a series of simple and disjunctive sentences, Lincoln patiently exhausts all alternatives. Beginning his sentences with repeated "If"s (anaphora), Lincoln rings all changes on the concessive clause (granting irrelevant assertions or assumptions for now) and the hypothetical clause (posing case after case for its own treatment). The analysis of every permutation of the subject seals off misunderstandings as if Lincoln were quietly closing door after door. The points are advanced like a series of theorems in Euclid, as clear, as sequential, as compelling:

> I have just read yours of the 19th instant, addressed to myself through the *New York Tribune*.
>
> If there be in it any statements or assumptions of fact which I may know to be erroneous, I do not now and here controvert them.
>
> If there be in it any inferences which I believe to be falsely drawn, I do not now and here argue against them.
>
> If there be perceptible in it an impatient and dictatorial tone, I waive it, in deference to an old friend whose heart I have always supposed to be right.
>
> As to the policy I "seem to be pursuing," as you say, I have not meant to leave anyone in doubt. I would save the Union. I would save it the shortest way under the Constitution.
>
> The sooner the national authority can be restored, the nearer the Union will be—the Union as it was.
>
> If there be those who would not save the Union unless they could at the same time save slavery, I do not agree with them.
>
> My paramount object in this struggle is to save the Union, and not either to save or destroy slavery.
>
> If I could save the Union without freeing any slave, I would do it; if I could save it by freeing all the slaves, I would do it; and if I could save it by freeing some and leaving others alone, I would also do that.
>
> What I do about slavery and the coloured race, I do because I believe it helps to save the Union; and what I forbear, I forbear because I do not believe it would help to save the Union.
>
> I shall do less whenever I shall believe that what I am doing hurts the cause; and I shall do more whenever I shall believe doing more will help the cause.

> I shall try to correct errors where shown to be errors, and I shall adopt new views as fast as they shall appear to be true views.
>
> I have here stated my purpose according to my views of official duty, and I intend no modification of my oft-expressed personal wish that all men everywhere be free.[28]

This is the highest art, which conceals itself. The opening sentences perform the classical role of an exordium, limiting one's task, disarming hostility, finding common ground with one's audience. The traditional *captatio benevolentiae* (claim on good will) could not be better exemplified than in Lincoln's address to his old friend's heart.

While making his own position clear, Lincoln professes a readiness to alter course if he is proved wrong. But he promises to do that only within the framework he has constructed. (He will change *only* if the change saves the Union.) He sounds deferential rather than dogmatic, yet he is in fact precluding all norms but his own. It is the same kind of rhetorical trap he used in his most famous statement of alternative possibilities:

> "A House divided against itself cannot stand."
>
> I believe this government cannot endure, permanently half *slave* and half *free*.
>
> I do not expect the Union to be *dissolved*—I do not expect the house to fall—but I *do* expect it will cease to be divided.
>
> It will become *all* one thing or *all* the other.
>
> Either the *opponents* of slavery will arrest the further spread of it, and place it where the public mind shall rest in the belief that it is in course of ultimate extinction; or its *advocates* will push it forward, till it shall become alike lawful in *all* the states, *old* as well as *new*—*North* as well as *South*.
>
> Have we no *tendency* to the latter condition? [SW 1.426]

Lincoln's own underlinings reinforce sentence structure in suggesting that these two and only these two outcomes are possible.

The language seems stripped of all figurative elements—though Lincoln has begun with a biblical figure that seems to pre-empt criticism of its premise. Lincoln's logic can be, and has been, challenged; but the ordering of the words *seems* logical, perspicuous. It is also, in its clipped quality, urgent. The rapid deployment of all options seems to press on the reader a need to decide. Lincoln's language is honed to a purpose.

Looking back to the nineteenth century's long speeches and debates, we might deplore the more disjunct "blips" of communication in our time. Television and other modern developments are blamed for a shortening of the modern attention span. But a similar process was at work in Lincoln's time, and he welcomed it. The railroad, the telegraph, the steamship had quickened the pace of events. Thoughts and words took on new and nervous rhythms. Lincoln, who considered language the world's great invention, welcomed a cognate invention, telegraphy. He used the telegraph to keep up with his generals—he even experimented with telegraph wires strung to reconnaissance balloons.[29] As president, Lincoln worked intimately with the developer of telegraphy in America, Joseph Henry, the president of the Smithsonian Institution.[30] He had praised the lightning "harnessed to take his [man's] tidings in a trifle less than no time" (SW 2.3). Lincoln spent long hours in the telegraph center at the War Department, and was impatient with the fumbling and imprecise language still being used on this instrument, which demands clarity as well as concision.[31] Hay reflects Lincoln's relief when he found an efficient user of modern language in one of his military engineers:

> This is Herman Haupt, the railroad man at Alexandria. He has, as Chase says, a Major General's head on his shoulders. The President is particularly struck with the business-like character of his dispatch, telling in the fewest words the information most sought for, which contrasted strongly with the weak, whiney, vague, and incorrect dispatches of the whilom General-in-Chief [McClellan]. [P. 46.][32]

Lincoln's respect for General Grant came, in part, from the contrast between McClellan's waffling and Grant's firm grasp of the right words to use in explaining or arguing for a military operation. Lincoln sensed what Grant's later publisher, Mark Twain, did, that the West Pointer who once taught mathematics was a master of expository prose. Sitting his horse during a pause in battle, Grant could write model instructions for his subordinates—a skill John Keegan compares to the Duke of Wellington's. Keegan even says: "If there is a single contemporary document which explains 'why the North won the Civil War,' that abiding conundrum of American historical inquiry, it is *The Personal Memoirs of U. S. Grant.*"[33] In an answering hyperbole, James McPherson has claimed that Lincoln won the war by his language.[34] The two half-truths contain at least one whole truth —that well-focused words were the medium through which Grant and Lincoln achieved their amazing degree of mutual sympathy and military accord.[35]

There was no possibility of misunderstanding a dispatch like Lincoln's of August 17, 1864, "Hold on with a bull-dog gripe, and chew & choke, as much as possible"—a message that made Grant burst into laughter and say, "The President has more nerve than any of his advisers."[36] Lincoln's telegraphic eloquence has a monosyllabic and staccato beat:

Have none of it. Stand firm. [SW 2.190]

On that point hold firm, as with a chain of steel. [CW 4.151]

Watch it every day, and hour, and force it. [SW 2.615]

Events were moving too fast for the more languid phrases of the past. As a speaker, Lincoln grasped ahead of time Twain's insight of the postwar years: "Few sinners are saved after the first twenty minutes of a sermon."[37] The trick, of course, was not simply to be brief but to say a great deal in the fewest words. Lincoln justly boasted, of his Second Inaugural's six hundred words, "Lots of wisdom in that document, I suspect."[38] The same is even truer of the Gettysburg Address, which uses roughly half that number of words.

The unwillingness to waste words shows up in the Address's telegraphic quality—the omission of most coupling words—that rhetoricians call asyndeton.[39] Triple phrases sound as to a drum-beat, with no "and" or "but" to slow their insistency:

we are engaged . . .
We are met . . .
We have come . . .
we can not dedicate . . .
we can not consecrate . . .
we can not hallow . . .

that from these honored dead . . .
that we here highly resolve . . .
that this nation, under God . . .

government of the people,
by the people,
for the people . . .

Despite the suggestive images of birth, testing, and rebirth, the speech is surprisingly bare of ornament. The language is itself made strenuous, its musculature easily traced, so even the grammar becomes a form of rhetoric. By repeating the antecedent as often as possible, instead of referring to it indirectly by pronouns like "it" or "they," or by backward referential words like "former" and "latter," Lincoln interlocks his sentences, making of them a constantly self-referential system. This linking up by explicit repetition amounts to a kind of hook-and-eye method for joining the parts of his address. The rhetorical devices are almost invisible, since they use no figurative language or formal tropes.

Four score and seven years ago our fathers brought forth on this continent, *a new nation*, *conceived* in Liberty *and dedicated* to the proposition that all men are created equal.

Now we are engaged in A GREAT CIVIL WAR, testing whether *that nation*, or any nation *so conceived and so dedicated*, can long endure.

We are met on a great <u>*battle-field*</u> of THAT WAR.

We have come to <u>dedicate</u> a portion of <u>*that field*</u>, as a final resting place for those who here gave their lives that *that nation* might live. It is altogether fitting and proper that we should do this.

But, in a larger sense, we can not <u>dedicate</u>—we can not <u>consecrate</u>—we cannot hallow—this ground.

The brave men, living and dead, **who struggled here**, have <u>consecrated</u> it, far above our poor power to add or detract. The world will little note, nor long remember, what we say here, but it can never forget what they did here.

It is for us, the living, rather, to be <u>dedicated</u> here to the unfinished work which they **who fought here** have thus far so nobly advanced. It is, rather, for us to be here <u>dedicated</u> to the great task remaining before us—that from **THESE HONORED DEAD** we take increased devotion to that cause for which they gave the last full measure of devotion —

that we here highly resolve that **THESE DEAD** shall not have died in vain—that this nation, under God, shall have a new birth of freedom—and that government of the people, by the people, for the people, shall not perish from the earth.

Each of the paragraphs printed separately here is bound to the preceding and the following by some resumptive element. Only the first and last paragraph do not (because they cannot) have this two-way connection to their setting. Not all of these "pointer" phrases replace grammatical antecedents in the technical sense. But Lincoln makes them perform analogous work. The nation is declared, again, to be "consecrated" and "dedicated" before each of these terms is given a further two (separate) uses for individuals present at the ceremony, who repeat (as it were) the national consecration. By this reliance on a few words in different contexts, the compactness of the themes is emphasized. A similar linking process is performed, almost subliminally, by the repeated pinning of statements to *that* field, *these* dead, who died *here*, for *that* (kind of) nation. The reverential touching, over and over, of the charged moment and place leads Lincoln to use "here" six times in the short text, the adjectival "that" five times, "this" four times.[40] The spare vocabulary is not impoverishing because of the subtly interfused constructions, in which Charles Smiley identifies "six antitheses, six instances of balanced sentence structure, two cases of anaphora, and four alliterations." "Plain speech" was never *less* artless. Lincoln forged a new lean language to humanize and redeem the first modern war.

Some have claimed, simplistically, that Lincoln achieved a "down-to-earth" style by using short Anglo-Saxon words rather than long Latin ones in the Address. Such people cannot have read the Address with care. Lincoln talks of a nation "conceived in Liberty," not born in freedom; of one "dedicated to [a] proposition," not vowed to a truth; of a "consecrated" nation whose soldiers show their "devotion"—Latinate terms all. Lincoln was even criticized, in the past, for using so "unliterary" a word as "proposition."[41] These criticisms are based on a misunderstanding. Though Lincoln used fertility *imagery* from the cemetery movement, his *message* was telegraphic (itself a Latin term, from the Greek). He liked to talk of the theorems and axioms of democracy, comparing them to Euclid's "propositions" (SW 2.19). He was a Transcendentalist without the fuzziness. He spoke a modern language because he was dealing with a scientific age, for which abstract words are appropriate. His urgency was more a matter of the speech's internal "wiring" and *workability* than of anything so crude as "calling a spade a spade." He was not addressing an agrarian future but a mechanical one. His speech is economical, taut, interconnected, like the machinery he tested and developed for battle. Words were weapons, for him, even though he meant them to be weapons of peace in the midst of war.

This was the perfect medium for changing the way most Americans thought about the nation's founding acts. Lincoln does not argue law or history, as Daniel Webster did. He *makes* history. He does not come to present a theory, but to impose a symbol, one tested in experience and appealing to national values, with an emotional urgency entirely expressed in calm abstractions (fire in ice). He came to change the world, to effect an intellectual revolution. No other words could have done it. The miracle is that these words did. In his brief time before the crowd at Gettysburg he wove a spell that has not, yet, been broken—he called up a new nation out of the blood and trauma.

---

1. Actually, Hemingway derived "all Modern American literature" from Twain's novel, but he seems to have been thinking of novels as coterminous with literature (*Green Hills of Africa* [Charles Scribner's Sons, 1935], p. 22).

2. Hugh Kenner, "Politics of the Plain Style," in *Mazes* (North Point Press, 1989), pp. 261–69.

3. Hay used the "Pike County" dialects that Twain also deployed. Hay regretted the change of his birthplace's original name to the more genteel Warsaw.

4. Hackett, an American who several times took his most famous role to Shakespeare's homeland, was "undoubtedly the best Falstaff of his time both in America and England" by the time Lincoln saw him play the role in the actor's sixties (*Dictionary of American Biography*, s.v. Hackett).

5. Robert V. Bruce, *Lincoln and the Tools of War* (University of Illinois Press, 1989), p. 14. Lincoln told Lewis Gallatin, the Harvard paleontologist, about this lecture during a White House visit, increasing the likelihood that he discussed it with Hay in their philological sessions. Cf. George Bancroft, *Literary and Historical Miscellanies* (Harper & Brothers, 1855), pp. 481–517.

6. Herndon says Lincoln labored to vary the length of his sentences, using Calhoun's speeches as models (Herndon-Weik, p. 421).

7. For Seward's role in the drafting of the First Inaugural, see Earl W. Wiley, "Abraham Lincoln: His Emergence as the Voice of the People," in William Norwood Brigance, *A History and Criticism of American Public Address* (McGraw-Hill, 1943), vol. 2, pp. 866–69.

8. SW 2.377, letter to General McClellan: "His route is the arc of a circle, while yours is the chord."

9. Hugh Blair, *Lectures on Rhetoric and Belles Lettres* (Edinburgh, 1783), in the facsimile edited by Harold F. Harding (Southern Illinois University Press, 1965), vol. 1, pp. 226, 189. For Blair's importance in nineteenth-century American rhetoric, see Brigance, *American Public Address*, vol. 2, pp. 202–4.

10. Herndon-Weik, p. 421.

11. Don E. Fehrenbacher, *Prelude to Greatness: Lincoln in the 1850s* (Stanford University Press, 1962), p. 180. Lincoln may have taken his Bible verse from Webster as well. Speaking on May 22, 1857, Webster said: "If a house be divided against itself, it will fall, and crush everybody in it." *Writings and Speeches of Daniel Webster* (Little, Brown, 1903), vol. 4, p. 244.

12. *The Papers of Daniel Webster: Speeches and Formal Writings*, vol. 1, *1800–1833*, edited by Charles Wiltse and Alan R. Berolzheimer (University Press of New England, 1986), p. 287.

13. Richard N. Current, "Lincoln and Daniel Webster," in *Speaking*

of Abraham Lincoln (University of Illinois Press, 1983), pp. 11–15. Cf. Hertz, p. 118: "Lincoln thought that Webster's great speech in reply to Hayne was the very best speech that was ever delivered."

14. Blair, *Lectures*, pp. 232–36. Especially p. 236:

> But whether we practice inversion or not, and in whatever part of the sentences we dispose of the capital words, it is always a point of great moment that these capital words shall stand clear and disentangled from any other words that would clog them.

15. Twain's attitude toward "crash-words" is Blair's toward "capital words." Hank Morgan criticizes the King's swearing: "the profanity was not good, being awkwardly put together, and with the crash-word almost in the middle instead of at the end, where of course it ought to have been" (*A Connecticut Yankee in King Arthur's Court*, ch. 35).

16. Blair, *Lectures*, pp. 243–44.

17. Ibid., pp. 245–46. This is, of course, the classical view: "Rhetoric plays a counter part [a term from dance moves] to logic" (Aristotle, *Rhetoric* 354 1).

18. Herndon-Weik, p. 248. F. B. Carpenter, *The Inner Life of Abraham Lincoln: Six Months at the White House* (Riverside Press, 1877), pp. 314–15.

19. David C. Mearns, *Three Presidents and Their Books: Fifth Annual Windsor Lectures* (University of Illinois Press, 1955), p. 54. Mark Twain, known like Lincoln for his mastery of the vernacular, was nonetheless a stickler for grammar, and satirized Southern deficiencies in the matter (*Life on the Mississippi*, ch. 44, in *Mississippi Writings*, p. 489).

20. Herndon-Weik, p. 35.

21. Twain, Letter of Oct. 15, 1888,

22. Blair, *Lectures*, pp. 189, 195.

23. Twain, "William Dean Howells," in *Complete Essays*, edited by Charles Neider (Doubleday, 1963), pp. 400–401.

24. Herndon-Weik, pp. 475–77.

25. Attention to the real force of a word like "with" is characteristic of Blair's criticism:

> *With* expresses a more close and immediate connection, *by* a more remote one. We kill a man *with* a sword; he dies *by* violence. The criminal is bound *with* ropes *by* the executioners. The proper distinction is elegantly marked in a passage of Dr. Robertson's history of Scotland. When one of the old Scottish kings was making an inquiry into the tenure *by* which his nobles held their lands, they started up and drew their swords: "*By* these," said they, "we acquired our lands, and *with* them we will defend them." [*Lectures*, p. 201.]

26. Parker, "The Political Destination of America," in Cobbe edition 4.91. Twain would later rewrite in this spirit the "Battle Hymn of the Republic": "Christ died to make men holy, He died to make *white* men

free" (*Mark Twain Fables of Man*, edited by John S. Tuckey [University of California Press, 1972], p. 418).

27. Blair, *Lectures*, p. 186.

28. SW 2.357–58. I print the text as Charles N. Smiley did in *Classical Journal* 13 (1917), pp. 125–26. Smiley, a classical rhetorician, counted in this letter "six completely balanced sentences, eight cases of anaphora, six instances of similar word endings [homoeoteleuton], six antitheses."

29. Bruce, *Tools of War*, pp. 85–88.

30. Samuel F. B. Morse just developed the code to be used on Henry's transmitter: Robert V. Bruce, *The Launching of Modern American Science, 1846–76* (Alfred A. Knopf, 1987), pp. 141, 150–57, 275–76.

31. See the memoirs of the War Department's telegrapher, David Homer Bates, *Lincoln in the Telegraph Office* (Century Co., 1907). By setting up telegraphic liaison with his generals, through Henry Halleck, Lincoln created what T. Harry Williams has called the first "modern system of command for a modern war," one "superior to anything achieved in Europe until von Moltke forged the Prussian staff machine of 1865 and 1870" (*Lincoln and His Generals* [Vintage, 1952], pp. 302–3).

32. Lincoln used Haupt to circularize scientists for suggestions on war-related research (Bruce, *Tools of War*, pp. 215–17). Haupt's reciprocal esteem for Lincoln is expressed in the *Reminiscences of General Herman Haupt* (Wright and Joys Co., 1901), pp. 297–301.

33. John Keegan, *The Mask of Command* (Penguin, 1987), p. 202.

34. James M. McPherson, "How Lincoln Won the War with Metaphors," in *Abraham Lincoln and the Second American Revolution* (Oxford University Press, 1990), pp. 93–112. Not all the language McPherson adduces is metaphorical, but it is all clear and most of it is brief.

35. For evidence of that accord, see *The Papers of Ulysses S. Grant*, edited by John Y. Simon (Southern Illinois University Press), vol. 9 (1982), pp. 196–97; vol. 10 (1982), p. 381; vol. 11 (1984), pp. 45, 263, 280, 360, 425, 441; vol. 12 (1984), p. 185.

36. SW 2.620. Horace Potter, *Campaigning with Grant* (1897, reprinted by Da Capo, 1986), p. 279.

37. Hannibal *Courier-Post*, March 1, 1835.

38. Francis B. Carpenter, *Six Months at the White House* (Riverside Press, 1877), p. 234.

39. Lane Cooper, the classicist, noted Lincoln's striking asyndeton in *The Rhetoric of Aristotle* (Appleton-Century, 1932), p. xxxiii.

40. Lincoln, conscious of the repeated "here," took out a seventh use in the phrase "they [here] gave the last full measure of devotion" (CW 7.23). The frequency of "that" in the speech was criticized by William E. Barton (*Lincoln at Gettysburg* [Bobbs-Merrull, 1930], p. 147).

41. Cf. Barton, *Lincoln at Gettysburg*, p. 148; Louis A. Warren, *Lincoln's Gettysburg Declaration* (Lincoln National Life Foundation, 1964), p. 106. Lincoln's fondness for the word "proposition" is apparent at SW 1.277, 683, 732, 741.

Richard Slotkin

A professor of American studies at Wesleyan University, Slotkin (b. 1942) is the author of an influential trilogy of books on the mythology of the American frontier—*Regeneration Through Violence*, *The Fatal Environment*, and *Gunfighter Nation*—as well as three historical novels—*The Crater*, about the failed Petersburg mine assault of 1864; *The Return of Henry Starr*, the story of an Oklahoma outlaw; and *Abe: A Novel of the Young Lincoln* (2000), a fictionalized account of the first 23 years of the future President's life. Undaunted by the sparse documentary record of his early years, or by Lincoln's well-known reticence on the subject, Slotkin brings to his task a shrewd eye for what historian Geoffrey Ward has called "the small details that make imagined past events immediate and real." In his boldest move, Slotkin combines the historic Lincoln's two flatboat trips down the Mississippi into a single mythic journey that owes much to *Adventures of Huckleberry Finn*, including the appearance of Sephus, a runaway slave. The final chapter of the book, printed below, finds its hero emerging into the milieu that will transform him, and ultimately allow him to transform his country: politics. A reinvigoration of the romantic tradition that ascribed great importance to Lincoln's frontier origins, *Abe* also draws from the opposing tradition that emphasized how hard Lincoln strove to escape from the rough, crude world that helped make him.

FROM

Abe: A Novel of the Young Lincoln

The Candidate

New Salem, June 1831–March 1832
He had found the stage he was looking for. All he wanted was the part to play on it. He didn't know at first what the part would be—he knew it would have to be big, that's all. *When I was a child I thought there was just two ways for a man to get things done. The story-book way, which an ordinary living man could never do, of Moses and Washington; and the ornery bully-boy way of Pap,*

and the Grigsbys, and Allen Gentry. But now I'm a man I see differ-
ent. Between Sephus, Ruby, and the Old Man I have learned a thing
or two. There's ways between *the impossible of Washington and*
Moses, and the low-down skunk-eating meanness of Grigsby and Jones
and Starkey, and Uncle Mordecai. And Pap.

And it ain't Judge Davis's way neither. I don't want a world of my
own making, and every man and woman in it smiles to my face and
wishes he could stick a knife in me.

So he didn't care if, at the start, New Salem took him for
"Offutt's man." He was himself alone. Nobody, not even himself, knew all of what he was, let alone what he might be. New
Salem's laughter just gave him a blind from which to take in the
lie of things and make his plans. He would earn the respect of
men like Graham, Rutledge, and Kelso; find what they valued
and show them he had it, or knew where he could put his hands
on it. And he would catch the eye, and whatever else there was
to catch, of Annie Rutledge, because she was the finest, clever-
est, sharpest, prettiest, most hot-eyed red-headed girl he ever
met. And he'd whup Jack Armstrong, have to, because there can't
be but the one Big Bull to a lick.

Not a year since he first saw New Salem, and he had got
nearly all the things he wished for. Then Offutt went and put
him in the way of a brawl with Jack Armstrong.

Rutledge and Graham were very much afraid the scrap would
hurt him with respectable folks, the election only six months
away. "If you win they will think you are one of the rowdies, and
if you lose . . ." Graham beseeched him.

"Why would I lose?" As if the idea was outlandish. Besides,
Abe had his own calculation as to the consequences of wrassling
Jack Armstrong, and was set on it, pig-headed, no matter *what*
the best heads in the county might think.

The best heads had to ask themselves if they hadn't made a
mistake after all. And that was the moment Dr. Allen picked to
spring his long-laid ambush on the candidate.

New Salem, March 25, 1832
At the end of the evening's debate, the Doctor proposed a subject for their next encounter: "Resolved: that the institution of

negro slavery is contrary to the law of nature, and of nature's God."

The subject made Rutledge uneasy. He did not want the Club divided with the election approaching, and this was an issue on which honest men—*these* honest men—differed strongly. Not that any of them had the least interest either in owning negroes or setting them at liberty. But the lack of material interest somehow made their difference more intense: a question of conscience and moral character. Rutledge expected the Club to shun Allen's proposal. But to his surprise, there was a rumble of support for the notion—and from his nephew-in-law Camron too! albeit with a hang-dog look. Graham looked puzzled. Kelso looked grim.

"Well then, gentlemen, since you will have it so," Rutledge said ruefully. "Who will contest the palm?"

There was a silence. Herndon cleared his throat. "How about you, Lincoln?"

"Yes indeed," said Camron—refusing to meet his Uncle's eye. "It would be good practice for our candidate."

Rutledge's lifted eyebrow told Graham his friend was alarmed. Graham smelt conspiracy. Kelso *harumphed*, and lowered like a fat thunderhead. Lincoln looked cool enough. "That suits me." There wasn't anything else a man could say under the circumstances, not without backing down.

"And who to oppose?"

"Well," said the Doctor, "since it was my suggestion, I suppose it is only fair . . ."

Rutledge gave him an empty grin. "Then all that remains is to determine who shall argue the affirmative, and who the negative." It was bad business that would cost Abe votes either way.

"Oh, I don't mind arguing the affirmative," said the Doctor with elaborate off-handedness.

"And Lincoln the negative?"

Abe shrugged carelessly, "I don't mind."

There was a silence while Rutledge, Graham, and Kelso took in the fact that they had been circumvented. The only question was, how deep did the malice go? Were their colleagues just aiming to make Abe sweat a little, for his too-easy winning of the prize? Or did they mean to do him in?

Lincoln seemed neither to notice nor to care. After the meeting broke up, Graham took Abe aside and said he was sorry it turned out so. But Kelso said there was nothing to worry about. "What a man argues in here is secret and sacred. That's our rule. So have no fear, my son, but let her rip!"

Graham and Rutledge exchanged looks: Kelso was too sanguine. Nothing was secret very long in this town. If you were to switch from a right- to a left-hand hold, taking a piss in your own outhouse, the town would hear of it inside a week.

"I'm not worried," said Abe. "I've argued him down before." He grinned wolfish: "I've seen the institution first-hand. If I can't argue against it, I don't know—"

The three men were took poorly at the same time. "Abe?" said Graham. "Don't you know what 'the negative case' is?"

He got it, sudden: his brownish skin went janders-yellow, his slab-lips bloodless. His eyes winced.

"Resolved: that slavery *is* against the law of nature, and of nature's God," Kelso recited grimly. "You have got to argue that it *ain't*."

Rutledge was stern: "And fight Jack Armstrong the day after that."

New Salem, March 31–April, 1, 1832
The day before the debate he went off into the woods, to his secret clearing on the other side of the Sangamon, to puzzle out his argument. He meant to stay all night if he had to: packed a cut of meat and some corn bread, and a flask of Elixir against the night chills and paludals. He took his *Orator* and *Elocution* and his Grimshaw too, but they weren't help enough. What he wanted was a book that did for *thinking* what Cradok's *Western River Pilot* did for the River: something to map the shoals and snags and teach you how to run the bends. This argument had a doubleback in it as bad as any the Old Man had ever thrown him.

He ate supper for strength, a sip of Elixir against the chill as evening came down. The Elixir warmed his chest and belly, and made his thoughts squirm more energetically without helping them make more sense. The only thing that got clearer were his wishes and hankerings. He wished he had Ma here: she had a sharp-eyed way of listening at him that woke him up and helped him hone a sharp edge on his thinking. A small bright-eyed blackbird flipped into the pignut tree and perched, looking down at him speculatively. *All right then, you stand up there for Ma and let's see what comes of it.* Konkapot would have liked him talking things out with a blackbird. *But Konkapot is dead.*

The law of nature and of nature's God. Ma would say the same as Mam: *There can't a sparrow fall but the Lord is in it.* The bird bobbed her head, to signify that suited *her* notions.

"I don't like to be the one to say it," he told the bird, "but seems to me the Lord is a little careless when it comes to birds." And not just birds. *Everyone and everything dies, and I'm hanged if I can see the reason or justice in it. Not that it makes a difference what Abe Lincoln thinks.* Abe took another sip and stretched out on his blankets, the Elixir had a kind of softening effect on the knobby ground. "Here lies poor Lincoln 'neath the sod," he said. "Have mercy on his spirit, God. As he would have, if he was . . ."

The blackbird cocked her head at Abe. Abe's campfire made orange points in her bright eyes. While he'd been talking to her the dark had come down. He took another sup of Elixir against the chill. The sang-roots loosened the cramp in his brains and made it easier to talk to the blackbird.

Listen, he told her, *in my experience Providence don't take account of nothing smaller than the United States of America. Don't care for sparrows nor pigeons, don't care if Mam dies of Milk-sick, don't care if Uncle Mordecai kills a million Injuns and their camel and their ass, don't care if you buy dis 'ooman Catrun Massa—don't care if Gentry sells Sephus to be seasoned or whipped or worked to death on Red River. Providence ain't reasonable, nor kind, nor even mean the way a man or a woman would be: if there's any justice in it, it's cold and slow as drip-water wearing at a rock or tree-roots working at a fault in the stone till they pick it apart. Or it gathers blind like the River and drives downstream by its own heedless rule, busting out this levee and flooding the bottoms, raising up that levee for a man to grow sugar and sell niggers behind, drownding babies and floating steamboats with naked women painted on the sides full of actors and merchants, but always driving down and down and down the ways it is bound to go . . .*

. . . and he was adrift on the River, rushing swift and silent towards the rising shadows. A black ball bobbed in the welter alongside, a face—

Sephus! His eyes were white . . .

The River foaming rolled Sephus under and he was gone in the terrible hurl of dark water that still rushed Abe headlong towards the shadows, lifting him sailing him into the . . .

. . . Sunlight?

Sunlight flickering through leaves. There was a tree-root sticking in his back. Ouch.

Abe lifted his head—his brains bulged a little and his eyes watered. The Elixir: it was greased lightning going down, but heavier'n a sack of lead shot waking up next day.

It wasn't till he had gone down to the Sangamon and washed the sleep out of his eyes that he realized the gravity in his brains was more than the dregs of the Elixir. Whether it was the bird, the books, the sang-roots, or something else that gave it to him, his head was full of argument—pretty *heavy* argument too, if he was any judge.

That was a signifying dream that come to him: he reckoned it meant Sephus was dead. And it was on him how Sephus died—maybe not the whole of it, but a good piece of it. It was the dead weight of the man Sephus that give his argument that leaden heft in his mind. It was almost more than he could carry—almost. But it was his best holt, and if it wasn't good enough for the work . . . ? Then he'd take his whupping. And first thing next morning get out of bed and whup Jack Armstrong in front of Clary's Grove and New Salem both. And if he lost that one too . . . ?

Well, he'd done what he could. Whup, die, or go to Texas— he was never more ready for anything in his life.

New Salem, April 2, 1832

The Clary's Grove Boys, hilarious, clad every one in his finery and foofaraw, hailed their champion to the goose-pulling ground. The crowd opened up to make way for the Boys, who bullied up half the wide circle of bodies that framed the wrassling ring.

From the opposite side here came Long Abe Lincoln, head and shoulders above the crowd he waded through.

Every man in New Salem district, and every boy who could get away from chores, was in the crowd. The women were supposed to keep away, but most found places at the upstairs windows of the Herndons' house and Onstott's cooper shop, which had a view of the grounds. Of the Club only Fat Jack Kelso stood with Abe and Denton Offutt. Rutledge and Graham took their stand in sight of the ground where a man was free to suppose they had come in the ordinary course of business. If they joined the crowd they would appear to countenance a spectacle that could do their candidate no good. But to stay at home might suggest they did not support Abe. Besides, they were as het up as every other man woman and child in the county to see who would come out on top.

Offutt and Uncle Clary shook hands and gave their wagers (ten dollars silver, each) to Babb McNabb to hold. Ten dollars was the least of it: the wagering had gone on for days, odds running from even-up to Armstrong, five against three.

Jack glowered at Abe. His retainers, Royal Clary and Pleasant Armstrong and Bully Bob Kirby, stripped off his cockfeathered hat, fringed hunting-shirt, and white undershirt. Jack swelled up his chest so the muscles rolled across his breast and back and upper arms. He roared like a bear, bulging his eyes out. The Clary's Grove Boys hollered for Jack to go on and show that Bean-pole who was boss! The whole crowd bellowed its joy, and Armstrong felt his strength swell with it.

Jack stomped up to meet Lincoln and McNabb in the middle. He was shorter than Lincoln by a head, but a good bit wider in the shoulders and hips, heavy-boned, heavy-muscled. At the first look, Abe was just that bean-pole the Boys had called him, lean and narrow throughout his whole extraordinary length, so narrow his head looked oversized. But Armstrong had a closer sight of what Lincoln had hid under his ragged shirt and pants: his chest was solid, lean twists of muscle showed in his neck and shoulders, his arms were like braided cable. Those arms were plenty long too—sort of freakish long, as if Lincoln had unfairly spliced on an extra foot of reach. It gave Jack Armstrong to think about that story of the ax held straight out while a man counted one hundred.

Little McNabb was dwarfed by the two wrasslers, but he had the law to lend him dignity. "This here's straight wrasslin', not a scuffle. No kickin' no buttin' no gougin'. No *grabbin'* holts below the belt, but you kin hip-throw an' bang shins all you're a mind to." He looked from one to the other to see he'd been heard. "Shake hands, and git at it."

The Boys hollered for blood. The two men hunched their backs and circled, swiping for a hold first with this arm, then that. The Boys were screaming for Jack to close and whup that son of a mule, but they didn't have to get past that pair of long-handled scythes Lincoln was swinging at him—grinning all the time so goddamn calm and pleasant.

Lincoln let his hands drop. Jack saw his chance and jumped in roaring, charging the center of Lincoln's chest in a bull-rush with arms wide.

He must have blinked, because instead of busting through Abe's ward to slam chests grapple and throw him back, Jack only bumped him—spoiled his own balance—and suddenly found he had run his neck into the crook of Abe's left arm, and Abe was slamming him across the belly with a thigh hard as a log of wood trying to get a hip-throw, and then Abe's other arm like some horrible giant snake come grappling around him, squeezing and scrunching up under the edge of his ribs to drive the wind out of him, to start his feet . . .

Jack felt his ground snatched away, he was horribly light in the air, then the earth slammed him head-to-heels.

"That's a fall!" hollered McNabb, and the Boys groaned jeered and complained. But there was a lot of hollering for Abe now, Fat Jack Kelso howling, "A touch a touch! O think not, Percy, to vie with me in glory any more!"

Abe offered Jack his hand. Jack batted it off and hauled himself up. Offutt was bowing to the crowd as if it was himself had made the throw. Clary was purple with chagrin, crying foul, promising vengeance, the Boys clamoring like wolves over the corpse they would make of Longshanks if he didn't wrassle fair.

Jack stood straight, trying not to show he was sucking wind, flinching the muscles across his back to feel if they were hurt. The hollering of the Boys was like dogs barking at him, *Git 'im Jack Git 'im Jack*, dang if you think it is so easy whyn't *you* come try it and let *me* do the hollerin'? He wished they'd let him alone, but they wouldn't. They barked him back into the center of the ring.

Abe's long ugly face was solemn, and the white-blue eyes met Jack's straight and calm. Jack had the sense Abe knew what he was thinking, and knew Jack knew it too. It was almost funny: the two of them out here. Might have been better if there wasn't nobody around, but only the two of them, man to man.

"If you're ready," said McNabb, "then git at it!"

This time Jack was careful. No bull-rushes. They hunched and circled, reaching and slapping arms away, Jack easing in a little bit each time around, a quarter-step, a half—he banged Abe's forearm aside and closed, his left shoulder digging into Abe's breast. They clinched, freeing an arm to snatch for a hold, quick leg-kicks as they risked their balance to hook a leg behind. Then they gave that over and stood grappled, front to front, legs braced and straining, arms locked. In the crowd the betting swung to Jack, he looked heavy and solid against Offutt's whip-lean boy, and you had to like his weight and low position in a straight grapple.

Only Jack couldn't budge him. It wasn't reasonable. The Clary's Grove Boys were howling, Uncle Clary beside himself with rage. But Jack couldn't budge him. He was straining every muscle in his body full out, his toes clawed in the ground, pushing with his legs, spine stiff as a musket, the muscles of his neck swole with the force of his pressure, arms bulging, hands going numb. But inside his head he was nothing, he was light as air, wondering as if it was happening to someone else, *I can't budge him no more than if he was a rooted tree.* It wasn't reasonable.

Lincoln's brown skin was nearly black with straining: but his white eyes looked very cool and steady. Jack felt Lincoln gather himself a little—then felt Lincoln begin to bear down slow and steady, felt himself begin to bend down under it, to bend back . . . *I am going to lose*, Jack's thought blew around inside his head, *and there ain't a goddamn thing I can do about it.* He wished the Boys would quit their yapping and leave him alone. *Get mad*, he told himself, *get mad get strong.* He was losing the match, losing Uncle Clary's bet, he'd have to eat his brags and the brags of all his friends and kinfolk too, the Boys piling it on his head even now with their goddamn yapping and bellering, Uncle Clary yelling: *"For Christ's sake, Jack, throw the son of a bitch any way you can!"*

Done by God! Jack loosed his right arm, dropped, and slammed his hand between Lincoln's legs, *crutch-hold goddamn you*! heaved him off his feet, then throwed him sideways and down. *"Got you you son of bitch!"* he roared blind mad, next thing he would knee-drop and bust his ribs . . .

But hands were grabbing him, Kelso, McNabb, his brother Pleasant . . . The crowd was hooting, cries of "Foul!" popping off like scattered shots. The crowd was mad enough for some hardy souls to push against the Boys—and the Boys abashed enough so they didn't push back.

It came down hard on Jack Armstrong right then and there, in the middle of that crowd, standing over Abe Lincoln with every eye in New Salem on him. He had showed out shameful. Fouled a man he couldn't whup fair. He knew it, so did Abe, and all the people there—even the Boys knew it. His eyes pinched, he shook his head, he couldn't make out what to do, what a man was supposed to do in such a fix. He looked down at the man he had throwed.

Lincoln met his eye: not mad, not jeering, just earnest. He reached out his hand. Jack got the idea. He reached down and hauled Abe back up onto his legs. Abe nodded thanks, but it was Jack that was grateful. Lincoln turned and lowered his head at Uncle Clary. "If you want a scuffle, Clary, why don't you come get one *yourself*."

Clary turned red. The Boys eased away from him. Lincoln wouldn't let him off: stood there staring him straight in the eye. He had to answer. "Naw," he said, trying to wave off his shame with a swipe of his hand, "go on an' wrassle."

A sigh ran through the crowd. Some no doubt sorry there

would not be a grand riot, Abe Lincoln versus the Clary's Grove Boys. Some satisfied to see Clary put in his place.

McNabb took his stand in the center and beckoned Abe and Jack to him. "Let's go ag'in, boys. Whenever you're ready."

Abe and Jack stood looking at each other, as if each waited for the other to hunch his back and start to circle. Abe grinned. "Jack, if we keep on we are liable to find out who is the best wrassler in Sangamon County." Jack nodded. Abe lifted his eyebrows like a pleasant notion just come to him: "On the other hand, if we stop now New Salem can boast she is home to the *two* best wrasslers in Sangamon County."

Jack Armstrong considered. Then he smiled. He felt as light and clean and peaceful as ever he felt in his life. He stuck out his paw, and when Lincoln took it clapped him round the shoulder and give him a bear hug—a tight one, to show his strength. Then he rounded on his Uncle, pointed a finger at him and cried, "Drinks on Uncle Clary!" The Boys mobbed them, whopping Abe and Jack and themselves on the back, and swept off to the Grocery shouting victory.

McNabb, Offutt, and Kelso were left like flotsam in the backwash. McNabb took the twenty dollars out of his pocket and gave them to Offutt. "One fall for Abe, the second a foul. I reckon you win the bet."

Offutt hefted the coin. "That's my boy Abe," he said.

"Not for long," said Kelso.

McNabb looked after the mob. "By Josaphat," he said, "I can't believe he done it. That was the coolest thing I *ever* see."

Kelso said, "Maybe. But I have seen one to match it."

New Salem, April 1, 1832
What Kelso had in mind was the debate the night before, "Resolved: that the institution of negro slavery is contrary to the law of nature, and of nature's God," Dr. Allen arguing the affirmative and Abe Lincoln the negative.

James Rutledge regretted the necessity of going through with the debate, which could only harm Lincoln's prospects. Even Mentor Graham—who held slavery was a providential institution, given to bring the benighted heathen of darkest Africa into the Gospel light—Graham felt a grievance with Dr. Allen. "It was a trick, and a mean one at that, to put the boy where he must defend a principle obnoxious to him."

Oddly, Jack Kelso, who held views opposite to Graham, was willing, even eager, to see how Abe would handle himself. "It don't signify what the boy says, or even thinks, about the question. If a man is to get on in politics, and serve his people, he must argue for things that aren't near to his heart—maybe even for that which his soul abominates, if his constituents adore it."

So be it then. Abe put on a clean shirt for the evening, and had worked upon the pitifulness of some good woman to such an extent as to get her to darn up his elbows and patch his knees. Dr. Allen's face was buffed to a cleanly pink shine, his collar and shirt-front crisp and white, he wore a soft woven coat of gray wool.

The Doctor rose up, and spoke for the half of an hour by the glass. He reviewed the Scriptures on the question of Christian holding Christian in bonds, and Graham (with sinking heart) heard him anticipate Abe's possible citation of "servants obey your masters." Then reviewed the Natural Law, showing its consistency with the Moral Law, a thing evil in the one producing with mathematical certainty evil in the other. And wound up with a grand review that took in manufacturing and shipping statistics, fluctuations in the price of the staple, the British Empire, the soaring flight of Freedom's Bird, and the Declaration of Independence. He even managed to condemn slavery without conceding an inch to the superstition of negro equality. Graham judged the arguments sound enough that John C. Calhoun himself might have "nullified," but could not have answered them.

Then Abe got up on his legs. His shoes were a misfortune, and he had destroyed by nervous rumpling whatever hope of decency he had combed into his hair. He had a paper in one out-size fist, clinched hard enough to fuse it in a crumpled mass. He never even tried to look at it. He looked off over the head of every man, into the far unlit corner of the Rutledge tavern's main room. What he said was spoke in an ordinary conversational way—except he was talking past them, to those shadows in the corner. He said: "Well, I ain't got all that much to say. I was taught, when a boy, that the natural world is in the Lord's keeping. It is writ so in Scripture, I believe. My understanding of what is meant by 'the law of nature and of nature's God,' is that the Lord made the world; and being good He made it good, and meant it to be kept so. I was taught, and read it in Scripture too, that there can't a sparrow fall in the wilderness but the Lord will see—and take keer of it—make good the evil done to it."

He paused, and pressed his lips into a grim line. He looked sad, his white eyes burned off into the shadows.

"But when I 'came a man," he said quietly, "and come to look at the world, what did I see? Weasel eats the sparrow, wolf eats the weasel, man kills 'em all—I can see the sense of that, I can see the *nature* of it: what I can't see is the *providence*, or the justice, or the law of it. They say a sparrow can't fall—but I've seen pigeons fall out of the trees in their thousands, shot, knocked down with poles, busted on the ground with clubs, more killed than we could have et in a year—listened hard all through it, and never heard a word spoke for their sakes. I seen Milk-sick . . . I seen . . . I've seen Milk-sick take off the best and kindest woman ever breathed a Christian breath, and leave a mean selfish squint-eyed bully to track his boots across the world. I don't see the justice in that; I don't see the providence.

"I see one man lord it over another, by his strength or riches. I see one man make another crawl, and *smile* crawling. I see one man buy another, buy a woman away from her child, and sell them like they was hogs—and I see men and women beg for a kind man to come buy them, to save them being worked or seasoned to death on the Red River. If you was to ask, every one of those men—the proud and mean and the crawling poor and shameful, the buyers and the boughten—every one would say he was a Christian—say it was the Lord's providence he should be who he was, where he was, doing what he's doing. I can't deny that that is nature. That is the world as it is give to us."

He stopped. He lowered his eyes, and leveled them at Dr. Allen, then Rutledge, then Graham, then Kelso. "I can't deny that that is nature. But I don't see the providence in it. Nor the *law*: leastways, not no law that takes account of sparrows—or poor men—or women—or niggers."

He looked off into the corner, and nodded to his shadowy interlocutor. Looked down at the crumpled unread paper in his hand. Then he took his seat.

There was a horrified stunned silence.

Dr. Allen rose, hesitantly, unsure whether to begin rebuttal. "I'm sorry," he offered, ". . . is that all? I mean, is that your argument?"

Abe signified it was.

Allen cleared his throat, and glanced uneasily around. There was some trick, he was certain, but for the life of him could not tell what it might be. Perhaps Kelso . . . but no—the fat blacksmith was wringing his hands, Graham looked nauseated, Rutledge bereft. Camron gave the Doctor a grim nod. "Well then," said the Doctor, "I'm afraid, my boy, you've made my rebuttal rather difficult"—he laughed a little—"or rather easy, I'm not sure which! You haven't offered a single argument in favor of the proposition that slavery is consistent with the law of nature, and of nature's God. All you have done—and I cannot believe this was your intent—all you have done is offer evidences that the moral law, and the providence and justice of God, have no relation to nature—none whatever."

"Yes," said Abe, "you have understood me about right."

"By thunder!" cried Camron. "That is blasphemy!"

Dr. Allen reached out a hand as if to snatch Camron back, the outburst had broken the thread of his rebuttal. But it was no use, they were all hollering and shushing each other at once, Camron castigating Fat Jack for filling the boy's head full of Bad Tom Paine, Kelso denying he had but defending his right to do so if ever he . . . Rutledge was a Deist when feeling respectable and an Epicurean when feeling his oats—but Abe had just about took *his* breath away. But he recovered himself, pounded his stick on the floor-boards, and demanded they hush and let Abe and the Doctor finish.

Dr. Allen was sweating now. He was either about to win the debate and show up Rutledge for his choice of a buckskin as candidate, or he was about to fall through the smartest trap one debater ever laid for another. "Then Lincoln," he demanded, "you admit all you have offered in argument is a denial that nature is governed by the law of God?"

Lincoln was cool. "If by *law of God* you mean justice for the critter and the man—yes, I have said I don't see evidence such a law exists."

"Why man," said the Doctor, "that isn't an argument! It is simply blasphemy."

"Yes," said Lincoln. "The root of any law has got to be justice. So if slavery *ain't* against the law of nature and God, that can only be because there *ain't* any justice in nature—and so there can't be no God, neither."

Camron rose in outrage, all he could hear ringing over and over again was Abe Lincoln denying the existence of the Lord! Rutledge and Graham jumped between, hauled Camron off, trying to get him to see it. He *wouldn't* see it.

Meanwhile Dr. Allen slumped in his chair, stunned. Kelso loomed over him: "Play it square after this, won't you? If you want to hurt him, you can spread this around."

Allen met Kelso's eye. "I'm honor-bound by our rules— what's said here is for argument only."

"Damn the rules and you too," Kelso growled. "You know, don't you, it wasn't any blasphemy."

The Doctor looked like he needed a dose of something. "No, you're right. It wasn't meant for blasphemy."

But it took a lot longer than that to convince Camron, long after the others had left, and Abe too—Kelso giving him a comforting pat on the shoulder and a promise to make it good with Camron. The persuasion was complicated by the fact that one of the persuaders, Graham, thought what Abe said *was* blasphemy —only spoken thoughtless, and not out of heathenism. That mollified Camron, and Rutledge would have settled for that.

But not Jack Kelso. "You don't see it, do you? Not any of you." He shook his head wonderingly. "Young Abraham went and found the only way there was to win that debate, without arguing against his own principles." The others objected, but Jack overrode them: "Of course he won. He won on *rebuttal*. He tricked Doc Allen into asking him that question, so *he* could answer: The only way slavery *ain't* against the law of nature and nature's God, is if there ain't neither law nor God."

The light dawned, but slowly. Rutledge saw it first: "So if there *is* a law of God . . ."

"If!" cried his nephew-in-law.

"My word," said Graham, "he argued the negative, while maintaining the truth of the positive." The joke suddenly dawned on the schoolmaster: "He turned Allen's rebut into his own summation! Hee hee hee!"

"He won the debate without compromising his principles," said Kelso, "and risked all his prospects with us to do it—and you know danged well he ain't got anything *but* those prospects. Now you tell me: have you ever seen anything *cooler* than that?" Kelso shook his head, and gave Rutledge a look. "Remind me in future: if young Mister Lincoln ever raises my bet, I will call or fold my hand."

Rutledge mused, "You're right, Jack. He has got *some* iron in him, anyways. Too bad this ain't the kind of thing you can set before the people."

"No," said Kelso, "people prefer Jack Armstrong's sort of iron. I hope Abe whups him tomorrow—whups him as good as he whupped Allen tonight."

Rutledge shrugged, "I'd rather it was something more honorable than a brawl."

"Pray for war," said Kelso.

Camron sniffed. Graham had a notion, and said: "Mind what you pray for."

New Salem, April 18–20, 1832

The mounted courier, two days out of Vandalia, spatterdashed into town on the puddle track from Springfield just before noon. He called James Rutledge out of his tavern and handed him the Governor's call to arms: "Fellow Citizens! Your country requires your services. Black Hawk and his Indians have assumed a hostile attitude, and have invaded the State . . ." Then he rented a fresh horse on the Governor's credit and pounded off westward to Beardstown. Rutledge clanged the iron triangle that hung by the door, summoning all in earshot to assemble and pay heed:

"The militia of New Salem is hereby called out. All able men will meet here—mounted, with arms, accooterments, and five days' rations—day after tomorrow, as near first-light as may be. They will march for Richland, where the Sangamon County troops will assemble and elect officers. They will then proceed to Beardstown, for swearing-in. Any man who does not come to muster will be fined one dollar, cash money."

The day of the muster Abe was up before first-light. Offutt snored in his room off the store. Abe had a good buckskin hunting-shirt to wear, decent pants (an old pair of Jack Armstrong's, repaired for him by Jack's wife, Hannah), and boots refurbished gratis by the cobbler. New Salem would not send a soldier off looking discreditable. The new rifle he shouldered was only half his—he was partners in the piece with Offutt. Abe had all the other accooterments for service but the horse. The animal he shared with Offutt was spavined, so Jack Kelso had said Abe might borrow one of his.

Jack had the animal ready in his stable, a stumpy brown mare with hairy hocks and ears like a jackass. They talked horse while the street outside got loud with militiamen, and dozens of men women and children who came to send each of them off. "War fever," said Kelso, "the whole district is down with it. Symptoms plain enough: patriotism, with whiskey complications. I'm hoping you ain't caught it."

Abe grinned: "Well I'm goin', ain't I?"

"Oh, you don't want that fever to be a soldier. Can't tell what fever will make you do: whup the world, run away, or do bloody massacre." He gave Abe a shrewd look. "So keep a cool head. We don't want a hero, what we want is a man for legislature. 'The paths of glory lead but to the grave.'"

Abe gave him a straight look: "What paths don't?"

"Here he comes!" hollered Jack Armstrong, and waved Abe to join him at the head of the column. The other troopers were already mounted. The chosen twelve were, most of them, sons of the town fathers—the new generation off to fight the Indian as their fathers had done in their day, and their grandfathers before them. They yipped and waved Abe up to the head of the column, glad he was with them—as if his being with them was a guarantee of good luck and a good time for all.

Annie Rutledge's pale face flashed in the crowd, framed in a blaze of hair. From the height of Kelso's horse Abe gave her a straight look and touched off a blush that took her like fire in dry brush.

Then with Abe and Jack at the head the New Salem contingent of Mounted Rifles went clop-jouncing out Main Street. Miss Warburton remarked to Miss Potter that Mr. Lincoln could use shorter legs or a taller animal: his feet hung so low it looked like he was riding a six-legged horse. Miss Potter wished to know, What did Miss Rutledge think?

Miss Rutledge had never took no notice of Abe Lincoln in the first place.

Misses Warburton and Potter rolled their eyes, they knew what *that* signified.

Once they cleared the town the company slowed to a lazy horseback amble. It was a fine, sweet-aired spring day. Abe felt himself *growing*, expanding. The broad reaches of the sky were about his limit. He was on the road to History at last, armed and friended and hot on Black Hawk's trail. Tonight they would join up with the rest of the County and elect officers. *With Jack and Clary's Grove to politick the other towns, I will bet Jack Kelso's horse I can get myself elected captain*. This was how all of them started: Columbus and Boone and Washington, Mordecai and Moses, they all went out after Injuns, or in the case of Moses *Egyptians*, which was nearly the same thing.

The sun drew a moist haze out of the tall prairie grasses through which they rode. Saddles squeaked, canteens sloshed, tin pans panked and ponked. Usil Meeker rattapanked his drum, Royal Clary's Jew's-harp boynged and boybadadded, and the New Salem troop sang,

"Old Black Hawk may be bold as brass,
　　But we're the boys to chop his ass—
　You Injuns *git*—and start to-*day*!
　　O'er the hills and far away.

"O'er the hills and crost the plain,
　　Through burnin' sun and pourin' rain,
　Our country calls and we obey,
　　O'er the hills and far away."

Abe was happy—as happy as ever he had been since Mam. He wasn't afraid of the war, not a bit. It come to him, like prophecy, that it would be easy, much easier than the River had been. He wasn't but a boy when he took on the River. Now he was a man growed. A man respected. A man followed by the strongest and roughest, the finest in New Salem. He'd lead his people to the war and through it, and when he came back he'd ride his horse right up to that stump on the edge of the goose-pulling grounds where the candidates gathered to address the people.

I will look out over New Salem, and they will be watching and waiting on me, all of them: James Rutledge the best man in town, and dour Camron, and Doc Allen that used to think he was the smartest man in New Salem but now he knows different. Jack Kelso with his wise grin: will he think I have come back a hero? Well Jack, a man's a man for a' that. Maybe Denton Offutt will still be there, I hope so, he's the only one knows how far I've come. And Jack Armstrong that used to be the Big Bull of Sangamon County? He'll be there, and Clary's Grove with him, to whoop for me and see I don't lack parade.

And she'll be there: Miss Annie Rutledge, her clever head her quick tongue her cat-green eyes, red-haired girls is randy girls and I am her hankering or if I ain't yet I will be soon enough—the same as she is mine. All it needs is her to see me standing up there on the stump, New Salem's favorite son. And when she hears what I will say she will rise to me and shine love in her green eyes, and open me her secret self like a book of a thousand and one stories . . .

This was dreams of course. He knew that when he did stand up on that stump what he said would be the same he had agreed with Rutledge Graham and Kelso, the same as in the letter they put in the *Sangamon Journal*: River improvements. Steamboats. Relief of debtors. "That every man be enabled by education to read the histories of his own and other countries, by which he may duly appreciate the value of our free institutions." And the laws of estray. "I am young and unknown, have no wealthy or popular relations . . ."

Oh, but in his heart and spirit he would be speaking a different speech altogether, suiting the word to the action the action to the word, and he wondered and he hoped, and under that huge open sky and grass-billowing prairie his heart rose to a certainty: that She would hear the speech underneath his speech, and see behind his ugly face and candidate's smile the truth of what he was:

I am Abraham Lincoln—the Bull of the Lick from Pigeon Crick! Half-horse, half-alligator, and blood-nephew to the meanest son of a bitch west of the mountains. The universal sky is my shake roof and I stake my claim to the whole American republic.

I've been mothered twice and not fathered even once. I pass for quality with the b'iled shirts and a rowdy with the coon-hats. I have seen the elephant and heard the owl hoot. I can track like an Injun, dance like a negro, shoot like a Kaintock, lie like a drummer, and cipher past the Rule of Three. I can out-chop out-wrassle out-talk and out-think any man in this district. I can shoot or hold fire, according to my need. I have wrassled the Old Man, rode his back, and made him tote my goods. I've measured rivers with a stick and made their currents run to rule. Sparrows may fall, but if they fall in my district I will see it don't happen regardless. I've read the books, now I'm fit to have the books read me.

I've been to the bottom of the River and come back to tell the tale. I ain't afeared of Nothing. I can smile and murder whiles I smile, change colors with the chameleon and set the murd'rous MacIvell to school. Can I do all this and cannot get elected to the General Assembly of the sovereign state of Elanoy, that earthly Eden garden-spot of the West? that paradise of speculators rattlesnakes Milk-sick patriots and sangroot whiskey?

The blue sky stood high and spread creation wide around

him. Islands of trees misted with haze stood like tow-heads in the rippling flow of the tallgrass prairie. Abe stood tall in his stirrups, balancing tipsy and waving his hat like a daredevil on a fence-rail.

"*Whoo-hoo!*" he hollered at the open sky. "*Whoo-hoop!*"

2000

Adam Braver

Another provocative contributor to the new golden age of Lincoln fiction, Braver (b. 1963) creatively structured *Mr. Lincoln's Wars*, his first novel, as a series of vignettes that use stream-of-consciousness storytelling and an almost discordant vernacular style to portray the doomed President as a grieving father and exhausted, fatalistic husband, well aware that there can be no rest for him, even at the war's end. Although most of the book takes place during the Civil War, the final chapter below shifts back in time to the spring of 1849, shortly after Lincoln finished his one term in Congress and returned to Springfield with his political career at a dead standstill. When he was interviewed on National Public Radio, Braver explained that he employed "a contemporary style, meaning using contemporary rhythms and language, and some tone, mostly because I wanted to locate a reader in a familiar place." In "A Rainy Night in Springfield, Illinois" that place seems to be a decidedly 20th-century zone of hardboiled, neo-noir cynicism, in which an angry and despondent Lincoln recoils from taking on another "greed-based" legal case. Published at the beginning of the 21st century, *Mr. Lincoln's Wars* raises a provocative and timely question: if Americans are to continue to see themselves in Abraham Lincoln and celebrate him as a representative American, must we also see Lincoln in who *we* have become, and imagine him as one of us, for better or worse?

FROM
Mr. Lincoln's Wars

A Rainy Night in Springfield, Illinois—1849

If any personal description of me is thought desirable, it may be said, I am, in height, six feet, four inches, nearly; lean in flesh, weighing on an average one hundred and eighty pounds; dark complexion, with coarse black hair, and grey eyes—no other marks or brands recollected.
—DECEMBER 20, 1859

The rain seems to fall harder in Springfield. Maybe the clouds are thicker. The sky's ceiling hangs a little lower, and the gray rain clouds mix heavy and brutal, like the mind of a condemned man. It can kind of sneak up on you. A morning blue sky teases with the promise of a cheerful day, and then by mid-afternoon the day turns mysteriously darker, yet there isn't really a visible cloud on the horizon. Then without warning the sun hides or is kidnapped or just doesn't care anymore, and a cannon boom thunders that not only rocks your house, but rocks your nerves. Next come the electrical flashes, dangerously aimed at your window. A tinkling of rain follows that initially sounds melodic, but builds to an evil crescendo that seems full of motive and malice. And just when you finally come to terms with that, the thunder cannon booms again, and the lightning rods spear straight at you, and the best that you can do is curl yourself into a ball on the couch in your sitting room, too afraid to go near the windows and draw the curtains, waiting and hoping for the terror to pass.

Mary Todd Lincoln sat on the couch in her sitting room, wrapped in a blanket that was drawn up around her neck, her knees pressed tightly together, while her taut fingers cinched the wool. The wind outside whistled ghost songs, accompanied by the shivering leaves and percussive banging of the oak branches. The kerosene lamps clouded the room in yellow. A big burst of lightning lit up the room, leaving electric shadow outlines as it receded, then returned the room to its faded burning color.

It seemed like it would never end. The rains hitting the flower bed outside like the stamping of angry feet. Then all around the house. Angry feet dancing all around her. She pulled the blanket tighter. And waited.

She had sent her son Robert down to her husband's law office with the urgent message that she needed him to come home, while her three-year-old was long asleep in the back room. "Tell him I don't trust the threatening rain," she told the boy, insisting that he look up at her while she spoke.

"I don't get it," Robert replied.

"Just tell that to your father."

Robert had run out the door, slapping it shut behind him. His mother watched him dash across the lawn, shielding his hand over his forehead for cover, and out through the picket gate that he carelessly forgot to close, leaving the rusted metal latch to bang with each new burst of wind. His feet managed to find every puddle, stamping up waves of dirty runoff water that spotted his trouser legs in thick dark spots. Sometimes that boy didn't consider the importance of what's around him. Or even care. A lot like his father in that way.

Mary cuddled herself on the couch to wait. Thinking to herself that it was strange that she had never feared the future nearly as much as the here-and-now.

Abraham Lincoln leaned forward into the scattered papers on his desk, resting his cheek in the palm of his left hand. He looked up at the uneven molding tacked around the ceiling while listening to the tapping of the rain. Before him lay the briefing for a typical greed-based case that involved some combination of land, cattle, and resale shares. He had taken the case on behalf of a witless middleman named Earl Muncie who claimed to have been boned by a big landowner called Toots Johnson over near Tuscola, just southeast of Springfield near the Indiana border. This Muncie turned out to be a real jackass, and hardly the underdog that he had presented himself as when Lincoln first met him on one of his consulting junkets. He sang some *poor me the little guy gets fucked again* tune, drawing upon all the sympathies of this visiting lawyer. But since then it appeared that Muncie had his own lines of illegal networks, including a little side business that cashed in on the dead-or-alive rewards for runaway slaves gone north, specializing in the "dead" part. But Lincoln had already taken the case. Accepted the retainer, an unusually large sum, in retrospect, from a plaintiff in an I-got-screwed case.

The Lincolns could use the money now. His law practice was off the ground, but he still needed to take any case that came in. They had the house at Eighth and Jackson all dressed with its precise decor, the furniture designed in sharp angles, and parlor chairs handcrafted after the classic European styles, a stark contrast to the split tree trunks that his father, Thomas Lincoln, had called furnishing. A showcase for Springfield, where many of the prestige class of the city had milled the single-floor home with a cocktail in their hand at one time or another, making toasts to one another, while Mary individually reminded them that their assistance to her husband's political career would soon be required. He had almost left his Kentucky roots far behind. And one day he would save enough to put a second story on the house, and he would sleep on the top floor, snoring down over the white-trash childhood he had been forced to endure.

But here he sat in the not quite dark, a candle nearly burnt to the tabletop, its spitting wick only threatening light. The thought of this Earl Muncie made him sick—the same kind of bastard grin as his father's, pulled back long and slim in ignorant righteousness over mismatched teeth, spilling out sour breath as he heaved a throaty laughter in quick spurts. Exactly like his father, whose main source of power was the unsubstantiated belief that he had in himself. But unlike Thomas Lincoln, Muncie had one more secret weapon—a load of cash that he used to hypnotize the unsuspecting into willing conscripts.

But what did Lincoln care? Take the money and run. Right? It wasn't as if this Toots Johnson character was any great prize worth saving. He too was a conniving piece of shit who used his pocketbook and its complement of political influence to ensure that things worked out his way. Plus if Lincoln won the case he'd really be taking both of their moneys in the end. A form of philanthropic assistance in burying his past, and molding a future that would one day leave him more empowered than both of them combined.

He filed through the notes that he had taken, deciphering the tall angles of his handwriting. The case didn't really make sense from a legal standpoint, but he was sure that if he dedicated himself he could manipulate some precedent to his advantage, and out-orate any country sap attorney that Johnson would employ. But each time he read a direct quote from Muncie, he would see that bastard face, and his gut would tighten when he spun a justification to himself on behalf of that clown.

He wished he could just chuck the case. Tell Muncie to stick the cattle, the contract, and the retainer up his bony ass. But Abraham had promised Mary a new dining-room table, long, smooth red mahogany with beveled edges. It was the last piece of furniture that they needed to complete their home, and she had already met with a woodworker named Sam to start the carpentry.

Maybe he could become more selective after this case. As soon as the verdict was rendered, and Earl Muncie slapped his overgrown gritty fingernails into Lincoln's palm in celebration, Lincoln could pull his hand away and say that he quit defending shit cases just for the money. He had his dining-room table. His house. His past successfully plowed under and suffocated so it could never rise again. He could then take cases based on his own sense of right and wrong. Become a true defender.

Sure.

He dropped the papers, watching them fall to the floor. His chest tightened, and he found it hard to breathe, as if the air in his lungs had turned thick and humidly weighted in sadness.

He listened to the rain fall harder. Mary would be waiting for him. The rain terrorized her almost as much as the fear of ordinariness.

The Muncie papers were scattered at his feet. He couldn't go on like this. A new life didn't mean anything if it came at the expense of more assholes like his father. Wasn't that why he'd left Thomas Lincoln in the first place? He thought to himself that he was no better than a sonabitch slave who keeps working the same plot of land with the bullshit promise that it will one day be his.

Robert burst through the door, and let his slick soles slide across the hardwood. He landed in front of his father's desk, a thick-lipped grin rising from his fresh, boyish face between flushed cheeks. His dark curls were matted flat and wet, dripping a perfect circle of spent rain around him on the floor. The water ran in a downward stream under the desk, and quickly soaked into the Muncie notes, leaving only splotches of black ink blood.

A smile rose from Lincoln's face as he looked up from the drenched papers. "I'm glad you got the looks of the Todd family."

Robert stared at him, unsure of what to make of that, waiting to see if his father would be mad at him for ruining the papers on the floor.

"You are a handsome boy is all I'm saying. Got a nice round face."

Robert smiled at the compliment, then turned serious. "Mother sent me here."

"Because of the rain."

"She said she doesn't trust it."

"It scares her."

"I don't get it. I told her I didn't get it."

"It's okay, I do."

"She said you would."

"And I do."

Robert remained in place. His arms flat at his sides, looking like he was melting under the dim candlelight. He wore a baffled expression, one that his father recognized as resignation to the logic of his parents. Reluctantly accepting their manner of conducting family business.

"Are you just going to stand there and make Lake Bob?" Lincoln grinned at his son. He reached into a cabinet behind him and pulled out a towel and a blanket. "Put this around you after you've dried off, and just hold tight a few minutes while I finish the last of my business."

As Robert dried his hair, Lincoln bent over and pried the Muncie notes off the floor, the corners of the logged paper disintegrating in his fingers. He balled it up into a mass of pulp and threw it against the back wall, where it stuck with a thud before loosening and sliding down to the floor into a pile that looked like splattered bird shit. And he really should have thanked Robert for his boyish carelessness in ruining those notes, unwittingly stopping the Lincoln tradition of miserable fathers dead in its tracks. Because tonight, on this miserable spring evening of 1849, Abraham Lincoln quit. The ghost of old Thomas Lincoln was howling somewhere deep in the night. There was nothing left to prove. Abe had run from his past, and now that he was a million miles away he was going to quit charging forward with a nervous look over his shoulder. He was sorry for what Mary might think, and the angst it might initially bring her, the shortage of money and the delay of status, but he knew in the end she would be happier with a husband who lived by his own convictions. They were more likely to be where they wanted to be if that place was borne of strength. There really was no choice.

Lincoln ground his toe into the white pulp, mashing it into the floor until it nearly disappeared, and then he kicked it in a thin ragged line along the baseboard.

"What was that?" Robert peered out from under the blanket, his eyes wide and excited.

"Just some junk lying around."

"Do you have any more?" Robert asked, as if intrigued by the new game.

"I hope not."

Robert donned the familiar baffled expression.

Lincoln stood to get his coat and hat. He turned around to face his son. "Let me ask you a question, Robert."

"Dad."

"Do we need a new dining-room table?"

"What's wrong with the old one?"

"I don't really know. Do you like it?"

"It's fine." He shrugged. "It's just a table to me."

"It doesn't make you think of anything?"

"Just eating."

Lincoln leaned over and kissed his son on the crown of the head. "Thank you, Robert. You have been a tremendous help."

"Sure thing," Robert said, his expression even more mystified.

Lincoln leaned over and blew out the candle. A flash of lightning cracked outside the window, and in the silver light he saw the remains of the Muncie papers, and thought to himself that he felt like he was loading bullets into someone else's suicide shotgun—hopefully his father's.

Mary looked relieved when she saw her husband and son come through the front door. She didn't rise from the couch, but instead held her hands out as though she needed assistance in regaining her balance. Lincoln shooed his son off to his room, instructing the boy to get out of those wet trousers and into some dry nightclothes and straight into bed. Robert ran off in a burst of exhausted energy, his shoulders clumsily banging side to side against the hallway walls, as another round of thunder rocked the night.

"Dear God, Mr. Lincoln," Mary cried out. She dug her nails into his wrists and pulled him down against her. She moved her grip over his forearm. "Make it go away."

"Weather always passes. You know what I tell you about that."

She reached up and stroked his hair. "You're all wet," she said. "Go dry yourself off."

"I'm fine, Mother."

"You'd never leave me, would you, Mr. Lincoln?"

"I don't know who else would accept a mug as ugly as mine."

"No." She scooted in closer. Her eyes half closed in momentary solace. "I mean you'll always be with me."

"Mary"—he laughed—"I'm not going anywhere. At least not for another seventy years."

"Because I couldn't handle it. I'd fall apart if you weren't here to hold me when it rains."

He took her hands off his wrist, and held them in his. Her eyes, those bright blues that sometimes looked so lost and gone, stood attentive, maybe on account of the electrical storm. "I came to a decision tonight," he said softly. "A big one."

She laid her head on his shoulder. The rain had stopped pounding, and turned to steady drizzle. "It's so damp," she whispered.

"I can't keep doing what I don't believe in."

Mary dropped her hands and caressed his thigh in short tender strokes.

"I'm not going to lawyer for thieves just for the money." He stiffened briefly, bracing for the reaction. But Mary just reached up and kissed his neck. Her lips felt thin and dry.

"Did you hear me, Mother?"

"I don't know what it is about the rain that frightens me. Maybe it's the thunder."

"We may not have the same amount of money for a while. I'll need to build a new clientele."

"Oh, Mr. Lincoln, it's like you just told me, and always tell me: the weather always passes, and sure enough the sun will shine again."

"We won't be able to get the dining-room table for a time."

"I like the one we have."

Lincoln leaned in and nuzzled her neck, tasting the dry salt that was left over from her fearful sweat. He dropped his hand between her legs, and ran his fingers in short little tickles on her inner thigh, feeling the smooth and spongy flesh that made his mouth water and his teeth ache. She pulled him on top of her and gripped his protruding hips.

He glanced up to the window, at the trickling streams running unevenly down the panes. Lincoln felt good, as strange as that was. Free of his father, and free from the endless burden of escaping him. He wanted to inventory this feeling. Catalog every nuance, from the lightness in his toes, to the thrusting of his pelvis, to the tingling of his brain. It was so foreign, and he wanted to be able to recall it in case he became lost to the darkness that routinely fueled him.

As if reading his mind, Mary cooed in his ear, "I am so happy right now, Mr. Lincoln."

"Me too."

"Let's make another baby right now," she said. "Someone who can capture all of this happiness."

Lincoln started to kick off his trousers. "If it's a boy," he said, "let's call him William—after Shakespeare."

"And every time we look at him, or think about him, we will just know happiness."

"I do love you very much, Mary."

"I'd fall apart if you weren't here to hold me when it rains."

Abraham Lincoln made love to his wife on the couch that night. Thankful that his pain was behind him.

In praise of happiness.

2003

E. L. Doctorow

A dazzling literary craftsman, Doctorow (b. 1931) has written several novels that have been hailed for successfully integrating history and fiction, including *The Book of Daniel*, *Ragtime*, and *Billy Bathgate*. His first Civil War novel, *The March* (2005), follows several soldiers and civilians, black and white, caught up in General William Tecumseh Sherman's relentless campaign through Georgia and the Carolinas. In the excerpt printed here, Lincoln is seen through the eyes of Dr. Wrede Sartorius during his meeting in March 1865 with Grant and Sherman at City Point, Virginia. (Sartorius is an imaginary character who first appeared in *The Waterworks*, an earlier Doctorow novel set in New York in 1871.) To the battle-hardened doctor, the President initially seems oddly deferential and almost womanish as he frets over the hard hand of war, but Sartorius soon comes to see "a sort of ugly beauty" in Lincoln, as well as an immense sadness and weariness, "the amassed miseries of this torn-apart country made incarnate."

FROM

The March

General Grant's residence was not elaborate but well situated on the bank of the James River, with a view of the harbor. It was a place. It stood still. Sartorius found himself sitting in a tufted parlor chair with his knees together and his hands in his lap while Mrs. Grant sat opposite him and gallantly attempted to deal with his silences. Somewhere along the march, he supposed he had lost the talent for polite conversation. She was a charmingly homely woman, Mrs. Grant, a thoughtful hostess, and he appreciated her effort to entertain him while her husband and General Sherman were secluded. But she did ask him his advice about Ulysses, who was having some trouble with his back. Then she herself admitted to some difficulty breathing when walking up a stairs.

Grant, when he appeared with Sherman, was almost shockingly unprepossessing—rather short, stocky, brown beard of a thick texture, a quiet man clearly not interested in making any kind of impression, unlike Sherman, who didn't seem to be able to stop talking. Grant's color was good, and his eyes only slightly bloodshot.

Wrede was included in the luncheon, an affair of about twelve, mostly Army of the Potomac staff, with Mrs. Grant at one end of the table and the General at the other. His tunic unbuttoned, Grant sat slumped in his chair, not eating very much, nor drinking anything but water. Uley, Mrs. Grant called to him, Dr. Sartorius has a liniment for your back, if you would consider it. I think that is so very kind of him, don't you?

After lunch everyone stood up from the table and Wrede didn't know what to do when Grant and Sherman walked out of the room and made to leave the house, but Sherman came back and beckoned to him, and he joined the two generals as they strode down to the wharf and went aboard the *River Queen*, a large white steamer with an American flag flying at the stern. After the bright light of day, Wrede needed a moment to acclimate himself to the dim light of the aftercabin, where a tall man had risen from his chair to receive them. He had the weak, hopeful smile of the sick, a head of wildly unmanageable hair, he wore a shawl over his shoulders and house slippers, and Wrede Sartorius realized with a shock, this was not the resolute, visionary leader of the country whose portrait photographs were seen everywhere in the Union. This was someone eaten away by life, with eyes pained and a physiognomy almost sepulchral, but nevertheless, still unmistakably, the President of the United States.

After these many months of nomadic life in the Southern lowlands, Wrede could not quite accept his proximity to Abraham Lincoln. The real presence and the mythic office did not converge. The one was here in a small space, the other unlocatable anywhere save in one's own mind. Lincoln's conversation was deferential, too much so. You could not imagine any European leader appearing this self-deprecatory before underlings. The President at moments had about him the quality of an elderly woman, fearful of war and despairing of its ever ending. General Sherman, he said, are you sure your army is in good hands while you're away? Why, Mr. President, General Schofield is in command while I'm gone who is a most able officer. Yes, Lincoln said, I'm sure he is. But we'll have our little talk and we won't keep you.

Sherman was ready to speak of the war as if it were over. He thought that, for the peacetime regular army, new regiments should not be commissioned but, rather, that existing regiments should be replenished from the ranks. Ah, General Sherman, Lincoln said with a faint smile, so you think we have a future? Sherman, humorless in this situation, replied, General Grant will agree with me that with one more good battle the war will be won. One more battle, said Lincoln. How many would that make, now? I think I have lost count, he said, bowing his head and closing his eyes.

General Grant asked after Mrs. Lincoln, and the President excused himself for a moment to summon her, at which point Grant came over to Sartorius. The President appears to me to have grown older by ten years. What do you have in the nature of a nostrum to brighten him up? Do you have anything? It is hard for all of us, but we are in the field. He can only wait on our news, sitting in Washington without the hell-may-care that comes from a good battle.

Before Wrede could reply, the President returned and announced that Mrs. Lincoln was not feeling well and had asked to be excused. The President's heavy-lidded eyes suddenly widened with an alarmingly self-revealing glance directed at Sartorius. An embarrassed silence ensued.

At this point the President and his generals retired to another cabin. Sartorius paced about and tried not to interpret the sound of their conversation as it drifted through the wall. He did not hear the actual words but the voices—the baritone murmurs of the President, the occasional gruff utterance of Grant, and the louder exclamations of Sherman, who sounded the upstart assuring his elders that he had everything in hand.

Finally the cabin door opened and Sartorius, standing upon their return, was able to see now how tall the President was. His head almost brushed the cabin ceiling. He had enormous hands and large, ungainly feet, and the wrist where his shirtsleeve was pulled back showed curled black hair. The long head was in proportion to the size of the man, but intensifying of his features, so that there was a sort of ugly beauty to him, with his wide mouth, deeply lined at the corners, a prominent nose, long ears, and eyes that seemed any moment about to disappear under his drooping eyelids. Sartorius thought the President's physiognomy could suggest some sort of hereditary condition, a syndrome of overdeveloped extremities and rude features. Premature aging might also be a characteristic. That would explain the terribly careworn appearance, the sorrows of office amplified by the disease.

What is most important, the President was saying, by way of conclusion, is that we not confront them with terms so severe that the war will continue in their hearts. We want the insurgents to regain themselves as Americans.

At this moment Mrs. Lincoln appeared, after all, a stout woman with her hair tightly bound to frame a round face, and eyes filled with undifferentiated suspicion. She seemed barely conscious of the visiting generals, to say nothing of Wrede, but went right to her husband and spoke to him of some later plan for the day as if nobody else were present. Then, frowning in response to some invisible disturbance, she departed as suddenly as she had arrived, the cabin door left open behind her, which Lincoln moved to close.

The generals, who had risen to greet her, could only think to resume their conversation.

Wrede was startled to find the President looming up. The odd exhilaration one felt in being directly addressed by Mr. Lincoln made it almost impossible actually to attend to what he was saying. One had to not look at him in order to listen. General Sherman tells me you are the best he has, the President said. You know, Colonel, this war has been as hard on Mrs. Lincoln as on the longest-serving battle-worn soldier. I do worry about her nerves. I sometimes wish she could have the advantage of the latest medical thinking, the same that is available to any wounded private in our military hospitals.

It was only a few minutes later, as Wrede Sartorius accompanied General Sherman to the steamer waiting for the return voyage, that he was made to understand of what a presidential wish consisted. I'm sorry, Colonel, Sherman said, but you're off the march. You are reassigned to the Surgeon General's office in Washington. You will embark with the President's party.

Sherman made to go aboard but turned back. There can be tragic incongruities in a man's life, he said. And so a great national leader suffers marriage to a disagreeable neurasthenic. They did lose a son. But so did I, so did General Hardee. All our Willies are gone. Yet my wife, Ellen, is steady as a rock. She does not plague me with her fears and suspicions while I attend to the national crisis. I will have your things sent to you. Good luck, Sherman said, and ran up the gangplank.

In City Point, Sartorius bought some clothes and a bag to put them in and repaired to the *River Queen* for the trip to Washington. He had to accept his situation, there was nothing else for it. Mr. Lincoln may be under an illusion about the quality of care in army hospitals, he thought. If so, it is his only illusion.

I have no nostrums—none. I have a few herbs, and potions, and a saw to cut off limbs.

He could not stop thinking of the President. Something of his feeling was turning to awe. In retrospect, Mr. Lincoln's humility, which Wrede had descried as weakness, now seemed to have been like a favor to his guests, that they would not see the darkling plain where he dwelled. Perhaps his agony was where his public and private beings converged. Wrede lingered on the dock. The moral capacity of the President made it difficult to be in his company. To explain how bad he looked, the public care on his brow, you would have to account for more than an inherited syndrome. A proper diagnosis was not in the realm of science. His affliction might, after all, be the wounds of the war he'd gathered into himself, the amassed miseries of this torn-apart country made incarnate.

Wrede, who had attended every kind of battle death, could not recall having ever before felt this sad for another human being. He stood on the dock, not wanting to go on board. Life seemed to him terribly ominous at this moment.

2005

Epilogue:
Barack Obama at Springfield

In April 2005 the new junior senator from Illinois traveled to Springfield to speak at the opening of the Abraham Lincoln Presidential Library and Museum. In his remarks, Barack Obama addressed a question that Americans have asked themselves time and again: How is it that Lincoln, a "homely and awkward" man "given to depression and wracked with self-doubt, might come to represent so much of who we are as a people, and so much of who we aspire to be?" For Obama, the answer lay in Lincoln's sheer energy, his rise from poverty, his determination to master the law, his ability to overcome loss and defeat:

> In all of this—the repeated acts of self-creation, the insistence that with sweated brow and calloused hands and focused will we can recast the wilderness of the American landscape and the American heart into something better, something finer—in all of this Lincoln embodies our deepest myths. It is a mythology that drives us still.

Yet he judged Lincoln's most important contribution to be his unflinching confrontation with the nation's greatest moral challenge. "In the midst of slavery's dark storm and the complexities of governing a house divided, he kept his moral compass pointed firm and true," in part through his refusal to demonize those who fought on the opposing side. The lesson the recently elected senator drew was one of humility: rather than evoking "our common God to condemn those who do not think as we do," we should "seek God's mercy for our own lack of understanding."

Obama returned to the subject of Lincoln in his book *The Audacity of Hope*, and, like many of the writers in this anthology, encountered paradox. While he considered Lincoln to be rightly remembered for the "firmness and depth of his convictions," his presidency was nonetheless "guided by a practicality that would distress us today" that led him to "test various bargains" with the South before the war, to discard generals and strategies during the conflict, and to "stretch the Constitution to the breaking point" in the pursuit of victory. This time the lesson Obama drew was about the necessity for both reflection and action in politics: Lincoln sought to maintain within himself "the balance between two contradictory ideas—that we must talk and reach for common understandings, precisely because all of us are imperfect and can never act with the certainty that God is on our side; and yet at times we must act nonetheless, as if we are certain, protected from error only by providence."

In light of his continuing engagement with Lincoln memory, it was surely no accident that Senator Obama chose a day very close to Lincoln's 198th birthday in February 2007 as the date for the announcement of his presidential candidacy, or that he selected as the setting the restored Old State Capitol in Springfield, "where Lincoln once called on a divided house to stand together, where common hopes and common dreams still live." Braving the frigid weather—as did the thousands who filled the square to hear him, as some of their forebears had likely once gathered to hear Lincoln—he evoked the memory of the past, acknowledged the challenges of the present, and summoned a future that seemed the natural fulfillment of the promise of the victorious Union, emancipation, and the guiding presence of Lincoln. Against the inevitable doubts concerning the feasibility of his presidential aspirations and his call for fundamental change, Obama deployed the inescapable example of another relatively inexperienced, yet unquestionably ambitious, former state legislator from Illinois who had also defied expectations (and a powerful senator from New York) to seek the very same office:

> By ourselves, this change will not happen. Divided, we are bound to fail.
> But the life of a tall, gangly, self-made Springfield lawyer tells us that a different future is possible.
> He tells us that there is power in words.

He tells us that there is power in conviction.

That beneath all the differences of race and region, faith and station, we are one people.

He tells us that there is power in hope.

As Lincoln organized the forces arrayed against slavery, he was heard to say: "Of strange, discordant, and even hostile elements, we gathered from the four winds, and formed and fought to battle through."

That is our purpose here today.

Barack Obama's closing words echoed Gettysburg, striking, as so many before him have, and so many to follow undoubtedly will, our most powerful and enduring chord of national memory: "Together, starting today, let us finish the work that needs to be done, and usher in a new birth of freedom on this Earth."

CHRONOLOGY

SOURCES AND
ACKNOWLEDGMENTS

INDEX

Chronology

1809   Born February 12, in log cabin on Nolin Creek, three miles south of present-day Hodgenville in Hardin (now Larue) County, Kentucky, second child (sister is Sarah, b. 1807) of pioneer farmer and carpenter Thomas Lincoln (b. 1778) and Nancy Hanks Lincoln (b. circa 1784). Named Abraham after paternal grandfather.

1811   Moves with family to 230-acre farm (only about thirty acres of which are tilled) on Knob Creek, eleven miles northeast of Hodgenville.

1812   Brother Thomas born. He dies in infancy.

1815   Attends school with Sarah for short period in fall. (Neither parent can read, father can write only his own name.)

1816   Briefly attends school with sister in fall. Father, who is involved in suit over title to his land, moves family across Ohio River to southwestern Indiana in December. There they settle in backwoods community along Little Pigeon Creek in Perry (later Spencer) County. Family lives in three-sided shelter for several weeks until log cabin is built.

1817   Helps father clear land for planting on 80-acre plot. Family is joined late in the year (or in early 1818) by great-aunt Elizabeth Hanks Sparrow, her husband, Thomas Sparrow, and 19-year-old cousin Dennis Hanks, who becomes Lincoln's close companion.

1818   Sometime after his birthday Lincoln is kicked in the head by a horse and is momentarily thought to be dead. Thomas and Elizabeth Sparrow die of milk sickness in September. Mother dies of milk sickness on October 5 and is buried near Sparrows on knoll a quarter mile from cabin.

1819   On December 2, father marries Sarah Bush Johnston, 31-
        year-old widow with three children (Elizabeth, b. 1807,
        John, b. 1810, and Matilda, b. 1811), during visit to Eliza-
        bethtown, Kentucky. (Father and stepmother knew each
        other when Lincolns lived in Hardin County.)

1820   Attends school briefly with sister Sarah.

1822   Attends school for several months.

1824   Helps with plowing and planting and works for neighbors
        for hire. Attends school in fall and winter. Reads family
        Bible, and borrows books whenever possible (reading will
        include Mason Locke Weems's *The Life and Memorable Ac-
        tions of George Washington*, Daniel Defoe's *Robinson Crusoe*,
        Aesop's *Fables*, John Bunyan's *Pilgrim's Progress*, William
        Grimshaw's *History of the United States*, and Thomas Dil-
        worth's *A New Guide to the English Tongue*).

1827   Works as boatman and farmhand at junction of Anderson
        Creek and the Ohio River, near Troy, Indiana.

1828   Sister Sarah, now married to Aaron Grigsby, dies in child-
        birth on January 20. In April, Lincoln and Allen Gentry
        leave Rockport, Indiana, on flatboat trip to New Orleans
        with cargo of farm produce. While trading in coastal Loui-
        siana sugar-growing regions, they fight off seven black men
        trying to rob them. Returns home by steamboat. Watches
        trials at county courthouses.

1830   In March, moves with family to Illinois, where they settle
        on uncleared land ten miles southwest of Decatur in Macon
        County. Makes first known political speech, in favor of
        improving navigation on Sangamon River, at campaign
        meeting in Decatur.

1831   Builds flatboat with stepbrother John D. Johnston and
        cousin John Hanks in spring and makes second trip to New
        Orleans, carrying corn, live hogs, and barreled pork. Re-

turns to Illinois in summer and moves to village of New Salem, twenty miles northwest of Springfield in Sangamon County (family has moved to Coles County, Illinois). Clerks in general store, where he sleeps in the back, helps run mill, and does odd jobs. Accepts challenge to wrestle Jack Armstrong, leader of the "Clary's Grove boys," local group of rowdy young men, and stands his ground when they rush him to prevent Armstrong's defeat. Match is agreed to be a draw, and Lincoln gains respect and friendship of group. Becomes friends with tavernkeeper James Rutledge, his daughter Ann, and schoolmaster Mentor Graham. Learns basic mathematics, reads Shakespeare and Robert Burns, and participates in local debating society.

1832   Borrows and studies Samuel Kirkham's *English Grammar*. Announces candidacy for House of Representatives, lower chamber of Illinois General Assembly, in March. Volunteers for Illinois militia at outbreak of Black Hawk Indian War in early April and is elected company captain. Reenlists as private when his company is mustered out in late May and serves until July 10 in Rock River country of northern Illinois, covering much ground but seeing no action. Loses election on August 6, running eighth in field of thirteen candidates seeking four seats. Becomes partner in New Salem general store with William F. Berry.

1833   Store fails and leaves Lincoln deeply in debt. Works as hired hand and begins to write deeds and mortgage papers for neighbors. Boards with different families, moving every few months. Appointed postmaster of New Salem in May (serves until office is moved to nearby Petersburg in 1836); regularly reads newspapers in the mail. Studies surveying with Mentor Graham's help after being appointed deputy surveyor of Sangamon County.

1834   Makes first known survey in January and first town survey on site of New Boston, Illinois, in September (works as surveyor for three years). Elected as a Whig on August 4 to

Illinois House of Representatives, running second in field of thirteen seeking four Sangamon County seats. Begins to study law, reading Blackstone's *Commentaries* and Joseph Chitty's *Precedents in Pleading* and borrowing other law-books from attorney John T. Stuart. Takes his seat on December 1 at capital in Vandalia. Rooms with Stuart, who is elected floor leader by Whig minority in House. Meets Stephen A. Douglas, 21-year-old lawyer active in Democratic party politics.

1835   Serves on twelve special committees and helps draft bills and resolutions for other Whigs. Votes with the majority to charter state bank and to build canal linking the Illinois River and Lake Michigan. Death of former store partner William Berry in January increases Lincoln's debt to approximately $1,100, which he repays over several years. Returns to New Salem after legislature adjourns on February 13. Ann Rutledge dies on August 25 from fever at age twenty-two. Attends special legislative session in December, called to speed up work on Illinois and Michigan Canal and other internal improvements. Votes for bill pledging credit of state to payment of canal loan.

1836   Returns to New Salem after legislature adjourns on January 18. Wins reelection on August 1, running first in field of seventeen candidates contesting seven Sangamon County seats in lower chamber. Receives license to practice law on September 9. Begins halfhearted courtship of Mary Owens, 28-year-old Kentucky woman visiting her sister in New Salem. Has episode of severe depression ("hypochondria") soon after returning to Vandalia in early December for new legislative session.

1837   Lincoln and other members of nine-man Whig delegation from Sangamon County (known as the "Long Nine" because they average over six feet in height) lead successful campaign to move state capital from Vandalia to Springfield, a shift that reflects population growth in central and northern counties. Supports ambitious internal improvements program. With fellow Whig representative Dan Stone, enters protest against anti-abolitionist resolutions adopted in their chamber. Legislature adjourns on March 6. Moves to Springfield on April 15, rooming with storeowner Joshua F. Speed, who becomes a close friend. Becomes law partner of John T. Stuart and begins extensive and varied civil and criminal practice. (Lincoln occasionally acts as prosecutor, but appears for the defense in almost all of his criminal cases throughout his career.) At special legislative session in July, votes with majority to continue internal improvements despite national financial panic. Mary Owens rejects his proposal of marriage, and courtship is broken off in August.

1838   Delivers address on "The Perpetuation of Our Political In-stitutions" to the Springfield Young Men's Lyceum on Jan-uary 27. Helps defend Henry Truett in widely publicized murder case, delivering final argument to jury; Truett is ac-quitted. In May, debates Douglas, who is running for Con-gress against Stuart. Reelected to the legislature, August 6, running first of seven successful candidates in field of seventeen. Nominated for speaker by Whig caucus when legislature convenes on December 3, but is defeated by Democrat W.L.D. Ewing. Serves as Whig floor leader.

1839   Legislature adjourns on March 4. Lincoln makes first ex-tensive trip on Illinois Eighth Judicial Circuit, attending court sessions held successively in nine counties in central and eastern Illinois. Chosen presidential elector in October by first Whig state convention. Debates Douglas in Spring-field on issue of national bank. Assumes greater share of legal partnership when Stuart leaves for Congress in No-vember. Admitted to practice in United States Circuit Court on December 3. Legislature convenes in special ses-sion, December 9, meeting at Springfield for the first time. Becomes acquainted with Mary Todd, 21-year-old daugh-ter of prominent Kentucky Whig banker, sister-in-law of Illinois Whig legislator Ninian W. Edwards, and cousin of John T. Stuart.

1840   Votes in minority against repeal of internal improvements
       law of 1837, which has caused financial crisis (state defaults
       on its debt in July 1841). Legislature adjourns on February
       3. Campaigns for Whig presidential candidate, William
       Henry Harrison, debating Douglas and other Democratic
       speakers. Argues his first case before Illinois Supreme Court
       in June (Lincoln will appear before it in over 240 cases).
       Reelected to the legislature, August 3, polling lowest vote
       of five candidates elected from Sangamon County. Becomes
       engaged to Mary Todd in fall. Legislature meets in special
       session on November 23. Lincoln is again defeated by Ewing
       in voting for speaker. In parliamentary maneuver to protect
       failing state bank, Whigs attempt to block adjournment of
       special session by preventing quorum. When plan fails on
       December 5, Lincoln and two other Whigs jump out of
       ground-floor window in unsuccessful attempt not to be
       counted as present; incident causes widespread derision in
       the Democratic press.

1841   Breaks engagement with Mary Todd on January 1. Is se-
       verely depressed for weeks and absent from legislature for
       several days. Legislature adjourns, March 1. Dissolves part-
       nership with Stuart, who is often absent on political busi-
       ness, and forms new partnership with Stephen T. Logan,
       prominent Illinois Whig known for methodical legal work.
       Wins appeal before Illinois Supreme Court in case of *Bailey*
       v. *Cromwell*, successfully arguing that unpaid promissory
       note written by his client, David Bailey, for purchase of
       slave was legally void in Illinois due to the prohibitions
       against slavery in the Ordinance of 1787 and the state con-
       stitution. Visits Speed at his family home near Lexington,
       Kentucky, in August and September. On return trip by steam-
       boat, sees twelve slaves chained together "like so many fish
       upon a trot-line."

1842   Delivers address to local temperance society on February
       22. Does not seek reelection to legislature. Resumes court-
       ship of Mary Todd during summer. In September, accepts
       challenge from Democratic state auditor James Shields, who

is angered by four published pseudonymous letters ridiculing him (one was written by Mary Todd and a friend, another by Lincoln). Lincoln chooses broadswords as weapons, but duel is averted on September 22 when Shields accepts Lincoln's explanation that the letters were purely political in nature and not intended to impugn Shields's personal honor. Marries Mary Todd on November 4 in parlor of her sister's Springfield mansion, then moves with her into room in the Globe Tavern.

1843   Unsuccessfully seeks Whig nomination for Congress, then tries to establish arrangement with John J. Hardin and Edward D. Baker for each of them to be nominated in turn to serve for one term. Son Robert Todd Lincoln born August 1. Lincolns move into rented cottage.

1844   Lincolns move in May into house, bought for $1,500, at Eighth and Jackson streets in Springfield (their home until 1861). Campaigns as Whig elector for Henry Clay in the presidential election. Visits former Indiana home in fall. Partnership with Logan is dissolved in December so that Logan can take his son as new partner; Lincoln establishes his own practice and takes 26-year-old William H. Herndon as junior partner.

1845   Works to assure himself Whig congressional nomination when Hardin refuses to abide by principle of rotation. Income from law practice is approximately $1,500 a year.

1846   Second son, Edward Baker Lincoln, born March 10. Wins congressional nomination at Whig district convention held on May 1. Speaks on May 30 at mass meeting in Springfield that calls for united support of recently declared war against Mexico. Helps prosecute manslaughter charge in June; jury deadlocks and case is never retried. Elected to U.S. House of Representatives on August 3, defeating Democrat Peter Cartwright, a Methodist preacher, by 6,340 to 4,829 votes.

1847   Makes first visit to Chicago in early July to attend convention protesting President James K. Polk's veto of bill for river and harbor improvements. In October, represents slave-owner Robert Matson at habeas corpus hearing in Coles County. Lincoln argues that Bryants, slave family Matson had brought from Kentucky to do seasonal farmwork on his Illinois land, were not state residents and thus were not freed by antislavery provisions of Illinois law. Court rules against Matson and frees Bryants. After visit with wife's family in Lexington, Kentucky, travels with wife and sons to Washington, D.C., and moves into boarding house near the Capitol. Takes seat in the House of Representatives when Thirtieth Congress convenes on December 6. Presents resolutions on December 22 requesting President Polk to inform the House whether the "spot" where hostilities with Mexico began was or was not on Mexican soil.

1848   Serves on Expenditures in the War Department and Post Office and Post Roads committees. Attacks Polk's war policy in speech on floor of the House, January 22 (almost all fighting had ended with the American capture of Mexico City in September 1847, but peace treaty had yet to be signed). Ridiculed as "spotty Lincoln" by Illinois Democratic press. Wife and children leave Washington to stay with her family in Kentucky. Attends national Whig convention at Philadelphia in early June as supporter of General Zachary Taylor, who is nominated for president. Abides by his own rule of rotation and does not seek second term in Congress. Rejoined by family in late July. House adjourns on August 14. Campaigns for Taylor in Maryland and Massachusetts; meets former New York governor William H. Seward at Whig rally in Boston on September 22. Visits Niagara Falls before taking steamer to Chicago. Campaigns in Illinois until election. Returns to Washington, December 7, for second session of Thirtieth Congress. Supports the principle of the Wilmot Proviso by voting to prohibit slavery in the territory acquired from Mexico.

1849   Votes to exclude slavery from federal territories and abolish slave trade in the District of Columbia, but does not speak in congressional debates on slavery. Congress adjourns on March 4. Makes only appearance before United States Supreme Court, March 7–8, unsuccessfully appealing U.S. circuit court ruling concerning application of Illinois statute of limitations on nonresidents' suits. Applies for patent (later granted) on device for reducing draft of steamboats in shallow water. Returns to Springfield on March 31. Visits father and stepmother in Coles County in late May. Goes to Washington in June in pursuit of position as commissioner of the General Land Office, but fails to receive appointment from the new Taylor administration. Resumes law practice in Illinois. Declines appointment as secretary and then as governor of Oregon Territory.

1850   Son Edward dies on February 1 after illness of nearly two months. Lincoln returns to Eighth Judicial Circuit (now covering fourteen counties), making 400-mile, 12-week trip in spring and fall. Becomes a closer friend of David Davis, who had practiced law with Lincoln on the circuit before becoming its judge in 1848. Delivers eulogy of Zachary Taylor at Chicago memorial meeting in July. Studies Euclidean geometry. Third son, William Wallace (Willie), born December 21.

1851   Learns that father is seriously ill in Coles County. Writes to stepbrother John D. Johnston that he cannot visit because of wife's health. Father dies on January 17.

1852   Wife joins First Presbyterian Church in Springfield. Lincoln rents a pew and attends at times but never himself becomes a member of any church. Delivers eulogy of Henry Clay at Springfield memorial meeting in July. Serves as Whig elector and makes several speeches in support of Winfield Scott during presidential campaign.

1853   Fourth son, Thomas (Tad), born April 4. In May, Lincoln serves as court-appointed prosecutor in child-rape case and wins conviction (defendant is sentenced to eighteen years in prison). Accepts retainer from Illinois Central Railroad in October in suit to prevent taxation by McLean County, a case crucial to railroad's claim that it could be taxed only by the state government.

1854 Helps argue McLean County case in Illinois Supreme Court, February 28; court orders that it be re-argued. Lincoln's declining interest in politics is revived when Congress passes the Kansas-Nebraska Act on May 22, repealing anti-slavery restriction in the Missouri Compromise. Completion of direct railroad link increases Lincoln's practice in U.S. district and circuit courts in Chicago. Runs for Illinois House of Representatives to help campaign of Richard Yates, a congressman who opposed the Kansas-Nebraska Act. Speaks against the act at Bloomington, September 26, Springfield, October 4, and Peoria, October 16, appearing before or after Stephen A. Douglas, its principal author. Elected to legislature, but declines seat to become eligible for election to the United States Senate.

1855 Legislature meets to elect United States senator, February 8. Lincoln leads on first ballot, but eventually throws dwindling support to anti-Nebraska Democrat Lyman Trumbull, who is elected on tenth ballot. Goes to Cincinnati in September to appear for defense in *McCormick* v. *Manny*, federal patent infringement suit originally scheduled to be tried in Illinois. Is excluded from case by other defense attorneys, including Edwin Stanton of Pittsburgh, and does not participate in trial, but stays to watch arguments. Lincoln's earnings now total about $5,000 a year.

1856 Re-argues McLean County tax case before Illinois Supreme Court, January 16–17 (court later rules in railroad's favor, but Lincoln is forced to sue railroad for payment of his fee). Attends meeting of anti-Nebraska newspaper editors, held in Decatur on February 22, that calls for convention to organize new free-soil political party. Joins in founding Republican Party of Illinois at convention in Bloomington, May 29, and inspires delegates with address that goes unrecorded (later known as the "Lost Speech"). Receives 110 votes from eleven delegations on first ballot for vice-presidential nomination at the first Republican national convention, held in Philadelphia, June 19. Makes more than fifty speeches throughout Illinois as presidential elector for Republican candidate John C. Frémont.

1857   Helps prosecute murder case in which defendant is acquitted for reasons of insanity. Wins suit against Illinois Central Railroad over his fee in the McLean County tax case on June 23 (receives $4,800 in August as balance of $5,000 billed, his largest legal fee, and continues to represent Illinois Central in important litigation). Delivers major speech against Dred Scott decision in Springfield on June 26. Visits New York City, Niagara Falls, and Canada with wife in late July. In September defends Rock Island Railroad in the *Effie Afton* case, involving steamboat destroyed by fire after striking the first railroad bridge across the Mississippi River. Trial ends when jury deadlocks 9–3 in railroad's favor, a significant setback to riverboat interests in their efforts to block railroad expansion.

1858   In May, wins acquittal for William (Duff) Armstrong, son of New Salem friends Jack and Hannah Armstrong, by using almanac to discredit testimony of key prosecution witness as to height of the moon at time of alleged murder, and by suggesting that deceased had died because of a drunken fall from his horse. Charges no fee for defense. Accepts endorsement on June 16 by the Republican state convention at Springfield as its "first and only choice" for Senate seat held by Douglas and delivers "House-Divided" speech. Attends speech by Douglas in Chicago, July 9, and replies the following day. Begins following Douglas through state, occasionally riding as ordinary passenger on the same train that carried Douglas in his private car. On July 24, invites Douglas to "divide time" on the same platform for remainder of campaign. Douglas declines, but agrees to seven debates, which are held on August 21, 27, September 15, 18, and October 7, 13, 15. Audiences at debates probably number between 10,000 and 15,000, except for about 1,200 at Jonesboro on September 15 and perhaps as many as 20,000 at Galesburg on October 7. Both candidates also deliver scores of speeches throughout state, concentrating on counties of central Illinois. Republicans win a plurality in the election on November 2, but they do not gain control of the legislature because of Democratic holdovers and an unfavorable apportionment of seats. In December, Lincoln assembles newspaper clippings of debates and major campaign speeches in scrapbook.

1859 Legislature reelects Douglas to the Senate on January 5 by vote of 54 to 46. Lincoln begins negotiations in March for publication of debates. Son Robert fails Harvard College entrance exams and enrolls at Phillips Exeter Academy in New Hampshire. From August to October Lincoln makes speeches for Republican candidates in Iowa, Ohio, and Wisconsin. Begins to be mentioned as possible presidential candidate. In fall makes last trip through Eighth Circuit (reduced to five counties in 1857). Speaks in Kansas before its territorial elections in early December.

1860 Delivers address on slavery and the framers of the Constitution to audience of 1,500 at Cooper Union in New York City on February 27. Visits Robert at Exeter and speaks to enthusiastic crowds in Rhode Island, New Hampshire, and Connecticut before returning to Springfield. *Political Debates between Hon. Abraham Lincoln and Hon. Stephen A. Douglas in the Celebrated Campaign of 1858, in Illinois*, printed from Lincoln's scrapbook, published in March by Follett, Foster & Co. in Columbus, Ohio. Republican state convention, meeting at Decatur on May 10, instructs Illinois delegation to vote for Lincoln at national convention. Lincoln remains in Springfield while team of supporters, led by Judge David Davis and Norman B. Judd, chairman of the Illinois Republican state central committee, canvasses delegates at Republican national convention in Chicago. Wins nomination for president on the third ballot, May 18, defeating main rival Senator William H. Seward of New York as well as

Senator Simon Cameron of Pennsylvania, Senator Salmon P. Chase of Ohio, and Edward Bates of Missouri. Learns of his victory and of nomination of Senator Hannibal Hamlin of Maine for vice-president at office of *Illinois State Journal.* Studies platform, which opposes the extension of slavery, vaguely endorses a protective tariff policy, and calls for homestead legislation, internal improvements, and a transcontinental railroad. Following established practice, Lincoln does not campaign and makes no formal speeches, but corresponds extensively with Republican leaders. Makes one of his last court appearances on June 20 in a federal patent case. (At conclusion of legal career has net worth of approximately $15,000.) Hires 28-year-old John G. Nicolay and 22-year-old John Hay as personal secretaries. Son Robert is admitted to Harvard College. Follows election returns in Springfield telegraph office, November 6. Defeats Stephen A. Douglas (Northern Democratic), John C. Breckinridge of Kentucky (Southern Democratic), and John Bell of Tennessee (Constitutional Union) to become first Republican president. Receives 180 of the 303 electoral votes while winning plurality of 40 percent of the popular vote. Meets with Republican leaders in Springfield, considers Cabinet appointments, and is beset by office-seekers. South Carolina secedes from the Union on December 20 (Mississippi, Florida, Alabama, Georgia, Louisiana, and Texas follow within two months).

1861 Works on inaugural address. Sees stepmother for the last time at her home in Coles County, January 31–February 1. Leaves Springfield by train on February 11, making brief speeches and appearances in Indiana, Ohio, Pennsylvania, New York, and New Jersey. Warned in Philadelphia that he might be assassinated in Baltimore, travels secretly to Washington on night of February 22–23; trip is ridiculed by opposition press. Finishes selecting Cabinet that includes the other major contenders for the Republican presidential nomination: William H. Seward (secretary of state), Salmon P. Chase (secretary of the treasury), Simon Cameron (secretary of war), and Edward Bates (attorney general), as well as Gideon Welles (secretary of the navy), Montgomery Blair (postmaster general), and Caleb B. Smith (secretary of the interior). Inaugurated on March 4. Decides, after much discussion with Cabinet, to send naval expedition to resupply Fort Sumter in Charleston harbor. Confederates open fire on the fort, April 12, and its garrison surrenders two days later. On April 15, Lincoln calls forth 75,000 militia and summons Congress to meet on July 4 in special session. Meets with Douglas, who supports Lincoln's efforts to preserve the Union and advises calling for 200,000 troops. Virginia secedes on April 17 and is followed within five weeks by North Carolina, Tennessee, and Arkansas, forming eleven-state Confederacy. On April 19, Lincoln proclaims blockade of Southern ports, and on April 27 he authorizes the military to suspend the writ of habeas corpus along the Philadelphia–Washington railroad line. Issues proclamation on May 3 directing expansion of the regular army and navy. Consults with various members of Congress, including Massachusetts senator Charles Sumner, beginning a personal friendship. Suffers first sense of personal loss in the war at the news of the death on May 24 of his young friend Colonel Elmer Ellsworth, shot while removing a Confederate flag from a building in Alexandria. Disregards *Ex parte Merryman* opinion of Chief Justice Roger B. Taney, finding his suspension of habeas corpus unconstitutional (Taney had sought unsuccessfully to enforce a writ issued by himself, not the full Court, which did not hear the case). Has White House draped in mourning after Douglas dies in Illinois on June 3 while rallying support for the Union. Follows progress of battle and Union defeat at Bull Run, July 21, from War Department telegraph office (will receive news and send orders from there for remainder of war). Appoints George B. McClellan commander of the Department (later Army) of the Potomac on July 27. Sees visitors, including Cabinet members, senators, congressmen, military officers, office-seekers, and ordinary citizens, for several hours each weekday. Often takes carriage rides in the afternoon. Writes letters and signs commissions in the evening. Enjoys attending theater, opera, and concerts. Reads

Shakespeare, the Bible, and humorous writings of Artemus Ward, Orpheus C. Kerr, and Petroleum V. Nasby. On September 11, revokes General John C. Frémont's proclamation of emancipation in Missouri, bitterly disappointing many antislavery advocates. Saddened by death on October 21 of friend and former Illinois Whig colleague Edward D. Baker in skirmish at Ball's Bluff, Virginia. On October 24, signs order relieving Frémont of his command. Replaces him with General David Hunter. On November 1, appoints McClellan commander of the Union army after Winfield Scott retires. In message to Congress, December 3, recommends program of emancipation and colonization for slaves confiscated from Confederate owners. After Cabinet meetings on December 25 and 26, agrees to the release of two Confederate envoys seized from British ship *Trent* in November, resolving serious Anglo-American crisis.

1862   Reads General Henry Halleck's *Elements of Military Art and Science*. Meets with congressional Committee on the Conduct of the War and rejects demand of its chairman, Ohio Republican senator Benjamin Wade, that McClellan be dismissed for inaction. On January 13, replaces Simon Cameron with Democrat Edwin Stanton amid charges of widespread corruption and incompetence in the War Department. Nominates Noah Swayne of Ohio to the Supreme Court. Issues General War Order No. 1 on January 27, calling for a simultaneous Union advance on several fronts beginning February 22. Is frustrated by McClellan's unwillingness to take offensive action in Virginia. Recommends promotion of Ulysses S. Grant to major general after capture of Fort Donelson in Tennessee by Grant's army on February 16. Son Willie falls ill in early February (probably with typhoid fever) and dies on February 20. Wife is overcome with grief and never recovers emotionally. Lincoln relieves McClellan as general-in-chief on March 11 and assumes direct command of the Union armies (retains McClellan as commander of the Army of the Potomac). Appoints Halleck as commander of western armies. Reluctantly agrees to McClellan's plan for an advance on Richmond by way of the peninsula between the York and James rivers and is frustrated by its slow progress. Signs act on April 16 abolishing slavery in the District of Columbia. Refuses to dismiss Grant, who is widely blamed for heavy Union losses at battle of Shiloh. Visits Peninsula, May 5–12, and directs successful Union attack on Norfolk, Virginia. On May 15, approves legislation establishing the Department of Agriculture, and signs the Homestead Act on May 20. Visits General Irvin McDowell's corps at Fredericksburg, May 22–23. On May 24, concerned about safety of Washington, cancels planned movement of McDowell's troops to join McClellan's army near Richmond and orders that McDowell launch an attack on Thomas (Stonewall) Jackson's command in the Shenandoah Valley. To escape the heat, moves with family in early June to cottage at Soldiers' Home on hill four miles northwest of White House (will live there each summer). On June 19, approves legislation prohibiting slavery in the territories. Issues order on June 26 that consolidates Union forces in the Shenandoah Valley and northern Virginia as the Army of Virginia, under General John Pope. Signs Pacific Railroad Act and bill providing land grants for agricultural colleges on July 2. Visits Peninsula, July 7–10, conferring with McClellan and his corps commanders in aftermath of the Seven Days' battles. Returns to Washington and appoints Halleck general-in-chief on July 11 (does not name new overall western commander to replace Halleck). Nominates Iowa Republican Samuel Miller to Supreme Court. On July 17, signs Second Confiscation Act, authorizing seizure of slaves and other property of persons found by federal courts to be supporting the rebellion, after Congress appends resolution satisfying most of his reservations. Reads draft of preliminary Emancipation Proclamation to Cabinet on July 22, but delays issuing it, apparently agreeing with Seward that it should follow a Union military victory to avoid being seen as an act of desperation. Agrees with Halleck's decision to abandon Peninsula campaign and withdraw Army of the Potomac (order is issued on August 3); move is widely criticized, with campaign's failure attributed to Lincoln's withholding of troops for defense of Washington. Relieves Pope after his defeat at the second battle of Bull Run, August 29–30, and places his army under McClellan's command, despite distrust of McClellan in the Cabinet and Congress. Union victory at Antietam on September 17 ends Lee's invasion of Maryland. Lincoln issues preliminary Emancipation Proclamation on September 22, to take effect January 1, 1863, in all territory still in rebellion against the national government. Worried by significant Democratic gains in fall congressional and state elections. Nominates his friend David Davis to the Supreme Court. Removes Don Carlos Buell from command of the Army of the Ohio, October 23, and replaces him on October 30 with William Rosecrans (command becomes Army of the Cumberland). Replaces McClellan with Ambrose Burnside as commander of the Army of the Potomac on November 5, and confers with Burnside at Aquia Creek, Virginia, on November 27. In annual message to Congress, December 1, recommends constitutional amendment authorizing gradual, compensated emancipation. Extends clemency to 265 of 303 Sioux Indians condemned to death after summer uprising in Minnesota. Army of the Potomac suffers costly defeat at Fredericksburg on December 13. Lincoln holds lengthy meeting on December 19 with Cabinet (excluding Seward) and nine senators from Republican caucus seeking Seward's dismissal and greater Cabinet role in running government. Meeting results in submission of resignation by Chase, Seward's chief Cabinet critic; Lincoln rejects it, along with previously submitted resignation of Seward, thereby resolving crisis. Signs bill on December 31 admitting West Virginia to the Union.

1863   On January 1, issues the Emancipation Proclamation freeing all slaves in Confederate-held territory. Responding to protests, on January 4 revokes Grant's order of December 17, 1862, that expelled all Jews from the Department of Tennessee. John P. Usher succeeds Caleb B. Smith as secretary of the interior. Appoints Joseph Hooker to succeed Burnside on January 25. Approves bill on February 25 creating a national banking system, and signs act on March 3 introducing military conscription. Nominates California judge Stephen J. Field to the Supreme Court. Concerned by allegations that Grant is incompetent and frequently drunk, is reassured by reports of Charles A. Dana, Stanton's special emissary at Grant's headquarters. April 4–10, visits Army of the Potomac at its winter quarters in Falmouth, Virginia, and views Fredericksburg battlefield from Union front line. Battle of Chancellorsville, May 1–4, ends in Union defeat, and Lincoln returns to Falmouth on May 7 to confer with Hooker. Replaces Hooker with George G. Meade, June 28, during Lee's invasion of Pennsylvania. Greatly encouraged by Lee's defeat at Gettysburg on July 3 and by capture of Vicksburg, last major Confederate stronghold on the Mississippi, by Grant's army on July 4. Discusses recruitment and treatment of Negro troops with abolitionist Frederick Douglass at White House on August 10; Douglass is impressed by seriousness with which Lincoln receives him. Encouraged by victories of administration supporters in Ohio and Pennsylvania state elections. With Chattanooga under Confederate siege after the Union defeat at Chickamauga, September 19–20, appoints Grant to command of all operations in the western theater and authorizes him to replace Rosecrans with George H. Thomas as commander of the Army of the Cumberland. Delivers dedicatory address at the Gettysburg Cemetery on November 19 to audience of 15,000–20,000, following two-hour oration by Edward Everett. Ill with varioloid (mild form of smallpox) for three weeks after return to Washington. Issues proclamation of amnesty and reconstruction, a program for restoration of the Union, on December 8. Retains Chase in Cabinet despite Chase's willingness to challenge him for the Republican nomination.

1864   "Pomeroy Circular," a letter produced by radicals supporting Chase's candidacy and distributed to influential Republicans, is published in late February. It embarrasses Chase and rallies support for Lincoln. He receives endorsement for second term from Republican caucus in Ohio, Chase's home state, and in early March Chase withdraws from campaign. On March 12, appoints Grant general-in-chief of the armies, Halleck chief of staff, and William T. Sherman as Grant's successor commanding in the West. Grant makes his headquarters with the Army of the Potomac while retaining Meade as its commander. Responding to a recommendation from Lincoln and Stanton, Congress repeals provision in conscription law that allows payment of $300 in lieu of service. Signed by Lincoln on July 4, the act retains the provision that permits hiring a substitute. Nominated for president June 8 on first ballot by nearly unanimous vote of the National Union Convention, a coalition of Republicans and War Democrats. Convention nominates Democrat Andrew Johnson, military governor of Tennessee, for vice-president and endorses proposed constitutional amendment abolishing slavery. Lincoln accepts Chase's resignation on June 30 and names Republican senator William P. Fessenden of Maine as his successor. Pocket-vetoes the Wade-Davis bill, congressional reconstruction plan he considers too severe, on July 4. Observes fighting on outskirts of Washington from parapet of Fort Stevens during unsuccessful Confederate attack, July 11–12, and comes under fire. Writes private memorandum on August 23, acknowledging that he probably will not be reelected. Feels less pessimistic about his election prospects after capture of Atlanta by Sherman's army on September 2 and General Philip H. Sheridan's decisive victory in the Shenandoah Valley at Cedar Creek on October 19. Appeases Republican radicals by replacing conservative Montgomery Blair as postmaster general with William Dennison on September 23. On Grant's advice, approves Sherman's planned march from Atlanta to the sea. Follows election returns at War Department telegraph office on November 8. Defeats Democratic nominee, General George B. McClellan, winning 55 percent of popular vote and 212 of 233 electoral votes. Appoints James Speed (brother of friend Joshua F. Speed) as attorney general to replace retiring Edward Bates. Nominates Salmon P. Chase as chief justice of the Supreme Court on December 6.

1865   Uses influence to gain some Democratic support in House of Representatives for resolution proposing submission of Thirteenth Amendment, abolishing slavery, to states for ratification (Senate had approved amendment in April 1864). House passes resolution by three-vote margin on January 31. Meets with Confederate representatives in unsuccessful peace conference at Hampton Roads, Virginia, on February 3. Signs bill on March 3 creating bureau for relief of freedmen and refugees. Inaugurated for second term on March 4. Names Comptroller of the Currency Hugh McCullough as secretary of the treasury when Fessenden returns to Senate. Leaves for City Point, Virginia, on March 23 and confers with Grant, Sherman, and Admiral David D. Porter on military and political situation, March 27–28. Visits Richmond on April 4 after its evacuation by the Confederate army. Returns to Washington on April 9, the day of Lee's surrender to Grant at Appomattox Court House. Makes last public speech on April 11, devoting it mainly to problems of reconstruction. Shot in the head by well-known actor John Wilkes Booth while watching performance of comedy *Our American Cousin* at Ford's Theatre shortly after 10 P.M., April 14. Dies in nearby house without regaining consciousness at 7:22 A.M., April 15. After funeral service in the White House on April 19, casket is viewed by millions as it is carried by special train to Illinois before burial in Oak Ridge Cemetery, outside Springfield, on May 4.

Sources and Acknowledgments

James Agee. *From* Abraham Lincoln—The Early Years: *The Lively Arts: Four Representative Types*, ed. Rodney E. Sheratsky and John L. Reilly (New York: Globe Book Co., 1964), pp. 403–16. Copyright © 1952 by the James Agee Trust. Reprinted with permission of The Wylie Agency Inc.

Anonymous. *From* Abraham Africanus I: *Abraham Africanus I* (New York: J. F. Feeks, 1864), pp. 9–12.

Anonymous. The Federal Phœnix: *Abraham Lincoln: A Press Portrait*, ed. Herbert Mitgang (Chicago: Quadrangle Books, 1971), pp. 422–23. Originally published in *Punch*, December 3, 1864.

George Bancroft. Oration in Union Square, New York City: *Obsequies of Abraham Lincoln in Union Square, New York, April 25, 1865* (New York: D. Van Nostrand, 1865), pp. 9–20.

Jacques Barzun. Lincoln the Writer: *On Writing, Editing, and Publishing* (Chicago: University of Chicago Press, 1971), pp. 57–73. Copyright © Jacques Barzun. All rights reserved c/o Writers Representatives LLC, New York, N.Y. Originally published as "Lincoln the Literary Genius" in *The Saturday Evening Post*, February 14, 1959.

Henry Ward Beecher. Sermon Preached in Brooklyn: *Our Martyr President, Abraham Lincoln. Voices from the Pulpit of New York and Brooklyn* (New York: Tibbals & Whiting, 1865), pp. 33–48.

Rosemary Benét. Nancy Hanks: *A Book of Americans* (New York: Farrar and Rinehart Inc, 1933), p. 65. Copyright © 1933 by Rosemary and Stephen Vincent Benét. Copyright renewed © 1961 by Rosemary Carr Benét. Reprinted by permission of Brandt & Hochman Literary Agents, Inc.

Stephen Vincent Benét. *From* John Brown's Body: *John Brown's Body* (Garden City, N.Y.: Doubleday, Doran, 1928), pp. 72–74, pp. 111–12, pp. 177–78, pp. 211–22, pp. 325–26, pp.362–63, pp. 371–72. Copyright © 1927, 1928 by Stephen Vincent Benét. Copyright renewed © 1955 by Rosemary Carr Benét. Reprinted by permission of Brandt & Hochman Literary Agents, Inc.

Lerone Bennett Jr. Was Abe Lincoln a White Supremacist?: *Ebony*, February 1968, pp. 35–42. Copyright © 1968. Reprinted by permission of the Johnson Publishing Company, Inc.

Adam Braver. *From* Mr. Lincoln's Wars: *Mr. Lincoln's Wars: A Novel in Thirteen Stories* (New York: HarperCollins, 2003), pp. 289–303. Copyright © 2003 by Adam Braver. Reprinted by permission of HarperCollins Publishers.

Noah Brooks. Personal Recollections of Abraham Lincoln: *Harper's New Monthly Magazine*, July 1865, pp. 222–30.

William Cullen Bryant. Introduction of Abraham Lincoln at Cooper Union: *New York Evening Post*, February 28, 1860. The Death of Lincoln: *Poems* (New York: D. Appleton and Company, 1876), p. 446. Originally published in 1865.

Witter Bynner. A Farmer Remembers Lincoln: *Grenstone Poems* (New York: Frederick A. Stokes Company, 1917), pp. 20–21.

Dale Carnegie. *From* Lincoln the Unknown: *Lincoln the Unknown* (Dale Carnegie & Associates, Inc.: Garden City, New York), pp. 20–31. Copyright © 1932 by Dale Carnegie, renewed 1959 by Dorothy Carnegie. Reprinted by permission of Dale Carnegie & Associates.

Winston Churchill. *From* The Crisis: *The Crisis* (New York: The Macmillan Company, 1901), pp. 499–515.

Sir Winston Churchill. *From* A History of the English-Speaking Peoples: *A History of the English-Speaking Peoples*, vol. 4: *The Great Democracies* (London: Cassell, 1958), pp. 169–72, pp. 206–7. Copyright Winston Churchill. Reproduced with permission of Curtis Brown Ltd, London on behalf of The Estate of Winston Churchill.

Norman Corwin. *From* The Rivalry: *The Rivalry* (New York: Dramatists Play Service, Inc., 1960), pp. 54–58, pp. 69–74. Copyright © Norman Corwin. Reprinted by permission of the author.

Mario M. Cuomo. Abraham Lincoln and Our "Unfinished Work": *More than Words: The Speeches of Mario Cuomo* (New York: St. Martin's Press, 1993), pp. 87–99. Copyright © 1993 by Mario M. Cuomo. Reprinted by permission of Mario M. Cuomo.

E. L. Doctorow. *From* The March: *The March* (New York: Random House, 2005), pp. 330–35. Copyright © 2005 by E.L. Doctorow. Used by permission of Random House, Inc.

John Dos Passos. Lincoln and His Almost Chosen People: *Lincoln and the Gettysburg Address*, ed. Allan Nevins (Urbana: University of Illinois Press, 1964), pp. 15–37. Copyright © 1964 by the Board of Trustees of the University of Illinois. Reprinted by permission of the Dos Passos Estate.

Frederick Douglass. Oration in Memory of Abraham Lincoln: *American Speeches: Political Oratory from Abraham Lincoln to Bill Clinton*, ed. Ted Widmer (New York: Library of America, 2006), pp. 74–84. Reprinted from *The Frederick Douglass Papers*, Series One, Volume 4, ed. John W. Blassingame and John R. McKivigan (New Haven: Yale University Press, 1991), pp. 428–40. Copyright © 1991 by Yale University. Reprinted by permission of Yale University Press. *From* Reminiscences of Abraham Lincoln by Distinguished Men of His Time: *Reminiscences of Abraham Lincoln by Distinguished Men of His Time* (New York: North American Publishing Company, 1886), pp. 185–95.

W.E.B. Du Bois. *From* The Crisis: *Writings*, ed. Nathan Huggins (New York: The Library of America, 1986), p. 1196, pp. 1197–99. Originally published in *The Crisis*, May and September 1922.

Ralph Waldo Emerson. *From* The Journals: *The Journals and Miscellaneous Notebooks of Ralph Waldo Emerson*, vol. XV, ed. Linda Allardt and David W. Hill (Cambridge: The Belknap Press of Harvard University Press, 1982), pp. 186–87, pp. 194–95, p. 218. Copyright © 1982 by the President and Fellows of Harvard College. Reprinted by permission of the publisher. Remarks at the Services Held in Concord: *Miscellanies* (Boston and New York: Houghton, Mifflin and Company, 1883), pp. 305–15.

John Gould Fletcher. Lincoln: *Breakers and Granite* (New York: The Macmillan Company, 1921), pp. 159–63.

Shelby Foote. *From* The Civil War: A Narrative: *The Civil War: A Narrative*, vol. 3, *Red River to Appomattox* (New York: Random House, 1974), pp. 973–86. Copyright © 1974 by Shelby Foote. Used by permission of Random House, Inc.

James Sloan Gibbons. Three Hundred Thousand More: *New York Evening Post*, July 16, 1862.

Richard Watson Gilder. On the Life-Mask of Abraham Lincoln: *The Poems of Richard Watson Gilder* (Boston and New York: Houghton Mifflin Company, 1908), pp. 117–18. Originally published in 1886. To the Spirit of Abraham Lincoln: *The Poems of Richard Watson Gilder* (Boston and New York: Houghton Mifflin Company, 1908), p. 163. Originally published in 1888.

Allen Ginsberg. Adapted from Neruda's "Que despierte el leñador":

Collected Poems 1947–1997 (New York: HarperCollins, 2006), pp. 704–06. Copyright © 2006 by the Allen Ginsberg Trust. Reprinted by permission of HarperCollins Publishers. Originally published in *Plutonian Ode: Poems 1977–1980* (1982), with the following note: "Adapted Summer 1978–Spring 1981 by Sidney Goldfarb and Allen Ginsberg from Waldeen's Tr. of *Let the Railsplitter Awake and Other Poems, by Pablo Neruda*. New York: Masses and Mainstream, 1950."

Ulysses S. Grant. *From* Personal Memoirs of U. S. Grant: *Personal Memoirs of U. S. Grant*, Vol. II (New York: Charles L. Webster, 1886), pp. 121–23, pp. 142–43, pp. 420–24, pp. 522–23, pp. 532–33, pp. 536–37.

Horace Greeley. The Prayer of Twenty Millions: *Dear Mr. Lincoln: Letters to the President*, compiled and edited by Harold Holzer (Reading, Massachusetts: Addison-Wesley Publishing Company, 1993), pp. 156–61. Originally published in the *New York Tribune*, August 20, 1862.

Edward Everett Hale. Sermon Preached in Boston: *Sermons Preached in Boston on the Death of Abraham Lincoln* (Boston: J. E. Tilton and Company, 1865), pp. 267–75.

Marsden Hartley. American Ikon—Lincoln: *The Collected Poems Marsden Hartley, 1904–1943*, ed. Gail R. Scott (Santa Rosa, CA: Black Sparrow Press, 1987), p. 197. Copyright © 1987 by Yale University by permission from the heirs of Marsden Hartley. Reprinted by permission of Yale University as Literary Executor.

Nathaniel Hawthorne. *From* Chiefly About War-Matters by a Peaceable Man: *The Centenary Edition of the Works of Nathaniel Hawthorne*, volume XXII, *Miscellaneous Prose and Verse*, ed. Thomas Woodson, Claude M. Simpson, L. Neal Smith (Columbus: Ohio State University Press, 1994), pp. 410–15. Copyright © 1994 by the Ohio State University Press. Reprinted by permission of the Ohio State University Press. Originally published in expurgated form in *Atlantic Monthly*, July 1862.

William H. Herndon. Abraham Lincoln, Ann Rutledge, and New Salem: A Lecture: *Abraham Lincoln, Miss Ann Rutledge, New Salem, Pioneering & the Poem* (Springfield, Illinois: 1910), pp. 7–50. Originally published in 1866.

William H. Herndon & Jesse W. Weik. *From* Herndon's Lincoln: The True Story of a Great Life: *Herndon's Lincoln*, ed. Douglas L. Wilson and Rodney O. Davis (Urbana, Illinois: University of Illinois Press, 2006), pp. 246–52. Originally published in 1889.

Julia Ward Howe. "Crown His Blood-Stained Pillow": *Poetical Tributes to the Memory of Abraham Lincoln* (Philadelphia: J.B. Lippincott & Co., 1865), pp. 15–16. Abraham Lincoln: *At Sunset* (Boston: Houghton Mifflin Company, 1910), pp. 3–4.

William Dean Howells. *From* Life of Abraham Lincoln: *Life of Abraham Lincoln* (Bloomington: Indiana University Press, 1960), pp. 56–76. Originally published in 1860.

Langston Hughes. Lincoln Monument: Washington: *The Collected Poems of Langston Hughes*, ed. Arnold Rampersad (New York: Alfred A. Knopf, 1994), p. 103. Copyright © 1994 by The Estate of Langston Hughes. Used by permission of Alfred A. Knopf, a division of Random House, Inc. Originally published in 1932.

Victor Hugo. Notebook entry: *Europe Looks at the Civil War*, ed. Belle Becker Sideman and Lillian Friedman, translated by Tina du Bouchet (New York: The Orion Press, 1960), p. 306.

Henrik Ibsen. Abraham Lincoln's Murder: *Ibsen's Poems: in versions by John Northam* (Oslo: Norwegian University Press, 1986), pp. 92–94. © Universitersforlaget AS 1986. Originally published in *Fædrelandet*, May 15, 1865.

MacKinlay Kantor. *From* If the South Had Won the Civil War: *If the South Had Won the Civil War* (New York: Bantam Books, 1961): pp. 40–49, pp. 55–69, pp. 82–85. Copyright © 1960 by MacKinlay Kantor. Renewed © 1988 by the Estate of MacKinlay Kantor. Reprinted by permission of the Kantor Estate and the Estate's agent, Donald Maass, 157 West 57th Street, Suite 703, New York, NY 10019, in association with Forge, an affiliate of Tom Doherty Associates, LLC.

William Kennedy. *From* O Albany! An Urban Tapestry: *O Albany! An Urban Tapestry* (New York: Viking Press, 1983), pp. 67–71. Copyright © 1983 by William Kennedy. Used by permission of Viking Penguin, a division of Penguin Group (USA) Inc.

Donggill Kim. Lincoln and Confucian Virtues: *Abraham Lincoln: An Oriental Interpretation* (Seoul: Jungwoo-sa, 1983), pp. 34–45, pp. 205–07. Copyright © 1983 by Donggill Kim.

Stanley Kunitz. The Lincoln Relics: *The Poems of Stanley Kunitz, 1928–1978* (Boston: Little, Brown and Company, 1979), pp. 22–25. Copyright © 1979, 2000 by Stanley Kunitz. Used by permission of W. W. Norton & Company, Inc.

Vachel Lindsay. Abraham Lincoln Walks at Midnight: *The Congo and Other Poems* (New York: The Macmillan Company, 1914), pp. 145–47.

James Russell Lowell. The President's Policy: *North American Review*, January 1864, pp. 234–60. *From* Ode Recited at the Harvard Commemoration: *Poets of the Civil War*, ed. J. D. McClatchy (New York: The Library of America, 2005), pp. 40–42. Originally published in *Atlantic Monthly*, September 1865.

Robert Lowell. Abraham Lincoln: *Selected Poems*, Revised Edition (New York: Farrar, Straus & Giroux, 1977), p. 175. Copyright © 2003 by Harriet Lowell and Sheridan Lowell. Reprinted by permission of Farrar, Straus and Giroux, LLC.

Edwin Markham. Lincoln, the Man of the People: *Lincoln and Other Poems* (New York: McClure, Phillips & Company, 1901), pp. 1–3.

Karl Marx. On Events in North America, Address of the International Working Men's Association to President Johnson: *The Karl Marx Library, Volume II: On America and the Civil War*, edited and translated by Saul K. Padover (New York: McGraw-Hill Book Company, 1972), pp. 220–23, pp. 241–42. Copyright © 1972. Reprinted by permission of the McGraw Hill Companies. Originally published in *Die Presse* (Vienna), October 12, 1862, and *The Bee-Hive* (London), May 20, 1865.

Edgar Lee Masters. *From* Spoon River Anthology: *Spoon River Anthology* (New York: The Macmillan Company, 1916), p. 220, p. 229.

Herman Melville. The Martyr: *Battle-Pieces and Aspects of the War* (New York: Harper & Brothers, 1866), pp. 141–42, p. 252.

H. L. Mencken. Abraham Lincoln: *Prejudices: Third Series* (New York: Alfred A. Knopf, 1922), pp. 171–75.

Marianne Moore. Abraham Lincoln and the Art of the Word: *The Complete Prose of Marianne Moore*, ed. Patricia C. Willis (New York: Viking, 1986), pp. 529–34. Copyright © 1986 by Clive E. Driver, Literary Executor of the Estate of Marianne Moore. Used by permission of Viking Penguin, a division of Penguin Group (USA) Inc. Originally published in *The Marianne Moore Reader* (1961).

Honoré Willsie Morrow. *From* With Malice Toward None: *Great Captain: Three 'Lincoln' Novels* (New York: William Morrow and Company, 1930), pp. 284–90. Originally published in 1928.

Robert Russa Moton. Draft of Speech at the Lincoln Memorial: Typescript marked "Address as originally written," box 11, folder 13, Moton Family Papers, Manuscript Division, Library of Congress.

Petroleum V. Nasby. Has an Interview with the President: *The Nasby Papers* (Indianapolis: C.O. Perrine & Co., 1864), pp. 45–47.

John G. Nicolay & John Hay. *From* Abraham Lincoln: A History: *Abraham Lincoln: A History*, vol. IV (New York: The Century Company, 1890), pp. 136–53.

Reinhold Niebuhr. The Religion of Abraham Lincoln: *The Christian Century*, February 10, 1965, pp. 172–75. Reprinted by permission of the Estate of Reinhold Niebuhr.

James Whitcomb Riley. Lincoln—The Boy: *Morning* (Indianapolis: The Bobbs-Merrill Company, 1907), p. 87.

Edwin Arlington Robinson. The Master (Lincoln): *The Town Down the River* (New York: Charles Scribner's Sons, 1910), pp. 3–7.

Theodore Roosevelt. Centenary Address at Hodgenville, Kentucky: *The Works of Theodore Roosevelt*, National Edition, ed. Hermann Hagedorn, volume XI, *The Rough Riders and Men of Action* (New York: Charles Scribner's Sons, 1926), pp. 210–14.

William Safire. *From* Freedom: *Freedom* (Garden City, N.Y.: Doubleday, 1987), pp. 797–803, pp. 1087–88. Copyright © 1987 by William Safire. Reprinted with permission.

Carl Sandburg. Journey and Oath, "Paint His Head Against Lavender Shadows": *Selected Poems*, ed. George Henrick and Willene Henrick (San Diego: Harcourt, Brace, 1996), pp. 95–96, pp. 96–97. Copyright © 1996 by Maurice C. Greenbaum and Philip G. Carson, reprinted by permission of Houghton Mifflin Harcourt Publishing Company. *From* Abraham Lincoln: The Prairie Years: *Abraham Lincoln: The Prairie Years*, vol. 1 (New York: Harcourt, Brace, 1926), pp. 19–43. Copyright © 1926 by Houghton Mifflin Harcourt Publishing Company and renewed 1953 by Carl Sandburg. Reprinted by permission of the publisher. *From* The People, Yes: *The People, Yes* (New York: Harcourt, Brace and Company, 1936), pp. 134–39. Copyright © 1936 by Houghton Mifflin Harcourt Publishing Company and renewed 1964 by Carl Sandburg. Reprinted by permission of the publisher. Mr. Lincoln and His Gloves: *Selected Poems*, ed. George Henrick and Willene Henrick (San Diego: Harcourt, Brace, 1996), pp. 92–95. Copyright © 1996 by Maurice C. Greenbaum and Philip G. Carson, reprinted by permission of Houghton Mifflin Harcourt Publishing Company. The Long Shadow of Lincoln: A Litany: *Complete Poems* (New York: Harcourt, Brace & World, Inc., 1950), pp. 635–37. Copyright © 1950 by Carl Sandburg and renewed 1978 by Margaret Sandburg, Helga Sandburg Crile and Janet Sandburg, reprinted by permission of Houghton Mifflin Harcourt Publishing Company. Originally published in *The Saturday Evening Post*, February 1945.

Carl Schurz. *From* Abraham Lincoln: An Essay: *Abraham Lincoln: An Essay* (Boston: Houghton Mifflin Company, 1891), pp. 1–36.

Delmore Schwartz. Lincoln: *Summer Knowledge* (New York: Doubleday Company Inc., 1959), pp. 236–37. © 1959 by Delmore Schwartz. Reprinted by permission of New Directions Publishing Corp.

Robert E. Sherwood. *From* Abe Lincoln in Illinois: *Abe Lincoln in Illinois* (New York: Charles Scribner's Sons, 1939), pp. 141–85, pp. 235–50. Copyright © 1937, 1939 by Robert Emmet Sherwood, copyright renewed © 1965, 1966 by Madeline H. Sherwood. Used by permission of Robert A. Freedman Dramatic Agency, Inc. All inquiries for performing rights should be addressed to author's agent Robert A. Freedman Dramatic Agency, Inc.

Richard Slotkin. *From* Abe: A Novel of the Young Lincoln: *Abe: A Novel of the Young Lincoln* (New York: Henry Holt, 2000), pp. 455–75. Copyright © 2000 by Richard Slotkin. Reprinted by permission of Henry Holt and Company, LLC.

Edmund Clarence Stedman. Abraham Lincoln: Assassinated Good Friday, 1865: *The Poetical Works of Edmund Clarence Stedman* (Boston: Houghton, Mifflin and Company, 1884), p. 293. Originally published 1865. The Hand of Lincoln: Edmund Clarence Stedman, *Poems Now First Collected* (Boston: Houghton, Mifflin and Company, 1897), pp. 5–7. Originally published 1883.

Adlai E. Stevenson. Remarks at Gettysburg: *The Papers of Adlai E. Stevenson*, vol. 3, *Governor of Illinois, 1949–1953*, ed. Walter Johnson (Boston: Little, Brown, and Company, 1973), pp. 468–71.

Richard Henry Stoddard. Abraham Lincoln: An Horatian Ode: *Abraham Lincoln: An Horatian Ode* (New York: Bunce & Huntington, 1865), pp. 4–12. Abraham Lincoln: *The Poems of Richard Henry Stoddard* (New York: Charles Scribner's Sons, 1880), p. 434.

William O. Stoddard. *From* Inside the White House in War Times: *Inside the White House in War Times* (New York: Charles L. Webster, 1890), pp. 9–36.

Bram Stoker. *From* Lecture on Abraham Lincoln: "Bram Stoker's Lecture on Abraham Lincoln," ed. Robert J. Havlik, *Irish Studies Review*, vol. 10, No. 1 (2002), pp. 14–15, pp. 26–27. © 2002 Taylor & Francis Ltd.

Irving Stone. *From* Love is Eternal: *Love is Eternal: A Novel About Mary Todd and Abraham Lincoln* (Garden City, N.Y.: Doubleday & Co, 1954), pp. 135–46. Copyright © 1964 by Irving Stone.

Used by permission of Doubleday, a division of Random House, Inc.

Harriet Beecher Stowe. Abraham Lincoln: *The Living Age*, February 6, 1864, pp. 282–84.

George Templeton Strong. *From* The Diaries: *Diary of the Civil War*, ed. Allan Nevins (New York: The Macmillan Company, 1962), pp. 281–84, pp. 582–87. Copyright © 1952 by Macmillan Publishing Company. Copyright renewed © 1980 by Milton Halsey Thomas. Reprinted with the permission of Scribner, a Division of Simon & Schuster Adult Publishing Group.

Ida M. Tarbell. *From* The Life of Abraham Lincoln: *The Life of Abraham Lincoln*, vol. I (New York: The Doubleday & McClure Co., 1900), pp. 241–56.

Tom Taylor. Abraham Lincoln: Foully Assassinated, April 14, 1865: *Abraham Lincoln: A Press Portrait*, ed. Herbert Mitgang (Chicago: Quadrangle Books, 1971), pp. 487–90. Originally published in *Punch*, May 6, 1865.

Melvin B. Tolson. The Dictionary of the Wolf: *Rendezvous with America* (New York: Dodd, Mead & Company, 1944), p. 70. Copyright © 1944. Reprinted by permission of Melvin B. Tolson, Jr.

Leo Tolstoy. Tolstoi Holds Lincoln World's Greatest Hero: *New York World*, February 7, 1909.

Mark Twain. A Lincoln Memorial: *The New York Times*, January 13, 1907.

Mark Van Doren. *From* The Last Days of Lincoln: *The Last Days of Lincoln* (New York: Hill and Wang, 1959), pp. 107–41. Copyright © 1959 by Mark Van Doren. Reprinted by permission of Hill and Wang, a division of Farrar, Straus and Giroux, LLC.

Gore Vidal. *From* Lincoln: *Lincoln* (New York: Random House, 1984), pp. 19–27. Copyright © 1984 by Gore Vidal. Used by permission of Random House, Inc.

Henry Villard. *From* Lincoln on the Eve of '61: Henry Villard, *Lincoln on the Eve of '61*, ed. Harold G. Villard and Oswald Garrison Villard (New York: Alfred A. Knopf, 1941), pp. 13–20. Copyright © 1941, renewed 1968 by Henry H. Villard and Vincent S. Villard. Reprinted by permission.

Artemus Ward. On His Visit With Abe Lincoln: *Vanity Fair*, December 8, 1860.

Booker T. Washington. Address on Abraham Lincoln Before the Republican Club of New York City: *The Booker T. Washington*

Papers, volume 10, ed. Louis R. Harlan and Raymond W. Smock (Urbana: University of Illinois Press, 1981), pp. 33–39.

H. G. Wells. *From* The Six Greatest Men in History: *The American Magazine*, July 1922, p. 148.

Walt Whitman. *From* Leaves of Grass: *Complete Poetry and Collected Prose*, ed. Justin Kaplan (New York: Library of America, 1982), pp. 459–68. Originally published in 1881. *From* Specimen Days & Collect: *Complete Poetry and Collected Prose*, ed. Justin Kaplan (New York: Library of America, 1982), pp. 732–34, pp. 763–64, p. 765, pp. 1036–47. Originally published in 1882. *From* November Boughs: *Complete Poetry and Collected Prose*, ed. Justin Kaplan (New York: Library of America, 1982), pp. 1196–99. Originally published in 1888.

John Greenleaf Whittier. The Emancipation Group, Boston, 1879: *The Poetical Works of John Greenleaf Whittier* (Boston: Houghton, Mifflin and Company, 1882), pp. 513–14.

Tom Wicker. *From* Unto this Hour: *Unto this Hour* (New York: Viking Press, 1984), pp. 219–25, pp. 335–38. Copyright © 1984 by Tom Wicker. Reprinted by permission of the author.

William Carlos Williams. *From* In the American Grain: *In the American Grain* (New York: A & C Boni, 1925), pp. 234–35. Copyright © 1933 by William Carlos Williams. Reprinted by permission of New Directions Publishing Corp.

Garry Wills. *From* Lincoln at Gettysburg: The Words that Remade America: *Lincoln at Gettysburg: The Words that Remade America* (New York: Simon & Schuster, 1992), pp. 148–75, pp. 288–91. Copyright © 1992 by Literary Research, Inc. Reprinted with the permission of Simon & Schuster Adult Publishing Group.

Edmund Wilson. *From* Patriotic Gore: *Patriotic Gore: Studies in the Literature of the American Civil War* (New York: Farrar, Straus, and Giroux, 1962), pp. 99–130. Copyright © 1962 by Edmund Wilson. Copyright renewed © 1990 by Helen Miranda Wilson. Reprinted by permission of Farrar, Straus and Giroux, LLC.

Woodrow Wilson. Address at Hodgenville, Kentucky: *The Papers of Woodrow Wilson*, volume 38, ed. Arthur S. Link (Princeton, N.J.: Princeton University Press, 1982), pp. 142–45. Copyright © 1982 by Princeton University Press. Reprinted by permission of Princeton University Press.

Index

This book is set in 10 point Janson, a faithful re-creation of a seven-teenth-century Dutch typeface designed by Nicolas Kis. The display type is Bodoni Condensed. The paper is acid-free lightweight opaque and meets the requirements for permanence of the American National Standards Institute. The binding material is Pearl Linen, an aqueous-coated cloth made of 100% cotton fabric and manufactured by ICG/Holliston, Tennessee. Composition by Dedicated Business Services. Printing by Malloy Incorporated.

A limited first printing of this volume, with Smyth-sewn binding and a ribbon marker, was finished by Dekker Bookbinding exclusively for Library of America subscribers.

THE LIBRARY OF AMERICA SERIES

The Library of America fosters appreciation and pride in America's literary heritage by publishing, and keeping permanently in print, authoritative editions of America's best and most significant writing. An independent nonprofit organization, it was founded in 1979 with seed money from the National Endowment for the Humanities and the Ford Foundation.

1. Herman Melville, *Typee, Omoo, Mardi* (1982)
2. Nathaniel Hawthorne, *Tales and Sketches* (1982)
3. Walt Whitman, *Poetry and Prose* (1982)
4. Harriet Beecher Stowe, *Three Novels* (1982)
5. Mark Twain, *Mississippi Writings* (1982)
6. Jack London, *Novels and Stories* (1982)
7. Jack London, *Novels and Social Writings* (1982)
8. William Dean Howells, *Novels 1875–1886* (1982)
9. Herman Melville, *Redburn, White-Jacket, Moby-Dick* (1983)
10. Nathaniel Hawthorne, *Collected Novels* (1983)
11. Francis Parkman, *France and England in North America*, vol. I (1983)
12. Francis Parkman, *France and England in North America*, vol. II (1983)
13. Henry James, *Novels 1871–1880* (1983)
14. Henry Adams, *Novels, Mont Saint Michel, The Education* (1983)
15. Ralph Waldo Emerson, *Essays and Lectures* (1983)
16. Washington Irving, *History, Tales and Sketches* (1983)
17. Thomas Jefferson, *Writings* (1984)
18. Stephen Crane, *Prose and Poetry* (1984)
19. Edgar Allan Poe, *Poetry and Tales* (1984)
20. Edgar Allan Poe, *Essays and Reviews* (1984)
21. Mark Twain, *The Innocents Abroad, Roughing It* (1984)
22. Henry James, *Literary Criticism: Essays, American & English Writers* (1984)
23. Henry James, *Literary Criticism: European Writers & The Prefaces* (1984)
24. Herman Melville, *Pierre, Israel Potter, The Confidence-Man, Tales & Billy Budd* (1985)
25. William Faulkner, *Novels 1930–1935* (1985)
26. James Fenimore Cooper, *The Leatherstocking Tales*, vol. I (1985)
27. James Fenimore Cooper, *The Leatherstocking Tales*, vol. II (1985)
28. Henry David Thoreau, *A Week, Walden, The Maine Woods, Cape Cod* (1985)
29. Henry James, *Novels 1881–1886* (1985)
30. Edith Wharton, *Novels* (1986)
31. Henry Adams, *History of the U.S. during the Administrations of Jefferson* (1986)
32. Henry Adams, *History of the U.S. during the Administrations of Madison* (1986)
33. Frank Norris, *Novels and Essays* (1986)
34. W.E.B. Du Bois, *Writings* (1986)
35. Willa Cather, *Early Novels and Stories* (1987)
36. Theodore Dreiser, *Sister Carrie, Jennie Gerhardt, Twelve Men* (1987)
37a. Benjamin Franklin, *Silence Dogood, The Busy-Body, & Early Writings* (1987)
37b. Benjamin Franklin, *Autobiography, Poor Richard, & Later Writings* (1987)
38. William James, *Writings 1902–1910* (1987)
39. Flannery O'Connor, *Collected Works* (1988)
40. Eugene O'Neill, *Complete Plays 1913–1920* (1988)
41. Eugene O'Neill, *Complete Plays 1920–1931* (1988)
42. Eugene O'Neill, *Complete Plays 1932–1943* (1988)
43. Henry James, *Novels 1886–1890* (1989)
44. William Dean Howells, *Novels 1886–1888* (1989)
45. Abraham Lincoln, *Speeches and Writings 1832–1858* (1989)
46. Abraham Lincoln, *Speeches and Writings 1859–1865* (1989)
47. Edith Wharton, *Novellas and Other Writings* (1990)
48. William Faulkner, *Novels 1936–1940* (1990)

To subscribe to the series or to order individual copies,
please visit www.loa.org or call (800) 964.5778.